The Bonanza Trail

BY THE SAME AUTHOR

Ghost Cities of Colorado
Cloud Cities of Colorado
Stampede to Timberline

BY Muriel Sibell Wolle

The Bonanza Trail

GHOST TOWNS AND MINING
CAMPS OF THE WEST

Illustrated by
the author

INDIANA UNIVERSITY PRESS

This book is a publication of

Indiana University Press
Office of Scholarly Publishing
Herman B Wells Library 350
1320 East 10th Street
Bloomington, Indiana 47405 USA

iupress.indiana.edu

The paper used in this publication meets the minimum requirements of
the American National Standard for Information Sciences—Permanence
of Paper for Printed Library Materials, ANSI Z39.48-1992.

Manufactured in the United States of America

LCCN: 53010019
ISBN 978-0-253-03327-7 (pbk.)
ISBN 978-0-253-03328-4 (ebook)

1 2 3 4 5   22 21 20 19 18 17

DEDICATED TO all the patient, long-suffering, mistreated beasts—the horses, mules, burros, and oxen—without whose help man would have been unable to conquer the West

Acknowledgments

THIS BOOK, which covers such a vast area and such an amazing variety of terrain, was accomplished only through the assistance of many people: oldtimers who were willing to talk to me, and writers of books, pamphlets, diaries, and newspaper articles, who made vivid the human as well as the historical development of the great West.

I am grateful to the filling-station attendants, storekeepers, newspaper editors, housewives, and waitresses who gave me road directions, bits of history, and the names of pioneers still living in the community. I appreciate the picturesque reminiscences recounted by dozens of old men, who identified mine properties, historic sites, and the original status of remodeled buildings, and who often rummaged through trunks and drawers to find faded photographs taken when a town was in its prime. Without this help, I should not have been able to visit many remote places, to identify what I saw nor to sketch important relics as they appear today.

I am deeply grateful to the host of librarians who dug up forgotten material and who often saved me time by having it ready upon my arrival. At the University of Colorado in Boulder Mary Lou Lyda, Elizabeth Selleck, Virginia Holbert, Louise Black, and Frances Binkley were my mainstays. The bulk of my research preparatory to my long trips through the West was done in the Western History Department of the Denver Public Library, where Miss Ina M. Aulls, Alys Freeze, Opal Harber, and Louisa Ward Arps put piles of books before me. Additional material was supplied by Margery Bedinger, Science and Engineering Librarian of the same library, and by Frances Shea, Librarian of the State Historical Society.

Outside of Colorado my thanks go to the following librarians: In *Arizona* to Mrs. Alice B. Good, Department of Library and Archives, at Phoenix; in *California* to Caroline Wenzel, State Library, at Sacramento; in *Idaho* to Mrs. Gertrude McDevitt, Historical Society, at Boise; in *Montana* to Mrs. Anne McDonnell, State Historical Library, at Helena; in *Nevada* to Mrs. Constance C. Collins and Mrs. Katherine Raycraft, State Library, at Carson City; in *New Mexico* to William Reed, Historical Society, Palace of the Governors, and to Mrs. Irene S. Peck and E. Anne Amison, State Extension Library Service, at Santa Fe, and to William M. Speare, New Mexico School of Mines, at Socorro;

in *Oregon* to Lancaster Pollard, Historical Society, and Evelyn Robinson, Public Library, at Portland, and to Pearl Jennings, Public Library, at Baker; in *South Dakota* to Mrs. George Brewster, Jr., Public Library, at Deadwood; in *Utah* to A. R. Mortensen, State Historical Society, at Salt Lake City; in *Washington* to Mildred M. Hill, State Library, and to Mrs. Ida N. Burford, State Capitol Historical Museum, at Olympia, and to Mrs. Gilbert, Public Library, Spokane; in *Wyoming* to Mary E. Cody, State Historian, and to May Gillies, State Library, at Cheyenne.

In each state certain individuals were especially helpful. In *Arizona* Miss Maurine E. Sanborn and her uncle George Upton told me of their town, Stanton; Mrs. Alfred Nelson, nurse, did the same with Oatman; Fred Gibson, curator at the Thompson Southwest Arboretum, owned photographs of Silver King; Jay Lowe, Superior, directed us to the town; and Mrs. Olsen, schoolteacher, the Sargents and Virginia and Allen Cheves showed us the remains of the place. In *California,* Mr. Hill, North San Juan, showed me old photographs and books, and Mrs. Gildo E. Solari talked of Mokelumne Hill. In *Colorado* Frances Dorrell and Arlene Wolfe typed the manuscript. In *Idaho* Mr. Dundas, merchant of Pierce, and John Grete, oldest inhabitant of Silver City, discussed the old days and identified buildings, and John Fairchild, Boise lawyer, gave valuable tips on roads. In *Montana* Mrs. Katharine Sullivan of Marysville and Harry Bouton of Garnet knew their towns and shared their information with me. In *Nevada* Bob and Paul Cornelius, proprietors of the Ghost Casino, were full of stories of Rhyolite's past, and W. H. Brown, ex-sheriff of Death Valley and butcher at Beatty, drew me a map of Rhyolite; Mrs. Berta Reed, postmistress, and Ollie Thompson, veteran miner, were goldmines of local lore in Searchlight, as was ex-State Senator James A. Caughman of Hawthorne, who acted as my guide to Aurora and Bodie, and Gary Barton, also of Hawthorne, who got me to both places in spite of washouts. In *New Mexico* Howard E. Sylvester and William L. Long, faculty members, New Mexico School of Mines at Socorro, started me on my New Mexico tripping; Mr. Leslie A. Gillett, mining expert of Santa Fe, gave me a list of important old towns; and Mr. McCall who owns a garage in Hillsboro, Mr. and Mrs. R. H. Chandler, who run a filling station in Silver City, Mr. and Mrs. Johnson, the only people I saw in Mogollon, Mr. Bentley, veteran storekeeper at Organ, Effie Jenks, owner of the ghost town of Bland, and Mr. Jackson, oldtime resident of White Oaks, all contributed to my growing fund of information. In *Oregon* Amos E. Voorhies, editor of the *Grants Pass Courier,* put early papers at my disposal; Oscar E. Coombs of Baker was a walking encyclopedia of dredge and placer mining; Mr. Snyder of Cornucopia described the town as it had been in his boyhood, and Mrs. Binns, postmistress of Sparta, showed me old relics she had collected. In *South Dakota* Mrs. Camille

Yuill, staff writer for the *Deadwood Pioneer Times,* laid out an itinerary of the Black Hills towns; Mrs. Charles Bentley of Rapid City showed me her girlhood home at Galena, and Mrs. Ted Browne, postmistress, and James Cosgrove, prospector of Silver City, pointed out mines. In *Utah* Helmer L. Grane, watchman and caretaker at Mercur, and Tim Sullivan, oldtimer in Eureka, both knew tales of boom days. In *Washington* Chapin D. Foster, director of the Washington State Historical Society, Tacoma, obtained permission for me to quote two elusive sources and Mr. and Mrs. Tim Kelly, formerly of Seattle, gave me names of persons to contact. In *Wyoming* Robert D. Martin, editor of the *Saratoga Sun,* gave me access to the old files and George Baker, one of the first residents of Encampment, told me of the mines in the Sierra Madre.

I am grateful to the following for permission to quote from copyright material: The Automobile Club of Southern California, Los Angeles, Philip Johnston, "Lost and Living Cities of the California Gold Rush"; the Keystone Press, Butte, Montana, Professor Thomas J. Dimsdale, "Vigilantes of Montana"; the Torch Press, Cedar Rapids, Iowa, R. E. Twitchell, "Leading Facts of New Mexican History"; Alfred A. Knopf, Inc., George W. Fuller, "A History of the Pacific Northwest"; Kate B. Carter, "Heart Throbs of the West"; Pressly Watts, editor of the *Okanogan Independent,* writings by O. H. Woody, deceased; *Great Falls Tribune,* Mary J. Pardee's article on Beartown; *New Mexico Magazine,* Manville Chapman's article on the E-town dredge; *Casper Tribune-Herald,* reminiscences of George Carpenter; *Rock Springs Rocket,* article about South Pass; the John F. Hiskey Unit No. 45 of the American Legion Auxiliary, Austin, Nevada, from its historical leaflet; the *Pacific Northwest Quarterly,* reprints from the *Ruby Miner* from Loretta Louis' article on Ruby; Mrs. Persis Gunn Ulrich of Index, Washington, for reminiscences printed in "Told by the Pioneers."

But if it had not been for five particular companions who cheerfully accompanied me on the long trips of exploration, I could not have completed this work. Although these five are referred to in the text simply as "my companion," "my driver," or "my friend," they of all people deserve to be named here and to receive my deepest thanks. The trip to southern Wyoming I owe to a friend of long standing, C. K. (Budd) Arnold; the circle of the Black Hills of South Dakota to a former trooper on Colorado trips, Victoria Siegfried (Mrs. Gordon) Barker; the days in the deserts of southern California, Nevada, and Arizona to my exuberant friend and colleague on the faculty of the Department of Fine Arts, Leslie O. Merrill; the "pilgrimages," one of six weeks and the other of three, through all the rest of the territory in eight big states, to my steady friend and splendid driver, Hazel Townley (Mrs. Frank) Potts; and most of all I owe the initial trip through New Mexico and Arizona and the impetus and encouragement for the whole project to my husband, Francis Wolle, whose patience, understanding, and help make this book his as well as mine. To the constant support and confidence of these five during years of research and months of traveling are really due the sketches, the history, and the anecdotes of the pioneering for hard metals that make up this volume.

MURIEL SIBELL WOLLE

Professor of Fine Arts
University of Colorado

Boulder, Oct. 5, 1952

Contents

Illustrations

Maps

The Bonanza Trail

WASHINGTON TERRITORY

OREGON TERRITORY

1853–1859

WASHINGTON

OREGON STATE

TERRITORY

1859–1863

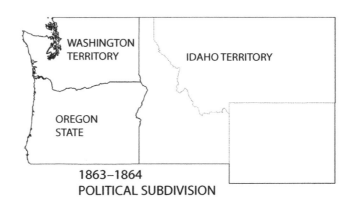

WASHINGTON TERRITORY

IDAHO TERRITORY

OREGON STATE

1863–1864
POLITICAL SUBDIVISION

Map created by Mia Partlow. Data from Steven Manson, Jonathan Schroeder, David Van Riper, and Steven Ruggles. IPUMS National Historical Geographic Information System: Version 12.0 [Database]. Minneapolis: University of Minnesota, 2017. http://doi.org/10.18128/D050.V12.0

Introduction

WITH DUE apologies to the geologists, I am convinced, after having read nothing but mining history of the West for the last three years, that mines are discovered by accident. Had it not been for Indians who showed glittering stones to eager prospectors, and for burros which broke their hobbles and strayed away while their masters slept, the gold rushes would not have occurred. The number of Indians who wore silver and turquoise ornaments, yet refused to divulge the sources from which they came, or who dangled sparkling specimens of rock before greedy white men's eyes and then gave sketchy directions as to where the stones could be found, cemented the determination of the explorers to search for the hidden wealth. The number of pack animals that perversely wandered off and were trailed by their owners up some mountainside has become folk legend. The prospector always picked up a stone to heave at the beast and discovered that he had a piece of blossom rock or float in his hand. Instead of throwing it, he began digging and the result was a gold or silver rush, which usually netted him nothing.

For more than three centuries the West attracted restless and curious white men. The first ones were the Spanish explorers, who searched avidly but unsuccessfully for the fabled Seven Cities of Cíbola, said to be so rich in gold, only to find that they were the seven adobe pueblos of Zuñi, gilded by sunlight. They became a symbol of the lure which for more than three centuries beckoned men and made them crazy, while they searched and killed, and found and lost the gold and silver and copper. Sometimes the quest made them millionaires; sometimes, paupers. But even when they lost, their eyes kept searching the sandy banks of rivers and the rocky sides of mountains for the "strike" which they knew was ahead of them, and as they grew older the glitter in their eyes grew brighter and their efforts became more determined. Tomorrow they would strike it rich; tomorrow was another day.

3

Álvar Núñez Cabeza de Vaca heard of the golden cities in 1528; Fray Marcos de Niza and the Negro Estevan discovered them in 1539; and Coronado went north to conquer them in 1540. Antonio Espejo is credited in 1582 with discovering silver in the Cerrillos Hills of New Mexico and also west of Prescott, Arizona. Juan de Oñate, who colonized the Rio Grande Valley in 1598, brought with him settlers and padres to establish missions and christianize the Indians. In 1692 Father Eusebio Francisco Kino began a similar missionary task in what is now Arizona, working north from Sonora, Mexico. The California missions, founded by Father Junipero Serra, were the last great chain and were not begun until the middle of the eighteenth century.

Authorities differ as to the amount of mining accomplished by the padres and their Indian slaves, but a sufficient number of old workings and primitive tools have been discovered to prove that some was done. The neophyte Indians submitted nominally to the padres, but they were restive and finally rebelled—the Pueblo tribes in 1680, and the Pimas and Papagos in 1751. The Spaniards came in contact with only a fraction of the Indians living in the vast desert land. Priest, soldier, settler, and miner were all intruders, whom the Indians bent their efforts to exterminate, never letting up until the middle 1880's when the last of the Apaches were placed on reservations and nearly all their great chiefs were dead.

After 1821, when Mexico gained her independence from Spain and set up the provinces of California and New Mexico (which included Arizona), Spanish and Mexican colonists were attracted to the vast new territory known as Pimeria Alta. In it they built many pueblitos near rivers or near the mountains, especially if ore outcroppings had been discovered nearby. Those who survived the murderous raids of Apaches and Comanches developed the little settlements and prospered on the gold and silver wrung so hazardously from the forbidding land. Gold placers and silver lode-mines were discovered in the part of Mexico which now comprises New Mexico and Arizona; but large-scale mining activities did not begin until prospectors arrived from the States during the 1860's.

Trappers, scouts, and guides were the most persistent of the restless men who roved over the uncharted mountains and deserts in the early years of the nineteenth century. In their wanderings they discovered passes and waterholes and they hacked out trails across the deceptive mountain ranges. Years later these trails became the much traveled roads over which thousands of emigrants, with their lumbering ox-drawn wagons, crept toward the gold camps of the west coast.

During the years when Indians in different areas were on the warpath, army posts or forts were set up for the protection of settlers and miners and were manned with small companies of soldiers who scouted and patrolled the

The black portions are the mining areas covered in the chapters on the individual states.

territory under their jurisdiction. The soldiers were often men who had mined in California or on the Fraser River; consequently, in their spare time they prospected the hills or the stream beds in the vicinity of the forts and often made important discoveries.

After the United States acquired vast quantities of land—through the Louisiana Purchase in 1803, through the Mexican War of 1846-1848, and through the Gadsden Purchase in 1853—and after the settlement of the Oregon border dispute in 1846, the government sent surveyors and geologists to study the new possessions and to map and chart the country. Their reports often made the first mention of mineral deposits to be found.

Everyone knows the story of Marshall's discovery of gold in 1848 on the American River at Sutter's Mill and of the gold rush that followed. This stampede to the coast was only the first of many which caused men and beasts to cover countless miles of virgin country and to endure incredible hardships on the way.

After the cream of the California diggings were staked, disappointed miners or those still searching for richer ground drifted north. In 1851 they found placer deposits in what is now southwest Oregon. All through the fifties they panned their way through the present state of Washington, although part of the area was not open to settlement until 1858. Just as they were settling down, a gold rush to the Fraser River in British Columbia sent them scurrying farther north. When that boom was over, in the early sixties, back they came to placer the gravel ledges of the upper Columbia River and to fan out south and east to Oregon and to the areas now included in Idaho and Montana.

While the "forty-niners" were the advance guard in the California rush, all through the fifties and early sixties men from the East and Middle West continued to stream to the fabulous gold camps, taking either the Santa Fe Trail or the Overland route to the coast. Many found what they were looking for. Others stopped on the way to prospect and discovered new diggings. Some arrived in California, found no fortune, and started back east, lingering to try their luck again in the newly found gold fields of Nevada, Colorado, and Arizona in the south, or of Montana, Idaho, and Wyoming in the north.

The movement which began in California spread to the north, from there turned east, and finally flowed south where it fused into the streams of newcomers who were crowding west, thereby completing an endless circle over which hundreds of thousands traveled during the next fifty years. In the meantime the discovery of the Comstock lode in Nevada was sending waves of men across the Sierras from the California camps to Washoe, the newest of the bonanzas. The same year (1859) another rush farther east took swarms of men to the Rocky Mountains, drawn by the slogan "Pikes Peak or Bust."

The sixties, seventies, eighties, and early nineties saw more rushes, to the

Boise Basin in Idaho, to Butte, Montana, to Tombstone, Arizona, and to Creede, Colorado. The 1900's produced Tonopah and Goldfield, Nevada. Each new rush was certain to be the biggest yet and the best.

All hard-rock mining followed the same pattern and all prospectors were drawn to the mountains by the lure of gold. In fact, gold was the only metal sought in the initial "rushes." In many instances gold was found only in modest quantities, while appreciable silver and copper deposits were thrown to one side as worthless rock and their very presence was cursed by the men who could see fortunes in only one glistening metal.

The first prospectors were placer miners, who worked their way up the streams in search of "colors" and, when they found minute yellow grains and nuggets, staked off claims and began to pan the stream beds and banks. Other miners left the streams to scramble up the mountainsides looking for float or exposed ore deposits. This ore was also profitable, but within a few months, or a few years at best, most of the easily obtained gold, both in the stream beds and at the grass-roots, had been found and shipped out by pack train.

Lode mining followed, the miners sinking shafts and tunneling into the mountainsides to get at the veins. This ore when found was not pure but was combined with quartz and other minerals. To extract the gold from it required the erection of stamp mills, which crushed the ore and thus freed the precious metal from the worthless rock. The deeper the mines were dug the more varied and refractory the ore became, and when stamping no longer released the gold, other methods of extraction were tried. Smelters and reduction works were then built, each equipped to cope by chemical processes with the complex ore bodies.

With each new "strike" a camp sprang up and, as a result, thousands of western mining camps exist today. Many are deserted, overgrown sites; others have become bustling cities that give no hint of their raw boom days, and hundreds are quiet little towns tucked away in the hills.

Most camps grew up around a single mine or group of mines, all producing one metal, perhaps gold. The camp flourished until the ore played out. Then the miners left and the camp became dormant or deserted. Later on, other prospectors came and found traces of another metal, and another boom began, which, if the metal were silver, usually lasted until the silver crash of 1893. Again the camp slept, until some other mineral was found in its mines or until it became a summer resort, a stock-raising center, or a lumber town. During the years its population fluctuated with each strike, swelling on the crest of each wave of discovery into the thousands, then shrinking to mere handfuls of determined or stubborn men who refused to leave and whose eyes were fixed on a mirage—the next boom, which they were sure would inevitably come.

Frequently in the course of developing a given lode, the metal content of the underground deposits changes. Gold may be found at or near the surface, but below a certain depth silver or copper ore may predominate. A mine may even become a "bonanza" through the discovery of mineral which it was not suspected to contain. Many a camp was deserted long before its paying ores were exhausted, simply because imperfect methods of milling failed to extract all the values from the diverse ore bodies.

Miners' Delight, the tiny cluster of tents and log cabins in the mountains of Wyoming, built around a mine of the same name, whose promise brought men from all directions scurrying to the remote hillside to claw at its surface and dig into its rocky soil for gold, is a ghost town today. Its eager founders have long since drifted away and died and only a handful of people live in the once busy camp, but Miners' Delight is a symbol of the thousands of mining camps which dot the western half of the United States, some flourishing, some forgotten, but all rich in history and fascinating to visit.

In spite of similarity of architecture and location each is unique, and it has been my good fortune to visit hundreds of such towns, to make a pictorial record of them as they exist today, and to try in my mind's eye to visualize them as they were at the peak of their mining booms. Each camp grew up around a mine or group of mines, and each mine was discovered by some intrepid individual whose greed for gold led him to the streams and mountains of the uncharted West.

Ghost towns may be grouped into certain categories:

First, mining towns that are still alive, like Tombstone, Arizona, and Jacksonville, Oregon, which started as mining camps but today are largely dependent on other industries. They have a permanent population and contain some of the original buildings.

Second, towns which are partly ghost, such as Telluride, Colorado, and Goldfield, Nevada, where many of the early buildings, both commercial and private, stand unoccupied, although a portion of the town is inhabited and is still carrying on a normal life, the chief industry still being mining.

Third, mining towns which are true ghosts—completely deserted, although buildings still line their streets. Bodie, California, and Gold Road, Arizona, are of this type. To avoid fine distinctions I include here also those towns in which only one or two families still live. Mogollon, New Mexico, and Mercur, Utah, are typical examples.

Fourth, mining towns which have disappeared and whose sites only re-

WHITE HILLS, ARIZONA. TOWNSITE AND DESERT VIEW

SILVER KING COALITION MINES, PARK CITY, UTAH

main. Beartown, Montana; Silver Reef, Utah; and Battle, Wyoming, are in this class.

In addition to these groupings are the camps which have become modern cities—Butte, Montana; Globe, Arizona; and Deadwood, South Dakota.

Architecturally, camps follow the same pattern. First, tents were pitched; next, dugouts or log cabins were built. As soon as a sawmill was packed in, and dressed lumber was available, frame structures were erected, including many with imposing false-fronts. If the camp continued to flourish, brick, adobe, and stone buildings were constructed, and it is these that have most successfully weathered the years, although some false-fronted "emporiums" have also withstood the ravages of wind, rain, and snow. Each camp reflects the combined tastes of its early settlers. The men built in a style reminiscent of their homes "back east" in so far as they could duplicate them with the limited material at their disposal. Individual camps therefore unmistakably reveal the Southern or New England or Middle Western background of their founders.

The search for ghost mining towns or for vestiges of early camps in the twelve great western states covered in this book, all of which owe their development to the efforts of prospectors and miners to find gold in their streams and mountains, is a most fascinating hobby. In crossing the vast areas of plains, deserts, and mountains which comprise the states, a traveler ignorant of the history contained in each settlement may pass through old mining communities on main highways unaware of their glamorous boom days. If side roads and twisting trails lure him off the pavement, he will see not only more of the country's magnificent scenery but also hundreds of now neglected places around which still lingers the fabulous history of the pioneer West.

The material in this book is grouped by states, and the illustrations picture the towns as I found them in 1951 and 1952 when I toured these states by car. Of necessity descriptions are limited to typical camps and those with rich historical backgrounds. Each chapter contains a map, which indicates the relative location of the places mentioned therein. By comparing these maps with any state road map, one can check existing places and trace roads or trails which lead fairly close to abandoned sites.

Such side trips take one over good, graded, "maintained" thoroughfares which anyone can drive, and also onto forgotten wagon roads with steep grades, high centers, deep ruts, and washed, rocky surfaces, where a car creeps and bounces in low or second gear, and where only expert handling prevents scraped fenders and bruised oil pans. Most mountain roads are built wide enough for passing, although they may not look so until a car approaches and slips safely by. Extremely narrow roads have turnouts where cars wait for others to pass.

Many a road is cut into a mountainside high above a stream or valley; such roads are equally safe to explore, although nervous and giddy people often prefer to look up rather than down while traveling along the well-built, rocky shelf. Second gear is the driver's friend both in climbing and descending a grade, for it gives power and security and eliminates worn-out or smoking brakes. Mountain driving is really safer than other types, for no one can hurry on the winding roads and the driver on the upgrade has the right of way.

Tips for the novice in the hills include leaving the car in gear, and cramping a rock against a wheel when parking on a hill to prevent the car's rolling if the brake should slip out. It is a good idea to have the emergency brake carefully checked before starting. Extra water for the radiator, a shovel with which to repair a washed roadbed cut by a sudden mountain cloudburst, and a reserve quart of motor oil in case some hidden rock damages vital underpinnings of the car are all safeguards to pleasant motoring although they will probably seldom be needed. To prevent being delayed by vaporlock after a long, stiff, hot climb, be sure that the car is heading downgrade before shutting off the motor.

Above all, ask questions of those living on the highway nearest to the town or site you plan to visit. They can provide information about local road conditions and from them one often learns interesting bits of history and folklore. I always ask at least two persons the same questions and tally their replies (which seldom agree). Then regardless of what they say, I go on.

Lest the foregoing cautions discourage some of you, let me say that in over 70,000 miles of back-road explorations I have never had an accident, never damaged my car, and only once had to resort to a shovel. If the road peters out, park your car and hike to your destination. If you hesitate to drive to some remote spot, it is usually possible to hire someone with a jeep or a truck who will bounce you to your goal. If you like riding, rent a horse and let him take you up the trail while you enjoy the vistas.

Partly because I know nothing about the "innards" of a car, but chiefly because it would have been unwise to risk driving the endless miles, day after day, across mountain passes and desert wastes without a companion, I have always taken some willing and adventurous person with me. Each one—whether a friend, a student, or my husband—has done most of the driving and taken complete care of the car, so that I could concentrate on sketching, interviewing old-timers, and ferreting out research in libraries or in newspaper offices along the way.

Half the fun of this hobby has been the adventurous trips connected with finding each place, and it is these, together with bits of the picturesque history of the early days, that I share with you in the following pages.

I'm an amateur where geology and mining are concerned, and such terms as "rocker," "adit," and "stope" meant nothing to me when I began looking for ghosts. The methods of mining and the processes for reducing ores were equally obscure, yet even a little understanding of such things helped to bring each camp to life and showed clues which would otherwise have been overlooked. Denuded hills mean that forests were destroyed to supply timbers and fuel for hoisting-engines; abandoned mills are symbols of increased labor costs, which could not compete with the decreasing market values for low-grade ore; torn-up stream beds full of boulders prove that golden nuggets once lay beneath the water's surface.

Mining history is exhilarating and depressing. It is full of violence and faith, of bravery and chicanery. It is built on extremes—a boom, a crash; a strike, a shut-down. It begins with the search for gold and with placering; it ends with concentrates, the search for strategic metals, and improved scientific methods of extraction.

Of the two kinds of mining—placer and lode—the first is wet, the second dry. Placering comes first; lode mining later. Placering needs little equipment; lode mining requires expensive machinery. Placering removes the free-milling, easily removed deposits with the aid of water; lode mining exhausts the free-milling surface deposits quickly, and then encounters ore surrounded by "country" or non-metal-bearing native rock, which is often excessively hard and therefore difficult to remove even by blasting.

PLACERING   Gold deposits are found in mountains in hard rock. Only oxidized, surface gold is washed away by seasonal flood waters and deposited in the beds of streams, in crevices of rocks, on LEDGES beside a stream or in BARS, formed by changing currents. Since gold is heavier than rock, it sinks to the bottom while being carried downstream and, when deposited, lies below the loose sand and gravel at BEDROCK.

The placer miner works upstream, knowing that the source of the gold is above, in some hill. Each creek or gully down which water flows may be the channel which leads to the VEIN or LODE. He therefore pans sand or gravel as he goes, searching for COLOR or minute particles of DUST, or for NUGGETS. He digs away surface gravel till he reaches bedrock, which may be only a few feet below the stream's surface, or as much as thirty or forty feet. Where it lies deep, he dams or deflects the stream for a short distance above his CLAIM and sinks pits into the wet earth so as to examine the exposed gravels in which he expects to find gold.

Whenever he finds gold, he needs plenty of water to wash away the worthless residue with which it is combined. Most Western streams and rivers are

PIPER'S OPERA HOUSE AND MINERS' UNION HALL, VIRGINIA CITY, NEVADA

TOWNSITE OF SILVER REEF, UTAH

dry or at low water the greater part of the year, except during the spring run-off of melted snow from their high mountain sources. Ranchers and miners are therefore dependent on the spring floodwaters to fill their reservoirs and to provide irrigation surpluses for the dry months ahead. As the miner needs a constant supply of water, he builds a ditch to bring it to his DIGGINGS. It must be gravity fed and must enter above his diggings.

Next he begins to wash his gold by means of arrastres or sluices. An ARRASTRE, the most primitive method of crushing ore, is a shallow, circular basin, constructed of stones in such a way that water can flow into it. In its center is a pole with a shaft attached to it at right-angles. Several large rocks are chained to the shaft; and a horse (or a man or mule) hitched to it, walks round and round, dragging the rocks to pulverize the ore, shoveled in by the miner. Water flows over the crushed rock and washes the waste material away; quicksilver catches the gold, which sinks to the bottom. SLUICES are long boxes, placed end to end on a slight slope so that water will run through them. On the bottom of the boxes are nailed cleats called RIFFLES, and at the lower end of the sluices is a piece of cloth or carpet called an APRON, which catches the fine particles of gold that have washed over the riffles. Because quicksilver has an affinity for gold, a little of it is poured into the boxes above the riffles. One man shovels sand and gravel from the pile beside him into the first box, water is turned into it, and the resulting grey mud flows through to the end.

At the end of each day or at other stated intervals, a CLEAN-UP is made. The accumulation of gold, sand, and gravel is carefully scraped from the riffles and apron into a GOLD PAN, partly filled with water. The worthless material is then washed away by a circular motion called PANNING. The gold dust, gold scales, and nuggets that remain are placed in a small buckskin pouch. This is tightly squeezed so that the quicksilver which has picked up the gold will be forced through the porous skin, leaving only the gold. The contents of the sack is placed on a shovel and put on a redhot stove where the remainder of the "quick" passes off as vapor. A button of gold is left.

If the water supply is inadequate or if the placer is at a distance from water, a ROCKER is built. It is smaller than a sluice and is portable, and the bottom is mounted on curved cleats. Two men operate a rocker. One shovels, and the other pours in water and "rocks" the contraption by means of a handle.

HYDRAULICKING Where a stream has cut its way through high banks or BENCHES, which may also contain gold, the washing and digging is done by means of high water-pressure. The water brought by the ditch is stored in nearby reservoirs and from there is piped to the diggings, where it is run into smaller pipes. To these are connected flexible rubber or canvas hoses, ending in nozzles, called GIANTS. These can be played in any direction, and the

CALICO, CALIFORNIA, LOOKING ACROSS DRY LAKE BED TO DAGGETT

BUFFALO BOY TRAM HOUSE, CUNNINGHAM GULCH, COLORADO

enormous pressure from them eats away the earth, undermines it, and washes it down to the large wide sluice which has been put in place at the lower end of the diggings. From this point the process is the same as placering, only on a larger scale. The men engaged in hydraulicking stand knee-deep in water; men at the nozzles are continually drenched with spray.

DREDGING Dredges rework old placers and the valleys and lands bordering the streams where gold has been found. A dredge is a flat-bottomed boat, floated on an artificial pond, dammed from the stream down which it cuts its way. It is equipped with an endless bucket chain which gouges out the earth ahead of it and delivers it in dripping mouthfuls to the machinery which mechanically separates gold from waste. The waste is spewed from another long bucket chain at the back of the boat, called the STACKER. Each dredge leaves in its wake mounds of boulders, which remain stark and unsightly for years, until enough earth blows over them to support vegetation. The DRAGLINE is a small dredge which works the edges and banks of streams.

QUARTZ MINING Quartz mining is dry mining. The prospector, with pick and pan, finds OUTCROPPINGS or FLOAT—exposed mineralized rocks—which he recognizes as containing gold, silver, or copper. He breaks off samples, tests them, and if they prove valuable, digs a prospect hole. It must be ten feet deep to entitle him by law to keep it, and he must stake his claim, record his location, and do a certain amount of assessment work upon it each year to retain possession of it; otherwise another prospector can "jump" it.

He digs his hole until it is deep enough to require timbered or CRIBBED sides, by which time it is known as a SHAFT. Or he may TUNNEL into the FACE of the mountain to cut a VEIN or LEAD of ore. After he has piled up enough ore at the mouth of his shaft or tunnel, he builds an arrastre.

If the mine continues to produce, the prospector takes a load of ore to a SAMPLING WORKS, where it is tested chemically and its average value per ton estimated. If the ore is rich, he and his partners erect a STAMP MILL, in which heavy metal pestles drop constantly on the ore, battering it into powder. When stamping fails to extract the gold, chemical processes are tried. The pure gold recovered is BULLION; the pulverized waste is TAILINGS. It is poured into retaining or SETTLING PONDS to keep the chemically impregnated earth from polluting the streams, whose waters are used not only in the reduction processes but by farmers and ranchers as well.

Certain ores respond best to SMELTING, a roasting and melting process, in which the metal sinks to the bottoms of crucibles and is run off into bars, while the lighter particles of rock and waste or SLAG, float on the surface and are drawn off, loaded on cars, and poured over the edge of dumps.

Mining has a vocabulary of its own. To aid in understanding it, a glossary is included on page 477.

1. *Indian Turquoise and Spanish Gold*

New Mexico

FROM THE MOMENT we left Albuquerque and drove toward Socorro I was excited, for this was new country. Town after town slipped by—Los Lunas, with its fabulous, pillared mansion, built by the Lunas family when the entire area was part of their land grant; Belen, once the "Bethlehem," or sanctuary, where hundreds of freed Indian slaves lived side by side with the early Spanish settlers. Jarales, Sabinal, Polvadera—the names themselves were musical invitations to explore this country of cactus and greasewood, tamarisk and mesquite.

Except for the rim of distant mountains, the only break in the level plain was Ladrón Peak (once a rendezvous for horse thieves) which rose out of the desert and grew bigger and more sinister as we approached it.

SOCORRO

SOCORRO, once an active mining camp, is a drowsy place with a Spanish plaza shaded by big trees, many old adobe buildings, and the church of San Miguel, one of the oldest in the country. But there is nothing drowsy about the School of Mines, and from the moment we met our faculty friends things began to hum. Sitting in the canteen over coffee, I listened to a bewildering number of stories and facts, most of them told by Mr. William L. Long, whose fund of mining information is profound and delightfully human.

He told the story about Russian Bill, who was really a nice guy but who liked to pose as a bad man. The camp grew tired of his pranks, and one Christmas Eve, when he became boisterous in the midst of a poker game and playfully shot off the finger of one of the players, they hanged him right there in the dining room of the hotel. The charge against him read: "Hanged for being a damned nuisance."

17

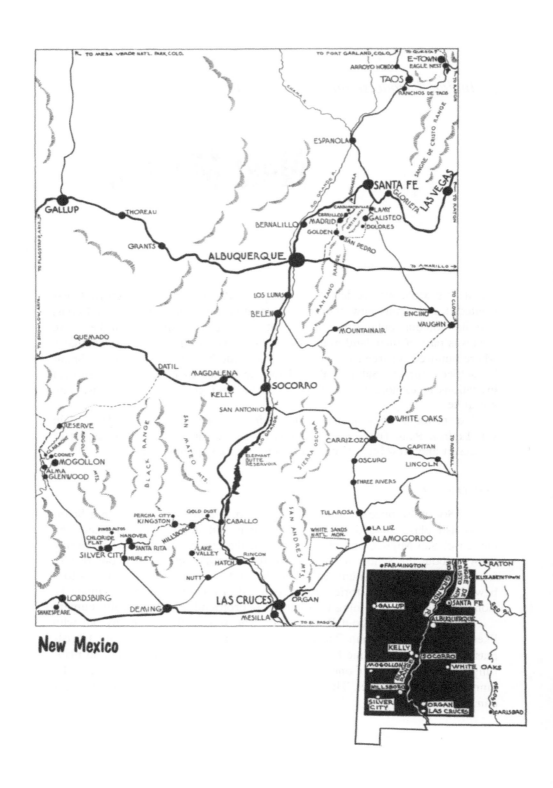

New Mexico

"Be sure to see Organ—it's a real ghost town," said Mr. Long. "Don't miss Hillsboro and Kingston and Mogollon, and of course go to White Oaks and Kelly."

That very afternoon Howard E. Sylvester, of the English faculty, drove us to Kelly, a ghost camp so close in color to the mountainside against which it is built as to be almost invisible. The road from Socorro to Magdalena, the railroad town three miles below Kelly, winds back of Socorro Mountain into sagebrush country. After a gradual one-thousand-foot climb, the road crosses a desert park or llano, with the Magdalena Mountains on the left, Strawberry Peak on the right, and Ladrón Peak, a blue cone, far away in the distance.

Magdalena is a newer town than its neighbor. In 1880, when Kelly was booming, it was only a handful of tents and adobes at a stagecoach stop called Pueblo Springs; in 1884 it began to take shape; in 1885 the Santa Fe railroad completed a spur as far as the town and then found the next three miles of grade to Kelly impossible to engineer. From that time Magdalena began to grow, both as a terminus and as a shipping point for the mines. But it was primarily a roaring cow town, and even now it is a wool- and cattle-shipping center for the surrounding country. We drove through Magdalena and across the tracks to a big mill, beyond which begins the deceptively steep two-mile grade that climbs one thousand feet more to Kelly. To the right, on the highest mountain, is the Virgin of Magdalena, a formation of bare rocks so interspersed with a natural growth of shrubbery as to resemble a gigantic head with a woman's profile. The likeness became a symbol first to the Indians and then to the Spanish-speaking residents, who see in it benign protection and look upon it with awe.

KELLY

AT THE end of the two-mile pull we saw houses in the chamiso and cedars and, turning a corner, began the final climb up a winding main street to the largest mine on the mountainside. Skeleton buildings, chimneys, and abandoned machinery, all surrounded by huge dumps, showed that big-scale mining was once carried on here.

I sketched, slowly working down the steep main street with its many ruined adobe stores, one below the other like a flight of steps. No roofs remained, only crumbling walls with gaping holes where doors and windows had been. Cracked concrete slabs in front of a dense growth of chamiso and piñon indicated the location of sidewalks. A few frame houses with porches hidden in vines, a frame church with a cupola and cross, and a number of tumbledown shacks and stables dotted the two or three side streets. Debris was strewn everywhere—rusty, rattling sheets of corrugated iron, old bed springs, broken fences, and cellar excavations filled with trash. Everything but the street was overgrown with sage, chamiso, greasewood, and cedar. Behind the town rose the mountain, covered with squat piñon pines and scarred by mine workings. To one side, on a low hummock, was the cemetery, every grave fenced in with weathered pickets.

The view from the upper end of Kelly out across the valley was tremendous: far below lay Magdalena, its buildings looking like pins in a pincushion; and clear to the horizon stretched a wide plain broken by ripples of ranges and isolated peaks. In our wanderings around the empty streets we saw three men some distance away, and once a dog rushed out to bark at the car. Only two families lived in Kelly at the time of our visit, though the town once had a population of 3,000.

J. S. Hutchason went prospecting in the Magdalenas in 1866, after receiving a specimen of ore from a miner friend who had picked it up while marching through that territory with the Union army in 1862. Hutchason never found any rock that resembled his sample, but he staked out two mining claims, the Graphic and the Juanita, and the oxidized lead-zinc ore he hacked and blasted from them he smelted in a crude adobe furnace. He shipped the pigs of lead to Kansas City by oxcart over the Santa Fe trail, and made enough to carry on his work.

In his gophering he found another outcropping, not far from the Juanita, and showed it to a friend, Andy Kelly, who ran a sawmill in the vicinity. Andy gave the claim his name and worked it for a time; but one year, when he failed to do the necessary amount of assessment work, Hutchason, who had watched its development with acute interest, jumped the claim and thereafter worked it himself. The Kelly ore was low-grade carbonates containing some galena and averaging 50-60 per cent of lead, ten ounces of silver, and a small amount of copper to the ton.

By 1870, miners who had staked claims in the lead-silver belt near the Graphic and Kelly properties laid out a townsite and called their mountainside settlement Kelly. Between 1876 and 1880, Col. E. W. Eaton leased the Juanita claim and in developing it struck a richer concentration of silver ore than had yet been found. This discovery encouraged more prospecting, and many new mines were located.

In the late seventies Hutchason sold his Graphic mine to Hanson and Dawsey for $30,000 and the Kelly mine to Gustav Billings for $45,000. Billings built the Rio Grande smelter on the southern edge of Socorro in 1881 and, during the twelve years it operated, hauled Kelly ore to it for treatment. For several years the Kelly produced the greatest amount of lead mined in New Mexico.

The town's first boom began in the eighties when people swarmed in, some interested in mining and others in farming, ranching, and lumbering. Even

KELLY. MAGDALENA ON PLAIN IN DISTANCE

ORGAN CAMP AND ORGAN RANGE

as late as 1885, the year the railroad reached Magdalena, Indians roved the hills, attacking settlers and stealing horses and cattle. Once, rumors of their approach so upset both camps that an engine, coupled to a train of cars, was kept ready in case of attack, to carry the women and children to safety in Socorro. During Kelly's period of increased mining activity, several rooming houses, two churches—Methodist and Catholic—two hotels, seven saloons, three stores, and two dance halls were well patronized. As the town continued to grow, living quarters became increasingly scarce and both hotels rented beds in three shifts, with no patron allowed to buy space for more than eight hours!

All-night dances drew crowds, not only of miners but of cowboys, who would ride fifty miles to attend them. Magdalena's cowboys frequently galloped up to the dances, but Spanish-Americans were discouraged from participating, although Kelly's young bloods often crashed the "bailes" in Magdalena and swaggered down its wide streets looking for trouble. In the early days everyone in Magdalena wore guns, and a favorite cowboy sport was to ride furiously down the main thoroughfare whooping and yelling and shooting out every light in town. These cowboys sometimes went to Kelly to shoot out lights, and, on one such occasion, so many men dived under the table for shelter that they raised it a foot from the floor. One old-timer insists that the citizens of Kelly were law-abiding and never carried guns, and that when they fought, it was only with fists, bottles, or bricks.

Jonas Nelson had a short lease on the Hardscrabble mine. Since he didn't have enough tools to keep a force of men employed full time, he made them work in relays at top speed, until they were exhausted. As each man threw down his tools, a member of the next crew picked them up and started working in the same frantic way. By this unique system Nelson obtained an immense amount of ore before his lease expired. Toward the end he struck a rich deposit of silver-lead ore. When he received the check from the smelter for the shipment he was so overwhelmed by its size that he threw a party such as Kelly had never seen. From Los Angeles a special train brought delicacies of food and drink and a group of captivating girls. Before the train arrived, Nelson built a big platform in front of the mine workings and held his party there. By the time it was over he was dead broke.

In the nineties, Cony T. Brown, of Socorro, who had seen greenish rocks on the Graphic dump-pile, sent some of them east to be tested. Next, he and J. B. Fitch took a lease on the Graphic property and began to ship the green rock from the dump and to blast additional tons of it from the mine. Everyone thought the men crazy until the rock was found to be zinc-carbonate, or Smithsonite—a rare and valuable deposit. Kelly's second boom resulted from this discovery, as every dump was stripped of its greenish waste and new companies leased old properties and developed them. In 1904 the Sherwin-Williams Paint Company bought the Graphic from Fitch and Brown for $150,000. The same year the Tri-Bullion Smelting & Development Company bought the Kelly from Billings for $200,000 and built a smelter at Kelly. Zinc recoveries increased until the Kelly district became the leading zinc producer in the state. Its total mineral output between 1904 and 1928 was $21,667,950.

The big Kelly smelter at the head of the main street was finally dismantled by the Empire Zinc Company in 1922, and its machinery was sent to the company's other plant in Canon City, Colorado. All through the twenties the Graphic and Waldo mines were active, but by 1931 the Smithsonite deposits in them seemed exhausted; during that year only one carload of ore was shipped from the entire district. In 1943, the American Smelting and Refining Company bought out the Sherwin-Williams interests and worked the lead-zinc sulphides of the Waldo-Graphic mines, but even their plant is idle today. Some mining is still done in the hills around Kelly, but the camp itself is dead, and its few miners now live comfortably in Magdalena.

Kelly was my first New Mexico ghost town, and I found it different from the deserted camps I had explored in Colorado. The country and the vegetation were different; the use of adobe instead of logs changed the appearance of the towns themselves; and the manner in which adobe crumbled was quite unlike the way in which wood weathered and rotted. If Kelly was a sample of what I was about to undertake, I knew that I had an exciting and challenging project ahead.

New Mexico's mines cover a greater span of years than those of other states. Near Santa Fe in the Cerrillos Hills are the remains of ancient Indian turquoise workings dating back to pre-Spanish days; and in the southwestern part of the state, at Santa Rita, another ancient site, is one of the largest open-pit copper mines in the country. The Spanish forced the Pueblo Indians to work in the mines, and as a result of the mistreatment they received, thousands of Indians died. When, therefore, the natives succeeded in expelling the Spaniards from their territory, they hastily hid the mines and refused to reveal them to subsequent Spanish masters. In the nineteenth century American prospectors were seriously hampered by the Utes and Apaches, who resented the destruction of their hunting grounds and the invasion of their land. The Indians harassed and intimidated and killed so many miners that they retarded by several years the development of certain areas where precious minerals were known to exist. Turquoise, silver, and copper were mined by the Indians or were at least located by them; gold, silver, and copper were mined by the Spaniards and Mexicans, and later by the Americans, whose scent for minerals was especially keen during the last quarter of the nineteenth century. Most of

New Mexico's mining towns are in the mountains, with Elizabethtown north-east of Taos, and the others much farther south in several distinct ranges.

The view from any hill in Santa Fe is of a vast desert panorama broken here and there by isolated hills and edged with distant mountain ranges. The bulk of old Sandia, over fifty miles away, rises hazily from the valley floor; but much closer are a group of low, conical hills silhouetted against higher peaks. The pointed cones are the Cerrillos Hills; behind them lie the Ortiz Mountains. In this small area the oldest mines of New Mexico are found. To Indians the turquoise is a sacred stone and a talisman against evil. Turquoise deposits far south in the Burro Mountains of the state, as well as those in the Cerrillos district, were worked by them long before the arrival of the Spanish, as the discovery of stone hammers, sledges, wedges, and ancient pottery sherds in old mine workings proves.

Coronado's search for the seven fabled cities of Cíbola uncovered no golden towns but, instead, a handful of mud pueblos in which turquoise, not gold, was used for ornaments. Espejo, Oñate, and other explorers learned from the natives of deposits of turquoise, and also of silver and lead, that lay hidden in the Cerrillos Hills; and Espejo is credited with assaying these metals in the year 1582. The mine from which they came is thought to be the Mina del Tiro, or Mine of the Shaft, which was worked by Indian neophytes under the direction of Spanish priests. The underground levels were reached through a shaft cut in the rock, with landings every few feet. Notched logs served as steps for the Indians, who carried the ore to the surface on their backs in skin sacks or in baskets. The lower portion of the mine was below water level, and the remains of a skin canoe were for many years visible at the water's edge. Old Spanish records tell of many expeditions from Mexico to the Rio Grande missions, for the purpose of obtaining silver, copper, and turquoise from the Cerrillos area. In time, Spanish oppression caused the Indians to rebel; and in 1680 the Pueblo tribes killed all the Spaniards in the area or drove them back to Mexico. They then concealed the mines in which they had suffered, and in some cases filled them with earth and rocks. By 1692, when De Vargas re-entered the valley to reconquer the rebels, the locations were effectively lost, and for a century and a half no mining was done.

Placer gold was found near the Ortiz Mountains in the early part of the nineteenth century by Mexicans, and in 1879 the Cerrillos mines were redis-covered by Americans who were looking for gold and silver. In the old mines they found stone axes and other indications of early workings. The new mining boom lasted only a few years, but it was long enough to cause the town of Cerrillos to grow and to produce two new silver camps—Bonanza and Car-bonateville—in the Cerrillos Hills. During the first part of the twentieth century the turquoise mines in these hills were also extensively worked, and quantities of fine stones were mined. Archaeologists, who have uncovered quantities of turquoise at Chaco Canyon and in other Indian ruins, are certain that the stones came from these same mines centuries ago. Only a few miles from Cerrillos are the sites of the Old and New Placers—mining districts from which millions in gold were washed in the first half of the nineteenth century.

OLD PLACERS (DOLORES)

TO REACH the site of the Old Placers, one goes from Santa Fe to Lamy and then to Galisteo, an old Spanish pueblo which has retained more of its early charm than most adobe towns. Beyond Galisteo the road winds to the still older town of Dolores, where the Old Placers were located. Though this whole area was visited by the Spanish as early as 1540, the placer deposits were not found until 1828, when they were discovered by a Mexican herder who, while searching for lost cattle on Ortiz Mountain, found rock similar to that he had seen in the gold fields of Sonora. The thick bars of sand and gravel which had washed down from the mountain were worked diligently until the middle thirties, when they were deserted for the New Placers just discovered on the opposite side of Ortiz Mountain. Even with crude wooden bateas, $60,000 to $80,000 worth of gold was obtained annually from the channel of the Galisteo River and what is now Cunningham Canyon.

In 1833 a vein of gold-bearing quartz, the probable source of the placer deposits, was found on the Santa Rosalia Grant, which belonged to José Francisco Ortiz. The Ortiz mine, as it is called, which is half a mile above the town of Dolores, is one of the oldest lode mines in the country. Since its owner knew nothing about working it he took a partner, Don Demasio López, a Spaniard, whose successful operation of the mine made it a substantial source of income. Ortiz was delighted and talked so extravagantly of its wealth that several unscrupulous men persuaded him to get rid of López and form a partnership with them. By unearthing an obsolete decree which forbade Castilians from living in Nuevo Mexico, they forced López to leave. Under their management the mine stopped producing entirely. Since then the Ortiz and other mines on the mountain have been developed by different companies, but the boom days of the Old Placer district are over.

NEW PLACERS (GOLDEN)

THE Cerrillos-Madrid road turns south from the Albuquerque highway about ten miles southwest of Santa Fe and cuts across rolling country toward the New Placers, near Golden on the western side of the Ortiz Mountains. The road skirts the Cerrillos Hills with their eroded, piñon-studded rock formations, and it passes through Cerrillos, the railroad center for the busy towns of Dolores, Golden, and San Pedro in the days when placer mining was in full swing and children panned gold in the arroyos. The fire of 1890 destroyed part of the town but spared the two-story Palace Hotel, whose faded elegance still lends an air to the less imposing adobes which form a large portion of its buildings.

The night before my visit to the site of New Placers it stormed, and the highway was powdered with fresh snow. Beyond the coal town of Madrid the road climbs gradually to the sprawling adobe village of Golden, most of which lies along one street. Adobes dot the slopes above the business center and across the arroyo, which cuts a gash below and to the right of the road.

A church, surrounded by a cemetery, fills a nubbin of hill at one end of the town, and the remains of placer mine workings dominate the other end. One new mill, in which copper concentrates are stored, stands on the brink of the arroyo; the ruins of a stamp mill sag beside the road. The one store, "Ernest Riccon, General Merchandise," in front of which men and boys sun themselves against the warm adobe walls, displays a sign reading, "Open Every Day, also Sunday."

In 1839, eleven years after the first diggings at Old Placers, some prospector or herder found rich deposits in the San Pedro Mountains on Lazarus Gulch and in the tributaries of Tuerto Creek. To Tuerto, the new town which grew up just north of the present town of Golden, flocked the miners from Old Placers. They sank small shafts into the gravel to cut a streak of pay ore and followed it laterally until it pinched out. Only the crudest of equipment was used: dry washers and bateas, round wooden bowls in which the earth was placed, submerged in water, and stirred until the heavy gold particles sank and the residue could be floated away. By 1845 Tuerto was the center of the district and contained twenty-two stores; yet today no trace of it remains. Placering continued sporadically in the district during the next forty years, but Golden's boom did not come until the late eighties and nineties. In 1900, when its population was 3,000, the town contained a bank, a stock exchange, a newspaper, and many saloons. Its mines were east of the townsite and were worked for their gold, although some copper was recovered and processed at San Pedro, a nearby camp. Pockets of gold are still found at bedrock, especially after heavy rains have washed fresh gravel into the stream bed.

SAN PEDRO

THE road between Golden and San Pedro became progressively narrower, and the higher it climbed into the mountains the deeper the snow lay on the ground. The old town was shown on maps as four or five miles beyond Golden, but we found no trace of it, even after struggling up a

SAN PEDRO

STORE AND MAIN STREET,
GOLDEN

ELIZABETHTOWN.
INTERIOR OF POOL HALL

steep, winding hill whose slippery surface was a mixture of snow and sticky
adobe. High on the mountainside I spied a mine and some buildings but no
town; so we turned back. As the road swung left at the bottom of the hill, we
found the empty pueblo, which on our way up had been hidden by a low
mound. It was truly a ghost town in 1951, full of ruined adobes, foundations,
one or two frame or corrugated-iron shacks, and an adobe church whose windows were shrouded with sheets of rusty tin. Behind it was a long, black dump,
and near it some useless machinery.

Gold and copper properties were first opened at San Pedro by the Spaniards in 1832; by 1845, when José Serafín Ramirez secured a Mexican land
grant of more than 31,000 acres which included the gold placers and the copper mine, the area was full of men panning gold.

When Lieutenant J. W. Abert visited the San Pedro district in October,
1846, it was alive, and his report to Congress says in part:

> In the evening we visited a town at the base of the principal mountain; here,
> mingled with houses, were huge mounds of earth, thrown out of the wells so that the
> village looked like a village of gigantic prairie-dogs. Nearly all the people there were
> at their wells, and were drawing up bags of loose sand by means of windlasses.
> Around little pools, men, women and children were grouped, intently poring over
> these bags of loose sand, washing the earth in wooden platters or goat horns. [R. E.
> Twitchell, *Leading Facts of New Mexico History*.]

A formal townsite was not laid out until 1880, when the San Pedro Milling
Company began large-scale development of the mineral region by constructing reservoirs in the nearby canyons and laying pipes from them to the placers.
Both the big copper mine on the hill and the placers on the flat were worked
for some time, until several consecutive years of drouth cut off the water supply and litigation shut down the smelter. A gold strike in 1887 again woke
the village to action. I knew nothing about the town until I was handed Volume I, Number 1, of a small, yellowed newspaper, the *Golden 9*. This ten-page
weekly was published at San Pedro, and copies of only its first two issues—
July 18 and July 25, 1889—are extant. It was hard to picture the completely
deserted and almost nonexistent town as ever needing a newspaper. The first
number quotes a paragraph from the *Albuquerque Democrat*:

> So far as the prosperous condition of San Pedro is concerned at present, the
> greatest credit is due to half a dozen men. . . . To Thomas Wright belongs the
> credit of giving the camp a starting point from a four years' sleep. To Messrs. Webb
> and Wright belong the credit of standing by the miners in adversity and prosperity
> for over nine years. Since Mr. Wright opened the famous Lucky, hundreds of
> miners have been attracted to the rich fields. . . . Had the Lucky not been dis-

covered and its wealth exposed to the world by Thomas Wright the many thousands of dollars now circulating at San Pedro and Albuquerque would be a hidden treasure in the mountains instead of, as it is, lining the pockets of operator, merchant and miner—everybody, in fact, but the newspaper man, whose only duty is to attract the attention of other people to the place where they can make a fortune and fare better . . .

The San Pedro Copper mine, high on the mountain beyond the town, produced several million pounds of metal between 1889 and 1892, and the *Golden 9,* in the first flush of mining hysteria, accurately reflected the exuberance of the reactivated camp:

July 18—Everybody is coming to San Pedro and the rest of the world will be used as pasturage.

Timely Remarks.
People from afar contemplating removing to San Pedro will do well to ponder on a few hints we have compiled for their benefit. Bring a tent. If this is not possible, then bring along wagon sheets, canvas, table covers, door mats, gunny sacks, umbrellas, etc. with which to improvise a tent-shack or tepee in which to live until you can make a dug-out or build a house. . . . There are no vacant houses in town. . . . There are families here living in coke ovens. Others have nothing but a town lot.

Some idea of the number of homeless people pouring into San Pedro may be formed [from] the hillside late in the evening on looking around upon the hundreds of camp-fires brightly burning.

Possibly a more varied assortment of residence buildings have never before been seen as are now going up in San Pedro. Unprecedented demand has exhausted the supply of building material. Log houses, frame houses, adobe houses, sod houses, pole houses, stone houses, conglomerate houses, mixed houses, and dug-outs are going up by hundreds.

When a man buys a San Pedro town lot at a nominal figure, washes out about $1000 in placer gold in his back yard, and strikes a lead in his cellar, he isn't taking long chances.

Mr. Kelly of Golden, yesterday dropped into the hand of our local scribe a little gold button which only weighed 23 ounces and was worth only $425. He took it right away again too.

A case was tried before our local justice yesterday, wherein a saloon keeper had knocked an unruly customer through his window and then sued him for the price of it. The case got too deep for the local legal talent, and it was declared off.

All during the early part of the twentieth century San Pedro had spurts of activity, especially during World War I, when a copper shortage reopened its mine. Today a new copper exploration project, partly financed by a government Defense Minerals Administration loan, has stirred the ghost town back to life.

ELIZABETHTOWN

NOT quite thirty years after the discoveries at New Placers, gold was found in the mountains far to the northeast of Santa Fe, and Elizabethtown, five miles north of Eagle Nest Lake and easily reached from Taos over good mountain roads, sprang up near the mines. If I hadn't read about Elizabethtown, I might have driven through it without stopping, for the scattering of houses and stores on the bare, sloping hill hardly looks like a settlement that in 1868 contained 7,000 persons; yet, from its placer and lode mines $5,000,000 worth of gold was recovered.

The wide, rich fields of the Moreno River valley were Apache and Ute hunting grounds, secure from the prospector's pick and pan until the middle sixties, when an Indian went to Fort Union to trade hides and furs and displayed some copper float to a few of the men stationed there. W. H. Kroenig and William H. Moore paid the Indian to guide them to the outcrop from which the float came; it proved to be close to the top of Baldy Mountain, the highest peak in the vicinity. There in 1866 they drove location stakes and began to develop the Mystic Lode copper mine.

Later in the same season, while a group of prospectors from Fort Union were camping on Willow Creek, one of them began washing gravel from the edge of the stream and discovered particles of gold in his pan. Since it was too late in the year to work the sands, he marked the spot, swore his comrades to secrecy, and then returned to the Fort for the winter. Long before spring the news was out, and as soon as the weather permitted, scores of men were off to Willow Creek to stake claims and begin panning. Two of the men, Mathew Lynch and Tim Foley, crossed to the south side of the gulch and, while exploring the east slope of Baldy, discovered the Aztec lode. Others found gold on the west slope of the same mountain a few hundred yards east of the present townsite of Elizabethtown, and named their location Michigan Gulch. When the placer field was found to extend for nearly ten miles along the foot of Baldy, prospectors tripped over one another to reach the northern Moreno River valley, where they were soon washing colors from every gulch and creek bed. Grouse and Humbug proved the richest of all, and their gravels were easily washed because of the water in both creeks; but the other gulches— Pine, Big Nigger, Anniseta and Mexican—and Spanish Bar, in front of Grouse Gulch, were all black with men and bristling with location stakes.

Charles P. Clever, delegate to Congress from the Territory, said of the diggings in 1868:

One company of five men with a sluice ninety feet long were taking out $700 in gold per week, others were just commencing and were realizing less, but a fair remuneration. . . . By October, 1867, the company of five . . . were taking out $100 apiece per day. . . . One company is now constructing a ditch or canal to bring water upon portions of these fields. This ditch will cost $100,000. . . .

A town has been laid out near the principal washings: it is called "Virginia City" and will without doubt soon be a place of much importance. There is hardly a day that *new* discoveries of gold are not made in that portion of New Mexico.

If Congress will only give some help to these hard working men, by constructing a good wagon road from Maxwell's ranch to Virginia City—and it can be done for the small sum of $30,000-$40,000—all kinds of supplies can be readily got in at cheap rates; when more and more poor people will flock thither and will soon give back to the government in return, the gold now so much needed. [Quoted by Ralph E. Twitchell in *The Leading Facts of New Mexican History,* Vol. III.]

After John Moore and T. G. Rowe laid out and surveyed the townsite early in 1868, the rapidly growing settlement chose a new name, Elizabethtown, in honor of Moore's oldest daughter; and almost before Colfax County was sliced off Mora County in 1869 and the Territorial Legislature designated the gold camp as county seat, the name had been shortened to E-town. The first few years of the camp's life were its boom days. Gold brought twenty dollars an ounce just as it came from the dripping gravel, quartz veins yielded ore which assayed $2,000 a ton, millions were skimmed from sandy bars, and only the richest and most easily obtained gold was considered worth mining.

The years 1868 and 1869 were the most productive in the district; but as the number of active placers increased and the population soared to 7,000, the need for more water, both for the town and for the mines, became apparent. The only solution was to build a ditch which would tap mountain water and lead it to the dry river valley. Some attempts of this sort had already been made: Thomas Lowthian brought a ditch from the north side of Baldy to his claim in Grouse Gulch, and miners on Spanish Bar dammed the Moreno River above their diggings. But the supply provided was not enough. Finally, businessmen from Fort Union and Las Vegas became sufficiently interested in the project to undertake it, and the construction of the forty-two-mile E-town or Big Ditch began. It was completed late in 1868 at a cost of $280,000, and the first water was delivered to Humbug Gulch on July 9, 1869. When still more water was needed, additional ditches tapped Moreno Creek and the Ponil River; the surplus water was held in reservoirs or lakes high in the Red River Mountains. The ditch had a capacity of 600 miners' inches of water, but

because of its great length and the consequent amount of seepage and evapo-
ration, a much smaller amount was delivered to its several users than was anticipated. Although it was never the paying investment its backers had hoped
it would be, it saved the miners during its several years of operation.

All this time the camp was growing. Henri Lambert, once cook for Grant
and Lincoln, drifted into E-town to try his hand at placering. Within six
months he was running a hotel. In 1871 he left for Cimarron to open another
hostelry, the famous St. James, which is still in existence. By 1869, when
E-town's first newspaper, the *Lantern,* appeared, the camp contained seven
saloons, five stores, one drugstore, two hotels, and three dance halls; and
gamblers, gunmen, and hangers-on had flocked to the noisy, lusty, false-
fronted settlement. Guns were the law, claim jumping became a common
practice, and when things got too hot, the Vigilantes held a necktie party,
after which the rough element quieted down or slipped out of town. When a
frightened woman confessed that her husband killed and robbed everyone who
spent the night at their wayside hotel, the sheriff and his deputies rode off to
arrest the murderer. They found him burning the bones of his patrons and
took him back to town to stand trial. Fearing that his cronies might pack the
jury, the miners took him from the courtroom and dragged him through the
streets at the end of a rope until he was dead.

By the seventies three stage lines—one from Springer, one from Trinidad
via La Belle, and one from Questa—rolled into town; but travel was still hazardous. In 1873 Coal-Oil Johnny and Long Taylor held up a coach in Cimarron Canyon and robbed it of $700.

By the middle seventies the placers were wearing thin, and Indians, who
still claimed the country as theirs, were so troublesome to the miners that most
of the population drifted away. A few die-hards remained and even brought
their families into the surrounding valley, where they built homes and pastured
cattle on the grassy meadows, and a few lode miners stayed on and worked
their properties, the War Eagle, Red Bandana, Paragon, Puzzler, Only Chance,
Bull of the Woods, and Heart of the World. But it was not until H. J. Reilings'
big dredge began to tear up the Moreno valley in 1901 that E-town boomed
again and its hotels and saloons overflowed with people.

Reilings, who had been operating a dredge in Bannack, Montana, built
the big boat on the lowlands below E-town for the Oro Dredging Company
at a cost of $100,000. Its capacity was 4,000 cubic yards of earth a day, and
each cubic foot sucked into its hungry maw yielded from thirty cents to three
dollars. At first no one would risk hauling its heavy machinery from the railroad at Springer through Cimarron Canyon to E-town, for the boilers alone
weighed 21,000 pounds each, and the danger of their rolling off the wagons
and injuring drivers and animals was great. When Jack Bennett and Charles

Webber of La Belle took the contract, bets were placed as to how long delivery would take. As soon as Webber got the first boiler chained on his wagon, he phoned that he was starting his fifty-five-mile trip. Two weeks later, after he and his crew had widened roads and built bridges, he arrived!

The big gold-boat was completed by the summer of 1901, and on August 20 everyone from E-town and vicinity, as well as a carload of eastern stockholders, stood beside it while speeches were made. Mrs. Mougey of Ohio christened it with champagne, saying as she did so:

> With the authority given me by the powers that be, I christen thee Eleanor. May thy wheels never turn without profit to thy owners; may there be no loss of gold in thy boxes; no leakage of water in thy seams. May harmony and success prevail. May our kind host gather wealth and comfort from thee and ever continue to be one of us—a good fellow. [Manville Chapman, *New Mexico Magazine,* November, 1937.]

For four years, except during the coldest months when the stream was frozen, the dredge worked two shifts of men a day. It paid for itself within a year. Then it was mortgaged to raise funds for the company's new dredge in Breckenridge, Colorado, and when the mortgage was foreclosed it was sold at a sheriff's sale. Its new owners did little with it except keep a watchman in its cavernous hull. Year by year, after he left, it sank lower and lower into the sand and ooze until only its pilothouse was visible. Now even that has disappeared.

E-town was deserted when I visited it, and the wind blew in cutting blasts across its treeless streets. On the crown of one low hill is a church, built of stained and weathered boards; on the top of another hill is the cemetery. Below the church, which dominates the townsite, stands a schoolhouse, and in front of that are two or three terraced, grass-grown streets, reached by rutted roads. Tall sagebrush hides many of the foundation holes, in which debris and fragments of sun-tinted lavender glass lie jumbled together. In one the carcass of an upright piano lies flat upon its back. The entire rear wall of a stone-and-adobe pool hall has been torn away, and in it only a billiard table and part of a bar are left. The false-fronted store in which George Greely, its proprietor, was shot to death in 1886, can be identified by the dim letters which spell "George's Place." E-town may come alive in summer, when fishermen and tourists roam the mountains and cattlemen drive their herds into the fertile valley and up the slopes of Old Baldy, but in February it is only a rattling husk.

WHITE OAKS

Now that I had seen E-town, the most typical northern camp in the state, I was ready to explore the southern and western mining towns, beginning with White Oaks. The drive south from Albuquerque to Socorro was familiar ground by now, but the seventy-five miles between Socorro and Carrizozo, across a barren desert and over sinister lava beds, were both tedious and lonely.

In Carrizozo we inquired the way to White Oaks and were told to drive three miles toward Vaughn, then cross the railroad tracks and go "up the lane" till we reached it. Each mile the "lane" grew narrower and steeper and finally turned into a bed of rocks from which all top surface had washed away. However, at the end of nine miles we saw buildings and the Cedarvale Cemetery and knew that we were getting close. Just before we entered the wide main street, lined with ruined buildings, crumbling adobe walls, and foundations and cellar excavations filled with trash, we crossed an arroyo on a decrepit wooden bridge which gave a loud crack as we drove off it.

Farther up the street, surrounded by sagebrush and chamiso, two or three brick and stone buildings stood in stately isolation; and at the far end of the thoroughfare was a tiny adobe marked "Post Office," in which two or three people were waiting for the mail to be sorted. They could tell me nothing about the place in its prime, but one of them suggested that I find Mr. Dave Jackson, who "has been here since the year one. Only the mountains have been here longer." As we started across a ravine toward his house, we met him coming for his mail. He was an elderly Negro and rather deaf, but he knew White Oaks, and his stories of it brought the town to life.

Cowboys discovered the first glittering particles of gold in a stream bed in the Jicarilla Mountains not far from White Oaks in 1850, while they were searching for stray cattle. Lone prospectors searched the gulches thereabouts for years afterward and placered a little here and there, but found nothing spectacular.

Thirty years later, Jack Winters and another prospector whose name differs according to the source (Harry Baxter, George Wilson, or John Wilson), were panning gold in a gulch on Baxter Creek, ten miles south of the Jicarillas, when a stranger, also named Wilson, rode into their camp and joined them at lunch. He was restless, however, and while the others were eating, he took a pick and his food and said he was going to the top of the mountain to find a gold mine. Part way up he stopped to rest and sat on a big blowout of rock at which he chipped idly as he ate. The fragments which broke off glittered, and he put one or two in his pocket. It was nearly dark when he reached camp again, but his samples of rock still glittered. Both the other men let out loud

WHITE OAKS. EXCHANGE BANK ON RIGHT

INTERIOR OF DESERTED CHURCH, WHITE OAKS

whoops when they saw them and insisted that, tired as he was, he guide them to the place from which the specimens came. They set their stakes by lantern light on August 14, 1879. When they asked Wilson what his full name was, in order to record it with theirs, he countered by saying that he didn't want a share in the mine, he wasn't interested in gold, and as soon as his horse was rested he'd be on his way again. Some accounts of this story add that a Texas sheriff was not far behind Wilson and that he climbed the mountain, not to look for ore, but to scan the surrounding country for posses. The two prospectors then offered him all their ready cash—forty dollars—a pony, and a bottle of whisky, and, completely satisfied with the deal, he rode away and was never heard of again.

The lode which he uncovered became the famous North Homestake, from which large amounts of ore were taken even before systematic development released its deeply hidden treasures; its total yield up to 1904 was $525,000. In November, 1879, the property was divided, Winters retaining the North Homestake and John Wilson taking over the South Homestake. The latter, too, was a great success, as it also produced slightly more than half a million dollars by 1904. In 1880 the men sold both properties to a St. Louis company for $30,000 each, and the newly created Homestake Company began at once to develop the mine. A twenty-stamp mill was built in the gulch below the new townsite and was supplied with water from White Oaks Spring.

The discovery of the Homestake started a stampede, first to Baxter Mountain, which was soon covered with prospect holes, and then to the surrounding hills. Many other lodes were found: the Comstock, Little Mack, Smuggler, Rip Van Winkle, and Old Abe. The Old Abe is said by some authorities to be the original strike in the district and to have been found by Abe Whiteman, who was one of the first to explore the area, attracted to it by the placer gold occasionally found in the gulches. He staked a claim a few hundred feet down the gulch from the North Homestake; but before it "proved up" he disposed of it, so the story goes, to William Watson for one dollar. Watson developed the mine and found, to his amazement, that he had a bonanza which during its first year of operation occasionally produced $35,000 in a single week, much of its ore averaging $100 a ton. In 1890 one of the richest veins of high-grade ore was opened, and during the next twenty-five years, as the shaft sank farther and farther into the earth, gold continued to pour from its depths. Even when the shaft reached 1,400 feet, no trace of underground water hampered mining operations. After John Y. Hewett and his associates became owners of the mine, another $1,000,000 was taken from the spectacular property.

The North and South Homestake mines and the Old Abe brought thousands of people to Baxter Mountain and the vicinity, and before the end of

1880 the booming camp of White Oaks was laid out and surveyed, and the townsite was covered with tents. The plat showed several streets—White Oaks Avenue and Livingston and Jicarilla Streets—but at first only tents, log cabins, adobes, and hitching racks lined the muddy, rutty tracks with the imposing names. The "Western Klondike" lasted twenty years, and within that period a solidly built town replaced the hurriedly constructed shelters of the early eighties. Stores and homes of red brick or of native stone increased in numbers, and a large $10,000 brick schoolhouse on one side of town balanced an equally large brick residence on a knoll on the opposite side.

During the eighties and nineties White Oaks was the "liveliest town in the Territory," and its Exchange Bank, which still stands, was one of the busiest in New Mexico. Its second-floor offices were used by several lawyers, soon to be well known politically: W. C. McDonald, first Governor of New Mexico under statehood; H. B. Fergusson, delegate to Congress; and John Y. Hewett, attorney and the town's leading businessman.

As the population grew, three churches, two hotels, a planing mill, and a newspaper office were added. In fact, four weekly papers were printed in the busy little city between 1880 and 1905: *The Golden Era* (1880-1884), *The Lincoln County Leader* (1882-1894), *The Old Abe Eagle* (1885-1905), and the *New Mexico Interpreter* (1885-1891). Emerson Hough, author of *The Covered Wagon* and many other novels, was a reporter for the *Golden Era* and practiced law for a short time while the town was growing up. The locale for his *Heart's Desire* is White Oaks, and Abe Whiteman is one of its characters.

Although on June 10, 1882, the *Red River Chronicle* reported that "The White Oaks Vigilantes took a horse thief from the jail and hung him," the town soon settled down to a more humdrum existence. On June 24, 1887, the *New Mexico Interpreter* remarked smugly,

> There is no more orderly city west of the Allegheny Mts. than White Oaks. . . .
> Our Supreme court, M. H. Bellomy presiding, held a session Wed. and Thurs. White Oaks is too peaceable to make this court a financial success and we hope it may continue so.

Advertisements in the tattered, crackling, brown sheets of the *New Mexico Interpreter* for 1887 and 1888 mention Ah Nue, a Chinese cook for the Bar W Ranch during the seventies, who came to town during the boom, opened a restaurant, and sold Oriental goods on the side. Ah Nue's songbirds, which comprised one shipment of merchandise, were described as

the best in the country, and his
cages the most beautiful. Those desiring a
lovely singer should give him a call.
His prices are very low.

Ah Nue remained in White Oaks sixty-five years and was a great favorite with the townspeople. When he died at the age of 101 years, "The businessmen paid tribute to him."

The town enjoyed its celebrations. One year on the Fourth of July it turned out in such numbers for a picnic at which "the Declaration of Independence was well read," that a table 130 feet long, "loaded with the good things of life," was needed to serve the hungry throng. In September, 1888, a three-day tournament was held, at which the chief attractions were the baseball game between the White Oaks Club and the Lincoln Club for a purse of twenty-five dollars, the dance held each night in a new store building, and various races. These included a fifty-yard foot race, a first-class horse race of 400 yards for a purse of fifty dollars, a second-class race for "cowponies and horses with no records," and a "Fast and Slow Burro Race" with a purse of five dollars and an entrance fee of fifty cents for each participant.

When 4,000 persons lived in the hidden mountain valley and floundered through the mud and dust of its main street, the *Interpreter* inquired pointedly, "Has not the time arrived when White Oaks Avenue should have sidewalks its entire length?" "And how about a railroad to move our gold bricks?" asked the mining companies, which were getting tired of shipping bullion by stage across the Oscura Mountains to San Antonio, over seventy miles away. The *Interpreter* joined in the clamor and during 1887 crusaded for a road by frequent allusions.

July 8—White Oaks is bound to be one of the best towns in the territory. It has the precious metals and immense beds of coal right at its doors and when railroads reach that portion of the country, White Oaks will grow rapidly.

July 8—President Detwiler of the El Paso and White Oaks railroad has succeeded in successfully negotiating the franchise to New York parties, and the sale will be completed if the El Paso people ratify the terms. It is generally understood that just as soon as work begins from El Paso into Lincoln county, the Santa Fe road will push work on the proposed line from Socorro and Carthage to White Oaks, and it is a certainty that the Santa Fe will get there first.

October 5, 1888—Over 60 carloads of ties and timbers for the White Oaks road have been received and are being unloaded. The Kansas City, El Paso and Mexican Railway, known as the White Oaks road is being pushed with great vigor. . . . But where is the A. T. & S. F. Railway that have so constantly made the assertion that they would build the first road to White Oaks?

As negotiations went on, a meeting of the town's property holders was called, for the purpose of considering "a right of way and depot grounds." Hewett and the other businessmen were so certain that the railroad would have to come through White Oaks that they demanded too high a price for the land and would make no concessions. The road officials then decided to by-pass White Oaks and lay their track through Carrizozo and Capitan instead; whereupon the local committee changed its tune and begged for the road on any terms. But they were too late, and White Oaks' big moment was past. The best they could get was stage connections with Carrizozo, ten miles away. At first the loss did not affect the town, and it continued to boom. The *Interpreter* for October 21, 1891, mentions that

Several wagons loaded with men, women, children, poultry and furniture arrived in town Wed. afternoon. The prospect now is that they will be obliged to become dwellers in tents and wagons, for there is hardly a vacant house in White Oaks.

But shortly afterwards, as Mr. Jackson put it, "The people's heart went out of their business and the town began to go down." One by one families drove away with their possessions piled around them, and the number of empty houses grew. Cattle wandered once more over the hills, pitted now with prospect holes and scarred by ore dumps, and the few remaining families tore down deserted sheds and cabins for fuel. Building after building disappeared until whole blocks were razed. Only a few brick and stone structures are now left to watch, with sightless eyes, ultimate destruction creeping toward them. Hewett's big house is one of them, and his bank is another.

Behind White Oaks Avenue stands a one-story stone building, well-proportioned and enriched by a pilastered façade. I crossed the rough, sage-dotted ground of the ghostly town to reach it. The double doors were barred, but the north wall had been torn open, leaving a gaping hole many feet in diameter. Climbing on a pile of toppled rocks and debris, I looked inside. The building was a church, and its interior was in a sad state of ruin. At one end a raised platform ran the width of the room; on the plaster-strewn floor lay a chest of drawers and a blackboard; in one corner, leaning rakishly against the wall, was a large wooden cross; and painted on the wall was the faded inscription, "They that seek . . . shall find me."

According to Mr. Jackson, twelve families lived in White Oaks in 1951. The day of our visit we saw but six people, and as we left the quiet place, the

tinkle of a cowbell sounded musically in the distance. What a contrast to White
Oaks' days of deafening stamp mills and bawdy gaiety issuing from Mme.
Varnish's Little Casino!

ORGAN

BETWEEN Carrizozo and Organ black lava beds and white gypsum
sands break the monotony of the dry, cactus-studded desert. Just before sunset we started the climb over Organ Pass, and a short distance beyond
the crest we reached the ghost town of Organ. Its one street is lost beside the
highway where cars streak by, their occupants unaware that a few old false
fronts and Bentley's stone store mark the site of a once-prosperous mining
camp. Mr. Bentley, an elderly man who now owns the town, has seen it grow
and fade since his arrival in 1903. We found him in his store surrounded by
merchandise, some old, some new. Going to the door with us, he pointed out
the various mining properties, especially the Torpedo across the road and the
Stephenson-Bennett to the south.

Organ's lead-silver vein was discovered in 1849 by a prospector whose
name has since been forgotten. Hugh Stephenson, who was living near the
Rio Grande at the time, was interested in the property from the start and later
acquired it. Although he had little capital with which to develop the mine, it
produced steadily under his supervision, and its ore was packed by burros to
his small adobe smelter by the Rio Grande to be processed. He sold the mine
to army officers from Fort Fillmore in 1858 for $12,500. By this time it had
produced $90,000, and by 1904 its total output was $500,000.

Other lodes were opened in the vicinity in 1863 and again in 1881. Of
this second boom the *Rio Grande Republican* of July 23 says:

Two months ago not more than a dozen prospectors were camped in the Organ
Mountain mining district. Now this whole territory is as full of busy life as an ant
hill and all are enthusiastic over their prospects.

Another spurt of mining took place in the early years of the twentieth
century. The Torpedo, which was only a prospect in 1900, is said to have
produced $1,000,000 in copper and silver when its shaft was only 300 feet
deep. In 1905 it was closed by litigation, or, as Mr. Bentley put it, "It was
a freezeout." While the boom lasted, Bentley ran a boardinghouse as well as
his store. When the Torpedo company asked him to install a bar, he refused.
The company officers then explained that, unless he did so, "The miners would
go to Las Cruces to get drunk and be gone three or four days—too much time
lost from work." He put in the bar.

Below his store, overlooking the wide Rio Grande valley, is the stone schoolhouse he built. "There used to be eighty scholars and two teachers in it," he said proudly. "All miners' children, too. This camp will come back when the mines pay again. We've got the ore."

Across the highway from the little oasis, so full of memories to Mr. Bentley, stand the concrete foundations of the Torpedo mine buildings; above them loom the bare and frightening teeth of the Organ Mountains. Somewhere in those barren, upthrust pillars of stone was Father La Rue's legendary lost mine.

In 1797, Father La Rue and his parishioners in Chihuahua, Mexico, were facing starvation after a period of drought. A dying stranger, to whom the father had recently administered the last rites, had described a gold-bearing vein he had worked in the mountains two days' journey north of El Paso del Norte. Recalling the man's description, Father La Rue decided to lead his emaciated people into this northern territory, find the mine, and establish new homes for them in kindlier terrain. The serrated turrets of the Organs were easily recognized from the stranger's description, and Father La Rue turned east toward them. Following his directions, the men found placers and gold lodes and for a short time lived comfortably.

When Mexico City authorities learned that a priest and his parishioners had disappeared from Chihuahua, a party of soldiers was sent north to find them. Father La Rue, realizing that the mine and its treasure might cause greedy men to attack the little community and steal the gold, kept guards posted along the trail leading to the settlement. On the day the sentinels reported the approach of soldiers, the priest led his men to the mine entrance and ordered them to hide all the gold they had mined and conceal the opening. By the time the soldiers arrived no trace of mine or gold was to be found. The priest explained the reasons for his departure from Mexico but refused to point out the mine. That night he was murdered, and his followers were tortured and killed when they, too, refused to disclose the treasure and its source. Since then many futile attempts have been made to locate the mine.

GOLD DUST

KNOWING that the Black Range was full of mining camps, we left Las Cruces early one morning and drove up the Rio Grande to Caballo, where the scenic highway across the range to Silver City begins. A few miles to the west is Gold Dust, a small, modern camp where dry dredging is recovering considerable quantities of gold from each day's take. The site of Gold Dust was the scene of a raid by Victorio and his band of Chiricahua Apaches in 1881.

In 1868 the Chiricahua Indians had been moved by the government to Ojo Caliente, near the northern end of the Black Range. In spite of government supervision, however, small bands would slip away from the reservation to hunt in the country in which they had previously lived. The growing number of settlers in the hills requested that the Indians be moved to the San Carlos reservation in Arizona for Victorio, Geronimo, and Mangas Colorádas (Bloody Sleeves), with their bands of warriors, continually harassed the mining communities on the east side of the range, picked off lone prospectors or unprotected farmers, and stole horses and cattle pastured in the surrounding brush-covered hills. Although neither Indians nor army officers thought the move advisable, the government ordered it made. Victorio, the leader of the Chiricahuas, escaped from the Arizona reservation more than once. In 1879, with thirty followers, he headed for Ojo Caliente, where he killed several men and took nearly fifty horses in an engagement with U. S. troops. The next morning 150 Chiricahuas from the San Carlos reservation joined him. From then on until his death in 1883, he and his warriors evaded the troops and endeavored to wipe out all miners and settlers to avenge the death of Torribeo, his son-in-law, who had been killed by white men near Alma.

For the protection of the settlers, small army posts were set up throughout the territory; but the garrisons were small and the area patrolled by each so vast that the townspeople were left much on their own when sudden danger approached.

On the occasion of the 1881 raid, Victorio was being chased by a company of Negro troops under Captain Schmitt. The Indians, who knew the country, led the cavalry as far as the river and then back toward the mountains and the placer camps. Thirty men were at work in Flap Jack Gulch at the time of the raid. Their families were living in tents half a mile away from their diggings, on the mesa where Gold Dust is now situated. One of the women, seeing the ominous cloud of dust approaching, took charge at once and ordered everyone to lie flat on the ground in the tents. The yelling band of Apaches galloped round and round the little settlement, shooting at the tents but aiming too high to hit the terrified women and children who were pressed against the sandy soil. The miners heard the yells and came running up, but the Indians by then were off toward Hillsboro. Victorio, circling back, then ambushed Captain Schmitt and his hundred men in Gavilan Canyon, where, according to old-timers' tales, camp kettles, canteens, and buttons from uniforms could still be found fifty years after the massacre.

HILLSBORO

WEST of Gold Dust the road to Hillsboro winds up and down and around sage-covered hummocks until it crosses Percha Creek and enters the shade cast by the giant cottonwoods which arch over the streets and houses of the quiet little community.

BANK AND ALARM BELL, KINGSTON

MAIN STREET, HILLSBORO

In April, 1877, Dan Dugan and Dave Stitzel, who were prospecting on the east side of the Black Range, picked up some float but decided it was no good. Stitzel, however, slipped a few pieces in his pocket and took them to a quartz mill on the Mimbres River. As the assay on them ran $160 in gold to the ton, he returned to the spot in May and located the Opportunity and Ready Pay mines. The first five tons of ore he hauled in brought him $400. By August, therefore, he was back at his prospects and built a cabin. As other prospectors gravitated to the hills, the cluster of tents became a camp whose name was selected from suggestions written on slips of paper and shuffled in a hat. Hillsborough (later changed to Hillsboro) was the winning title. All through the eighties and nineties the camp teemed with life, in spite of its isolated location and frequent Indian raids. Its mines produced over six millions in gold and silver.

At the edge of town, on the road to Lake Valley, crumbling adobe and stone walls mark the remains of an old stagecoach corral; it dates from the days when Sadie J. Orchard drove four to six mules every day between Kingston and Lake Valley by way of Hillsboro. She and her husband owned a stage line which served Silver City, Pinos Altos, and Mogollon. For two years he managed its runs while she operated the new line between Kingston, the silver camp deeper in the mountains, and Lake Valley, fifteen miles to the south, where the railroad touched the silver belt.

The Orchards, who ran their stage and freight line when the towns were at their height, owned two Concord coaches, an express wagon, and more than sixty horses and mules, many of which Sadie broke herself. Certain passengers preferred to ride with her, possibly because her coach was never in a holdup. And yet the run between Kingston and Hillsboro was through narrow, rugged Percha Canyon, full of splendid hideouts for footpads; even between Hillsboro and Lake Valley no stage was safe. The coaches often carried large shipments of gold or equally large payrolls, and on more than one trip road agents, as the highwaymen were called, relieved the vehicle of its valuables.

Bill Holt, one of Orchard's drivers, had a hunch that he would be held up the day he was taking $75,000 from a Kingston bank to the railroad at Lake Valley. Several miles out of Hillsboro he asked a passenger to hold the reins while he got out to see what was wrong with one of the horses. Taking the money with him, he skillfully removed some hay from the horse's collar and inserted the money in the cavity. He then re-buckled the pad over the collar and drove on. Only a few miles farther a number of masked men stepped into the road, stopped the stage, and demanded the treasure. "You're a day too late," Holt said evenly. "The Madam took the money down yesterday." At Lake Valley an astonished railway agent watched Holt "milk" the horse collar and drop silver and currency into a tub placed on the ground to receive it.

Although the drive to Kingston through Percha Canyon was often made dangerous by Indians or highwaymen, it was a picturesque and popular one, especially on Sundays. One summer afternoon Mr. Loomis, a Kingston jeweler, his wife, and two children were driving briskly behind a span of mules in their light wagon, in which Loomis had rigged up an extra seat across the back end. On the homeward trip, just as the wagon reached the narrowest part of the canyon, the boy, who was beside his father, looked up and yelled, "Indians!" Loomis saw at the top of the cliffs several feathered and painted heads peering around rocks. As Mrs. Loomis screamed, he whipped up his mules and dashed for Kingston.

"Indians!" he shouted as his lathered animals galloped up the main street, where rows of dozing cow ponies were hitched in front of the saloons, "Indians in the canyon!" A posse of men was quickly formed. Just as they were ready to ride down the canyon, the boy asked his father, "But where's Ma and Sis?" In Loomis' mad dash for home the extra wagon seat had come loose and catapulted his wife and daughter into the road. The two were found unhurt but furious and were brought safely back. The men scattered through the cliffs to hunt the Indians, who turned out to be ten small boys from Hillsboro playing redskins in paint and feathers. That was the Loomises' last pleasure drive in the spring wagon!

Hillsboro still contains many old stone and adobe buildings with recent veneers, especially in the east end of the town and along the main street. On a hill above the trees is another street with a church, a school, several homes, the ruins of a large stone jail with barred windows, and the lower story of a still larger brick ruin with arched windows and doorway. A man was busy resetting some bricks when I walked by, and I asked him what it was.

"The old Sierra County Courthouse, Ma'am," he replied. "The last trial held here was in 1938. Now that the county seat's at Hot Springs we don't need this building, but it's a shame they tore it down. They'd ought to have kept it as a landmark. Here's the cornerstone, laid in 1893." I was delighted to see even the shell of the courthouse, for in it the trial of the Fountain murder, one of the most famous unsolved crimes in New Mexico, was held.

Judge Albert J. Fountain lived in Las Cruces and had to travel 150 miles to the sitting of the midwinter term of Court in Lincoln. In January, 1896, he made the trip, taking with him his nine-year-old son, Henry. During their first night's stop someone cut the halter rope, and the horses returned to Las Cruces. Nevertheless, the Judge got other horses and continued his journey. He was distinctly unpopular in Lincoln, where his fearless decisions had made many enemies among the cattle rustlers and their friends. During the session he secured indictments against a number of cattlemen, including William McNue, a cowhand, and Oliver Lee, the owner of several ranches. When court was over, on January 31, he and Henry started for home and stopped for the night at La Luz. While there the boy bought some candy and put the change, a nickel and a dime, back in his pocket. The next morning the Judge delayed his departure for a couple of hours, and when he did drive off he carried his gun across his knees. At Luna's Wells he stopped to ask if three men, who had been trailing him all day, had ridden by, and learned that three horsemen had been seen at a distance. Farther on he met the mailman, who, upon learning that the three unidentified riders still flanked the buckboard, urged him to return to La Luz; but the Judge impatiently drove on. Neither he nor Henry was ever seen again.

The following night the mailman stopped at the Fountain home to inquire if the Judge had arrived. His story of meeting the Judge on the road threw the household into commotion. Soon a posse was formed which rode through Organ Pass and up the valley towards Luna's Springs. Horse tracks, leading up an old road from Chalk Hill, brought them to the abandoned buckboard. Some distance farther a camp site was discovered, with the imprint of a child's shoe, a nickel and a dime, and grass that had been crushed flat by a heavy weight. More hoofprints led over rough country toward one of Lee's ranches, but they were soon lost in a welter of cattle tracks, which cut across and entirely obliterated the trail. Other posses, and even individuals, continued for some time to hunt for the bodies or clues of any kind. Feeling ran high in both Lincoln and Las Cruces as people took sides and advanced theories, plausible and fantastic, as to the fate of the Judge and his son. Many of Fountain's friends were positive that Lee was back of the disappearance, and they said so, loud and often. Then one day Lee sauntered into the Sheriff's office, saying he had heard the charges and here he was. The startled sheriff pressed no charges.

Two years later, however, a new sheriff issued warrants for the arrest of Oliver Lee, James Gilliland, and William McNue for the murder of Judge Fountain and his son. By this time factional feeling was so acute that the trial could not be held in the home county and was moved to Hillsboro in Sierra County. Sadie Orchard, who had given up her stage-driving and was running a hotel, sent up meals to the prisoners in the adobe jail. The trial lasted for three weeks in May, 1898, and during that time every restaurant and hotel was jammed and cowboys camped beside chuck wagons on the edge of town. In the course of the trial a piece of vital evidence was "lost"; so the crime of murder could not be proven against the suspects, and the verdict was "not guilty."

A still earlier courthouse, the first one in Hillsboro, is an adobe building on the main street now doing service as a garage. Mr. McCall, the proprietor, led me through his shop to the windowless adobe cell which once served as the jail.

KINGSTON

HILLSBORO is in a pocket between low hills, but Kingston, eight miles to the west, is on a mountainside, its buildings hidden in thickets of walnut, cedar, and pine trees and its foundations overgrown with mesquite and cactus. The excitement bred by the Hillsboro mines led to the discovery of silver farther west along North and Middle Percha creeks. Two parties of prospectors scoured the hills and accidentally met at the present site of Kingston in October, 1880. One party is said to have found the first silver on Thief Creek in November. Phillips and Elliott, prospectors with the other party, located the Empire and Iron King lodes, also in November, and cast lots as to which each should take. Phillips drew the Empire; Elliott, the Iron King, the mine from which Kingston is said to have gotten its name.

Other groups hurried to the hills but almost immediately scurried out again to escape the fury of Victorio and his band, who during the next year roved through the Black Range, killing scores of prospectors. In spite of this, enough men had filtered back into the Kingston area to establish a mining district there in the spring of 1881. Then, in 1882, Jack Sheddon discovered rich silver float at the head of North Percha Creek, three miles north of Kingston, in the Solitaire or Blackie mine. Almost immediately a trading post was opened at the new location and a townsite platted; it consisted of 300 lots, of which 120 were sold for from fifteen to forty dollars apiece. J. M. McCuiston, a merchant from Chloride, learning of the strike, packed his stock on burros and crossed the mountains carrying 300 cigars, five gallons of whiskey, six bottles of champagne, and eighteen bottles of beer. He was followed by A. D. Osborne, who opened the Ore Saloon, dealing in "wet groceries."

Percha City, as the camp was called, was soon connected with Hillsboro by a wagon road; although its population never exceeded 500, the camp flourished as long as the Solitaire continued to produce. A piece of its float, exhibited in Denver, resulted in press notices which boomed the entire district and caused Kingston to expand overnight.

Within a few weeks of the Solitaire discovery, Kingston, the camp on Middle Percha, had begun to grow. Its townsite was surveyed in October, 1882, and by the end of the year 1,800 miners and merchants had arrived there by the canyon trail from Hillsboro. Lots on Main Street were already selling for $500. It was a tent city at first, with plenty of saloons and dance halls and a tent lodginghouse with bunks three tiers high. The lower tiers cost more but were safer from the stray bullets that often ploughed through the canvas late at night, in the midst of drunken brawls and fights. At the first shot those in the top tiers would dive for the floor and lie there till morning.

During the first winter, which was exceptionally cold, a wagon road was

hacked through the pines from Hillsboro, and supplies were hauled in at exorbitant prices. That same winter smallpox did its best to wipe out the struggling new camp. Dr. Guthrie, the only physician, was drunk too much of the
time to do more than have a large tent pitched in a grove of juniper at the edge
of the settlement to serve as a pesthouse. As nurses he hired two old topers,
who craftily offered to care for the sick if given a daily jug of whisky. After
several patients had died and the women of the camp, who were cooking for
them, found that little food and less care were being given the invalids, the two
drunks were fired. Three women from the red-light district offered to replace
them, and under their care no more patients were lost.

Mine after mine was located—twenty-seven paying properties around Kings-
ton alone—and, as each was developed, long pack trains twisted over the trails.
Later, wagons heaped to the brim with high-grade ore creaked down to Lake
Valley and the railroad. Most of these were drawn by ten-mule teams and
accompanied by armed guards carrying double-barreled shotguns. The Iron
King was the most widely known property; but the Grey Eagle, Brush Heap,
Gypsy, Lady Franklin, Bullion, U. S., Cumberland, Calamity Jane, Keystone,
Superior, Comstock, Mountain Chief, Miner's Dream, Black Colt, Savage, and
Little Jimmie all helped to make of Kingston a unique mining camp, built for
permanency by men who believed the mines would be a steady source of income. Had silver not been demonetized in 1893, their predictions would have
been correct; as it was, the mines produced $7,000,000 in silver, and unknown
deposits were left unexplored after the companies shut down and families
moved away.

But in 1883 no one foresaw the "crime of '93." A handbill, widely distributed in the earlier year, read:

HO! FOR THE GOLD AND SILVER MINES
OF NEW MEXICO

Fortune hunters, capitalists, poor men,
Sickly folks, all whose hearts are bowed down;
And Ye who would live long, be rich, healthy,
and happy; Come to our sunny clime and see
For Yourselves.

In 1883 Charles E. Greene published a pamphlet called "The Mines of
Kingston, New Mexico," which contained the following paragraphs:

Its society is characteristic of the frontier, but contains a greater number of re-
fined and educated people than one would expect to find so far from the comforts
and conveniences to which they have been accustomed in eastern homes. . . . The

rough house is often furnished in far better style than its exterior betokens, and probably there is as much real enjoyment and family contentment amid such surroundings as in the brown stone or marble palaces of the great cities.

As to churches, this has not seemed to be a specially inviting field for missionaries. No church buildings have been erected, nor have any societies been organized. . . . Although it is by no means unpopular to take a drink of beer or whisky, and temperance societies would not secure a large membership in the camp, there is but little drinking to excess, and no more drunkenness on the streets than is usual elsewhere.

In the first excitement more prospectors tumbled into town than could find claims to work, and an excessive number of merchants jockeyed for footage on the main thoroughfare; crowds in the streets were said to be so great on pay nights that a person could progress only ninety feet in half an hour! But the excitement passed, the floating population left, and Kingston settled down to a steady, but far from drab, existence. It had everything a brash new town needed—a brewery which shipped beer all over the Southwest, a dancing school, a theatre in which Lillian Russell's troupe of entertainers twinkled before a noisy but appreciative audience, and a meat shop which sold beef, bear, venison, pork, wild turkey, antelope, and goat. Seven sawmills provided lumber for frame buildings, and a brick kiln and stone quarry produced materials for the better homes and business establishments.

Within five years the town had a population of 7,000, and its long, curving main street, which continued to grow down the canyon high above Middle Percha Creek, was edged with boardwalks and solid with brick and stone buildings, housing twenty-two saloons (some accounts say thirty-six!), fourteen groceries, and three hotels. Three newspapers supplied the reading public; a G.A.R. post and Masonic, Odd Fellows, and Knights of Pythias halls took care of lodge members. The Percha Bank, a stone building which is still standing, was the backbone of business. As soon as men brought their families to town, a schoolhouse was built. When someone noticed that, despite all its enterprise, Kingston had no church, hats were passed in the saloons and dance halls as well as in less colorful establishments; and with the $1,500 of nuggets, jewelry, and silver collected, a stone chapel with a belfry was constructed. The camp had no jail, only a snubbing post to which offenders were tied (and gagged if they were noisy) and held until removed by the proper authorities.

Kingston lore includes the tale of "Pretty Sam's" Casino, which had been under construction for months and whose opening on Christmas Eve was anticipated by the entire town. Sam sent invitations to all the bigwigs and planned all details of the blowout: everything was to be on the house! Since the gulch was narrow and the ground fell away on the "down" side of the street, only

Sam's front entrance was at street level; the rear of the building was supported on stilts, thirty feet above Percha Creek. A bridge across the creek from the back exit was not finished in time for the opening, and for safety Sam bolted the back doors and nailed down the rear windows.

The orchestra from El Paso was playing, all the girls from Shady Lane were present, and Big Annie, who ran the Orpheum, arrived with her bevy of beauties to dance with the miners. Suddenly a drunk pushed into the hall looking for his woman and began shooting out the lights. Big Annie led the stampede to the back exit, where her efforts and the pressure of those behind her burst open the doors and dropped her into the dry creek below. She was pulled out bruised and breathless.

On a flat a mile below the town was Toppy Johnson's slaughterhouse. Tall stories are told about Toppy—that he rustled the steers he butchered and was the leader of a gang of counterfeiters—but no one could hold him responsible for the unexpected outcome of a Fourth of July footrace between Green, the gamblers' contestant, and Crowley, the local favorite. Crowley left Green behind from the first and was close to the finish when a bear jumped out of the brush ahead of him. By the time he and the bear were disentangled, Green had crossed the tape. The bear was believed to have been nosing around the offal from the slaughterhouse until the noise of the race startled it and sent it bolting across the track.

As late as the spring of 1885, Geronimo and his band made raids on the Black Range camps. At Fort Bayard, near Silver City, Lieutenant John Pershing was perfecting the heliograph, flashing sunlight from mirrors to stations a hundred miles away, and the people in the mining camps learned enough code to read the signals. While Geronimo and his warriors were thought to be still in Mexico, signals flashed a warning that two bands of Indians were headed toward the hills. Men rode hurriedly to the mines and ranches to spread the warning and bring the women and children to towns or to the nearest fort. Tom Page, who was out cutting wood for the Kingston smelter (which by 1884 was running steadily on ore from the Iron King) did not get the warning. When he started to town with his loaded wagon, one of his mules, which was Indian-shy, kept looking to the south, and soon Page saw ten braves riding toward him. Jumping down from the wagon, he unhitched a mule and rode off toward Kingston surrounded by thudding bullets. Dashing into camp, he gave the alarm and started another man off to Hillsboro for reinforcements. No attack followed; but when Tom returned next day for his wagon, it was burned and the remaining mule was dead.

Warning of another raid sent people into the timber behind the town with food, blankets, and guns. All night they huddled in the trees, with no telltale campfire to reveal their hiding place. In the morning, scouts scoured the foothills but found no Indians. On their return to deserted Kingston, however, they discovered the doors of a saloon wide open and heard hearty snores issuing from inside. On the floor lay an old fellow, surrounded by empty bottles, who, when awakened, instead of looking sheepish, yelled at the group: "Cowards, all of ye! Run off, ye will, like sheep and leave me alone to defend the town!"

Kingston seemed absolutely deserted the February day we explored it. Many of its cabins, both old and new, are summer homes, and a big stone lodge caters to hunters and fishermen; but it was the old buildings for which I was looking, and the first one I saw was the Victorio Hotel. It does not look much as it did in 1882, when it was three stories high and its sturdy stone walls served as protection for the women and children during Indian raids; a recent owner has ripped off its two upper stories and boarded up its windows. Still, above its double doors, on a glass transom, is the name VICTORIO.

Farther up the street is the alarm bell, hung from sturdy posts and used today to announce the arrival of the mail. Across from it is the bank, now the post office. Scattered through the growth of Spanish bayonet, live oaks, junipers, and willows are other buildings—landmarks from the days when Sheba Hurst, whom Mark Twain immortalized in *Roughin' It,* made jokes on Kingston's streets; when Albert B. Fall worked in its silver mines; and when Edward L. Doheny staked out the Miner's Dream, one of the less successful prospects in the camp. After the miners left, the cattlemen came in to graze their herds on the hills.

SILVER CITY

UPON leaving Kingston the road turns sharply up the mountain, past the little cemetery tucked in among the trees, and climbs by long loops over the crest of the Black Range. After miles of mountains and stretches of canyon it emerges in farm country and rolls past Santa Rita, with its great open-pit copper mine, to Silver City, once a hell-raisin' mining camp and now the business and agricultural center of southwest New Mexico.

James and John Bullard reached the site of Silver City in the spring of 1868, after unsuccessfully searching for a lost mine along the Frisco River. After crossing the Burro Mountains, they began to search for outcroppings. Two miles west of the present city they uncovered silver float on a strip of land two miles long and half a mile wide. From this placer area, known as Chloride Flat, millions of dollars' worth of silver were taken from the grass roots. Chloride Flat today shows a few dumps and mounds of earth, but most of its workings have been obliterated by frequent floods.

The silver from Chloride Flat was hauled to the new town of Silver City, which by 1870 enveloped an older Spanish settlement known as San Vicente de Cienaga. All through the seventies and eighties and even into the nineties, freight outfits and pack trains filled its streets, and twelve-horse teams delivered loads of gold and silver bullion to the express offices. The numbered bricks were piled in stacks on the sidewalks, where they might remain a day and a night in perfect safety, for early attempts at robbery had been discouraged by sure, swift hangings. Gamblers, miners, and merchants crowded into pretentious bars—the Red Onion, the Blue Goose, and others—which ran three shifts of bartenders to cope with the constant trade.

From its founding until 1885, Silver City was always menaced by Apaches. John Bullard, who had discovered silver in the area, became tired of these constant raids and organized a company of citizens to drive the Indians out of the vicinity. He and his men succeeded in chasing them across the Arizona border, but the Indians counterattacked and Bullard was killed. All roads were unsafe for travel, and the soldiers from Fort Bayard, near Silver City, were constantly called upon to protect the whites or to avenge some act of violence.

In 1883 Geronimo sent a few warriors from Sonora, Mexico, across the border to the San Carlos reservation, to induce the rest of the tribe to join him. The Indians split into three bands and started south, killing any whites they met.

Among many others, they attacked and killed Judge McComas and his wife, of Silver City, as they and their six-year-old son Charlie were driving through the Burro Mountains toward Lordsburg. The Indians carried the boy away with them, and rumors persisted for some time that he had been seen south of the border. In 1938 an archaeological expedition in Mexico discovered a tribe of Indians, thought to be a part of Geronimo's band that had escaped at the time of his capture. Their chief had red hair and blue eyes. Was he Charlie McComas?

In 1885, Geronimo and his warriors were finally captured and removed from the region, and the citizens of Silver City and the entire area drew a breath of relief. But Silver City's troubles were not over. As early as 1868, when the Bullard brothers had camped on the site of the present city, flood debris could be seen caught in trees along San Vicente Creek, twenty feet above the ground. This fact was pointed out to those who laid out the present city, and it was suggested that a location farther from the canyon would be safer; but no attention was paid to the idea, and the town grew up beside the stream. Small spring floods were an almost annual nuisance. They were not serious, however, and everyone was too engrossed in business to notice that overgrazed hills and rapidly depleted forests were reducing the natural watershed.

Main Street had grown to be a solid line of one- and two-story business blocks when the big flood hit it on the night of July 21, 1895. About midnight a second wave, twelve feet high, rushed down the gorge upon the already tottering buildings and swept everything before it. Even after this disaster, people did nothing to prevent a recurrence. The flood of 1903 was so severe that a piano from a second-story room was found, days afterwards, seven miles downstream. Finally, the creek carved a channel for itself, fifteen feet deep, in what had been Main Street. North Bullard Street is now the chief thoroughfare, and San Vicente Creek is known as the Big Ditch.

We found the Ditch and the oldest house, which stands on the brink of the deep arroyo and from which the piano plummeted into the boiling floodwaters, and we saw the old Southern Hotel, with its second-story balcony surrounding the building; but most of the landmarks have disappeared or are crowded in between new buildings.

MOGOLLON (PRONOUNCED MUGGY-ÓWN)

FROM the time I first planned to visit New Mexico's old mining towns, everyone to whom I talked said, "Don't miss Mogollon. It's a real ghost town, the best one you'll find." Eighty miles from Silver City the forgotten camp hides in the bottom of an almost inaccessible canyon.

Four miles beyond Glenwood, a small resort town in a cottonwood grove, we left the highway and turned right on a narrow mountain road which climbed a steep hill until we could look out over the entire valley. Below was Alma, the small farming center in which Torribeo, Victorio's son-in-law, was lured into ambush and killed by irate settlers. His death resulted in years of warfare and terrorism for the entire area over which Victorio and his braves roamed.

At the top of the hill the road twisted through a forest, always on the edge of the slope and affording frequent glimpses through the trees to the next ridge. There, on a level with us but separated by a deep valley, perched a mine with many buildings and a huge dump. Far below the mine, in a gap in the hills, was a schoolhouse. It was our first glimpse of Mogollon! The descent was much sharper than the ascent and the country wilder and more densely wooded. All the way to the foot of the hill were the remains of mining operations: mill foundations, tunnel openings, and broken machinery. The road was just wide enough for one car and had no turnouts that I can recall. At the bottom of the canyon, with its high, rocky walls and dense vegetation, was Silver Creek. Still no sign of a town; but then a sharp turn and—Mogollon!

Its buildings were wedged in on either side of one long, twisting street, beside which ran the nearly dry creek bed several feet below the road level. Two large stone buildings—"Holland's Furniture and Notions" and "J. P. Holland, General Store"—stood facing each other, like gates, at the lower end of the canyon. Beyond them were ruined adobe and frame buildings, vacant lots where buildings had stood, their foundations barely showing through the underbrush, and frame houses supported on stilts and reached by steep flights of steps or bridges over the creek. Farther up the street another store with a second-story wrought-iron balcony stood behind empty gasoline pumps. On the hillside was a church, and above it the school we had seen from the top of the hill. Near the church a road broke from the main street and disappeared around a shoulder of the mountain. It led to the big mine we had seen across the canyon, and it was lined with mills and miners' shacks. By climbing up behind the church and peering through a crack in its boarded-up windows, I could see a white-and-gold altar; the rest of the building was empty. Patches of wooden sidewalks remained here and there; more cabins and rooming houses, their porches and balconies overgrown with vines, bordered the creek as far as we could see. Except for a few steers grazing on one of the upper streets, there was no sign of life. On the way back to the car we met one of the two families still living in the deserted place. Mr. and Mrs. Johnson came out of their house and talked to us.

To one of my questions Mr. Johnson replied, "Gosh no, Mogollon wasn't the first camp around here. Clairmont over on Copper Creek was, and the second camp was Cooney on Mineral Creek. Mogollon, here on Silver Creek, wasn't laid out until 1889. The camps ain't far apart, but there's lots of high mountain between; so you've got to go a long way round to get to them. Mogollon's a name that belonged to the mountains long before this camp cropped up." Mr. Johnson knew the history of Mogollon from beginning to end, and what an exciting story it was!

In 1712, the Spanish crown appointed Don Juan I. Flores Mogollón Governor and Captain-General of a vast area which included present New Mexico and extended west to the Pacific coast. The mountain range, described by the Jesuit Fathers in the seventeenth century as rugged and inaccessible, was named in his honor. With the exception of occasional foolhardy trappers or prospectors, only Indians were familiar with its bare cliffs, dense forests, deep canyons, and wild life.

In the late 1860's, small companies of cavalry from U. S. Army posts began to explore the rugged terrain of the Mogollon Mountains. In 1870, Sergeant James C. Cooney, who was stationed at Fort Bayard, commanded a detachment which mapped trails and waterholes in the area. On this scouting trip he found rich ledges of gold-bearing ore on Mineral Creek; but he kept the discovery a secret until his term of enlistment was over. A month after his discharge in 1876, Cooney, with Harry McAllister and other prospectors, returned to the area. Despite Indian raids, they made several locations. As hostility increased, they abandoned their diggings and returned to Silver City. In 1878 Cooney, William Chick, and several other men set out again for the rich bars, taking with them two ox-drawn wagons full of equipment and supplies. They relocated their claims, laid out the first settlement in the Mogollons at Clairmont on Copper Creek, and organized a mining district. In spite of Indian raids, miners continued to explore the ledges of Silver Bar all during 1878 and 1879 and to prospect deeper into Cooney Canyon and along Mineral Creek. The first shipment of gold from the Mogollons came from the Cooney mine and was sent to Silver City in 1879 for treatment; it netted $200 per ton.

Simultaneously with the Cooney expedition, Jim Keller, Maurice Coates, John Roberts, and other ranchers entered the Frisco Valley with their families and settled where Alma is now. Both settlements built stockades for defense against Indian attack and, except for minor brushes, no serious trouble developed until 1879.

In May of that year five Apaches fired on some men who were plowing and clearing a field at Alma. Two of the men went to warn the occupants of outlying ranches; the others trailed the Indians to the site of Glenwood, where, staking out a horse in a field as a decoy, they hid and waited for the Indians to return. In a short time the Apaches were seen approaching the horse on foot. The settlers fired, wounding or killing three of the savages. One of the Indians killed was Torribeo, Victorio's son-in-law.

To avenge this killing, Victorio went on the warpath. Late in April, 1880, he attacked the Cooney mine, killed two of its men, and burned the miners' cabins. Fearing that he would attack Alma next, James Cooney and William Chick set out to warn the settlers in the valley, and during the ensuing fight both men were shot and scalped. Cooney Canyon is named for James Cooney, and his body is buried in a rock tomb near its entrance.

As soon as Captain Michael Cooney heard the news of his brother's death, he resigned as Customs Inspector at New Orleans, reached New Mexico during the summer of 1880, and went at once to Silver Bar (or Cooney) in the Mogollon Mountains to take over his brother's mining interests. A letter from James Cooney, written not long before his death, had mentioned the Silver Bar mine as having $150,000 of ore in sight and enough copper available to pay all running expenses of the property. As a keen businessman, Michael Cooney was eager to explore it. During the next ten years he and his associates developed the mines of the district, built the first mill, and opened new lodes on Mineral and Silver Creeks. Cooney held controlling interests in all his properties until 1896, when he sold his holdings to a Colorado company.

In the spring of 1883, a man named Turner asked Cooney for a grubstake in order to go prospecting in the district. Cooney staked him and never saw him again. The following year Cooney by chance met Turner's uncle, and learned that the older man had come west at the request of his nephew to share in a mine the latter had discovered on Sycamore Creek in the Mogollons.

The uncle had sold his business in the East and arrived in Silver City to meet his nephew, who never appeared.

In 1889 a skeleton, believed to be Turner's, was found by cowboys in Sycamore Canyon. The empty cartridge shells surrounding it indicated that the victim had been attacked by Indians and had put up a fight for survival. With the discovery of the skeleton, Captain Cooney determined to find the lost mine. He and a group of men made one attempt in 1889, but all they found were blazed trees. The Captain and his son Charles made a second fruitless search; but each disappointment added to Cooney's determination to locate the mine which was rightfully his. In the fall of 1914, he arranged for another trip, although his wife and son tried to prevent his going to the mountains so late in the season. He left his home in Socorro on October 26, 1914, with two horses and a wagon. On the thirtieth he camped at a ranch, where he left the wagon. Packing supplies on his horses, he started into the mountains. When he did not return on Thanksgiving, as he had promised, a search party was organized, but deep snow and new storms drove it back. His body was not found until February 14, 1915. With it was the diary which he always kept on mountain trips. He had encountered much rain and cold and toward the last was feeling "poorly," owing to exposure. The entry of November 12 concluded: "Two of the worst nights, matches all wet; can have no fire." The final entry, written on November 15, read: "It let in a little sun and feels better." His body lay only 100 yards from the spot where Turner's skeleton had been discovered.

When a road was built through Cooney Canyon in 1882, the miners drifted away from Clairmont, on Copper Creek, and settled on Mineral Creek near the working mines, calling their new location Cooney Camp. All through the eighties the tent and log settlement, with its general store, post office, and one saloon, was the center of mining operations in the Mogollons. The saloon keepers, Penny and Shelton, had no competition and developed a bad reputation by charging exorbitant prices for their tangle-foot and bug-juice, and then beating up their customers and kicking them out.

By 1889, just as mining activity in Mineral Creek was slowing down, mines in the next gulch began to attract attention, and within the year a new camp, called Mogollon, sprouted in the bottom of Silver Creek Canyon. The first mines developed were the Maud S. and the Deep Down; the steadiest producers were the Little Fannie and the Last Chance. As these and other properties were located and worked, a succession of companies hauled heavy machinery over terrific grades to the mines and brought water and electricity to the many mills whose foundations were blasted into the canyon walls.

The big mine on the hill is the Little Fannie, from which immense amounts of both high-grade and low-grade ore have been shipped. Its huge tailings

SILVER CREEK
FLANKS
MAIN STREET,
MOGOLLON

CATHOLIC CHURCH, MOGOLLON

dump slid into Silver Creek in August, 1914, after torrents of rain had saturated it and weakened its retaining timbers. As it descended, it sheared off timber over a half-mile swathe, turned the Maud S. mill into kindling wood, and
buried its sleeping watchman in silt. The slide dammed the narrow gorge of
Silver Creek and threatened to flood the lower portion of Mogollon. Crews
of men dug tons of sand in a futile effort to cut a channel through the packed
debris and to recover the watchman. Two days later, a cloudburst sent so
much additional water raging down Silver Creek that it cut its way through
the tailings and allowed the pent-up stream to escape.

The Last Chance was located in 1889 by John Eberle in his prospectings
on the South Fork of Silver Creek. In 1899 it came into the possession of
Ernest Craig, an English mining engineer. Craig was convinced that the mine
could be made highly productive, and for years he experimented with different
methods of ore treatment, losing two fortunes in the process. His third attempt
was successful and brought him a fortune; whereupon he returned to England
and in 1910 became a member of the British House of Commons.

Since 1889 the Last Chance, the Little Fannie, and such mines as the
Confidence, Champion, McKinley, Little Charley, Pacific, Crescent, and Deadwood have produced gold, silver, and copper in excess of $15,000,000; but,
as in many mining districts, rising costs and diminished returns have caused
the mills to close. In 1950 the Little Fannie was still being worked by lessees,
but, so far as I know, the other properties were idle.

John Eberle, the discoverer of the Last Chance, built the first cabin in
Mogollon. A few weeks later, Harry Hermann, pioneer lumberman of the
Cooney District, moved his sawmill from Mineral Creek to the new camp. For
five years its whine was constant, as the demand for lumber to build the growing town exceeded the supply. Cabins, tents, and stores straggled up Silver
Creek, close to the water or crowded against the hills on either side of it. A
frame school was built, and in 1892 a post office was opened. The tinder-dry
camp was licked by flames in 1894, and even the forest was threatened by
sparks. The town was rebuilt with adobe and stone, which saved portions of
it from destruction in the fires of 1904 and 1915. The concrete schoolhouse
on the hill was built after the last blaze, and the citizens boasted that it cost
$15,000 and included equipment for courses in manual training, drawing, and
music.

When the Fannie mill was built in 1909, the population rose to 2,000. By
1911, when fourteen saloons, seven restaurants, five stores, and two hotels
were open, it was even larger. Perhaps its isolated location made Mogollon
wilder than other camps; whatever the cause, at first gamblers and gunmen
made the laws and enforced them. The stage from Silver City had just arrived
one afternoon and delivered a sizable mine payroll to the Mogollon Mercantile
Company to be placed in its vault, when two Mexican laborers held up the

manager of the place and demanded the $14,000 which the strongbox contained. As he tried to push them out, both he and his clerk were killed. The terrified bookkeeper then pointed to the box, and the men helped themselves and left. A posse followed hot on their trail and overtook them. One was killed and the other captured.

Mogollon in those days was not a healthy place for the police; and when four of them arrived at the Governor's orders to arrest a deputy sheriff who was known to favor the toughs of the town, they found themselves looking into the barrel of the sheriff's gun. Their quick shooting wounded him, however, and when they left the saloon where he lay, the street was strangely quiet. Not until they noticed rifle barrels behind several windows did they hurry to leave town. But in 1914, when Mogollon was incorporated and a Mayor and councilmen elected, law and order had been established. Speaking of the election, the "Sixth Annual Edition, Mogollon Mines" comments that:

The new Mayor and Town Council are broad guaged liberal men and will stand for the best interests of the town and townspeople. . . . There is not a more peaceful quiet town within the limits of the United States than Mogollon. Disorder will not be tolerated and the offender, be he American, Mexican, Italian, Indian or Negro is promptly arrested, tried and fined or imprisoned.

The same publication urged the formation of a Humane Society:

There is room and there's an absolute necessity for the establishment of a Humane Society for the Prevention of Cruelty to Animals in Mogollon. Scarcely a day passes but what a cruel and heartless driver abuses his animals, whether in a team or as a burro heavily laden with wood, both are subjected to knock-out blows with cordwood or loaded whips. It is not uncommon to see an animal devoid of one eye, and frequently this in a bleeding condition, and the poor suffering brute has no way to relieve itself of the constant annoyance of myriads of flies. . . . Two or three arrests will check and teach the heartless drivers that they will be held responsible for their actions.

By 1915, when the camp's monthly payroll was between $50,000 and $75,000, gold and silver bullion was shipped regularly to Silver City by stage or in eight-team freight wagons. The Silver City and Mogollon Stage Line ran a daily service between the towns, leaving Silver City at 5:00 A.M. and arriving at Mogollon at 7:30 P.M., leaving the canyon town again at 1:00 A.M. to arrive in Silver City at 3:30 P.M., "in time for outgoing trains."

It was late afternoon and long shadows were creeping up the canyon walls when we left the Johnsons and their fascinating stories about the once teeming town. If you really want to see an exciting ghost town go to Mogollon, and if you're a good hiker, go to Cooney, too.

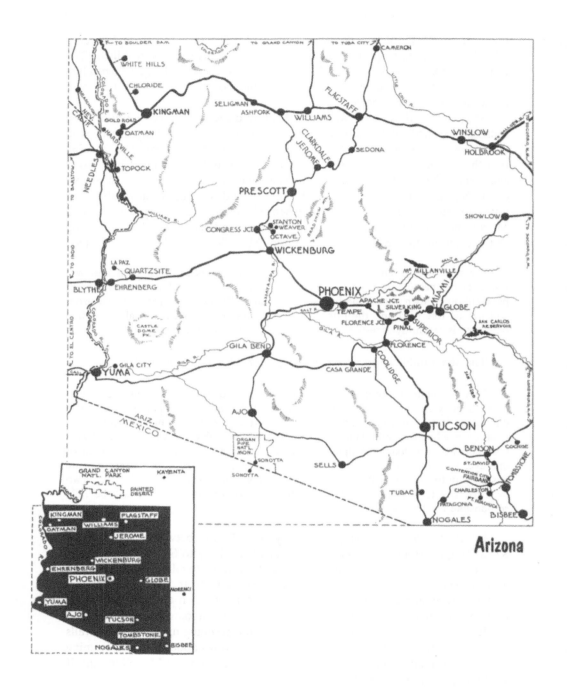

Arizona

2. *Desert Mines in Cactus Hills*

Arizona

To visit the mining areas of Arizona means to cover all but the northeast corner of the state, where the Navajo and Hopi Indians live in a magnificent land of eroded cliffs and flaming sunsets. Arizona's mountains are full of minerals, and copper mining is one of its chief industries today. But the copper mines were not developed until the 1880's, while gold and silver had been pried from the earth since early Spanish and Indian times. The camps are so widely scattered that no single itinerary can include all of them without a tremendous amount of backtracking.

TUBAC

Tourists driving between Tucson and Nogales pass three historic sites —the chalk-white mission buildings of San Xavier del Bac to the west, the ruins of Tumacacori mission close to the road, and the sleepy little town of Tubac a scant mile east of the highway. The two missions, one ruined and one active, attract many visitors, but Spanish-speaking Tubac dozes in the hot sun and gives no indication of its age or its important past.

During the twenty-four years that Father Eusebio Francisco Kino was building a chain of missions north of the state of Sonora, Mexico, the tiny settlements were entirely without military protection from marauding and hostile Indians. Father Kino died in 1711, and during the next forty years, although the missions he established were maintained, the Pima and Papago Indians in whose country they stood chafed under the restrictions and demands made by the padres. In 1751 they rebelled and drove the priests back into southern Sonora or killed them before they could escape. The following year a presidio, or garrison, was established north of Tumacacori at Tubac, and in 1753 a new group of priests took up the work left unfinished by their predecessors in the several missions.

Tubac, with its watchtower and mission church of St. Gertrude, was the most northerly fort until 1776, when a presidio was established at Tucson. Both towns were garrisoned in 1854, at the time of the Gadsden Purchase, whereby the United States acquired 20,000,000 acres of land from Mexico. Tubac immediately became the center of the newly acquired territory, largely because exaggerated accounts of its silver mines caused Eastern corporations to send engineers to the desert outpost to investigate the mines and open new properties.

When Charles D. Poston and Hermann Ehrenberg reached Tubac shortly after the signing of the treaty, they found that the Mexican garrison had abandoned it. They therefore took possession and used it as headquarters while they prospected the surrounding country for gold and silver. Their explorations took them as far west as Ajo, where they discovered the copper deposits that have since been developed on such a gigantic scale. Convinced that the entire area was rich in minerals, Poston, who was a promoter at heart, launched a mining boom which brought men, backed by capital, to the dilapidated buildings of the dozing Spanish village. With his help Tubac was rebuilt, until by 1859, when the first issue of the *Weekly Arizonan* appeared on its streets, it contained 1,000 persons, five-sixths of whom were Mexicans.

Several large companies were represented in the mining boom—the Santa Rita Mining Company in the mountains east of Tubac, with H. C. Grosvenor in charge of development and Raphael Pumpelly as geologist; the Sopori Land and Mining Company, in which Sylvester Mowry was a shareholder; the Aztec mines, which Professor Rickard, an Englishman, operated; and several properties west of Tubac in the Cerro Colorado Mountains, owned by Hermann Ehrenberg, Samuel P. Heintzelman, and Poston. Engineers and prospectors were now making new trails into the mountains in their search for gold and silver. Since the Apaches were very troublesome, Fort Buchanan was established thirty-two miles east of Tubac, to give added protection to the whites.

As the mines began to yield, merchants from Hermosillo and Guaymas, Mexico, drove pack trains up the long valley, loaded with the necessities and luxuries demanded by the expanding community. Papago Indians settled on the fringes of the town and found work in the *tiendas* and mines. Before long, sinuous processions of mules loaded with sacks of ore began to wind through the desert and across mountain ranges to distant Kansas City, the nearest railroad. And then, just as the mining boom was well under way, came news of the Civil War. No sooner had the soldiers left Fort Buchanan and the other garrisons than the Apaches increased their attacks upon the hated white intruders. Ranchers moved to Tubac to escape being massacred, and just in time, too; for the Indians raided the valley and besieged Tubac for three days, retreating only when reinforcements from Tucson came to the town's rescue.

Mine after mine was attacked, and drivers of ore and supply wagons were murdered. Only the toughest men stayed at the lonely workings and attempted to keep them running in the face of threatening Apaches and sullen Mexican laborers who were as anxious as the Indians to rid the country of these unwanted strangers. Pumpelly and Poston stayed for a while, but in 1861 even they fled to California.

Toward the close of the Civil War, when Poston returned to Tubac and resumed his mining, he was accompanied by J. Ross Browne, the correspondent for *Harper's Magazine,* who visited all the boom camps and wrote colorful accounts of what he saw.

What they found is summed up by Browne as "mines without miners, forts without soldiers . . . all without means." Even the plaza was deep in weeds and surrounded by crumbling buildings. During their absence mining machinery and valuable equipment had been destroyed by Apaches, or by Sonorans who had looted the abandoned properties. All the other camps—Patagonia, Calabasas, and Arivaca—had fared the same. In time the mines were reopened and mining resumed, but the threat of Indian ravages continued. On March 30, 1872, the *Weekly Arizona Miner* commented:

> The Patagonia and other mines paid well and will do so again but not until the Apaches and other bad Mexicans cease to be the evil power they are and have been in this unfortunate Territory.

YUMA

IN THE extreme southwest corner of Arizona is Yuma, whose site on the Colorado River was first visited in 1540 by Hernando de Alarcon, a Spaniard who ascended the river from its mouth 150 miles below. Padre Kino crossed the muddy waters several times while searching for a way to California; he even established a mission, which was destroyed in 1697 by the Apaches. Years later Father Garcés established another mission on the west bank of the river. He was rejoicing at his progress with the hostile Yumas when a party of soldiers and colonists settled on Indian land without permission. To make matters worse, in 1781 a detachment of soldiers pastured their horses on planted fields, destroying the food supply of the Indians. In retaliation the outraged Yumas attacked while everyone was at Mass, killed the men, and clubbed Father Garcés to death.

In 1849 California-bound emigrants reached the banks of the Colorado River in ever-increasing numbers; during 1850-51 an estimated 60,000 persons crossed it on their way to the gold fields. Some left the desert at that point and continued by steamer down the Colorado and around the Isthmus of Southern California to San Francisco, but the greater number crossed laboriously on the ferry operated by the Indians, and continued across the desert wastes. A garrison was placed at the junction of the Colorado and Gila rivers early in 1850 to protect travelers; but the Indians not only continued to kill emigrants but also attacked the fort so persistently as to cause its abandonment. Two years later the post, manned by six companies of soldiers, was re-established on high ground overlooking the river. In 1853, with the fort as protection, the village of Colorado City was laid out below it. The settlement was first renamed Arizona City and finally Yuma. It was never a mining town, but through it passed all the southern emigrant trains, and past it sailed the river traffic to the camps of La Paz, Ehrenberg, Hardyville, and Gila City. When it was made county seat in 1870, supplanting La Paz, the records and other official paraphernalia were moved downstream on the steamer *Nina Tilden*.

GILA CITY AND LA PAZ

THE first placer gold rush in Arizona occurred in 1858, when rich sands were found on the banks of the Gila River just east of its junction with the Colorado. Gila City mushroomed at the site, and crumpled in 1864, when the placers became washed out. Its 1,200 miners then moved up the Colorado River to La Paz, where gold had been discovered in 1862 by the famous trapper and scout, Pauline Weaver.

Pauline, Paulino, or Powell Weaver—the name appears in all three forms but most often as Pauline—whose gravestone on the old capitol grounds in Prescott reads, "Pioneer, Prospector, Scout, Guide, Free Trapper, Fur Trader, Empire Builder, Patriot," was born in 1800 in Tennessee. The son of a pioneer father and a Cherokee mother, he went west as a young man and joined the Mountain Men, spending years in trapping and trading pelts. It was 1831 before he reached the area of Arizona as an agent of the Hudson's Bay Company. In 1847, during the Mexican War, he guided the Mormon Battalion from the headwaters of the Gila River across the deserts into California. For the next few years he lived on a ranch in California, but in 1853 he disposed of his property and began prospecting in Arizona, then a part of the Territory of New Mexico. His discovery of placer gold on the Colorado River precipitated the rush to La Paz.

In the camp which emerged overnight everything was confusion and excitement. Packing boxes served for furniture and for coffins, card games were played with nuggets as stakes, and drinking water was hauled in from distant springs and sold for two dollars a gallon. Dry diggings away from the river were supplied with water carried in rawhide bags by pack animals. During the seven years that La Paz flourished, both as a gold center and as a river port, $8,000,000 was washed from its sands and many large "chispas," or nuggets, were found in the bateas with which the miners washed the gravels.

From 1852 until the completion of the Southern Pacific railroad in 1878, clipper ships and steamships brought cargoes to Puerto Isabel at the mouth of the Colorado River. There light steamers reloaded the freight and started upstream to Yuma, Ehrenberg, La Paz, and Hardyville, at the head of navigation, 337 miles from the Gulf of California. Since murderous attacks by Indians made overland shipment of gold and silver to the East a hazardous procedure, ore was shipped down the river to Mexico instead. Early in the Civil War the government realized that it was sending coin out of the country, and to rectify this leak it sent troops to La Paz and the other mining camps to protect freight shipments east through Indian-infested territory. When the new settlements of Prescott, Wickenburg, and Congress Junction sprouted in the Hassayampa Valley, La Paz became a supply base to which river boats brought cargoes and from which freighters hauled the produce to these inland settlements.

Then, during a spring rise in 1870, the river cut a new channel and left La Paz a mile inland. It was ruined as a port, and, since the placers were about worked out, La Paz began to fade. Ehrenberg, six miles downstream, became the new distributing center.

EHRENBERG

This river town, called Mineral City when it was founded in 1863, was later named for Hermann Ehrenberg, who had prospected in the vicinity in 1856. It was set back from the water's edge in a grove of willows. Like most new settlements, it started as a group of adobes surrounded by a stockade, but by 1872 it had grown to such an extent that it contained the River View Hotel, a bank, a stage office, an excellent steamboat and ferry landing, and several merchandise establishments. One of the latter offered to pay the highest prices for "Hides, Bullion or any other marketable article produced in the country."

Sandbars and low water often upset the steamer schedules. Although the round trip from Yuma to Hardyville was usually run in ten to twelve days, at low water it might take as much as two months. The arrival and departure of riverboats was always news:

Miller's train brought 218 sacks of Tiger ore for San Francisco which go down on the *Mohave*. Capt. Miller is expected tomorrow. [*Weekly Arizona Miner*, April 13, 1872.]

Gila City, La Paz, Ehrenberg, and Hardyville have long been deserted, and year by year their roofless adobe walls wash slowly away and sink into shapeless mounds. Mesquite and willows push up around the ruined enclosures that were homes and stores and corrals and hide them from sight. Lonely roads lead from the highway to each town, but little remains at the end of the trail.

QUARTZSITE

TWENTY miles east of Ehrenberg, on the highway to Wickenburg, is Quartzsite, an early stage stop and mining camp. Formerly called Tyson's Wells, it is known today chiefly as the place where Hi Jolly is buried. Tourists spin through the town and glance curiously at the silhouette of a camel balanced on top of a stone pyramid in the cemetery, but few know its significance.

Lieutenant Edward F. Beale's idea that camels would be useful in the southwest desert for transporting army supplies appealed to Secretary of War Jefferson Davis, who in 1855 persuaded Congress to appropriate $30,000 for the purchase of seventy-five animals. They were bought in Egypt and Smyrna; and natives, including one named Hadjii Ali, were hired to drive and care for them. The caravan landed in Texas in 1856 and, led by Lieutenant Beale, plodded across Arizona, plotting a military road to California. The camels might have been a success, as they could carry 600 pounds at a time and travel thirty miles a day. But the soldiers on the whole disliked them, and their strange appearance stampeded every animal they met. When the journey to California was completed, all the camel drivers but Hadjii Ali had quit. So the Army abandoned the camel project. Some of the mistreated beasts were turned loose in the desert; some were used to haul ore from the mines; some were shot or worked to death by cowboys and freighters; and a few were killed and sold for jerked meat to the men at the Gun Sight mine. The desert wanderers continued to startle prospectors for years, appearing unexpectedly over a hill or moving silently across a moonlit stretch of cactus-studded ground like silver ghosts. Hadjii Ali liked the desert and never returned to his home; instead, he started prospecting near Quartzsite, where he was known to everyone as Hi Jolly. When he died in 1902, he was buried in the cemetery; more recently the camel monument was placed over his grave.

WICKENBURG (THE VULTURE MINE)

HENRY WICKENBURG would be lost in the gay desert playground which bears his name today; for guest ranches and swank motels line the Hassayampa River, where his little adobe mill once stood. Wickenburg is a resort town, lively, attractive, full of new homes. From its cattle brands to the glistening stagecoach that rattles into town, filled with fresh young Eastern visitors in chaps and ten-gallon Stetsons, it is dripping with western ranch atmosphere. But in 1871 the "village" which grew up nearly a mile below the Vulture mill complained of "dullness," for "when the mill or mine stops the residents feel it particularly."

Heinrich Heintzel fled from Austria with the government after him, because he had innocently sold coal from a vein on his father's land instead of turning it over to the state. As soon as he reached America he changed his name to Henry Wickenburg and struck out for the West to begin prospecting in the Arizona desert. In 1862 he went to Yuma to look for gold, and then on to La Paz, where he expected to join a party bound for Peeples Valley and the Hassayampa River country; but the steamer up the Colorado was delayed by low water, and by the time he reached La Paz the party was gone. Determined to find them, he started alone across 200 miles of unfamiliar desert and miraculously reached Major Van Bibber's camp in Peeples Valley. The men prospected south along the Hassayampa, and after making an unsuccessful expedition west as far as the mountains, where Henry had heard of a vein of surface gold, they left the area.

In October, 1863, the group returned to the same locality and prospected for another two months, still with no success. Everyone was discouraged but Wickenburg, who started off one day with his burro toward a mountain west of the river. It was farther away than he thought, so he spread his blankets on the ground and rolled in early. The next morning his burro was gone, but he trailed it to the base of the peak he had seen. Late that afternoon he rode excitedly into camp, exclaiming that he had found gold and had posted a claim in the names of his five companions and himself. He named it the Vulture, for while he was tramping across the desert, one of the black scavenger birds had circled above the peak at whose foot the deposit lay. After ten weeks his companions lost faith in the find and left him. Wickenburg remained, however, and spent the winter taking out ore and packing it on the backs of two burros to the river twenty miles away.

Early the next summer Wickenburg and Charles Genung built an arrastre, or crude ore-mill, on the Hassayampa. On the Fourth of July, 1864, they crushed the first ton of Vulture ore. Wickenburg could not work his mine and his arrastre too; so he devised a plan whereby others should develop the mine and bring him the ore to crush, paying him at the rate of fifteen dollars a ton. As he was not aware of the quality of ore the Vulture was producing, his estimate was too low, and unscrupulous miners high-graded the best pockets and stole more than they paid him to grind.

In 1865 he sold his rights in the mine to the B. Phelps interests of New York for $85,000 and received a down payment of $20,000. The company immediately improved the property by piping water from the river, installing new machinery, and constructing a small settlement of native rock buildings for the workmen. A technical dispute soon arose between Wickenburg and the company, and Henry spent his $20,000 financing litigation to settle the issue. The company won and then refused to pay him the balance of the sales price. By 1872 it had taken out $1,850,000 in bullion and had forgotten all about the argumentative German who lived in an adobe house on the river.

The history of the mine is too complex to give in detail. The property has changed hands many times. The main vein has been lost and found again. One of the first companies used the "room and chamber" method of mining, leaving pillars of rock to support the excavated areas; the next company shot out the pillars, and the whole roof dropped in, creating a glory hole. The old stone buildings of Vulture town were torn down and run through the mill, and the walls averaged twenty dollars to the ton in gold. During some years the mine has been idle; at other times it has buzzed with activity. It is known to have produced $17,000,000, and no one attempts to estimate how much high-grade was carried off in lunch buckets.

During the 1880's, the mine superintendent and two guards were held up shortly after they started for Phoenix with a bar of gold bullion valued at $7,000. They were attacked and murdered not many miles from the mine by three Mexicans, Inocente Valenzuela, his brother Francisco, and a third man whose name is forgotten. At the Gila River, after trying unsuccessfully to hack the bar in half, the three separated. With a posse hot on their trail, there was nothing to do but bury the loot and make a dash for the border. Francisco crossed the line, and the third member of the gang turned state's evidence. When Inocente foolishly returned to the cache, he was followed and killed, and the bullion was recovered.

From the time he sold his mine and began the development of a 160-acre farm (covered today by the townsite of Wickenburg) until his death, Henry Wickenburg lived quietly in an adobe cabin near his mill on the Hassayampa River. As he grew older he became philosophic, spending long hours contemplating the changing colors of the desert and the cloud shadows that drifted across its brassy surface. Year by year he became more feeble, and his meager savings dwindled away. On July 4, 1905, his body was discovered in a mesquite thicket back of his house with a bullet hole in the temple. An old-style revolver lay by his side. Since he had no money and no enemies, it was thought to be a case of suicide.

I was anxious to visit the mine, even though I expected to find nothing but modern buildings on the property. The desert drive to the Vulture was invigorating in the crisp morning air, and the sun, as it rose above the strange black rock forms between which we wound, caught the clumps of cactus and yucca candles that grew beside the road and gilded them momentarily. The country was nearly level, and after driving some miles I could see ahead several hoists and tin-roofed sheds above the cactus and mesquite. The gate to the property was closed, and a sign said, "Positively No Admittance Without Caretaker." We knocked on the door of the lone cabin beside the gate, but no one appeared. We noticed that the door was padlocked. But surely no one could object to our looking at the glory hole and the few old buildings! Leaving the car outside the gate, we walked up the forbidden road to a sort of compound, around which adobe and stone buildings were grouped. I began to draw one especially picturesque shed while my chauffeur wandered off to see the Hangman's Tree. The screech of car brakes broke my spell, and a man leaned out of a truck and asked me what I thought I was doing. I explained. "Didn't you see the sign?" he asked gruffly. I admitted that I had but that the watchman was not around.

"You bet he isn't; he's gone fishing. But you read the rules, didn't you?" he continued. "Where's the other party? I saw a man with you."

"He just stepped around the building," I replied, sketching like mad to make the most of my remaining time. The motor raced and the truck disappeared, but only for a minute. When it returned, "the other party" was in it, and shortly afterward so was I. We were deposited at the gate, and the efficient deputy-Vulture watched us leave before he started back up the road.

RICH HILL DISTRICT (OCTAVE)

CONGRESS JUNCTION is north of Wickenburg. As it was once a supply point for a prosperous mining district, I stopped at the general store to inquire if any of the old camps still existed. The proprietor walked to the door with me and pointed north to the dump of the Congress mine, one of the oldest producers in the state, and east to a high mountain which he called Rich Hill. At its foot were three old camps, Stanton, Octave, and Weaver; and after he had shown us which road to take, we started toward them. We drove to Octave first and were surprised to find that every building had been razed. Nothing remained except stone foundations, cellar pits, two powder houses, a few fences, and skeleton door and window frames embedded in concrete.

Octave, laid out as a placer camp in 1863, was claimed by eight men. The

Octave mine, which was developed at a later date, was worked through two shafts 1,300 feet deep, and from its quartz veins $8,000,000 worth of gold was recovered. The mine was still working during World War II, but at the close of the war it shut down, and the buildings in the camp were razed to reduce taxes on the property. From the skeleton before us, it was hard to realize that its peak population had been 3,000.

WEAVER

AT WEAVER (or Weaverville), close to the east base of Rich Hill, little is left except ruined stone houses. Jumbled in a mass of mesquite and saguaro cacti are the broken rock walls of burro corrals and remnants of the town's Boot Hill cemetery. The camp was named for Pauline Weaver, who, with Major A. H. Peeples, Jack Swilling and other gold-seekers, left La Paz, after the discovery of gold there in 1862 and pushed east into central Arizona on another prospecting expedition, with Weaver acting as their guide. Although this area was new to him, his knowledge of the desert and his ability to negotiate with Apache Indians and speak many of their dialects made him a valuable scout. The party, after crossing long stretches of arid country, reached a range of mountains near which they shot some antelope. They named the stream on which they were prospecting Antelope Creek, and the mountain north of it Antelope Peak. A creek in the vicinity they called Weaver in honor of the veteran pioneer.

A Mexican who was with the Peeples party was crossing the mountain to Weaver Creek when he stumbled upon a deposit of coarse gold in a depression on the summit; from it he took a large quantity of gold nuggets. Peeples hurried to the spot and, according to one story, picked up $7,000 worth before breakfast! The mountain was named Rich Hill. After its surface gold was skimmed off, some of the men who had rushed to the strike stayed beside Weaver Creek to pan the gravel bars. The placers, which were rich in coarse gold, were soon being worked by about a hundred Americans and thirty Mexicans; and since the ground was extremely productive, each claim was limited to 200 feet square. The placers alone are said to have yielded $1,000,000; the gold-bearing veins on the mountain behind them poured out additional riches. By the 1890's the population at Weaver Camp was made up entirely of Mexicans, and the place developed an unsavory reputation as a hangout for desperadoes, who, it was said, divided their time between Weaver and the penitentiary. The town was so tough that law enforcement officers made no attempt to track down outlaws and criminals inside its limits. According to one story, the towns of Weaver and Prescott both bid for the Territorial capital, and Weaver lost the election because the men were too engrossed with the saloons and dance-hall girls to take time out for voting.

.By 1896 the camp was through. The surface of Rich Hill is still a network of mine trails to prospect holes, and old-timers will tell you they are still full of ore. But the rowdy camp of Weaver is only a memory.

STANTON

As THE ghosts of Octave and Weaver were almost invisible, we drove to Stanton up a narrow, sandy lane hemmed in by a high growth of mesquite and greasewood. The first buildings we spotted were old ones, made of adobe and brick, with generous, shaded porches. An eighth of a mile beyond them a group of remodeled frame houses with corrugated-tin roofs came into view. Behind them were a few weathered and dilapidated cabins and barns. On top of a low hill, in the middle of a lawn whose grass looked excessively green in contrast to the desert sage beyond it, stood a trim white house surrounded by fruit trees and flower beds.

Just as I was about to knock at the screen door, a woman, followed by a collie dog, came around the corner. She was Miss Sanborn, and when I told her of my interest in the old camps she informed me that she and her uncle, Mr. George Upton, owned Stanton and had lived there for a number of years. At her invitation, we joined her uncle on the porch and, as first one and then the other talked, we watched Stanton and the neighboring camps come alive before our eyes.

Stanton, like Octave and Weaver, started as a placer camp in 1863 and was originally called Antelope Station. In its thriving days, the district had a population of 2,000, and two other camps stood below it on the same trail. The main stage road ran through the town, past Wilson and Timmerman's store and the other adobe and brick buildings.

The town is named for Charles P. Stanton, a deputy county recorder with vicious ambitions, who lived near Wilson and Timmerman's place of business. He was greatly disliked in the district and was said to have been expelled from a monastery on charges of immorality, while studying for the priesthood. He was in league with the cutthroats over at Weaver and called upon them from time to time to assist him in carrying out his treacherous plans. Envious of Wilson's and Timmerman's success with their store, Stanton hired Mexicans to murder them, laying an elaborate scheme which would remove any suspicion from himself.

One day hogs broke into the cabin of William Partridge, one of the few white men in Antelope Station, and ate some of his provisions, whereupon

Timmerman sent Wilson to tell Partridge that he would replace the stolen grub. Stanton, however, sent a Mexican in his employ to warn Partridge that Wilson was out to get him. Partridge therefore got his gun and shot Wilson on sight. Stanton wrote Partridge's "confession" and kept referring to himself as Partridge's friend. As a result of Stanton's influence and craftiness Partridge was sent to the "pen." At this point in the story, Miss Sanborn disappeared into the house and returned with a cribbage board that Partridge had made while serving his sentence. A little later Stanton disposed of Timmerman and then changed the stage road to run by his place, cornered the trade that his victims had built up, and renamed the town Stanton.

Each time a murder occurred he was arrested but as it was always done by accomplices, no direct evidence was ever pinned on him. His most wholesale crime concerned the Martin family. Barney Martin, stage agent at Stanton, kept a red-brick store that we had seen upon entering town. Probably because he was honest, the toughs and Stanton hated him. During the summer of 1886 they told him to get out or he and his family would be the next victims. Martin sold his store, pocketed the cash it brought, loaded his family in a wagon, and drove away toward Phoenix. As he left, he sent word to Captain Calderwood, a friend of his, that he would soon arrive at the captain's home at Coldwater Station. After several days had gone by, Calderwood became concerned and started a search for the party. Not far from Hot Springs, wagon tracks led into the hills, and about a mile from the road the remains of the vehicle and the charred bodies of the entire family were discovered. When the Martins left Stanton they had been followed by some Mexicans, who forced their wagon off the road and killed them all. The murderers had then piled the bodies and plenty of brush in the wagon and set it on fire. The same Valenzuela gang that had killed the men from the Vulture mine was accused of the mass murder. Stanton, who by that time was believed to be the leader of the outlaws, was charged with complicity in the crime; but, as usual, no evidence was produced to convict him.

Later in the same year Stanton was shot by Lucero, the oldest son of a Mexican from Weaver, who headed a tough gang of desperadoes and was known as their "King." The murder was committed in Stanton's store to avenge an insult received by Lucero's sister. Stanton was sitting with his chair tipped back against the counter, when Lucero rode up and fired one shot through the open door. The same day Tom Pierson, coming to town over the mountain from the Crown King mine, met Lucero on the trail.

"I've just killed Stanton and I'm heading for the border," Lucero called as he passed.

"You don't have to pull out," said Pierson. "If you stick around, you'll get a reward."

OLD STORE BUILDINGS, STANTON

OLD STORE, WHITE HILLS

GOLD ROAD

TWENTY-FIVE miles southwest of Kingman an excellent highway crosses Sitgreaves Pass, climbing in long loops up the face of the dry, cactus-studded mountain and clinging to the bare rock walls on the western side of the divide. Just below the summit, caught between mountains on a barren, washed-out flat, lies Gold Road. The camp had burst into fame in 1902 and burnt itself out so completely that its buildings, like those at Octave, were razed in 1949 to save $38,000 in taxes on the dormant mine properties. The flat where the houses had stood was Mexican Town; the rest of the people had lived in homes all over the hills. Houses used to extend all the way to the top of the pass, and one house had 100 steps leading up to it.

When José Jeres asked Henry Lovin of Kingman for a grubstake, Lovin gave him one and saw no more of the man until, three months later, he returned with samples of gold ore. Lovin asked him where they came from, and Jeres described a vein that had already been sampled by scores of prospectors and was too lean to be worth developing.

"Forget about it and get out," said the busy Lovin, going back to his work; but the Mexican was insistent and urged Lovin to return with him and see for himself. To Lovin's annoyance, the man hung around for a week and continued to beg him to go look at the prospect. Finally, to get rid of him and avoid having to give him another grubstake, Lovin got a buckboard and rode out with Jeres. Where the old trail through the mountains crossed the well-known vein, they stopped by the ironwood tree to which Jeres, on his first trip, had tied his burro. While he was resting under its shade, he had chipped away with his pick at a rock and had knocked off its top layer, uncovering an outcrop—the top of an ore chute that had worked to the surface. Before leaving the spot, Jeres had set up a monument and staked the Gold Road claim.

Lovin, on seeing the prospect, became as excited as Jeres. Seizing a pick, he began to dig the required ten-foot hole. The vein was as strong at the bottom as at the top. Lovin was almost afraid to go deeper for fear he "would pick the eye out of it," but he dug to twenty feet and the vein still held. Taking a sackful of samples, he drove back to an assayer in Kingman and found that the ore contained forty ounces of gold to the ton. News of the discovery started a rush to the mountainside, and in the flush of the boom Lovin and Jeres sold the mine for $50,000 to a Los Angeles company.

According to the *Mohave County Miner:*

By one of those strange coincidences peculiar to mining, this lode [Gold Road] is within a thousand feet of the first road constructed in Mohave county, which

DESERT COUNTRY. APPROACH TO OATMAN

GOLDROAD, ARIZONA. RUINS OF "MEXICAN TOWN"

parallels it for two miles, hence the name of Gold Road. There was no excuse for the hundreds of experienced prospectors who have gone over this road not having discovered it, as the ledge did not hide its light under a bushel by any means. [Sept. 15, 1900.]

Besides the $25,000 which Lovin received as his share of the property, he obtained freighting and store concessions in the new camp of Gold Road and from these combined interests reaped a fortune. Jeres drank up his share of the mine and in 1906 committed suicide by taking Rough on Rats. The Nevada *Searchlight* of August 24 reported his death and added:

Whatever may have been the shortcomings of José Jeres the giving to the world of the great Gold Road mines wiped the slate clean.

Other mines were discovered close to the initial property, the Billy Bryan and the West Gold Road producing most heavily. In 1905 a gold bar worth $45,000, the result of a fifteen-day run in the company's mill, was shipped from the Gold Road mine; in 1906 the company declared its third dividend to the amount of $15,000; and in 1912 the bar of bullion from the regular weekly cleanup averaged $23,000.

Stores lined both sides of the main street in its prime. Several mine buildings with hoists rose out of the jumble of tents, adobes, and shacks which filled the townsite and crept up the sides of the surrounding mountains. The camp reached its peak in 1905, when, according to the December 16 issue of the *Mohave County Miner:*

The people of Gold Road have decided to celebrate Christmas with Christmas trees and to dance on a scale never before attempted in the county. The trees are to arrive in a few days and will be handsomely decorated. Every child in the camp will be remembered and the few older folk will presumably be in on the distribution of the good things.

The festivities concluded with a "free" ball for which the music was provided by Eller's Orchestra from Needles, said to be "one of the best . . . this side of Los Angeles."

As I looked out across the layers of ragged, paper-thin mountains to the west, I wondered how John Moss and his party, the pioneer prospectors in the district, ever found free gold among the myriad dry and forbidding hills. Yet in 1863, from a hole ten feet in diameter and ten feet deep, situated just four miles northwest of the Gold Road of forty years later, Moss took out $240,000 and then put it all back in developing the property. About the time the Moss mine was found, the Miller (also called the Parsons or Hardy) mine was also located. Its ores were treated in the seventies at the Moss Mill near the Colorado River. Then silver was discovered north of Kingman in the Cerbat Range, and the district around Gold Road was deserted until the sensational discovery of José Jeres.

OATMAN

A SHARP curve three miles southwest of Gold Road brought us to Oatman, a fair-sized town filling the bottom of a cup above which rise gaunt and jagged peaks. Oatman is a town of contrasts: a barren, taffy-colored tailings pond; rows of houses surrounded by flower beds and shaded by straggling palm trees; a main street filled with new and old stores; above and below it, side streets reached by trails and steps; above and behind the town, Elephant Tooth, a jagged white prong of rock silhouetted against the gray mass of the Black Range; and, in the far distance, Boundary Cone, a fantastic black pyramid silhouetted against hazy blue ridges of distant mountains.

One tiny white false-fronted store from which swung a sign—"Western Union, Barber Shop, Magazines, Justice of the Peace"—caught my eye, and I went inside to send a wire. In the middle of the small room, in the barber chair, a man was being shaved by the Justice himself. The Justice's wife is the storekeeper. She had me sit at a card table to write my message and then asked me to listen while she phoned it to Kingman, in order to be sure she got it straight. When she was through, she sat down beside me and answered my questions concerning Oatman and Gold Road.

She had lived in Oatman only six years, but her husband, Alfred Nelson, had been there thirteen. They were both busy all the time, she as a nurse and he as barber and Justice. Oatman wasn't what it had been when it had 8,000 inhabitants; last November there were only 111 registered voters! Two bad fires had destroyed many of the buildings and left holes and vacant lots along the main street.

The most imposing mine property in Oatman is the Tom Reed mill. Its breastwork of cyanide tanks stands silhouetted against the mountains, just below chalky Elephant Tooth. The mine, first called the Blue Ridge, was located in 1900 and passed through a series of ownerships. Shortly after its discovery it was sold at a sheriff's sale for $30,000. The two main shafts, the Ben Harrison and the Tom Reed, were sunk early in its history. Year after year, new ore bodies were uncovered and worked, although the amount of gold left in the tailings showed that substantial profits were being thrown away. Still, in 1912 the average monthly cleanup was $70,000, and in November of that year "five yellow bars," obtained from a single month's run and valued at $133,000, were taken to Kingman.

A mining man, George W. Long, succeeded in interesting a few men with capital in his theory that the ore body here followed a branch vein which ran north. He then formed the United Eastern Mining Company and obtained three claims adjoining the main property. Within three hundred feet of the surface the major vein was cut, revealing "stringers" that ran as high as $2,100 a ton. This discovery, made in February, 1915, started a gold rush which centered at Oatman. The *Mining and Engineering World* of January 1-June 24, 1916, gives a givid picture of the boom:

Where twelve months ago there was a sleepy little village supported almost entirely by the Tom Reed Mining Co., which employed 200 miners, and a few hardy prospectors. . . . today [stands] a booming town of 3500. As yet, this is a camp of no regrets. The time has been too short and the development too much in its infancy for it to have produced any losers. . . . Stocks that are selling up to $4 were purchased, in the main, at around ten to twenty-five cents. Real estate values have doubled and trebled since the boom started a year ago. . . . Where two stores found it difficult to make it pay last February, there are twenty today, all doing a thriving business. Hotels and lodging houses have had a mushroom growth and still accommodations are unequal to the demand. There are 36 auto stage lines running into camp daily, and the landscape is dotted with tents and shacks.

Here gasoline is king. All passenger travel is done by automobiles. Every so often a barker walks up and down the main street of Oatman calling through a megaphone "passengers for automobile stage to Needles" or "passengers for automobile stage to Kingman." All the freight but the heaviest is done by automobile trucks which carry 10,000 pounds each trip.

Only once in a while is a prospector seen going into the hills walking behind two or three packed burros.

If only part of the stories told prove true, Oatman will not only become the capital of an important local mining district . . . but . . . the main center of a mining area twenty times larger. This will be the result of the advent of the automobile which has made a hundred mile trip today easier than a trip twenty miles long was fifteen years ago.

Oatman is named for a pioneer family whose daughters were hidden by Indians at a spring just north of the present townsite. The Oatmans were part of a large emigrant train that reached Arizona in January, 1851, and then, because of disagreements, split in two. The Oatman wagon and seven others chose to follow the Cooke-Kearny route across the territory. Some of the party stopped at Tucson, but the Oatmans and several others went on, even though their animals were jaded and their provisions low. It was late February before they reached the Pima Indian villages, where reports of Apache trouble ahead made all but the Oatmans decide to remain until travel was safer. Royse Oatman was afraid to delay, because his two yoke of cows and one of oxen were already so weak and gaunt that they could not last much longer. Furthermore, a Dr. Lecount arrived from Yuma and reported no Apaches in sight. In sheer desperation, the weary family left the Pimas on March 11. They crept westward for seven long days before they were overtaken, south of Gila Bend, by Lecount and a Mexican, who were returning to Fort Yuma. Already the family and the animals were near starvation; Lecount, realizing their plight, agreed to hurry ahead and send back help from the Fort, which was still ninety miles away.

That night Apaches attacked Lecount and his guide and stole their horses. Before the men set out on foot, Lecount left a sign on a tree for the Oatmans, telling them what had happened and warning them to watch out for Indians. Although the Oatmans camped near the tree, they either missed the warning or Oatman destroyed it in order not to alarm the others. On May 18 the party camped on a sandbar in the Gila River; the next day the animals gave out. By lightening the load and pushing the wheels, they covered a few more miles. In the late afternoon the exhausted pioneers stopped at the edge of a steep bluff, unloaded the wagon again, and started to make camp for the night. Just at sundown a band of Apaches rode up and surrounded them. Oatman greeted them in Spanish and gave them tobacco and a small amount of bread. Nevertheless, they attacked the helpless group and killed all but a boy and two girls. The boy, left for dead, was later found by a rescue party. The girls were taken captive and carried off to the north. One died in captivity, but the other was released five years later and was reunited with her brother at Fort Yuma. Although a detail of troops from the Fort trailed the Indians in the hope of rescuing the girls, and once passed close to the spring where the Apaches had carefully hidden the captives, the soldiers failed to discover them.

WHITE HILLS

ABOUT fifty miles northwest of Kingman, White Hills, a small but most satisfactory ghost town, lies bleaching at the edge of the foothills of the Cerbat Range. For six years it flourished, and when its boom was over it died. White Hills had the ore, but it was also a promoter's dream, and the ruins of its main street with battered false fronts are therefore the more appalling.

We were looking so hard for a road sign that didn't exist that we passed the turnoff to the camp and had to stop at a filling station to get our bearings. When I asked the gas dealer's wife if she had any postcards of White Hills for sale, she replied, "No. People take their own pictures of that kind of place." We found the camp only five miles east of the highway, after following a road that cut straight across the desert.

The Indians knew of the mineral deposits near the Secret Mining District, from which they dug red iron oxide for face paint; but they carefully withheld the information from the white men who gophered the mountains so ruthlessly. Yet in 1892, Henry Shaffer, who was mining some twenty miles away, at Gold Basin, found the silver deposits in the White Hills through the help of an Indian: Hualpai Jeff showed him some pure silver ore and pointed out the source from which the tribe obtained red oxide. The location turned out to be the site of the Hidden Treasure mine.

Shaffer made several locations in the hills before returning to Gold Basin to report his discoveries to his friends, John Burnett and John Sullivan. The three went back to the hills, worked their separate mines, and were soon shipping out ore that averaged $1,000 a ton. As news of the discoveries spread, many lessees arrived at the diggings and made small fortunes from surface workings.

R. T. Root was the promoter of the district. He visited it, tested the ores, and determined to make the camp the center of a rich mineral district. His plans culminated in the formation of the White Hills Mining Company, of which he was president and for which D. H. Moffat, of Colorado, provided much of the working capital. Root lost no time in building the first mill and excavating the first deep shafts; by 1894 his company owned the town. During the few years in which White Hills "lived," its streets were honeycombed by twenty-seven miles of tunnels, its population rose to 1,500, and its many mines returned to their owners between $3,000,000 and $12,000,000. Supplies were hauled by freight wagons from Kingman or from the nearest boat landing on the Colorado River, and no expense was spared to make the town attractive and substantial.

In 1895 the White Hills Company was sold for $1,500,000 to an English concern, which immediately built a forty-stamp mill, installed an electric light plant for both town and mines, piped water from a spring seven miles away to a huge concrete reservoir, and placed pipes and iron hydrants along the streets to distribute the water. Coal for mine boilers was hauled from Kingman; fuel for steam hoists was provided by Joshua trees or yucca palms, which were cut and stacked beside the heads of shafts. The spring was never able to supply the community's needs, and water was still hauled in wagons and peddled on the streets. If water was scarce, however, liquor was not, as the twelve popular saloons on Main Street testified. A schoolhouse, a church, and a laundry were added to the town, most of whose buildings were situated in the southern portion of the district along White Hills Wash.

The fifteen mines were less than a mile from the center of town. The Prince Albert, a heavy producer, paid royalties amounting to $30,000 in an incredibly short time; the Hidden Treasure, the discovery property, continued to pay off; and such mines as the Grand Army of the Republic, the Occident, the Garfield, the Bryan, and the Grand Central were not far behind. But even with its mines producing, the English corporation was unable to make its final payment, and the property it had so lavishly developed was put up at sheriff's sale. Root and Moffat bought it back and began to boost it again. The *Mohave County Miner* for January 16, 1897, quotes a mining man, R. J. Patterson, as stating that "White Hills is destined to become one of the greatest camps in Arizona and possibly on the Pacific Coast." The *Miner* went him one better on February 6 by predicting that White Hills would be "the scene of the greatest excitement ever witnessed in a mining camp on the American continent."

The Arizona Stage Company provided daily mail and passenger service, and the W. H. Taggart Mercantile Company, as well as Gaddis & Perry, ran beer and ice wagons to the desert metropolis. More buildings were erected, the Independent Order of Good Templars organized a lodge with twenty-seven members, and Root announced that a railroad would soon reach the isolated paradise in which he so firmly believed. In 1898 the peak of production was reached. Thereafter the rich veins began to play out, and the "floating" population, seeing what was coming, hurried off. All through 1899 the plucky camp hid its disappointment by optimistic notices in the *Mohave County Miner:*

January 28: The cabins are filling up again. School is running smoothly with a full attendance. White Hills is a good place to come back to. You are welcome, returning prodigals.

February 4: The attendance at the White Hills free reading room is increasing. The big building is given rent free by the White Hills Company and an occasional subscription by the boys pays for fires, lights, stationery and periodicals. $14 was contributed in January.

February 18: As the warmer days come there arises here and there a drifting odor, not of new mown hay or opening flowers—for the smell of coal smoke from the big mill is incense compared to it—an odor of stables, dishwater, outbuildings and dead cats. In the palmy days of the camp . . . cats were at a premium and have been drawing compound interest ever since. . . . The camp has had its ups and downs but the cats have been entirely oblivious of these things, holding caucuses and conventions every spring, nominating Tom-a-row or Bob Scratch for mayor and contesting the election fiercely with long harangues and street parades, every cat with torch in each eye. . . . Finally game being scarce, a few of them were tried as targets. . . . Though they are pretty tough, sharpshooting and lots of ammunition sickens them, and as the funeral rites are neglected, they are neither gone nor forgotten. . . .

Moreover on a windy night big oil cans come galloping down the streets, booming like heavy guns, to the musketry of a swarm of smaller ones. Or a man crossing the street by day may be swooped down upon by a pair of discarded overalls which twine affectionately around his neck.

Early on the morning of August 5 a cloudburst in the hills "took the desert by surprise" and poured water down the town's streets.

A shanty in its path bade good-bye to the town and started for the valley and by 9 o'clock the whole town was in danger. . . . Water came tossing down like the rapids above Niagara, the waves seeming to run four or five feet high.

Luckily the water took a path to one side of the business section. . . . A cabin in which Mr. Shallenberger was sleeping was lifted and whirled end for end. After much floundering in the water he managed to pull ashore with his blankets. The foundation was washed from under the east side of the schoolhouse and it lies tilted toward the sunrise with mud piled inside.

At the Grand Army Extension the men got out just as the water filled the shaft "to the collar." At the African mine, with water and rocks streaming down the shaft, the men were unable to climb the 200 feet of ladders until "a trench turned the main sheet of water and the men escaped." Two feet of soil was deposited on the road surfaces, and six horses were needed to pull one wagon through the silt. The account in the *Miner* concludes:

We might call this affair "Too Much of a Good Thing" for water sells at one dollar a barrel in White Hills . . . we had a million dollar bath.

In 1900 the forty-stamp mill was running half time, and because of lack of water it was dropping only ten of its stamps. By 1904 several smaller mills were operating on ore from the many huge dumps that overshadowed each mine and mill. Root and Moffat retained their holdings in White Hills for a number of years, but even they could not sustain the camp's life indefinitely.

The morning of our visit the camp looked empty, although a truck stood at the edge of town, in front of a big house whose porches were partly hidden by smoke tree and bird-of-paradise plants. Every building on the street was askew and sagging, with crooked door and window frames wide open to the weather. An iron safe lay on its back beside the road, and behind the few buildings that are gradually being crowded by creosote bush and barrel cacti rose low, gray hills spilling whitish dumps down sage-covered slopes. The only sounds were those made by the wind as it rattled loose tin or rustled water-stained canvas. Then down the draw came the pulsing throb of a gasoline engine, accompanied by the nasal grind of a truck in low gear. Even this wasn't a true ghost town! The truck stopped when it reached us, and one of the men in it said he'd been up in the mountains looking for stock. "Sure, you hear an engine. There's an outfit working a mine above here. It went in six days ago. I don't know what mine they're working; I'm a cattleman," he said, and the truck droned on.

Before leaving the town we walked down a winding side road, past Joshua trees and yucca, to one of the two cemeteries. On the rocky flat most of the untended graves were outlined with two or three tiers of stones, or hemmed in with bleached and broken fences, through whose split palings grew sparse but persistent desert vegetation. On a few wooden headboards I made out dates—1893, 1899, 1905—but the names were so weathered as to be illegible. Behind the cemetery were the somber hills; in front of it the wide valley stretched west to the next range of mountains, almost invisible in the hazy atmosphere. Yucca, barrel cacti, rocks, weathered wood, a century plant, and silence. How different from the noise and life and brief prosperity that made Jim Twiggs, the livery-stable proprietor of White Hills, weave up and down Main Street after a few too many drinks, shouting, "Hooray for Jesus Christ, George Washington, and R. T. Root, the three best men in Mohave county!"

SUPERIOR

SOME of the most beautiful scenery in Arizona is found on the highway between Phoenix and Globe. Superstition Mountain, beyond Tempe, is a majestic and haunting mass of rock; and, even before one reaches Apache Junction, saguaro cacti, the candelabra of the desert, rise in contorted forms from the valley floor. In the midst of yucca and cactus, at the foot of a rugged range of mountains, lies Superior, a mining town that sprang up in 1875. The Silver Queen, directly above the town, was opened as a silver mine, but its ores were hard to work, and the silver proved only a capping for the copper which lay beneath in limitless amounts. The mine, now known as the Magma, is one of the state's rich properties, and the Magma Copper Company's big smelter stack is visible miles away.

Superior is built on a mountain slope, and its main street is one of the newer avenues of the busy industrial center. The older portion of the town is higher up the hill, where adobe homes and stores and frame cottages with enclosed, vine-covered porches crowd close together on the steep streets.

SILVER KING AND PINAL

BEFORE leaving Superior we inquired about the road to the Silver King mine, for, although it is only five miles from the highway, it is so hidden by rolling foothills as to be invisible from the town. We were soon on a dirt road, which passed the city dump and a small power station and dwindled to a twisting trail that rounded the shoulders of hills and dropped into dry washes. Its meanderings took us closer and closer to the wall of mountains over which the first wagon road to Globe was built. General Stoneman was

sent out by the army in 1872 to build a road over the Pinal Range. After he
had set up headquarters at Camp Supply, two miles south of Superior, and a
work camp on top of the ridge, he started blasting a trail up the side of the
rugged mountains. When completed it was known as Stoneman's Grade.

During its construction, the term of service expired for two of the soldiers
who were stationed at the camp on the crest of the range. As soon as they
were discharged they started on foot for Florence, a valley town on the San
Pedro River. They had stopped to rest on a projecting ledge of rock near the
foot of the Grade when one of them, named Sullivan, began picking up small
lumps of heavy black rock and crushing them with larger stones. To his surprise, they refused to break, but flattened like lead. When he reached Florence,
he showed the black nuggets to Charles G. Mason without saying where they
came from, and then left the area. Mason had the ore tested and found it almost solid chloride of silver.

Attempts to find the source of the nuggets were unsuccessful until 1875.
In March of that year Mason, accompanied by Benjamin W. Regan, William
H. Long, Isaac Copeland, and another man, went to the Globe area to pack
out some ore. On the return trip the jack train was attacked by Apaches, and
during the fight one of the men was killed. His body was buried on top of the
pass in one of the old bake ovens used by the road camp, and the remaining
four men descended the mountain. While they were watering their mules at
the stream, one of the animals strayed away, and either Copeland or Long—
the accounts differ—was sent to find it. He discovered it standing on a knoll
on which lay some outcroppings identical with those Mason had in his possession. The source of Sullivan's silver was found at last!

The four men claimed equal shares in the mine, which they named the
Silver King. Copeland and Long sold their shares not long after for $80,000.
Mason was the next to sell. He disposed of his interest to Colonel S. M. Barney
of Yuma for $250,000. Even though the best ore was said to average $8,000
to $20,000 a ton, Regan began to suspect that such riches could not last and
sold his quarter interest to Barney for $300,000.

A camp called Silver King soon covered the mountainside around the
mine, its main street crowded with business houses, saloons, eating places, and
hotels, and its water piped in from across the Pinal Mountains. In 1876, shortly
after the discovery, a five-stamp mill was built ten miles southwest of the mine
on Queen Creek. Before long, a second mill of twenty stamps was constructed,
and around these buildings a camp called Picket Post sprang up. Troops were
stationed near it to protect the miners from the Apaches; for Picket Post Butte,
which rose straight up behind the camp, was one of several signal stations for
the Indians. From it they watched every movement of the men and the troops.
By 1880 Picket Post was as busy a camp as Silver King, and its name was

changed to Pinal City. In 1886 its population of 2,000 was crammed into a small, compact space, crowded with tents, shacks, adobes, a few wood and stone buildings, a bank, fourteen saloons, two hotels, and the office of the weekly paper, *The Pinal Drill.*

The activity of the camp depended on the fabulous amounts of silver that constantly poured from the throat of the Silver King mine. The ore lay in a vertical pipe, or chimney, and the richest deposits were uncovered below the 250-foot level. By the time the silver was exhausted, the shaft had been sunk more than 1,000 feet. During the early eighties, when the silver seemed inexhaustible, the mine superintendent wore a strand of wire silver several feet long twisted around his hat. Native silver was sent to the mint, and the silver dollars made from it were brought back to the mine and distributed as souvenirs to visitors. Every day long processions of ore wagons, four hitched together to make a train, each train pulled by ten or more spans of mules, hauled the rock down the steep grade to the Pinal Mill.

Ore stealing was a common practice, especially as several assayers acted as "fences" and received the stolen highgrade without asking questions. Swampers on the ore wagons threw off big chunks of rich ore on the way down to the mill, so that their confederates could pick them up and hurry them to the "fence" for refining.

The heaviest single shipment from the mine was twenty-two bars valued at $70,000, the result of a fifteen-day run. Besides the bullion, concentrates valued at as much or more were produced during the same period; they usually ran $2,000 to the ton. By 1882, when the mine and mill were in full operation, bars and concentrates were shipped to the Casa Grande station on the Southern Pacific railroad, and thence to San Francisco. The stage that carried the bullion was robbed twice, each time not far from the Pinal mill. The first coach to be held up carried but one bar; the second contained three. These bars were recovered, and the robbers sent to prison. After these incidents, the Silver King company cast the bars of such a weight that no mule could pack one.

Sometime in the eighties an old man walked into Pinal City, looked with surprise at the mills and the hum of activity, and asked the way to the company office. He said he was Sullivan, the original discoverer of the vein, and that he'd been in California all this while trying to save enough money to return to work it. He was given employment in the mill.

When we visited the Silver King, all we could find of the town were several small stone buildings half hidden in cactus. Beyond them the road was so steep and rough that we left the car and started on foot up the curving trail. Part way up the hill I was surprised to hear chickens cackling, but at the top of the rise I was even more surprised by an amazing two-story house, surrounded by sheds, a mine shaft, and a cabin in which lived the owners of the chickens.

The woman who answered my knock on the cabin door told me that her husband was working a lease on the old property and that their dwelling was made from lumber salvaged from the Silver King shaft house. She showed me King's Crown, the high peak behind the camp. An indistinct trail on the mountainside she pointed out as Stoneman's Grade, the road over which stagecoaches had once rattled.

"There were streets and houses all over the mountain, on the ridge across from the mine as well as below it," she reminisced. "The old foundations are still there."

"Two hundred families once lived here," she continued. "But by 1886 the pay rock was thinning out, and by 1888 the big days were over. For years, though, the mine paid $25,000 a month in dividends, and its total output was $17,000,000. The ore was lousy with silver, and lots of it ran $2,000 to $4,000 a ton. The mine's half full of water now, but there's silver in it yet. If you go up to the big building, the woman up there—she's the schoolteacher at Superior—will show you through. It was one of the old company houses and used to be a boarding house or a hotel or some kind of headquarters—I don't know just what."

We walked to the big house, and the nearer we got the more fantastic it looked. It was square and too tall for its width, and it wore its overhanging roof like a broad-brimmed hat pushed down on its head. It sat perched high on a stone foundation, and its front porch was reached by a steep flight of steps, at the top of which stood a dog growling and wagging its tail.

Mrs. Olsen, the teacher, hospitably invited us into the living room, which boasted a fourteen-foot ceiling, explaining how she and her husband had lived there for two years while he and the other men worked a lease on the mine. She drove back and forth every day to her school in Superior, taking with her Allen and Virginia, the children of the third lessee. When we left, Allen walked back to the car with us to point out the sights and tell us stories about the mine. One concerned a man who, the day before his lease on the Silver King ran out, took all the silver bricks he had made and hid them in an outdoor toilet. He expected to return for them after the new lessee was on the property, but that night a torrent swept the gulch and washed everything down the creek, including the bricks. Only a few were recovered; the rest were never found.

GLOBE

JUST outside of Superior the highway to Globe, the oldest camp in the district, climbs and carves its way through the Pinal Range on a road that only modern engineering could conceive or construct. Twenty miles to the east, Miami, a larger, newer smelter town than Superior, made up of com-

SILVER KING BUILDINGS

MCMILLANVILLE AND THE STONEWALL JACKSON MINE

pany houses and the huge plants of the Inspiration Consolidated and Miami Copper companies, sprawls over a flat through which runs Bloody Tanks Wash.

The Bloody Tanks Massacre occurred in 1864, when Col. King S. Woolsey and his soldiers attacked a band of Apaches who had been summoned to attend a peace parley, killed nineteen of them and injured others. Both Indians and troops brought weapons to the conference in violation of their agreement and, although the Apaches outnumbered the soldiers, they were easily overcome by the superior rifles of the military. Some authorities insist that Woolsey, a veteran Indian fighter, invited the Indians to a feast in connection with the parley and then fed them "pinole" to which strychnine had been added and that as the stricken and dying men crawled painfully to the creek, gasping for water, their blood stained the deep pools in the stream and gave it its name.

In general, however, Apache Indians guarded their mountains and desert streams so well that prospecting was impossible prior to 1874, when they were temporarily subdued. In the lull which followed, Mason and his group of prospectors crossed the Pinal Mountains from the west and located the Globe claim; but little attention was paid to their discovery, for on their return trip to Florence they stumbled on the Silver King outcroppings, and its fabulous silver deposits became the only topic of conversation for some time to come.

The Globe mining district was organized in 1875, and by 1876 a frontier camp called Globe was laid out along Pinal Creek, only six miles from the Apache reservation. Within a year it had a population of 1,000; four years later it had two newspapers, the *Arizona Silver Belt* and the *Globe Chronicle*. Nearly all the silver discoveries were made by 1876, and at first the men mined the rich benches only for the native silver they contained. They continued to throw away the copper ore even after 1877, when the first copper from the district (ore from the Hoosier mine) was smelted in an adobe furnace by Venarsdell and Garrish. The *Arizona Silver Belt* of July 1, 1878, mentioned the "abundance of copper ore revealed by superficial workings on the Globe and Globe Ledge claims," but the metal was not generally regarded as important until 1881. At that time the Hoosier mine was sold on the strength of its copper deposits. Fortunately for the miners, the change from silver to copper mining was so gradual that copper ore from several mines was being smelted before the production of silver bullion ceased.

The original Globe and Globe Ledge claims became the property of the Old Dominion Company, which erected its first small furnace six miles west of Globe, close to the site of the Bloody Tanks massacre. This smelter was later moved to Globe. As the company expanded, it also built two larger plants on Pinal Creek, just north of the town. Globe's history, beginning with 1881, is built around its many copper mines; yet in 1886 the low price of the metal and high operating costs compelled most of the mines to shut down. Lack of railroads was the prime factor. All supplies and ore had to be hauled 120 miles by ox team between Globe and Wilcox, the nearest rail connection. Even the Old Dominion was unable to meet the rising costs, and its property was sold at auction in 1886 for $130,000. In 1888 the company was reorganized, and the property produced steadily until the middle nineties, when it shut down again to await the arrival of the promised railroad. The United Globe Company, organized in 1892 and active until 1896, also suspended operations and awaited the much-needed railroad.

The track to Globe had to cross the Indian reservation, and the Apaches, who were not at all eager to see it pass through their land, were slow to give permission for its construction. When they finally consented, the railroad officials staged a big meeting and celebration at which the Indians were given food and trinkets, received $8,000 for the right of way, and were promised free transportation over the road for thirty years. On December 1, 1898, the first train reached Globe, ending the twenty-year period of freighting by ox team and mule train and beginning Globe's second period of prosperity. Since the town is still flourishing, its further story does not belong here.

Broad Street, the main thoroughfare, follows the snake-like meanderings of treacherous Pinal Creek, which more than once flooded the lower parts of the town. Today the creek is a dry wash, and Broad Street, once the mule and ox trail through the camp, is a paved highway, lined with modern stores, hotels, and a grandiose courthouse built in 1907. Along it saunter Apache Indians, cowboys, and tourists; above it on the side hills perch row upon row of homes, to which the miners and merchants climb after work. North of the town are the huge black slag piles and the concrete foundations of the Old Dominion smelters.

Globe is so alert today that I could not picture it when it had no water supply except a town well and when, to avoid the summer heat in a town without an ice plant, women with sick children camped in tents on the mountains, risking Apache raids for the sake of the healing breezes.

McMILLANVILLE

THE roofs of a few adobe buildings at McMillanville are just visible from the highway, but no one except a ghost hunter would look for them. McMillanville, eighteen miles northeast of Globe, was a short-lived town, and its bonanza was concentrated around one mine, the Stonewall Jackson. The mine was discovered in February, 1876, by T. H. Harris. He and Charlie McMillan had traveled north across the hills from Globe on a prospecting trip, and McMillan insisted on taking a siesta under a piñon tree in a ravine.

Harris, impatient to get on with the journey, wandered to a ledge of rock and, while sitting on it, hit it repeatedly with his pick. This action split open some of the rock and revealed a core of silver. The men staked a claim, naming their mine the Stonewall Jackson. Upon further investigation they discovered that not only were the surface deposits rich but that certain pay streaks contained silver so pure it could be cut out with a chisel. Almost before their assessment work was done, scores of prospectors had found their way to the ravine and were busily pecking at the rocky ledges.

Shortly after their discovery, McMillan and Harris sold the Stonewall Jackson for $160,000 to a California company. Had they known its value they might have kept it longer. While it was by far the best property, eight other claims were located on the same lode—Lady Franklin, Lady Washington, Robert E. Lee, Abraham Lincoln, Hannibal, Little Mac, 220, and Florence. The original five-stamp mill that handled most of the ore was enlarged to twenty stamps in 1880, and the bars of bullion it produced were shipped over the mountains to Casa Grande.

The town of McMillanville, a conglomerate jumble of tents, adobe saloons, gambling casinos, stores, and hotels ranged on either side of the sandy gulch, reached its peak in 1880. It was a lusty man's camp with a population of 1,500. Freight wagons, filled with merchandise from Globe, clogged the one long street whose six saloons never closed. Old-timers like to tell about the proprietor of the Hannibal saloon who, on the opening night, dramatically threw away the key; and they always describe the Christmas celebration at which a tree was hung with nothing but cigars and tobacco, dynamite and fuses, grub and bottles of whisky.

A few of the miners brought their families to the growing town and built adobe homes among the trees and bushes that covered the townsite. How could they know that by 1882 the ore would begin to thin out, and that by 1885 the paystreak would be exhausted? As early as 1883 water was beginning to fill the shafts faster than it could be pumped out, and when the price of silver started to fall, mine after mine shut down.

McMillanville lay in the San Carlos Indian reservation, and the Cibecue Apaches watched resentfully as the miners tore up the hills. Finally, they rode through the country attacking lonely ranches and then swept down on the half-empty and unsuspecting mining camp. The women and children were rushed to the tunnel of the Stonewall Jackson mine, and the men fought from behind adobe walls and hastily constructed barricades. The raid lasted all day, and when it was over the miners boarded up the buildings, covered the mine shafts, and moved to Globe, leaving McMillanville to old Charlie Newton, who spent the rest of his life in the empty camp waiting for it to come back.

McMillanville's few adobes are better preserved than most, and not one of them has as yet lost its roof. The gallows frame above the mine shaft on the hill still stands, a black silhouette against the sky, but nothing remains of the stamp mill except its stone foundations.

TOMBSTONE

ARIZONA has two mining camps of which everyone has heard; yet two more different places cannot be imagined. Tombstone is in the middle of the desert; Jerome is high on a mountain. Tombstone is far to the south, and Jerome is in the northern part of the state. Tombstone reached its peak in the 1880's, Jerome in the 1920's. Tombstone lives on tourists, Jerome on copper. Tombstone is reviving; Jerome is struggling to keep alive.

The approach to Tombstone from Benson is dreary except for St. David's, a farming community whose wide green fields, bordered with trees, none but Mormons could have coaxed out of a dry desert. Tombstone lies on a flat mesa, surrounded by rolling plains which are hemmed in by the Whetstone, Burro, Mule, Huachuca, and Dragoon Mountains. The first settlement was at Watervale, two miles from the Tough Nut mine, but it soon disappeared in favor of Tombstone. When that townsite was laid out in 1879, lots on Allen Street sold for five dollars each, and the population of a hundred lived in forty tents and cabins. By the spring of 1880 four townsites dotted the mining district: Tombstone, by far the largest, was close to the Tough Nut group of mines; Richmond was one and a quarter miles southeast of it; and Contention City and Charleston were eight miles away on the San Pedro River.

Ed Schieffelin discovered the mining district, although in a way the Apaches led him to it. Schieffelin, who had prospected all his life for the excitement of it, started for Arizona in January, 1877, with two mules and a pack outfit. It was dangerous country, for the Apaches were on the warpath and United States troops were after them. Schieffelin reached Fort Huachuca, where the troops were stationed, in April, and made it his headquarters. At first he went out with scouting parties, using their presence as protection against Apache attacks and prospecting while they scanned the countryside. As he became more acquainted with the lay of the land, however, he began going out all day by himself and returning to the fort by dark. Each night the soldiers would chaff him and ask if he'd found anything. "Someday you'll find your tombstone," they warned him; but he paid no attention and continued his solitary trips.

On one of his wanderings to the hills bordering the San Pedro River, he met two men who were inspecting the old Brunckow mine. They hired him to stand guard while they worked, but he was impatient to get on with his own prospecting and before long left to scour the hills to the east. In August, 1877, he found a ledge of silver ore. Recalling the soldiers' jokes, he called his claim the Tombstone and his second location the Graveyard.

He took his samples of ore to Tucson, but no one was interested in them, and by the time he got back to his diggings it was October. By then both his money and his grub were gone, and he was forced to live by whatever he could shoot with his rifle. When he had accumulated a bagful of specimens he set out for the Silver King mine, where his brother was working; but when he reached there, he found that his brother had gone to the Signal mine near the Colorado River. Ed set off again and finally reached his brother, who was as unimpressed as the others had been with his samples. An assayer and mining engineer named Richard Gird, however, was excited when he saw them, and ran an assay. He found that the ore from the Tombstone claim was low-grade but that the specimen from the Graveyard assayed $2,000 a ton. Gird then proposed to grubstake an expedition to the hills east of the San Pedro and to form a partnership with the brothers, participating equally in whatever they found.

The three men left Signal in February, 1878, and returned to Ed's diggings, where they discovered that the ledge which had tested so well contained only a pocket of ore. Their Graveyard claim was well named. But Gird and Ed Schieffelin were positive that the country contained silver, and they continued their investigations until they uncovered a lode which assayed $15,000 a ton. This they named the Lucky Cuss. Their next location was the Tough Nut.

When these discoveries became known, the rush to the region began. Hank Williams and John Oliver, who arrived with the first wave of prospectors, promised Gird that if he would assay their samples, they in return would include him in their discoveries. Their strike was so good that they forgot their part of the bargain. He reminded them of it, however, and after some disagreement he received his share of the mine, which he appropriately named the Contention. Their portion was called the Grand Central. In April, 1878, the Schieffelins and Gird sold their rights in the Contention for $10,000 cash. Later that summer, as capitalists became interested in the mines, A. P. K. Safford, third Territorial Governor of Arizona, offered to finance a reduction plant and further develop the Tough Nut and Lucky Cuss mines for a quarter interest in the properties. Under this satisfactory arrangement, the brothers and Gird formed the Tombstone Mining and Milling Company, and Gird supervised the construction of a ten-stamp mill on the banks of the San Pedro, not far from the abandoned Brunckow mine.

The Lucky Cuss, Tough Nut, Contention, and Grand Central were the mines from which millions were taken between 1880 and 1886. While they were yielding so abundantly, Tombstone grew to be a rip-roarin', prosperous

SCHIEFFELIN HALL, TOMBSTONE

INTERIOR OF THE BIRDCAGE THEATRE, TOMBSTONE

silver camp whose population reached 14,000 and whose principal industry, next to mining, was gambling. Gambling was profitable, not only in itself, but because the taxes collected from the sale of licenses supported the public schools. Allen Street became the main thoroughfare, and the Crystal Palace and Oriental saloons threw open their doors to increasing crowds of patrons.

Scores of tales are told about Tombstone's lawlessness. One concerns Frank Leslie, who was tending bar at the Oriental the day Billy Claiborne threatened him. He finished the "killer cowboy" by slipping out a side door and covering him just as he was about to re-enter the saloon. Leslie called Claiborne's name and, as he turned, dropped him with a bullet in his heart. Returning to the bar, Leslie commented, as he picked up his unfinished cigar, "He died nice."

"The liveliest street battle that ever occurred in Tombstone" took place on October 27, 1881, in front of the O.K. Corral. In the few seconds that guns barked three men were killed and two others wounded. The fight climaxed a long-standing feud between certain outlaw cowboys led by Ike Clanton and the three Earp brothers. The drunken cowboys, who were armed, openly bragged they were out to get Virgil Earp, the City Marshal; to put an end to their threats, the Marshal enlisted the aid of his brothers, Wyatt and Morgan, and of Doc Holliday in an attempt to disarm the men. About 2:30 P.M.

they started toward the O.K. Corral on Fremont street, and a few doors below the Nugget Office saw the Clantons and the McLowery brothers talking to Sheriff Behan, who had requested them to disarm. The marshall called out, "Boys, throw up your hands; I want you to give up your shooters."

At this Frank McLowery attempted to draw his pistol when Wyatt Earp immediately shot him, the ball entering just above the waist. Doc Holliday then let go at Tom McLowery with a shotgun, filling him full of buckshot under the right arm. Billy Clanton then blazed away at Marshall Earp, and Ike Clanton, who it is claimed was unarmed started and ran off through the corral to Allen street. The firing then became general, and some thirty shots were fired, all in such rapid succession that the fight was over in less than a minute.

When the smoke cleared away it was found that Frank McLowery had been killed outright. . . . Tom McLowery lay dead around the corner on Third street. . . . Billy Clanton lay on the side of the street, with one shot in the right waist and another in the right side near the wrist, and the third in the left breast. He was taken into a house and lived half an hour in great agony.

Morgan Earp was shot through both shoulders, the ball creasing the skin. Marshall Earp was shot through the fleshy part of the right leg. Wyatt Earp and Doc Holliday escaped unhurt.

The shooting created great excitement and the street was immediately filled with people. Ike Clanton was captured and taken to jail. . . . The feeling of the better class of citizens is that the marshall and his posse acted solely in the right in attempting to disarm the cowboys and that it was a case of kill or be killed. [*Tombstone Epitaph* Oct. 27, 1881.]

With every other building on Allen Street a saloon, with 110 liquor licenses paid in 1880 alone, and with fourteen faro banks which never closed, perhaps the Episcopal bishop who visited Tombstone was justified in saying that it was not yet ready for a resident rector. Yet in 1881 Reverend Endicott Peabody arrived fresh from divinity school, so full of enthusiasm that on Saturday nights he visited saloons and dives and invited the patrons to attend services on Sunday. The men liked him, listened to his sermons, and contributed liberally toward the church which he succeeded in building.

From Fifth and Tough Nut streets one gets an unobstructed view of the mines. Far to the left are the Grand Central, Contention, and Tough Nut properties, and to the right is the Lucky Cuss. Almost at one's feet is the gaping mouth of the Million Dollar Stope, down whose black throat every tourist gazes. This, more than anything else, convinces the visitor that the city is honeycombed with mine tunnels.

Each property was developed by sinking deeper and deeper shafts, but water was struck at the 500-foot level. To combat it, huge Cornish pumps were installed by the Grand Central and Contention companies, and these drained the lower mine levels. The Grand Central pump cost $300,000 and operated with a huge walking beam that stood thirty feet above its foundations. Both companies soon discovered, to their annoyance, that they were draining the district; but the other companies which benefited from the pumping refused to pay for the service. The Grand Central continued pumping, however, until 1885, when a fire in the pump house stopped all work. A year later the Contention hoist and pumping works burned, and, with both systems disabled, the two mines closed down.

The years 1880 to 1890 saw Tombstone rise and ebb as a silver camp. After the mines became flooded in 1886, most of the people for whom the town had laid silver eggs moved away, and its population of 20,000 had shrunk by 1890 to 2,000. With the big pumps idle and the natural water table only 500 feet below the surface, sporadic and shallow leasing operations were all that could be carried on; most of those were on No Account Hill, whose deposits had thus far been overlooked.

In 1891, A. L. Grow, an agent for two of the big mining companies, conceived the idea that by consolidating all the mines in the district into one corporation, the pumping problem could be handled satisfactorily and the flooded lower workings again be made accessible. The necessary capital was raised, and in 1901 the Tombstone Consolidated Mining Company began operations by sinking a boom shaft to a depth of 1,080 feet, building a cyanide mill, and installing boilers to provide steam for the pumps. These in time began to raise 8,000,000 gallons of water a day, and during this period Tombstone enjoyed a flurry of activity. It was short-lived, however, for the cost of operating the pumps was high—fuel oil alone cost $700 a day—and before long the company was in debt. Pumping went on, however, until 1909, when, through careless-ness, water entered the fuel pipes under the boilers. The fires went out, and in an hour the water in the shaft had submerged the pumps. After fifteen months of work the flow of water was reduced and the pumps repaired, but the ex-pense had been too great for the company. On January 19, 1911, the fires under the boilers were pulled, and the water in the mines returned to its natural level. That August the company, which had fought a losing battle for years, went into bankruptcy. On June 23, 1914, the entire Tombstone Consolidated Mining Company was bought by the Phelps Dodge Company for $500,000 at a receiver's sale.

Tourists, not mining, are now the city's main industry. Tombstone has wisely taken stock of its assets and preserved so much of its past appearance that visitors can enjoy a vicarious thrill by walking its history-laden streets and investigating its historic sites. Not that Tombstone is intact—for two bad fires in the early eighties leveled the business area—but its adobes and brick build-ings, whose wood or metal awnings cover the sidewalks and shade pedestrians from the fierce summer sun, are those which replaced the original flimsy tents and shacks. Only where buildings have been torn down for the lumber they contained (for Tombstone is in a desert and the nearest forests are miles away) are there gaps in the few compact blocks which comprise the nucleus of the city.

Tombstone is built on level ground, and as most of it is only one story high, only a few buildings stand out from the others. The Cochise County Courthouse on Tough Nut Street and the City Hall on Fremont Street, both built in 1882, are imposing red brick structures with carved white trim. Schief-felin Hall, on the corner of Fremont and Fourth streets, is a large two-story adobe. It was built in 1881 by Al Schieffelin, who felt that the raw new camp needed entertainment other than that provided by Joe Bignon's Theatre Co-mique, which had opened in 1879. Upon the Hall's completion, it was said to have the largest stage between Denver and San Francisco.

The Tombstone Dramatic Association, an amateur group, opened the build-ing on September 15, 1881, by presenting *The Ticket-of-Leave Man*. The proceeds from the performance were donated to the Rescue Hook and Ladder Company for the purchase of a bell. The first professional traveling troupe, the Nellie Boyd Dramatic Company, played in the Hall on December 5 and pre-sented *The Banker's Daughter*. Tombstone in those days was on the dramatic circuit, and troupes which were booked for Denver and El Paso stopped off to play the town, bumping in coaches over Indian-infested roads from Benson to the expectant camp. The Hall was seldom empty, and its performances drew a better class of audience than did the variety theatres on Allen Street.

The Bird Cage, the most famous of the latter, was opened on December 26, 1881. Where Schieffelin Hall was big and respectable, the Bird Cage was small and intimate; and it, too, was rarely empty. The building was a story-and-a-half adobe, and the theatre, with its suspended, curtained balcony boxes, was behind the barroom. The stage was small, the scenery was made by the various performers, and the girls who sold drinks to the patrons sang as they worked—hence its name. The Bird Cage is a museum today, filled with relics and trinkets of the gaudy past when "people were crazed with delight" at the arrival of a "new company of twenty first-class artists" and paid twenty-five cents for general admission. Boxes varied in price "according to location." Visitors are shown the dumb-waiter that conveyed drinks to the suspended balcony, where rival factions occupied opposite sides of the theatre. If one side hissed the actor, the other side. applauded, and if the applause was too enthusiastic, guns barked from both sides.

Not only variety shows, but also masquerades and balls, were held in the cosy little auditorium where the actresses danced with the audience—which, according to the management, "made for friendship between the performers and the public." Respectable women and the more cultured strata of Tomb-stone's society never attended the Bird Cage. To lure them to it, a Ladies' Night was announced; but, as no ladies responded, the idea was abandoned after the first program. That the theatre has survived is due to the faith and almost superhuman efforts of its several managers, especially the Hutchinsons, who opened it, and the Bignons, who ran it during the precarious years be-tween 1886 and 1892.

Visitors to Tombstone hunt up the *Epitaph* office, partly because its name fascinates them and partly because they want to get a copy of the paper which is still being published in the remarkable camp that advertises it is "too tough to die." John P. Clum founded the paper and named it *Epitaph,* because he felt that "any town named Tombstone should have an epitaph." Even hurried tourists are now able to read excerpts from the paper, for Douglas D. Martin's book, *Tombstone Epitaph,* published in 1951, contains expert cullings from the old files.

Tombstone covers so few blocks today that it is possible to walk over the entire town, visit all the old sites, and pick out the buildings which, in spite of new coats of stucco, show that they were built when thick walls and iron shut-ters stopped bullets and fan lights over windows and doors were the last word in architectural elegance. On one edge of town is the Boothill Cemetery, which for years was a forgotten rubbish dump where only cactus and yucca grew. In recent years the place had been cleaned up, its graves outlined with stones, and legible headboards placed on each. Where but in Tombstone could one find so many inscriptions which read, "Killed by Indians," or "Died of Wounds," or such odd ones as, "John Blair, died of Smallpox. Cowboy throwed Rope over Feet and Dragged Him to His Grave."?

Dutch Annie, queen of the red light district, died in 1883, and her funeral was attended not only by the underworld but by businessmen and city officials. The procession to the cemetery consisted of 1,000 buggies and was second in size only to that of Ed Schieffelin.

John Heath's gravestone reads: "Taken from County Jail and Lynched by Bisbee Mob in Tombstone, Feb. 22, 1884." Heath and four others who had robbed and killed in Bisbee were brought to Tombstone for trial. Heath was the first to be tried, and, although the acknowledged leader of the gang, he was convicted of only second-degree murder. The next morning his body dangled from a pole, and the jury was advised to think more carefully before rendering similar verdicts for the remaining murderers. His confederates were sentenced to be hanged, and a gallows was erected on which all four could swing together. Invitations marked "Non Transferable" were issued for the spectacle, which took place on March 28, 1884. Some ghoulish but enterprising person built bleachers near the scaffold, but they were torn down by a shocked and civic-minded mob before the hangings occurred.

Tombstone's most notable figure, Ed Schieffelin, is buried on a hill overlooking the town, close to the site of his first discovery. A monument erected over his grave is inscribed: "This is my Tombstone." Around it grow cholla cactus and prickly pear.

CONTENTION CITY AND CHARLESTON

THE mill towns of Contention City and Charleston, on the banks of the San Pedro River, are in ruins today and can be reached only by unimproved roads across the desert. Contention City, on the west side of the river north of Fairbanks, was miles from Tombstone; but, as it had the closest available water, it was selected as the site for the Contention mill. Broken adobe walls and heaps of ruins choked by willows and cacti are all that remain of it now.

Charleston (formerly Millville) is south of Contention City and nine miles southwest of Tombstone. When Governor Safford helped Richard Gird and the Schieffelin brothers to finance the Tombstone Mining and Milling Company in 1879, Gird chose Charleston as the location for the company's mill. The place was familiar to Ed Schieffelin, for the abandoned Brunckow mine, at which he had worked in 1877, was nearby. Frederick Brunckow, a scientist exiled from Germany, had found his way to the trackless desert in 1858, built a home, and begun to dig; but before he could develop his mine, he was killed by an Indian arrow. Others relocated the property in 1880, but nothing of value was discovered.

Gird built not only the company mill but also the Big House, a huge adobe office building with walls three feet thick, in which the bars of silver produced by the smelter were placed for safekeeping while awaiting shipment. Holdups were so common in Charleston that Gird installed an immense steel safe in which to stack the bullion. Actually, the safe was a blind, for, instead of using it, Gird dug hiding places in the thick walls of the building and covered the holes with movable panels papered to match the rest of the room.

Charleston, though in a sense a suburb of Tombstone, had an independent life of its own. Through its streets roamed many colorful characters, none more dynamic than Justice Jim Burnett, who ruled the wild river camp during the early eighties. Burnett's salary as Justice of the court was a fixed percentage of the revenues received from fines. During his term of office he rendered only one quarterly report to the Board of Supervisors at Tombstone, and with it he demanded $380 from the county as due him from unpaid fees. When notified that the Supervisors had cut the amount he replied, "Hereafter the justice court of Charleston precinct will look after itself." Only once did the county officials attempt to audit his books. Burnett greeted the men by saying, "This is a self-sustaining office. I never ask anything from the county and I never give the county anything."

Burnett was the law in Charleston, and he held court and imposed fines when and where he pleased. Once, when a drunken rancher was riding down the street shooting up the town, Burnett yanked the armed man from his horse and fined him twenty head of three-year-old steers. A Mexican stole a horse from a man named Curry and was foolish enough to drive it into town shortly afterwards hitched to one of his wood wagons. Curry recognized his animal and demanded it back. While he and the Mexican were arguing, Burnett came along, listened to the story, and fined the Mexican nine cords of wood, to be delivered to the Gird mill. To the discomfiture of its owner, the wagon train contained exactly nine cords, and Burnett made a good profit by selling the wood to the mill.

A man named Durkee freighted ore between Tombstone and Charleston. One year, when his profits were big, he decided to throw a party in the biggest saloon in the camp. He hired dance-hall girls and an orchestra for his guests, bought the saloon's entire stock of liquor, and put stacks of silver dollars on the gaming tables. Though only miners and freighters were invited, the men so greatly outnumbered the girls that the latter were danced into a state of coma. Guns were checked at the door, but by the time the guests got roaring drunk and pugnaciously aggressive, bottles, chair legs, and any movable object served as weapons. Durkee's bill, which included replacement of plate-glass mirrors and bar fixtures, cleaned out his profits. The party did not become an annual brawl.

Charleston was smaller but tougher than Tombstone. Its four saloons never closed, and, since Fort Huachuca was only a few miles away, paydays brought the soldiers to the camp to drink and gamble. As one old-timer put it, "When the thermometer gets up to 124 degrees you have to drink a lot to keep the sweat rollin'. The water ain't safe to drink, so you don't drink water." No one seemed disturbed when dead men lay in the street. If the corpse had a gun on it and the shot had been from the front, you didn't look for the killer.

Guns made the law, and men had to react in a split second. A faro dealer and a customer once got into an argument and the customer left. The dealer sat down at the bar to read his paper. He heard someone approaching and, pulling out his .45, shot between the eyes the figure who entered the saloon. The dead man was, of course, the former customer, who had gone for his gun. The faro dealer had known he would return and that whoever fired first would survive. He returned to his paper.

With five big mills along the river all turning out bullion and gamblers raking in coin in each saloon, Charleston was a center for holdups. The mill whistles blew for fires and for bandits, but the robbers often escaped by obliterating their tracks in the stream bed of the shallow river.

Every now and then the Galeyville gang galloped into Charleston. Galeyville, some fifty miles east of Tombstone on the eastern slope of the Chiricahua Mountains, though a boom silver camp in 1881, was better known as a hangout for rustlers, murderers, and smugglers. One Sunday evening the gang swaggered into the church in Charleston, followed by a few local toughs. When the collection plate was passed they contributed lavishly, but when the minister, sizing up his congregation, shortened his sermon, one of the armed men spoke up: "We've paid our dough and we want a full-length spiel, and throw in a prayer too." The minister complied. Just as he concluded, another voice inquired, "Now, how about a little music and singing?" The minister hesitated until the speaker continued, fingering his gun, "Or perhaps you'd rather dance for us?" The pastor played and sang until the men were satisfied.

Next morning a constable fined one of the local bums for disturbing the peace at a religious gathering. The man objected, saying he had done his best to keep the visitors from getting rough. "Then I fine you for being in bad company on Sunday," snapped the resourceful officer.

The adobe and stone buildings of Charleston, though ruined, are still recognizable. The Big House has lost its roof and most of its walls, but the safe

STEEP GRADE
MAIN STREET, JEROME

JEROME TERRACES

OLD STONE BUILDING,
VULTURE MINE, WICKENBURG

is embedded in the corner of one room. Another mass of crumbling adobe is pointed out as the House of the Whore; but for all its rowdy past, the river town is only a bawdy memory. If any ghosts linger in it, Jim Burnett's is among them.

JEROME

WHETHER you approach Jerome from above or below, the first sight of the city is fantastic; for it is precariously balanced on Mingus Mountain, midway between summit and base, and in pictures it looks completely unreal, a sort of mirage on a mountain. The drive from Flagstaff to Jerome is full of variety: first, spectacular Oak Creek Canyon; then side roads luring the motorist to the Indian ruins of Montezuma's Castle and Tuzigoot; then the neat company town of Clarkdale, with its great black smelter stacks; and, last, the serpentine climb to Jerome, 1,800 feet above the Verde Valley floor.

The city is only seventy years old, but the mineral deposits which caused a town to blossom on the steep mountainside were known as early as 935 A.D. by the Tuzigoot Indians, who used the vivid oxidized surface outcroppings for body paint and pottery decoration. Centuries later the Spaniards, while hunting for gold and silver in the Southwest, visited the area and found on the mountain a shallow shaft which the Indians had dug in their search for blue, green, and brown pigments. When Al Sieber, an Indian scout, first saw the mine in the early 1870's, he too found proof of Indian workings: rock tools and ladders made of juniper logs.

John O'Dougherty, Captain John Boyd, and a small party of prospectors from Nevada were the next to see the location from which such unguessed wealth was to be dug. The men reached Prescott in January, 1876, pushed on to the Verde River, and followed it until they were close to the Black Hills. Here, near the head of a stream they called Bitter Creek, they began to prospect. They found outcroppings and marked several locations but did not stay in the area to develop their claims. Later in the year, John Ruffner and August McKinnon, ranchers, visited the Verde Valley and prospected the same area. Ruffner is usually credited with staking the claim which became the United Verde, but some authorities name McKinnon or Al Sieber as the initial discoverer. Other claims were made, and mines were opened up on the mountainside between 1877 and 1882 by prospectors who located likely sites, gophered at them for a while, and then abandoned or traded them.

Ruffner, whose chief interest was ranching, willingly sold his claim to Territorial Governor Frederick A. Tritle for $500 in cash and a balance of $1,500 to be paid six months later. Tritle, unable to develop the property alone, found in Eugene Jerome, a New York lawyer, a backer who agreed to finance the project on condition that the town which was sure to grow up around the mine be named for him.

Little was done to develop the property until 1882, when the railroad reached Ashfork. Tritle was then able to ship in a small smelter, although he had to build his own road for the freight wagons from Ashfork to the mine. In 1883 the United Verde Copper Company was incorporated, and the town of Jerome was born. At that time its fifty houses, three stores, six saloons, and population of four hundred gave no indication of the city it would become. In 1892 it was still a camp of log and tent houses, to which long pack trains brought wood and water. In 1900, when the contract to supply water was held by Pancho Villa, 200 loaded burros driven by swarthy Mexicans made regular deliveries to the town.

The United Verde began to pay dividends in 1884, and shortly afterwards Senator William A. Clark of Montana became interested in the property. First he leased it; then he bought it. During the next twelve years he spent a million dollars developing it, and, consequently, no dividend checks were paid to stockholders until 1900.

The great success of the United Verde, the richest copper mine in Arizona from the time he bought it in the middle 1880's until its sale to the Phelps Dodge Corporation in the middle 1930's, was the result of Senator Clark's vision, capital, and management. As soon as he acquired the property, he built several tiers of frame houses on the mountain, to accommodate miners with families, and the Montana House, a big stone hotel, for the bachelors.

When the smelter near the mine proved too small and cave-ins on Woodchute Mountain (the one adjoining Mingus) prevented its enlargement, Clark built a great new smelter in the valley. To house its employees, he laid out the model town of Clarkdale beside the Verde River, and to keep the mill regularly supplied with ore he constructed a squirming narrow-gauge railroad down the mountainside. From the day the plant opened in 1915, its black stacks belched smoke day and night. To facilitate the shipment of ore, he built a standard-gauge road to connect with the main line. Before he was through, eighty-five miles of shafts and drifts undermined Mingus Mountain, and double tracks more than a mile long ran from the 1,000-foot level in the mine to the tipple at the smelter. In 1920, United Verde began digging its big open pit on Woodchute Mountain, and by 1940, when the pit operations ceased, $80,000,000 had been recovered.

All through the twentieth century United Verde and Jerome have been synonymous, for without the mine the city could not have existed. Fire destroyed the business section three times, and fumes from the first smelter killed all the vegetation on the mountain; a little of it is beginning to grow back, but trees are not one of Jerome's beauties.

In its prime the city was not lacking in variety of entertainment. One week Miss Hollister, of Phoenix, lectured under the auspices of the WCTU, and Jack Fanning, the "World's Greatest Trap Shot," gave a demonstration of his skill at the Jerome Gun Club, which also held a "shoot" during his visit. The Knights of Pythias, the Jerome Fire Department, and other organizations gave annual balls, described by the *Jerome Mining News* as "most enjoyable and swell affairs." Tickets to the Firemen's Ball cost $1.50 and admitted "Gentleman and ladies . . . so gentlemen may bring as many ladies as they wish without incurring extra expense." In 1903 the Fashion Saloon and Gambling House, by opening an addition to its already popular quarters, made available a beer and German lunch hall and a bowling alley. Those wanting less exhilarating sport could attend the box sociable of the Ladies' Guild of the Episcopal church, where, incidentally, the chances sold on a "handsome pillow" cleared eighty dollars. The Fourth of July festivities included a Boilermaker's Riveting Contest.

The town reached its peak in the twenties: in 1921 alone the "yearly diggings" totaled $25,000,000. Its population in 1929 was 15,000, of whom 4,000 were miners—Italians, Mexicans, Yugoslavians, Swedes, Bohemians, and Welshmen—each group living in its own section of the crazy city whose houses were propped on stilts and reached by interminable flights of steps. A blast of 250 pounds of dynamite set off in the Black Pit in 1925 started a landslide in Mingus Mountain which nothing has been able to retard. Since then the town has moved half an inch a month toward the valley. Buildings have cracked, many are propped up, and some have collapsed or have been torn down. The concrete city jail slid 300 feet across the highway and lies on its side below the street level; a movie theatre, the post office, and the J. C. Penney store skidded down the slope. Yet the residents of the town are unperturbed and continue to drive their cars into garages on their roof-tops and climb up to their braced basements. It was shortly after 1935, when United Verde had closed down due to the depression, that the Phelps Dodge interests acquired the property and reopened it. Since then the population of Jerome has fluctuated according to the demand for copper. During World War II the town had a spurt of activity, but since then its decline has been gradual but steady.

In 1951 I drove down Yaeger Canyon from Prescott and stopped on the topmost shelf of highway overlooking the valley. In the distance were the fantastic blood-red cliffs of Oak Creek Canyon; in front of them, the wide, level Verde Valley. Far below, darkened by cloud shadows, was Clarkdale, a toy village tucked in between the base of the mountain and the immense plain. Directly below lay Jerome, a jumble of buildings glued in place and ranging from four- and five-story brick and concrete structures to frame and metal sheds built on shelves overhanging the thirty-three-degree slope of the mountain.

Jerome is 5,435 feet above sea level, and its top layer of buildings is 1,500 feet higher than its lowest. The highway down the mountain and through the town has a nine-percent grade, except where it is fourteen percent. The city has no level ground except one compact area that contains the tallest buildings and a diminutive city park, the size of a back yard. Most of the stores are boarded up and empty. Big concrete buildings are hollow, perforated shells without roofs, doors, or windows. Some buildings are protected by heavy iron shutters; in others circus posters, displayed inside the dirty glass panes, date back twenty years. In one dusty shop I found photographs of Jerome when its buildings were new and its mines active; the proprietor was Chinese. Nevertheless, Jerome was not a ghost town; for music and voices issued from the taverns, washing flapped on lines, and children played about the streets. Even though its bank opens only on payday and its last hotel and chain store have been closed, the bars, the filling station, the groceries, and the school are still running. At present Jerome is but a shell of its former self; once it was the fifth largest city in the state.

From the foot of the grade I took a last look at Jerome, perched so tenaciously on its mountain. I had seen Tubac, where big-scale mining began before the Civil War; Tubac is dozing. I had seen White Hills, where mining flared and died out; White Hills is dead. Now I had seen Jerome; if it is dying, I saw it just in time. But Jerome hasn't died yet!

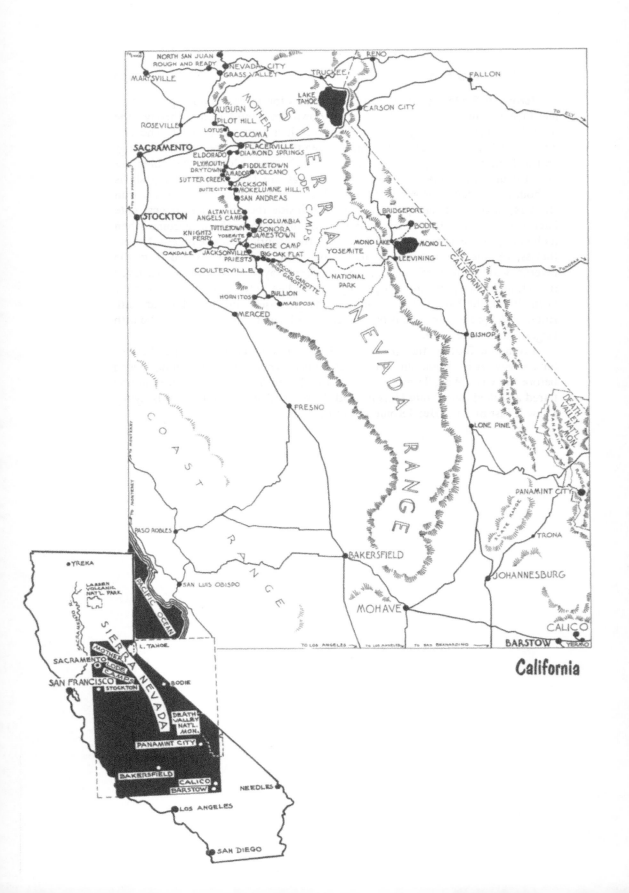

California

California

THE FIRST and most fabulous of all the gold rushes was the one to California during 1848 and 1849—the rush which started men hurrying from all parts of the world, by whatever routes or conveyances were available, to the remote western slopes of the Sierra Nevada Mountains, each man straining to be the first to reach the gulches and so win quick and easy wealth by finding the rich flakes and nuggets which lay hidden there. The gold came from a mammoth lode of quartz 162 miles long, which through the centuries had disintegrated into fragments, until exposed particles of it were carried down the mountainside by swift freshets and were deposited in sand bars and stream beds or were caught between crevices of rock. The discovery of gold in this "Mother Lode," as it was called, was an accident and brought ruin to James Marshall and John Sutter, the two men most closely concerned with it.

During the early 1840's, while the southwestern portion of what is now the United States was part of Mexico, a few trappers and scouts found their way across the mountains and through passes in the high Sierra, only to be imprisoned or packed back across the mountains by the resentful Mexican officials responsible for the territory. After the Mexican War, scouts, emigrants bound for Oregon or California, and bands of Mormons bent on colonizing, began wearing trails across the trackless western country, suffering extreme hardships, doggedly enduring desert heat and mountain storms in their relentless drive to the green valleys along the Pacific coast.

Among these hardy pioneers was John A. Sutter, who ventured across the Sierras in 1838, became a naturalized Mexican citizen in 1840, and obtained a grant of seventy-six square miles from the Mexican governor of California, Juan B. Alvarado, in 1841. On this land, which lay in the fertile Sacramento River Valley, he built his fort and his trading post. All through the forties it served as a supply center for the northern frontier and as a haven for the

travel-wracked wagon trains which succeeded in crossing the barricade of
the high Sierra. The fort covered five acres and was surrounded with eighteen-
foot walls with bastions and cannons at the corners. Within the walls, in addition to the large two-story central building, were the shops and storehouses.

Year by year Sutter's empire (which he called New Helvetia) prospered
as his fields, tended by Indians, grew profitable crops, his herds provided beef
and hides, and his mills produced flour and lumber. As trade increased, Sutter
needed more lumber, and in August, 1847, he hired James Wilson Marshall to
construct and operate a sawmill near a source of timber. After several expeditions in search of a site, Marshall chose a spot on the south fork of the
American River about fifty miles from the Fort and, with the help of several
Mormons and Indians, began the construction of the mill. On January 24,
1848, Marshall inspected the mill and found on bedrock in the tailrace a few
flakes of gold. Putting them in his hat, he showed them to the men at the
mill and then tested them. They stood the test. He then hurried to the fort
and showed the flakes to Sutter, who also tested them. Sutter was somewhat
appalled by the discovery, for he feared what would happen to the fertile
country when it was known to contain gold. Not only would his employees
quit work, but the whole countryside which he had developed would be torn
up by ruthless strangers, and his years of labor would be lost. As soon as
the news leaked out, his worst fears were realized—he and Marshall became
pawns to be pushed aside by greedy men who killed his cattle and spoiled his
crops in their headlong rush for the precious metal. During 1848 it was men
from Oregon and California who trampled down his wheat and destroyed his
property. The real rush occurred in 1849.

There were but three ways to reach the gold fields from the east, and each
was an ordeal which only the hardiest survived. The longest, safest, and most
comfortable (if such a word can be used) journey was by ship around the
Horn. The shortest way was by ship to the Isthmus of Panama and thence
across the fever-ridden strip of land to the Pacific, where passage on a second
ship had to be obtained before arrival at San Francisco. This route was difficult because the ships were always crowded, the trip across the Isthmus was a
nightmare, and the supply of vessels on the west coast was never sufficient for
the impatient hordes of men, haggling for passage on the beaches.

The overland trip started at the Missouri River from St. Joseph or Independence, and before the rush was over thousands of covered wagons with
"California or Bust" painted on their flapping canvas sides had crawled west
mile after mile toward the parching deserts and the mountain barriers, for
which the adventurers were as a rule completely unprepared. In spite of disease, Indians, broken wagons, exhausted and dying oxen, sun-crazed travelers,
dry water holes, and lack of food, streams of men converged upon the Sacra-

mento and American River valleys until the river beds and gulches were
glutted with prospectors. Kanakas, Mexicans, Chileños, and Chinese, as well
as Americans and Europeans, were soon hard at work at the diggings. An-
tagonistic to the Chinese because of their utterly different appearance, language, and mode of living, the other miners continuously ousted them from
any rich bar they uncovered. With characteristic patience the Chinese miners
ferreted out new locations or reworked claims abandoned by less industrious
Anglos.

From every promising diggings a camp emerged. Most of them are now
prosperous towns or sleeping villages; only a few are piles of crumbling foundations lost in vegetation. A trip through the Mother Lode today on paved
highways is so easy that the miles slip away and camp after camp passes by
in a blur of new and old buildings, neon signs, and filling stations.

In the midst of the bustling, beautiful city of Sacramento stands Sutter's
Fort. Although surrounded by apartment houses and private homes, it is easy
to find. The Fort has been preserved as a state Historical Monument and is a
site of extreme interest. Within its high walls the present is shut out, and hours
can be spent inspecting the many exhibits and workshops housed in the hollow
square of buildings which surround the original, restored structure. From the
fort it is an easy drive to the site of Sutter's Mill and the camps which mushroomed all along the narrow 120-mile strip of the Sierra foothills, known today
as the Mother Lode country.

AUBURN

FROM Sacramento a wide freeway leads directly to Auburn, one of the
northern Mother Lode towns in which the old and the new stand side
by side. Two Chileños found gold in Rich Ravine in 1849, where the town
now stands, and almost before they were aware of it, John S. Wood, an ex-
soldier from Stevenson's regiment, moved in on them and modestly called the
place Wood's Dry Diggings. He then sent word to his soldier-friends to join
him at the rich ground, and it was one of them that, inspired by Goldsmith's
"loveliest city of the plains," named the camp Auburn.

Auburn was built in three successive tiers, with the old section, which soon
became the foreign quarter, at the foot of the hill; a second settlement on the
side of the hill; and a third, select portion on top of the hill in the shadow of
the gilt-domed courthouse. The old section lies close to Highway 40. I found
the cupola-topped fire station, one of the best preserved of the wooden buildings, next to the charred fronts of three frame stores, still smoking from a fire
that had gutted them that very morning. Across the street were more land-

marks—brick stores and warehouses, with sheet-iron awnings shading the side-walks. Only a block away stood a row of one-story brick houses—a remnant of the old Chinese quarter.

The buildings on the steepest street were set one above another, and the sidewalks and awnings ascended in steps to the highest tier. Ailanthus trees made thickets of green in gutters or in cracks between walls—wherever a patch of earth provided a footing. This portion of town is an excellent place to begin a study of the old camps, for nearly every kind of structure typical of the Mother Lode is represented.

The Forty-niners developed such a distinctive style of architecture that it is easy to spot the old buildings in each community, even when their façades are coated with a fresh layer of stucco or are hidden behind garish and hideous signs. In most of the towns the old buildings are treasured; in others they are in a state of decay or, worse still, they have been so extensively remodeled that little of their original construction remains. The architecture of the Mother Lode is important, for it set a style which was followed all through the West wherever California miners gravitated and wherever similar building materials were available.

The first settlements were tent colonies. These soon became platted town-sites filled with frame shacks; but, as fire leveled camp after camp in the early fifties, the flimsy cabins and lean-to's were replaced by more permanent struc-tures and a style was born. It was designed to resist fire, and the very fact that so many of its buildings survive proves that, to a large extent, it suc-ceeded. Its buildings were made of adobe, brick, and native stone and had plain, massive walls. The adobes were unrelieved by any ornament. The brick buildings showed great ingenuity in bonding, in recessed paneling, and in dentil moldings and cornices, which produced patterns of light and shade above and about doors and windows. The stone structures were unadorned except for carefully dressed and fitted door and window trim and arched portals. Door and window shapes were simple rectangles except for those topped with fan-lights.

To fireproof the buildings further, all doors and windows were fitted with iron shutters. These were solid sheets of metal and were often reinforced with vertical and horizontal strips of iron painted a contrasting color. Each store originally had a wooden sidewalk in front, sheltered by a wooden or sheet-iron awning, the awnings supported on slender wood or iron columns. The majority of the buildings were one or two stories high, but in a few of the larger settle-ments three-story hotels were not uncommon. The taller structures were en-riched with wrought-iron or wooden balconies of considerable intricacy of design.

Frame buildings were not so original, as they followed as closely as possible the latest trends of domestic architecture found in the towns back east from which the miners came. The gable-roofed, gothic-windowed home with its carved, spindled, and shaded porch was merely transplanted from its Ohio or New England setting.

GRASS VALLEY

AFTER my friend and I had inspected Auburn's landmarks, we drove north on Highway 49 (the Mother Lode Highway) expecting to go as far as Downieville, but road construction delayed us so long that we never got beyond North San Juan. Grass Valley, twenty-four miles north of Auburn, was our first stop. Since I knew something of its history, I looked forward to seeing the portion of town known as Gold Hill, where George McKnight, in chasing a cow that had slipped its tether, stumbled over an outcropping of ore streaked with gold—the first quartz gold found on the Lode. Shortly after his discovery hundreds of men swarmed over the hill, digging the rich rock out with shovels and ultimately taking $1,500,000 from its gold-ribbed soil.

I remembered reading of the three men who, during a fire, shut themselves in a brick store with iron shutters. When the flames were spent, the townspeople returned to the wreckage and called to the men within the building but received no answer. They forced open the iron doors and found the three were dead, roasted by the searing heat that had enveloped them.

Would I see the gravestone of the innocent man who was hanged for stealing a horse? The identity of the real thief was discovered after the hanging, hence the inscription of the victim's tombstone:

Lynched by Mistake
The Joke's on Us.

Perhaps the home of Lola Montez, the actress, would make an attractive sketch. The famous beauty came to Grass Valley in 1852 and lived for seven years in a vine-covered cottage with her pets—a new husband, fierce dogs, and grizzly bears. Here, too, she trained sprightly little Lotta Crabtree, teaching her to dance and sing and, if the stories are true, took the child to the camp of Rough and Ready, and there placed her on an anvil in the blacksmith's shop to entertain the miners with her capers. For years Lotta was the toast of the camps.

I drove expectantly into Grass Valley looking for landmarks and, after cruising about, we pulled up to the attractive stucco Bret Harte Inn. Cars were bumper to bumper along every curb. The streets and stores were full of people. It was Saturday, and everyone had come to town. Right then I received a shock, as I realized that this was 1951 and I was searching for places built one hundred years ago. The lower half of the old buildings were hidden by cars or trucks; the upper half showed little but cornices or roofs and up-to-the-minute signs. On the surface, there was little for my sketch pad. So I contented myself with driving about and "spotting" the old places and with glancing at Gold Hill, and then I hastened on four miles to Nevada City.

NEVADA CITY

THOUGH Nevada City has a brand new courthouse perched on top of one of its many hills, the town gives the impression of age and of a nostalgic reverence for the old buildings and the history that surrounds them. The location was known to the trappers and hunters of the forties as Deer Creek and to the earliest prospectors as Caldwell's Upper Store. It was christened Nevada (or Snowy) by the miners in March, 1850, and after lode as well as placer mines drew men to the settlement and Wells Fargo opened an express office in the camp, the word "City" was added to its name. It has always been a mining camp. The placer workings of the fifties and sixties gave way to hydraulic operations in the seventies; and deep quartz mines in the hills overlooking the city are still producing.

Nevada City's growth was so rapid that in 1850, a year after its founding, the population numbered 12,000, and in 1856 it cast the third largest vote in California. The first samples of ore from the Comstock Lode were brought in 1859 to J. J. Ott for assaying, and other samples were taken to Melville At-wood in Grass Valley. The reports of these men were almost identical; and after the Nevada City *Herald* printed the first sensational news of the great silver bonanza, the bulk of the population joined the mad race across the high Sierra to windy Washoe, and by the middle sixties the town was nearly deserted.

It is far from deserted today, but it is the kind of place that invites leisurely inspection. Its streets are narrow, winding, and hilly, and at least three of its seven hills have picturesque names. Aristocracy Hill housed the prominent citizens, judges, and officials. Lost Hill may have received its name for any of three reasons: a small boy disappeared from home and was discovered asleep on it; a drunk, attacked by robbers, refused to give them the $20 gold piece in his pocket and instead threw the money into the muddy street where it disappeared in the ooze; a mining company lost a lead it was exploring somewhere within it. Piety Hill was named for its streets—Jordan, Calvary, Zion, Gethsemane, and Tribulation Trail—as well as for an old flight of wooden steps leading to its summit, known as Jacob's Ladder.

Each street is full of old brick buildings or of modern structures built in

OLD QUARTER,
AUBURN

FIREHOUSE (LEFT),
NEVADA CITY

the early style, and any number of commercial blocks have wrought-iron balconies, metal shutters, and corrugated-iron or tile roofs. The three-story National Hotel on Broad Street, an important hostelry during the sixties and seventies, is one of the oldest landmarks and was once headquarters for the stagecoaches which drew up in front of its balconied façade. In the residential portion of the town are many pretentious old homes shaded by big trees and shrubs and surrounded by carefully tended gardens. Nevada City has an allure that is intoxicating.

The city had five major fires during its first ten years of existence; so it is not surprising to learn that three fire companies were established to protect it from further destruction. Two of the firehouses are still standing, one on Broad Street and the other on Main Street. The latter, Nevada Hose Co. #1, has been converted into an excellent historical museum. Of the many exhibits, I remember most clearly the fearful din made by a miniature stamp mill when its stamps began to drop and the magnificent altar salvaged from the Chinese Joss House at Grass Valley. The altar fills the entire end of the building and is a mass of carved and gilded wood, silk hangings, fringes, lamps, and gongs. By the time I left the museum, I was so much a part of the gold rush that I went to a hardware store and bought a gold pan as the most suitable souvenir I could find.

NORTH SAN JUAN

THE drive to North San Juan, although only fifteen miles, was up hill and down dale all the way, and much of the road lay in forested areas. From the top of one hill I looked down to the bed of the Yuba River, far below. The stream was filled with huge gray boulders and showed the scars of hydraulic washing.

North San Juan was just the kind of place for which I had been looking. Its homes were spread over rolling hills, and its main street still contained a number of old brick buildings. The people on the streets all knew each other, and no one was in a hurry. When I went to a store that seemed "alive," I found the door locked. "Come back later, lady," called a man, sitting in the shade of a walnut tree. "It'll be open this afternoon."

Christian Kientz, a veteran of the Mexican War, named the hill where he discovered gold in 1853 "San Juan," for to him it resembled San Juan de Ulloa in Mexico. The Grizzly Ditch Company brought water to the diggings; but it was not until the following year, when the Middle Yuba Canal Company was able to supply large quantities of water to the miners, that the real boom began. The town reached its peak population of 10,000 in the seventies, when it became the center for the tremendous hydraulic mining operations on San Juan

Ridge, in which huge monitors or hydraulic hoses cut a gash through the hills several hundred feet deep, half a mile wide, and seven miles long, loosing thousands of tons of pay gravel, "lousy with gold." Through North San Juan the first long-distance telephone line in the West was strung in 1878, to provide communication between the big mining companies in the region; and this sixty-mile line had its main office in the town.

According to Philip Johnston, in his *Lost and Living Cities of the California Gold Rush:*

There was a time when the town extended much farther to the north than it does today; but those who lived in that section were unfortunate in having built their houses on "pay gravel." As mineral claims took precedence over all other titles, the huge monitors swept all before them, carrying away the ground where the houses stood. . . .

A menace lurks in the yawning precipice at North San Juan. In days when the town was populous, mothers cautioned their children against playing near its brink. . . . Old residents tell of a small boy who, with his companions, was flying a kite near the pit. Holding the string in his hands, he ran backward in order to watch the ascent of the kite, and stepped off into empty space! . . . although seriously injured, he lived to tell of his experience.

One day, the Downieville stage was standing in front of the express office. The driver was unloading the mail, and the passengers had alighted to stretch their legs. Suddenly, one of the horses took fright, and lunged forward in his harness. His mate, startled by the sudden movement, sprang forward with him, and the stage moved rapidly down the street in a cloud of dust. Several men dashed out in front of the runaway, waving their arms; but their efforts only changed the course of the terrified animals, and the stage careened around a corner, heading directly for the pit. Rearing back on their haunches, the horses tried to stop at the brink; but the momentum of the heavy vehicle pushed them over the edge and they plunged downward, snapping the traces. . . . When the driver, accompanied by half the town's population, arrived at the pit, they saw one horse lying motionless below with a broken neck, and the other trotting unconcernedly away. [Copyright, 1948, by the Automobile Club of Southern California, and here reprinted by permission.]

I could see no traces of mining from where I stood on the main street, but an old building with an ornate iron balcony girdling its second-story made a fine subject for a sketch and I started drawing it. Before I had even blocked it in, a white-haired man, carrying a large envelope, crossed the street to see what I was doing and said, "I see you are interested in buildings just as I am. See what I received through the mail?" Opening the envelope, he drew out an old photograph of the very building I was sketching. When the picture was taken, a large flume supported by a trestle crossed the highway, passed behind the building, just clearing the roof of a frame hotel, long since burned, and ran up the slope back of the Methodist church to the brink of San Juan Hill. This was one of the immense flumes installed by the hydraulic mining companies to provide water for their operations in cutting down the ridge.

The white-haired man, Mr. Hill, introduced himself and urged me to come to his house where he had more views of North San Juan and also a library of historical material. He suggested that I also visit the Methodist church, where his daughter was conducting a summer Bible school for boys and girls: "It's the white one up the street at the top of the hill. It was built in 1856."

I reached the church just as the Bible class raced out of doors for recess and, while they whooped around the lawn, I sketched the auditorium. Later on, in his cool living room, surrounded by photographs and books dealing with the Mother Lode, Mr. Hill talked to us about North San Juan, and pointed to a void that had once been the summit of the Hill before it was gouged away. He showed me pictures of the Odd Fellows Hall, dedicated in 1860, and he identified the meat market on the main street as the Masonic Hall, the Forty-Niner Liquor dispensary as How Chi Tung's Chinese store, and the two-story brick structure with the handsome iron balustrade and classic cornice as an office building dating from the early fifties. Several hydraulic mining companies had offices on its second story; a men's clothing store occupied the first floor. He even marked the following passage in Johnston's book, which described landmarks he feared I might miss:

Anachronous is the sign "Garage" painted upon the side of a two-story brick structure with iron doors and windows yet in place; but within until recently there was a quaint horsedrawn hearse, with windows and black curtains still intact. A few doors beyond is the firehouse—a small shed in which reposed an ancient hose-cart that was brought around the Horn, and transported hither by ox-drawn wagons. At the end of the street stands the Odd Fellows Hall, its lower story a repository for junk from two generations, and the upper story—where brothers of the lodge once foregathered—long unoccupied. In disarray the old furniture is scattered about, and official forms and documents litter the floor. [Copyright, 1948, by the Automobile Club of Southern California, and here reprinted by permission.]

As I left the town, I noticed the Chinese cemetery and a larger burying ground on a knoll beyond the highway, completely shaded by huge trees.

ROUGH AND READY

Mr. Hill had suggested that we visit Rough and Ready on the way back to Auburn, as it was only a four-mile detour out of Grass Valley.

Captain Townsend was the leader of a group of prospectors from Wisconsin who, in September, 1849, reached the green valley where Rough and

WELLS FARGO OFFICE
AND OFFICE BUILDING
WITH IRON BALUSTRADE,
NORTH SAN JUAN

OLD STORE BUILT
ABOUT 1855.
ELDORADO

ST. GEORGE HOTEL,
VOLCANO

Ready now stands and found placer gold there. In the Mexican War, Townsend had served under Zachary Taylor—"old Rough and Ready"—and the words "Rough and Ready" were painted on the canvas sides of the covered wagons that brought the men to the diggings. They naturally called their placer camp by the same title. Townsend lost no time in building a cabin that served as courthouse, saloon, and gambling establishment; and on more than one occasion, while a case was being tried, the judge would caution the faro-dealers to "call their games low."

Rough and Ready grew up around its placer diggings and was soon known as the most independent camp on the Lode. In April, 1850, one of its citizens called a mass meeting to protest against Federal mining taxes and so incited the men with his oratory that they agreed to secede from the Union and set up the independent State of Rough and Ready. They even went so far as to elect a President and a Secretary of State! The republic existed until July 4, when deep-rooted patriotic sentiment caused the miners to dissolve the new state, of which the government had never heard.

The camp hit its stride in 1851 with a population of 6,000 and boomed throughout the fifties. By the middle of 1859, the placers were exhausted, no quartz leads had been found, and a bad fire destroyed all but six of its 300 buildings. It was never completely rebuilt. Few of its old buildings are left today except the Odd Fellows Hall and a weathered, false-fronted shed beside the "Slave Tree." According to local tradition, a slave girl arrived in Rough and Ready in the early fifties and stuck her riding switch into the ground at that spot. It took root and is now an immense cottonwood tree. But far more exciting than the buildings, is the pulverized stream bed below the town, with its mounds of worthless rock and hummocks of earth, out of which have grown so much chaparral and shrubbery that they almost completely conceal the many acres of placer ground.

COLOMA

RETURNING to Auburn, we started south to see the rest of the camps on Highway 49, as well as certain ones which lie east or west of the main road. I did not intend to explore or sketch this area in detail, because it has been so well covered in many previous volumes, especially the books which appeared at the time of California's centennial celebration; but I was on the lookout for interesting tangible remains of the gold-rush days.

Coloma, less than twenty miles south of Auburn on the South Fork of the American River, is important as the site of Marshall's discovery. A stone monument marks the location of Sutter's Mill, where California's first gold was found in the tailrace, and a hill overlooking the town is crowned with a statue of Marshall, pointing to the spot where the discovery flakes lay. Coloma is a quiet little town, so buried in trees that only the buildings along the highway are easily seen. Marshall's home, a frame house with a roof of shakes, is preserved, as are two boxlike stone buildings beside the road—the China Bank dating from 1850 and a Chinese store built the following year. On the opposite side of the highway are the brick walls of Robert Bell's store, erected in 1856, its roof and porch gone, its iron doors ajar, and its interior a green tangle of weeds and ailanthus trees. Set back among more trees are two churches: one Roman Catholic, the other Emmanuel Episcopal—the first Protestant church in the mining camps.

PLACERVILLE

A SATURDAY afternoon in August is no time to visit Placerville if you are bent on exploring its past. The streets are narrow, traffic is heavy, the pavements are crowded, and the place is so completely modern that had I not known its early, colorful history I would have driven through it without a glance.

Few camps on the Lode have had so many names. The region around Coloma was quickly staked off by eager prospectors, so that latecomers were forced to seek unclaimed ground elsewhere. On the bank of Weber Creek three prospectors, Perry McCoon, William Daylor, and a man named Beaner discovered gold during the summer of 1848. The stream had so little water in it that their camp was called Dry Diggings. In time other localities were spoken of as "dry diggings" and, to avoid confusion, the settlement in the ravine was renamed Old Dry Diggings. When more men pushed up the gulch and the town grew, its name was changed to Ravine City. Its rapid growth attracted gamblers and criminals and initiated a period of lawlessness that lasted until its steady citizens took effective means to curtail crime by stringing three men from the limb of a tree; whereupon Ravine City became Hangtown. By the time law and order were established the miners adopted its present name of Placerville. But the name Hangtown persisted and even inspired a dish—the "Hangtown Fry"—still found on menus in the Mother Lode. A miner just in from his claim walked into the Cary House in 1849, threw a poke full of gold on the counter, and asked what was the most expensive meal the cook could produce? "Oysters are dearest and eggs come next," said the waiter. "Fry a mess of both and throw in some bacon," ordered the miner. The result was a Hangtown Fry.

Although the surface gold in the immediate region played out by 1851, the town became a crossroads for the Overland Stage route, the Pony Express, and the transcontinental telegraph, and its status as a mining and trade center made it the lively town it is today. Among its early merchants were Mark Hópkins, Philip D. Armour, and John M. Studebaker. Hopkins peddled groceries from door to door; Armour ran a butcher shop, and Studebaker made miners' wheelbarrows until he had saved enough money to return East and found his wagon factory, the forerunner of his automobile industry.

EL DORADO TO JACKSON

THERE are at least half a dozen towns on Highway 49 south of Placerville, between El Dorado and Jackson.

We scouted each one for its old buildings—the frame hotel with rickety balcony and the window-perforated stone façades of three imposing stores in El Dorado; two frame store-fronts, braced like scenery "flats" in Plymouth; a little brick gem of the late 1850's with twin arches and a recessed entrance at Drytown, and the two-story frame hotel at Amador City. From Plymouth we drove six miles through rolling hills to Fiddletown, curious to see the source of Bret Harte's "An Episode of Fiddletown."

Although settled in 1849 by a group of miners from Missouri and named by one of them "because the boys were always fiddlin'," its boom came in 1852, when a party of Frenchmen took a quarter of a million dollars from French Hill. Judge J. A. Purinton, a prominent citizen, was so embarrassed by being known in metropolitan circles as "the man from Fiddletown" that he sponsored a movement to rename the camp Oleta. The change was made in 1878 but, in spite of the judge, the old name clings. Fiddletown's three oldest buildings are well preserved and stand in the former Chinese section. A store, an adobe office with steep-pitched roof of shakes, in which Dr. Yee prescribed for his patients, and a brick and adobe Joss House flank the narrow main street. The rest of the town is almost invisible, so dense are the shrubs, trees, and tangled gardens that envelop every dwelling.

We drove through Sutter Creek to Jackson, a delightful place in its combination of old and new and with so much to see that we wandered its hilly streets until dusk.

VOLCANO

NEXT morning we made a very early start in order to avoid logging trucks and set out to the east for Volcano. After winding nine miles, we turned off the highway onto a side road which led through a grove of tall trees and dove down a steep hill to a flat, crossed it and dove again into Volcano. It was Sunday morning and not yet seven o'clock, and the place was asleep.

The town lies in a hollow filled with big white limestone boulders and ringed with conical, wooded hills. It was once thought to be in the crater of an extinct volcano, hence its name, but geologists have exploded that theory. It is said to antedate Coloma; a party of soldiers from Stevenson's regiment were already camped on the flat and were prospecting, when a passing trapper brought them news of Marshall's discovery. Most of them started at once for Sutter's Mill, but the ground they found was poorer than the diggings they had left. So back they came to join the few who had stayed on, and built a camp called Soldiers' Gulch, soon renamed Volcano.

Miners of all nationalities drifted into the diggings and worked peaceably together until a hot-headed Texan lost a pick, accused an Indian chief of stealing it, and shot him. The Indians retaliated by killing several miners but, after several skirmishes, they were driven away. The winter was unusually severe, and storms prevented supply wagons from getting through to the men in the hollow. The first wagon loaded with provisions arrived in the spring, just in time to "save Volcano from becoming a graveyard."

The claims yielded lavishly, the richest gravel paying $500 a pan. For a man to wash $100 a day was usual; some took out as much as $1,000 a day for a month. Hydraulic mining followed the hand-washing methods and so thoroughly cleaned out the bowl where the town lay that many of the oldest buildings were undermined and destroyed. The St. George Hotel, built in 1854 and now at one edge of the camp, was originally near its center! Volcano's miners never lacked water; in fact, they had too much of it and had to devise ways to store and divert it so as to avoid flooding the town as well as their diggings. While the area was productive, a total of $90,000,000 in gold was extracted from it, and during those years Volcano boomed.

Large quantities of bullion were sent out of the camp by both Wells Fargo and Adams Express companies; but after several treasure boxes were stolen by road agents, it was suspected that someone was tipping off the highwaymen. To test this, boxes filled with rocks were shipped out and these were never touched; so, after a few more holdups, the express offices closed.

The quiet town today, with its scattering of old stone buildings and frame houses, is a mere ghost of its boom days. Then it contained 8,000 people, 47 saloons, 2 breweries, 12 restaurants, 5 hotels, an Odd Fellows and Masonic Hall, a jail made of steel plates set between two-inch planks, and a church. Preacher Davidson, who was well liked, held services under a big tree until the miners constructed a frame building and obtained a bell for it in San Francisco from a ship that was being dismantled. The bell was then hauled by ox-team to Volcano.

The three-storied, balconied St. George Hotel, with its vine-covered columns, dominates the town and dwarfs the diminutive post office beside it. I walked between parked cars in front of the hotel and tried the front door, for I wanted to see the lobby and its stone fireplace; but at that early hour the building was locked. Farther down the street were the stone walls of the two saloons side by side in a duplex building, the jail, one or two other stone shells, the Adams Express office with its iron-paneled doors, and the Odd Fellows and Masonic Hall. Volcano established a Miners' Library Association and a Thespian Society in the early days, but where these organizations were housed I could only surmise, as not a soul was around whom I could question. Back of the houses and old stores I caught glimpses of huge, washed boulders and of acres of turned-up earth left by hydraulicking—all that remains visible of the mining operations that made the town so rich. The sun was just peeping over the hills when we left Volcano and started back to Jackson.

JACKSON TO SONORA

THE drive from Jackson to Sonora, through a succession of famous old camps, is similar to the stretch between Placerville and Jackson, for each town has one or more old landmarks or sites where historic events occurred. A solitary stone skeleton, the Ginocchio store, marks Butte City; the three-story I.O.O.F. Hall in Mokelumne Hill is by no means the only old structure left, but it is the most imposing. Erected in 1854 by the Adams Express Company, its third story was added by the Lodge in 1861. In Altaville, Prince's balconied store of cut stone is especially handsome and well preserved; Angels Camp and Tuttletown have several brick and stone monuments dating from the fifties. On the outskirts of Sonora I realized how hungry I was; so instead of taking the left-hand road to Columbia, I drove on into the larger town to get breakfast. But it was still early and Sonora was sleeping late. The best breakfast we could find was a lemon coke in a cigar store!

Sonora like Jackson is a captivating mélange of the old and the new. Its narrow streets and garden-trimmed homes invite leisurely inspection and admiration. A group of Mexicans from the state of Sonora opened the first placer and quartz veins in these southern mines during the summer of 1848, and for some time after Americans came to the diggings the majority of the population was Mexican—hence its first name, Sonorian Camp.

After our sketchy breakfast we drove back along the main street past St. James Episcopal Church, a Gothic structure, whose tall red steeple rose above the dense shrubbery and arbor vitae trees of its churchyard, and continued for four-and-a-half miles to the reawakened camp of Columbia.

COLUMBIA

FOR years the camp had been almost deserted; then in 1945 California purchased the whole town and made it a State Park as a memorial to the spirit of the forty-niners. Pride in historic mining camps is growing until today at least one is preserved in each of several Western states: Tombstone in Arizona; Virginia City in Nevada; Jacksonville in Oregon; Idaho City and Silver City in Idaho; Virginia City in Montana; Central City in Colorado; and Calico and Columbia in California. The moment one drives into the narrow shaded streets of Columbia the twentieth century disappears, for even newly restored buildings, shops catering to tourists, and modern cars parked in streets laid out in the days of carriage trade, cannot destroy the languor, the charm, and the sense of detachment that emanates from this appropriately named "Gem of the Southern Mines."

Although the gold in the southern camps was located first by Mexicans, their presence was resented by the Americans who followed them to every diggings. So strong was this intolerance that during 1850 a state law was passed taxing all foreign-born miners twenty dollars a month. This was designed to rid the gold fields of the many industrious and competing Mexicans, Chinese, Spaniards, Chileans, Peruvians, Italians, and Kanakas. It was only partially effective.

Columbia was one of the last of the gold-rush camps to materialize. It was March, 1850, before a group of Mexicans, driven from their claims in Sonora by American miners, found placer gold on the present site of the camp. They were successfully pounding the ore in mortars and washing it in the stream, when a party of men led by Dr. Thaddeus Hildreth camped at their diggings. A heavy rainstorm during the night drenched the men and their belongings, so the following morning they had to wait for their blankets to dry out before moving on. While they waited, they prospected on the hillside, and John Walker, one of the group, made a strike. Hildreth and his companions then ran the Mexicans out of their rightful diggings on Kennebec Hill and set up what was soon known as Hildreth's Diggings. The Americans took out fifteen pounds of gold a day during the first half week. So rich was the ground that within a month 6,000 persons had taken up claims in this phenomenally productive camp.

Now that the Mexicans were gone, the place was called American Camp, and later Columbia. As it grew, its tents and shacks began to follow an orderly pattern, and its streets were given names reminiscent of thoroughfares in well-known cities—Broadway, State, Fulton, Washington, and Jackson; and Gold and Silver were inevitable.

Mrs. Denouille was the first American woman to arrive in the camp. The miners were so eager to welcome her that they decorated the streets with arches and marched four miles down the road to escort her into town, preceded by a brass band. On October 25, 1851, when the camp's first newspaper, the *Columbia Star,* appeared, Mrs. Denouille, who by then was running a successful boardinghouse, bought the first copy for one ounce of gold dust. The paper was published for only five weeks; its successor, the *Columbia Gazette,* which first appeared on October 22, 1852, survived for six years.

At first the placers yielded abundantly, but they were dry diggings, with water available only at certain seasons. Production, therefore, did not reach its peak until after 1852, when ditch companies constructed flumes and canals, many miles in length, to provide a constant water supply to the camp. When one company completed a sixty-mile ditch, a procession, led by the Sonora Band and including the fire companies of both Sonora and Columbia, the men who built the flumes carrying banners, and the Miners Union four abreast, marched out the Gold Springs road to the high flume crossing. The festivities concluded with fireworks, a ball, and the "streets illuminated with candles."

The high flume served as a gallows on more than one occasion. A murderer named Barclay was taken from jail by a mob late one night in 1855 and hurried to a spot under the flume. A hasty miners' trial was held by the light of pine torches, with the newspaper editor acting as judge. When the sheriff arrived and tried to cut the noose, already around the prisoner's neck, he was hit over the head by one of the mob and was "out" until after Barclay was safely hanged. A similar event took place in December, 1858. A gang of thieves were raiding the community all too frequently, and the sheriff and the constable, John Leary, were determined to wipe them out. The men eluded every trap set for them, but finally two of the robbers were cornered in a lumberyard. In the gun battle that followed, Leary was killed and the robbers escaped. But shortly afterward one of them was captured and strung up on the Ditch Company's flume. Leary's funeral procession was half-a-mile long and was composed of the members of all the lodges of both Sonora and Columbia, as well as of hundreds of citizens on horseback or in carriages. By 1856, when sluicing failed to release gold from the gravels, hydraulic giants began to clean away the rich red soil from the limestone formations surrounding the town. Acres of mammoth gray boulders, completely denuded of earth, still reveal the extent of hydraulicking carried on.

Columbia, which by 1853 was the third largest city in California with a population of 15,000, prepared a petition with 10,000 signatures attached, to be presented to the State Legislature, urging that the capital be moved from Benicia to Columbia. A committee was appointed to take the document to the legislative session; meanwhile the petition was locked in a bank vault in Columbia. While the important paper lay in the bank, a group of citizens en-

I.O.O.F. HALL, BUILT 1854, MOKELUMNE HILL

COLUMBIA

deavored to secure the release of a man who was under a death sentence for
a crime of which he was thought by many to be innocent. A request to the
Governor that he pardon the accused murderer was refused. Frustrated but
inventive, the prisoner's friends saw in the "capital" petition a chance for his
pardon. One of them (some accounts say it was Senator J. W. Coffroth himself) broke into the bank vault and cut off the petition for the capital from
the list of 10,000 names. In its place he attached an appeal for their friend
and sent the paper by special messenger to the Governor. Impressed by the
number of signatures, the Governor signed the pardon, and the pardoned man
disappeared before the ruse was discovered.

In a second version of the story, the original petition was on its way to
the legislature when the committee carrying it met another group from Columbia, hurrying to plead for the pardon of the condemned man. The two delega-
tions mingled and in the course of heated discussion decided that an innocent
man should not die. The men sponsoring the petition then allowed a "slight
substitution" to be made, and thus lost Columbia's chance to become capital. Yet in 1945 the town realized its ambition for one day when, on July
15, Governor Warren, sitting in a plush-covered barber chair in the shop that
was delegated as his office, signed the document that made Columbia a State
Park.

When fire almost obliterated the camp in July, 1854, it promptly replaced
its flimsy canvas and wooden shacks with brick and adobe buildings and
widened its streets in an effort to prevent recurrent disasters. By the end of
the year the settlement possessed 143 faro banks with a capital of $1,500,000,
4 regular banks, 30 saloons, 27 stores, 7 bakeries, a brewery, a theater, and a
stadium for bull and bear fights. Dust and bullion were shipped from any of
three express offices. By 1856 a daguerreotype studio, 3 drug stores, and 6
laundries had been added, as well as St. Anne's Catholic church on Kennebec
Hill. The three rich mining claims donated for the site of the church are said
to be the only "unwashed acre" in the entire town. In 1857 a $1,500 bell was
shipped from New York around the Horn to Columbia and installed in the
newly built belfry.

In August, 1857, fire again swept the town. Indians who were gathered in
the nearby hills for a pow-wow helped the miners fight the fire and save property; but at that season the amount of water in the streams was so low as to
be of little use. In spite of every effort the flames continued to spread. They
licked their way into a hardware store and ignited forty kegs of powder, and
the explosion that followed scattered fragments of flaming debris in all directions. Finally, when nothing seemed able to halt the flames, the Tuolumne
Water Company opened its ditches and flooded the town.

Columbia's Firehouse #1 contains two old engines, one of which, called

Papeete, is claimed to be the oldest in the United States still in active duty. It was built in Boston in 1850 for King Kamehameka of the Sandwich Islands, and shipped around the Horn to San Francisco. There it lay unclaimed and unpaid for until its owners, fearing they'd never collect from the king, gladly sold it to Columbia Fire Company #1. Its progress to Columbia was slow, since it was sent by boat to Stockton and then to Bensonville by ox-cart. At Bensonville a committee met the engine and dragged it to the town in spite of rough and muddy roads. Two days after Papeete reached Columbia, its powers were demonstrated at a fire where it threw a stream of water "nearly as high as the new Liberty Pole." Fire Company #1 was made up solely of Yankees. A rival company was immediately formed which admitted French, Irish, and Germans to membership. Both organizations gave fashionable balls; and the one held by Company #2 on December 3, 1860, provided "a most beautiful supper saturated with champaign" and, as entertainment, a portion of the opera "Lucy de Lammermore," sung by Mr. Hirschel.

On the quiet Sunday morning when we drove through the shaded streets of Columbia, we found parking space not far from the one-story building, built in 1857 as a shop and bought by the members of Fire Company #1 to house the hand-pumper Papeete. Next to it stands John Duchow's printing office, with its lace-like iron balcony and three paneled doors. In it the *Columbia Gazette* was published. Every building has its history, and although some of the oldest were torn down in the sixties to mine the gravels under them, several blocks of brick and stone structures remain with their wooden or corrugated iron canopies shading the sidewalk.

Every street has its important edifices. The I.O.O.F. Hall is plain and massive; on the fringes of the little city are the ruins of old fandango halls and Chinese stores; near the entrance into town stands the Fallon Hotel and Theater. The first theater on the site was a wooden structure built in 1850. In 1854 Fallon bought the property, and within a few weeks the building burned. He rebuilt with wood, and the structure burned again in 1859. He then built the present brick building and hotel, which opened in 1860. The theater is operated during the summer by Stockton's College of the Pacific, which produces melodramas in the spirit of the rip-roarin' gold-rush days.

The Pay Ore Saloon is now an artist's studio, and the City Hotel, hidden in vines, has an ornate balcony; but nothing approaches in artistic perfection the Wells Fargo building (dating from 1857), with its cast-iron tracery from Troy, New York. In the days when its scales weighed out $50,000,000 in dust, Adams & Company, Page Bacon & Company, D. Ogden Mills & Company, and an agent representing Rothschild's of England also handled the swelling city's banking business.

The Stage Drivers' Retreat, built in 1854 and once the stage office and the most popular saloon, is now a museum chock full of valuable Columbiana. Of especial interest were several certificates of shares in the various water companies which once supplied the diggings. The Tuolumne County Water Company, incorporated September 4, 1852, with a capital stock of $550,000, offered shares at $250 each; the Columbia Gulch Fluming Company, with a capital stock of $30,000 and "chartered for fifty years from December 18, 1854," certifies that "W.O. Sleeper & Company is the holder of one share of the Capital Stock" and dates the transaction "May 2nd 1857."

In another case a naturalization paper issued by the "State of California, Tuolumne County" on February 14, 1855, states that Edward Quigley, a "subject of the Queen of Great Britain . . . made application to be admitted a citizen of the United States of America." Near it lies a notice describing a theft of "Gold Dust stolen from the office of Thos. Conlin, at Columbia, June 10, 1889," the total weight of the dust being about sixty ounces and its value $1,200. Any information concerning it was to be sent to Thos. Conlin or to Curtin's Detective Agency in San Francisco. A reward for its return was offered.

Before we left the town, we climbed Kennebec Hill to St. Anne's red brick church to see the altar murals painted by James Fallon, son of the hotel-keeper, and the ornamentation covered with gold leaf taken from the Columbia mines. The view from the church porch was extensive. On top of a hill at the northern edge of the camp is the two-story schoolhouse, erected in 1862; next to it is a cemetery. From this vantage point, the heart of town was hidden by trees, but below and on all sides were acres of naked rocks and only partially overgrown pits and hummocks, where husky men once dug with knives and picks and where great Monitors tore the topsoil from the lime formations in the mad but profitable quest for gold. Columbia as a State Park is dreamy and nostalgic where once, as a teeming camp, it was vibrant and filled with the sounds of industry and of men and beasts. Fortunately for the twentieth century, its architectural husk retains a visual fragment of those days.

SONORA TO COULTERVILLE

IN A FEW HOURS we were back in Sonora, and this time we saw more of its old houses with wooden lace eaves and carved and ornamental porches, as well as several remodeled brick buildings whose iron shutters had disappeared long ago. At Yosemite Junction we detoured west a number of miles to Knight's Ferry, clattering across the covered wooden bridge over the Stanislaus River, to the quiet town.

William Knight, a scout and fur trader, settled on the bank of the river in

1849 and, since the Stanislaus was dangerous to ford, established a ferry and built a trading post to serve the swelling flood of prospectors who were pouring into the Southern mines. Thousands of men and pack animals crossed the 150-foot-wide river on the ferry, until it was replaced in 1852 by a covered wooden bridge. A grist mill was erected near the bridge, but both were washed away in a torrential flood in 1862. As soon as the waters subsided a new mill of stone and a second covered bridge with massive abutments were built by an English stonemason, T. Vinson, under the direction of Dave Tullock.

During its heyday Knight's Ferry was a gay but rough camp, in which a most impregnable jail was constructed during the fifties. It was made entirely of iron plates, its foundation was bedrock, and the small peephole in each cell door could be closed with an iron plate fastened with a bolt. A frame lodge-hall dating from the eighties stands on one side of the street, and the ruins of the grist mill stand on the other, close to the bridge.

When we had retraced our way to Yosemite Junction and driven on to Chinese Camp, we were much disappointed to find so little of it left. Even the old Wells Fargo building was completely screened by foliage. A winding road beyond it twists down to the Tuolumne River and on to Jacksonville, whose old hotel, the sole survivor from a fire in the 1850's, was being torn down when we drove by.

Beyond Jacksonville Highway 49 follows Moccasin Creek for several miles. The entire creek bed shows the result of goldwashing, even though bushes and grasses have gradually grown over endless rows of clean-washed boulders. The road leaves the valley, corkscrews over a saddle, and then winds through ranch land to Coulterville, tucked away in a pocket of the hills.

George W. Coulter came into the valley with a pack train of goods early in 1850 and opened a tent store on Maxwell's Creek. When he hung a flag in front of his store, the Mexicans called the camp that mushroomed around the diggings Banderita, or "little flag." Before long the name was changed to Maxwell's Creek and then to Coulterville. Several old buildings are grouped around an open plaza. Some are roofless wrecks, survivors of fires, and a couple still do business as store or hotel. The three-story Jeffrey Hotel, barricaded by umbrella trees, though not the oldest, is the largest of the buildings. The sleepy town has charm, but it is hard to picture it with 3,000 white miners and 1,000 Chinese, the latter quartered on its northern fringe.

Back at the junction just south of Jacksonville we left Highway 49, to climb Priests Grade to Big Oak Flat and the few camps between it and the edge of the Yosemite Valley. As we snaked up the grade, the extent of the placerings in Moccasin Creek lay spread out below—a corrugated strip of waste gray rock, cut by a trickle of stream and bordered by thickets of greenery.

The camps of Big Oak Flat, First Garrotte, and Second Garrotte have one to two landmarks each, and the last has the dead stump of the Hangman's Tree from which sixty men are said to have swung.

From Second Garrotte we drove east into the high Sierra, leaving behind the Mother Lode with its historic towns, all so well photographed, sketched, and described in dozens of books. The drive across Yosemite, through groves of trees in which Giant Sequoias tower above the biggest pines and where bare granite rocks overshadow green forests, is scenically indescribable. So is the view from the summit of Tioga Pass, where the magnificent sweep of Leevining Canyon unfolds, its rocky walls so sheer and high that cars crawling along the shoulder of the yawning gorge are colored dots on a hairline of roadway. The flat, high line of the horizon is desert—the endless, barren, eroded mountains and sinks that form Panamint and Death valleys and the huge Mohave Desert farther to the south.

BODIE

EAST of the rocky ledges of Leevining Canyon we stopped in the town of Leevining, near Mono Lake, to inquire about the condition of the road to Bodie, one of the most colorful of the California ghost camps. The gas station attendant discouraged our taking the road out of Mono Lake across the desert and up the face of Bodie Bluff, saying it was very rough and that much of its surface was washed away. He suggested that we drive north almost to Bridgeport and take a shorter road to Bodie on which the county grader had recently worked. From the time we made the turnoff south of Bridgeport, we had a steady twelve-mile pull up the western slope of the mountain to its crest. Here we were above timberline, and as we started down the east side, we passed a few old mine properties before we reached the barren flat in a high mountain hollow, where the skeleton camp of Bodie bleaches and rots away. The ground was covered with sage and bunch grass and a stiff, raw wind blew steadily from the west.

Gold was known to exist in the region by 1852; for by then the Mother Lode was saturated with miners. Streams of disappointed prospectors began scouring the nearby ranges for "colors," crossing the Sierra toward the east over Tioga, Sonora, and Ebbets passes. Discoveries near Mono Lake in 1857 resulted in a small settlement known as Monoville.

William S. Body (or Bodye or Bodie) was one of a party of placer miners who left Monoville and explored the desolate mountains east of the Sierra, where they found gold in a high, hidden valley in 1859. When supplies began to dwindle, Body started for Monoville with a poke of dust to exchange for the men's winter rations. On the return trip he and E. S. Taylor were caught in a blizzard, and Body became too exhausted to travel farther. Taylor carried the helpless man as far as he could, then left him wrapped in a blanket while he fought his way through the storm in search of help. When Taylor returned, he was unable to find the spot where Body lay, although he spent the entire night searching for his companion. The body was not discovered until the following spring. It was then taken to the camp and buried on top of the hill overlooking the embryo town, which the men immediately christened Bodie in honor of the unfortunate prospector.

The Bunker Hill mine, later known as the Standard, was discovered high up on Bodie Bluff in July, 1861; and all through the sixties the windswept camp attracted miners, who worked the placer ground or traced the outcroppings up the mountainside and pitted the Bluff with prospect holes and mine shafts. Practically all freight was brought in by ox- or mule-drawn wagons from the valley town of Hawthorne, Nevada, forty miles below. The road had been extended through difficult terrain for almost ten miles west of the booming camp of Aurora, also in Nevada. Mine owners were soon in need of capital, and to raise the necessary funds they consolidated their holdings and issued stock. By July, 1864, most of Bodie's mines had merged and were held by the Empire Company of New York.

Soon after this transaction J. Ross Browne, travel correspondent for *Harper's Monthly,* visited Bodie, and in August, 1865, an account of his "Trip to Bodie Bluff and the Dead Sea of the West" was printed in the magazine. Browne reached the high mountain camp by the road from the Nevada side of the range. He describes

. . . the base of a conical hill, surmounted by a range of reddish-colored cliffs, very rough, jagged and picturesque; a capital looking place for a den of robbers or a gold mine. This was the famous Bodie Bluff. The entire hill as well as the surrounding country, is destitute of vegetation, with the exception of sage-brush and bunch grass—presenting even to the eye of a traveler . . . a wonderfully refreshing picture of desolation.

We reveled in dust along the road that skirts the Bluff; it was rich and unctuous, and penetrated us through and through, so that by the time we arrived at the Judge's cabin, where he had some workmen employed, we were permeated with the precious metals of Bodie. A fine spring of water, aided by a little snake-medicine, set us all right. . . .

In the undeveloped condition of the mines, which are yet but partially opened, much is left to conjecture; but from the direction of the various lodes I should judge them to be ramifications from some great principal vein or Veta Madre, as the Mexicans call it. Loose quartz in disconnected masses is found on the surface of the hill. . . .

I descended several shafts. . . . This thing of being dropped down two hundred feet into the bowels of the earth in wooden buckets, and hoisted out by blind horses attached to "whims," may be very amusing to read about, but I have enjoyed pleasanter modes of locomotion. . . .

There are several companies engaged in working the principal veins that extend through Bodie Bluff. . . . the largest interests are held by the "Empire Gold and Silver Mining Company of New York." . . .

There are [also] placer diggings in the Bodie range which have yielded during ordinary seasons of rain as high as sixteen to twenty dollars a day to the head. In fact the "color of gold" as the miners say, can be obtained from the surface dirt taken at random from any part of the hill.

In the illustration he made of Bodie, Browne shows a barren hill and a flat on which stand a handful of frame shacks. Of the town he reports:

There are now some fourteen or twenty small frame and adobe houses erected for the use of the workmen; a boarding house is already established; lots and streets are laid out by means of stakes; new houses are springing up in every direction, and speculation in real estate is quite the fashion.

It was amusing to witness the enthusiasm with which the citizens went into the business of trading in lots. Groups of speculators were constantly engaged in examining choice locations, and descanting upon the brilliant future of the embryo city. A pair of boots, I suppose, would have secured the right to a tolerably good lot. . . . Some of the city dignitaries, however, duly impressed with the importance of having a view of their town appear in the illuminated pages of *Harper*, paid me the compliment to attach my name to the principal street; and thus, in future ages, I confidently expect my memory will be rescued from oblivion.

In the middle seventies the Fortuna vein was opened, exposing stringers of gold richer than any heretofore discovered, and when successive strikes uncovered other large veins, a new gold rush started. The most extensive operations were carried on during 1876-1877 in the Standard mine, whose property included the Fortuna, Incline, and Burgess veins. This mine became the bonanza of the camp, producing in its first twenty-five years $14,500,000 and paying $5,000,000 in dividends. The Bodie mineral belt was two-and-a-half miles long and three-quarters of a mile wide, and although the average value of the ores ran only $35 to $60 a ton, while the boom lasted the mines produced $400,000 of bullion a month and kept thirty companies actively engaged in mining the lucrative metal.

Advertised as "Bigger than the Comstock," the camp drew men of all kinds to swarm over the mountains and stake claims for miles around and swell the population, until sixty saloons and gambling halls and quantities of hotels and lodging houses were hastily thrown together to accommodate the sudden influx. Since the slopes above Bodie were treeless, timber for mines, for buildings, and even for fuel, was freighted in and sold for outrageously high prices.

During the winter of 1877, when winds whirled around the barren bowl where the town lay and when snow piled twenty feet deep in drifts, the mines closed down and, as one miner wrote, "There's nothing to do but hang around the saloons, get drunk and fight, and lie out in the snow and die." But by early spring the noise of hammers mingled with the clatter of the mills, and Bodie became a "wooden town of 250 buildings" with additional cabins near the mine shafts. As the population increased, first to 13,000 and then to 15,000, wildcat promoters began to push the Bodie mine by selling stock at twenty-five cents a share. For a time the camp was flooded with stock certificates instead of money; then, unexpectedly, large deposits of gold were found in the mine and the worthless stock jumped to $55 a share.

By 1879 the camp had struck its stride and its many streets were solid with buildings. A Miners' Union and an Odd Fellows' Hall; a church, constructed from funds collected in a single night's soliciting of the many saloons and gambling dens; three breweries; and a bank established by Mark Hopkins were added to the little city. Three newspapers, the *Bodie Standard,* the *Esmeralda Union,* and the *Bodie Free Press,* reported the colorful life of the raucous camp, whose days were punctuated with shootings, brawls, and stabbings. The *Free Press* is credited with the story of the child whose family was moving from Aurora to Bodie and who, on the night before their departure, concluded her prayer by saying: "Goodbye God, we're going to Bodie." The *Press* contended that she had said, "Good, By God, We're going to Bodie!"

Bodie soon became known as a "Shooting Town" in which few criminals were brought to trial. Its two adjoining cemeteries, one neatly fenced and the other, the more popular burying ground, reserved for gamblers, gunmen, and fancy women, were soon populated with those who died from bad whisky or "poor doctors." Six men died in shooting scrapes within a week in 1879; and two gunmen, who while drunk got into an argument as to which was the better shot, staggered out behind the saloon to test their marksmanship. The following day Bodie had a double funeral. Road agents seized so much bullion from the coaches that rattled out of town that Wells Fargo was forced to protect the shipments with the best of its sharp-shooting guards.

Bodie's boom began to peter out by 1883; but as long as any of its mines produced, the city clung tenaciously to its windy site in spite of its dwindling population. All through the eighties the *Esmeralda Herald,* published at Hawthorne, Nevada, carried a column headed "Bodie Mines Clippings" which included such items as:

August 18, 1883: Andy Donohue, a miner was killed on the 16th, four miles from Bodie. He was riding on a load of copper bullion when the wagon turned over, crushing him to death.

January 26, 1884: *The Sloggers.* The prize fight in Bodie between Skewes and Roughan was won by the latter in twenty-four rounds when Skewes' second threw up the sponge, stating that his man's arm was too badly injured to continue the fight."

March 15, 1884: Bodie has more dogs to the acre than any other camp on the coast. China Charley, who used to work at Wagner's corner is now pronounced by his countrymen to be a leper.

Year by year the population fell away and when, in the early 1900's, the pumps in the Standard mine, from which a total of $50,000,000 had been extracted, were removed and the fires under the boilers were pulled, Bodie began to atrophy. Not that it died, however; for the Roseclip mine was reopened briefly in 1936, and the Standard was worked intermittently by lessees up to World War II. Now nothing but low-grade ore remains in the mines, whose total output is estimated at $70,000,000, and for the last few years the many properties have been idle.

A fire in June, 1932, destroyed the bank and a portion of the business district; but the church, the schoolhouse, the firehouse, and the greater percentage of the tinder-dry wooden buildings remain, blistering and cracking under each successive summer sun. Eight people lived in Bodie in 1946; but there is no one in the mummified town today, except in summer. Then a few hardy men live in its barren houses, and curious tourists wander through the empty streets, peering into the brick vault of the bank, photographing the blocks of boarded-up houses and stores, or visiting the small museum, housed in the Miners' Union Hall. The rotting wooden sidewalks echo their footsteps and the wind carries the sound to the barren hills, whose treasure drew so many men to the high and desolate basin.

PANAMINT CITY

THE eastern portion of southern California is desert—not mile upon mile of drifting sand, but range after range of desolate, eroded mountains, separated by salt and alkali "sinks." Between the bony ribs of the barren mountains are ghost mining-towns, dead and bleaching under the torrid sun, or enjoying a lengthy siesta between capricious booms. Death Valley has at least a dozen of them, and Panamint Valley, just west of it, has more.

Of recent years, since over two million acres of primitive, untouched desert have been set aside as Death Valley National Monument and a de luxe inn awaits travelers at Furnace Creek, many persons, fascinated by the ma-

ADOBES, CALICO

BODIE, FROM THE CEMETERY

cabre country, visit it during those seasons when the heat and humidity make exploration of its lonely, colorful mountains safe; but to the emigrants of '49, it was a Stygian nightmare from which many never awoke.

In seeking routes to the California gold fields, thousands of pioneers and adventurers journeyed southwest from Salt Lake City across endless sandy wastes, stunned by the extent of the desert and hopefully scanning the western mountains for a break in their massive walls over which jaded oxen could pull the creaking, heavily loaded wagons. Guided by scouts or provided with crude maps and quantities of inaccurate information given them by survivors of earlier parties, the wagon trains moved toward the coast in an alkali-laden pall of dust. Those who stuck to the proven trails had hardships enough; those who struck out to find shortcuts courted death by thirst or starvation. Many went insane as their wagons fell apart in the blistering heat, their oxen weakened and died, and their own tongues became black and swollen for lack of water. They seemed to make no progress, for every mountain scaled revealed another and another to be crossed before the lush green fields and the mountain streams of California could be reached.

Typical of those who broke away from the long, tested, but comparatively safe trails was the Bennett-Arcane party, which, as part of a large wagon train, left Salt Lake City in September, 1849. Each day's travel across the desert was slow, and before long arguments developed over the route chosen by the wagonmaster, and one after another the disagreeing parties pulled their wagons out of line and struck off for themselves. The main column crawled south, but after some days more of alkali dust and brackish water, three groups, impatient to get away from the desert, struck west toward the mountains. The first of these consisted of thirty young Jayhawkers, who abandoned most of their equipment and hurried ahead, crossing the Panamint Range and the Mohave Desert and finally reaching California. The second party tried to keep up with the Jayhawkers and forced their oxen ahead. The Bennett-Arcane party, which consisted of two women, four children, and thirteen men, among whom were Lewis Manly and John Rogers, traveled more slowly and were soon left behind.

Manly scouted the country for water holes, camp sites, and routes that wagons could travel, but few springs existed in that part of the valley and, day by day, the supply of food and fodder dwindled. The Amargosa River was a welcome sight, and both men and stock drank greedily of the bitter water, only to discover that its acrid content was Epsom salts. By the time the wagons reached Furnace Creek Wash, the oxen were spent, and, frantic at the thought of dying in the desert, several of the men in the party went on alone. Only the two families and Rogers and Manly remained and, realizing the desperate situation, these two men agreed to go ahead, try to find a way out of the valley, get provisions and return to the stricken emigrants. Bennett believed they could be back in fifteen days and accordingly rationed what little food remained. An ox was slaughtered and the flesh dried and packed in the men's knapsacks and, after they disappeared into the unknown mountains, those left behind made camp and settled down to await their return, subsisting on tea, rice, and jerked ox-meat.

Fifteen days went by and then twenty, and still the men had not returned. Believing that they had reached California and had no intention of struggling across the mountains again, the famished families on the twenty-fifth day decided to move on, leaving their wagons and using the few remaining oxen as mounts for the women and children. Just before they started, the desert silence was shattered by a shot; and, looking in the direction of the sound, the dazed survivors saw Manly and Rogers leading a mule whose pack bulged with provisions. Led by these already weary men, who had crossed more than two hundred miles of desert before finding a ranch where they could buy food, the emaciated party struggled on, over the Panamints and the Slate Range to the California valley. On the summit of the Panamints, one of the women looked back into the terrible sink that had so nearly claimed them and unconsciously named it when she whispered, "Good bye, Death Valley."

On the west side of the Panamint Range, at the head of a narrow and treacherous canyon, is the ghost of Panamint City. In 1860 and 1861 more than one prospector explored the canyons leadings into the range, and William Alvord tried repeatedly to find again the cliff he had seen up a deep ravine, south of Telescope Peak. He described the entrance to the canyon as a broad fan of gravel—the debris from cloudbursts—and he named the narrow gorge itself, with its mile-long passageway of high rock wall, no more than fifteen feet wide, Surprise Canyon. Beyond this narrow defile and 6,000 feet above the valley floor, there was a sloping basin at whose head rose the high gray cliffs that he had seen. On a third trip to the forbidding canyon, Alvord took a partner along who, oppressed by the overhanging 500-foot cliffs in the gorge, went beserk and killed him. In 1861 a party of prospectors entered Wildrose Canyon (north of Surprise Canyon), and when they discovered signs of antimony and silver, they drove a tunnel into the mountainside. The Panamint Indians watched them curiously and then, resenting this intrusion of their territory, crept stealthily down upon the miners and killed them.

No further digging in the area was attempted until December, 1872, when Richard C. Jacobs, W. L. Kennedy, and Robert L. Stewart struggled up Surprise Canyon searching for the source of the silver float they had found at its mouth. After climbing up 5,000 feet in five miles, they reached a basin walled with greenish-blue cliffs. Here they hastily built a furnace in which to test samples of the rock and, when their crude assays showed copper-silver values up to $2,500 a ton, they staked two claims, one of which was the Wonder. They then placed notices on bushes and under rocks throughout the area, calling a meeting on February 10, 1873, for the purpose of organizing the Panamint mining district and for formulating laws to govern it. On the appointed day the three discoverers and a handful of men, some of whom were "hiding out" in the mountains, established the district, twenty miles long on the crest of the range and extending east to the center of Death Valley and west to the center of Panamint Valley.

The first load of ore from the Wonder claim was packed down Surprise Canyon to Los Angeles in December, 1873, where it was displayed in the Clarendon Hotel, in the hopes of interesting men with capital in the Panamint claims. John Percival Jones and his partner, William Morris Stewart, both of whom had made fortunes on the Comstock, were the first to back the properties by buying a group of claims and by organizing the Surprise Valley Mill and Water Company. Word that Jones and Stewart had invested in Panamint mines started a rush to the canyon, and by October, 1874, four hundred men had struggled to the high, hidden valley and were living in tents or shelters made of piles of stones.

It was a violent camp from the first because of its inaccessibility. No road led to it—only sand trails hardly fit for horses or pack mules—until R. C. Jacobs and a few other enterprising citizens fell to work with picks and shovels and filled and smoothed the roughest stretches. Even after a wagon road of sorts was built through the valley and a toll road up the gash of the canyon, the population was made up largely of men with notorious pasts for whom more than one sheriff was hunting. It was said that so many of the population were "wanted" elsewhere that their unclaimed mail at Pioche, Austin, and the many other towns they had hastily vacated, was just naturally forwarded to the raw, new camp atop the Panamints. The first vehicle to reach the camp was a two-wheeled butcher's cart, which in a surprisingly short time was pressed into service as a hearse and was carrying the corpses of those killed in gun battles to the cemetery in Sour Dough Gulch.

Many of the claims were owned by the desperadoes. Two road agents sold their location for $25,000 and went to San Francisco to collect the money. Wells Fargo & Company, learning of the transaction claimed $12,000 of the sales price to cover their losses from the holdups that the robbers and their gang had staged. The ringleader was given a choice of paying or being arrested. He paid—and demanded a receipt! As mine after mine was discovered and tunnels were driven into the solid cliffs above the town, two hundred Chinese laborers were brought in to improve the toll road and to chip trails to the mines along the ledges and benches of the cliffs, and promoters were busy organizing stock companies, until by December, 1874, seven such were operating. By late fall, pony express riders, freight wagons, and swaying stage-coaches were toiling up the appalling grade to Panamint City, the center of all this activity, and Meyerstein's Panamint Freighting Company was making regular trips to and from the valley, hauling machinery, merchandise, lumber, and food.

The town, laid out at the head of the sloping valley, consisted of one street a mile long, flanked by more than two hundred stone houses, between which crowded merchants' tents and shacks. The head of the street was 1,000 feet higher than the foot, and from it branched smaller canyons, one of which, known as Maiden Lane, was occupied by Martha Camp and her bevy of girls. Dave Neagle was the first to lay a board across two barrels, set out two glasses, and open a saloon. Others followed his example until Main Street had twenty whisky mills.

As the town prospered, the merchants built more permanent quarters, and Neagle's Oriental Saloon boasted a black walnut bar, separate card rooms, $10,000 worth of fixtures, and a bullet-proof wall to separate it from the Occidental Saloon next door. The Dexter was the most elegant of the establishments. It was built of milled lumber—a great extravagance—and its interior was covered with "silver gilt paper." To complete its furnishings Fred Yager, its proprietor, ordered a large mirror to place behind the bar. It was shipped from the East around the Horn and hauled across the desert by mule-team. Travelers reported its progress on the road, and the entire camp went a mile down the trail to escort into town the freight wagon that was carrying it. The mirror was taken from the wagon and carried into the saloon. There its bearers, elated by anticipatory celebrating, stumbled, and the mirror fell with a shattering crash!

Panamint with a population of 5,000, reached its peak during the winter of 1874-1875. Lots sold for $2,500, a much-needed boardinghouse was completed, a Masonic Lodge was formed, and the first white child born in the camp was presented by the citizens with a case of champagne. Several hundred mining claims were staked off, eight properties were tunneled, and the Wonder, Hemlock, and Wyoming mines were producing heavily. Ten tons of sacked ore were ready for shipment each day and, even though they had to be sent all the way to Britain for smelting, the ore was so rich in copper and silver that its owners netted a neat profit.

On July 4, 1875, when Jones and Stewart's mill and furnace were completed, the occasion was celebrated by a parade, led by a band and graced by a float (the butcher's cart again), on which rode a Goddess of Liberty and three little girls decked in bunting. In August the thirty stamps of the mill began pounding on ore from the Wyoming and Hemlock tunnels; and day by day, as the 2,600-foot cable from the Hemlock mine delivered buckets of ore to the mill and the pile of bars awaiting shipment grew higher, John Small and John McDonald, two of the town's desperadoes, waited expectantly. Everyone could guess what the gunmen were planning, as they were known to be equal to any crime. Only the preceding New Year's Eve, they had gone down the grade to where several hundred Chinese lived and had thrown rocks at the hovels, until the frightened Orientals fled down the canyon. They then burned the miserable shacks, and so strong was anti-Chinese feeling in the camp that when they returned to Panamint they were cheered for their actions. Altogether Panamint had the reputation of being such a tough camp and holdups occurred with such inevitable frequency, that Wells Fargo simply refused to handle bullion shipments. Late in the fall the two men learned that the silver was about to be sent out. Anticipating that it would be shipped at night, they hid in the narrowest part of the canyon and waited until the freight wagon came jingling down the grade. As it came abreast of them, the men jumped from the shadows and demanded that the driver hand over the silver it contained.

"Help yourself," was the unexpected answer and, looking into the open wagon, the men saw that the silver was cast into five 750-pound cannon balls and that they were helpless to lift even one of them. Stewart had devised a safe method of delivery, and thereafter all shipments were made in this form.

But even while the stacks of the big furnace belched black smoke and the stamps thudded in the mill, Panamint's boom began to fade. In 1875 the silver veins began to pinch out, and the limestone surrounding them was extremely hard and expensive to work. After the financial panic hit Los Angeles and the bank of Temple and Workman, the heaviest underwriter of Panamint's stocks, failed, the population began to hurry down the canyon trail to the new camp of Darwin. T. S. Harris, editor of the *Panamint News,* who set up his office in a tent and printed the first issue on November 26, 1874, had announced that the aims of the paper were "To furnish the people of Panamint with the latest news; to give to the 'outside world' accurate and truthful information regarding the mines and district; and to make money." On October 21, 1875, he printed the last issue. He then shipped his press to Darwin and hurried down the road after it. Even after the first exodus the big mill continued to run, pounding away on $50,000 worth of ore from a newly discovered vein in the Hemlock mine. Encouraged by this new strike, the few miners and merchants who stayed on were confident that Panamint would "come back."

And then, on the morning of July 24, 1876, it began to rain and continued to pour until noon. The sun shone briefly but was soon obscured by a new bank of heavy black clouds. While thunder rumbled, a cloudburst struck the head of the valley, sending tons of whirling water in waves fifty feet high down the main street. The terrified inhabitants, warned by the roar of the flood, rushed up the mountainsides to safety, or formed human chains, after the crest of the water had passed, so as to rescue persons who had miraculously escaped drowning and were marooned by the swirling eddies. Huge boulders and tree trunks, swept along by the tremendous force of the water, battered frame buildings into kindling wood and demolished stone walls. The main stream was swelled by new floods pouring down side canyons, until the immense volume of water, piling up at the entrance to Surprise Canyon, catapulted through the narrow ravine and out onto the desert floor below, carrying with it the debris that twenty minutes before had been half of the town of Pana-mint, and the bodies of fifteen persons lost in the boiling waters.

That was the end; and, although occasionally some miner has gone into the lonely deserted valley and made a few dollars from its abandoned mines, scarcely anyone has lived in the town since the deluge. The last unsuccessful attempt to tunnel under old properties was made in 1925.

Panamint City can be reached by truck or jeep, and it is best to travel up Surprise Canyon with someone who knows the country and is weatherwise; for cloudbursts have ripped through the gorge more than once, leaving scars high on the rock walls and adding tons of silt to the fan-shaped delta at its mouth. If you reach the site of the city, you will see the tall brick stack and the foundations of the big mill, and the cellars and ruined stone walls of a few stores and other buildings, scattered far apart on the once busy thoroughfare. Even a few of the graves in Sour Dough Canyon are intact; but the rest of the city is gone.

CALICO

THREE years ago, while visiting friends in Los Angeles, my husband and I were driven to Buena Park for dinner at Knott's Berry Farm. "With your interest in old camps you must see the ghost town he has assembled," they insisted. I was skeptical about the ability of transplanted and reconstructed buildings to convey anything resembling the atmosphere of a real ghost town; but the remarkable collection assembled by Mr. Knott succeeds in making vivid a vital part of American history to hundreds of thousands of people who cannot go farther afield. While we were enjoying the chicken dinner served in the tremendous dining room, Mr. Knott told me that he had his eye on a real deserted site, which he was planning to restore. This one was to remain a deserted town in its original setting.

A year later I read that Walter Knott had purchased old Calico town, near Yermo, California, and was making extensive plans for its restoration to boom-day appearance. Walter Knott's interest in the town is partly sentimental; for he grew up on a homestead in the Mohave desert and worked in the Calico mines during the summer of 1910. Now that he owns the seventy-five-acre tract containing the townsite, he intends, with the help of Paul V. Klieben, to reconstruct the place as he knew it. To date little has been completed but the clearing away of debris and the reinforcing and labeling of old buildings; but Knott's plans are intended to cover many years.

Charles Mecham, John McBride, and Larry Sylva are credited with finding horn silver in Wall Street Canyon in the Calico Mountains in 1881, and their discovery started a stampede to the gaudy hills. The Silver King, in Wall Street Canyon above the townsite, was the earliest discovery; and Walter Knott claims that his uncle grubstaked the prospectors who found it, but that in the mad rush to the diggings he was pushed aside and others developed the property from which $10,000,000 was later taken. During the eighties a narrow-gauge road was built from the mine, and also from the Waterloo mine in the next canyon to the west, down to the stamp mills on the Mohave River, north of the supply town of Daggett. Silver ingots from the mills were shipped to the San Francisco mint.

More than one hundred properties were opened and worked by seven hundred miners during the boom days, and most of the mines were self-supporting from the start. The district was a "poor man's bonanza," for the deposits were shallow and could be worked at little expense. Furthermore, the bullion obtained from the mines scattered in Bismarck, Occidental, Odessa, and Wall Street canyons was "exceptionally pure." Before the high-grade veins began pinching out and the price of silver dropped to sixty-three cents an ounce, a dozen mills with a total of 170 stamps were pounding away on Calico ore. Express company receipts covering the fifteen-year period of the camp's activity show that $65,000,000 of silver was shipped from the district.

In addition to its silver deposits, borax was found during 1883 high up in Odessa and Mule canyons, east of Calico townsite.

Borax had already been discovered in Death Valley in 1873 by Aaron and Rosie Winters, and the claims they staked sold for $20,000 in 1880 to W. T. Coleman, the pioneer producer of the rare white substance. The following year "cotton ball" borax was refined by Coleman at the Harmony Borax works north of Furnace Creek and was freighted in specially constructed huge-wheeled wagons, drawn by twenty mules, miles across the desert to the nearest railroad. Up to 1883 borax was found only in fibrous "cotton ball" form. That year a solid type was discovered in the ledges of Mule Canyon, northeast of Calico, and the product was named Colemanite in honor of the Death Valley manufacturer. The Pacific Coast Borax Company, of which Francis Marion (Borax) Smith was president, explored the deposits near Calico and decided to develop them. "Borax" Smith built a narrow-gauge road from Marion Station, on the flat at the foot of the mountains, up the steep canyon to the mines at Borate, and even built a guest house close to the workings. The grade from the camp to the valley was so steep that, after leaving Borate, a loaded train could not stop until it reached Marion. After several years of steady production, the price of borax fell and the property was forced to shut down. Smith then loaded the expensive furnishings of the guest house on one of his trains, intending to ship the valuable pieces to his own home. As the train started down the long incline to the valley, sparks from the engine set fire to the load, and by the time the cars could be slowed down at Marion everything was consumed by the flames.

The town at the mouth of Wall Street Canyon was named by a miners' committee. The choice was between "Silver Gulch" and "Buena Vista," until a vociferous and persuasive speaker campaigned for "Calico" and won. By 1882, five saloons, three restaurants, several stores, assay offices, hotels, boardinghouses, a school and a community hall lined busy Wall Street. In addition to the frame and adobe homes and lodginghouses in the town, tents, shacks, and caves housed the miners in the hills. The Cornishmen lived in dugouts to escape the strong winds that raked the canyons. Water was scarce and was hauled from wells near Calico Lake. It sold at ten cents a gallon and was used sparingly; even with the greatest care two men used a dollar's worth each day.

Dr. A. R. Rhea, the village physician, was busiest during the typhoid epidemic of 1883. The disease struck so suddenly that the supply of drugs in his store was soon exhausted, and an order for acutely needed medicines was placed with the freighters, who made regular trips between Calico and San Bernardino. Meanwhile many died, and the blacksmith was kept busy making coffins and covering them with black cloth from the local stores.

The return of the supply wagons was anxiously awaited, and when the cloud of dust on the valley floor announced their approach, one of the men galloped out to meet the slow-moving vehicles and get the box of medicines. He questioned the driver of each wagon and learned that each thought the other had attended to the commission. Even when the wagons reached the town and were being unloaded, the dazed people stood around waiting for the precious box of drugs to be lifted down, so sure were they that it must be somewhere in the load. When the last wagon was empty, Mary Ryan, the only registered nurse in the camp, spoke to the stunned crowd, asking that someone volunteer to go to San Bernardino for drugs as rapidly as possible. From the many volunteers she chose two dependable men, borrowed a buggy, and accepted the loan of Dr. Rhea's fast team. More deaths occurred during the days that the men were away. When they finally got back and patients received the proper medicines, the epidemic lessened and gradually died out.

Calico did its best to prevent the Chinese from entering the town; but since they were the only cooks available for restaurants and mine boardinghouses, they were soon a part of the community. Perhaps it was Yung Hen who settled the question of Chinese labor in the camp by announcing calmly, when a group threatened to hang him and threw a rope around his neck, "Go ahead. Plenty more Chinamen to take my place." Yung Hen remained in Calico as long as the camp lasted, running several boardinghouses successfully, grubstaking many a miner and feeding others until they got jobs.

The camp was at its height in 1886, with a population of between three and four thousand, a new schoolhouse, a cemetery, two dozen saloons, and gambling houses which never closed. The following year fire destroyed 135 of its buildings, but the new town which rose on the debris of the old was planned to withstand fire: every third or fourth structure was made of adobe to serve as a firebreak. It is these buildings which still remain.

By 1892, when the price of silver first began to drop, some of the camp's richest veins were exhausted, and by the end of the year the Waterloo, the Silver King, the Bismarck, and the Thunder mines had shut down. By 1897 mining had ceased entirely, and the bulk of the population had drifted away. In 1902 Calico's wooden houses were hauled down to Yermo and Daggett and set on new foundations in those swiftly building railroad towns.

In 1885, when the citizens of Calico applied for a patented townsite, the request was refused, as the site had never been officially surveyed. Some years later a survey was run on this site and others in the vicinity, and a notice was sent to the county judge that the patent could now be issued. The judge sent back word that there was no longer any need for a patent, as the town had ceased to exist.

Certain mines were reopened in 1917 and again in the 1920's, and attempts to tap their deep ore bodies were made; but the depression of 1929 and another decrease in the price of silver put an end to all work.

In the spring of 1951 I persuaded a friend, who has piloted me to several out-of-the-way old towns, to drive me to Calico. As it is hot in the desert even in early June, and we wanted to reach the place and explore it before the sun was high, he beat upon my door in the Yermo tourist camp at five o'clock. After a sketchy breakfast in a café catering to truckers, we started toward the brightly colored Calico Mountains where, hidden in one of the corrugated folds of rock, lay the deserted camp.

The road from Yermo crossed the desert and climbed gradually for six miles toward the bare, sculptured mountains, across whose tops the sun was just beginning to creep, throwing the canyon walls into deep contrasting shadow. For the last half-mile it ran through a cut which framed the view ahead, revealing the few buildings of Calico's main street silhouetted against an immense backdrop of mountains and mine dumps. Not a soul was around when we parked the car and started toward the handful of adobe-walled ruins.

While I was leaning against one old building and sketching another, a long, black nose appeared at the end of the wall, and a friendly mule ambled up to see what was going on. He trailed us all over the town, until the door of the largest house opened and Fred Noller, the long-haired, bewhiskered custodian and host of Calico, brought out a pan of food for the animal. Spying us across the street, he called out, "You folks must have come up here before you had breakfast. I'm going to get mine now." With that he whisked into the house and shut the door.

As we explored the buildings, many of which are identified by signs as having been a certain store, saloon, or restaurant, I remembered stories I'd read about the camp of Bismarck, across the ridge in the next canyon—a much smaller camp, contemporary with Calico, that grew up around the Bismarck and Humbug mines. Since it had no schoolhouse, the children trudged back and forth over a high trail between the two places to attend classes in the larger town. It also had no post office, and for three years, from 1883 to 1886, the only mail carrier between it and Calico was Dorsey, a dog, trained to wear leather pouches in which the letters were placed.

One building in Calico is a museum, and while my friend climbed up to the nearest mines and investigated the old ore-bins and shaft houses, I looked at the assortment of relics it contained—the fragment of a letter dated from Calico on May 2, 1886; an envelope with a Calico postmark addressed to Charles J. Perkins, Atty. at Law, Calico Mining District, Daggett; faded photographs of people and ore wagons and mines, and several framed and water-stained copies of the *Calico Print,* the town's first newspaper. Its advertisements told me more than anything else about the once busy mining center:

Sunday, October 12, 1884.
Fine Horses, Calico Stage Line.   Wm. Curry
Concord Coach put on
Trips made Twice a Day
between
Calico and Daggett.

———————

Quinn & Sutcliffe
opened a Beer Hall July 18th at Calico
Boca Beer 5 cts. a glass
No Jaw Bone.

Ice! Ice! Ice!
Furnished at Daggett
at the following rates
Under 100 lbs. @ 3 cts.
Over 100 lbs. @ 2¾ cts.
Furnished at Calico
Under 100 lbs. @ 4½ cts.
Over 100 lbs. @ 4 cts.

———

Kirwin & Flynn
dealers in
Wines, Liquors & Cigars
Barber Chair in the Rear.

By July, 1885, the paper was being issued at Daggett, California. The issue of July 19 contained the following items:

LOCAL NEWS.
Bullion Report.
. . . shipment from Calico mining district through Wells Fargo & Co.'s Express

———

Barber's Mill 2 shipments $7000
King mine 1 shipment $3224
Total since Jan. 1, 1884 $1,484,884
and still Everyone Goes
to the Capital.

———

Calico Colors
All the Calico boys who were in San Bernardino as witnesses in mining suits have returned and quiet once more reigns supreme.

———

Now that the 4th of July is a thing of the past, what are we to do to amuse ourselves? We would suggest a moonlight picnic, instead of having one in daytime, sweltering under the hot rays of *Old Sol*.

On the way out of town we detoured to the cemetery, a patch of rocky ground across a gully from the main road. Although the graves are outlined by piles of stones, the barren ground is so strewn with rocks and boulders that except for the bleached wooden headboards, it is hard to tell where the individual plots lie. We drove back to the valley across the bed of a dry lake, and as we crossed it I glanced back for a last glimpse of Calico; but, like a mirage, it had disappeared again into the folds of the range.

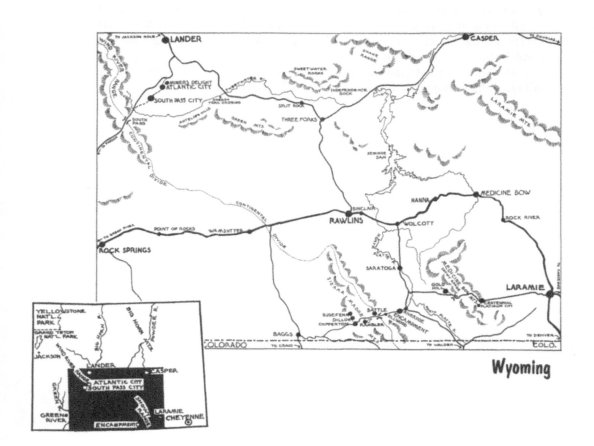

4. Copper and Gold in the Sagebrush

Wyoming

THE OLD mining camps tucked away in the mountains of Wyoming are nearly all deserted, for the state's industries today are oil-refining, stock-raising, farming, and coal-mining, not the production of gold and copper. The camps are found in two portions of the state—in the Medicine Bow and Sierra Madre Mountains near the Colorado line, and in central Wyoming south of the Wind River Range, not far from Lander.

CENTENNIAL AND PLATINUM CITY

THIRTY miles west of Laramie, Centennial presses against the aspen-covered slopes at the foot of Sheep and Corner Mountains, in the Medicine Bow Range. Although most of its buildings are new, one or two old ones stand a little apart and make good sketches. Just as I finished drawing the weathered boards and curling shingles, a woman invited me into her home, moving a pile of freshly pressed clothes from the chair which she offered me, and continuing her ironing as she talked.

"Sure, this was a mining town once," she said. "The boom was in the seventies when high-grade ore came from surface diggings. One old feller dug up a boulder full of gold and got $700 for it, and once they took $48,000 from a trench 125 feet long and 65 feet deep. Maybe you've heard of Stephen Downey? He found a gold lode near here which was so good he wouldn't sell it, even when he got an offer of $100,000 for it. Maybe he wished he had when the vein pinched out. He and lots of others have tried to find it ever since, but it's gone.

"You should drive to old Platinum City while you're here," she went on.

"Just take the dirt road behind that barn and go south two miles. You'll go past a ranch and you'll have to open a couple of gates to get there. Some of the prospectors who were hunting all over Centennial Mountain for the lost Downey lode found platinum in the ore they turned up. Right away, promoters bought the meadow at the foot of the mountain and started to sell lots. They brought in mine machinery and did a little building, but the mine didn't pay expenses. That was in 1920, and in 1938 the government took the property for taxes.

"There's always a little mining boom at Centennial every spring and summer, but the fellers who pick away at the hills now don't find much."

We took the dirt road and at the first ranch gate met a cowboy; he cautioned us to keep to the upper tracks over the hill in order to avoid a marshy stretch ahead. We covered more than the two miles, but all we ever saw to show that Platinum City had existed was a mine property high on the mountain and one pile of bricks in the meadow.

GOLD HILL

FROM Centennial we climbed over the Snowy Range of the Medicine Bow Mountains toward the valley to the west. Although it was mid-July, snowbanks lay under the trees as we neared the top, and at the summit, where grim granite cliffs rise straight up behind several deep, clear lakes, deep snow covered the ground on both sides of the highway. On the horizon were distant ranges, and below and ahead was the fertile valley of the Platte, bordered by the Medicine Bow and Sierra Madre Mountains. Not far below timberline on the west side of the Snowy Range, a forest trail, marked "Gold Hill 3 mi.," led north into the trees. Some miles farther on we reached the North Platte River and drove on to Saratoga, one of the oldest valley towns. When I inquired about Gold Hill, I was directed to the office of the *Saratoga Sun* and to its editor, Mr. Robert D. Martin, an authority on the history of the entire region.

Rich outcroppings of ore at Gold Hill sent prospectors by the dozens to the mountainside throughout 1890, but only a few of the 200 or more locations made were developed beyond the ten-foot hole required by law. The Acme, Leviathan, Occidental, Wyoming, and Little Giant are said to be the only properties "sufficiently exploited to determine their values as prospects"; their ore was treated first in arrastres and then in Colonel Downey's small quartz mill, which dropped stamps from 1891 until lack of funds forced it to shut down. Early in the boom, indications of silver caused mining men to predict that Gold Hill might end up as a silver camp, but neither gold nor silver was found in large enough amounts to produce bonanza diggings.

Several townsites were laid out by land companies in the first season, until different sections of the mountainside were spoken of as Gold City, Greenville, Golden Courier, and Altamont. At one time two post offices existed, one at the upper and the other at the lower end of the camp; but before long Gold Hill became the recognized name of the entire settlement.

During its brief boom, six-horse Concord coaches ran between Rawlins and the Hill, via Saratoga. The first twenty miles of road, from Saratoga to Headquarters station, were such that "vehicles for passengers can trot all the way," but from there the remaining eight miles were stony and rough. On one such trip "a package containing a broadcloth cape, a testament . . . an autograph album . . . some seashells and other articles" was lost and a reward of five dollars offered for its return. Although the camp was never a large one, it contained three hotels, three saloons, a blacksmith shop, a school for its fourteen children, and a barber shop which

The boys have to patronize . . . at night because Joe's days are taken up by wood chopping.

What Gold Hill needs just now is a laundry. A good washer woman would find business brisk. [*Saratoga Sun,* Nov. 6, 1891.]

To liven things up, Mrs. Ainsworth, wife of the landlord of the Acme Hotel, held a dance "that was largely attended—eight ladies being present"; and in February, 1892, the Ainsworths held a christening party for their "boy baby," the first child born in the camp.

Except for the initial rush, the place grew slowly, for it was a "poor man's camp," the properties being developed by individuals rather than by outside capital. Furthermore, since the ore was not rich enough nor found in sufficient quantities to warrant thirty to forty dollars' transportation charges per ton, little was shipped out. Each year optimistic promoters assured the world that this was the year that Gold Hill would "forge to the front," but their prophecies never materialized.

In 1901, when the ore bins were piled full of high-grade ore, there were only sixteen people in camp, and even after the railroad pushed all the way to Encampment in 1905, shipping costs remained so high that the camp was no nearer to a boom than it had ever been. The ore is still there, but the old-timers who know the deposits say it lies deep and will take capital to release it. So, until such time as big business takes a hand in the mines, Gold Hill sleeps.

ENCAMPMENT

WE LEFT Saratoga early in the morning and drove twenty miles down the valley to Encampment, reaching that ranch center before many of its citizens were about. Its streets were wide; its houses were spread over a considerable area of prairie; and its stores were a jumble of false fronts, two-story brick buildings with ponderous cornices, and modern one-story frame or cement-block structures with garish signs.

By the time we had driven all over town, people were beginning to appear on the streets. I inquired about local history of three men sitting on a bench in front of a store. They had little to tell, and I was walking away when one of them shouted after me, "Lady, you should talk to George Baker. He's lived here all his life. He's in the barber shop across the street right now."

At that, the barber stuck his head out of his shop and called, "Do you want George?"

"No, but she does," said one of the men, pointing to me. As I climbed the wooden steps to the shop, an elderly man stepped outside and introduced himself. When I explained what I wanted, he held the door open and waved me inside. For the next half hour I listened to his reminiscences.

Grand Encampment, as the place was first called, was a trappers' rendezvous and campground to which the Indians came each year during the hunting season to barter with the traders. Ranchers did not settle in the valley until 1877, and minerals were not discovered in the vicinity until 1879. These were in such small quantities, however, that no rush resulted; and it was not until after 1897, when Ed Haggarty, a prospector, found his copper mine, that the real boom started. This mine was twenty miles across the mountains to the west, but it brought prosperity to Encampment as well as to the five towns in between. According to Mr. Baker, Ellwood was nothing but a stage and freighting station; then came Battle, on top of the Divide. Next was Rambler, down in the hollow beside Battle Lake, and then Copperton, a sheep camp with two saloons (but a right lively place), and last was Dillon, just half a mile below the mine itself. Mr. Baker knew Dillon well, for he had run one of the four saloons there when the town had two stores, a post office, and a $30,000-a-month payroll. It was quite a place while it lasted, but that was only seven years. He was the last man to leave when the town folded up. He seemed pleased when I said that we were going to drive up to Battle and Rambler, and he invited us to stop by his house when we drove back through Encampment, as he had a scrapbook full of old clippings which might be helpful.

Haggarty got three men to grubstake him and, after scouring the hills, located two claims on the Sandstone. In the spring of 1897, he and a small

FALSE FRONTS AND WOODEN SIDEWALKS, ENCAMPMENT

DESERTED BUILDINGS, RAMBLER

party of copper-miners camped on the shores of Battle Lake, west of the Continental Divide; Haggarty listened while one of the men described a certain red, spongy iron ore, or "gossan," which indicated the presence of copper deposits. When he started off to do assessment work on his claims, he saw on the mountain ahead of him a quartzite dyke toward which he climbed; but deep snowbanks prevented his reaching it. He detoured, crossing the mountain along a bare slope which he had not traveled before. Upon examining the bare rock, he found it red, spongy iron ore, and, returning the next day, he set up location stakes, laying off a twenty-acre tract.

Dead timber lay so thick on the mountain between his discovery and his camp that he could not ride a horse to his claim. He therefore moved to Deal's sheep camp, which was nearby, and spent the rest of the summer working his mine. By fall he had dug out several hundred pounds of copper ore.

The following spring he returned to the mountain and located new claims above his first one, sinking a shaft so as to catch the vein on the dip. After only three months of work, $300,000 worth of metal was in sight; at the peak of production, $10,000 worth of ore a week was shipped. While he was absent one day, Ferris, one of his partners, visited the property and was so impressed with what he saw that he told Haggarty to build a much-needed wagon road to the mine. That September logs were cut for a bunkhouse, for timbering the shaft, and for a corduroy bed to lay over marshy stretches of the wagon road. In October, 1899, the first load of ore was hauled over the mountain to Fort Steele, sixty miles away on the railroad; when deep snow closed the road, the ore was hauled on sleds. The four partners called their mine the Rudefeha, a name consisting of the first two letters from each of their names—Rumsey, Deal, Ferris, and Haggarty. Following this strike, sixty or more mines, including the Golden Eagle, the Portland, the Tully, and the Doane Rambler, were located in the Sierra Madre Mountains. To handle the ore from these properties, the Boston-Wyoming Company built a smelter with a capacity of 100 tons a day beside Grand Encampment Creek.

As soon as the Rudefeha mine proved to be a producing property, some promoters surveyed a townsite and laid out lots on the prairie close to the river; but few were attracted until a second company bought the townsite, where six lonely buildings stood, and began to advertise it in a big way. Willis George Emerson, promoter, financier, and author, was the leader of this scheme; to get things started he sent Grant Jones, a reporter, to Encampment to write a glowing account of the town and of Purgatory Gulch, where the ore was found. His article was printed in every paper in the nation that received telegraphic news, with the result that hundreds flocked to Wyoming. The first issue of the *Grand Encampment Herald,* on March 18, 1898, also advertised the town by screaming:

GRAND ENCAMPMENT
THE WORLD'S STOREHOUSE OF GOLD, COPPER, and COBALT

.   .   .   .

THE COMING METROPOLIS OF THE ROCKIES
TANGIBLE GOLDEN WEALTH that SURPASSES the PHANTOMS
of the KLONDYKE.

————

Wonder of the Age!
Grand Encampment has no Equal on the Globe, Says Noah Seiver.
Days of '49 to be Repeated in Wyoming;
Thousands Soon to Take the Trail

Emerson and his associates next formed the North American Copper Company, bought the Rudefeha mine in 1903 for a reputed half million, renamed
it the Ferris-Haggarty, and sold thousands of shares of stock. The company
also bought and enlarged the smelter and built an aerial tramway from the
Ferris-Haggarty to the reduction works. The construction of this tram was a
great engineering feat, for in its twenty-mile length it had to cross the Continental Divide. Its cables were supported by 304 towers, its buckets held 700
pounds of ore, and it could deliver 98 tons a day to the furnaces on the river.

Between 1903 and 1908 the town's growth was phenomenal. Its resident
population was 2,000, and its streets were crowded with freight teams, ore
wagons, and the men and women who found relaxation—according to their
tastes—in literary clubs or in saloons and dance halls. As long as the several camps in the mountains flourished, Encampment was the center which
supplied them with mining equipment and provisions. Fine homes and substantial business houses, a water system, and an electric-light plant made it a
most enterprising place. In 1905 the Pennsylvania-Wyoming Company bought
the smelter and enlarged it, and an independent company began the construction of the Saratoga Encampment railroad to link the town with the main
line of the Union Pacific at Wolcott.

Encampment's decline began in 1906 when the concentrating mill at
the smelter was completely destroyed by fire. In 1907 another portion of the
smelter burned; even so, the Ferris-Haggarty continued to tram ore to the
charred site in order to have a supply on hand when the mill was rebuilt. By
1908 the railroad was completed; but by then the smelter was closed, and
the drop in the price of copper caused mine after mine to shut down. That
same year the Ferris-Haggarty Company was indicted for "over-capitalization

and fraudulent stock sales," and within three years Encampment's population had shrunk to 200. Since then the town has become a ranch center, and the last population figure I have been able to find is 288.

Mr. Baker had come to Encampment in 1898, when the town had contained only one store and one hotel, down near the present railroad station. "The streets were named for pioneers—McCaffery Avenue and Rankin Street— but the people today have even forgotten the names. Before the mines closed down, the town had thirteen saloons and several hotels. The tram from the Ferris-Haggarty was taken out in 1910 or 1911. It was the longest tram in the world at the time it was built. The mine itself has ore in it yet. It was simply 'oversold and undermined.' "

I thanked Mr. Baker for his help and was soon on the gravel road westward to see what remained of the five copper towns he had mentioned. The climb from the sagebrush valley was abrupt and led through forests to the 9,916-foot pass at the top of the Sierra Madres.

BATTLE

BATTLE was named after the Battle Mountain Massacre between soldiers and Indians which took place years before on this same site. Even in its early mining days, prospectors carried guns to protect themselves against the ever-lurking enemy. The first mineral deposit to be found was the copper vein west of the Continental Divide, the lode which in 1879 became known as the Doane Rambler. Then other properties were opened, and before many years a small camp named Battle perched among the rocks and timber close to the pass. The increased need for copper during the Spanish-American War sent men hunting it feverishly all through the southern mountainous portion of Carbon County, and during this period the camp reached its peak.

With the Rudefeha mine beginning to send ore down to the valley and the Doane Rambler producing, Battle became the overnight stop for the freight teams which traveled back and forth to the smelter. The town was also a center for the miners, teamsters, gamblers, and promoters who frequented its five saloons, read its newspaper, took specimens of ore to its assay office, and assembled in its false-fronted town hall to denounce sheepmen. The *Saratoga Sun* in 1931 reprinted a "puff" from a Denver paper of 1899, which stated that Battle was brand new and that "a traveler must pay fifty cents to sleep in a garret." It also mentioned the four general stores, hotel, feed stable, barber shop, and restaurant, and it concluded by describing the sawmill which "right in town furnishes the best music—the music of industry."

The fact that Battle occupied grazing land infuriated the sheepmen and caused more than one bloody fight. One night a sheepherder and his friends entered a certain saloon where Kid Blizzard, a gambler, was tending bar. When they began to curse him, Blizzard struck the herder over the head with his gun. In a moment the place was in an uproar, as townsmen and herders fought in a melee of flying fists and barking guns. When it was over several of the miners were badly injured, and the herder who began it left the place mortally wounded and was found dead the next morning, slumped behind the school-house.

After the Ferris-Haggarty bubble burst, the camp became a ghost. In 1933, CCC camp workers demolished it and turned the site into a public campground. The only remains on the flat and in the trees among the fallen timber are foundation holes, a few old shafts, a couple of mine dumps, an old cemetery containing thirteen untended graves, and a Forest Service marker on which is carved: "Townsite of Battle. Established 1898. Abandoned 1907."

RAMBLER

Two miles farther along the shelf of mountain road west of the Divide was a narrow dirt road which "took off" suddenly and pitched down 1,000 feet to Battle Lake. The grade was steep—40 per cent at least—and the roadbed was stony and badly washed. At the bottom of the hill, just before entering the townsite of Rambler, it forded a stream and disappeared in a marsh close to several dilapidated buildings which sagged drunkenly on the squashy flat. Long, straight ruts in the meadow indicated streets, and piles of flattened boards showed where houses had once stood.

On our way down the hill we passed a mine whose yellow dumps cascaded over the mountainside. This proved to be the historic Doane Rambler, the oldest producing property in the district, which had been located in 1879. Shipments up to January 1, 1904, totaled half a million pounds of copper, several carloads of which averaged 51 per cent pure metal.

Ed Haggarty and his party stayed at Rambler beside its tiny lake in 1897 on the occasion of his discovery of the Rudefeha mine. But the place contains no life today, except in summer, when sheep outfits make it their headquarters or fishermen pitch their tents by the beaver dam.

A few miles west of Rambler, at the turnoff to Haggarty Gulch and the Rudefeha mine, stood Copperton, a teamster's stop for the continuous string of wagons hauling freight to and from the mine. But today the old five-mile wagonroad to the neglected mine property is only a foot trail.

DILLON

A MILE this side of the mine are the remains of the camp of Dillon, built rather defiantly by the barkeepers of Rudefeha when the Ferris-Haggarty Company banned saloons from that camp. As soon as Millica Dillon opened his saloon and laid out a townsite, others followed his example and moved their businesses down the hill. The men followed, so as to be near the bars, and built themselves new cabins in the timber. Dillon's own saloon provided free meals for a year, depending on liquor receipts to pay expenses.

To this town came Grant Jones, the reporter whose extravagant account of the Encampment boom first publicized the district. He was an author and contributor to the *Chicago Daily Mail,* and until his death in 1903 he wrote many wild tales about the region, describing the strange birds and beasts of his invention (such as the Cogly Woo and the Rackaboar) which inhabited it. He also published the *Dillon Doublejack,* which he dedicated to:

the most distinctive brotherhood whose members see the word "welcome" on fewer doormats, and know more about hospitality, travel over more miles of land, and see fewer cows, worship nature more and see fewer churches, regard women with more chivalry and see fewer of them, judge men better and wear fewer starched shirts, undergo more hardships and make fewer complaints, meet more disappointments and retain more hope—than any other class of men in the whole wide world—to the brotherhood of quartz and placer prospectors and miners.

Dillon is now a jumble of decayed and roofless cabins and shacks, strewn over a mountain park. Broken bottles, parts of stoves, bed springs, even an old safe, hide in the deep grass and underbrush. Unique relics of the winters whose snows lay many feet deep are the tall outside toilets, propped up on cribbed log bases, which stand like chimneys; their doors are eight feet above the ground and are reached in summer only by flights of broken, rotten steps.

Now that we had investigated the state's copper camps, we were off to the site of Wyoming's first gold rush—South Pass City, the town through which so many thousands of emigrants traveled in the days of the wagon trains. As we neared the Sweetwater River, the long line of majestic, snow-covered peaks crowning the Wind River Range rose out of the distance on our left. Somewhere in those forbidding but impressive mountains the Lost Cabin mine may still be hidden! Although the legend connected with the mine is generally laid in the Big Horn Mountains, northeast, one version mentions the Wind Rivers as its locale. Each variation is plausible, and each has sent credulous men into uncharted terrain in search of treasure.

According to the legend, Allen Hurlburt caught the gold fever in 1863, while in Walla Walla, Washington, and persuaded two men to go with him into the Rocky Mountains to prospect. The men took horses and a month's supply of grub and set out for the Yellowstone River, down which they floated on rafts until they reached the Big Horn River, where they camped. Realizing that they were in hostile Indian territory, they traveled by night into the Big Horn Mountains and, after considerable prospecting, found pay gravel so rich that they cleaned up $100 a day per man. Since they had sufficient ammunition to last some time and game was plentiful, they built a cabin and spent the winter at their diggings.

In the spring, as soon as the ice melted in the stream, they worked their sluices until the day Hurlburt heard shots near the creek and saw Indians kill his two partners. Horrified, he hid until the Indians left. Then, creeping to the cabin, he took what few things he could carry and left on foot; for the Indians had taken the horses. To escape capture, he detoured far to the south, passing through country which he was too hurried and too terrified to notice in detail. After eighteen days of wandering he reached a settlement and collapsed.

After recovering from his harrowing experience, he joined a large party which was starting for the gold fields of Montana; but when the men heard about his mine and saw the nuggets he carried with him, the party split. Over five hundred emigrants with 150 wagons chose to go with Hurlburt in search of his mine, following him through the mountains until he admitted that he was lost. Angry and exasperated, they would have lynched him had not one of the men, said to have been Jim Bridger, held them off with his revolver. Shortly after this, Indians so harassed the party that it left the country.

Another story describes how three men prospected the headwaters of the Little Big Horn, where they found a body of rich ore. One version says they packed a quantity out on horses to Fort Laramie, where it brought $26,000. Another version states that they built a boat, loaded it with nuggets, and buried what they could not take with them. They planned to float down the Yellowstone River until they reached civilization, traveling by night to avoid detection by the Indians. They slipped successfully through several native villages; but one night a barking dog roused the Indians and caused their capture. Two of the men were immediately killed. The third escaped and wandered until he met some white men to whom he told his story; but his details were vague, and shortly afterwards he went insane.

Still another variation tells how a white man wandered into Fort Washakie in 1877 and babbled that he and others had been mining in the Wind River Range, where they had a cabin. All had gone well until Indians killed everyone but himself. No one paid any attention to him, and he wandered away. After he was gone, a few men recalled his story and tried unsuccessfully to find his cabin. In 1884, however, a cabin like the one he had described was discovered in those mountains by a prospector. It had portholes for windows and an underground passage for an entrance, and near it lay the skeleton of a white man with a bullet in his skull. Other human bones were scattered about, and tools and giant blasting powder lay hidden under the cabin's rotting floor. The prospector and a man named J. B. Osborne staked claims in the vicinity and planned to return to the location in 1885. I have been unable to discover whether they made it or not.

SOUTH PASS

EIGHT miles before we reached Lander we took a road that veers to the west and after nearly forty miles crosses the Wind River Range at South Pass, the long, low saddle, 7,500 feet above sea level, over which thousands of men and women and animals plodded during pioneer days. Some say it was discovered in 1812 by Robert Stuart, on his way east from Astoria, Oregon, and others say that it was found in 1824 by one of Ashley's Rocky Mountain Fur Company men. In 1827 Ashley dragged a small cannon over it on the way to his fort at Utah Lake. The next whites to use it, with the exception of fur trappers, were probably missionaries.

The Presbyterians and Congregationalists sent Reverend Samuel Parker and Dr. Marcus Whitman to Oregon in 1835 as missionaries to the Indians. The task was enormous, and the following year Whitman and two Nez Percé Indians went back east to plead for more missionaries to help with the work. On the way back to Oregon, Whitman stopped at St. Louis for his young wife, who gladly accompanied him into the wilderness. When the couple began their long, grueling journey, they were accompanied by Reverend and Mrs. H. H. Spalding. For safety they traveled with a group of traders from the American Fur Company.

On the Fourth of July, 1836, while the main party continued, the four missionaries paused on the summit of South Pass to hold a religious service. Affected by the experience, Mrs. Spalding wrote in her journal: "Is it a reality or a dream that after four months of painful journeying I am alive and actually standing at the summit of the Rocky Mountains where the foot of white woman has never before trod?" At the conclusion of the service the travelers hurried after the fur caravan. Years later a monument was erected on the spot and inscribed:

Narcissa Prentice Whitman
Eliza Hart Spalding
First White Women to Cross This Path,
July 4, 1836.

In 1843 wagon trains rolling to Oregon began to wear deep ruts in the prairie soil, and in 1847 the first company of Mormons coaxed 72 wagons and 175 horses over the long, gradual slope. By 1849 a steady procession of white-topped wagons crossed the pass; because the people in them were going west to settle, their loads were heavier and harder to pull. Consequently, as the wagons were lightened to save the straining oxen, the trail became littered with discarded treasures—bureaus, chairs, trunks, anything which could be spared. The South Pass became a favorite route because it provided grass and water for stock, and its long three-mile grade was less steep than others.

SOUTH PASS CITY

GOLD was first discovered in the Sweetwater district in 1842 by a Georgian who had journeyed west with the American Fur Company in the hope of recovering his health. At the end of a year he started home, telling his trapper friends of his plan to return the next season with a company of men and begin mining. Indians must have waylaid and killed him, for he never reached home. Thirteen years later, in 1855, a party of forty men prospected the length of the Sweetwater and found traces of gold everywhere. Blizzards sent them out of the country for the winter. In the spring, eager to get back to work, they stopped at Fort Laramie to get tools and provisions, but when they were two days away from the post a company of soldiers overtook them and escorted them back to the fort. The party was disbanded on some flimsy charge and their equipment confiscated. Three years later the leader of the group again prospected along the Sweetwater; in 1860, accompanied by eight others, he commenced work in Strawberry Gulch. For years afterward traces remained of the old sluices and rockers they had used.

During 1861 most mining was abandoned, for the prospectors found that they could earn more by putting up hay and cutting poles for Creighton's telegraph line than by washing gravel. The first man to do placering in the gulch where the great Carissa lode was to be discovered a few years later was H. G. Nickerson, a mountaineer. Soldiers guarding the construction of the telegraph line in 1863 saw him packing dirt on an ox to Willow Creek and washing gold in its waters. Because he worked alone and was open to Indian attack, the soldiers persuaded him to leave the country.

During the summer of 1864, Lieutenant William H. Brown and his company of men, who were guarding the telegraph line and the wagon trains which passed along the Sweetwater, did some prospecting in the same neighborhood. They found rich dirt in a dry gulch, filled gunny sacks with it, and packed it on their horses to the nearest stream. They also found a rich lead north of

Rock Creek and named it the Buckeye. This claim probably made them the real discoverers of gold on the future site of Atlantic City. Lieutenant Brown and his men developed the Buckeye until Indians destroyed their tools; whereupon the men decided that soldiering was a healthier occupation than mining. Several other groups of men entered the Sweetwater vicinity during the next two or three years, but they were either driven out by the natives or were never seen again. Each year the persistent stream of prospectors increased, attracted to the country by the stories of those who had been forced out of it.

While a detachment of troops from Fort Bridger was patrolling the country during the summer of 1866, some of the men who had been miners in California and Nevada detected the mineral characteristics of the land. Tom Ryan, one of the soldiers, spotted the outcrop of gold quartz which became the Carissa lode, but he had no time to examine it. He reported its location, however, with the result that a few of the men, as soon as their term of military service expired in the fall, organized a prospecting party and returned to the South Pass country, camping on Willow Creek until run off by Indians. In June, 1867, Captain Lawrence and his party from Salt Lake found the Carissa lode of which Ryan spoke, a lode richer than any other in the district. Their excitement made them forget the constant danger of Indian attack, and a band of savages swooped down on them when they had no weapons but picks and drills with which to protect themselves. In the fight which followed, one man was killed and Captain Lawrence was critically wounded. The Indians ran off their horses and stock, leaving the men to stumble back on foot toward Fort Bridger. On the way they met a well-armed party from the post, headed for the diggings they had so recently left. Returning with this group to their property, they continued mining, but always with their guns beside them and one of their number on guard on top of a hill.

News of the Carissa discovery touched off a stampede, and men converged from all directions upon the diggings. By fall more than seven hundred prospectors had pitched their tents or built log cabins with dirt floors and sod roofs along Willow Creek, and many claims had been staked and recorded. By October, 1867, a townsite called South Pass City was laid out, and the men who planned to dig in for the winter near their mines cut huge quantities of wood for fuel and hunted buffalo, elk, and deer to provide food for the months when they would be shut off from the outside world. A crude shelter was built at the Carissa mine, and all through the cold months when the creek was frozen the men crushed the richest of the ore in hand mortars, accumulating $15,000 by the end of the season. Late in the year the miners held a meeting and set up Carter County, named for W. A. Carter of Fort Bridger. Their action was ratified on January 3, 1868, by the Dakota Legislature, for the land was in Dakota Territory.

By February, 1868, the *Sweetwater Miner*, published at Fort Bridger, circulated such encouraging reports of the gold field that constant streams of men crowded into the already swollen camp. By summer the city comprised hundreds of buildings, including five hotels—the South Pass, U. S., Eclipse, City, and Kidder—three meat markets, two bakeries, four law firms, and thirteen saloons, of which the most popular were the 49er, the Keg, the Magnolia, the Elephant, and the Occidental. Worden Noble opened the first store to furnish miners' supplies. By the end of 1868 the population had reached 4,000!

Many of the best mines were discovered that year—the Young America, the Carrie Shields, the Mahomet, the Oriental, and the Lone Star. Tom Ryan, the discoverer of the outcrop, finally returned to find that his mine had been relocated by others. After some prospecting he uncovered another strike, the Carter lode, later known as the Robert Emmett. Placer discoveries on Carissa Gulch and Strawberry Gulch and on Rock Creek and Big Atlantic Gulch proved as rich as the lode mines. All the gulches for ten miles around were auriferous, and, as a result of locations discovered at some distance from the town, the new camps of Atlantic City and Miners' Delight sprang up. During that year the Carissa mine at South Pass City was developed to a depth of 400 feet, and a steam hoist, pumping machinery, and a six-stamp mill were installed on the property. After this investment proved satisfactory and other mines added hoists and mills, boom conditions prevailed in the district until 1872.

The Indians resented the white men who had entered their hunting grounds. They watched the slow ox-teams lumbering across the prairies, and they crept silently up to the isolated, unprotected camps and often destroyed them. The miners who tore up the soil and disturbed the streams were their special targets, and they haunted their diggings, waiting patiently until a single daring raid could wipe out one or a dozen of the hated intruders. An effective way of harassing the whites was to steal their horses and stock, for the Indians knew that the miners, though armed, could not pursue them on foot.

A band of Indians scalped William Rhodes and made off with the four-horse team he was driving. They found an old Frenchman digging potatoes in his garden, tortured him to death, and mutilated his body. A freighter known as Uncle Ben Hurst was returning with his four-ox team to South Pass City with a load of merchandise when Indians attacked his wagon and wounded his driver. Although hurt himself, Hurst drove off the Indians and then placed the driver under the wagon, wrapped him in blankets, and piled rocks around him to form a barricade. Leaving his gun and ammunition with the injured man, he unhitched his cattle and drove them into South Pass, where he assembled a posse and hurried back to the wounded teamster. During his absence the Indians had returned, killed the man, and stolen the goods from the wagon. The rescue party was attacked on the way back and had to hide in the willows. One of the men, who was riding a swift horse, attempted to dash ahead for more help but was chased by one of the savages and shot through the head. A group of nearly thirty men rode after the Indians but could not find them.

In September, 1869, a band of Sioux near Miners' Delight killed a man who was hauling lime and stole his three yoke of oxen. Riding over the hill to Atlantic Gulch, they killed another man, who was cutting wood. No one felt safe even when, for the protection of the settlers, Fort Stambaugh was established between Atlantic City and Miners' Delight. The issue of the *South Pass News* for April 9, 1870, is devoted to "The Indian Outrages" and states that it is "largely taken up with the details of the recent murders committed by Indians upon numbers of our peaceful citizens." An excerpt selected from several columns of grievances states the attitude of the people to the crucial problem:

. . . these depredations are known to have been committed by Indians whose title of original possession of these lands has long since been extinguished by treaties with the Government of the United States, wherein said Indians agreed to refrain from their murderous hostilities, which treaties are continually violated by them, and have been thus far strictly observed by the citizens of the Sweetwater district. . . .

The town welcomed Governor Campbell's authorization of Lieutenant Colonel J. W. Anthony to raise four companies of volunteers, "irrespective of party, class or creed," to fight the Indians. He raised the companies with no difficulty; but when he received instructions to proceed against the savages without killing any of them, he refused to accept his commission.

Yet, according to reminiscences of Dr. George A. Carpenter, a pioneer in the district:

Firearms were needed in self-defense against whites as well as Indians. . . . The man I worked for was slain from ambush one night just outside my shack on Rock Creek. Everyone knew who did it. The killer was taken before a justice of the peace. He raised his right hand and swore innocence. That was all. He was freed. . . . One day I was riding to town . . . and saw buzzards circling over a clump of brush. I investigated. A miner, shot through the head, lay in the brush. We went on into town and never heard anything further about it. [*Casper Tribune*, Feb. 23, 1934.]

The year 1869 was an important one. Iliff and Company opened a private bank managed by Judge Amos Steck, who bought gold from the miners and shipped it to New York. The second Masonic Lodge in the Territory was organized, holding its meetings in the upper part of a two-story log building; a five-column newspaper, the *South Park News,* appeared; and the business houses included two breweries with beer gardens, a livery and feed stable, a jewelry store, a fur store, and (possibly because Indian scares made the miners carry arms at all times) a shooting gallery and a gun store.

South Pass City became the seat of Sweetwater (formerly Carter) County in 1869 and remained so until 1874, when it was succeeded by Green River. But the event of the year which had the most far-reaching results was Mrs. Esther Morris' tea party. Mrs. Morris, who was a suffragette, invited forty prominent ladies of the community and two men, W. H. Bright and Captain H. Nickerson, the Republican and Democratic candidates for the Territorial Legislature, to her home. After entertaining them with tea and cakes she announced that she wanted a pledge from both candidates that the one who was elected would introduce and work for the passage of a bill conferring suffrage on women. Mr. Bright, who won the election, kept his pledge and introduced a measure which not only granted the ladies the right to vote but also permitted them to hold office and receive equal compensation with men. When Mrs. Morris was elected Justice of the Peace in South Pass the same year, the rough element tried to force her withdrawal, and her predecessor refused to turn over the court docket to her. Instead of haggling with the man, she got a "new clean" docket, and her decisions were so fair that none of the forty cases brought before her was appealed to higher courts.

South Pass continued to boom; in 1872 it was the second largest city in the Territory, and its main street extended for half a mile along the gulch. Then the rich pay streaks in the placers disappeared, and the deeper ore in the lode mines became refractory. As a result of these unfavorable conditions, almost all the properties were abandoned and the bulk of the population moved away. By 1878 the city was full of vacant homes and stores, grass-grown placers and rotting sluices, and not until 1885, when further development in the Carissa mine caused a temporary flurry of mining, did it show any signs of life. In the middle nineties the Carissa was further developed by lessees, and a large body of ore was opened up. A twenty-stamp mill was built; it saved up to 90 per cent of the ore values, in contrast to early-day operating, when both rusty and brittle gold were lost in the tailings. In July, 1933, came the next boom, when the dredges began to cut their way through the old placer grounds, and the headlines in the *Rock Springs Rocket* read:

Hundreds Now in South Pass Hunting Gold
Present Revival May Eclipse Past Peak

The article continued:

That the ghost mining cities of Atlantic City and South Pass at the crest of the Continental Divide in Fremont County are heading to a revival that will eclipse the palmy days of the region when Miners' Delight and other million dollar operations, with but crude equipment turned out hundreds of thousands of dollars in yellow metal and contributed to two of the wildest mining camps of the early days, is seen in present activities at several modernly equipped plants, where showings of heavy gold recovery both in lode and placer mining have been attracting the attention of hundreds of people who visit the district daily.

But again the spurt of activity was short-lived, and South Pass dropped back into lethargy.

I had no idea what we would find when we turned west on Highway 28 and drove more than twenty miles over high, rolling hills to the gravel road that cuts across the prairie straight to the Carissa mine. Beyond it stood a few frame houses scattered on a hill. A curve in the road swept around the next bare hill to the center of town, with its wide street flanked by sagging frame structures and weathered log cabins with sod roofs. One block was still full of buildings—several false-fronted stores and the balconied South Pass Hotel. Only one store is open today, but in it I found photographs of the town in its lively days, and from its proprietor I learned the way to our next stop, Atlantic City.

We reclimbed the hill past several newer homes, one of which had Gothic windows in its chinked log walls, until we again reached the Carissa mill. From it a four-mile drive brought us to a gorge, at the bottom of which lay Atlantic City.

ATLANTIC CITY

THE Atlantic Ledge was discovered in 1867, and by the following April a new mining camp with a population of 300 had grown up on Rock Creek, four miles from South Pass City, in the midst of gold-bearing quartz lodes and placers. Almost immediately, Eugene Amoretti, a merchant at South Pass, opened a store at the diggings, and others hurried in to give him competition. At first the camp threatened to overshadow its neighbor, but it soon settled down to a slower but more permanent development.

Advertisements in the *South Pass News* of 1870 mention the Atlantic Hotel as the "only first class" stopping place in town. For briefer visits the Eldorado Billiard Hall, Saloon, and Club Room on Main Street, and the Democratic Club Room, run by Hank Smith, where "Hank always has a good fire and a warm home for his patrons," held attractions. Leighton and Company were "House, Sign and Ornamental Painters" as well as "Dealers in Paints,

HOTEL AND STORES, SOUTH PASS CITY

ATLANTIC CITY, WITH DREDGE DUMPS

Oils and Window Glass"; and the sawmill's owners informed the public that log huts were "played out" and that "frame houses were better and warmer," adding, "Now is the Time to Build While Materials and Labor are Cheap."

The mines that boosted the camp were not only the placers but the lodes; these included the old Buckeye claim, rediscovered in 1868; the Alice; the Caribou, which produced $50,000; the Rose; the El Dorado; the Northern Light; the Jim Crow; the Hoosier Boy; the Copperopolis; the King Solomon, discovered by Tom Ryan; and the St. Lawrence, located by Dr. Leonard, a miner and surgeon. Quartz mills were built to handle the output from the many properties; and in order to haul the ore to shipping points, a wagon road was constructed whose articles of incorporation read:

To All Whom This Shall Concern

Greeting

Be it known that for the purpose of constructing, furnishing, maintaining and enjoying a wagon and toll road from Atlantic City, Carter County to South Pass City in said county, by the most direct, feasible route between the two points aforesaid and within said county of Carter and Territory of Dakota, we whose name and seals are hereunto subscribed and affixed, have . . . incorporated a company.

. . . in witness whereof we have hereunto set our hands and seals at South Pass City in the County of Carter, Dakota Territory this 15th day of May A.D. One Thousand Eight hundred and Sixty-Nine.

JAS. W. MANEFEE

CHALETON   C. H. FRY

Mining continued to some extent after the first boom quieted down. In 1884 Emile Granier, who represented a French company, obtained title to several miles of placer ground along Rock Creek and installed hydraulic pipes and an elevator for handling tailings. After several years of work and the expenditure of large sums of money on ditch construction, the ditches were found to be completely impracticable because of the slight percentage of fall in the streams tapped. The elaborate plant was disposed of by the company and lay idle until 1904. Then the Dexter Mining and Milling Company obtained 1,100 acres of placer ground in the Atlantic district, brought water from the Wind River Range in a twenty-five-mile ditch, and controlled the supply by constructing several storage reservoirs. This company was also unsuccessful, because the mill they built at a cost of over $200,000 was "so designed as to insure its failure." In the 1930's the E. T. Fisher Company brought in a dragline which employed twelve men and recovered $67,000 in gold its first season. The dredge worked a strip of ground 120 feet wide, from which one of the three shifts of men removed dirt and brush while the other two operated the machinery on the boat.

The first thing one notices about Atlantic City is the dredged-out stream, whose symmetrically stacked ridges of scoured boulders extend far beyond the ends of the townsite. This debris is bordered by dense thickets of brush, beyond which, on a gently sloping ridge, stands the town itself. Its log, frame, and stone houses, its barns, its lone hotel, and its church cover quite an expanse, and it is obvious that other buildings once filled the gaps between these survivors.

Robert McAuley, the camp's first postmaster, came to Atlantic early in 1869 and lived there until 1898. During that time he lived in three counties, two territories, and one state; yet he never moved his residence or business! When he arrived, Atlantic City was in Dakota Territory. A month or two later, on April 15, 1869, the area, which had been designated Wyoming Territory in July, 1868, was formally recognized, and J. A. Campbell was inaugurated as its first governor. Carter County, as set up by the miners, had been recognized by the Dakota Legislature in 1867. In 1869 its name was changed to Sweetwater. In 1884, by a rearrangement of boundaries, Atlantic City and the adjacent towns fell within newly created Fremont County. The Territory of Wyoming became a state in 1890.

MINERS' DELIGHT

WHEN Herman G. Nickerson felt crowded by the rush to South Pass in 1868, he ranged over the hills to Spring Gulch, four miles east of Atlantic. So did other prospectors, who, after gophering around for a while and finding valuable outcroppings, laid out a camp which they called Hamilton and settled down to work. That fall a mine was discovered on Peabody Hill, just west of the new town, and was named Miners' Delight. Its ore was free-milling and ran as high as thousands of dollars to the ton; after the installation of a ten-stamp mill on the property, $300,000 was recovered in six months. The mine had many owners, and before its shafts filled with water it yielded $5,000,000.

After its discovery, merchants hauled supplies to the new camp, whose name had been changed to that of the bonanza mine, and opened stores in tents on the banks of the creek. The next spring a small army of men mushed in early through deep snow to work their findings of the preceding season and to prospect Red Canyon and Strawberry creeks, both of which were close to the camp. A young teacher who went to Miners' Delight late in the sixties used to ride horseback two and a half miles through the snowdrifts to the schoolhouse throughout the winter, with two of her pupils behind her on the horse. Her salary was fifty dollars a month, and twenty of it went for board.

The town's boom population reached 2,000, and prospects in the vicinity continued for years to attract miners. Today little remains but the foundations of a church, a few cabins, and a graveyard.

As we left Wyoming's old mining camps and picked up the first of the many long miles which would take us into Montana, I began to think about Joseph A. Slade, the notorious desperado and stage agent who had operated over these wide stretches of country.

Jules Reni was station-keeper for the Overland Stage Line at Julesburg, Colorado, when he and Slade first met. He was a hot-tempered French Canadian who ran the station to suit himself, appropriating company property as he saw fit. The Overland needed a competent agent, and in Slade they saw their man. Reni naturally resented being discharged, and he looked upon Slade as a sworn enemy. Some authorities say that the men had quarreled before the dismissal; certainly they often quarreled after it, until Reni emptied a load of buckshot into Slade, hoping to kill him. Instead, the resilient Slade recovered from the peppering and swore that he would live to kill Reni and wear his ears in his pocket.

Reni left the vicinity, and Slade settled down to his work of keeping the stages moving. His methods were drastic and ruthless, and stories of shootings, stabbings, beatings, and even hangings became legends of the stage line; but, regardless of how many were true, the coaches went through on schedule. Typical of his methods is the story of the rancher with whom he bargained for a stack of hay. After paying for it, Slade discovered that the stack was made of worthless brush, covered over with a thin layer of fodder. He dragged the rancher to the stack and roared, "I'm going to chain you here and set the stack on fire." He lighted the brush but let the man go on the promise that he would leave the country.

When Slade heard that Reni was coming after him with a gang intent upon killing him, he consulted the officers at Fort Laramie as to what he should do. They replied that, under the circumstances, he had the right to kill Reni on sight. That was what Slade had intended them to say, and, knowing that he was now secure from arrest if he killed the man, he sent his henchmen to capture Reni. The Frenchman was cornered at Chanson's Ranch and held until Slade arrived. Slade then dismissed his men and, standing Reni against a corral wall, shot at him repeatedly, killing him by inches. After his victim was dead, Slade cut off his ears and put them in his vest pocket. In time his tactics of running the stage station came under suspicion, and he too was dismissed.

After his discharge he drifted into Virginia City, Montana, in the spring of

1863. By then he was drinking like a fish, and when he was drunk he was a desperate and dangerous character who rode his horse into saloons, shot up bars, and beat and threatened friends, enemies, and innocent bystanders with equal impartiality. Storekeepers hearing that he was on a spree would hastily bar their doors and put out the lights in the hope that he would by-pass their places. When he was sober he was kind and gentlemanly and willingly reimbursed the merchants for the damage he had done. Around him gathered an armed band of roughs and cut-throats who did whatever he ordered and upheld him in his crimes. On the other hand, he also had a following of solid citizens, who liked him when he was at his best and respected him as a member of the Vigilante Committee.

The night before his arrest in 1864, he shot up the town again, and his gang terrorized the citizens. The issue became that of Slade and his followers versus law and order, for Virginia City was fed up with his actions. He offered no resistance when Sheriff Fox took him into court to read the warrant ordering his arrest; but during the reading he became abusive, seized the paper, tore it up, and tramped upon it. At this display his friends, who had followed him into the building, cocked their revolvers, and the sheriff, realizing what would follow any restraining action, allowed him to leave.

One of his respectable friends, foreseeing what would happen, begged him to get out of town; instead, Slade hunted up the judge of the court and held a pistol to his head. The gesture was ill-timed, for the Vigilantes, realizing that they must settle matters if Virginia City and the surrounding country were to have security, agreed to do away with him at once. As soon as the miners learned what was brewing they gathered in the streets "armed to the teeth," the contingent from neighboring Nevada City ready to hang him on sight.

As soon as he realized that the committee meant business, Slade sobered up and even apologized to the judge, but the committee went grimly ahead with their preparations. A stout beam on top of a corral gate held the noose and a dry-goods box was the platform. One of his cronies rode off to Slade's home in the Madison Valley to notify his wife of his arrest. According to Thomas J. Dimsdale's account in the *Vigilantes of Montana:*

In an instant she was in the saddle, and with all the energy that love and despair could lend to an ardent temperament and a strong physique, she urged her fleet charger over the twelve miles of rough and rocky ground that intervened between her and the object of her passionate devotion.

Fearing that her arrival would stay the execution, the committee kicked the box from under Slade's feet with dispatch, cutting off his last words—"My God, must I die? Oh, my dear wife."

The body had hardly been laid on a table in the Virginia Hotel, when the lady galloped into town and upbraided the Vigilantes, not for killing him but for not shooting him. "I would have done it myself if I'd been here. He should never have died by a hangman's noose," she protested. Rumor says that she not only took the body home with her but placed it in a metal coffin filled with alcohol. When she left the valley for Salt Lake City, the sloshing coffin went with her.

Montana

MOST OF MONTANA'S mining camps, and all of its oldest, are in the mountainous western part of the huge state. Though copper mining is the great industry today, with Butte as its center, copper ore was the last metal that the early prospectors wanted or expected to find. It was gold they were after—first as "colors" in the stream beds and then as veins hidden in the hills. When they found greater deposits of silver than gold they quickly decided that silver was the metal they were seeking. But when the surface ores were exhausted and the deeper layers of rock revealed copper, they became discouraged, and the majority pulled out for other places. It was not until Marcus Daly discovered how to treat the despised copper that another boom was on—one which continues to this day.

Although many of the old camps later became known as silver or copper towns, their early history is one of gold. Some, like Silver City and Beartown, are gone; some, like Marysville, are alive but full of relics from the past; some, like Bannack, Elkhorn, and Garnet, have so few people that they are spoken of as "ghost towns"; and some, like Helena and Butte, have become important cities.

Although gold dust had been found in Montana at Gold Creek as early as 1856, the first big strike was made at Bannack, on Grasshopper Creek.

BANNACK

BANNACK was, therefore, our first goal. Although older than Virginia City, it is far enough away from a main highway to have retained much of its early quality and appearance. To reach it from Dillon, we left the pavement and turned west on a wide graveled road which ran mile after mile across rolling hills covered with sagebrush. Not a tree nor a ranchhouse broke

173

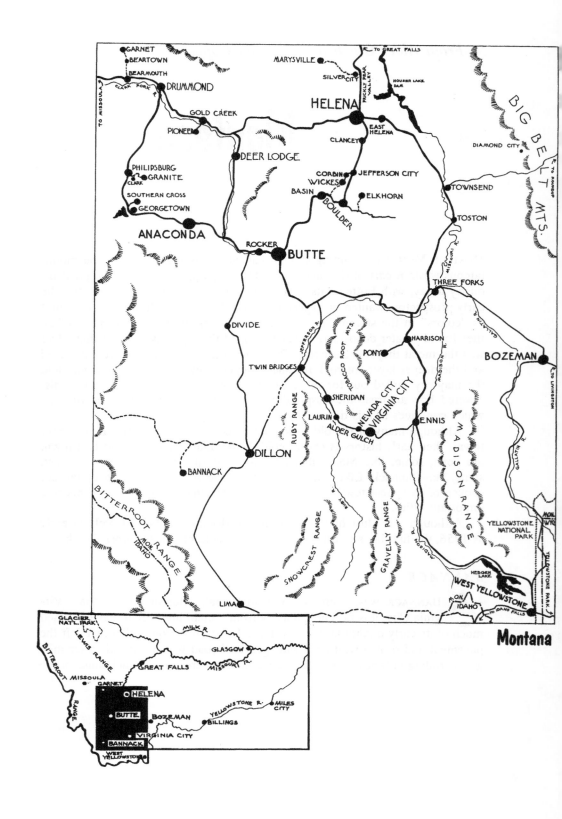

Montana

the lonely stretches of gray-green sage; but every few miles an inconspicuous sign, obviously hand-lettered, read "Ox Bow Bar, Bannack," and gave the distance we had still to go. It reminded me of the crudely daubed signboard which in 1862 had stood south of Dillon at the junction of Beaverhead River and Rattlesnake Creek. It read:

> Tu grass Hop Per digins
> 30 myle
> Kepe the Trale nex the bluffe.

Our map showed two roads to the town, but the first proved to be nothing but dim wagon tracks disappearing through the brush. Trusting that the second would be in better shape, we drove several miles to a fork where the now familiar "Ox Bow Bar" sign read: BANNACK 8 MILES.

Most of the remaining distance was downhill, winding around or over one sage-covered hump after another to the valley. From the time we left Dillon till we drove up the main and only street of Bannack, we had seen no sign of life, not even a jack rabbit. And Bannack looked deserted, too.

Big trees shaded weather-beaten one-story log cabins, whose untended yards were knee-deep in grass. Picket fences surrounded some of the individual properties, but both fences and houses were partly hidden by sagebrush and greasewood five to six feet high. Beyond the first few cabins and barns were a number of false-fronted stores, most of them boarded up. Farther up the street were a church and more cabins, built of square-hewn logs and decorated with bleached fragments of scrolls and pendants, the remains of carved bargeboards that had once framed their eaves.

On either side of the street was one large building: on the right stood a two-story frame schoolhouse painted white, with ornamental trim and staring empty windows like eye sockets in a skull; almost opposite it was a historic red brick structure—the first Territorial Capitol of Montana. We found the Ox Bow Bar, and from its proprietor, who seemed delighted to talk to someone, we learned a good deal about Bannack's past.

During the summer of 1862 a party of prospectors, bound for the Idaho gold camps, turned back into the Deer Lodge Valley when they heard that the Idaho diggings were already overcrowded. Working their way south, they stopped on July 28 at Willard's (now known as Grasshopper) Creek to pan for colors. John White and William Eads made the lucky discovery which touched off the first big strike in Montana. It drew to the banks of the little stream not only swarms of prospectors, eager to get in on the first rush but roughs and gamblers from the California and Nevada camps as well. Within a few months a roaring camp of tents and shacks, named Bannack after the

Indian tribe of that name, stood in the sagebrush ravine, its population swelling as each stagecoach deposited another load of dusty passengers in front of the log hotel.

Before the end of 1862 five hundred men were placering Grasshopper Creek, and five hundred more came early in 1863; but the discoveries on Alder Gulch later that year quickly emptied the camp, as the gold-crazy men rushed over the bare hills to the new Eldorado.

For two or three years Grasshopper Creek and Bannack were almost deserted. Then, in 1866, Smith and Graeter built a miner's ditch to increase the water supply essential for placer operations. The company charged seventy-five cents a miners' inch for its water, but it could not furnish enough to work the bench gravels above the stream bed. Next, the Bannack Mining and Ditch Company constructed a thirty-mile ditch at a cost of $35,000; and later a third ditch, the Pioneer, was built to handle the benches north of the town. By 1870 two other ditches were in operation, both taking water out of Grasshopper Creek: White's ditch brought water to the bars below town, and Canyon ditch fed the Bon Accord placers.

"Just remember," said the proprietor of the bar, "that these ditches were all pick-and-shovel work and that the longest of them was forty-four miles!"

With the completion of the ditches, placer mining was resumed, and the benches and bars were worked and reworked until no more colors showed up in the sluices. Bannack dozed again until the spring of 1895, when Fielding L. Graves launched the first electric gold dredge near the sleepy town. From the richest ground the dredge gouged $22,000 and $38,000 in two successive weekly cleanups. Another dredge, the Mollie Gibson, was put into operation that same fall, north of the Excelsior mine, and a third was launched in 1896. A fourth was installed to dig at the Bon Accord placers a short time later; a fifth, several miles below, capsized as it was being launched.

The hills above Grasshopper Creek are full of prospect holes and mine dumps, for placering was not the only type of mining carried on. Bannack claims the first quartz mine in the territory—the Dakota—which was located in 1862 and for whose ores a six-stamp mill, "entirely hand-made and driven by water power," was built. The first steam-operated stamp mill was completed in 1864 at a cost of $25,000, and before 1870 three more mills stood in the gulch. As late as 1914 a cyanide mill, which ran a short time, was built by the Bannack Gold Mining and Milling Company.

When the Grasshopper diggings were discovered in 1862, they were in Oregon Territory. In September, 1863, Sidney Edgerton, Chief Justice of the newly created Idaho Territory (which was cut out of the Oregon tract), was on his way to his post in Lewiston, with his family. Rather than risk traveling across the mountains so late in the season, he decided to winter in Ban-

HEART OF TOWN WITH SCHOOLHOUSE, BANNACK, MONTANA

FIRST TERRITORIAL CAPITOL, BANNACK. GALLOWS (RIGHT) WHERE ROADAGENT PLUMMER WAS HANGED

nack. The following spring he wrote to Washington, urging the creation of still another territory—Montana. This was voted by Congress on May 26, 1864, and Edgerton was made Governor. Bannack became the temporary capital. On December 12, 1864, the first Legislative Assembly of Montana met in the brick building which we had noticed upon entering town. But during 1864 Virginia City, a rival camp with a population of 10,000, overshadowed Bannack, and no sooner had the legislators convened than they voted to hold their next session in Virginia City.

From the time the placers were exhausted until the dredges began to tear at the gravels in the nineties, Bannack's population was small, and only a few quartz mines were worked from time to time. In 1938 its post office was closed, and Montana's oldest town went back to sleep; but it kept one eye open for visitors, and it dusted off its relics and labeled them.

Next to the Capitol is Skinner's Saloon, once headquarters for the road agents and murderers who kept Bannack terrorized during its first year of existence. These fugitives from justice flocked to Bannack, especially after Henry Plummer arrived there and became sheriff; for Plummer's record was like their own, and with him as their leader they could rob and kill and still be protected by the law. Plummer was even smooth enough to persuade the Virginia City sheriff to resign in his favor, and thereafter he ran both camps to suit himself.

The highwaymen's operations were confined, for the most part, to the ninety-mile stretch of road between Bannack and Alder Gulch. Their victims were systematically robbed, and, if not sufficiently cooperative, they were killed. The gang was well organized and had as its password, "I am innocent!" At every one of the stage stations a member of the band was "planted." He used the station as his hangout and passed tips to the gang whenever individuals were known to be carrying "dust" on them or stages had treasure boxes heavy with bullion. One of their rendezvous was Robbers' Roost, near the town of Sheridan. This weathered log stage station, just a few feet from the present highway, was originally run by Pete Daly; it was a favorite meeting place for Plummer and his henchmen.

After Plummer's men had killed over a hundred persons, a group of citizens from Bannack and Virginia City decided to put an end to their exploits. They formed a Vigilante Committee similar to those that had brought law and order to California and took as their signature the symbol 3-7-77. Within a year they rounded up the desperadoes, tried them before miners' courts, and hanged or exiled the most notorious offenders.

For some time Plummer's association with the gang of highwaymen was not known. So that his evil deeds might not be discovered, he had posed as a conscientious officer of the law. Shortly before his death he entertained a group of notables in his home, among them the Governor and several of the

Vigilantes. His duplicity might have gone undiscovered had not so many stages been held up and robbed of their treasure just after he had been told the time of their departure and the amount of bullion each carried. Once, when a stage was robbed, he rashly removed his gloves to place the stolen sacks of bullion in the strongbox. A passenger recognized the hands of the masked road agent as Plummer's.

A well-worn path leads through the sagebrush to Hangman's Gulch, where a replica of the gallows, complete with nooses, has been erected. Here Plummer and two of his deputies were hanged on January 10, 1864. Plummer was arrested in a cabin while he was washing his hands. "I'll come with you as soon as I put on my coat," he said evenly; but his captors were not deceived. "I'll hand your coat to you," replied one of them, removing a pistol from the pocket as he did so. At the gallows Plummer's bravado deserted him and he groveled and begged to be spared. "Cut off my ears, strip me naked and let me go, but spare my life," he cried. "I want to live for my wife. I am too wicked to die." Finally convinced that his time had come, he became calm and said: "As a last favor, gentlemen, let me beg that you will give me a good drop."

Overlooking Hangman's Gulch and Boot Hill cemetery are two other burying grounds with weathered headboards and forgotten graves. The inscriptions show that many children and young women were buried in them, as well as numerous veterans of the Civil War who were later attracted to the diggings. These ex-soldiers, while alive, had shown their opposing loyalties by naming a nearby gulch Jeff Davis, and a residential section of the town Yankee Flats.

The jail at Bannack still stands. It is a stout wooden building with a sod roof, a dirt floor, small barred windows, and tiny individual cells. In the older portion of the building are several rings embedded in the ground, to which prisoners were chained. Ironically enough, it is said to have been built by Plummer.

It was late afternoon when we left Bannack, and the sun's rays stained the barren hills a warm rose. We had seen no one in the lonely town except the bartender, but an exuberant collie and several cows pastured in one of the larger front yards indicated that a few other people must live there.

ALDER GULCH (NEVADA CITY)

FROM Bannack we drove to Alder Gulch, from which $70,000,000 was washed. For miles we followed the stream bed, much of which is hidden by thickets of alders and willows or by high mounds of boulders— the tailings left by the dredge which worked the already much-sifted sands between 1910 and 1920.

In the sixties several smaller camps lined this stream—Centerville, Nevada City, Adobe, Junction, and Ruby—and back from the creek was Central City. Alder Gulch had been solid with miners' claims then; yet today hardly a trace of the old places remains.

Nevada City is the only one which is at all recognizable as having been a town, and it has shrunk to a handful of eight or ten weathered cabins.

An old photograph of Nevada City in its prime shows a long street literally crammed with cabins and one- and two-story false-fronted stores and hotels, a thoroughfare filled with stages, freight outfits, pack trains, and milling crowds. Just such a boom town it must have been when George Ives was hanged.

Ives was the first of Plummer's men to be killed. He had waylaid Nicholas Tiebalt, stolen his money, killed him, and hidden his body in the brush along Alder Gulch. Days later, Tiebalt's body was discovered and brought to Nevada City. Then a man, who had heard the shot and who had shortly after met Ives with Tiebalt's mules, told about it, and a posse of twenty-five men rode out to capture Ives, whom they had little difficulty in tracing. On the way back to Nevada City, Ives tried to escape by betting that his horse could outrun all the others. The wager was taken, and Ives broke from the trail and hit for the hills. By the time the astonished posse realized what was going on, he was out of sight. It took two hours to overtake and recapture him. His trial was held after dark, by the light of a big bonfire. A jury of twenty-four men deliberated half an hour and then pronounced him guilty. His friends stood in the shadows on the outskirts of the crowd but had no opportunity to rescue their crony. Before the fire died down Ives' body "swung in the night breeze, facing the pale moon that lighted up the scene." The Vigilantes had hanged their first man!

Ives, however, was not the only villain to be done away with at Nevada, as the following account from the *Montana Post* shows:

Execution at Nevada, M. T.

Saturday Evening Sept. 17, John Dolan, *alias* Coyle, *alias* The Hat, . . . paid the penalty of his crimes at Nevada.

Shortly after sundown, a strong body of armed citizens marched from Highland, Pine Grove, Junction and Virginia, and joining the force already on the ground, formed on each side of the entrance to the ball room next to the Jackson House where the prisoner was confined. In a few moments, the culprit, pinioned and guarded, made his appearance, when the procession moved on in military array to the place of execution. The prisoner was in the center. . . . At the ground, a circle was instantly formed with the prisoner standing on a board supported [in such a way] that a touch of the hand only was required to convert it into a drop.

The citizen's guard, with revolvers ready for instant use, faced outwards, and confronted the crowd of 400-500 individuals.

The prisoner admitted that he had committed the crime but that he was drunk when he did it. He requested that some of his friends would bury his body. . . . The plank fell and in a moment the prisoner was swaying in the night wind. He died without a struggle.

A stern order to fall back, enforced by the click of 500 revolvers, startled the dense crowd, and a stampede of the wildest description took place. . . . After ascertaining that life was extinct, the body was delivered to Dolan's friends. [Sept. 24, 1864.]

VIRGINIA CITY

In 1863 a party from Bannack, led by Henry Edgar and Bill Fairweather, was turned back by hostile Indians from a prospecting trip to the Yellowstone Valley. Discontentedly camping beside a creek overhung by alder bushes, Fairweather panned gravel from the stream bed and on May 26 found gold. Some days later Fairweather and his friends were forced to return to Bannack for supplies. Sure that they had kept their discovery a secret, they were amazed to find several hundred prospectors at their heels, when they slipped out of town and started back to Alder. The first year's yield from Alder Gulch, whose sands held so much more dust than the shallow gravels of Grasshopper Creek, was $10,000,000, washed from over a thousand claims by the husky men whose cabins fringed the precious waters.

When the town which sprang up in the diggings needed a name, the many southerners among the miners proposed "Varina," in honor of Jefferson Davis' wife. The judge who was asked to record the name was a northerner, however; he refused to write it, substituting, with appropriate remarks, "Virginia," which proved agreeable to both factions. This town, which was incorporated in January, 1864, and one year later supplanted Bannack as the second Territorial capital, is graphically described by the *Montana Post* of August 27, 1864, as follows:

Virginia City.

On arriving at this place what astonishes any stranger is the size, appearance and vast amount of business that is here beheld. Though our city is but a year old, fine and substantial buildings have been erected, and others are rapidly going up. One hundred buildings are being erected each week in Virginia City and environs. Nevada and Central cities are equally prosperous. Indeed the whole appears to be the work of magic—the vision of a dream. But Virginia City is not a myth, a paper town, but a reality. . . . The placer diggings will require years to work out. . . . Many persons are taking out $150 per day to the hand. . . . Wages are high,

$6 to $12 per day. Old miners have the preference as they are worth much more than green hands. . . . The other side of the picture is this—we desire not to deceive, but to give facts. All the claims, as a matter of course, around our city, have long since been taken up. These must be purchased, and that too at very high figures. A "pilgrim" must work for somebody else or purchase a claim, or strike out for other diggings. . . . An ordinary laborer can get $6 per day, and this in gold, making it equal to $12 in greenbacks. He can board himself for $1.00, thus receiving $11 in greenbacks per day. . . . The abundance of gold makes everything high.

This information was given in the first issue of Virginia City's first paper, a six-column sheet, the 960 copies of which were snapped up at fifty cents apiece by news-hungry men who read every word, from the slogan: "My country, may she always be right, But my Country Right or Wrong," through the "Introductory" paragraph—

The interest of the miner, agriculturist and business man will be carefully looked after. . . . The latest telegraphic news will be given up to the time of going to press, so that our readers may be aware of what is passing in the outer world. . . .

—to the final advertisement on the back page.

Interesting items gleaned from the files of the *Montana Post* fill out the picture of Virginia City during its early years:

During the past week Gold Dust has been offered freely, but amounts sold are in small lots; mainly for remittance to the States. Coin is plenty, while Treasury Notes are very scarce, and as there is no safe way to get them from the States, the demand will exceed the supply until another season, when we trust our *circulation* will be entirely Treasury Notes or Coin; until that time we shall, of necessity, have to stick to that very interesting article known as "Trade Dust." . . . Exchange on all parts of Europe 10¢ premium, payable in Coin. [Aug. 26, 1865.]

Bartenders were not averse to payment in gold dust, for by the simple process of keeping their fingernails longer than necessary they were often able to scoop up more than they deserved while weighing out a payment from a miner's buckskin poke. Chinese laundrymen always panned the wash water after doing the miners' wash and profited thereby.

As Virginia City grew, its business houses increased in number and variety, and the *Montana Post* is filled with advertisements of the many merchants and hotelkeepers who catered to a cosmopolitan trade. The City Bath Rooms, with their Shaving and Hairdressing Saloon attached, were patronized by the men in from the gulches, where no such niceties existed. Dr. H. N. Crepin, Physician and Surgeon, advertised his office as "Opposite the hay scales on Main

St." In the second issue, the publishers, John Buchanan and M. M. Manner, introduced a column whose title showed how remote Virginia City was from the rest of the country. It was headed "News from America." Before the third issue slid from the press, the publishers sold out for $3,000, but the paper went on and became one of the state's leading journals.

Many colorful items appear in the early files of this newspaper, such as a warning to the public of the danger from stray bullets, and the following advertisement:

William Fairweather lost last week in Virginia City a valuable nugget of gold, being the first taken out of Virginia Gulch. The finder will be amply rewarded. [Sept. 3, 1864.]

A "Fatal Accident" was reported which occurred eighty miles east of Virginia City, when a

coach upset and a double-barreled shotgun was caused to go off, two balls entering the driver's thigh, and one ball through a passenger's arm and entering his left breast. Our informant further states that he could not say whether the wounds were mortal or not, until a physician could be procured. [Sept. 24, 1864.]

Early in the city's existence a Lyceum committee was organized to bring "touring musicians and lecturers" to the raw, new town. The programs were held in the Stonewall building, where "the woodwork was richly grained . . . and the ceiling about to be frescoed." When the Montana Theatre opened in December, 1864, its *première* bill contained the play, *Faint Heart Never Won Fair Lady,* followed by "comic and sentimental songs and a grand ouverture by the orchestra." For good measure the program concluded with a "roaring farce, 'The Spectre Bridegroom!' "

A bigger crowd than gathered at the theatre attended the

PRIZE FIGHT—BETWEEN RILEY OF VIRGINIA CITY AND FOSTER OF BANNACK . . . the men are under heavy training. We see by the cards of admission that no weapons of any kind are allowed around or outside the enclosure. [Sept. 3, 1864.]

The ground was well chosen—being a nice level spot, among the hills. In the center of the corral a most substantial ring was formed.

Riley's colors were green and he wore the stars and stripes around his waist. Foster hoisted blue stripes on a white ground, with blue and red spots.

Precisely at thirty-one minutes past three, Foster shied his castor into the ring. He was speedily followed by Riley. [Sept. 24, 1864.]

Fire was a constant threat to every mining camp, and even organized fire companies and bucket brigades were unable to prevent periodic ravages. Virginia City had its fire-laddies, but often the "red monster" was not discovered soon enough for them to save the buildings in its path. The *Post* therefore inaugurated a plan on October 29, 1864, which met with general approval.

FIRE! FIRE! It appears to us that a night watch should be instituted. One good, sober, vigilant man could be found to patrol from sun to sun, over all the town, and to give the alarm of fire. . . .

Having secured a watchman for the city, the paper next investigated the water supply. "Let someone look to the WATER," began an article on November 12, 1864. "Without it buckets are as useful as thimbles to thirsty men."

The most important additions to the tools of a fire company, without an engine are two or three troughs holding about a barrel of water each. Such a trough laid on the ground and worked by a stout fellow throwing up water with a large wooden shovel, can do more than twelve bucket men—the direction, quickness and amount delivered being all on the side of the shovel.

A good man can throw water with it on top of almost any house in town, except the two-story buildings and the side walls of these can be kept safe by water thrown from the ground, where no man can stand the heat and smoke on a ladder.

Soon after the preceding article appeared, reservoirs were built above the town and waterworks constructed. "Starting from the mountain slope, the water is conveyed in wooden tubs to the town. The price is $2 per month, per family."

Governor Edgerton visited Virginia City and was serenaded by the enthusiastic citizens at the conclusion of his speech.

He remarked at the growth of our beautiful city . . . beckoning the emigrant to this "Switzerland" of America. His remarks were conservative, no political harangue was indulged in. This was right. Saturday he returned to Bannack. [Aug. 27, 1864.]

On February 7, 1865, Virginia City was voted the temporary capital of the Territory by the second Legislative Assembly, succeeding Bannack. She was not to hold her supremacy long, however, for gold had been found in the Prickly Pear Valley, Confederate Gulch, and Silver Bow Creek. The more restless men, who were always "rarin' to go," had already been lured to the newest strike. Furthermore, Alder Gulch was showing signs of washing thin, after two

WOODEN SIDEWALKS AND OLD STORES, WALLACE ST., VIRGINIA CITY, MONTANA

MORRIS-ELLING MILL, PONY

years of terrific and systematic sifting. But the "Future Prospects of Virginia City," as stated in the *Montana Post* of February 18, 1865, were bright:

In view of the recent discoveries at Last Chance Gulch, Silver Bow and elsewhere, some people ventured to prophesy that Virginia City is "gone up." This elegant phrase, in our opinion, applies only to property, which has, decidedly gone up, and is still increasing in value. . . . Stone houses, architecturally imposing, are scattered in all directions.

Notwithstanding other strikes the "Golden Arrow" points steadily to Virginia City as the future Queen of the Mountains.

The population in 1870 was listed as 2,555, "including whites, chinese and negroes"; between 1880 and 1900 it stayed close to 600; in 1940 it was 380. At the close of 1903, the *Madisonian,* the newspaper still published at Virginia City, gave a detailed description of the many quartz mines that were operating in or near Alder Gulch and concluded by stating: "The prospect is brilliant that ere long she will be producing wealth from her rock-ribbed veins in greater abundance than ever she did from the auriferous sands in her gravelly beds. . . ." Mining is still going on in the vicinity; the U. S. Grant Mining Company's office is on the city's main street, and miners' supplies are carried in the stores.

The *Historical Directory-Montana,* published in 1879, evaluated the town's status by saying: "Now that she has become a steady business city she is not compelled to depend on the former placers, but looks with pride at the strides made in the agricultural valleys that contribute the elements of life and prosperity." Much the same statement could be made today. Only to mining and ranching must be added a new source of income—tourists; for in the last few years Virginia City has been bidding for their trade.

Charles A. Bovey, rancher, state senator, and millionaire, has done excellent work in restoring the historic town. From the moment one sees the lower end of Wallace Street, with its false-fronted stores, wooden sidewalks, and old-fashioned street lamps, one forgets that this is the twentieth century. Every store is a museum, with windows displaying antiques and interiors stocked with merchandise which dates back many years. Some, like the Wells Fargo Express Office and the Dressmaker's shop, contain life-sized figures dressed in the fashions of the boom days. The smallest store is the barber shop, built in 1870, with shelves full of shaving mugs and a wooden barber chair with carved "swan" armrests. The interior of the shop is so dark that both the figures of the barber and the customer in the antiquated chair look startlingly lifelike.

Many of the older buildings are built of brick or native stone, with Gothic windows set deep in their massive walls. The Territorial Capitol and the building that housed the *Montana Post* both have such windows.

When we visited Virginia City, Wallace Street was full of visitors, as wide-eyed as ourselves, peering into every doorway and reading aloud the historical descriptions tacked to each building. We were drawn to the Bale of Hay saloon by tinkling music which an old man was grinding out of an ancient piano organ on its colonnaded porch. Inside the saloon were nickelodeons and peep shows, large clanging music boxes with metal discs the size of circular buzz saws, and room after room hung with paintings salvaged from old bars.

After dark Virginia City is even more believable than by daylight, for the soft glow cast from windows and lamp posts picks out pools of light and causes the trees that line the street to cast grotesque shadows over the façades of buildings.

Just beyond the Bale of Hay stands an old stone barn, now used as a theatre, in which melodramas are presented during summer months by the Virginia City Players, a group of students from Montana State University. After dinner we sauntered down the street to the lantern-lighted auditorium. While we waited for the curtain to rise on *Miriam's Crime, or Innocent Sin,* we compared notes on the places we had visited during the afternoon. I had gone to the Memorial Museum to see its excellent historical collection, and from there to the old brewery with its huge vats and its beer garden alongside the stream. My friend had climbed the slope to Boothill to see the graves of five of Plummer's road agents—Boone Helm, Jack Gallagher, Frank Parish, Hayes Lyon, and Club-foot George Lane—who were hanged on January 14, 1864, by Vigilantes.

The most desperate of the five was Boone Helm, who drifted into Virginia from the gold camps of Idaho. He and five companions had left there in midwinter and started east, but only Helm reached Montana. A half-starved Indian who shared a meal with him somewhere en route licked his lips after tasting the meat which Helm gave him and asked what it was. Helm unwrapped the bundle in which he kept his provisions and held up a human leg! It was his custom to swagger down the street, roaring drunk, with a gun swinging from each hip. "Look out, Boone Helm's coming," people would warn each other, ducking out of sight until he had gone by. Even on the scaffold he protested his innocence, asking for a Bible on which to swear. This was too much for the Vigilantes, who promptly tightened the noose and cut short his last words: "Hooray for Jeff Davis!"

A more appealing local character was Bummer Dan, whose chief fault was his apathy toward work. He stole food, begged drinks, and skillfully avoided any exertion until the day when the miners, who resented his indolence, caught him eating a stolen pie. Outraged by his shiftlessness, they put a pick and shovel in his hands and insisted that he get busy. He was shown a worthless-looking claim, high above Alder Gulch and told to work it or get out of camp. Reluctantly, with the men standing over him, he began to peck at the soil, stopping frequently to rest but each time forced to resume digging by their well-directed boots. Finally, they left him and returned to their work. Hours later a few of the men returned to see how Dan was making out. To their surprise, they found him digging like a gopher, surrounded by pay dirt. Bummer Dan's bar proved to be one of the richest in the area, and after panning several thousand dollars from it, he sacked his dust and started by coach for the States. Road agents, tipped off that he was aboard, relieved him of his fortune; whereupon he returned to Virginia City and became a bum again.

The sun was just peeping over the Madison Range the morning we left Virginia City, and before we had pulled halfway up the long grade out of town we looked down upon the tree-shaded cemetery where Bill Fairweather lies buried. It seems appropriate that he should rest there, overlooking the gulch which he made famous and to which his body was brought in 1875 after his death at Robber's Roost.

At the top of the long hill we stopped for a last glimpse of the city. Beyond it, to the west, were mile upon mile of rounded hills, then the wide, flat Ruby Valley, and back of it a barricade of mountains. How easily we were traveling over territory that once was so hazardous and tedious to cross! I had recently seen a handbill, dated 1863, when Virginia City and Bannack were part of Idaho Territory, which was phrased to catch the eyes of restless men.

HO! for the IDAHO GOLD FIELDS.

I will dispatch on or about April 1, with a large mule train from Nebraska City, Nebraska Terr. to Bannock and Virginia Cities, Idaho, going through in about 45 days, gaining nearly 40 days over the great spring emigration.

I have been in the business for fifteen years, have crossed the Plains twenty-two times, and flatter myself that I understand the wants of emigrants, as well as any and can take a party through with as great speed, safety and comfort as any man in the West. All danger from Indians will be avoided by going in my train, as there are 150 men going with me, all Well-armed.

I can take out 100 passengers and 200,000 lbs. of Freight. For Terms etc. address me at the Adams House, Chicago, Ill., where I remain till the 20th inst. after that date at Nebraska City.

Refer to G. LeFevre, 167 S. Water St. Chicago. S. M. Dunn, Pacific House, St. Joseph, Mo.; A. P. Byram, Atchison, Kansas

D. D. White

Passengers will rendezvous on March 31 at Nebraska City so as to be ready to start at once.

Just a year later, the Virginia City newspaper contained a notice which further emphasizes the great distances that had to be covered to get into or out of this outpost town.

Overland Stage Line
        Ben Holladay, Prop.
Line connecting with daily coaches between Atchison, Kansas and Placerville, California. Tri-weekly coaches between Great Salt Lake City and Walla Walla via Boise City, West Bannack, and Tri-Weekly stages between Great Salt Lake City and Virginia City, Montana via Bannack City carrying the United States mail. [*Montana Post,* Aug. 27, 1864.]

PONY

"IF YOU are ever in Montana be sure to go to Pony," said a friend, years before I had thought of visiting that state. "It's a mining camp named for such a little runt that he was known all over Montana as 'Pony,' although his real name was Tecumseh Smith." "Pony" left Alder Gulch in the early boom days, wandered across the Tobacco Root Mountains, and worked his way up Willow Creek to the foot of Mineral Hill, panning the stream bed as he went. He found gold in the gravel and staked a claim—some say it was where the town now stands, others that it was higher up in the hills just below the Strawberry lode—but, always restless, he wandered off again. When he did return in 1868 he had a partner with him, and the two men began working the ground he had staked years before. Satisfied with the coarse gold it produced, they stayed several seasons and occasionally uncovered a nugget worth from three to five dollars.

Attracted by the stories of gold found in "Pony's gulch," other prospectors began to drift into the area; but no lode mines were discovered until 1875, when George Moreland pushed his pick through some wild strawberry plants, sunk a fourteen-foot hole, and uncovered the Strawberry lead. The vein, ten feet wide, produced free gold that occasionally assayed up to $1,000 a ton. This discovery attracted others, until the stream bed and hillsides of the gulch were full of men searching for pay gravel or quartz float and finding both.

Two partners, Walters and Reynolds, found quartz from which they pounded free gold with only a mortar and pestle. Others developed prospects on the extension of the Strawberry lode. To release the free gold from the quartz, mills were needed; the first, a ten-stamp mill run by water power, was moved over from the nearby camp of Sterling in 1875. Other mills followed— the Getchell and the Morris, both run by water power, and the Morain, run by steam—until six in all were dropping their stamps in a ceaseless clatter which reverberated through the narrow canyon. In addition to these, three arrastres were worked. But even before the stamps began to fall, "Pony," the weather-beaten little man who had drifted from gold camp to gold camp, found his gulch too crowded and noisy and quietly slipped away to prospect elsewhere.

Shortly after Moreland's discovery of 1875, the camp of Strawberry materialized. It was short-lived, however, for in 1877 the town of Pony was laid out two miles below, its cabins and tents bordering the stream from which most of the pay gravel came.

That same year, W. W. Morris and Henry Elling, the two men who were to be most closely identified with Pony's development, arrived from Virginia City. In 1880 they purchased the Clipper and Boss-Tweed mines, the bonanzas of the camp, which during forty years of continuous operation produced $5,000,000 in gold. In 1900, when Elling died, the mines, which were said to have $10,000,000 worth of ore still in sight, were sold to Boston capitalists who worked them up to their maximum output. Since then the property has changed hands several times.

Although the Strawberry and Boss-Tweed-Clipper properties were responsible for the initial fame of the camp, other mines in the vicinity were operated with success. The Fourth of July group of claims was developed with Butte money. The Keating-Strawberry group was acquired and successfully developed by a Helena syndicate in 1889 and as a result of this purchase the town of Pony boomed again.

In 1900 a spur of the Northern Pacific railroad was built to the camp. With its completion transportation costs on ore shipments were lowered, and the prospects looked good as men talked of other active mines—the Elephant and the Keystone, the Atlantic and the Pacific, the Gilt Edge and the Agitator, the Oro-Cache and the Saturday Night. Even in 1903, a mining expert who examined the properties prophesied that Pony would "eventually prove to be the most extensive and permanent gold mining district in the west." With new machinery and improved methods of mining, what could not be accomplished? But the boom was brief, and one by one the mines closed down.

If Pony Smith and W. W. Morris had driven into the quiet town as we did one bright summer morning, both would have been surprised at what they found, although their reactions would have been different. Pony would have stared with astonishment at the size of the place—the main street with its two-story brick and frame buildings, its many false-fronted stores, the big stone schoolhouse and the tree-shaded, comfortable homes set well back from the wooden sidewalks. To Pony his town would seem immense; but to Morris, former financier and leading citizen, the town would be too quiet, too lonely.

He would find people on the street, but their voices would carry far on the still air. Too few stores would be open, even though his "block," the Morris State Bank with its colonnaded stone entrance and corniced roof, still served as the Mines Sales Leasing Agency of the district. At the end of the street, just as it enters the canyon, he would see the stone shell of the Elling and Morris mill, its machinery gone, its mellow stone walls and weathered beams half hidden by bushes and vines. Pony is not a true ghost town, but it is quiet and many of its buildings are asleep.

DIAMOND CITY

TWENTY-THREE miles east of Townsend, at the head of Confederate Gulch in the Big Belt Mountains, is Diamond City, the fabulous camp of the sixties. From its stream bed and bars $10,000,000 in gold was washed. It received its name from the accidental location of its first four cabins, so placed that paths connecting them formed a diamond. Before any cabins existed, however, placering was being done near the mouth of the gulch.

The Civil War was directly responsible for the discovery of the diggings. After Sterling Price's army was defeated by the Union forces and its men scattered, a large number of its renegade members were rounded up and given their choice of surrendering and going back home or being banished to the wilds of Montana. Many chose the latter, partly, perhaps, because they had heard of Alder and Last Chance gulches and were anxious to try their hands at panning gold. Three of them, Jack Thompson, Washington Baker, and Pomp Dennis, began prospecting in the summer of 1864 near the mouth of a gulch which led up into the Big Belts. Thompson sank a prospect hole and got ten cents' worth of dirt in his first pan. Excited by his find, the men began to work up the gulch, and the farther they went the richer the gravel became.

Two weeks later, John Wells, another Confederate soldier, arrived at the mouth of the gulch with a party of prospectors and began work, testing the sands as he went. Wells uncovered the bonanza diggings; as news of them spread, hundreds of men rushed to Confederate Gulch and began picking feverishly at the earth. Nearly $2,000,000 was placered from the land at the junction of Montana and Confederate gulches; but richer deposits were still to be uncovered.

Gold was next found at the base of Gold Hill and just below Diamond City, where rich diggings were worked by men who got as high as $180 in a single pan. Then the gold bars were discovered: first Boulder, then, late in 1865, Montana, the richest of all. The gulches were forgotten as men washed $1,000 to the pan from the bedrock of the bar. Montana Bar was washed and re-washed and still yielded appreciable amounts of dust. Higher up on

Gold Hill was Diamond Bar, which, though not so rich as Montana, paid $100 a day per man.

Diamond City grew from a cluster of scattered cabins to a town whose long, straggling streets housed a population of 10,000. After a flume had been built to bring water from the mountains for hydraulic work, some of the houses had to be raised on stilts to prevent their being swept away or buried in the tailings that filled the gulch. All too soon the gold was washed out and Diamond City began to fade.

John Schonneman, Alex Campbell, and Charles Fredericks, the men who had located the richest portion of the great bar, sacked their million dollars' worth of gold dust, hired teams to haul the treasure to Fort Benton, and left town. From the fort they shipped their gold to the States and deposited it with a private banking house on Wall Street. This seemed to be the signal for others to pull out, until the city looked empty and footsteps echoed on its boardwalks. By 1870 its population had shrunk to 250, a year later it was only 64, and by the eighties only four families remained.

But Worcester Fox stayed on. He had arrived in 1865, and in 1899 he was still working his claim and reminiscing about the time he saw seven pans of gold, valued at $114,800, taken from the sluices at one cleanup.

Diamond City has disappeared and only a few foundations remain to show where it stood.

LAST CHANCE GULCH (HELENA)

IN JULY, 1864, John Cowan and three others were returning disconsolately to Alder Gulch from an unsuccessful prospecting trip into the Prickly Pear Valley. En route, they stopped to investigate one gulch they had neglected. It was their "last chance," and they fell to placering rather perfunctorily; but there was nothing perfunctory about the yells they let out when they lifted the dripping pans from the gravel and inspected the yellow particles. Last Chance Gulch was paying off in a big way.

News of the discovery brought hundreds to the diggings, until the banks of the crooked stream were filled with greedy men whose tents and rough cabins clung to the sides of the ravine. As more and more miners arrived, street above street began to line the gully in terraces, some crooked as cow's trails and all crowded as close as possible to the precious gravels.

Last Chance Gulch was the big discovery in 1864, and before the year was out John Somerville rechristened the settlement Helena after his home town in Minnesota; but to the lusty miners *H-e-l* spelt "hell," and *Hel*ena has been the pronunciation of the name from the first.

Just a year later the crowded, flimsily built "wooden town narrowly escaped destruction by fire," according to the *Montana Post* of August 26, 1865:

A pile of straw, surrounded by empty dry-goods boxes, in the rear of Walcot, Morse & Co.'s store, on Bridge street, was found in a blaze by some gentleman returning to his home, who instantly alarmed the slumberers and by their united exertion the fire was extinguished. This was undoubtedly the work of some incendiary, and we think it high time for our citizens to organize a regular system of fire night watch and not be satisfied with only talking about it. . . .

Last Chance is said to have yielded $16,000,000, most of which was placered before 1868. The placers were worked out by 1870, but by that time lode mines had been discovered in nearby Unionville and up toward Marys-ville. Helena, first as county seat and later as capital, became the center of wealth and culture. Long after white miners abandoned the diggings, Chinese washed fortunes from the discarded sands. Even today "colors" are found whenever excavations are made for new buildings along Main Street—which is still spoken of as Last Chance Gulch.

It is hard to believe that the wideawake main street the visitor sees today is the same gulch about which the *Montana Post* contained this item on August 26, 1865:

One of the dancers in the Gayety Saloon, being a new hand and not well posted as to the surroundings of the hurdy-gurdy house, on stepping out of the back door, made a sudden and unexpected descent of ten feet, falling on the bed rock, unfitting herself for business for a short time, but not sustaining serious injury. The house has been undermined, and is supported by stilts at the rear and on one side.

The old part of town, perched high above the gulch, is full of houses of the early mining era, while to the west are the big homes of later boom days. A drive over the entire city reveals three periods of growth: first, the brick and stone buildings in the southern end of town and along lower Main Street which replaced the first flimsy structures that were destroyed by fire; second, the massive stone mansions, with landscaped grounds and carriage houses in the rear, which housed the city's millionaires; and, third, the newer residential sections with their modern bungalow homes and drive-in markets. Helena is a fascinating city, historically and architecturally, and it is proud of its past; yet it is a modern city and lives in the present.

MARYSVILLE

NORTH of Helena in the Prickly Pear Valley are the invisible ghost towns of Silver City and Scratch Gravel, and in the mountains beyond Marysville, accessible only by trail, decaying cabins and abandoned mines mark the sites of more ghost settlements. Silver City, once the county seat of Edgerton (now Lewis and Clark) County has been dredged into oblivion— not a trace remains of the camp which sprang up along Silver Creek in 1862 and produced $3,000,000 in gold dust. In the days when their streams were placered, Silver City and Last Chance Gulch were rivals. Both were full of hard-working men who were cleaning up gold from the sluices, but the gold at Silver City was less fine than that at Last Chance and contained considerable silver. The gravels of the valley had been discovered in 1862, but the rich bars were not uncovered until 1864.

With the discovery of Last Chance Gulch, prospectors swarmed to the new diggings, and the right of Silver to remain the county seat was challenged. The contest ended in 1865 when Colonel W. F. Sanders, a citizen of Last Chance, rode horseback to the camp on Silver Creek and, before anyone could stop him, rode back with the record books in his saddlebags. Scratch Gravel, another placer camp in the same vicinity, is also gone.

From the site of Silver City we turned west into the hills. Six miles over a good highway laid on an abandoned railroad grade brought us to Marysville, one of the great gold-producing centers in the state prior to 1899. Below the highway, Silver Creek is lined with the remains of placering—mounds of gravel, now overgrown with brush. Higher up the gulch, nearer Marysville, are broken dams of settling ponds, old shacks, and rusted machinery, all once part of the town's great mining development.

When lode mines were discovered at the head of Silver Creek, a town sprang up in the level valley surrounded by the mineral-bearing peaks. Marysville, named for Mrs. Mary Ralston, pioneer woman of the district, never became a big camp—its greatest population is estimated at 2,000—but in its prime it was gay and lusty and had its colorful characters. Mike McDermott, or Mike the Butch, never drank water for fear it might rust him, and his pal, Larry Walch, wasn't sober for twenty years. When the town needed a Catholic church and no funds were in sight, Annie Dillon, boardinghouse keeper, put on a one-woman drive to raise the money. Her method was direct and effective. She stood at the mouth of each mine tunnel as the shifts came off work and asked every miner to donate a day's pay to the cause. Next she asked Mr. Cruse, wealthy owner of the Drumlummon mine, for two lots on which to build the church. He grudgingly gave her one; but when the building was completed half of it was found to be on the second lot! Cruse made no comment.

HOTEL AND FRATERNITY HALL, ELKHORN

MAIN STREET, MARYSVILLE

Until the railroads were built, everything was freighted into Marysville up the steep canyon grade, and swaying, creaking stage coaches carried passengers over the hair-raising shelf road. But in 1887, as the big mines began to pay and the town grew, the Northern Pacific and the Great Northern began a ruthless race to reach the town and corner the freight trade.

The Northern Pacific reached the head of Silver Creek, the only entrance to the Marysville valley, and built a high trestle across the canyon's mouth, sweeping around in a big arc and rolling into town at an altitude of 5,360 feet. The Great Northern built straight up Silver Creek to the canyon's head, where it was stopped dead by the Northern Pacific's refusal to grant a right of way under its trestle. The Great Northern had no alternative, therefore, but to build its station at the head of the gulch, a quarter of a mile from town. It was considered a dangerous road because of the steeper grade it had to maintain along the entire length of the canyon. An engine had difficulty drawing one coach at a time, and down-grade engines periodically went out of control and rolled over the bank. People therefore shunned it, and in less than two years it scrapped its rails and sold its ties for mine timbers. Even the Northern Pacific had a stiff grade of more than 125 feet to the mile, but it reached town by a series of switchbacks and operated into Marysville until 1924.

The mine which made Marysville was the Drumlummon. Though different stories are told about its discovery, the name of Thomas Cruse is most persistently linked with its history. Disappointed in his prospecting in California and Nevada, Cruse wandered to Montana and arrived broke in Helena in 1865. There he met William Brown, who had been placering on Silver Creek for more than a year. Brown offered Cruse a placer claim in the gulch, and the two men worked side by side. Cruse noticed that the gold he washed was often attached to bits of quartz, and this made him believe that the mother lode was nearby. He tried to interest Brown in prospecting the hillsides with him, but Brown was a placer miner. Cruse therefore began to divide his time between placering in the gulch and prospecting the hills for the real source of the gold.

He worked hard, dug a tunnel, cut into a vein of ore, sank a discovery shaft, dug a second tunnel to cut the vein where it was widest, sacked his ore, and trudged with it at night across the hills to an assayer in Helena.

Another story claims George Detweiler as the first owner of the Drumlummon. He staked out a claim in 1876 but failed to do the amount of assessment work required by mining law to hold his claim. After the first of the year, when his ownership lapsed, Cruse jumped the claim.

A third story states that Detweiler, after staking his claim, went east to the Centennial Exposition in Philadelphia and asked Cruse to do his development work while he was gone, but that Cruse did nothing on the claim and after the New Year filed on the property himself. Whichever of these three stories gives the true beginning, it is certain that Cruse very early owned the mine, which he called the Drumlummon after his birthplace in Ireland. For six years he took out high-grade ore from his workings and crushed it in a little five-stamp mill in Marysville. His total was $144,539 in bullion from 3,780 tons of ore. In 1883 he sold the mine for $1,500,000 to an English syndicate, the Montana Company, Ltd.

As soon as Cruse had made a fortune from his mine he began to live as became a man of his wealth. He moved to Helena, founded a bank, rode about the city in a carriage driven by a liveried coachman, and conscientiously attended board meetings, although he could not read and had only recently learned to write his name. Much of St. Helena's Cathedral was built with his money, and his timely investment in bonds for the state capitol facilitated its completion. After he sold the Drumlummon, he was unhappy until he bought the Bald Mountain property west of Marysville. He spent hours at the mine, climbing the shafts and sitting at the tunnel's mouth watching the cars clatter out to the dump. This was the life he understood and enjoyed.

The English company which bought the Drumlummon spent fortunes on the mine. Many of the stockholders were English aristocrats whose sons were sent to the mines to become engineers or mining experts. They were paid large salaries and were well housed. At one time there were more officials than miners! The company provided electric lights, steam heat, and hot and cold water to the officials' homes and furnished them lavishly. The grounds of the manager's house were landscaped by a trained gardener, and even the pump station resembled a Gothic chapel. When the company needed a new pump in 1890, they ordered a Cornish one at a cost of $55,000, paying an additional $33,000 in freighting costs. They sent for an expert from London to install it. The water in the mine was so low when he examined the property that he scornfully remarked that there wasn't enough water even to prime the pump, and hurried back home. Nevertheless, the pump was on its way. While it was being hauled up the canyon, however, the wagons carrying it broke down, the pump rolled into the bottom of the gulch, and the company never bothered to retrieve it. No wonder the firm went broke!

In 1889 the St. Louis Company, operating the adjoining property, discovered that the Drumlummon miners had crossed into their ground, while following a vein, and as a result of this encroachment the mine was tied up in litigation for nearly twenty years. The court finally decided in favor of the St. Louis Company, and the Drumlummon gave up rather than appeal the decision.

Fire, probably caused by defective wiring, broke out in the mine in 1892 and raced up the No. 1 shaft, destroying 800 feet of timbering which stood in its way. It was discovered by the night shift as they entered the mine. "Hose lines were run into the tunnel from fire pumps in the boiler room and by stretching a wet blanket across the tunnel and pushing it ahead, the men were able, several hours after the fire started, to get close enough to the shaft to put water into it." Five million gallons of water were pumped down the shaft, causing the water in the mine to rise to the 700-foot level.

In 1896 C. W. Merrill reworked the tailings from the Drumlummon by the cyanide process, and both he and the company profited by the venture. Finally, in 1911, the mine was sold to the St. Louis Mining & Milling Company. Altogether, under its several owners, it produced $20,000,000.

As soon as the Drumlummon lode was discovered in 1876, other veins were uncovered and mining began to boom. Nate Vestal invested the $12,000 worth of gold dust he had washed from Alder Gulch in quartz claims around Marysville. He developed his Snowdrift property, but he neglected the Penobscot, which adjoined it and which he had bought from the original owner in 1872. Finally two men asked permission to trace the Penobscot vein in the hope that it led beyond his property onto vacant ground that they could stake. Immediately they uncovered richer ore at the grassroots than he had found in the Snowdrift. From this mine Vestal took $80,000; from it also came a gold bar weighing 242 pounds and valued at $54,262.62, said to be the largest bar ever cast from a single mine. Vestal later sold his mine for $400,000 and went east to spend his fortune. After a year in Europe and the eastern cities of the United States, he wired a friend in Marysville for money to buy a ticket back home. Soon after his arrival he was back in his own mill working for $3.50 a day.

Very gradually the mines played out or their ore became too low-grade for profitable handling, and the properties closed down.

As we drove through the canyon gate into the town we passed the big, silent Drumlummon mill with its mass of buildings and dumps. In front of us lay the town, consisting of a main street, lined with substantial brick and stone buildings, and several streets of homes beyond. Two frame churches, Methodist and Catholic, stood, each in its little fenced-in yard, almost opposite a large, drab schoolhouse. Some blocks in the middle of the town had no houses at all and were overgrown with grass and edged with decaying wooden sidewalks. Only the stone foundations of the former buildings were visible.

Just as we were starting to explore the streets, a car pulled up at a corner and a man got out, carrying a bunch of dead marmots which he threw to the ground.

"Hey, Bill," he called to an old man who was slowly walking down the hill from an upper street, "here's what Jo sent you for your cats."

The old man picked up the marmots and, coming over to where I was sketching, he began to talk in a high, thin voice.

"That's the Drumlummon," he announced, pointing with his stick to the big mine on the hill. "Tommy Cruse got disgusted gophering around here, so he went out to Nevada and stayed three years, but he kept thinking about the Drumlummon ore. First thing you know he came back to the old claim and worked it. I knew him, and he used to tell me about when he first got to Helena—how poor he was, and how a friend of his, who kept a drugstore, used to let him sleep on the counter nights. He was dumb, too. Didn't know float when he saw it. He dug holes all over these mountains before he located the Drumlummon. After that he was in the money. He's been dead a long time. Most of the old ones are in the marble orchard now." With this the old fellow started slowly back up the hill.

"What's he been gaffering about?" said a woman with a strong Cornish accent who came out of a store and leaned on the window of the car. "You should have seen this place when the mines were running full tilt and the Cousin Jacks would swing along in groups to and from their shifts singing at the top of their lungs. We had no unions here, but the English company paid union wages so the men didn't gripe. How they loved to bet! The tram from the Belmont mine to the mill was rickety, and the ore cars coming down the grade would hit the weak section where the rails sagged, and often enough they'd tip over. You'd never be sure. So the men would bet as to whether a certain car would make it to the mill. Chances were it wouldn't.

"Then there was the time that Lily Jones—she was one of the girls from the row, you know—decided to drown herself in the pond down by the mill and she threw herself in just when a shift was changing. Right away the bets were on. Five hundred dollars would she drown. Six to one she wouldn't. One of the miners jumped in to save her. They bet on him, too. Oh, those were the days." A sudden squall of rain sent the Cornish woman scurrying back to her store and us back to Helena.

Between Helena and Butte a number of old camps lie either along the highway or on roads leading off from it. First comes the site of Montana City, easily seen from the highway, which was once the scene of extensive placer operations but now shows only weed-covered mounds of gravel and tailings. Clancy and Jefferson City, a few miles farther south on Prickly Pear Creek, began as mining camps but are now so modern and alive that they reveal few relics of the old boom days. Two miles west of Jefferson City, however, is Corbin, and four miles farther is Wickes; both are mining and smelting camps that have retained much of their original appearance.

WICKES

THE distinguishing landmarks of Wickes are the row of abandoned coke ovens and the three gaunt smelter stacks at the entrance of the little canyon. The hills behind the town are covered with dumps and prospect holes, a dilapidated shaft house, and a ruined and dismantled mill.

The town, which was settled in 1877, was named for George T. Wickes, a contractor and mining engineer from New York. His partner was J. Corbin. During the early eighties, when the Alta, Comet, Gregory, and Ninah mines were being worked, the Wickes district was the largest producer of silver-lead ore in Jefferson County. The biggest mine was the Alta, and for thirty years more than three hundred miners trudged up North Hill to its workings. The mine has been worked steadily, and the yield of lead, gold, and silver ores from its thirty miles of tunnels comes to more than $32,000,000. In 1884 the Helena Mining and Reduction Company built the smelter, and at about the same time concentrators for handling Alta ore were built at Corbin. The smelter ran successfully until 1893, when the new smelter at East Helena took its place.

By the time the Northern Pacific built its branch road to Wickes in 1886, the camp was a thriving place with 1,500 people, 5 dance halls, and 22 saloons. Fights were so common that "a man wouldn't rise from his chair to see who was fighting." For several years a man and team were hired to clear Main Street each morning of the cards and other debris that littered it.

Big fires almost cleaned out the town, in 1900 and 1902; but today there is still an outfit on top of the hill working the Alta.

ELKHORN

AFTER we left Wickes we climbed out of the Prickly Pear Valley, crossed a low divide, and entered the wide Boulder Valley, with its well-cultivated fields. Climbing up the valley to the mountain town of Elkhorn, we passed a few ranch houses and once had to maneuver our way through a bunch of mares whose wide-eyed colts dashed toward the fence posts and stood quivering until we had passed. Soon we saw signs of mining—prospect holes on the hills and the rusty roofs of mine buildings directly ahead.

Elkhorn is situated in a high, sloping meadow surrounded by timbered hills, above which rise, to the north, Crow and Elkhorn peaks. It is a real ghost town, big and well preserved, with several streets half overgrown with sagebrush but still traceable, and row upon row of frame or log houses, some with bay windows, some two-storied, and many with false fronts.

Not a soul was in sight as we drove up the steep main street toward the big, crumbling mill with its huge dumps; but as soon as we turned our engine off we heard a throbbing sound and noticed electric lights burning in some of the smaller buildings near the mill. A man in a miner's hat stepped to the end of the building where he was running the hoist, and from him I learned that this was the Elkhorn mine, which had shut down in 1912 and had only recently been reopened by lessees.

The district had been prospected and quartz locations made prior to 1870. Peter Wyes, a Swiss, is credited with the first discoveries in the area; but the lode, later known as the Elkhorn, did not become a producing mine until A. M. Holter bought it from the original owner and further developed it. Before long the history of the district was that of the Elkhorn mine. The original owner had built a "5 stamp, wet-crushing, free-milling" plant on the premises, a mill that was adequate for the surface ores but that lost 50 per cent of the silver values when the deeper ores proved refractory. By 1881 a new mill equipped with a chlorination process was needed; but lack of capital and disagreement among the owners resulted in the property being put up for sale. Even during this period of confusion, the mine yielded 4,285 ounces of silver.

The Elkhorn Mining Company bought it in 1883 and erected a new mill. By means of its chloridizing process 90 per cent of the value of the ores was saved, and "a bullion aggregating $188,375 in silver and $2,320 in gold" was obtained from the first ten months' run. There were other mines in the vicinity, the C. & D., the Midnight Bell, the Queen, the Golden Curry, and the Dalcoath; but, though at least one of them shipped ore daily as late as 1910, they were completely eclipsed by the Elkhorn.

The camp which grew up around the mine flourished all through the eighties and nineties; in addition to the miners, whose monthly payroll was over $15,000, an army of woodchoppers was kept busy cutting timber for the mines and providing fuel for the furnaces. In 1884 Elkhorn was paying into the First National Bank of Helena an average of $5,000 daily. A cleanup of ten days' run in the new mill produced three bars of bullion weighing 300 pounds and valued at $4,500.

Though the town was built and maintained almost entirely by the Elkhorn Mining Company, supplies were expensive and hard to obtain, especially salt, which was used by the mill in reducing the ores. As miners never have time to grow crops, the ranchers in the Boulder Valley found a ready market for their produce. The supply situation was relieved in 1889, when the Northern Pacific built a railway up the steep grade of the narrow gulch east of town, and provided tri-weekly service.

The Elkhorn property has changed hands several times and has been thought to be worked out more than once, but careful exploration has always revealed new ore bodies. In 1901, however, pumping costs were so high and the ore was so low-grade that mining became unprofitable, and the property was abandoned. Up to this time it had produced 8,902,000 ounces of silver, 8,500 ounces of gold and 4,000,000 pounds of lead. Since then it has been opened up occasionally by leasers, one outfit spending two years and $80,000 to pump out the lower levels and put the mine in shape for operation. During the summer of 1910 about a hundred miners were employed. In 1951, how-ever, only four families were living in the town.

We drove slowly down the main street between empty, gaping buildings, their panes of glass broken and their wooden porches so rotten that steps hung awry and boards were missing. Several boys were playing in the street near the biggest, most imposing false-fronted building, the Fraternity Brothers Hall.

"Come on in and we'll show you where we play," they called. Gingerly testing out the rickety front steps and edging through the squeaking door, we entered the dark, cool interior. The big hall was unfurnished, although later I read that until recently a full set of band instruments and two pianos had been left to collect dust in its dingy interior. At the far end was a raised stage, its painted scenery—a mass of classic columns, panels, and festoons—fastened to the rear wall.

"There's another room upstairs," chirped the littlest boy. "Want to see it?" It turned out to be a second empty auditorium. From the vestibule at one end I stepped out on the creaking balcony, suspended over the hall's main entrance, and tried to see the town as it had once been, with its hotel, its fourteen sa-loons and two pool halls, its shooting frays, which had left bullet marks on so many of the cabins, its mail stage from Boulder drawing up to the post office door, its Elkhorn Trading Company store, and its population of 1,500. Be-cause of the many buildings still standing, it was easy to imagine Elkhorn as a place that had shipped out $14,000,000 in silver.

BASIN

From Elkhorn we returned to Boulder and started west again. Nine miles west of Boulder we passed through Basin, where, in 1864 and the years immediately following, placer gravel had yielded hundreds of thou-sands of dollars. When the gravels were washed clean, outcroppings of ore were found on the hills; as a result, the town was alive and active between 1870 and 1890. Many old houses and false-fronted stores dating from this period are still occupied, though some have been remodeled to suit today's tastes.

After 1890 Basin lay dormant till 1917, when a mining revival began which came to a head in 1924 with the construction of a 300-ton mill by the

Jib Mining Company. This spurt of activity lasted only until 1929. Today the most conspicuous sights are the big brick stack and stone foundations of a dismantled plant, and the huge, silent buildings of the Jib mill, empty and deserted at the far end of town.

BUTTE

LESS than an hour after leaving Basin we crossed the Continental Divide and looked down upon big, sprawling Butte. In 1864, when G. O. Humphrey and William Allison found placer deposits of gold in Silver Bow Creek and Silver Bow City was born, Butte did not exist. Within a year, however, the *Montana Post* of February 18 announced:

The county recorder's offices are located six or seven miles above Silver Bow City, at a small cluster of cabins rejoicing in the name of Butte City.

Butte's silver boom did not begin until 1874, when William L. Farlin returned from Idaho to work the quartz outcrops he had discovered in the sixties. As soon as the ledges around Butte City were known to contain silver, men rushed to the camp to stake claims. Two of them, Marcus Daly and William A. Clark, became multimillionaires, not through silver but through the inexhaustible deposits of copper which they discovered, developed, and cornered; both are closely identified with the city's development. By 1880 copper mining had replaced silver mining, and the era of the smelters began. Marcus Daly chose as the site for his smelter a location some miles west of Butte. There he platted a town in 1883 and named it Copperopolis; but as there was already a place of the same name in the state, and as the Anaconda mine in Butte was one of the big producers, the postmaster of Copperopolis sent in a new name, Anaconda, for the budding smelter city.

Today Butte and Anaconda are the big copper camps of the Northwest. Both have fascinating and colorful histories, but they are too prosperous to have retained even a semblance of their original appearance, and they are anything but ghost towns.

We spent only enough time in Butte to look at the forest of gallows frames on the big hill, the Clark mansion, and Marcus Daly's statue in front of the School of Mines. Then we drove on toward Anaconda through Rocker and the present town of Silver Bow. From the summit of one of the barren hills that separate the two cities, our first glimpse of Anaconda showed a tangle of mills and ponds and tracks. Above it the smelter's great stack rose sharply into the sky and cut across the line of barren hills beyond. To this huge smelter plant are brought the ores from Butte's many mines.

GEORGETOWN AND SOUTHERN CROSS

WHEN we left Anaconda early the next morning, we went on to Georgetown, a small resort beside an artificial lake. The original Georgetown was a mile farther on; but as we drove toward it the road kept branching. Keeping in the most traveled ruts for two miles, we reached a mine dump and the end of the road. We retraced our route and tried another fork. This took us past a few new cabins and one deserted, false-fronted store with faded, torn green shades and peeling paint. Then we turned up the only road we hadn't tried, went through dense timber for a mile, and emerged on a high plateau overlooking the lake. Mine dumps and mine buildings stood all around us. It was early Sunday morning and not a person was in sight, but blue smoke curled from one cabin chimney and I stumbled through the deep, bunchy grass toward it. A weather-beaten man answered my knock, throwing open the door and letting out a fragrant aroma of frying bacon.

"Where am I?" I asked. "Is this Georgetown?"

"Hell, no," he replied. "This is Southern Cross. If you came up the forest road you went right through Georgetown. Didn't you see an old store as you went by?" he continued. "You're 7,000 feet high here, so the summers are cold and the gardens are late. I'm just getting my lettuce now. That is, all I can keep the rabbits from stealing. The mines haven't been working since 1941. This was a live gold camp in the seventies. It's owned by the Anaconda Company now. It was named by a sailor. The other big mine he called the Pleiades.

"There's lots of old camps around here in the hills," he continued. "You passed the road in to Cable coming into Georgetown. Over beyond here is Red Lion. The old stage road between Anaconda and Philipsburg used to go over the mountains through Cable and Georgetown, and by this place, too. Lots of the houses were moved out of here when the mines shut down. You see the store down there in the pines? They used to do business with five hundred people. There's only eight of us here now."

GRANITE

NORTH of Georgetown is Philipsburg, a silver camp settled in 1866 and still so active that it is hard to discover the old buildings, which lie hidden among the trim new homes and modern stores. When we inquired the way to Granite, an old miner told us that it was no use going there, as the

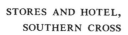

STORES AND HOTEL,
SOUTHERN CROSS

HOTEL, GARNET

SMELTER STACKS, WICKES

town has really disappeared. Even its wooden sidewalks have been torn up, and its last building, the Miners' Union Hall, is a ruin. Nevertheless, we decided that Granite's interesting history made it worth a visit.

The Granite mine was discovered in 1872. At first its yield was not too promising, and its backers grew panicky and wired the manager to close down. In the meantime, however, he had rushed a wire to them which read: "Have just struck pay ore."

On the strength of this bonanza, mills were built, machinery was freighted slowly up the mountainside, and a town grew along the one main street, which followed the contour of the hill. At its peak, Granite had a population of 3,000, and its stores and cabins were always in demand. A water wagon delivered a daily supply of five gallons from house to house at the rate of a dollar a month. There were three churches and considerably more than three saloons, outside of which lay a "carpet of disused playing cards and cigar butts."

Although the Granite mine was located in 1872, its title was allowed to lapse, and in 1875 it was relocated. In 1880, Charles D. McLure, superintendent of the Hope silver mill in Philipsburg, had a specimen of ore from the dump of the Granite mine assayed and immediately set about organizing a syndicate of St. Louis investors, who, believing in his judgment, advanced $132,000 to put into the property. All through the eighties the mine was developed, and its plant was enlarged as production expanded. Between 1885 and 1892, $20,000,000 was taken out in silver and gold, and dividends of $11,000,000 were paid.

Encouraged by the success of the Granite mine, other properties were opened, but only the Bimetallic, an extension of the Granite vein, paid off.

When we left Philipsburg, we turned east at the edge of town, by-passed a fork in the road which led to a big mill, and started up a steep mountain trail which twisted around the shoulder of the hill and never slackened its grade. It was extremely rough, had no turnouts, and was full of sharp corners. Dim tire tracks ahead encouraged us to go on for three miles, and then more hesitantly for a fourth, until we were brought up sharply by a locked gate blocking the road—Anaconda property, no trespassing. Could this be the location of the Granite mine?

We were 8,000 feet high and had climbed 3,000 feet since leaving the highway; as we eased the car around and started down, we occasionally cast glances at the tiny houses of Philipsburg, far below in the valley. Once safely off the mountain shelf, we drove in to the big mill we had seen on the way up. A man stepped out of the mine office just as we stopped the car. In answer to my questions he said, "Sure, you got to Granite, lady; and it's a good four miles. This place is Clark."

GOLD CREEK

FROM Philipsburg we drove north to Drummond and eleven miles east to Gold Creek. Here, in 1856, François Finlay, a quarterbreed Indian also called Benetsee, found the first gold in Montana. Three years later, James and Granville Stuart placered near the place from which Benetsee had washed his flakes; they too obtained colors from the sands, but insufficient supplies and tools, combined with threats from the Blackfoot Indians, drove them from the diggings, and they did not return until 1862. Then they set up sluices near the head of Benetsee, or, as it was later called, Gold Creek. A placer camp grew up at the diggings, but recent dredging has obliterated it.

Returning to Drummond, we continued northwest to Bearmouth, once a trading post for the nearby placer camps and still a shipping point on the railroad. We stopped at a house where a dirt road leads north from the highway and asked the woman who lives there about driving conditions to Beartown and Garnet.

"You'll have no trouble," she said. "The postmistress does it each Friday in her Ford. It's just a nice drive."

The first six miles were easy, although the roadbed was narrow and full of rock and gravel. The lower end of the creek was filled with smooth, clean pebbles and stones, the debris left by a dredge. Higher up, equally large piles of stones lay overgrown with weeds and low bushes—signs of the hand placering done in early days. Occasionally an empty, weathered cabin peered out from among trees and underbrush. When we reached the point where Deep Creek flows into Bear Creek, we knew we were on the site of Beartown.

BEARTOWN

BEAR CREEK is long and narrow, and the hills press in upon it on either side. Yet in November, 1865, Joe and Bob Booth, Charlie Hickey, and Jack Reynolds, who had been mining on Elk Creek, discovered gold in the sands of First Chance Gulch, which flows into Bear Creek; and just a few weeks later over a thousand men were jostling each other for space and attempting to stake claims in its once clear water. Because of the demand, claims were limited to 200 feet and each miner was responsible for dumping his tailings on his own ground.

Not only Bear and Elk creeks, but also Deep Creek, showed colors. Before long miners had spilled into the latter, panning their way to Top o' Deep, where a small temporary camp sprang up. Springtown, also on Deep

Creek, and Reynolds City, near the head of Elk Creek, were also temporary camps, consisting of a few shacks and a saloon-store. John Featherman ran the store at Reynolds City and charged his patrons twelve and a half cents for potatoes, fifty cents for salt, seventy-five cents for sugar, and eighty cents for bacon.

Beartown was not expected to last; so only the crudest cabins, lean-tos, and dugouts were prepared for shelter that first winter. Some of the men slept under wagons until driven into cosier lodgings by the first snowstorm. Living was rugged, with whisky the only drink and every fifth cabin a saloon.

The pay streak was narrow but rich, and claims were worked by sinking a shaft to bedrock, seventy feet below the surface, and "drifting" by means of lateral tunnels radiating from the shaft. When the individual workings were connected it was possible to walk eight or ten miles underground up Bear and Deep creeks without coming to the surface. The pay dirt was hoisted up the shafts in buckets and then sluiced. Miles of sluice boxes lined the creek. At one point the stream makes an ox-bow loop around a projecting cliff, and in order to avoid half-a-mile of sluice construction following this bend, the men dug a 100-foot tunnel through the mountain and laid their boxes in it. They built reservoirs at the heads of gulches to hold water for sluicing operations and released the water only two or three hours a day. Each miner used the water in turn as it flowed by his claim. By the time it reached those far down the gulch it was liquid mud. Many fights started over disputed water rights.

By the spring of 1866, when most of the discoveries had been made, the diggings were so well known that Deer Lodge, the county seat, was spoken of as "that village on the trail to Bear." On March 24, one enthusiastic miner wrote to Ben Dittes of the *Montana Post* as follows:

Friend Ben
You may "toot the old horn and blow the bazoo" as much as you please over Bear Gulch. It is enormously rich—claims are selling at $2000, and scarce at that. Pet Hall, Dave Thompson and L. C. May and other Virginia boys are here. The stampede is greater than ever known to any mines before.
The Elk creek mines are also thought to be big tho' not so well developed. This is reliable.

Within the year the new camp was the trading center for 5,000 miners, and its flimsy cabins lined both sides of the gulch in an irregular, straggling fashion, tucked into crevices under canyon walls and crowding out over the edge of the stream. Somebody drew a town plat, but nobody paid any attention to it; buildings faced whichever way their owners chose. Down one side of the main street ran a ditch, and "after the water had cleared it provided water for the town." Near the ditch each miner had a large hogshead which he filled with water each evening in order to have his next day's supply ready. The miners' cabins with their sod roofs and dirt floors were small, for most of the men were bachelors. Stoves were too hard to pack in, and cooking was done chiefly over open fires. In addition to the usual stores and saloons, Beartown had a brewery, a drugstore, a slaughterhouse, and Gee Lee's wash house. Ball's Hotel and Pelletier's saloon were among the few two-story buildings. There was always a gay crowd at Pelletier's, for the genial proprietor and Chicago Joe's dance-hall girls kept the "boys" entertained. At the lower end of town was a general store run by Joaquin Abascal, a Spaniard, and La Forcade, a Frenchman. Both were popular, for they gave credit to many of the men; in fact, nearly everyone in Beartown had at some time been grubstaked by them. Their bookkeeping was original, for each wrote entries in his own language and neither could read what the other wrote. Back of their store was a wine cellar dug into the mountainside, where the best liquors were kept; but for those whose tastes were less developed or whose poke of dust was lean, a barrel of whisky was kept in the store for free drinks.

One of the most welcome visitors to the gulch was Dr. Armistead Mitchell, who used to ride over from Deer Lodge whenever he got a hankering to see the "boys," or whenever his services were needed. "Mit" was a good surgeon when he was drunk, which was often, and his arrival in camp was always cause for a gathering, because he brought news from the outside world.

One morning he arrived at Abascal's store to perform an operation on Shorty, who had had the misfortune, while dead drunk, to stumble into his own fireplace and lie with his arm in the embers all night until it was burned to a crisp. As soon as "Mit" had sawed off the arm and bound up the stump in a soiled rag, Shorty, still fortified against pain by whisky, ran to the door and called in his friends for a round of drinks. While the boys crowded around the patient, "Mit" collected the scraps of flesh and bone and put them in a gunny sack to take home, with some fuzzy idea of using them in an experiment he was conducting. The board and two whisky barrels that had served as the operating table were put away, and Shorty, the doctor, and two or three cronies sat down to an all-day game of poker. That evening a dance was held at Pelletier's, and everyone went. It was daylight when it broke up, and the doctor lurched to his horse, carrying the sack of charred bones. Somewhere along the trail home he lost the arm.

Mary J. Pardee gives a vivid picture of Beartown's most colorful characters in her article of September 16, 1931, in the *Great Falls Tribune*. One of them was One-Eyed Mike Kelly, a grizzled miner who shaved infrequently with a rusty, chipped butcher-knife and who lost his eye when he attempted to jump a claim belonging to a Chinese. The two men went to "Fightin' Bar," the camp's regular prize ring, and agreed to shoot it out. Each got behind a tree and waited. Nothing happened. Kelly got impatient and peeped around the trunk, and the Chinese fired and hit his eye. According to Mike's story of the fight, he was hit with his own bullet. "You see, it was this way," he'd say. "We both fired at the same time and the bullets hit each other, and mine bounced back and landed in my eye. I'm a dead shot, I am."

Another was Old Greenwood, who worked a claim several miles down the gulch and had no partner except the one he invented, with whom he carried on constant abusive arguments. He would shovel gravel at the bottom of his shaft, and when he was ready to hoist the bucket, he would yell up to his "partner." After waiting awhile, he would climb to the surface and cuss out his nonexistent helper before proceeding to haul up the dirt himself.

One of the men who used to go to Beartown in 1866 to peddle jewelry, tobacco, and meat was W. A. Clark, who later became the great copper magnate of the state and represented it in the United States Senate.

Beartown had no city officers and earned the reputation of being the "fightingest" camp in Montana. "Judge" McElroy, an Irishman whose title was purely honorary, served as arbitrator in many local legal battles. When he was sober he was timid and his speech was halting, but, given whisky, his eloquence increased in direct proportion to the dose. Liquor also revived his memory, and he rolled out legal terms to the confusion of his opponents; therefore, whenever a case was to be tried, he was first taken to the bar and then led to the bench.

The following article from the *Montana Post* of April 6, 1867, describes both a celebration in camp and public sentiment toward the need for more law and order.

Beartown, Editor of Post:

Now and then we have an old-fashioned free fight and nothing is more common than to hear or see a man having a "head put on him," generally from exuberance of love and enmity. St. Patrick's day to the surprise of many who judged from the antecedents of the community, passed off without much fighting or serious casualties. This gratifying result is attributed to the wholesome influence of Fenionism. The day opened inauspiciously and a pitched battle appeared at one time to be imminent. The seat of war was at the lower end of town and the caucus belli was the old thing—a mining dispute. . . . The crisis so happily passed over, the parties adjourned to a large saloon up town, where a less bloody repast was spread forth. A stand was erected therein, from which, in the course of the day, several gentlemen *narrated*. The following named gentlemen worthily spoke the virtues of

St. Patrick and the Irish people with occasional references to the perfidy of Old England. . . .

Toward the end of the article, "Husky," the writer, describes a mining dispute which concluded with the aggressor jumping the owner's claim, and he deplores the lack of law enforcement in the territory with these words:

This country is actually destitute of the means of enforcing its most insignificant verdict on a charge of violation of its code. Notwithstanding the vast sums annually collected for the purpose of good government, there is not so much as a jail on the west side of the Rocky Mts. in Montana, or for that matter a free road, or trail, or footpath hardly. The general disposition of the community is law abiding.

Most of the pay dirt was washed out in three or four seasons, and when the men were no longer able to find the yellow particles of gold, once so plentiful yet no larger than grains of wheat, they pulled stakes and left. In 1916 some hydraulic work was done below Beartown, and as late as 1940 a dredge worked the channel. Altogether, the narrow gulch yielded $30,000,000.

GARNET

THE road continued to climb beyond Beartown to the foot of the "Chinee Grade," near the place where, years ago, the Chinese are said to have buried a five-pound baking-powder tin filled with gold dust. As we hit the grade I realized that never, save once in Colorado, had I encountered a steeper, nastier set of short switchbacks. Being unfamiliar with the road, unlike the postmistress, we drove it with less abandon and lost our speed beyond the hairpin turns; whereupon the car refused to pull the last steep rise—and vaporlocked. Taking my camera, sketch pad, and pencils, I started alone up the road between the trees.

The first signs of mining were dumps and prospect holes. I passed an old buggy in the marshy grass beside the road. Then, through a gateway of trees, I suddenly saw the town. It had many buildings, and its main street circled a hillside dotted with cabins and barns. The post office was crumbling, and its interior was full of broken and sodden debris. Two or three false-fronted stores lined the street, and at a crossroad stood the hotel, a large, three-story frame building with leaded glass doors. Peering through the dirty windows, I could see that some furniture had been left inside and that the walls were still papered. There was no sound in the town and no sign of life except a horse grazing on the meadow.

After making several sketches, I was about to start back when a car whizzed by in a cloud of dust. At the same time a man stepped out of a cabin on the hill above me and called out, "Was that the postmistress?"

"I wouldn't know," I shouted, "I'm a stranger here. Tell me where I am."

"Come up and I will," he answered.

"Garnet ores were all gold," he began. "First Chance Gulch—that's the gulch you're in—was all placering at first. Then they looked for the mother lode and they found good ore, but it was pockety. Most of the lode gold was found right here at Garnet. Even in 1867, while placer mining was going strong, the Lead King-Red Cloud, the Grant and Hartford, and the Shamrock veins were discovered. The whole country is pockmarked with mines. There are about fifty in this district alone."

"Which are the principal ones?" I asked.

"Well, there's the Mussigbrod and Mitchell about half a mile south of here, and the Magone Anderson—it yielded $300,000 in five years. The Grant-Hartford was where you passed the buggy. Then there's the Shamrock and the International and the Dewey. Ore from it ran $300 a ton."

"What about the Nancy Hanks? I've heard of it," I interrupted.

"I should think you would of," he replied. "They took $3,000,000 out of it. Sam Ritchey located the vein in the early seventies and in 1892 he found rich ore in the 'Old Shaft' of the property, but real production didn't begin till 1896, when he uncovered 'red ore' in the mine. After that this camp hummed. Other properties were opened up, and rich ore was shipped out for years. Garnet's never been entirely deserted, but its booms haven't ever lasted long. Most of the mines paid expenses from the start. The Dewey made regular shipments to the smelters right up to 1916. After that things slowed down, and some of the mines got tied up in lawsuits. None of them are really worked out, though.

"There used to be nine hundred men working here, and we had four saloons and everything that goes with a rough town. We had two fires before I came. The main street and the one that takes off from it were solid with houses then. The schoolhouse stood over there in the trees. Funny thing—it had no windows. In 1881 there were only eight children in school.

"You should see it snow up here. Last winter we had thirty-two feet. The most that fell in one storm was seven feet, but it sure piled up. My wife used to walk out on the porch roof to get to the clothesline. But that was nothing to the winter, years ago, when Garnet got snowed in. I've heard the old-timers tell about it. It snowed something awful, and no supply trains could get through the drifts. No one could get out, either. Provisions were getting mighty low and something had to be done. The placer mines all down the creek were tunneled to bedrock and the tunnels connected underground. Finally a man, with only a miner's lamp to light him, walked down to Bearmouth, eleven miles through the tunnels, and got some grub for the camp."

When I left, he insisted upon getting out his truck and driving me back to my car, and he waited to see us get started down the hill.

Slowly we crept around the switchbacks and down the gulch—the clutch jumping out of low on every steep grade! Garnet had been quite an adventure.

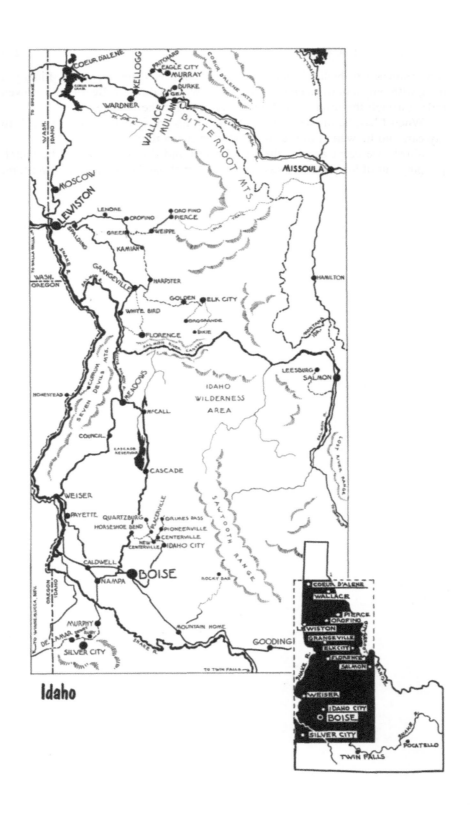

Idaho

6. *From Boise Basin to the Coeur d'Alenes*

Idaho

IDAHO from top to bottom is full of mining camps, most of them fairly accessible, a few reached only by trails. Oro Fino and Pierce City, the scenes of the state's earliest gold strike, are miles from a main road. The most direct approach to them is from Lewiston, once the closest supply point to the gold camps.

To this river town, in the spring of 1861, came Henry Plummer, the notorious road agent, fresh from California. He brought with him a wife, whom he later deserted, and he registered at the best hotel, awaking no suspicions as to his evil record. He used the bustling camp as headquarters until the spring of 1862, directing his nefarious campaigns secretly and often making stealthy night rides along the densely timbered trails to the mountains. He even established two roadhouses, called "shebangs"—one between Lewiston and Oro Fino and the other on the road to Walla Walla—each run by two agents, from which his deputies set out on designated raids. Plummer, in the meantime, stayed in Lewiston, sizing up the men and pack outfits that passed through its dusty streets and marking his future victims.

As I had seen the spot where Plummer was hanged in Bannack, Montana, in 1864, I was interested to learn his methods. He would obtain accurate details as to saddle, brand, color, and even date of purchase of each animal in a pack train or known to be carrying sacks of gold, then have a fake bill of sale made out in favor of one of his roadhouse keepers. A fast messenger would deliver the phony document to the innkeeper prior to the arrival of the owner of the pack train. When the victim reached the roadhouse, he was halted and asked where he got his animals. The fake bill of sale was pushed in his face, and he found himself looking down the barrel of a shotgun. If he were wise he left the shebang on foot.

215

Plummer and his gang were not the only desperadoes who lurked beside the lonely and unprotected trails which led from every mining camp. One of the grimmest stories centering around Lewiston is that of the Magruder murder in 1863. At the time of the crime Hill Beachy ran a hotel in Lewiston, and Magruder, who was a packer and trader, had his headquarters in the town. He and Beachy were close friends.

In August, 1863, Magruder loaded his train of seventy mules with miner's supplies and started for Virginia City, Montana, three hundred miles away. Several days after his departure, he was overtaken by a party of eight men who offered to help him with his packing in return for grub. Upon reaching Virginia City, four of the men left him and started mining. The other four hung around, helped him with his mules, and counted the money which he received for his goods. Three of these, D. C. Lowry, David Howard, and James Romain, were road agents; the fourth, William Page, was a trapper and scout.

By the middle of October Magruder, with $25,000 to $30,000 in gold coin and dust, was ready for his return trip. In need of help to get his large train over the road, he hired eight assistants—four strangers and the four who had worked for him all summer. One night the outfit made camp near a mountain top where the trail was close to a deep canyon. The road agents chose this spot as the place to kill Magruder and dispose easily of the evidence of their crime. Page was put on guard that night and was told of their plans, but was pledged to secrecy on threat of death. Lowry then stole up behind Magruder and killed him with an ax. The four new men, two of whom carried gold dust on their persons, were also murdered. After packing the money on the best mules, the three killers drove the rest of the animals over the high cliff. They rolled the dead men over the edge also, burned the camp equipment and then, with Page, went on toward Lewiston. All during the macabre incident the men wore moccasins so that their crime, if discovered, would be attributed to Indians.

If it had not stormed, the men would have avoided entering Lewiston, but the snow forced them there for shelter. They left their horses with a rancher and took the earliest stage to Walla Walla. From there they hurried to Portland, then by steamer to San Francisco.

Before Magruder started on his ill-fated trip, Hill Beachy had a dream that his friend would be attacked and murdered on the road. When Beachy saw the four men, whom he had seen the previous summer in Lewiston, leave by stage for Walla Walla, he had a hunch that they had done away with Magruder. So sure was he of their guilt that he got a warrant for their arrest and a "requisition from the Governors of Washington Territory, Oregon and California for the men wherever found." He wanted to follow them immediately, but since he had no actual proof he let himself be persuaded to wait for Magruder's return. Learning that the men had left their animals in Lewiston, he inspected them and recognized Magruder's mule and saddle. Next a group of packers who had left Virginia City three days after Magruder and had taken the same trail reported that they had not seen him on the way and that the four suspected men had been with him. Beachy set off at once to trail the murderers.

At Yreka, California, he telegraphed a description of the men to the San Francisco police, who located and arrested them. Beachy hurried to San Francisco and identified them. They were promised a fair trial. Then Page, the trapper, turned state's evidence and described the whole gory crime. The four men were returned to Lewiston to await trial before the District court which was to meet in January, 1864. Since snow prevented investigation of the site of the crime, Page's testimony could not be proved until the following summer; but enough evidence was produced to convict the men, and the three road agents were hanged March 4, 1864. Page, because of his confession and assistance, was freed. The gold dust, which the men had deposited in a San Francisco bank, was paid to Mrs. Magruder, and the First Legislature in Lewiston passed an appropriation of $6,244 to be paid to Beachy out of Territorial funds, reimbursing him for his services and for the money he spent in tracking down the criminals.

SPALDING

THE highway east from Lewiston follows the Clearwater River all the way to Orofino. At Spalding are the remains of the mission which the Reverend Henry Spalding established in 1836 for the Nez Percé Indians. Through his influence and teachings, certain of the natives became friendly toward the white men who were soon to invade their territory and strip it of game and timber. Across the river, about halfway between Spalding and Orofino, a small settlement named Lenore stands on the site of old Slaterville, once the head of steamer navigation on the Clearwater.

The Orofino of today is not the mining camp of the sixties; in fact, it is forty miles from the site of the gold discoveries which started men crashing through the timber and breaking trails over the mountains to the new diggings. Its good hotel made us decide to stay there for the night. While we were at dinner, a young man who knew the country into which we were going told us: "You won't find much at the site of old Oro Fino, but Pierce hasn't changed much in years. Down south of here are Elk City and Dixie. They're really old-timers."

PIERCE (CITY) AND ORO FINO

THE following morning we left Orofino while the fog hung over the river, and drove to Greer, where the road leaves the Clearwater. During the winding, ten-mile climb out of the valley to the high, rolling mesa land which we were about to cross, the car ducked in and out of ribbons of mist which clung to the steep hillside. The pavement ended at the top of the hill, and the rest of the drive to Pierce was over dusty roads flanked by huge wheat fields or by forests whose tall trees crowded both sides of the highway.

As we entered the town I was startled to find not the weathered log buildings and false-fronted stores I had anticipated, but instead a busy lumber camp full of modern buildings, neon signs, a bus station, and taverns, with dark interiors where juke boxes ground out the latest hits. Only a few of the old buildings are visible, tucked in between or behind those whose exteriors have been painted, stuccoed, and generally remodeled.

Nevertheless Pierce is the site of the earliest mining activities in Idaho, which at the time of the placer discoveries was a part of Washington Territory. Gold was known to lie in the beds of Idaho streams as early as the 1840's, for Father De Smet, pioneer Catholic priest to the northwest, had seen it. French Canadians found small quantities of it on the Pend d'Oreille River in 1852, and Captain Mullan had known of its existence in 1858 while building his famous road across the mountains; but no intensive exploration of the territory had been attempted because of Indian hostilities. By the terms of the Treaty of 1855, no white man was allowed on the Nez Percé reservation without permission of the Government agent and of the Indians themselves, and attempts to cross their land met with resistance.

The discovery of gold in appreciable amounts is attributed to Capt. E. D. Pierce, who in the autumn of 1859 washed colors from diggings on Canal Creek near Oro Fino. Pierce had heard in the early fifties that there was gold in the area, while he was on a trading expedition to the Nez Percés, but because of the Indians' belligerent attitude toward any encroachments upon their territory, he withdrew. In California he listened while an Indian, who watched him clean the riffles in his sluice box, described a strip of country to the east where similar glittering stones could be found and gave him instructions how to reach it. According to the story, several Indians had camped one night far up a river and watched the moon climb over the Bitterroot Mountains. Its light struck a canyon wall where a gleaming mass of rock shone like a star. Upon investigation, they discovered a "great shining ball" of metal which glittered but which they were unable to dislodge from the surrounding rock. Pierce also listened to Jean de Lassier, a trapper who in 1858 arrived in Walla Walla and reported that there was gold to be found on Oro Fino creek.

FIRST TERRITORIAL COURTHOUSE OF WASHINGTON AND THEN OF IDAHO, PIERCE, IDAHO

OLD CABINS WITH ROOFS MADE OF SHAKES, ELK CITY

Although Pierce realized that the location for which he was looking must lie somewhere on the reservation, he determined to try to find it. Accompanied by several men, he started for the territory described by the Indian, and on the south bank of the Snake River encountered a friendly band of Nez Percé Indians, led by Chief Timothy. Some of the natives, however, were not willing to let the white men go into their country and ordered them to leave. They pretended to do so, returned, and were again driven off. Then the chief's daughter, Jane, offered to guide them through the reservation, taking them by night up the North Fork of the Clearwater, to the junction of Canal Gulch and Oro Fino Creek. There Pierce and his men washed the first gold from the gravel. It was now late fall, 1859, and the men realized that they were not equipped to winter in the wilderness. They therefore returned to Walla Walla; but early spring found them stumbling back up the trail, with new recruits inflamed by their enthusiasm.

All summer they placered the stream, and by the fall of 1860 a handful of the hardier men made preparations to winter at the diggings. The rest returned to Walla Walla, carrying their dust with them and talking loudly of their strike. The next spring the rush began. During 1861 and 1862 streams of men hurried by all possible trails to the placer fields. Some came from Missoula, Montana, crossing by the Lolo trail to the further irritation of the Indians, who looked upon it as their personal property. Others followed the Clearwater. As soon as the spring freshets permitted, steamers paddled up the river as far as it was navigable, depositing their impatient passengers at Slaterville, forty miles from Pierce's diggings.

Here all freight was piled up around the five tents that comprised Seth Slater's camp, until pack trains could reload it and carry it into the mountains. Two of Slaterville's tents were stores, two others were cabins, and the fifth was a saloon in which one barrel of whisky, two bottles, and two glasses composed the entire stock. The Indians lined the river banks to watch the steamers, and one passenger in describing his trip by boat said that "on the entire journey up the Clearwater we were accompanied by Indians, riding along shore on horseback."

But the Indians still objected to the presence of the miners. Superintendent Geary, the Indian agent, knowing how impossible it was to keep the swelling stream of gold-thirsty men out of the reservation, made a new treaty, promising the Nez Percés "military protection and the enforcement of their laws." Before the treaty was signed, while the Indians listened to Geary's arguments, long processions of prospectors were converging upon the diggings, pushing past heavily laden supply trains all headed for Pierce City. The town had been named after the discoverer of the district (although one authority states that Wilbur Fisk Bassett was the real discoverer and that when he was an old man he would return to the abandoned diggings and shake his head over their decay).

By June, 1861, so many Idaho farmers had left their land and headed for the goldfields that few remained to harvest the summer's crops. By August, 7,000 men jostled each other in Pierce City, "2500 of whom were practical miners." During this boom Joaquin Miller was a mail carrier and pony express rider between Lewiston and the camp.

Pierce City already had a rival two miles upstream in Oro Fino City, a raw, new camp which stood closer to certain of the richer gravel beds. In no time it had sixty log houses, ten stores, and numerous tents and was selling lots for $200 and cabins for from $500 to $1,000. Carpenters made $10 a day and were much in demand, their hammers adding to the noise of the town, where at any hour of the day or night could be heard the brays of pack mules or the squeals of violins issuing from the saloons.

Patrick Ford, who ran a saloon at Lewiston and a dance hall at Oro Fino, was one of the few men who opposed the rough element which ran the camp, and the toughs resented him. One day he left Lewiston with six Spanish girls for his Oro Fino establishment and was smart enough to evade some men who were waiting to rob him on the trail. By the time the robbers rode up to his saloon in Oro Fino, Ford was in his back room. They stamped to the bar and began to shoot up the place. Ford demanded that they get off his property and roll out of town. As he followed them outside the demolished building, a pistol in each hand, the shooting commenced. Ford was fatally wounded, but he managed to empty eleven bullets into his opponents before slumping to the ground.

By 1868, the paystreaks in the vicinity began to dwindle, most of the miners drifted to richer fields, the few remaining merchants moved down to Pierce, and old Oro Fino was gone.

Captain Pierce, like all prospectors, had the wanderlust and long before the town he started was at its peak, he was miles away in the Boise Basin. When he left there in 1863, he wrote a farewell letter to the *Boise News,* which printed it on October 12 under the heading, "Here Today and Gone Tomorrow. Farewell Address of the Silver Fox."

What I have done for this Northern country, I leave for my friends to speak of when I am gone. Peace on earth, and goodwill to all mankind. Adieu, until you hear from me again. . . . As the Lord Giveth, saith my soul, never from this date will I imbibe any intoxicating liquors, let what may come and go. Wealth may pass away as the morning dew, friends forsake and foes unite—all will be the same for E. D. forever.

E. D. Pierce, Bannock City, I. T.

222 THE BONANZA TRAIL

The diggings at Pierce were especially rich in 1874 when $70,000 was washed from the sands; but most years were not so productive. By the early eighties the camp was virtually abandoned; then hordes of Chinese poured in to rework the denuded properties. They built a Joss House and held meetings in one of the two Chinese Masonic Lodges established in central Idaho. By 1884, so few people remained in the place that the county seat was moved north to Murray, in the Coeur d'Alenes. The total production of the placers at Pierce has been estimated at $50,000,000.

Of the few original buildings left in Pierce the most important is the two-story Territorial courthouse, built in 1860 and at present a private home. It is made of square-hewn logs which, as they seasoned, fitted tight without chinking, and it still contains the small barred window of its jail. As I examined the solidly constructed building, I wondered how many cases David Elliott, Probate Judge at Pierce City, had conducted within it. Elliott was just a young greenhorn from the East when he arrived in camp. The town bully immediately began to pick on the newcomer, shooting near his feet and ordering him to dance. With every shot the young man leaped into the air to the sadistic amusement of the crowd. As the bully repeated the performance every time Elliott appeared, the young lawyer decided to retaliate. Buying a brace of revolvers, he practiced secretly each day until he felt competent to get revenge. Then he sauntered into a bar where his tormentor was bragging as usual, and no sooner had he appeared than the bully started shooting at him. He danced a few times and then, without warning, whirled on the man and shot him, killing him instantly. At his trial the Judge fined him five dollars and took away his guns. The miners, delighted to be rid of such a worthless bully, took up a collection and bought Elliott two of the finest weapons available in the territory.

From Pierce we returned to Greer and drove for miles beside the South Fork of the Clearwater, the fork that the prospectors explored soon after gold was found at Oro Fino. At Grangeville, a prosperous agricultural center, once the outpost supply point for the Salmon River mining camps of central Idaho, roads radiate to a number of the old camps. The one we followed skirts the South Fork of the Clearwater for fifty miles as far as Elk City. Another leads to Florence, scene of the biggest gold stampede in the state and frequently described as the "richest, short-lived camp in western America." Farther to the southeast, across the Bitterroot Mountains, is Salmon, another outfitting and supply center, and high in the hills west of it is Leesburg, a true ghost town.

Each of these places burst into life overnight on the crest of a placer boom; each lived furiously for a brief time—a few months, or a few years at most. Then began a period of lethargy which has lasted up to the present, with spurts

of mining bringing brief flashes of activity from time to time. In each town a
few of the old buildings remain, but little else from the boom days.

ELK CITY

FOLLOWING the discoveries at Pierce, a group of fifty-two men, under
the leadership of Captain L. B. Monson, left Oro Fino in May, 1861,
to explore the upper South Fork of the Clearwater, as far as the Elk Creek
basin. This was Indian land and a favorite hunting and fishing place of the
Nez Percé tribe, who naturally resented this intrusion into their territory as
another violation of their treaty rights. A parley between their chief and the
prospectors was held, with the result that the greater portion of the party
grew afraid and turned back. The rest pushed on, with the grudging consent
of the Indians.

By July the men found gold, and by September Captain Monson, Moses
Milner, and a few others returned to Pierce for supplies, as well as to report
their discoveries. That month a townsite was laid out between Elk and American creeks, and forty cabins were hastily constructed to house and care for
the swelling population, which mushroomed from 300 to 2,000 before the
following season was over.

Two kinds of gold-bearing deposits were found—"skim diggings" and
"bench diggings." The lower deposits on the stream were the "skim diggings."
These were very rich but shallow concentrations of placer gold, found from
two to three feet below the surface and distributed over a wide area. The high
bars and gravel terraces were the "bench diggings." These were more expensive to work because water had to be brought to them through long ditches
and flumes, but their deposits were less scattered and paid well enough to off-
set the cost of such construction.

In 1864 the miners began to leave, partly because the diggings were believed to be worked out and partly because the gravels at Florence had been
discovered and were luring men there. Next came 1,500 Chinese, who, in the
seventies, bought out the few white miners who had resisted the Florence stampede. They made Elk City their own for a number of years, working the "skim
diggings" profitably and reworking old dumps and gravel that had already been
washed two or three times.

The Chinese liked their opium and ordered it by mail, disguised as tinned
tobacco, until an unforeseen incident put an end to the practice. During the
winter mail was brought in from Mt. Idaho, sixty miles away, on a carrier's
back. On one trip several tins of opium were included in the mailsack, and
since the cans had sharp corners, they caused the carrier great discomfort. He
therefore laid the locked sack on the ground and pounded it with a club until

every can was mashed flat. Opium is thick and sticky and the pounding sprung the cans so that their contents ran out over the letters. When the sack was opened at Elk City its contents was one gummy mess.

Most of the Chinese left in 1892, when white miners returned to rework the benches and to dig in recently located quartz mines. Next, hydraulics and dredges were introduced, with such success that in 1903 alone between $20,000 and $40,000 worth of gold was recovered. Dumps left by the dredges wall the creeks for miles below the city. Some are bare mounds of pebbles and boulders; others are partly concealed by strong young evergreens whose roots have thrust deep into the detritus. Elk City is credited with a total yield of $5,000,000 to $10,000,000. A little mining is still carried on in the vicinity, but most of today's activity centers around the summer visitors who fill its cabins.

FLORENCE

IN AUGUST, 1861, a large group from Elk City started south to prospect the Salmon River country. Five of the men left the main party and discovered the placers on Pioneer Gulch, after one of them had washed earth from around the base of an uprooted tree and found gold in his pan. One month later, a party left Oro Fino for the same area and made discoveries on Miller Creek. As a result of these strikes the country swarmed with prospectors, and then with the traders, who set up tents with wooden sides seven to ten feet high at the head of Baboon Gulch and supplied the miners with whisky and red flannel drawers. As the demand for goods increased, prices soared, until flour brought $75 a sack and bacon $3.00 a pound. Packers and merchants were frantic, trying to keep ahead of the rush of men who poured in a steady stream into the bursting log town until its population reached 10,000. Early in the fall a meeting was held; a townsite was laid out and the diggings christened Florence, after the adopted daughter of Dr. Ferber, one of the pioneers of the district.

Cold weather did not stop work until after the new year, the hardy miners "warming water with which to operate their pans and rockers." Then the snows came and lay ten feet deep on the level. The trails were blocked and supply trains could not get through. One of the last to succeed was G. A. Noble, who left Pierce City, 125 miles away, on December 21, 1861, and did not reach the isolated outpost until ten days later. He might never have arrived had not friendly Indians helped him battle through drifts and storms on the snow-packed path. By January, 1862, the only food left in camp was flour, selling for two dollars a pound. Incredible stories are told of men, weakened by illness or lack of food, who lived for weeks on flour and the inner bark of pine trees boiled in snow-water.

It was May before pack trains could stumble to within ten miles of Florence, their freight carried the remainder of the way on the backs of men who charged forty cents a pound for the service. Even they had their difficulties, for many went snowblind before reaching the camp. The leader, one of the few who could still see, carried a shovel under his arm, by the blade. The man behind him grasped its handle with one hand and the blade of another shovel with the other. In this way the line of twelve or more packers was able to plod single file over the trail, each clinging to the handle directly in front of him.

At first the placers at Florence seemed inexhaustible. Gold was plentiful, although the rich deposits were confined to an area of twenty-five square miles; still, everyone had money and spent it freely, especially those whose claims produced one hundred dollars to the pan. By 1862, a new town had been laid out a mile from the old one, so that the ground of the original townsite could be worked. The placers produced abundantly until late in 1863, and moderately until 1869; but as soon as the rich gravels gave out, the population dwindled, until by the spring of 1864 Florence was almost deserted. When the miners could pry no more bonanzas from the creek beds and benches, the Chinese were allowed to come in. With their usual persistence, they worked the depleted claims successfully until 1880. A second rush occurred in the middle nineties, when rich quartz lodes were uncovered and dredging units were brought in; but the excitement did not last, and although a little placer and lode mining is still carried on in the district, Florence's boom days seem to be over.

Like every mining town Florence had its bad man. When the diggings were at their peak, Cherokee Bob blew into town accompanied by Bill Mayfield, a fugitive from Nevada camps, and Bill's mistress, Cynthia. As soon as he reached Florence, Bob became proprietor of a saloon by the simple expedient of driving its rightful owner out of town. Bob's saloon was the headquarters for all the toughs and gamblers in camp. Before long, Bob began to make up to Mayfield's mistress. After a heated argument between the two men, Mayfield suggested that Cynthia be asked which of them she preferred. To his chagrin she chose Bob, leaving Mayfield to fade out of the picture. Sometime after this, a ball was held to which Cynthia wished to go. For some reason Bob could not accompany her and asked Willoughby, a friend of his, who was suspected by the miners of belonging to Plummer's band of outlaws, to squire her for the evening. Their attendance at the dance was objectionable to the ladies present, whether from outrage or jealousy is not clear, and the managing committee requested them to leave. Bob vowed revenge. The following morning he set out with Willoughby to find Jakey Williams, a saloon-keeper, and Orlando Robbins, the two who had ejected the pair. At first Williams tried to avoid trouble, but after Cherokee Bob fired at him he grabbed his shotgun, rushed into the street, and pumped lead into the two hotheads, killing them both. Cherokee Bob is buried in the Florence cemetery, where a weathered wooden headstone bears the words:

H. J. Talbotte
died Jan. 5th
aged 29 yrs.
Natv. of Ga.

LEESBURG

FIVE Southerners who had drifted to Deer Lodge, Montana, crossed the Continental Divide and discovered gold placers high in the Rocky Mountains of Idaho, on July 16, 1866. They had searched unsuccessfully for colors in every stream they crossed until they reached the Napias (the Indian word for gold), a creek that flows into a tributary of the Salmon River. Here the men sank a shaft to bedrock and took out dirt and nuggets valued at five dollars a pan. They staked claims and water rights, and while three remained to work their discoveries, the other two returned to Montana for supplies. They revealed their good fortune in confidence to a few trusted friends! Months later 3,000 men were working the gravels of the mountain settlement along the rich stream bed, and 7,000 were prospecting in the basin. The original locators, as loyal Southerners, named their camp Leesburg. But equally loyal Union ex-soldiers who had come to the diggings, with patriotic bravado laid out their own town one mile to the west and named it Grantsville. Ultimately each grew until they merged, and Grantsville became part of Leesburg's one long street.

The placers paid well—one miner recovered $1,000 from a single wheelbarrow load of gravel, and the five original prospectors "averaged $30,000 a week for several summers." By 1870 the town had reached its peak. One hundred "business firms," including a shoe factory, were operating, and four hundred miles of ditches carried water to the sluices. But even the richest placers play out, and by 1874, when the sand in the rockers was more sand than dust, most of the men loaded their pack mules and rode away to look for better prospects.

Salmon City, fifteen miles below Leesburg, was the trading center for the miners, and through its dusty streets crawled freight wagons from Montana, Utah, and Washington, piled high with merchandise and foodstuffs. After the white miners pulled out, the Chinese slipped quietly in, building for themselves a Chinese quarter, both in Salmon City and in Leesburg. They worked industriously until 1879, when all but one of them was massacred and robbed by

Sheepeater Indians; or so it was believed, until white men were suspected of instigating the crime and pocketing the gold obtained thereby.

Although the Leesburg placers yielded a total of $16,000,000 in gold, as the years passed they were worked less and less, until in 1930 hydraulics replaced hand processes of extraction. Gradually the population shrank—to fifty in 1940; to twelve; and finally, in 1946, to two. When these last inhabitants moved to Salmon, the post office and telephone exchange closed down. A few cabins still stand, but Leesburg became a ghost in 1946.

Boise, Idaho, is surrounded by old mining towns of which it is becoming increasingly proud. Each is within easy driving distance and each is distinct in its own way. A forty-mile drive northeast out of Boise brings one to Idaho City, and a few miles further on to Centerville, Pioneerville, Placerville, and Quartzburg. The paved road to Idaho City follows Moore's Creek, first between sagebrush foothills and tawny, eroded cliffs, and then through a portion of the Boise National Forest. Its grade, which I had expected to be tough, is so gradual, that we reached the dredged-out valley below Idaho City without realizing how much we had climbed. The roads from there to the other towns are not quite so easy. All of these places were laid out sometime in 1862, but Pioneerville is the oldest.

PIONEERVILLE

A BANNOCK Indian is responsible for the first prospecting expedition into the Boise Basin. Moses Splawn, an experienced miner, met the Indian first at Elk City and later both at Florence and the Salmon River diggings. At the third meeting, the Bannock confided to Splawn that he had seen chunks of yellow metal similar to those Splawn was washing, in a basin far to the south.

Egged on by this information, Splawn organized a small party of men in Walla Walla and set out to find the country the Indian had described. On the way he met George Grimes, who was also leading a group of men in search of gold. The two leaders combined their forces and tramped into the unknown territory, taking a roundabout course so as to avoid trouble with the Snake Indians, who were known to be hostile. One of the party washed out the first gold near the present site of Centerville. This so encouraged the rest that they continued upstream for several miles. The following day, while they were engaged in digging prospect holes, members of the party were fired on by Indians hidden in the dense timber above the creek, and Grimes was killed. He was later buried in a prospect hole, which is marked by a monument, not far from the highway. The prospectors, completely convinced of the richness of the gravels, hurried back to Walla Walla to reorganize.

Early in the fall of 1862 a large party led by J. Marion Moore started back to the discoveries, reached Grimes Creek on October 7, and founded Pioneer City. Before long they were in need of supplies, and a number of them started for Lewiston to restock. Those that remained, fearing an Indian attack, built a stockade fifty feet square, with walls twelve feet high, and stayed inside it the entire six weeks the supply train was gone. Upon its return, the men scurried out to the stream bed and staked out claims.

A week later, Jefferson Standifer with another party reached the diggings and discovered that Moore and his men had "hogged" all the best ground. In a rage, they christened Pioneer City with its stockade, Fort Hog'em, and stomped down Grimes Creek to the site of Centerville to begin explorations of their own.

At first the gravels at Pioneer City, or Pioneerville as it was later called, paid well. Even the poorest rock assayed at $62 a ton and better grades ran as high as $20,000! Although it never attracted as many citizens as its neighbor Placerville, its population reached 2,000, which made it, during its early years, the "busiest camp in the basin." Even the ebb and flow of mining booms have not succeeded in completely depopulating this first camp in the area—its population today is listed as 200.

IDAHO CITY

ALL that one sees on approaching Idaho City is the colorless debris left by the numerous dredges—the Boston and Idaho, the Estabrook, and the Idaho and Canadian, each of which since the nineties has reworked the rockpiles left by its predecessor. How much gold these hills of boulders have yielded will never be accurately known, although authorities say that between 1863 and 1869, the basin produced $40,000,000 and that since then its total has reached $100,000,000.

According to the historian Bancroft, Sherlock Bristol, one of the first men to arrive at the diggings, decided to spend the winter and spring on the creek. He and some other men built several log cabins in the trees and settled down to prospect the gulches in spite of deep snow. To avoid frequent tedious trips back and forth to the creek for water, they decided to dig a well closer to their claims. One of their number set to work shovelling through sand and gravel until, eighteen feet down, he struck not water but particles of gold. By evening you could not have bought the land where Sherlock's cabin stood for $10,000. The whole bench was rich and "bushels of gold were taken out of the gravel beds where Idaho City stands." The creek where the gold lay was named for

WELLS FARGO OFFICE AT END OF STREET, IDAHO CITY

PLACERVILLE

J. Marion Moore, and at first the camp itself was spoken of as Moore's Creek or Moorestown.

From December, 1862, until February, 1864, the place was called Bannock City, but confusion with Bannack, Montana, led to a further change, as noted in the *Boise News* of February 20:

The good people of Bannock—that was—were astonished on Sunday morning, to wake up and find themselves in a new city, but not among strangers; by some transmutation, the whole population, houses and all, were in Idaho City, and all this had been brought about by the receipt of a letter from Van Wyck, stating that Bannock was no more, but that the Legislature had incorporated our city under the name of *Idaho*.

During its first year Idaho City expanded beyond all expectations, its population reaching 6,000. Most persistent of all sounds were the blows of hammers and the whine of the sawmill, which never ceased day or night, for every foot of timber was gone the minute it was cut. The mill produced between 10,000 and 15,000 feet every ten hours, but the demand always exceeded the supply. And still people poured in. An advertisement of April 2, 1864, announced that

The Oregon and Idaho Stage Co. started two splendid four-horse coaches well laden with passengers for Idaho City yesterday. They go by the way of Portland, Umatilla, Placerville and Fort Hog 'Em and expect to reach the land of their longings in twenty-three days. Passage $100, each passenger to be allowed 25 pounds of luggage.

Each day packtrains wallowed through the muddy streets and dumped loads of goods in front of false-fronted shacks, while sweating merchants carried the stock to cellars dug into the hillsides back of their stores, safe from the constant threat of fire.

The Butler brothers hurried to the new camp in 1863, lugging their printing press with them. In the first issue of their paper, *The Boise News*, which appeared on September 29, they made a plea to the townspeople which, of course, went unheeded:

Don't cut down all the trees. One of the greatest ornaments to our city, is the forest that surrounds it, and in which a portion of it is built. We notice a disposition to destroy these noble outguards of creation, after having withstood the storms of a thousand years. It is not avarice, but convenience that has "laid the ax at the foot of the tree." Fuel is easily accessible at so short a distance from town that we hope a sufficient number within the city limits may be saved to screen it in some degree from the burning rays of the summer's sun. We shall need their generous shade.

On October 6 the paper reported the arrival of an unusual shipment of freight:

A wagon loaded with cats and chickens found its way into these "diggings" a month or so since, and found an excellent market. Cats brought $10 and chickens $5 each. Chickens have come down to $36 per dozen, but cats maintain former rates with an upward tendency. So long as ground-squirrels and ground-mice are as abundant as at present, cats will be in demand. Dogs are a drug on the market . . .

Another chatty bit appeared on October 12:

Obstinacy.
Coming up the mountain this side of Centerville, the other day, we met a whole stage load of passengers on foot, the stage having broken down on the mountain. Among others we recognized an old friend carrying a saddle, and perhaps, a little the maddest man in the diggings. He said there were eleven passengers aboard, and only four horses. He having the only saddle, concluded it should entitle him to a horse. Others, however, refused to accede to his demand, but insisted on using his saddle. This he utterly refused; and was actually carrying it on his back to Center-ville, a distance of four miles, rather than permit any of them to ride it; and they riding barebacked, rather than give up a horse. We glory in Joe's spunk, but rather think we should have weakened when it came to carrying the saddle.

Many of its citizens were veteran California miners, who introduced better methods of rocking and sluicing, conducted miners' courts, and nostalgically named the Bella Union Saloon and the What Cheer House for places they had previously frequented. So many came from Siskiyou County, California, that the *News* of April 2, 1864, printed the following excerpt from a "recent letter from Yreka":

There is a mighty rush of people passing through here (Siskiyou) for Boise. The signs of the times indicate a total depopulation of the State south of us, but while the men are leaving, children are coming into the world with great rapidity. . . . An old lady of Siskiyou, learned in such matters, confidently predicts an acces-sion of some thirty or more of the *infantry* ranks during the months of March and April. Bully for the women of Siskiyou! They are "Springing to the call for—thou-sands more,—To fill the vacant ranks of their 'husbands' gone before."

Not only placer bars and benches, but quartz lodes as well, added to the city's wealth. Gravel near bedrock paid five to twenty-five dollars a pan, and men worked "round the clock in three shifts as long as the water lasted," washing their dirt at night by the light of big bonfires which were kept burning near the ditches on Gold and East hills. Ditch owners often made more than claim owners, for water was expensive and an average claim used one hundred dollars worth of it a day. Even streets and houses were undermined by the human gophers as Johnny, the little son of Dr. J. B. Atkins discovered when he

fell from the back door of their residence, a distance of four to five feet into a cut being run under the house by the miners, and struck the edge of a board, fracturing his left knee. [*Boise News* June 18, 1864.]

Idaho City reached its peak in 1865. The main part of the town stood where it does today, but additional buildings stretched a mile up Elk Creek and two miles each way on Moore's Creek. A list of its 250 business houses includes 36 grocery stores, 20 drygoods and clothing establishments, 9 bakeries, 5 cigar stands, 5 drug stores, 1 saddle shop, 23 law offices, 15 restaurants, 5 billiard saloons, 4 hotels, 12 blacksmith shops, 4 breweries, 6 livery stables, 24 carpenter shops, 3 tailor shops, 2 music shops, 10 Chinese washhouses, 6 barbershops, and 41 saloons.

That same year and again in 1867, fire swept the town and destroyed most of the early landmarks; yet a few brick buildings with iron shutters survived the sixties. The Lunar House, built in 1868, replaced the hotels which had been lost in the blazes and, with its fine furnishings and excellent table prepared by Chinese cooks, became the center for the city's social life. When it burned sometime in the 1930's, another landmark was gone.

During the sixties and seventies theatrical troupes from New York, which played the western mining-camp circuit, always included Idaho City in their itinerary. The town had four theatres—the Idaho, the Temple, the Forrest, and the Jenny Lind. The Forrest, the biggest building in town, opened early in 1864 and announced in the *News* of February 27 that

Smoking is prohibited in the theater so that ladies can come and enjoy the performance without any apprehension of having their lungs inflated and inflamed with the fumes of tobacco. The Pleasant Neighbor, Two Gregories, and the Two Bonicastles have been performed during the week and other plays are in rehearsal.

The "most elegant" theatre in the Territory was the Jenny Lind, which opened in April, 1864. Its interior was gorgeously painted with frescoes, and its boxes, which sold from five to sixteen dollars, were equipped with chairs upholstered with plush.

In winter Sliding Clubs were the rage. Each of the Basin towns had at least one such organization which held competitive races for cash prizes. In January, 1864, the Placerville Champion Sliding Club challenged the Bannock Club to a contest, offering to run their cutter, *Flying Cloud,* against the Bannock's *Wide West.* The challenge was accepted, and early in February the club left Bannock "in one large sleigh, having in tow a whole fleet of smaller craft . . . the whole cavalcade led by Mr. Wallace in a small cutter drawn by his two Newfoundland dogs."

The tournament was decided when the *Wide West* won two out of three races. "After the punishment of the usual amount of tanglefoot," the Bannock club went home in their victorious *Wide West,* towing the *Flying Cloud* as a trophy.

A number of historic buildings can be identified in Idaho City today. The present courthouse was originally one of the old hotels, and three buildings that served as Wells Fargo offices remain. Another housed the *Idaho World,* the successor to the *Boise News;* and Weigle's Place, a modern tavern, was long ago the Miners' Exchange Saloon. The Chinese quarter, where hundreds of Orientals lived, was in the lower end of town along Montgomery Street, near Elk and Moore's creeks. No one could show me the site of the Poujade House where Poston's band serenaded ex-Governor Wallace and his "lady." The *Boise News* of September 10, 1864, reported the incident by saying that:

After two or three pieces had been performed, the Governor came out and stood on the balcony until they played the Star Spangled Banner, after which he addressed the crowd in a neat little speech. . . . Cheers were given with a will. . . . The meeting dispersed at twelve o'clock.

Idaho City is proud of its Lodge Halls, the I.O.O.F. and the Masonic, and claims that the latter is the oldest one standing west of the Mississippi. The Idaho Lodge No. 35, A. F. & A. M., was established on July 7, 1863, as the second in the Territory (the first was at Lewiston); and the Hall, which stands back from the main street, was built in 1865. It is still used, the upper floor for regular meetings and the lower for religious gatherings. The Pioneer Lodge of the Odd Fellows stands on a hill overlooking the city, and near it is the white frame building of the Catholic Church, which has stood since 1867. Its predecessor, built in 1863, was the first religious structure in the city.

Across Elk Creek is Buena Vista Bar, once connected with the main part of town by a swinging footbridge. On its slopes stood certain of the city's best residences, but its most famous building was the Territorial jail. This log structure, long since decayed, consisted of "two sturdy rows of cells." The acre of ground that surrounded it and served both as prison yard and cemetery was enclosed by a high stockade; not high enough, though, to conceal the limp figure swinging from the gallows when a hanging took place. Grim tales are told of Vigilante meetings held in the graveyard for the purpose of plotting the death of criminals still at large. The gallows was still standing in 1908, but since then dredging has churned up its site.

Simeon Walters was hanged in 1868 for murdering Joe Bacon, a rancher, and robbing him of his money. Walters was believed to have thrown the body in the Snake River. He was convicted after Bacon's false eye was found on an island. Another hanging, that of Herman St. Clair for the murder of John Decker, also became famous, because of the printed invitations which were issued for the event:

Idaho City
Boise County, Idaho
June 15, 1898

Mr. Henry Cross
You are requested to be present
at the execution of
H. C. St. Clair
on June 24th, 1898, at 10 A.
M; at Idaho City, Idaho.
J. A. Lippincott
Sheriff

Not Transferable

Idaho City today has a population of three hundred or so, and its industry is largely lumbering; but no one who visits it and walks along its shady streets or talks to its friendly people can forget its vivid past as a mining center.

Five towns which also flourished in the booming sixties lie beyond Idaho City. New Centerville is at a crossroads, with old Centerville three miles away and Pioneerville beyond it. Placerville is six miles northwest of Centerville on Granite Creek, with Quartzburg three miles higher in the hills. None of them is as well preserved as Idaho City nor as large, but all except Centerville and Quartzburg have populations that exceed one hundred.

Before we left Idaho City to visit these towns, we crossed Elk Creek and drove along Buena Vista Bar to the Masonic Cemetery, hidden deep in the timber. There, on the sloping hillside were graves, old and new, in plots fenced either by cast iron swags or sagging pickets. Some of the headboards were of marble, others were blistered wood, and some graves were mere hollows over-grown with wildflowers. Was this the cemetery of which I had been told, where only twenty-eight of the two hundred persons buried in 1863 died natural deaths?

And where was the spot where the three highwaymen who ambushed a stage as it rounded a curve on Moore's Creek hid the strongbox which they wrenched from the interior? It contained $90,000 in gold dust, and they must have buried it quickly; for they were shot down the same day as the robbery, by the Express messenger who accompanied the stage, and none of the dust was found on their bodies.

Road agents were so troublesome in the vicinity of Idaho City that Wells Fargo suspended its stage services for an entire year because of the losses it had sustained. The *Boise News,* as early as June 11, 1864, called attention to the fact that

> Theodore White, the Marysville urchin that proved such a terror to travelers last fall, has been seen on the road again. This boy is perhaps the most dangerous of all the outlaws that ever infested the upper country. . . . If it be true that he is really prowling on the way between here and the Columbia he will be very apt to get his wind shut off before fall.

CENTERVILLE

IT IS ONLY a few miles from Idaho City to Placerville, but the road is steep much of the way. Whenever it skirts a dry gulch, gravel mounds show where early placering was done. At Centerville, the road divides, the righthand turn leading up the creek to the site of old Centerville, once described as the "prettiest town in the Boise basin."

Like most mining camps it had its Masonic Lodge. When William Slade died, some "eighty odd Brothers, dressed in woolen shirts and patched pants" and wearing "pocket-handerchiefs in lieu of aprons," conducted his funeral rites. Afterwards, when the men returned to their hall, one of their number put a table in the center of the room, placed upon it gold scales and a purse and urged each member to "perform his duty" by contributing to a fund for the widow. As each man filed by the table, he selected a weight from beside the scales, placed it on one pan, and balanced it with gold dust from his pouch. He then poured his contribution into the purse and marched on. By this means a total of $3,000 was raised.

PLACERVILLE

PLACERVILLE, unlike most camps in this area, was laid out, not along one main street but around a hollow square or plaza. The square is a meadow today, and no flag flies from the pole erected in 1864 by the "Union men of Placerville," who ran up the Stars and Stripes, fired 34 guns, and gave three hearty cheers for Abraham Lincoln and Andrew Jackson. The flag was bought and paid for by all parties, Democrats as well as Lincoln men. [*Boise News* September 10, 1864.]

The townsite was selected in December, 1862, when only six cabins marked the spot; a city charter was procured from the first territorial legislature the following summer, when the population numbered 5,000.

On May 7, 1864, the *Boise News* remarked:

One of the benefits from the adoption of the city charter in Placerville is the fixing up of the public well on the plaza. The license tax on Hurdy Gurdy Houses alone will almost keep up the city government.

The chief saloon, the Magnolia, stood at one corner of the plaza, and across from it was the well, the scene of one of Placerville's early murders. The town's gamblers and killers frequented its many saloons and were a constant danger to such unsuspecting persons as the thirsty packer who stopped his mule train by the well. While he was drinking from the bucket, an ugly-tempered fellow, wishing to amuse his friends who were watching him from the porch of the Magnolia, threw water into the stranger's face and, before the man could draw his gun, shot him dead. The killer was acquitted on a plea of self-defense. Not far from town occurred the murder of the fiddlers of Ophir Creek. These men, while on their way to Centerville to play for a dance, were shot in the back and their bodies robbed.

At first, mail was brought in by horseback, with a charge of fifty cents or one dollar apiece per letter, depending upon the number of road agents who had to be evaded on the trail. A post office was established in 1864, when stage lines began to deliver passengers and letters, and the same year the Wells Fargo Express Company made its first shipment of dust from the Basin to Wallula, going through in four days. By 1865, the Oregon and Idaho Stage Company ran coaches from Umatilla to the camps by way of Placerville, with passenger fare one hundred dollars.

Though placering paid well, the water supply was never adequate for the needs of the miners. Their complaints were constant, especially when, long before the end of the season, the water became so muddy that it would scarcely run down hill. By 1870 most of the placers were exhausted, yet all through the years the town has held its own. As late as 1931 a forest fire, which burned most of Quartzburg, swept to the edge of Placerville, scorching the trees in the cemetery and dropping hot cinders on part of the town. Yet enough of the older buildings remain to give atmosphere to the quiet but by no means sleeping settlement.

BOONVILLE AND RUBY CITY

THE name Owyhee, an attempt to spell "Hawaii," was given by a Hudson's Bay Company trader to the big river that flows west of Boise into Oregon. He did it in memory of two of his employees who came from the Sandwich Islands (as the Hawaiian group was then called) and who were killed on the river bank.

The Owyhee Basin placers were discovered while Michael Jordan and twenty-nine other prospectors from Placerville were hunting for the Blue Bucket diggings, whose ephemeral location is as elusive as that of the Peg Leg Mine. Most of the Blue Bucket stories center in Oregon rather than in Idaho. According to one version, a wagon train, bound for Oregon in 1845, was attacked by Indians somewhere between the present sites of Pocatello and The Dalles. To escape from the Indians the pioneers hid in what proved to be an old mine tunnel, at the entrance of which lay an abandoned blue bucket. Since they were not miners, they went on without noting the location of the tunnel.

Another version of the traditional finding of gold at an early date is told by the veteran miner, D. H. Fogus. The nephew of a friend of his was one of an 1847 emigrant train that camped along a creek. Before starting to fish, the men picked curious stones from the bed of the creek, pounded them flat on their wagon tires, and used them as sinkers for their lines. After the discoveries in California, they realized that these stones had been gold nuggets. In the summer of 1862 Fogus and his friend searched the creeks of the Owyhee area trying to find the one the friend's nephew had described as "Sinker Creek."

Perhaps Jordan heard this story, too. At any rate he and his party made the long trip from Placerville, following the south side of the Snake River until they found a creek, which they named Reynolds Creek for one of their number. This they explored to its head; then, crossing a rugged divide, they discovered a creek running into a different basin. Here, on May 18, they camped for the night. One of the men, eager to test the gravels, scooped up some of the loose sand from the bank of the stream, washed it, and discovered "a hundred colors" in his pan! Yelling and shouting, the men grabbed picks and shovels and scattered along the creek, staking off claims and digging like gophers until dark. Next day they named the spot Discovery Bar and the stream, Jordan Creek, for the leader of their successful expedition. The party stayed in the vicinity for the next ten days, prospecting both Boulder and Sinker creeks, and then returned to Placerville.

Their news precipitated a rush of 2,500 eager and expectant men to the diggings. But upon reaching them, the newcomers found that the original discoverers had staked off practically all the ground and had drawn up mining laws which gave to each of them three claims, "one for discovery, one personal and one for a friend." Two days later, the same 2,500 men, angry and disgruntled, were home again. Further prospecting during the summer along the ravines and tributary creeks yielded some returns, but the real Owyhee bonanza was the discovery, late in 1863, of rich silver-bearing ledges along the smaller streams which emptied into Jordan Creek, some distance above Discovery Bar. Immediately a second stampede was off to the mountains, despite the lateness of the season and the hardships ahead for those who planned to winter in such high country.

The first camp to be built on Jordan Creek was Boonville, at the mouth of a canyon, but its location was so cramped between steep hills that a new camp called Ruby City was laid out farther up the creek where more space was available. By December a third town, named Silver City, was built one mile above Ruby, and from the first these two were rivals. By the following June, the streets of Ruby were noisy and bustling with

whips popping, hammers knocking, planes planing, saws sawing, augurs boring, anvils ringing, miners singing, horses running, (with fellows on 'em), and bulldrivers swearing. . . . The Pony Express made two successful trips from Humboldt to Ruby City bringing San Francisco papers only seven days old. . . . Horseback riding is a favorite pastime with ladies and gents of Owyhee. . . . Owyhee is a gay place. About the only seedy individuals are the lawyers. [*Boise News,* June 4, 1864.]

When, on December 31, 1864, Ruby City was made the seat of the newly created Owyhee County, the contest for supremacy between it and Silver City became acute. Although its population was now 1,000 and its townsite had ample space for expansion, its three streets were constantly swept by high winds, and the big mines were farther from it than from the upstart camp one mile away. Still, it held its own until 1866, when the county seat was moved to Silver City. Even the *Owyhee Avalanche,* the district's first newspaper, stayed only one year in Ruby, printing its first issue on August 19, 1865, and its last on August 11, 1866. The following week Vol. 2, No. 1, was run off the press from the Silver City office. Gradually the inhabitants of Ruby moved away, and the empty buildings were hauled to the larger town.

On October 15, 1881, perhaps the last burial ever to be made in the deserted cemetery at Ruby City was conducted in a blinding snowstorm. The "corpse," Henry McDonald, was alive when he left the Silver City jail and was driven to his grave, already dug beside the scaffold from which he was soon to swing. In spite of the storm three hundred people witnessed the execution.

Today only oldtimers, of whom very few are left, can point out the site of Ruby.

SILVER CITY

ALL during 1864 ranchers in Owyhee County were troubled by Indians, but not until the summer did they appear close to Silver City, on what was later known as War Eagle Mountain. Mines and buildings in which the women and children might gather in case of an attack were fortified, and a volunteer company was organized to protect the city. Ultimately a parley, held on Sinker Creek, resulted in the Indians being sent to a reservation in the eastern part of the Territory, and with their removal mining was resumed.

A more serious uprising, led by Chief Buffalo Horn, was directed against Silver City in 1878. Thanks to two friendly Indians, who rode through the country warning the settlers and miners of the approach of the war party, a company of volunteers pursued the Indians, but they were ambushed and forced to retreat. Buffalo Horn was killed in the engagement, however, and the Indians, with no leader to rally them, rode out of the country toward Oregon.

To reach the mining camp we skimmed over the highway to Nampa and from there south to Murphy, crossing the bridge over the Snake River at the site of the old Walters Ferry. For over fifty years this ferry was used by the stages which ran between Boise and San Francisco. Although today only a few adobe sheds mark the spot, it is said that rifle balls, arrowheads and even gold dust have been found hidden near the river bank. Murphy is such a diminutive county seat (the population of the town is given on the road maps as ninety), that we were in and out of it before we knew it and had to back up to inquire from the only man in sight the way to Silver City. He showed us a narrow, dirt trail leading off into sagebrush, and assured us that the road was good all the way.

For the first fifteen miles we seemed to be getting nowhere, for the twisty little trail wound up and down through the barren, sage-strewn foothills, climbing gently all the way. It was lonely country—no cattle, no houses, no cars—only startled jack rabbits which loped ahead of us or scuttled into the greasewood. Above us were bare, forbidding hills; yet instead of climbing toward them, we followed up a long draw beside a creek, and then climbed by a series of sharp switchbacks to a saddle high in the mountains. Finally, spread out before us in its high mountain valley, stood the many old buildings, mills, and mines of a sizable and really impressive ghost town, Silver City.

The first building we noticed as we entered the town was the Idaho Hotel. Except that it needs a coat of paint and some reinforcing of swaybacked porches and sagging columns, it looks much as it did in its prime, when all fifty rooms were filled with guests and its basement dining room and mahogany bar served the best refreshments of any in the city. The big frame building, made of whipsawed lumber, was built not in Silver but in Ruby City; but when that camp dwindled away, the hotel was hauled in three sections by ox team to its present location on Jordan Street. The Wells Fargo Company occupied office space in the hotel until they moved to quarters directly south of it.

Outside the Wells Fargo Company building; bars of silver bullion used to stand in stacks three feet high, awaiting shipment by ox team to Umatilla and thence by steamer to Portland and San Francisco. If bullion was sent by stage-coach, each bar was strapped in a separate, leather container and the coach was specially reinforced with iron bars so as to withstand the heavy load. Just south of Wells Fargo is the *Avalanche* office, which for sixty-seven years was one of the busiest places in town.

Nothing gives a better cross-section of the life and color of Silver City than these items culled from the paper's 1865 and 1866 files:

October 7 [1865]. . . . The saloons and Justice's office at Silver City have been doing a rushing business during the present week. Liquids and law take well in that burgh and the one seems to naturally follow the other. He who gluttonously patronizes the bar is liable to account to the bench.

Master Masons will observe . . . that a Lodge of Instruction has been formed in Silver City. We learn that a suitable hall has been secured.

October 28. . . . Mr. Cox recently of Silver City, was killed by the Indians on Wed. morning. Himself and family were moving in a wagon to Boise City, and when just beyond the summit, between Reynolds' Creek and the Snake River, they were fired on and Mr. Cox instantly killed. His wife drove on rapidly and escaped. A couple of teamsters with freight were near the place and abandoned their wagons and retreated to the river. These men and their mules came off with whole hides, but Lo inspected the goods, scattered them around, took a small quantity and marched off leisurely.

January 27 [1866]. . . . The Owyhee Debating Club meets every Thursday evening in the Sheriff's office. The subject of this week was "Resolved, That the immigration of the Mongolian race to this Coast should be prohibited by law." It was decided in the negative.

February 3. . . . According to an old woman's saying that "bread is the staff of life, but whisky is life itself" we are out of "life" just now, though there is flour enough to meet present wants.

July 14. . . . Nearly all the "Melican" boys who have been mining on Jordan, below Ruby and in the vicinity of Boonville, have sold out to Chinamen. Some have quartz on the brain and others the "gals they left behind." When really afflicted with either of these demoralizers, ye honest miner selleth his claim to Sam Yung, Ah Ping or Ye Whing without much regard to ye celestials' future profits.

"OWYHEE AVALANCHE" NEWSPAPER OFFICE (LEFT). MASONIC TEMPLE BY BRIDGE, SILVER CITY

OLD BUILDINGS, SILVER CITY

Up Jordan Street, half hidden by trees, is the Chinese Joss House, a weathered frame building with an ornate false front and spindle-trimmed porch. The Chinese also had their Masonic Lodge, and during Silver City's second boom they became merchants and cooks instead of miners. They also delivered water each day from door to door, carrying it in huge cans slung from a yoke across their shoulders and charging fifty cents a week for the service. When they died, elaborate funeral processions marched slowly down Jordan Street to their cemetery on the opposite side of town from the plots of the Masons and Odd Fellows, whose burying grounds adjoined each other "to the right of Slaughter House Gulch, one-quarter of a mile out of town."

Across from the Joss House is Sampson's Livery Stable, a big, red, barn-like structure, built in 1864. Silver had several livery barns in its busy days, but it was in this one that a hearse was kept "ready for a fast run to the mines." Many a time it returned with a mutilated body, crushed in some shaft or stope.

The Furniture Store and Undertaking Parlor, nearby, is said still to contain a few coffins. The cheap ones were used for gamblers, strangers, and the less opulent Chinese, while the expensive ones were special orders, freighted in from Portland. The hearse that bore the more elegant dead was probably the same one that dashed to the mines, for it is described as "an open spring wagon or hack" which was kept at "Samson's Annex to the War Eagle Hotel."

What is left of the War Eagle stands on Washington Street, a battered two-story frame house, completely surrounded with sagebrush. The hotel originally consisted of several buildings of various heights and sorts, each joined to the next in a straggling fashion but all facing Washington Street, where the stagecoaches and freighters deposited their loads. Winter snows were so deep that passengers, arriving at the hotel, had to descend a flight of steps, cut out of packed snow to reach the porch.

A block below the War Eagle stands the shell of the county courthouse, its upper stories and entire interior gone, and only the stone arches of its façade left to give an idea of its once imposing appearance. The *Owyhee Avalanche* of June 1, 1867, describes the building in detail:

The contract for building a Court House and Jail for Owyhee County was let last Wednesday. The jail is to be 30 feet by 22 feet, running back into the hill, built of hewn lumber set on end and lined with two inch planks spiked on; floors and ceilings to be of hewn timber. The Courthouse will be of two stories on top of the jail, running back ten feet further into the hill. . . . The first floor will contain offices for the county officers, lined and papered. The upper story will contain three rooms—the Courtroom, the District Clerk's office and a jury room. There will be two porches in front and stairs on the side.

Because the Masonic Hall spans Jordan Creek, many stories are told of Masons who, having entered the building by the front door, left it by the back and announced that they had just "crossed the Jordan." The jewels of the lodge are silver bullion taken from the mines on War Eagle Mountain and made by a local blacksmith.

A swaying footbridge, shaded by willows, crosses Jordan Creek beside the hall. On the far side of the creek are a church and a schoolhouse, and behind them, tier above tier, rise more steep streets and residences. The schoolhouse is in good repair, its porticoed windows unbroken and its carved balcony and balustrade untouched by vandals. The church, which stands alone on a knob of rocky ground, was built in 1896 by the Episcopalians and was sold in 1933 to the Catholics. Standing on the church porch, I looked over the city—at the business section crammed into the bottom of the ravine and at the homes dotting the lower slopes of the barren peaks which surround the town. Within six months of the city's founding, the thinly forested hills were stripped bare as one by one their trees were whipsawed into lumber for cabins and sluices.

For the first two years the placer deposits paid well and before they began to thin out, the important quartz lodes were discovered, so that mining went on uninterruptedly and with increased impetus. A small amount of placering was also done for some time by the Chinese, who succeeded in finding colors that the white man missed; in fact, occasional washing continued there until 1900.

The first period of vein mining lasted approximately ten years. The Morning Star and Oro Fino lodes were located almost simultaneously in 1864, the Oro Fino being the first of thirty locations made on War Eagle Mountain. Its quartz was so rich that it assayed $7,000 in silver and $800 in gold to the ton, and it was so easily worked that at first the men pounded up the ore in hand mortars. At the end of six years it had yielded $2,756,128. The War Eagle, located in 1864, and the Golden Chariot and the Poorman mines, located in 1865, were among the camp's best producing properties.

The history of the Poorman is a combination of fabulous production records and vicious disputes over ownership rights. Just which one of a group of men uncovered the vein is not known definitely, but two of them, Hays and Ray, staked the claim and did a minimum amount of development work upon it. Soon afterwards, C. S. Peck found a rich chimney of ore not far away. Uncertain as to whether his strike was on their land, he hid his discovery and even covered up the vein until he could investigate. When he found that the chimney was within their boundaries, without telling them of his bonanza he offered to buy the mine. As the price was too steep for him, he left the vicinity, planning to return later and make another bid for it. While he was gone, other prospectors rediscovered his chimney, recorded the location, and named it the Poorman. Hays and Ray at once contested their ownership by pointing out the overlapping boundary lines of the two claims. Secure in their possession of the chimney, the Poorman Company built a fort at the mouth of the mine, and while armed men guarded the property sent some of the highgrade ore to Portland to be assayed. To prevent endless litigation, both companies then agreed to sell, and thereafter the two mines were worked jointly first by a Portland, and later by a New York, syndicate.

The mine's production was phenomenal. From a solid mass of ruby silver crystals weighing 500 pounds, specimens were selected and sent to the Paris Exposition in 1866, where they won a gold medal. Its ore, which was so easily worked that it could be cut like lead, assayed $4,000 and $5,000 per ton; its total production, prior to 1875, exceeded $4,000,000. That year the secretary of the company absconded with the funds, and the Poorman was forced to close down. It lay idle until 1888.

The Golden Chariot and the Ida Elmore also staged a battle over boundary disputes. Both mines hired gunmen, and in the fight which took place at the Ida Elmore, the owner of the mine was shot through the head. Instead of halting the attack, this tragedy only served to incite the men to further violence. Fighting continued all that night and for three more days, until a squad of cavalry was sent from Boise to settle matters.

The miners of Silver City were a spunky lot. Although such drastic methods as those just described were infrequently used, the men often took matters into their own hands as is illustrated by a notice from the *Arizona Miner* of April 27, 1872:

A Muss Among Miners in Idaho.

The Owyhee *Avalanche* gives an account of an uprising of 300 miners, mostly from the Mahogany mine, under a foreman named John Jewell, who had become obnoxious to the men by his bad treatment of them. The men held a meeting and notified him to leave, but the acting-superintendent of the mine backed Jewell and sent up from town 40 armed men and 2 howitzers to keep the peace. Then the miners from 4 neighboring mines got together and agreed not to fight and not to go to work as long as Jewell remained at the mine. Jewell vacated the premises.

During the middle seventies most of the producing mines were forced to shut down because of a financial panic in San Francisco which affected all the incorporated properties. But slowly the camp came back as the men themselves continued developing properties that were no longer financed by outside capital. On February 24, 1875, the *Owyhee Daily Avalanche* printed an advertisement headed "Miners Wanted":

Twenty good miners to work in stopes of the War Eagle mine. It is estimated that fully 1000 additional men will be needed this spring to work the mines of this camp . . . $4 in coin per day is regular wages.

All the time the mines were being developed, the city was growing. The *Owyhee Avalanche,* now well established in its new location, installed in its office the first telegraphic news wire in the Territory, and so kept its subscribers informed not only of local events but of world affairs. This wire, which came from Winnemucca, Nevada, was laid direct to Silver City and from there to Boise.

Though Silver City may have slumped in the seventies, it came back with a rush in the late eighties and nineties, when the mines at the nearby camps of De Lamar and Dewey were active. During that period many of the present buildings were erected, including a brewery, which produced "Owyhee Beer" made from hops imported from the East. To convey the beverage from the brewery to the storage vats across the street, Fritz Schlefer, an ingenious man, built a pipeline under the road.

In 1942 the last of Silver City's mines shut down, and the following year post office and telephone services were discontinued. In 1948 the road from the valley was improved and the Kiwanis Club of Payette, Idaho, labelled the historic buildings. Each season since then many tourists visit the city. A couple who arrived the morning of our visit seemed to know the place intimately. I understood why, when the woman confided that she was born in Silver and that she and her husband were the last couple to be married in the church!

DE LAMAR

THE still ghostlier camps of De Lamar and Dewey are but five and nine miles respectively from Silver City. Both boomed in the nineties but De Lamar is the older. In the sixties, Wagontown was a small settlement and stage station eleven miles west of Silver City on the road to Winnemucca. Although the district in which it stood was explored shortly after the founding of Silver City, its real value was not known until 1888, when Captain De Lamar bought the Wilson mine and adjacent claims for $10,000 and began to develop the property by means of tunnels. The captain, a veteran mining man, built a town two miles east of Wagontown near his mine and named it for himself. In its center was the plant of the mining company, with its mills, shops, offices, hotel, and bunkhouses, and wriggling along the bottom of the gulch were several streets lined with houses and stores, assay offices, and at least one church. Such was the town and mine which De Lamar sold in 1891 to an English company for $1,700,000. It worked the mine successfully for years, at times producing as much as half a million dollars worth of bullion a month.

During the camp's prosperity a newspaper, the De Lamar *Nugget,* was published. These items from the first issue, on May 5, 1891, indicate its breezy personal tone:

Here We Are, Shake!

We are with you and have come to stay.

We are not as handsome and attractive as we expect to be later on but we hope you will good-naturedly overlook any imperfections in our make-up.

We want you to like us and we will do our best to be pleasant.

This is all the promises we have to make.

LAMB & YORK

"A man hastily entered a La Salle street bank recently and, approaching a teller's window carelessly threw down a check with the remark, 'I would like to deposit that; please credit the amount to my account.' The teller glanced at the check and winked very hard and vigorously to convince himself that his eyes were still all right. The bit of paper called for $463,000, and bore the signature of one of the most powerful syndicates in this country. It was accepted without a word, and the depositor left the bank within one minute of the time he entered it. The man was from Idaho."—*Chicago Mail.*

As neither of the editors of this paper have been in Chicago lately, and as Captain DeLamar has, our readers can readily guess who deposited this check.

Those who love a game of cribbage, solo sixty or seven up, but do not care to carry a jag home with them after they are done, can now find a fine place to play at Julius Isay's fruit and cigar store. He has fitted up a neat club room, with chairs and card tables, and the men now play for oranges, bananas, cigars, etc.

When the next presidential election comes off DeLamar will have a bigger vote than all the balance of the county. The Nugget don't care a continental whether that vote be Republican, Democratic, Alliance or all of them. One thing is certain, it will be sound on the silver question. The party showing a disposition to give the wheat and stock raisers of the West, the cotton producers of the south, and the silver miners of the country an honest deal in spite of the Wall Street and interest gathering influences of the East, will get every honest vote in camp.

DEWEY

SEVEN years after Captain De Lamar built his camp, Colonel William H. Dewey bought the site of Boonville, the first town on Jordan Creek, and replaced its crumbling old hotel, the only building left, with a new one so grandiose that it was the talk of the entire valley. Dewey has been called an "empire builder." Assuredly he was a man of vision and business acumen and he had a large part in the development of the Owyhee Mountain portion of

Idaho. He and Michael Jordan were business partners in San Francisco in the fifties, but Dewey became restless after a few years and went to Virginia City, Nevada, to mine. He was still there, but broke, when Jordan sent word to him of the rich placers he and his party had found in the Owyhee district. Dewey, eager to get in on the strike, immediately shouldered his pack and trudged the entire distance from Virginia City to the embryo camps on Jordan Creek.

First he helped lay out the townsite of Silver City, and next he built the toll road between Boonville and Ruby City. He constructed nearly every road in Owyhee county, and he built two railroads, one of which was to have reached his own camp of Dewey but never got farther than Murphy. In 1871 he bought the Black Jack mine on Florida Mountain, near the site of old Boonville. The following year he bought the Trade Dollar, which ultimately yielded more than $12,000,000 in ore. Many other mines in the Silver City area helped make him rich.

By 1896 he was ready to develop in a big way his large holdings in the Florida Mining and Milling Company. Where Boonville once stood, he erected a twenty-stamp mill, rated the "biggest and best in the west." Around it his money created a completely new and attractive town, which he modestly called Dewey. On the new hotel he spent incredible sums. It had three stories and was ornamented with a cupola and "double portico." It was steam-heated, had electric lights, and the most modern plumbing. Its rooms were handsomely furnished and its bar and "card rooms" were no more popular than the dining hall and the still larger third floor ballroom where dances and theatricals were given.

His superintendent of mines lived in a fine villa; for good measure Dewey added to his model town a steam laundry, a livery stable, a barber shop, and a city water system complete with fireplugs. Although this last utility was guaranteed to provide "almost perfect immunity from fire," it failed to save the hotel when a blaze ignited it in 1905. But by that time Dewey, who in 1900 had disposed of all his holdings in the mines, was in Nampa, playing host in his newest hotel, which eclipsed the former one both in size and elegance.

Dewey is a deserted town today, and so far as I can discover not even a postcard or a cream pitcher decorated with pictures of the hotel and superintendent's house exists.

The best known of Idaho's mining camps are those in the Coeur d'Alene district of Shoshone County. Most of them are busy industrial centers and do not belong in this study of old camps. None of them existed until the eighties, and therefore they cannot be classed with Pierce and Oro Fino and the other gold camps of the sixties. Their notoriety is due to their fabulous lead and silver mines and to the labor troubles which wracked them during the nineties.

Coeur d'Alene means "the heart of an awl." When the French fur trappers came into this area, they found the Indians not only unfriendly but shrewd in their bartering. The Frenchmen described them as having hearts no bigger than the point of a shoemaker's awl.

The mineral zone in the Coeur d'Alene Mountains is covered with such a dense growth of pine, cedar, and hemlock that the early prospectors complained of masses of fallen timber which hindered their progress through the forests. There is evidence that a man named Wilson entered the region in 1867 and found a little gold, and that Thomas Irwin located a quartz claim "near the Mullan road on Elk Creek" in 1878. But the man who did most toward opening the huge subterranean treasure chest was Andrew J. Pritchard.

In 1880 and again in 1881 Pritchard went north from the Mullan Road, crossed the mountains by way of the old Evolution Trail, and descended to a creek where he found a few particles of gold. On his second visit he followed the stream for some distance, panning its gravel at intervals and discovered more colors. By the fall of 1882, certain that gold in paying quantities lay at bedrock, he told a few friends of his discovery, binding them to secrecy, but at the same time urging them to join him in the spring of 1883.

Another version of Pritchard's story tells how, after he had shown specimens of gold to a group at a bar in Spokane, more than eighty men, many without blankets or tools, demanded that he lead them at once to Pritchard Creek. At first he refused, explaining that the snow was too deep and the water too high to permit any work so early, and suggesting that they delay this journey through the woods for a month or so. When they threatened to hang him, he went. At the diggings, the conditions he had predicted prevented their reaching bedrock where the gold lay. Cursing him for a liar, the men mushed back to civilization, telling everyone they met that the diggings were a hoax and that they had left Pritchard dangling from a tree. A few of the men remained with Pritchard, who was not dangling but digging, and in time found the coarse yellow flakes of which he had told them.

As the report of their discovery spread, hundreds of prospectors, including most of the original party, fought their way over impossible trails, eager to stake a claim before all were taken. Then hordes began to pour in from all directions. Every route to the mountains was difficult. Whether a man came by train to Belknap on the Northern Pacific or by steamer up Lake Coeur d'Alene and then up the river to the old Indian Mission, he had to complete the trip on foot, crashing through timber in summer or dragging heavily loaded toboggans in the winter and early spring, when the snow lay twelve to twenty feet deep.

Pritchard Creek was so full of activity between 1883 and 1885 that every foot of pay gravel for miles along its course was staked off. With the best placers gone, men began to fan out over the hills in search of new diggings. Some crossed the range to the south and staked out quartz claims along the creeks that fed the southern fork of the Coeur d'Alene River. When rich silver and lead deposits were found in immense ledges along this fork, the placer camps on Pritchard Creek were almost deserted.

Around each important mine a camp sprang up—Wallace in 1884, Wardner in 1885, Burke and Gem in 1886, Mullan in 1888, and Kellogg in 1893. The history of each town is closely related to that of its neighbors, and since nearly every famous mine that was discovered in the middle eighties is still producing, the towns are still active.

WALLACE

WE MADE Wallace our headquarters for the drives to the Coeur d'Alene camps of Gem, Burke, and Murray on the north, and of Kellogg and Wardner on the western edge of the belt.

When Colonel W. R. Wallace built a cabin and store in a dense cedar grove along the Coeur d'Alene River, the place he chose was known as Placer Center. An account of its founding, published in 1884 in the Eagle City newspaper, undoubtedly helped to attract settlers to the eighty-acre tract of land the Colonel was developing. Four years later, when the town was incorporated, it was named Wallace. Its location in the bottom of a deep, narrow canyon, whose walls are densely timbered, is most attractive, and its shaded streets show no evidence of the forest fire which in 1910 razed a large portion of the city.

GEM

WE DROVE up Canyon Creek, which is lined with mines, to the towns of Gem and Burke. Gem, three miles from Wallace, was once a rip roarin' camp with a population of 2,500 and more saloons than anything else. The Gem mine was the scene of violence during the labor riots of the nineties, in which nonunion men, brought in to break a strike, were driven out of town barefoot in midwinter. Others were taken into the hills, stripped naked, and left to freeze to death. Today the town is small, and its houses stand close to the main thoroughfare, which twists and climbs toward Burke, three miles away. Crowded into the narrow gulch between the creek and the highway, the railroad spur from Wallace serves both camps.

BURKE

AT BURKE the canyon narrows still more and the railroad runs up the middle of the town's only street. One side of the thoroughfare is filled with the million-dollar plant of the Hecla Mining Company. The other side is crowded with stores built so close to the tracks that their awnings have to be raised whenever a train goes by—or so they say! We drove the length of the town, with mills above and cribbing beside us and tramways over us. Finding a pocket or alley into which to squeeze the car in order to park it became a game. Everything in Burke is built layer upon layer and pushes tight against the hillsides. Even the Tiger Hotel, a four-story structure, has a tunnel through it to allow trains to travel up the gulch; and a large sign on the side of the building warns pedestrians in the narrow street under the cornice to beware of falling icicles!

The highway map shows a road leading from Burke to Murray by way of Thompson Pass. Before leaving town I went into the Tunnel Bar to inquire what shape it was in.

"She can't get to Murray from here, can she, Jim?" said the man behind the counter to his customer, who was having a beer.

"Hell, no," said Jim, looking at me over his glass. "That road's not fit for a jackass. She'll have to go down to Wallace and take Ninemile Creek."

Back we went, past the Hecla property and the Standard-Mammoth, the Tamarack and the Frisco mills. Beside us all the way was the torn-up creek bed, filled with stumps and boulders. Starting again from Wallace, we drove up Ninemile Creek toward Murray, an early placer camp as rich in history as it once was in gold. We crossed a divide and dropped down the far side to Beaver Creek and the North Fork of the Coeur d'Alene River. At the mouth of the famous Pritchard Creek we turned right and followed it some miles until we came upon a group of houses and an old hotel—all that remains of Pritchard.

EAGLE CITY

UP THE creek beyond Pritchard, a lumber camp and a sawmill stand on the site of Eagle City. When gold-bearing sands were found in Pritchard and Eagle creeks in 1883, a camp, known for a few months as the "Capital of the Coeur d'Alenes," sprang up at the junction of the two. Someone saw an empty eagle's nest high in a tree and suggested that the place be called Eagle City. Tents made of dirty canvas and ragged blankets served as shelters until a sawmill, hauled in on sleds through Fourth of July Canyon

MAIN STREET, MURRAY

TIGER HOTEL, THROUGH WHICH TRAINS RUN, BURKE

and by boat up the North Fork of the Coeur d'Alene River, began to turn out lumber for cabins.

By the spring of 1884, when the camp reached its peak, lots were selling for $2,000, stores and boardinghouses were crowded, supplies vanished as soon as they were unloaded from the backs of the pack animals that brought them in over the difficult trails, and the original townsite was extended until it stretched nearly a mile along the gulch. The miners did not even object when letters were brought in with a C.O.D. charge of fifty cents apiece. For such a raw, new community, Eagle City was amazingly peaceable:

Unlike most new excitements we are not called upon to record a long list of litigations and homicides. The camp thus far, though highly cosmopolitan in its population, adjusts its own difficulties and important questions by arbitration and public meetings. [From *The New Coeur d'Alene Gold Mines* by L. F. Butler, 1884.]

The "boys" were tenderhearted too, and when one of them died, the rest took time to pay their respects by going to his funeral. A. F. Parker gives the following account in the *Coeur d'Alene Eagle* of March 3, 1884:

Stumpy Wicks was sure dead. The mountain fever had laid its grip on 'im; . . . "gone over the range" the boys said. So they got together and made a coffin out of some boxes, and put Stumpy into it, with a flour sack over his poor dead face. There were forty men in the procession but no woman. Not a woman to drop a tear, as the ex-parson read a few lines of the burial service. If Stumpy's life had any history no one knew it. It was doubtless a sad enough one. In his pocket they found a woman's picture, faded and quite worn out. Maybe that was his history.

There was not a tear at Stumpy's funeral nor a sob. But neither were there any oaths or laughter. They rounded up the mound and put up a flat rock for a headstone. When the ex-parson stepped back from the grave he stumbled over the headstone of Billy Robbins, the gambler that Antoine Sanchez knifed.

The boys were quiet. They were thinking, perhaps. They looked up at the sky which, strangely enough, had no tint of blue. Then the sky, as if in pity that no tear was shed, wept some down on them.

The procession broke up and moved back to the saloons. One man said it was "the d——dst mournfullest plantin' he'd ever had a hand in." Men wondered what Stumpy was seeing. After a wretched, broken life, what is there for a man "over the range?"

The camp didn't get back to its normal condition until the next day.

But while the men could be sentimental over a dead partner, they could be ruthless where racial prejudices were concerned. At one time a noosed rope and a sign were fastened to a tree on top of Glidden Pass, one of the entrances to the district. The sign read: "This is for the first Chinaman who crosses this pass into Idaho."

But even while the placers around Eagle were being developed, richer diggings were found farther up Pritchard Creek in Dream, Buckskin, and Alder gulches, and the fluid population slipped upstream four miles to the new camp of Murray, which was closer to the new locations. It must have been about this time that Eugene V. Smalley arrived in Eagle; for in an article "Coeur d'Alene Stampede" he wrote:

Its rise and fall covered a period of only six months. Lots, with log buildings, which sold last February for one thousand five hundred dollars, can now be bought for fifty dollars. . . . When the quartz leads on Eagle and Pritchard Creeks are worked, Eagle will have a new growth. Just now its disconsolate inhabitants are eager to dispose of their huts, tents, and town lots, and their goods and whisky, at any price, and are only staying because they cannot get away. From Murray to Eagle, and on five miles farther to the Coeur d'Alene River, there is a pretense of a wagon-road. Vehicles are got over it, but the traveler finds it much more fatiguing to ride them than to go afoot. Pedestrianism in this somber twilight realm of dense foliage and trailing tree-moss has an especial charm when it leads out toward light and civilization. There it is but an easy walk to the river, and at the river you are done with sore-backed horses, dead-axle wagons, and tramping over tree-roots and through quagmires; for there you find the canoe, and can slide out of the wilderness on pea-green waters at the rate of ten miles an hour. [*Century Magazine*, October, 1884.]

Dream Gulch was discovered by an imaginative prospector named Davis, who dreamed of a heavily timbered ravine through which ran a stream, and of a gold ledge which lay at the forks of the stream. "From the ledge he chipped pure gold with a hammer and chisel." The next night he again dreamed of the place, and on the third night, he was loading pack animals with the gold he found. With considerable persuasiveness, he induced two friends to accompany him on his search for the mythical gulch. Several days of prospecting in the Coeur d'Alene hills brought him to a ravine which corresponded to the one in his dream; falling eagerly to work, he washed color from the stream. He then searched for the ledge and uncovered a quartz lode from which he took a nugget worth ninety-seven dollars. All spring and summer he and his partners worked the mine and ended the season with a clear $42,000.

MURRAY

THE creek bed between Eagle and Murray is full of debris left by hydraulicking and dredging operations; in places the mounds of smooth, gray boulders are so high that we could not see over them. The town of Murray is confined chiefly to the sides of its long main street. Hills close in the valley at the far end of the street and rise steeply behind the houses on the north side of the quiet camp. On the south side, Pritchard Creek cuts its way through the wide swathe of worthless gravel left by the hydraulic elevators and dredges. It is a wooden town, full of frame houses with wooden lace edging their eaves and with false-fronted two- and three-story frame store buildings facing each other all down the central thoroughfare. The homes look cosy, half hidden as they are by trees and vines and surrounded by flower beds and vegetable strips. Many of the buildings date from the town's boom years in the middle eighties, when gold placering yielded heavily and before the silver and lead deposits across the range lured away part of the population. All during its first years it grew, until it had twelve general stores, five or six restaurants, three drugstores, and a hotel. By 1885, less than a year after its founding, its population was 2,000. By the end of 1886 it had dwindled to 100. By 1888 the placering near Murray was almost abandoned; yet it was still the seat of Shoshone County, and as such it held an important position in the Territory.

The two-story frame courthouse is its most historic building; for in it the famous Bunker Hill-Sullivan mine case was tried in 1886, and from it the books and records were removed secretly in 1898 by zealous supporters of the "Wallace for county seat" crusade. Murray is still bitter about the removal; for it had served as county seat ever since it had succeeded Pierce in 1884.

"Murray was a better town than Wallace when they took the county seat away from us," mumbled an old man to whom I talked. "Stole it, that's what they did; just took the safe and the records and went off." He was convinced that the short cut from Burke to Murray over Thompson Pass remained "a terrible road and a fierce grade" as a result of this feud. "Wallace is afraid if we get that road fixed the camp will come back. By gosh, someday we'll show 'em."

The old man's pride was not shared by Smalley, who visited the camp in the summer of 1884:

It is composed of a hideous half-mile-long street of huts, shanties, and tents, with three or four cross-streets that run against the steep slopes after a few rods progress. . . . A more unattractive place than Murray I have seldom seen. The trees have been cleared away, leaving a bare gulch into which the sun pours for sixteen hours a day with a fervor which seems to be designed by nature to make up for the coolness of the short July nights, when fires are needed. Stumps and half-charred logs encumber the streets, and serve as seats for the inhabitants. . . . Every second building is a drinking saloon. . . . The town was full of men out of employment and out of money, who hung about the saloons and cursed the camp in all styles of profanity known to miners' vocabulary. Nevertheless, gold was being shipped out every day by Wells, Fargo & Co.'s express, and new discoveries were constantly reported. [*Century Magazine,* October, 1884.]

Smalley, like everyone else writing about the country in the eighties, was impressed by its dense forests. Of his journey from Thompson Falls to Murray he says:

Following a trail through the gloomy solitudes of this wilderness is not a cheerful proceeding. The sky is rarely visible, and there are no sounds to break the stillness, save the roar of a torrent. . . . In our case there was the adventure of running the gauntlet through a forest fire. The flames were on both sides of the trail. There was no way of getting around them with the horses, and it was a question of turning back or dashing through; so the little caravan was put to a gallop, and after an exciting minute in the smoke, came out with no damage, save some singeing of hair.

Farther on he mentions the forest again, saying that the trees stood so close together that a "pack-mule could not squeeze through between them" and that "away up in the air some two hundred feet was a little slit through which the sky could be seen. It was like looking out of a deep crevice."

KELLOGG AND WARDNER

WE RETURNED to Wallace through Eagle and Pritchard. As we turned west toward Kellogg and Wardner, we left the heavily timbered hills which make Wallace so attractive and cut through a wider valley, made ugly by dredge and mine debris, by dead trees and fire-blackened hills. Both Kellogg and Wardner are active today, and Kellogg looks particularly new and prosperous; but even up the gulch at Wardner we could locate but few old buildings.

Late in the summer of 1885, N. S. Kellogg, an elderly carpenter who lived in Murray, was out of work. The population of the camp was beginning to scatter across the mountains to the South Fork of the Coeur d'Alene River in search of silver ledges, and the building boom was over. Kellogg, therefore, asked two men for whom he had worked, O. O. Peck, a contractor, and J. T. Cooper, a doctor, to grubstake him, so that he too could turn prospector and comb the hills for outcroppings. They reluctantly agreed to give him a small outfit, and he resented its inadequacy. But with it packed on his jackass, he started across the mountains. South of the Coeur d'Alene River he found a deep gulch, up which he slowly worked his way for three miles. He made camp, tied his jackass, and went to sleep.

Next morning his pack animal was gone. He soon spotted it high on the mountain above him, but it took him hours to catch up with the beast. Kellogg was very tired after his taxing climb; while he got his breath, he sat on some rock and looked across the gulch at more wooded hills, and down to its bottom at Milo Creek spilling into the river. As he looked, his hand fumbled with the rock beside him. Automatically he picked up a piece, then examined it closely. It was almost pure galena! The ledge from which it came was part of a huge outcrop, and he was sitting on top of a silver mine such as had not been found in the entire region. He staked two claims, the Bunker Hill and the Kellogg, and posted a notice of location containing the names of the men who grubstaked him and his own. Then he returned to Murray with samples of ore. Still angry at the meager grubstake Peck and Cooper had given him, he did not tell them of his discovery. Instead, he looked up Phil O'Rourke, Con Sullivan, and one or two others and led them back to Milo Gulch.

Fearing that Peck and Cooper would squeeze him out of his share of the claim, he made no protest when O'Rourke and the others replaced the location notice with one containing only their names and his. The men then made new locations, the Bunker Hill and the Sullivan, and while they stayed to hold the property, one of their number hurried to Murray to file the fake location notice. As soon as the news was known two things happened: a rush to the gulch began, and Peck and Cooper filed suit against Kellogg for failing to include them in his discovery. They finally won their case, establishing their half-interest in the claim, and Kellogg later sold out his share. Since then, the two properties (which have changed hands more than once) have been consolidated and so greatly developed that official records in 1948 showed a total production figure of $300,000,000.

At Kellogg we left the main highway and climbed the long gulch street of Wardner, which winds up the canyon for three or more miles. Between 1892 and 1899, the years of the labor riots, it was a touch-and-go place in which much violence flared up. The riots were occasioned by wage disputes between the mine owners and the unions. In 1893, when wages were reduced in certain of the mines because of the nation-wide depression following the depreciation of silver, the union workers struck. The Frisco, Gem, and Bunker Hill-Sullivan mines then attempted to use nonunion labor. Fights ensued, and strike followed strike until 1899, when conditions became desperate. The greatest violence occurred at Wardner, where on April 29, several hundred men broke into the office building of the Bunker Hill-Sullivan Company and dynamited it and the mill. United States troops were sent into the district and martial law was maintained for more than a year. During part of this time

one thousand men were kept under heavy guard in a "bull pen." Gradually
the mines reopened with nonunion workers, and the union sympathizers and
strike leaders were forced to leave the area.

Many mines in the Coeur d'Alene district in the narrow neck of Idaho
continue to yield good returns, while farther south lumbering, agriculture, and
other industries have largely replaced mining. Idaho's early camps have not
been exploited like those of California, and, consequently, from north to south
the Gem State offers rich opportunities to the explorer of "ghost towns."

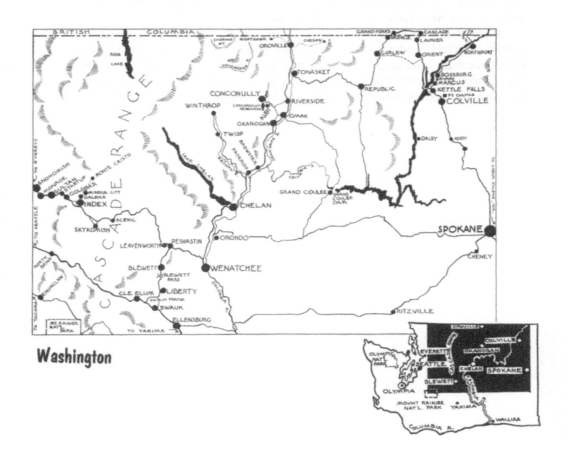

Washington

7. *Chief Moses Held the Key*

Washington

IN HUNTING ghost towns I have become accustomed to find them masquerading under several names. Three tents and a log cabin may be christened Metropolitan City, only to drop the "City" after a few seasons growth. Next, the place becomes Smithville, in honor of its leading benefactor. The years go by, the population drifts away, and by the time one inquires the way to the old site, no one in the vicinity has ever heard of it, or perhaps some old-timer will croak, "By gum, that would be old Metropole." Such experiences should, perhaps, have prepared me to find that states also change their identity. But it was baffling to find settlements mentioned as first in one and then in another of the territories of Washington, Oregon, Idaho, or Montana. I was confused until I found the following details about boundary changes.

1846. The United States-Canadian boundary was set at the Forty-ninth Parallel.
1848. Oregon Territory, which included all of the present states of Oregon, Washington, Idaho, western Montana, and western Wyoming, was created.
1851. Efforts were made to create a separate territory north of the Columbia River and call it Columbia, but nothing came of this until 1853.
1853. Washington Territory was created. It included all of its present area, the northern half of Idaho, and the western fringe of Montana.
1859. After repeated requests to Congress, Oregon, with its present boundaries, was admitted as a state. This increased the extent of Washington Territory tremendously, as it now absorbed all that Oregon had released.

    In the same year a gold rush began to the Oro Fino-Pierce area in eastern Washington. During the years 1860 to 1863 the Salmon River and Boise Basin mines were discovered in what was still Washington Territory.
1863. The Territory of Idaho was created, and thereafter Oregon and Washington assumed their present areas.

259

In searching for the mining towns of Washington, three things became evident: first, many of the earliest and most important ones are now in Idaho; second, many which started as placer camps are now either so dredged out that none of their early buildings remain, or else they have become lumber towns; and, third, the bony spine of the Cascade Mountains which cuts Washington into two distinct areas permitted little communication between the two portions until after 1887, and retarded the founding and development of camps except in sections situated in more accessible terrain.

Most of the early placer discoveries were made at approximately the same time—1859 or the early sixties. After the gravels were exhausted, the mining districts that had been organized were deserted for a number of years. In the seventies the lode mines were found, usually in the same areas that had already been worked, and new camps emerged. Many, however, materialized only in the nineties or early 1900's. Their development was often held back by the lack of transportation facilities, the rugged country, and the fluctuating demand for specific metals. Even today the mountains make it difficult for the hunter of old towns to get from one to another of the widely separated mining areas of Washington without considerable back-tracking.

FORT COLVILE

As early as 1826 the Hudson's Bay Company established a trading post in the wide valley between the Huckleberry Mountains and the Okanogan Highlands, far to the east of the Cascade Range. It was named Fort Colvile in honor of Andrew Colvile, a governor of the company in London. For thirty years this outpost was the chief trading center for a tremendous inland region. In the valley surrounding the fort were the farms of a few French settlers, and three miles away was a grist mill to which the farmers brought their wheat.

Angus MacDonald, chief clerk for the company from 1852 to 1871, and his twenty or more Canadian trappers and Iroquois Indians lived securely behind a high stockade which included a blockhouse that protected the huts, blacksmith shop, and storehouses from attack. The fort was located about fifteen miles northwest of the present town of Colville and a mile and a half south of Marcus, and by the middle fifties it had grown to such an extent that a portion of the stockade had been removed and several additional buildings had been placed outside the walls.

It was probably some French-Canadian mountain man who first found gold in the vicinity; but, if so, his discoveries were not considered important either by himself or by his companions. It is known, however, that the chief trader at the fort received a sack of dark sand from some passing Californian and that he showed it to his men. Soon after this, a thirsty teamster, while kneeling to drink on the bank of the Columbia River, noticed black sand similar to that in the sack he had seen; before leaving the river bar, he panned some of it in his hat and recovered a few flakes of gold. Thereupon Mac-Donald sent some of his men up the river to prospect. When they returned, days later, with several ounces of dust, he was so delighted that he celebrated the discovery by firing the fort's cannon and hoisting a buffalo hide and a bearskin to the flagstaff in lieu of a flag, which the fort did not possess.

As soon as the news traveled west, late in the summer of 1855, the first wave of prospectors started for the upper Columbia River, searching for gold not only in the streams of the Colville Valley but in many others; and reports of their strikes traveled nearly as fast as they did. Gold seemed to lie anywhere between the Spokane and Pend d'Oreille rivers, but the deposits were small and shallow. Still, a man could make three to six dollars a day.

The difficulties encountered in penetrating the wilderness were almost insurmountable. No roads existed from Puget Sound across the mountains; steamboat traffic up the Columbia had not yet started; supplies, limited to whatever the men could carry with them, were soon exhausted; and Indians were a constant menace.

For the benefit of the prospectors and settlers who began to trickle into the Columbia Valley, "Wild Goose Bill" Condon, a successful packer between Walla Walla and Fort Colvile, built and operated a ferry across the river and a trading post along its east bank. He had secured his nickname by firing into a large flock of tame geese, mistaking them for wild ones. The eggs from which the flock had been raised had been brought by a settler all the way from Oregon, and so furious was the woman at Bill's slaughter that she followed him clear to his cabin, scolding him and taunting the stupidity of a frontiersman who couldn't tell the difference between tame and wild geese.

As increasing streams of travelers began to stumble along the wilderness trails, bent beneath packs or leading heavily laden horses and mules, the Indians became frantic, for they feared the intruders would push them from their lands. With white men descending on them from the west and hostile tribes (pushed in turn from their own hunting grounds) pressing them on the east, where could they go and why should they go at all? In desperation, they defended their land.

Solitary prospectors were often killed or scalped before reaching their destinations, and as the number of massacres increased, volunteer companies were raised. These, under the leadership of Colonel George Wright, met the natives in a number of skirmishes throughout the year 1856. At the same time General Wool issued an order which read:

No emigrants or other whites, except the Hudson's Bay Co., or persons having ceded rights from the Indians, will be permitted to settle or remain in the Indian country, or on land not ceded by treaty, confirmed by the Senate and approved by the President of the United States.

These orders are not, however, to apply to the miners engaged in collecting gold at the Colville mines. The miners, however, will be notified that should they interfere with the Indians, or their squaws, they will be punished or sent out of the country.

Territorial Governor Isaac I. Stevens watched what was happening, and he feared, first, for the lives of the settlers and miners and, second, for the Indians who would ultimately be exterminated by the avalanche of white men. The only means of saving the Indians and preventing a costly war was to place them on reservations where they would at least be protected from intrusion. In May of 1855, therefore, he arranged a meeting of five tribes at Fort Walla Walla for the purpose of drawing up treaties.

From eastern Washington (now Idaho) came the Nez Percés, by far the largest tribe and the only one that was friendly to the whites. Under the able leadership of Chief Lawyer, their peace policies did much in restraining the violence of the other tribes. The Walla Wallas, Cayuses, and Umatillas gathered from the surrounding mountains and plains. From west of the Columbia River came the Yakimas, led by Chief Kamiakin. They were the most hostile of all, because the main passes to the gold fields led through their territory, and too many prospectors had already violated their women. They disliked all whites and were especially belligerent toward those with "ploughs, axes, and shovels in their hands." By the time the council opened, from 5,000 to 6,000 Indians had assembled to hear what General Stevens had to propose. Every tribe was suspicious of the motives that had prompted the council, fearing that by the terms of the treaties they would be stripped of their lands.

Chief Kamiakin opposed any cession of land. He tried unsuccessfully to show his people what they were sacrificing and how the reservations being offered them were inferior in size and quality to the lands that were rightfully theirs. But the trusting and friendly Nez Percés were willing to sign, and their example was followed by the others. By the time Chief Looking Glass, the war chief of the Nez Percés, rode into the conference grounds after an extended absence in the Blackfoot country, he was stunned to find that his arrival was too late to prevent the cession of lands to the whites. By the terms of the treaty, three reservations were to be set up and large payments made to each tribe in partial reimbursement for the ceded territory. The Nez Percés were to receive a tract between the Snake River and the Bitter Root Mountains; the Yakimas were to be restricted to the valley of the Yakima River, and the other tribes were assigned specific areas in eastern Oregon.

But army officials in Washington did not agree with Stevens that reservations would solve the Indian problem and delayed ratification of his treaties for four years. In the meantime, two years of Indian wars terrorized the country affected by the treaties and succeeded in further alienating each race from the other. Finally in August, 1858, Colonel Wright led another campaign against the Indians, so crippling to the natives that they agreed to his terms and scattered, a broken and bewildered people. These severe measures ended the Indian wars, except for sporadic outbreaks in southern Idaho. In the fall of 1858 the Walla Walla country was opened to settlers, although the treaties which permitted white men to enter the area were not signed until the following March.

But the Indians had been unable to keep the tide of determined and greedy men from attempting to slip through the forbidden country to the river banks where gold lay. Led on largely by Angus MacDonald's reports that gold had been found north of Fort Colvile, prospectors pushed into British Columbia as far as the Thompson River. In 1857 the rich bars on the Fraser River, in Canada, were discovered. Late in the same year, when a few prospectors drifted back to Washington and reported that the miners up there were making from eight to fifty dollars a day, and that the Indians were friendly, the Fraser rush was on. Experienced miners from California, Oregon, and Washington joined the gigantic stampede; and though they often clashed with the Indians, those who survived bound up their wounds, cocked their rifles, and plunged on.

COLVILLE

WHEN I went to Colville, I found that the old fort of the Hudson's Bay Company had disappeared. Not only are its buildings gone, but the site itself is submerged in the waters of Lake Roosevelt, which reaches miles up the Columbia River behind Grand Coulee Dam. There had been two forts of the same name, first the British Fort Colvile, later the American Fort Colville. The second was originally called Harney's Depot in honor of General Henry Harney, who opened the district north of the Snake River to white settlers in 1858. It stood three miles east of the present town of Colville, adjacent to Pinkney City, the first seat of Stevens County.

The town's reputation for lawlessness was due to the two companies of California volunteers stationed at Fort Colville during the early 1860's; they were sent to the fort to replace regular troops and were said to be cutthroats and jailbirds. Hardly had they arrived when they broke into the Chinese laundry at Pinkney City, ran the proprietor off the premises, and stole all his wash. The following year, one of their officers swaggered into town and with no provocation killed a man with a butcher knife. When he was brought to trial no one dared testify against him, and he was acquitted. To put a curb on crime and violence, Major Curtis, the commanding officer of the post, demolished the local distillery and confiscated the liquor. In 1874 a brewery was built three miles west of the fort, and for eight years it was the only building on the site of what in 1882 became the town of Colville.

The gold rush to the Cariboo Placers in British Columbia in 1860 brought miners through the Colville country and revived some interest in the region. Disappointed men returning from the Fraser River diggings explored the sands and benches of the Columbia. No gold- and silver-bearing quartz deposits were discovered in the district, however, until the 1880's.

In the spring of 1885, the Kearney brothers and A. E. Benoist were prospecting in the mountains east of Fort Colville. Benoist, who was an experienced prospector, climbed to the summit of the nearest peak and scanned the country to the north for outcroppings of ore. He was sure that deposits lay buried in a specific location that he pointed out in the distance. Although his companions disagreed, they were willing to follow him, and for two days they climbed up one mountain and down another. On the third day they camped on a slope at the south end of Colville Mountain, and W. H. Kearney, convinced that the whole trip was a wild-goose chase, told Benoist that he had decided to turn back. Benoist argued with him, and Kearney angrily swung his pick against a rock. The argument ceased as the men gazed at broken fragments of stone full of silver ore. Trembling with excitement, they drove location stakes and named their discovery the Old Dominion.

The mine paid from the grass roots, producing $500,000 in silver, lead, and gold during its first year. The highgrade ores were packed by horses to Spokane and shipped from there to Tacoma to be smelted. News of the strike started a silver stampede to the mountain on which the outcroppings had been found and to the flat, six miles to the west, where the town lay. Miners also flocked to Colville in anticipation of the restoration of Chief Moses' Reservation to the public domain; and were ready to rush in the moment it was declared open in 1886. In 1887 Major Moore, a former Indian agent on the Colville Reservation, built a small smelter on a hill near the town to treat the ores from the Old Dominion and other mines in the vicinity—the Daisy, Silver Crown, Bonanza, Young America, Eagle, and Kootenai properties. The smelted ores yielded an average monthly output of $33,000 and a monthly shipment of three carloads of bullion. Since the eighties the Old Dominion has been developed by several companies, and a mill and concentrator have been added to its property. Its total output up to 1892 was estimated at $625,000; and by 1916 no other mine in the state had produced such highgrade silver-lead ore. It is still producing: although Old Dominion Mountain, which overlooks the town of Colville, is heavily timbered and shows no signs of mining operations, trucks shuttle back and forth between the historic property and the railroad bringing down ore ready for shipment.

As the seat of Stevens County, Colville is today a thriving and attractive place; an air of prosperity and security surrounds its modern homes, stores, and public buildings. Fire destroyed some of its historic buildings in 1892, when the Dominion Hotel, built in 1885, as well as other picturesque structures, went up in smoke. Most of the residents of the town were attending a play given by the Ladies Aid Society in Meyers Opera House. At the alarm of fire, the men dashed out, formed a bucket brigade, and fought the blaze. Suddenly a miner shouted, "Stand back! Dynamite and giant powder!" He ran to the Rickey building, set fuses, and blew up a store in a vain effort to create a firebreak.

Since Colville is modern and Pinkney City and Fort Colville are mere sites today, we drove north along the Columbia River to see what was left of certain river towns and of Northport, a more recent mining center close to the Canadian border.

KETTLE FALLS, DAISY, AND MARCUS

LAKE ROOSEVELT, created by the Grand Coulee Dam, has backed so many miles up the Columbia River that a number of settlements along the banks have been submerged and the residents forced to move and build new towns high above the water level. Kettle Falls, nine miles north of Colville, is one of them. When its citizens learned that their townsite would be covered by thirty feet of water, they negotiated for consolidation with Meyers Falls, which was on higher ground, four miles farther north. Kettle Falls then annexed a sixty-foot strip of land completely surrounding Meyers Falls and began to move to its new home. When the formal vote for consolidation of the two places was taken, a majority also voted that the name Kettle Falls be used in place of Meyers Falls.

The original Kettle Falls consisted in 1888 of one small log cabin, hidden in the dense pines that grow close to the riverbank; but when the Columbia River bars were developed nearby and as far south as the camp of Daisy, it grew into a small but modern community with hotels and business blocks. In 1941 the threat of immersion started the negotiations with Meyers Falls.

The site of Daisy, though 1,500 feet above the Columbia River, is also inundated. Placer mining originally attracted prospectors to the location, and the discovery of two silver-lead mines, the Tempest and the Daisy, hastened the building of a small camp near the properties. A wagon road connected Daisy and Kettle Falls with Meyers Falls and was used in shipping ore from the mines to the railroad.

We passed through Marcus, named for Marcus Oppenheimer, its first settler and pioneer merchant. Like Kettle Falls, it is in a new location; for the original settlement, the oldest town in Stevens County, is now under sixty feet of water. During the sixties and seventies Chinese sluiced away the river bars below the town until nothing remained but huge boulders and exposed slabs of rock.

BOSSBURG

BEYOND Evans, where the American Gypsum Company has a large plant, we passed one boarded-up store, a filling station, and a weathered sign reading, "Bossburg." This was the last of the town's three names. Here the Young America Mining district was organized in 1885, after galena ore was discovered in the Young America and Bonanza mines. By 1888 a small village, called Young America, had grown up close to the mines and somewhat back from the Columbia River; by 1892 its population had doubled—from 400 to 800—and a stamp mill was completed. In 1893 the town was platted and recorded as Millington; but about 1896 it was re-christened Bossburg, in honor of C. S. Boss, one of its leading citizens. The community soon contained a substantial schoolhouse, a Congregational church, and a public meeting hall. Then it built a cable ferry across the Columbia, and as the valley prospered it shipped lumber, lime, and fruit as well as ore.

NORTHPORT

IN COLVILLE the preceding evening I had been fortunate enough to meet three mining men. When asked about ghost towns in Stevens County, they laughed and said, "Northport is the best ghost town around here. You'd better go see it."

"Tell me something about it first," I urged; and one of the three settled back in his chair and began.

"The big Le Roi mines up near Rossland and Trail, in Canada, are just north of the boundary, and back in the nineties they needed a smelter to treat their ore. The company which owned the mines built one in Northport and operated it until they ran into some legal trouble about mining ore in Canada and treating it in the United States. I don't know just what the trouble was, but the smelter shut down and everybody left. About that time the Hecla mine

REPUBLIC

MAIN STREET,
CONCONULLY

NORTHPORT

in the Coeur d'Alenes in Idaho decided it wanted a smelter; so it bought the Northport outfit and ran the plant for two years. But their mine wasn't a big enough producer to keep the smelter going, so it shut down again. Then the American Smelting and Refining Company bought it. They didn't want the property but they wanted the machinery; so they dismantled the smelter and shipped what they wanted to East Helena for their smelter there.

"Northport's a ghost town all right, in a way. There's people around, but they're not all mining. The U. S. Customs department has its port of entry in the town—has had since 1901, when they had lots of foreigners to check up on, especially Chinese who tried to slip in through Canada. While you're up there, why don't you run over the border and see the smelter at Trail? That's where they handle the Rossland ore now."

Northport may be a "ghost," but it is a very lively one indeed, and did not look at all as I had expected. To be sure, its streets are lined with buildings, both old and new; while many are empty, an equal number are fresh, new cabins. I felt the presence of two distinct generations, each seeming to ignore the other. Empty two-story brick stores stand apart on one street, while new one-story stores on another street are half hidden by the automobiles parked in front of them. There was life in the town, and the forgotten buildings looked vacantly at children playing in the streets and young women in bright housedresses hanging out wash. Lumbering has supplanted mining in Northport, and it is a profitable industry.

The smelter was what I expected—concrete foundations almost lost in the brush and young trees sprouting out of the debris. Only the big stack is untouched.

In the spring of 1892 three homesteaders' cabins stood where the city of Northport was being laid out by a townsite company. Neither railroad nor wagon road came within miles of the location; the only access to the "wooded flat" was by mountain trail. Yet within two months a printing press for the *Northport News* was somehow hauled to the site by ox team.

When the first issue of the new sheet appeared on July 4, 1892, the town contained two buildings, a few tents, and twelve persons. The paper introduced the new community to the world at large by saying:

Seldom in the annals of journalism has it been necessary for a new paper to explain for the benefit and enlightenment of its contemporaries where it exists and who are its expected patrons.

Yet . . . the most recently published map of the United States; the most comprehensive atlas; the very latest gazeteer, none of them indicate the location of Northport; none of them recognize its existence. The census taker has passed it by; . . . a month or two ago it was a beautifully wooded flat; today it is already a town; tomorrow—a few tomorrows hence, at any rate—it will be a city.

No sooner had the town been laid out than a forest fire threatened it. Though the fire had been burning for two weeks, no one had paid any attention to it, thinking it would die out; but when a strong wind whipped the flames toward the business section of the community, "the entire fire brigade was called out" to stave off the menace by back-firing. While they were at work the wind changed, and "nothing was lost."

By fall a schoolhouse had been added to the town's buildings; but the most exciting event took place on Sunday, September 18, when

. . . the railroad reached Northport and the sight of E. J. Roberts, the energetic chief engineer of the Spokane Falls and Northern railroad, clothed in a long duster and a regulation broad-brimmed army hat, walking with slow and majestic tread and commanding mien, giving his orders in a clear and forcible voice to a large crowd of men who were following him, putting ties in their proper places and laying rails, with the construction train slowly moving along behind the whole, was a pleasing and astonishing sight, and one that will never be forgotten by the pioneers of Northport, the future mining milling smelting and agricultural city of northeastern Washington.

The first passenger train ran two days later.

Northport's first post office has a unique history. When the town was first laid out it had none, the nearest one being six miles away at Little Dalles. As the community grew, and especially while the railroad was being built, the postmaster at Little Dalles, Cy Townsend, decided to accommodate the people of the new town by placing the office building on a flatcar and moving it to the end of the track, which by that time was only four miles away. In September, 1892, when the road reached Northport, Townsend again moved the building, set it up on Columbia Avenue, and began the regular distribution of mail. So far as Washington knew, the post office was still at Little Dalles.

Since his duties did not occupy all of his time, Townsend ran a saloon in conjunction with his post office. When the mail pouch was brought to him, he would open it, spill its contents on the bar and shout to the men to come up and claim their letters. Everyone liked the system, for it was quick and efficient. One day a stranger entered the saloon, and, after the men had taken their mail and left the building, he announced that he was a postal inspector. He asked Townsend if he customarily distributed the mail in that fashion, and he also inquired if registered mail was kept in a locked container.

"No," roared Townsend, "I keep it here under the bar, and when anyone has a letter I give it to him the next time he comes in."

This was too much for the inspector, who lectured the postmaster on proper procedures and insisted that he no longer mix drinks with government business.

Townsend bellowed, "I didn't ask for this job. I'm only doing it to accommodate the boys. They're satisfied, and if you're not, you can take the whole outfit with you when you go out." Then he snatched up a cardboard box containing a few unclaimed letters and hurled it into the street. Townsend continued as postmaster until the following year, when a regular post office was set up at Northport. During the remainder of his voluntary term his methods did not change.

One fire after another destroyed portions of the town during its first few years of existence. On May 8, 1893:

Fire . . . fastened its remorseless fangs on the best buildings of the town and laid them and their contents on the ground, a huge mass of ruins.

Only three months later, fire broke out in the front room of the International Hotel, and before the bucket brigade could quench the blaze, seven buildings had been gutted. The third fire, in March, 1896, was discovered by a patron who "opened the door leading upstairs in S. F. Bradbury's restaurant, opposite the depot," only to see "flames slowly licking down the stairway." Those at the tables, realizing they could do nothing, ran out to give the alarm. Many buildings were lost, and only through the concerted efforts of the firefighters was the big music hall across from the restaurant saved. After every fire the town immediately rebuilt.

By the time prospectors found silver deposits in the surrounding hills and river benches, Northport had begun to boom. The *Northport News* of January 5, 1893, boasted that:

Notwithstanding the roar and rush and bubble and life of Northport, there has not been a shooting scrape nor a highway robbery so far.

The next year, 1894, floods raised the river seventy-five feet above the low-water mark; since the townsite was not threatened, the newspaper jokingly suggested that "under the circumstances, we think it will be safe to build skyscrapers on the Northport business bench."

Next came the building of the smelter, which turned Northport into an industrial as well as a mining center. The company that erected the plant was English, and the Le Roi mines that were to feed it were located in Canada. The Canadians argued heatedly to have the plant constructed on their soil; but immense quantities of lime rock, suitable for flux, existed in the mountains near Northport, and the company estimated that the plant could be operated more economically there than in Canada. Apparently for business reasons, the property and the mines passed temporarily into the hands of Americans. Therefore, the smelter, which cost $250,000 and was blown in during the winter of 1897-98, was built by American capitalists. In 1899 the Le Roi mines, as well as the smelter, were resold to an English company and thereafter became known as the Northport Smelting and Refining Company, Ltd. During this period the entire output of the Le Roi, Kootenai, and Velvet mines was smelted at Northport, and some custom work was also handled.

Objections by the company to the formation of a Mill and Smeltermen's Union brought on a strike in 1901 that lasted for nine months. The company hinted that membership in the union would mean dismissal from the plant; since it could not afford to let all its trained men go at once, however, it did not suppress the union but pretended to ignore it. However, a few men at a time were discharged and replaced by nonunion workers shipped in from eastern cities. As soon as the union became aware of this it protested, claiming that the owners of the company were aliens. The company then reorganized under the laws of Idaho and obtained a restraining order prohibiting the union from interfering with the operation of the company. No violence resulted from this announcement; but when sixty-two men arrived from the East to replace union workmen, a delegation of strikers met them at the depot and marched with them to the plant in an endeavor to persuade them not to sign up for work. Their arguments must have been powerful, for thirty-five of the new-comers decided to leave at once. Twice the Sheriff of Colville was sent for to settle riots, and the strike dragged on until March 12, 1902. Its termination is best described in the *Northport Republican* of March 15:

At a meeting of the Northport Mill and Smeltermen's Union Tuesday night, March 11, a unanimous vote was declared in favor of continuing the fight to the bit-ter end, but hardly had the echo died from the loud cheering that followed the announcement of the ballot, when it was learned that the Western Federation of Miners with headquarters at Denver, had decided to cut off the weekly allowance of the Northport Mill and Smelter Union. This . . . nearly paralyzed the boys. . . . Next morning the free eating house, conducted by the Western Federation, closed its doors [and the men] began to realize their predicament. A mass meeting was called for Wednesday night.

The question of declaring the strike off was brought up and a vote taken. . . . The majority voted to call off the strike. . . . Finally it was decided to abandon the union and surrender the charter.

After 1902 the smelter's story is one of alternating production and idle-ness. During the eight years before 1905, the average monthly payroll was between $25,000 and $30,000, even including the period of the strike. In 1905 the plant became idle for a year; but two furnaces started up again in 1906, and the smelter ran at partial capacity until 1909. Then idleness again until 1916, when the "Day brothers and associates" purchased the plant, spent $500,000 on its development, added two lead furnaces, and "retained two of the most modern copper furnaces to meet possible custom demands." Under their management four hundred men were employed. When the American Smelting and Refining Company dismantled the plant, Northport gave up its interest in mining.

From Northport we drove back to Kettle Falls, crossed the bridge over the backwaters of Roosevelt Lake, and followed the west shore of the lake and the Kettle River toward the Canadian line.

ORIENT AND LAURIER

As WE entered the town of Orient with its broad main street, its big trees, and its widely spaced houses, I saw no signs of mining activity. While I was admiring the frame fire-tower, peering into the dark interior to see its hand-drawn hosecart, a middle-aged man came up the street. I began to ask him questions.

"Sure, this was a mining camp," he said, amazed at my ignorance. "It didn't get going until around 1902, when some businessmen formed the Orient Improvement Company and laid out the townsite. It was called Morgan at first, but as soon as the Orient mine was located they changed the name.

"There are plenty of mines around here—the First Thought and the Second Thought and the Titanic and the Copper Butte, and the Orient, of course. Some of them are two or three miles away, and the companies that opened them had to build their own roads to the properties. That's First Thought Mountain, east of town. The First Thought mine had the biggest payroll of any of them. It was a gold proposition, and between 1904 and 1909 it was a constant shipper. The mine was valued at $650,000, and in 1907 it shipped $35,000 worth of ore over this branch of the Great Northern railroad. We couldn't have made out here without the railroad.

"There's other camps near here. Rock Cut is three miles up the river, and Boyd's, where the big Napoleon mine is located, is twelve miles south.

"This town isn't what it once was. We had three hundred people here in the first boom and three hundred more miners in the district. The old Miners' Supply Company building was one of the first to be put up. We had a newspaper too, the *Kettle River Journal,* and two general stores and a hotel and planing mills. The high price they were paying for gold brought back the mines in 1935, but things are pretty quiet here now.

"If you're driving up to Laurier you'll see this whole valley wall is glacier-carved. The mines are back in the hills."

All the way to Laurier, I looked for mines. It was beautiful country, with layer upon layer of forested hills rising from both sides of the narrow river valley. Most of the way not even a trail broke the wild, green country, and once a buck crashed out of the trees and bounded across the highway. Just this side of Laurier, close to the Canadian line, the valley widened, and high, gray mountains rose abruptly to the west. Near the road a freshly painted frame building—the Talisman Mine Office—stood alone in a meadow, and opposite it a dirt road led to a mill at the foot of the gray cliffs; high above, on a pinnacle of rock, clung the buildings of the mine.

While waiting to go through Customs I wandered around looking for signs of what Laurier had been like in the days of mining excitement. All wagon and pack trains had to halt for inspection before crossing the boundary, and the settlement had had 2,000 inhabitants. Now its residents are the personnel of the United States Customs and Immigration Service. Once across the border, we skimmed through Canada from Cascade to Grand Forks, where we again entered the United States. We passed through Curlew, a town filled with big trees and weathered buildings, and then drove on to Republic.

REPUBLIC

JOHN WELTY'S discovery of gold on Granite Creek in February, 1896, touched off a rush which opened the northern section of the Colville Indian Reservation to white miners. Phil Creasor and Tom Ryan staked the Republic claim the same month, and by the end of the year more than a hundred locations had been recorded. In addition to the initial strikes, Dennis Clark and others uncovered excellent prospects during 1897, for although the ore was complex and refractory it lay in "well defined bodies and uniform veins."

As soon as the first discoveries were made, a lively little camp called Eureka sprang up among the dense trees along the creek—a typical "muslin town," for the stampeders were mostly single men who either camped in the open or lived in tents which could be taken into the hills when they struck out in search of claims. Larger tents and stores were merely wooden frames over which cloth was stretched, and at night the glow of lamps and candles within each one filtered through the transparent walls and lighted the otherwise pitch-black streets. J. C. Keller opened the first store in just such a tent and was soon receiving "large quantities of whiskey, flour and other necessities," packed in on Indian trails so poor that passage over them was almost impossible in wet weather.

By the fall of 1896 Eureka contained fifty log and canvas shacks, five stores, three blacksmith shops, two barber shops, four restaurants, two hotels, two fruit and cigar stores, two meat markets, three livery stables, three bakeries, three assay offices, a tailor, a shoemaker, a doctor, a lawyer, a jeweler, and several saloons in which gambling went on full blast. Dances sponsored by the Miners' Union were held in Patsy Clark's big boardinghouse, the only place large enough to accommodate the crowds which attended. After a young woman was strangled by an "unknown assassin," a cemetery was laid out under the big pines on the hillside.

The name "Eureka" was soon changed to "Republic" at the request of Patrick Clark, who operated the Republic Mining properties. Thereafter, the original buildings that comprised Eureka became known as "Old Town." The first school was held in a tent in Old Town "on the creek bottom in the brush." In 1900 a log house replaced the tent. Indians attended the school at no expense and at first outnumbered the white pupils.

As early as 1900 the town, which by then had an opera house and balconied, false-fronted stores, dance halls and 28 saloons, was "sixth in population among Eastern Washington cities," its Republic mine under Patrick Clark's management paid dividends aggregating $190,000, and stage service connected it with Spokane and with other supply points. Although the miners and merchants were skeptical as to whether the much discussed railroad between Republic and Grand Forks, Canada, would ever be built and joshed each other about the "Hot Air Line," the road was completed in 1902 and provided another outlet for Republic's growing industries. In recent years, half of the state's silver has come from mines in the vicinity. We found Republic, the seat of Ferry County, more modern and less historically photogenic than we had expected, for a fire in 1938 destroyed some of the most picturesque landmarks on the main street. But a careful survey of the town revealed a few of the old cabins, and a helpful storekeeper pointed out the location of Old Town.

OKANOGAN CITY, CHOPAKA CITY

FROM Republic the road winds west through the mountains to Tonasket, where it joins the main highway leading north to Oroville and to the site of the Similkameen placers. The discovery of gold just south of the forty-ninth parallel along the Similkameen River was made accidentally by the Boundary Commission which was in 1859 endeavoring to settle the Canadian-American border line. As soon as they found gold along the banks of the river, hundreds of miners rushed to the stream to placer the shallow deposits. Only a week after its founding, Okanogan City, their hastily constructed tent colony, contained 3,000 men. But news of the Cariboo and Fraser River placers soon reached the fluid population and off it went, leaving the camp deserted until the men began to dribble back and resume work on the river bars. Old Okanogan City has long since vanished and is not to be confused with the county seat of Okanogan, forty-six miles south of Oroville.

Hiram F. Smith, a native of Maine, reached the Okanogan Valley in 1858, having first tried his luck in the Fraser River mines. He liked the country at the southern end of Osoyoos Lake just below the Canadian border and built a log cabin close to the shore. He filed on 600 acres of land for a ranch and later bought 300 additional acres from Chief Tonasket. In 1862 he opened what is said to be the first private trading post in the Northwest and, according to tribal custom, he married Mary Manuel, the daughter of another Okanogan chief. But by far his greatest contribution to the development of the region was the planting of an apple orchard of 1,200 trees. He irrigated these and, through his care of them, taught the Indians in the vicinity practical methods of farming. "Okanogan" Smith, as he was called, was intelligent, fearless, completely honest, and a born leader. Without doubt he contributed more than any other individual to the development of Okanogan County. Shortly after his arrival in the West he was appointed to the United States Land Commission, and in 1865 he was elected to the Washington legislature. Since no roads had been built across the Cascades, he had to go north into British Columbia, then by steamer down the Fraser River and across Puget Sound to reach Olympia, the Territorial capital.

Smith and a few prospectors discovered gold-bearing rock on July 4, 1871, at the base of Mt. Chopaka some miles west of his ranch. Miners immediately flocked to the quartz mines on the mountain, established a mining district there, and named their camp Chopaka City. Next they started a miners' union and elected Smith president.

In 1873, however, Chief Moses claimed this land as part of his Reservation, and a company of soldiers came from the nearest military post and ordered all the miners to leave. But Alexander McCauley, an early settler who was friendly with Chief Moses, was allowed to remain on the tract, and that same year he built a cabin adjacent to the future townsite of Oroville. The Moses Reservation did not become public domain until 1886, and long before then Chopaka City had disappeared.

OROVILLE

WITH the opening of the Reservation in 1886, prospectors poured in to sift the sands at the junction of the Okanogan and Similkameen rivers, but the ore deposits were not sensational. The new camp was called Oro until the post office authorities added "ville" to its name to avoid confusion with the town of "Oso." By 1891 it contained one store. The following year when the town was platted, twenty saloons crowded its main street.

When the Great Northern Railroad extended its track through the town in 1905, Oroville enjoyed a boom, but in spite of its many new tents and wooden shacks it still had no calaboose. The town marshal therefore hand-cuffed drunks and fastened them with a logging chain and a padlock to a hitching post until they sobered up. The town is now a small agricultural and industrial center, engaged in stock-raising, canning, and mining, and few traces of its early days exist.

Okanogan County is full of old towns—small places half deserted today but originally mining camps—and anyone with curiosity and plenty of time can visit Nighthawk, Palmer Mountain, Weheville, Loop Loop, Bolster, Golden, Toroda, Bodie, Wauconda and Chesaw. Chesaw is probably the only settlement named in honor of a Chinese settler. He and his Indian wife lived in the area in the early days and opened their cabin to both whites and Indians traveling through the uncharted country.

RUBY

RUBY, thirteen miles northwest of Okanogan on Salmon Creek, is a true ghost town; yet in the middle 1880's, when 1,000 miners tramped its wooded streets, it was the noisiest, lustiest camp in the county. When a butcher added to his stock of beef by cattle rustling, a delegation of irate stockmen came to town dangling a rope and hunting for him. The miners immediately rallied to his defense and threatened the cattlemen if they touched him. As mob violence was feared, the butcher was hustled to Colville under guard, to stand trial there; but on the way over the guards became drunk, and the prisoner escaped. He was captured, and both he and the guards were then tried at Ruby—and all were freed.

Although a few "sooners," or prospectors too impatient to wait for legal entry into reservation land, investigated Ruby Mountain and staked squatter claims in the early eighties, the big rush came after March 1, 1886, when Chief Moses' land became public domain. A deputy sheriff and a county commissioner were among those who had discovered and worked locations prior to 1886, but on the day the reservation was opened for entry, both men were in Colville on county business. As soon as they could get away they rode night and day to reach their claims and protect them; but the trip took four days, and by the time they arrived their claims had been jumped. The four properties they lost were the Ruby, the Fourth of July, the First Thought, and the Arlington.

The ledges the prospectors uncovered carried silver and small amounts of gold, and as mine after mine was opened, Thomas D. Fuller in 1887 organized the Ruby mining district. As properties such as the First Thought, Second

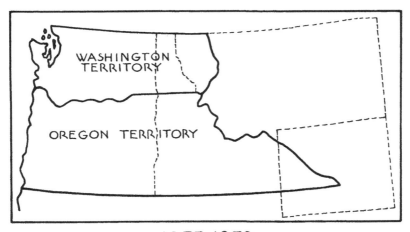

1853–1859

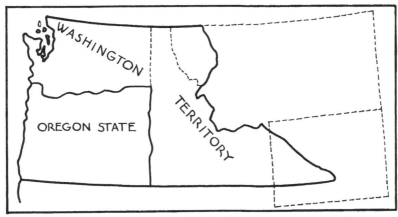

1859–1863

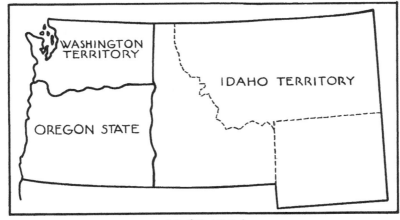

1863–1864
POLITICAL SUBDIVISION

From *A History of the Pacific Northwest* by George W. Fuller. 1949.
By permission of Alfred A. Knopf.

Thought, Ruby, Butte, Lenora, Peacock, Fairview, and Poorman began to pay off, Jonathan Bourne, Jr., United States Senator from Oregon, and investors from Portland, Tacoma, and Montana poured a million dollars into developing the district.

Ruby was laid out in 1886. Although still far from supply centers—Ellensburg, less than two hundred miles away was a four-day journey—and served entirely by freighters and packers, it grew rapidly until its stores and log houses lined both sides of a quarter-mile-long street. Occasionally in winter a slide ran into the gulch lifting a house from its foundations and shunting it down the slope or crushing it under tons of snow, and one year a teacher from the nearby camp of Conconully was caught and killed by an avalanche; but the citizens were from hardy stock and took everything in stride.

Their actions and reactions were forthright. When a miner held the hunting record of ninety-two deer in one season, another miner topped him by shooting ninety-six. A Chinese miner drifted into town one night, and certain of "the boys" dropped him into a dry well and, returning to the cosy saloon they had left to perform the deed, spent the rest of the evening drinking lager, chewing dried venison, and singing. After the men working at the Bourne properties demanded a raise in wages and were refused, they shot out all the front windows of Billie Dorwin's hotel as a protest against Jonathan Bourne, Jr., who was known to be staying in the hotel and who reputedly had a quarter-million investment in his Ruby holdings. When Ruby became the county seat and no safe-deposit vault existed in which to place the $1,800 in cash with which the new treasurer was entrusted, he put the money in an empty baking powder can and buried it on his ranch.

With each successive year the mines improved and the camp grew, and to advertise such progress the *Ruby Miner* printed:

As Virginia City is to Nevada so is the town of Ruby to the State of Washington. . . . Ruby is the only incorporated town in Okanogan County. It is out of debt and has money in the Treasury. . . . Public schools are open nine months every year, under the management of competent instructors, these furnishing unsurpassed educational advantages. . . .
LET US MAKE SOME MONEY FOR YOU IN RUBY, THIS DISTRICT IS APPROPRIATELY TERMED THE "COMSTOCK OF WASHINGTON."
Nature has endowed Ruby with the elements of a city.
MAN HAS SUPPLIED THE ADJUNCTS TO MAKE A METROPOLIS. [June 2, 1892.]

Every mine was working in 1893 until the silver crash. Then properties closed down and the population dropped to a few dozen. One rancher discovered that with no market left his horses and cattle were worthless. He therefore staked men who needed mounts with free horses and sold his cattle at a loss to a butcher. After the people cleared out, ranchers tore down and carted away empty buildings, and a fire in 1900 licked up most of those left. Today only a line of weathered foundations, hidden in brush and grass, straggle beside a dirt road, once Ruby's main thoroughfare.

CONCONULLY

FOUR miles higher on Salmon Creek than Ruby and separated from it by a low range of hills is Conconully, originally called Salmon City by the men who laid it out on the grassy plain at the mouth of a canyon. Although the first quartz lode in the vicinity was discovered in 1871, Foster and Pierce are the prospectors usually associated with the discovery of auriferous metals in this portion of the Salmon Creek area. Their claims, the Homestake and Toughnut, made in the fall of 1886, attracted others to the benches above the creek bed, so that by fall two stores marked the beginning of the camp in the newly organized Salmon Creek mining district. Only cold October weather drew the miners away from their pannings, washings, and diggings long enough to build cabins in which to hole up for the winter. The new camp grew fast, for the diggings were good and there was an abundance of water both from Salmon Creek and from Conconully Lake which bordered one end of the settlement.

By February, 1888, the camp was renamed Conconully and during the year, when the Territorial Legislature created Okanogan County from a part of Stevens County, and the commissioners of the new subdivision met in a log cabin to select a temporary county seat, both Conconully and Ruby bid for the honor. Although nothing had been said beforehand, a delegation from Ruby assembled by the cabin where the meeting was held and began to campaign for their town, promising the commissioners office space free from taxes if Ruby was the winner. At the same time representatives from Conconully offered the perplexed men five acres of land for county offices. The merits of both places were discussed all day long and still no decision was reached. By late afternoon the Ruby contingent began to shout "Good Old Ruby" and "Ruby for County seat" and, forming a large circle, danced around the cabin, whooping and yelling. When the vote was cast Ruby won, and her enthusiastic supporters sent up rousing cheers for the commissioners before stumbling happily home. Yet the following year by popular vote the county seat was moved to Conconully.

Like Ruby, Conconully was far from supplies, but from Charley Hermann one could order anything and be sure that from six weeks to two months later it would be unloaded by freighters in front of his store. Except for occasional bad winters, when stock froze for lack of feed, beef was plentiful and milk was peddled from door to door for ten cents a quart. Freight and passengers traveled up the Columbia on steamboats as far as Pateros or Brewster, the head of river navigation, and the rest of the way by wagon or coach. The Columbia and Okanogan Steamboat Co. advertised "Quick Time and Good Service" and promised to make "connection with all trains on the Great Northern R.R., at Wenatchee." When the river was blocked with ice, the mail came in on horse-drawn sleds.

The river boat season, which depended upon high water, was fairly short, and the arrival each spring of the first steamer was an eagerly awaited event. Everyone hurried to the landing to exchange news with the captain and the crew and to claim his portion of the long-awaited freight. To avoid whirlpools and tricky currents which made piloting an art, it was often necessary to "line" a boat across certain rapids. "Lining up" meant landing men below a rapid so that they could carry a big steel cable, one end of which was fastened to a capstan on the steamer's bow, up the shore and fasten it to a rock or cliff beyond the danger point. The windlass then slowly wound in the cable as the pilot directed, while the engineer forced the boiler to its utmost exertion and the boat creaked and groaned as it bucked the dangerous current. Frequently even this method failed to drive the boat beyond the pull of the rapid, and the process had to be repeated until "finally in the battle with nature, man wins."

Conconully and Ruby were involved in an Indian scare in January, 1891, which began with the murder of S. S. Cole, a freighter. One Indian accused of the crime was killed by a deputy sheriff, and a second Indian, called Steven, was placed in the Conconully jail. According to the *Ruby Miner:*

Last Thursday morning twenty horsemen swept silently through the town of Ruby. The soft white snow muffled the sound of their horses' hoofs and the slumber of the camp was not disturbed by their movements. Death was in their hearts and they sped remorselessly onward.

The jailer at Conconully was relieved of his keys by the cavalcade of miners and locked in the building while Steven was taken out and spirited away. A few days later the *Miner* reported that

Trouble is on foot and danger stalks abroad. It is principally owing to the lynching of Steven that this condition exists—but there are many supplemental reasons.

George Monk accompanied by Smitkin started to convey the body to the Indian Mission. The Indians claim that Monk, when he started out was sitting on the corpse, which was wrapped in a blanket and carried on a single bobsled. The appearance of the body was the signal for the commencement of a big dance. For two days the body was kept while the Indians stimulated themselves at the bier.

In fear that the Indians might retaliate, the women and children of Conconully were taken by night to Ruby where they could be barricaded in the Fourth of July mine in case of an attack. During this crisis the town, "with its congregation of temporary visitors," gave a dance which according to the *Miner* was:

Dancing Amidst Danger
Ruby Is Pretty Tough and Not Easily Scared

Some of the visitors were not in attendance, and therefore it is supposed that tumtums were out of order.

But the dance was great. If there is any idea that the Siwashes can keep Okanogan people from dancing they will have to quit. We dance and fight equally well. In fact Billy Dorwin says he is going to start a Messiah dance himself.

After a few days a conference was held with the Indians and trouble averted.

Conconully's first newspaper, the *Okanogan Outlook,* appeared in July, 1888. Its equipment was burned in the fire of 1892, and two years later its plant was destroyed in the flood; yet in July, 1894, it resumed publication for a time. In 1903 L. L. Work, pioneer banker of the county, established the *Okanogan Record,* a paper whose 1943 file reprints historical as well as current data.

Mail required three days to reach Spokane or Seattle in 1903: the first day it traveled by stage to Brewster, the second by boat to Wenatchee, and the third by train to its destination. A telephone call took almost as long, for it was sent in relays, and at times one or two days passed before the connection could be completed. By that year although grouse and prairie chickens were still abundant, state hunting licenses were mandatory with a fixed limit of ten birds a day.

In the fall a Literary Society was formed which by its third meeting "taxed the seating capacity" of the hall although the "room was poorly heated and badly lighted." A debate, "Resolved: That Washington achieved more for his country than did Lincoln," was so enthusiastically received that at the next meeting an even larger audience listened to the argument: "That railroads would be of more benefit to Okanogan County than irrigation." The affirmative view was upheld. By spring, attendance fell off at the meetings and by unanimous vote the society adjourned until the following season.

The winter of 1903 was one of heavy snows. All through March a nightly snowfall added five to six inches to the pile which already lay on the ground. When the fishing season opened on April 1, trout were snared through holes cut in the frozen lake. Thousands of head of stock died. Though baled hay was carried free of charge by Columbia and Okanogan steamboats to Brewster, it was impossible to get it from the landing to the town. Some ranchers tried driving their cattle south to the feed; but hundreds of animals died before reaching the bank of the Columbia. During the worst part of the winter the mail carrier between Conconully and Chelan abandoned his four-horse wagon and drove up the frozen surface of the big lake on a sled, quoting Shakespeare to any passengers who accompanied him on the long and lonesome trip.

"Indian Edwards," one of a hundred Indians for each of whom the government had set aside "one mile square of public domain," chose a plot in the Similkameen Valley and raised horses and cattle so successfully that he "rode in a wagon, wore store clothes," and owned property valued in 1899 at $3,000. By 1903 its value had risen to $8,650. At his death in February, 1904, he was said to be "one of the few men in the county who had more than $1,000 in cash."

Conconully suffered many major disasters. To the Indians the very name means "evil spirit" and the lake of the same name, nearby, is said to contain a fierce monster. Fire destroyed part of the town in 1892; next a flood swept away forty-two buildings and caused property damage estimated at $95,000. Toward the end of May, 1894, heavy rain began to fall in the hills and continued until both rain and melting snow turned the creek into a boiling torrent and the flat below the town into a lake. The second day, a cloudburst ten miles up the creek sent a wall of water seventy-five feet high rushing out of the canyon, which carried before it trees, huge boulders, and debris, and swept away everything in its path. By the time the flood had passed, water stood twelve feet deep in the shallowest places, and logs and other rubbish were lodged against the second stories of buildings. An iron safe that was swept out of the hotel was never found. A house containing an invalid floated out on the lake. When rescued, the man was still in bed and unhurt. Only one death resulted from the disaster, for a citizen, watching the rising waters, rode to every endangered property, warning people and insisting that they move to higher ground. One old lady had already reached safety when she missed her spectacles and, in spite of protests, went back home to get them. When her body was found wedged in debris, she was still clutching the fatal glasses. As late as 1903 signs of flood damage were still visible and a portion of the main street was blocked to traffic.

All the way from Omak, where we left the highway, to Conconully cars full of fishermen whizzed by us and, as we drove past the reservoir and lake on the edge of the town and up the main street, more fishermen in hip boots were busy unloading cases of beer and rods and creels from their cars. I had expected a ghost town, especially as on the way in I had seen the windswept cemetery. But instead of empty streets I found a small, active, and attractive place, whose few weathered false-fronts are almost lost among newer, freshly painted stores, churches, and homes. Even the old schoolhouse is being re-

STAMP MILL, BLEWETT

SCHOOLHOUSE ON MAIN STREET, LIBERTY

placed by a modern, more efficient structure. Perhaps the *Okanogan Outlook* was correct in saying:

here miners and prospectors have determined to make their homes and have brought the gentle and refining influence of women and home to the camp, which has had the effect of doing away with all lawlessness.

BLEWETT AND THE PESHASTIN MINES

THE Peshastin district in which Blewett is situated is one of the oldest producers of placer gold in the state. During the Indian wars of 1855-56, Captain Ingalls, in scouting the eastern slopes of the Cascade Range accompanied by an Indian named Colowah, followed the Wenatchee River to a tributary canyon and there found several gold nuggets. But because of their mission, they dared not stay to investigate the source. Later, when Ingalls returned, he was unable to find the place from which the gold came. Convinced of its value, he joined a party of prospectors and led them to the region; but he was accidentally killed, and the men, having lost their guide, left the area.

Charles A. Splawn was the next to search for the lost placer ground. In the spring of 1860, while searching for gold in the Similkameen, he met the Indian Colowah. Colowah refused to reveal the source of the gold he and Ingalls had seen, but he did draw a crude map of the region and say that the creek was called Peshastin. That fall Splawn and a small group of miners set out for the stream and at the mouth of the Wenatchee hired an Indian guide, who led them twenty miles up the river. There the Indian pointed out a big creek as the Peshastin and left them. Splawn worked up the stream and found promising colors. Hurrying to a prearranged rendezvous, he showed them to his companions.

While Splawn was still there, a messenger named Russell appeared at the camp on his way back to the west coast, having delivered the news of Lincoln's election to the men in the northern mines. He was so impressed with the gold that he took some of it back to Seattle, where exaggerated reports of the strike were printed. At the news a rush to the Peshastin began. Seventy-five miners spent the winter along the creek, many of them men returning from the Cariboo and Fraser districts of British Columbia. Although they found pay gravel near the junction of Peshastin Creek with the Wenatchee River until, as one pioneer expressed it, "the whole river was running through sluices," most of their placering centered farther up the creek at the site of the present town of Blewett. The settlement remained a small one, however, as it was extremely isolated and for years could be reached only by trail.

In 1879, after C. P. Culver, who stopped there on his way to the Columbia

River, found a gold quartz ledge—the first lode mine in the area—many miners moved into the district, not only to placer but also to crush in arrastres the oxidized ores found on the surface of the hills. With the building of a wagon road over the Wenatchee Divide from Cle Elum the same year, pioneer farmers were able to pack vegetables into Blewett and sell them to the miners, and freighters could more easily ship the crushed ore out of the camp. With this outlet and with the discovery of more gold ledges and lodes, large-scale mining was carried on for some time, especially after the Chelan Mining Company built a twenty-stamp mill on Peshastin Creek. A gold rush to Blewett Pass in 1890 brought more activity to the district until, at its peak, Blewett shipped 10,000 bricks a week! But the boom passed, fire destroyed most of the old saloons and cabins, and the big mill began to fall to pieces. When we took the highway up Peshastin Creek to the site of the gold camp, the few log and tinder-dry frame buildings were scattered about through the heavy underbrush, and the ruins of the old stamp mill stood out as the most conspicuous landmark. The mountainsides were riddled with tunnels, at the entrances of which there spilled dumps of waste ore gay with wildflowers.

THE SWAUK AND LIBERTY

SOUTH of Blewett Pass the highway enters the valley of the Swauk and for miles follows the meanderings of a creek whose bars once attracted hundreds of miners. Here in the fall of 1867 a prospecting party, who were following Indian trails through the eastern foothills of the Cascade Mountains to the Peshastin district, found particles of gold on the bar of the stream. Benton Goodwin, one of the number, although ignorant of its appearance, suspected that the yellow grains were gold; but his comrades were not impressed and went on, merely calling the location Discovery Bar. In the fall of 1873, Benton Goodwin, N. T. Goodwin, and others who had been with the discovery party six years earlier, returned to the Swauk. At first they were disappointed in their search; but Benton again found the first colors—a small nugget worth a few cents—and, forgetting his supper, panned gravel from a pothole in the river until, within an hour, he had five dollars worth of coarse dust and nuggets.

Next morning the party divided and began to work the creek both above and below their camp. They tried to keep their discovery a secret, but Indians passing back and forth along the trails spread the news, and within two weeks the usual pell-mell rush began. Before newcomers arrived, however, the original location party had recovered $500 to $600, and one of them, with no tool but a butcher knife, had dug out $150 in a single day. Before long the creek was staked for twenty miles; but the only gold found in quantity was in the vicinity of Discovery Bar.

The first winter all but fifty men left the placer camp. Although many returned in the spring, they were unable to strike any sensationally rich leads. At the end of three years during which an ounce a day per man was the average yield, most of the mines were abandoned. During the following years men trickled back and found the lost leads; and, when the district boomed in the early eighties, the placer camps of Liberty and Swauk Prairie became the centers to which the prospectors gravitated whenever they left their claims. Nuggets worth from $20 to $1,120 were not infrequently taken from the Swauk, and for a time there was such good pay in the coarse gold washed from the bars that the men discarded the fine gold as not worth saving. Near Liberty, on Williams Creek, nuggets worth $65 were occasionally turned up; old timers remember one pan that ran $1,365!

By the time a mining district was organized in 1884, many Chinese had followed the white prospectors to the profitable diggings and were hard at work recovering gold from the gravels. The *Engineering & Mining Journal* for May 31, 1884, shows the attitude of the whites toward them:

The miners of the Swauk Mining district have held a mass meeting and notified all Chinese that they must leave the diggings at once. It is not yet known what the Chinese will do. There are a large number of Celestials in the district, and should they refuse to go, trouble is anticipated.

We found Liberty a small and exceedingly quiet community hidden in a narrow valley near the head of Williams Creek, a stream whose banks and bed for several miles have been churned by placering into successive mounds of boulders, only partially overgrown with grass and hardy shrubs. Swauk Prairie, a few miles farther south on the Swauk, has melted away. Once beyond the endless piles of placered earth and stone, the country opens out into wide rolling farmlands—the Swauk prairie itself. Swauk Creek, the remains of its fabulous bars as yet uneradicated, is a monument to placering.

SULTAN

THE last of the important gold centers of Washington can best be reached from the west coast. We therefore drove east from Everett, straight toward the rugged Cascades. Sultan, or Sultan City as it was called by the fifty miners who petitioned for a post office in 1885, stands at the junction of the Sultan and Skykomish rivers, and was named for Chief Tseul-tud of the Snohomish tribe. Highway No. 2 streaks by its main street, from which the first unbroken view of the massive Cascades fills the horizon. The early settlers in

INDEX, WITH MOUNT INDEX RISING BEHIND THE TOWN

MAIN STREET, SULTAN, CASCADE RANGE AT RIGHT

Sultan had no such vista of the mountains, for the townsite was so smothered by dense forests that lamps were lighted by three o'clock every afternoon.

The sands along the river banks attracted placer miners in 1870, and all through the seventies locations were made by both white and Chinese prospectors. The Chinese, the first to arrive, were the last to leave, harvesting their meager washings of gold after the white miners had left. One claim, the Hong John, belonged to nine of them and was entered on the county records and signed in Chinese characters by each one.

John Nailor and his Indian wife, who were among the early arrivals, owned a claim at the mouth of the Skykomish River and near it built a cabin which for years served as a stopping place for travelers. In 1881 Nailor ran a ferry across the river and in later years, when the town boomed, built and operated the Pioneer Hotel.

The boom in Sultan did not begin until 1887-88, when mining companies began hauling in machinery, light draft steamboats pushed up the river as far as the camp, pack trains freighted to and from the mines, and stages brought in passengers and mail. The *Snohomish Eye* of July 27, 1888, tells of a mail stage, caught in a burning slashing. The driver escaped only by cutting the horses loose from the coach, fastening the mail pouch securely to one of the horses, then mounting and dashing ahead through the flames.

When the railroad was built through the valley, Sultan City became a supply station for the thousand men employed in construction crews. By 1892 the town was in full fling, with three steamers docking daily at its landing and seven stages rolling into town from Snohomish. The sawmill was turning out cribbing as fast as it could, and nine saloons and a host of eating houses were serving swarms of ravenous laborers. The railroad reached Sultan that fall, and with the departure of the work crews the peak of the boom was over.

Bolstered by the fur trade, which was unaffected by the silver question, Sultan weathered the 1893 panic; and, when in 1894 and 1895, the Sultan River Mining Company spent thousands of dollars at Horsehoe Bend to divert the course of the water and thus uncover the old river bed, placering, which had begun at the Bend in 1884, was resumed. Sultan, Startup, and the other towns along the river are lively communities today, with lumbering their major industry.

GOLD BAR

AT GOLD BAR, six miles east of Sultan, traces of dust were found in 1889. Later, when it became a construction camp for the Great Northern Railroad, many Chinese laborers were brought in. Anti-Chinese feeling ran high, and one night a serious riot was averted only by the quick action of a construction engineer, who shipped out all the Orientals, each hidden in a newly made coffin! Gold Bar is now a logging camp.

INDEX

FROM the time we left Sultan I had watched a jagged, saw-toothed mountain profile ahead—a section quite unlike the rounded summits and timbered slopes of the rest of the range. I was sure that Index lay at the foot of those rocky fingers, and just nine miles after we left Gold Bar we entered its wide, shaded streets. No better description of Index exists than that written by Mrs. Persis Ulrich, who saw the camp grow and fade.

When I came here with my parents and two sisters in 1889, we were compelled to travel by boat from Tacoma to Snohomish, and from there by smaller boats to Wallace (now Startup) and by pack train to the present site of Index, where my father had purchased a squatter's claim, upon which he filed a placer claim, to make sure that it would not be taken away from him. There was a small cabin on the claim but father soon built a larger place, to be operated as a hotel for the accommodation of prospectors headed for the diggings at Silverton, Galena and Monte Cristo, and the surveyors who were at that time blazing the trail of the railroad over Stevens Pass to the Sound.

By 1891, reported rich strikes of ore back in the mountains and the nearer approach of the railroad brought so many persons to Index, as my father had named the community, that he built a much larger hotel—quite a pretentious one for the time and place—and this became a very busy place.

I was then only 11 years old, but a very busy small girl. Few people today realize the amount of work that had to be done in an hotel in those days. There was, of course, no running water, and each room upstairs had its wash bowl and pitcher, to be cleaned and refilled every morning. And the kerosene lamps needed to be cleaned and filled, besides the making of beds and changing of linen. Every day was wash day—sheets, pillow cases, towels, table linen, etc.—and no washing machine either, just the good old wash board—rub-a-dub-dub. I helped, too, in the dining room at meal time. There was little time to play.

During the boom, with homes and business houses going up as rapidly as boards could be sawed and hammered into place by scores of carpenters, ours was an exciting town to live in. It was far from beautiful, however; for the streets were piled with lumber and the din of hammer and saw continued from early morning until late in the evening.

By 1893 the population had grown to 500 people, with from 800 to 1,000 prospectors and railroad men constantly coming and going. A tent hospital had been established and in that year my sister, Lena Gunn, taught the first school in a room of a private house. A small school house was built the next year.

As seemed inevitable in all pioneer towns, Index was visited in the summer of

1893 by a fire which destroyed virtually the entire town. The fire was started by a boy who, reading in bed, upset a candle. No lives were lost, but two little girls were badly burned. My father immediately rebuilt the store and hotel, and others also replaced the burned buildings.

But by now the railroad had been built and the workmen had departed, and the mining excitement died down.

About 1897-98, mining excitement again grew and the discovery and development of the Sunset copper mine brought renewed life to Index. Two new hotels, a drug store, and other mercantile establishments were built. A newspaper was established, giving us our first opportunity to read of local happenings in our own town. Many were the stories run in this little paper about the vast interests about to invest in mining—great concentrators and stamp mills to be built, railroads to carry the ore, etc.—but most of these rumors never materialized. [Belle Reeves, ed. *Told By The Pioneers.*]

Just as the mines were about ready to pay dividends, the Klondike rush depopulated the camp and it lay dormant for several years. With the revival of mining in the early 1900's, copper was mined as well as gold; and the Sunset (the largest of the old mines), the Index-Bornite Copper mine, and the Calumet were all worked. Index still has a population of about two hundred.

The striking snowcapped peaks—Mt. Index, Mt. Persis, and Gunn's Peak—rise so sharply from the valley on all sides of the town that I found it hard to concentrate on the houses, the stores, and the general appearance of the place. No doubt in the nineties, as Mrs. Ulrich says, it was far from beautiful; but of all the towns I have visited in the state Index is to me the most pictorially satisfying.

GALENA AND MINERAL CITY

YEARS before the town of Index existed, there was mining on Silver Creek. From Index we climbed the dirt road through timber nine miles to the Galena Guard Station, situated less than a mile from the site of Galena, the scene of mining excitement in the eighties, where a camp was finally platted in December, 1891. Left from the Guard Station, a forest road winds four miles farther up Silver Creek through a steep-walled canyon whose sides are pitted with abandoned mine shafts, to the site of Mineral City, another empty ghost town. There the road ends and only a faint trail fights its way the next nine miles to the ghost of Monte Cristo. All three camps rose quickly to a peak and then died out, but as late as 1898 ore from their mines was sacked and shipped to the Everett smelter.

Hans Hansen located the first gold on the west side of the Cascades on Silver Creek in 1874. Soon afterwards a prospector named Johnson discovered croppings of iron pyrites on the banks of the same creek and, believing them to be gold, hurried to Snohomish to report his strike, which he named the Anna. Excited by his news, men hurried back with him and at his insistence began to work the gravels with arrastres, but were able to recover only $2,000 to $3,000 from the sands. In 1882 Elisha Hubbard hacked a trail through the timber and relocated the Anna. As soon as it, the Trade Dollar, the Morning Star, and other mines were located, two camps, Mineral City and Galena, were laid out and flourished briefly.

On the trail to one of these camps a packer was leading a horse loaded with several boxes of dynamite, when the pack slipped and the frightened animal bucked it loose, scattering sticks of explosives all over the ground. The mules, which made up the rest of the train, stopped when they came to the sticks and began eating them greedily. The remaining miles to the camp were without mishap, but the bug-eyed packer kept well in the rear of his pack-string. He did not dare hit any of the animals all summer for fear of a delayed explosion.

MONTE CRISTO

SITUATED at the end of the trail, across a mountain range, in an extremely inaccessible primitive area drained by the Sauk River, Monte Cristo once outshone other nearby camps. The first mineral discoveries were made on July 4, 1889, by F. W. Peabody and Joe Pearsoll, who, while scanning with field glasses the view from the summit of Silver Tip, a peak in the Silver Creek district, detected a large vein of ore which they took to be galena cutting through a mountain range to the east. Breaking through timber to the spot, they located two claims and called them the Independence and the 1776.

By 1890 miners who had followed the two to the mountainside named their camp Monte Cristo and erected the first cabin on '76 Creek. During the summer they cut a trail to Silver Creek, thus connecting their isolated camp with Mineral City and Galena. By the end of the year the wealth of the district was recognized; for not only the Monte Cristo, Pride of the Woods, Pride of the Mountains, Mystery, Justice, Sidney, Philo, and Rantoul lodes had "proved up," but Peabody and Pearsoll had sold their holdings for $7,500 and $40,000 respectively. Investors then interested the Colby-Hoyt, or Rockefeller, syndicate in the mines. After the latter had obtained controlling interests in the properties, they began development on a big scale, building a railroad to the town in 1893 at a cost of $2,000,000, and the following year a 200-ton concentrator from which two carloads of ore a day were shipped to their smelter in Everett.

By June, 1894, Monte Cristo was a thriving town with a population of several hundred, a volunteer fire department, a school with thirty-four pupils, three hotels, and a partly built jail. Unknown parties tore down the jail just before its completion and threw the lumber in the river. In its place appeared a notice headed by a skull and cross bones and signed "4-11-44," the Vigilantes symbol: "We want no jail here. If you want to ride a rail go ahead."

All through the nineties and early 1900's the mines produced well. Even after the Rockefeller interests closed down other investors worked the best properties for a time. The Pride, Mystery, and Justice mines alone shipped ores valued at more than two and a half millions. Now only neglected trails lead to the camp from whose mines poured a total of over $6,000,000.

8. *Strikes Beyond the Siskiyous*

Oregon

OREGON'S MINES lie in two widely separated parts of the state, and their discovery occurred a decade apart. The southwestern diggings, in Josephine and Jackson counties, were located in 1851; the eastern Oregon mines, in Grant and Baker counties, in 1861. Of the southwestern towns Sailors' Diggings and Browntown have the most colorful history, but Jacksonville is the most picturesque to visit. In eastern Oregon, Auburn is only a site, but even its mounds of placered boulders take on meaning for anyone with a knowledge of the camp's history. Although Sumpter is half deserted, its surroundings offer a vivid picture of placering. Cornucopia is really two towns, each the result of a different mining company's regime. Sparta, which rests on a high, dry plateau, is no longer able to live by its mines, which produced only when water from the big ditch flushed the sluices and arrastres.

Sooner or later anyone discussing Oregon's mining history asks, "Where was the Blue Bucket mine?" All authorities agree on the main points of the "lost mine" story, but none is certain where the incident took place. So far as is known a party of emigrants, described as Meek's Cut-off Party, crossed central or eastern Oregon in the fall of 1845 on their way to the coast. While camping on their journey they found pieces of yellow metal in the stream bed or at the grass roots. According to one version they paid no attention to them, but some of the children in the party filled a blue bucket, such as was carried by wagon trains, with the yellow pebbles and took them along for playthings. A second variation states that the men in the party went fishing to replenish the company's larder and that, as they needed sinkers for their lines, they picked some yellow stones out of the stream and hammered them flat on their wagon tires. They threw them away after their fish were caught and next day broke camp and moved farther west. Not until they reached California and saw gold there, did they realize that the yellow pebbles were nuggets.

293

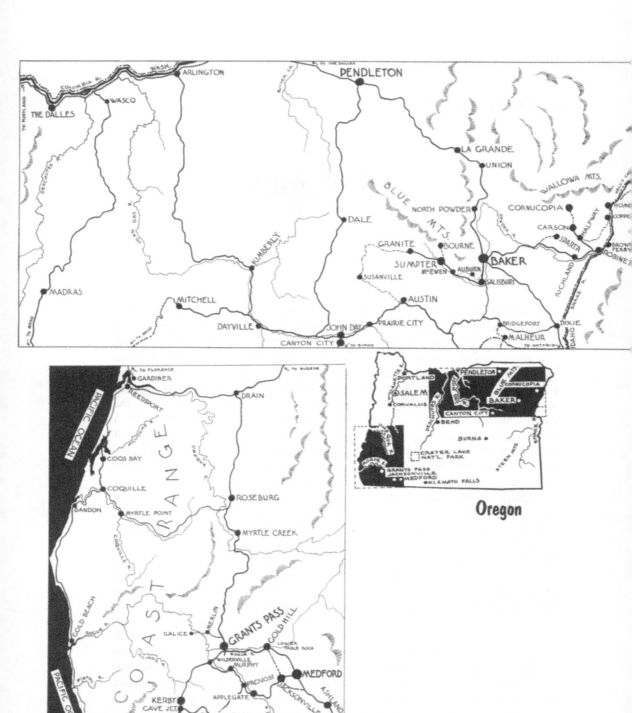

Oregon

Some say that the "blue bucket" comes into the story because the party, after finding the gold, discarded such a pail on the campsite. Still another version insists that a William F. Helm, whose family was part of the Meek party, had his wagon, ox yokes, and camp utensils painted blue, and that at the camp where the nuggets were found, one of the buckets was accidentally left behind. The stories agree that a party did camp, and did find gold, and either left a bucket by the campsite or took specimens of the gold with them in such a bucket. Later on in California they realized what they had overlooked.

The next phase of the story deals with the search for the gold, and here no two versions agree as to the exact location of the campsite. It is most often thought to be in the John Day country on a tributary of the river, or near Canyon City; but one version places it near the Snake River in Idaho. It is known that in 1868 Meek, the leader of the original party, led a group of thirty men back over the trail, searching for the diggings. Since then other expeditions and many lone prospectors have followed every clue, but the elusive nuggets and the battered bucket are still to be found.

The beginnings of mining in southwestern Oregon in the fifties are interwoven with the California gold rush and with Indian wars, which lasted until 1855. In 1848, when the Territory of Oregon was created, the Territorial Governor was also Superintendent of Indian Affairs, and thousands of Indians, many of whose tribes were unknown to him, came under his jurisdiction.

Prior to the California rush, the natives had seen few white men except trappers and solitary travelers, living just about as nomadically as the Indians. Settlers and prospectors, on the contrary, were intruders, and the Indians watched with mounting alarm the ever-increasing, crawling processions of men and beasts who fought their way through the wilderness into their domain. The races looked upon each other not only as intruders but also as enemies and sought to exterminate each other, with the result that the Indian attacks upon lone prospectors were no more savage than the white man's retaliation.

During the summer of 1851, when prospectors explored the valley of the Illinois River and found gold on Josephine and Canyon creeks, the Indians were temporarily quiet; for Governor Joe Lane, as Indian Agent, had called a council of the Rogue River chiefs in June, 1850, and had made a treaty with them which lasted a little more than a year. Lane gave them slips of paper which warned white men not to harm them. These the Indians showed to any traveler they met, saying at the same time, "Joe Lane," the only English they knew. But the truce was short-lived, and before the year was over, Indian raids caused a general exodus of miners from the valley.

Companies of volunteers from the mines joined those already assembled at Table Rock and went on what turned out to be a disastrous expedition against the hostile tribes. The Indians, as a rule, had rifles superior to those used by the small companies of troops, billeted in widely scattered forts. The government issue had a shorter range and was less accurate than the long rifles commonly carried by the pioneers. The Indians had equipped themselves with the longer type, either by stealing them from the settlers or by trading wives for them—the price of a woman was always reckoned in guns. The Indians were, therefore, a real danger from 1851 to 1855.

Josephine County was organized in 1851. Josephine Creek and Josephine County were named for Virginia Josephine Rollins, a girl of seventeen, who was the first white woman in that part of the country. She came with her father to the mines near Waldo, and when he returned east, she went on with her brother to California.

Another Josephine is sometimes confused with Rollins' daughter. This Josephine was the daughter of Leland Crowley, who in 1846 was moving north with his family and a party of emigrants into what is now southern Oregon. Josephine died en route and was buried under a large oak tree on the bank of a stream. The ground over her grave was trampled by oxen to obliterate all signs of the interment, for fear Indians might discover it and rob the body of trinkets. The party passed on, unaware that shortly after their departure Indians found the grave, dug up the body, and hung it from a limb of the tree. Another party of emigrants discovered it and reburied it. Nearly ten years later, during the Indian war of 1855, a fort was built near the bank of the creek and was named Fort Leland, after the Leland party. Six Indians who were captured during the skirmishes were hanged from the big oak tree and their bodies buried in the same grave with the remains of the young girl. The stream became known as the "creek where the graves were found," or Grave Creek.

SAILORS' DIGGINGS (WALDO)

SAILORS' DIGGINGS! The name has a gay and carefree sound, unlike Last Chance Gulch and Disappointment Creek. But, with the thousands of prospectors who filtered into the northwest after the California gold rush, why should sailors have been among the first to pan gold in what is now Oregon? So far, the answer had eluded me.

On the way south to Grants Pass we slowed the car near Myrtle Creek to make way for an old, bearded prospector riding a burro and leading a pack horse loaded with pick and pan. As we were about to pass him, he turned on to a trail leading into the hills. He was using what was the common means of travel through these hills just one hundred years ago, and I was delighted, though startled, to encounter him on a busy paved highway.

At the office of the *Grants Pass Courier* I asked the editor, Mr. Amos E. Voorhies, if he could tell me anything about Sailors' Diggings. He supplied me with the paper's Golden Anniversary edition, of April 3, 1935, which covered the history of the entire area. By the time we left Grants Pass to drive to the Diggings I was bursting with information.

Whether the sailors deserted a ship anchored at Crescent City, in northern California and fled inland, fired by stories of gold, or whether they left a wrecked schooner on the beach and worked their way across the Coast Range is uncertain; but there is no uncertainty about their discovery of gold in 1851 on the headwaters of the Illinois River near what is now the southern border of Oregon. Some authorities consider this the first discovery while others say that the first nugget was found on Josephine Creek, west of Kerby, a few months earlier by a party from California who had crossed the Siskiyou Range, and that the second was uncovered on Canyon Creek in the same vicinity. All agree, however, that the three finds were made in the summer of 1851, and that soon afterward prospectors swarmed up every gulch in the region.

Sailors' Diggings, later to be known as Waldo, was laid out near the Illinois River. Just as it was beginning to grow, the placers on Jackson Creek were discovered, and away went the men to the new strike. Then John and Philip Althouse washed pay dirt from a stream which lay between the two camps, and a new rush began. Next came the Fry brothers' discovery of gold on Sucker Creek; and so it went with almost every creek and branch in the area, until within two years camps had sprung up at Kerbyville, Althouse, Browntown, French Flat, Grass Flat, Allentown and Jacksonville.

During this period millions of dollars worth of gold were skimmed from the surfaces of flats and streambeds, by the most primitive methods of panning and sluicing; for not until the seventies were the higher banks washed down by hydraulics. To bring sufficient water to the placers, ditches were dug by hand. Though the one at Sailors' Diggings cost $75,000-$80,000 for its fifteen-mile length, it not only paid for itself within a year but also paid dividends to the stockholders who financed it. Dr. Watkins, an early resident of the area, said of the enterprise, "Many parties who live sumptuously every day owe their fortune to their connection with the Sailors' Diggings Ditch Company."

Sailors' Diggings was on the stage road to Crescent City on the coast and lay in a hollow between low hills. Like any boom settlement it was full of saloons, stores, hotels, cabins, and tents; yet it differed from most because patches of the hillsides were planted with peach and apple trees and grape vines, supplied with water from the near-by ditches. These green spots were in striking contrast to the barren, washed hills which surrounded them. By 1855

Sailors' Diggings, with a population of 500, was the largest town in the area, and in 1856 it was made the seat of Josephine County. Oregon's first mining code was drawn up at the Diggings and read:

Know all men by these presents: That we, the miners of Waldo and Althouse in Oregon Territory, being in convention assembled for the purpose of making rules and regulations to govern this camp. Resolved, 1st. That 50 cubic yards shall constitute a claim on the bed of the creek extending to high water on each side.

Resolved, 2nd. That forty feet shall constitute a bank or bar claim on the face extending back to the hill or mountain.

Resolved, 3rd. That all claims not worked when workable, after five days, be forfeited or jumpable.

Resolved, 4th. That all disputes arising from mining claims shall be settled by arbitration, and the decisions shall be final.

E. J. Northcutt,
Chairman.

During the fifties, when all the camps in the mining district were flourishing, the activities of Waldo (the later name of Sailors' Diggings) and Browntown, on Althouse Creek, were identical. Miners and gamblers went back and forth between the two and, on week ends especially, spent thousands of dollars worth of dust on the various pleasures which each camp afforded. Many Chinese were engaged in placering the creeks and were either ignored or mistreated by the white miners and merchants. "Packed like sardines," they were shipped into the camps in freight wagons and lived in abominable quarters close to their diggings.

A. B. McIlwain, who ran a store in Waldo, had many Chinese customers. They were wily purchasers. When they came to get gum boots, to wear when placering, they insisted on seeing at least one pair of every kind and size. More than once, when the store was crowded, McIlwain, impatient and angry, picked up a boot and beat his customer over the head with it. As late as the 1930's McIlwain's store and express office stood on the townsite, as well as his home and a livery barn. The store, which was the largest of the three buildings, was made of stuccoed concrete blocks, supported by a stone foundation. It had iron doors and shutters and a basement storeroom.

On our trip to Sailors' Diggings we drove south from Grants Pass to O'Brien, a small town almost on the California line. Here a marker indicated that the Diggings were four miles away. Turning east on a dirt road, we clattered over a plank bridge whose every board was loose, drove past several ranches, and finally saw beside us, on the right, a placered-out gulch. In the middle of the gulch, on an island of boulders and sod, stood one dilapidated building which I took to be McIlwain's store. As I sketched the concrete skeleton with its sagging, corrugated-iron roof, gaping doorways, and stone foundation, I was disturbed by the almost complete obliteration of Oregon's earliest mining camp.

ALLENTOWN

EVEN less remains of Allentown. Not far from Waldo, Allentown grew up at the same time, near the mouth of Allen Gulch. As the first winter approached, the men who expected to "hole in" until spring held a meeting and, realizing that their supplies would not stretch until packers could again reach the camp, decided that some of their number would have to leave. One man whom they ran out camped not far away in Butcher Gulch, and lived comfortably on the game he shot. In February he went over to Allentown to see how the camp was getting on and found most of the men starving. From then on he kept them supplied with meat, and they were more than glad to welcome him. During his exile he located the Deep Gravel mine at Butcherknife. Every time he left Allentown to return to the mine, some of the men tried to follow him to the location. When he knew they were watching for his departure, he pretended to get drunk and to fall into a stupor. Thus he remained until they grew tired of waiting or until the last man joined him on the floor. Then he sneaked out and hurried back to his mine.

The first church in the district was built at Allentown in the sixties. Not far from it, southeast of the Paterica mine, was the cemetery. Father F. X. Blanchard, a French-Canadian priest, came over the hills from Jacksonville on specified dates to conduct services. He was very popular with the "boys," and whenever he visited them, he smoked a pipe and carried a bottle of whisky from which he offered his friends a nip. He never urged them to join his church; yet when he held service, the place was filled, and he received larger donations from the visitors than from his own communicants.

During the sixties and early seventies the placers in Scotch, Butcher, Fry, Sailor and other gulches were worked to bedrock, the men standing in deep, wet pits and pitching shovelfuls of rock and gravel high above them into the flumes. In addition to the stream deposits, the men worked the surface material on adjacent slopes. By the middle seventies hydraulics replaced hand placering, and began to wash the deep gravels with considerable success. Once the giants (or big nozzles) started at the beginning of a season they never stopped, night or day. One giant could wash down more gravel in an hour than a man could placer in a week. With a good mine a profit of $60,000 could easily be made in a season. All the old channels were worked by hydraulics in the seventies and again around 1900. After the giants were through, no trace of many of the camps was left.

BROWNTOWN

I ASKED a garage man at O'Brien if we could reach the site of Browntown, another of the old camps that flourished when Waldo was at its peak.

"Sure," he said. "Drive to Holland. Then take the road that goes between the hotel and the store and go three miles. There's nothing left of the old town, but there's an outfit working up at the mine and they go in and out all the time."

At Cave Junction we swung east as far as the dirt road he had described, and then turned south until we reached the few buildings that comprise the heart of Holland. Three men sat basking in the late afternoon sun outside the store. I asked them about the road because I was not sure whether the narrow tracks that squeezed between two buildings and seemed to end in a barnyard were really the road we wanted.

"Yep, that's her," said one. "What's yer business up there? Do you want to see the boss at the mine?"

"No, just Browntown," I replied and drove off along the trail, which soon wound around the edge of a mountain, climbing steadily all the way. The roadbed was sticky where trickling springs had seeped into the red clay, and there were no turnouts for passing cars. Two miles, three miles, and still no town or flat on which a town could stand—only a steep mountain, and a gully below. Finally the road led into a clearing surrounded by buildings, obviously belonging to some mining company. There was no one around, so, a little baffled, we turned back toward Holland. Halfway down I noticed a big mine dump far below on a gravelly meadow. Perhaps that was the flat, consisting of several acres at the mouth of Walker Gulch, where Browntown once stood.

The camp was named for Webfoot Brown, a pioneer of the camp. It was the center to which the miners from Sucker and Bolan creeks and from Deadman's Gulch came to gamble and drink and spend their dust. All the other camps in the district were so close together that the miners constantly traveled the trails between them on business and pleasure. In the early fifties, when the boundary line between California and Oregon was still undetermined, the residents, to be on the safe side, voted in both places. A survey of the boundary was not begun until 1867.

Brown and DeLamater ran a general store in Browntown, and on days when they took pack trains, loaded with merchandise, to the mountain camps they left a young girl in charge of the business. Although she had orders to wait on all customers, the Chinese often outnumbered the other patrons, and, realizing that she could not handle them alone, she would lock the door when she saw them coming. Often swarms of angry Orientals milled around the building for hours waiting for it to open.

The Chinese were tireless workers, turning and removing large rocks left in the river channels, and cleaning the old gravels again and again. Even though they were forced to buy their claims from white owners and worked for twenty-five cents a day, they could save enough fine gold to make their existence worth while. They lived frugally on tea and rice and skunk cabbage, which they raised in little plots of sand along the bars. When one of them died, he was buried on a hillside and left there until his body could be shipped back home to China. Red candles lighted the spot, and offerings of food were laid beside the lonely grave.

A fort was built at Browntown, as protection against the Indians who were harassing miners on Althouse Creek and in the Illinois River valley. The Indians killed three men near Holland and two others in Deadman's Gulch. The latter had carried their rifles with them for protection and had placed the guns close to where they were working; but the Indians crept up stealthily, grabbed the guns, and killed the miners with their own weapons.

In 1858, when the camp was at its height, 500 men lived in or near it, and a smaller population occupied Hogtown, a sort of suburb. When one of the boys who had gone "outside" to be married returned with his bride, the women-starved miners gathered at the stage station to welcome the couple. As the bride stepped from the coach, the miners threw their hats in the air, fired their revolvers, and yelled like Indians so convincingly that she, not understanding the tribute, clung to her husband in terror.

If there were calm moments in Browntown, they are forgotten; for it was brawls and fights that I heard about from the three cronies at the Holland store. Bill Nicholas, a gambler from Waldo, was challenged to fight a duel by a gambler from Browntown. Both men faced each other in the street, held a handkerchief between them with their left hands, and carried their weapons in their right—Nicholas having a bowie knife and the other gambler a pistol. When the gambler fired, Nicholas dodged and escaped the shot, and at the same time drove his knife into the other man's shoulder. Miners then separated them and declared the duel over.

Nicholas was a small man, but even Waldo's bully did not faze him. The latter announced that he would whip Nicholas the next time they met in Waldo and, soon afterward, followed him into a store and tried to pick a fight with him. Nicholas coolly seized a ten-pound weight from a scale and threw it at the bully's head. The latter reeled but continued to taunt his victim until

Nicholas hurled another weight and struck him in the stomach. The blow knocked him down, and in the future he let the little man alone.

Tom Ryan was the terror of the gulch, and Maxwell, an Irishman, was a favorite among the boys because he sang well and often entertained them of an evening over their drinks. One night while he was singing, Ryan, who was in the same room, seized a stool and cracked a young chap over the head with it. Maxwell interfered; then he and Ryan fought until, after giving each other a bloody pommelling, the two men were separated. Ryan rushed to the door to get away as fast as possible but hesitated for an instant to look back at Maxwell. The latter then picked up a hot stove lid and threw it at him, splitting his lip and gashing his face badly. The miners again rushed to the aid of the men and cared for each of them—but in separate cabins.

GRASS FLAT

GRASS FLAT, three miles above Browntown on the west side of Althouse Creek, occupied a "grassy bench opposite the south end of Frenchtown Bar." Besides saloons, a butcher shop, cabins and tents, it had a small hotel from which General Joe Lane, the first governor of Oregon, made a political speech in 1859.

That winter it snowed almost constantly for seventy-two days. The cabins at the head of the creek were completely buried, and tunnels connected one with another. A miner who had been celebrating in Browntown staggered home over the crusted snow and fell down his own chimney just as his partner was cooking dinner!

FRENCHTOWN BAR

FRENCHTOWN BAR, or French Flats, was below Grass Flat and was famous for the amount of gold yielded in the fifties from a strip of ground thirty feet wide and twelve hundred feet long. On the bar stood a log hotel and store to which the miners and toughs went for relaxation after long hours at the rockers and in the pits. Large quantities of dust were sent out by mule train, and packers used every strategy to protect their precious cargos. On one occasion a packer was hired to carry a large amount of gold over the mountains to the coast, that it might be shipped out of the country. For several days before his departure, three suspicious looking strangers lounged around the Frenchtown hotel, and he felt sure they were going to overtake him on the road and rob him. One night he publicly told the innkeeper to be sure to wake him at 4 A.M., so that he could get away early. He went to his room, crawled out the window shortly afterwards and hurried to his mule, which, already packed, was hidden in a clump of trees. He reached his destination safely; and the three strangers, who had left town quite early, came back later in an ugly mood.

Two Frenchmen owned a claim on the bar and worked it together. One day, after a quarrel, French John quit and went to his cabin. When his partner, on his way home, approached, French John threatened to shoot him if he walked past the door. Amused at the absurd threat, he continued and was promptly killed. Two Browntown storekeepers, to whom French John owed $600, persuaded the justice of the peace not to bring him to trial, for they feared that a miners' court would hang him and that if he swung, they would not be able to collect their debt.

KERBY

As WE DROVE back to Grants Pass, we stopped at a small village some ten miles north of O'Brien. Kerby, or Kerbyville, as it was first called, was one of the early camps in the area. It was named for James Kerby, a pioneer who took up a donation claim there in 1855. Two years later the townsite was platted with the name Napoleon written on the plat, and the Territorial Legislature voted that the town be so known. No one liked the name, however, and in 1860 the Legislature voted to restore its former name.

In 1857, when the county seat was moved from Waldo to Kerbyville, the Masonic Hall was used as a courthouse. The same year bids were taken for a two-story jail, to be constructed of "hewn timber one foot square," with doors six inches thick. Kerbyville remained the seat of Josephine County until 1886, when Grants Pass won the honor. For a few years this camp was the mecca toward which thousands of miners gravitated. It had two hotels—the Eagle and the Union—two stores, a livery stable, a blacksmith shop, a barber shop, a billiard parlor and many saloons. Even when other camps overshadowed it, it was, as long as the circuit court met there twice a year, a place of importance, and its residents were proud of the saying, "There's no law the other side of Kerby."

Kerby had an unusual killing in 1864. By that time the town had two merchants whose stores were at opposite ends of the community and between whom a feud existed. Whenever Ephraim Hughey, who ran a hotel in conjunction with his store, saw his rival in his end of town, he ran him back into his own territory. One day he went so far as to draw a line in the dirt, beyond which he dared his opponent to go. This so infuriated the other man that he sharpened a cheese knife, stuck it in his trouser leg, and strode across the boundary. The men met and the usual chase began, but, as the two ran round and round a billiard table, the man with the knife stopped short, and holding the blade in front of him, waited until Hughey, unable to swerve in time, plunged into it. The next day the Kerby cemetery had a fresh grave.

One pioneer woman arrived by ship at Crescent City and from there made the trip overland to join her miner husband at Kerby. Since there was no wharf at Crescent City, passengers had to jump from a chair hanging over the side of the vessel into the bed of a wagon as it was driven through the water beneath the chair. In this case, because the captain was impatient to be off with the changing tide, the woman had to jump, with a three-year-old child in her arms, as the horses drawing the wagon went by at a trot!

GOLD HILL

SOUTHEAST from Grants Pass the highway follows the Rogue River, the scene of much early placering. Before bridges spanned the Rogue, prospectors forded the river to reach the bars. When the water was high, they swam across, holding tight to their horses' tails. For this reason, the crossing near the city of Rogue River was for many years called Tailholt. At Big Bar, above the town of Gold Hill, eight or ten men found pay dirt in 1851, and as miners from California straggled over the mountains into the Rogue and Illinois River valleys, the gold camps which we had just visited sprang into existence.

Gold Hill, a completely modern town today, grew fastest after the placering had stopped and the quartz lodes were discovered. White quartz deposits carrying free gold were located in 1859, and $400,000 worth of rich ore was extracted by 1860. But the ores were so "pockety" that even the twelve-stamp mill brought in at great cost from San Francisco could not pay expenses for long, and one by one the mines became idle. Later quartz properties include the Gold Hill Pocket, the Roaring Gimlet Pocket, and the Tin Pan.

JACKSONVILLE

AT MEDFORD we turned west for five miles to visit Jacksonville, the best preserved town dating from the 1851 discoveries. In December of that year, only a few months after gold was found on the tributaries of the Illinois River, two young men uncovered pay dirt on Jackson Creek. They reported their luck to James Cluggage and J. R. Poole, packers, who were traveling through that part of the country. These men did a little prospecting while their animals were feeding and washed gold from what became known as Rich Gulch, half a mile north of the original discovery. Little more than a month later, in February, 1852, so many men had poured into the region that the gulches were completely "staked out," and newcomers had to prospect the

CITY HALL (LEFT) AND OLDEST HOUSE (SLANT ROOF), JACKSONVILLE

OLDEST HOUSE AND MASONIC HALL (RIGHT), JACKSONVILLE

hills or work tributary streams. By midsummer a rush from northern California brought the total number of men in the vicinity to 1,000.

As a direct result of the discoveries on Rich Gulch, a mining district was organized; a second was formed in 1853, when placer discoveries were made along the Applegate River, ten miles south of Jacksonville; and a third was created in 1854, after coarse flakes of gold had been found in a small stream eight miles to the south, where the camp of Sterlingville sprang up.

As soon as the miners pitched their tents beside the creeks, two packers from Yreka, California, opened a trading post on Jackson Creek and brought in by mule train a small stock of tools, tobacco, whisky, and other essentials. By the end of the year cabins, and then houses built of clapboard, began to replace the miners' tents. But not a pane of glass was to be had, and cotton drill served to cover window openings.

On the heels of the miners came the gamblers and the sporting element, and with their arrival crime increased. In self-defense a people's tribunal was organized to try cases and administer swift justice to offenders. Its most drastic action was directed against a gambler named Brown, who had shot and killed a miner without cause. Brown was quickly convicted and hanged, and his grave is still under a tree near the Presbyterian church. The next spring the citizens elected an alcalde, who was to preside over criminal trials and to have unlimited power in settling disputes over mining and water rights. His biased verdicts made him so unpopular that the miners, in order to get rid of him, created a supreme court and overruled his decisions.

When the first child was born, on August 27, 1853, "every miner and trader considered himself a godfather" and presented the baby with lavish but inappropriate gifts. That same year Adams Express Company, of San Francisco, opened a branch office, and the first term of District Court was held in a wooden building which stood on the site of the present courthouse. During the cold weather pack trains could not get through the high-piled snow, and supplies of flour and salt ran very low. The people, however, shared with each other what little they had; and for years afterward, in remembrance of the "terrible winter of '53," they sent or brought small gifts to those in town who had divided salt with them.

The first years of Jacksonville's existence were colored with numerous Indian assaults. One summer afternoon a frightened horse with an empty, bloody saddle dashed through the dusty street of the town. A posse of men galloped off in the direction from which the horse had come and returned with the body of Thomas Wells, who had been shot by Indians. Panic followed, for no building was bulletproof, and the supply of arms and ammunition was low. That night guards were posted on the outskirts of the village, but no attack occurred. A few days later another man was shot. The first Indians to enter Jacksonville after these killings were two young boys. Their errand was innocent enough, but the spirit of revenge so inflamed the men of the town that they seized them as spies and hanged them.

Late in 1855, when the Rogue River Indian war broke out, all work was suspended, as ranchers and miners gathered with their families in fortified log houses. Many frightened settlers hurried to Jacksonville; but when the men began to leave, to fight in the volunteer companies which were being organized, and did nothing to fortify the town, where the women and children were congregated, the women held an indignation meeting from which all men were excluded. Just what went on at the meeting is not known; but the men resented it and after dark hung a petticoat from the top of the flagpole in front of the express office. In the morning, when the women discovered it, they demanded that it be lowered; but not a man would pull it down. Not until they threatened to chop down the pole was the petticoat returned to them. Grasping it triumphantly, they dispersed, having won round one of the fight. The next morning, two effigies—one male and the other female—hung high and out of reach from the branches of a large tree. The male had been hung higher than the female, to indicate male superiority, and the figures dangled there for weeks. The men had won round two!

In Jacksonville's Historical Society Museum is the picture of a pioneer woman, Mrs. George Harris, and an account of how she and her husband came to Oregon in 1852 and built a cabin near the new camp. On October 9, 1855, a group of about twenty Indians were seen approaching the house, and Mr. Harris rushed to get his gun. Just as he returned to the door, however, he was shot and killed, and his little daughter was shot in the arm. The mother seized a double-barreled shotgun, fired at the Indians through the cracks in the cabin, and temporarily stopped the attack on the house. In the meantime, the girl, feeling faint, climbed to the attic and lay down on a bed. Her mother did not know of the girl's wound until she saw blood trickling down through the rafters. She looked after her daughter and then went back to her task of defending the house. After dark, she and the child slipped into the chaparral and hid. In the morning a detachment of dragoons, under the command of Major Fitzgerald, came riding by after a band of Indians. Mrs. Harris left her hiding place, with the girl in her arms, and told them her story. She was given aid and was taken to Jacksonville by some of the company, while the others rode on, looking for the Indians and also for her son David, who had gone to a neighbor's before the attack and had not returned. He was never found.

The Indians were placed on reservations in 1855, and the warfare between them and the white men in the valley was over.

Jacksonville's first newspaper, the *Table Rock Sentinel,* appeared on November 24, 1855, and continued to publish under that title until 1858, when the name was changed to the *Oregon Sentinel*. It had as competitors the short-lived *Jacksonville Herald,* during 1857, and the partisan *Southern Oregon Gazette,* which in 1861 became "so disloyal to the United States" that it was barred from the mails.

Before 1857 only trails connected the growing little city with other towns in western Oregon and northern California, but that year "the demand for a road to Crescent City" made the legislature pass an act locating one between Jacksonville and the California line. A stage ran regularly over the route, and within two years a mail and passenger-coach service ran once a week between Jacksonville and Portland.

After the mines in eastern Oregon had been discovered, in 1861, and the camps established in the John Day, Powder, and Boise river valleys, enterprising farmers saw in these settlements a source of income for themselves and printed the following notice in the Jacksonville *Sentinel* of January 28, 1863:

Ho, For the John Day, Powder River and Boise mines! Now is the time to agitate the getting up of ox teams, loaded with flour, bacon, etc., for the mines above named. How many enterprising farmers in this valley will fit out from one to three ox teams, to go by way of the lakes, Lost River, etc., to start sometime in April? A number of loaded wagons passed over this route last spring. What has been done can be done again. If the northern mines are about to prove a permanent thing, now is the time for farmers of Southern Oregon to strike for a market for all their surplus products. If they do not look out for themselves, no one will do it for them. The millers are vastly interested in this enterprise, and will, no doubt do their share. All classes are to a great extent interested, but the farmer and miller more especially. Let us hear from some of the large farmers on this important subject.

Farmer

Each year the community grew until, by November, 1867, it was the "liveliest and most flourishing burg between Marysville and Portland," with a population of nearly 800 and a list of business establishments too long to enumerate. Such "extras" as Dr. Overbeck's Bathrooms, which supplied "Warm, Cold and Shower Baths on Sundays and Wednesdays," a photograph gallery, a milliner's shop, a soap "manufactury," a broom factory, and a first-class banking house set it apart as an up and coming city. According to the *Sentinel* of November 16, 1867:

What Jacksonville will be in the future, when the rugged 'Siskiyou' has been spanned with an iron girdle, and the iron steed comes snorting down the valley from across the mountains . . . it is hard to say; and if its prosperity and population increases as steadily as it has done for a few more years, we need fear no rival in this end of the state.

The Chinese population was large, and the *Sentinel* of April 22, 1868, tells how

Sheriff Reams, while collecting China taxes this week on the left hand fork of Jackson Creek, came to a cabin where he heard pounding on the inside. He broke the door open and found a Chinaman making bogus gold dust . . . dust so near the specific weight of gold that a casual observer would not detect the fraud. . . . Dealers will do well to be on their guard, Nothing can be done with the Chinamen, as our law attaches the punishable crime only to those who offer counterfeit coin or dust for sale or exchange.

At the next session of the Circuit Court the docket was "unusually long" and included the case of "Levins and Abrahams charged with riot and violent abuse of Chinamen."

A smallpox epidemic swept the town in 1868. At first it was thought to be only chickenpox, and many were exposed. Pitch logs were burned in the streets, in the belief that the dense smoke from them would provide protection against the disease; but after the first death, a pest house was set up south of the town, to care for the cases. As the disease spread and the number of deaths increased, many citizens fled, leaving most of the nursing to the Sisters of St. Mary's Academy (who had opened their school in 1865). For two months the epidemic raged and then, after forty had died, it wore itself out.

The following year a cloudburst tore down Jackson and Daisy creeks, flooding the business section of the town "waist deep in water 'till you could float a canoe anywhere." Two fires were the next catastrophes. The first, in 1873, destroyed $75,000 worth of property in less than an hour; the second followed the very next year.

After the placer diggings had been exhausted, quartz lodes were found, and the Opp, the Town, the Spaulding, and other properties were developed. Years later a dredge reworked the channels and bars that had already yielded so much. The early residents mined the gravels in their backyards or in the streets, and, when good pay dirt was uncovered, houses were moved or drifts were run under them. Beneath part of the town ran a labyrinth of tunnels dug by the Chinese between 1853 and 1880.

The oldest brick structure in the town, and one of the oldest in the state, is the J. A. Bruner block on Oregon Street, built in 1855 and used as a fort during Indian scares. Across from it stands the two-story I.O.O.F. hall, with its iron doors and shutters. It was built in 1856, was occupied as a synagogue in 1865, and is still used as a meeting place by Jacksonville's Lodge No. 10. To the left is a one-story brick building fronted by an arched colonnade, and just below the cornice in faded letters are the words "The Table Rock Billiard Saloon."

In its palmy days the United States Hotel on California Street boasted that it provided a stove or fireplace in every room. In the big two-story building President Rutherford B. Hayes spent one night during a stagecoach trip through the valley. Stories differ as to the amount the management charged the President, some fixing the sum at $75 and others at $150; but in any case it was an exorbitant sum, and the noted guest paid it under protest. C. C. Beekman's one-story, false-fronted, frame bank building, with its sagging, corrugated-iron awning extending over the sidewalk, looks much as it did in 1862. During the years when it was the leading financial institution in southern Oregon, its gold scales weighed $31,000,000 in dust, and its safe stored hundreds of thousands of dollars worth of gold awaiting shipment by Wells Fargo Express coaches to San Francisco and Portland.

The Wells Fargo office, on a side street, would pass for a brick residence if the sign over the door did not identify it. The old Brewery in the western end of town stands near the spot on Jackson Creek where gold was first discovered. Its beer was in great demand during the seventies and eighties, and its brewer was famous all over the state for his product. An old residence that is probably the least distinctive in appearance is the so-called Flag House, whose wooden exterior is completely void of ornamentation. When, on June 11, 1860, a Southern sympathizer displayed a Confederate flag, no man dared touch it for fear of a shooting fray between the Northern and Southern factions in the town; but Mrs. Ganung, a doctor's wife, walked resolutely from this house and cut down the banner.

Jacksonville resembles a New England village because of its white houses with ornamental barge boards, picket fences, and carved gateposts and because of its white, steepled churches, half hidden by big trees set out as seedlings when the meetinghouses were new. The Methodist church was built in 1854 with funds donated, according to one story, from one night's take at the gaming tables. It was the first Protestant church to be built west of the Rocky Mountains, and its melodeon was brought around the Horn to Crescent City and from there by muleback. Until the Presbyterians erected their church in 1881, this building was used by both denominations. Services were held for the first time in St. Joseph's Catholic church in 1858.

Several blocks from the heart of the business section, set back in a square by itself, is the imposing two-story courthouse. It was built in 1883, when the population was 1,200, and it served the county until 1927; but as Medford's population increased and Jacksonville's declined, the larger town became the county seat. The building was then closed for several years until a grange decided to use it for meetings and entertainments. In 1948 the voters of the county levied a tax of half a mill to raise money for the restoration of the building, that it might be used as a museum and as headquarters for the Jackson County Historical Society. Nevertheless, although Jacksonville is proud of its past, it lives in the present. Remove the automobiles from its streets and the neon signs from its stores, and it would seem to belong to the seventies and eighties; yet, although it is a quiet town today, its 800 citizens keep it very much alive.

The eastern Oregon mines lie in the area of the Blue and the Wallowa Mountains, and we made the town of Baker our "center" from which to explore them. By a happy accident, we chose a motel whose proprietor knew just the man I needed to show me the region. Mr. Oscar E. Coombs, a retired mining engineer, knew every foot of country for miles around and was delighted to revisit the places I needed to see.

AUBURN

AT SIX A.M. he picked me up, and we started for Auburn, the site of the first mining camp in that part of the state. A few miles out of Baker and before we turned off the highway to reach Auburn, Mr. Coombs pointed out Griffin Gulch, where the first gold was found, and beyond it, the hollow that held Auburn. Just a short distance from the road a historic plaque claims to mark the site of the camp; but Mr. Coombs scarcely paused in front of it and started down a steep, rough road to the bottom of the gulch. Through the trees I saw piles of gray stones and a few weathered boards. Old foundations and hollows showed where cabins had once stood, bushes grew from the old dumps, and underbrush and young trees hid the other relics of the past.

In August, 1861, Henry Griffin and a large group of prospectors left Portland for the Oro Fino mines, in what was then Washington Territory. When one of their number, a man named Adams, began to talk of the lost Blue Bucket mine and said he was certain he could find it, he was made captain of the expedition, and the others followed his trail over the Cascades and through dry deserts to the headwaters of the Burnt River. Suspecting finally that Adams did not know where the diggings were, they threatened to kill him if he did not find them within one more day. He tried to escape, but was caught, put on trial, and sentenced. He was to be stripped of everything but the clothes he wore and to leave the group. Furthermore, if he dared to follow them, the members of the party had the privilege of shooting him.

The next day the party divided. The majority went northwest and ultimately discovered the John Day mines; the smaller group worked northeast, prospected the head of the Burnt River, and crossed over into the Powder

River valley. On October 23, 1861, they crossed a ridge near Elk Creek and camped in a gulch where Griffin, who was a member of the party, sank a three-foot hole in the gravel and struck bedrock. He shoveled gravel from the hole into his pan and washed out a handful of gold flakes.

Griffin and three others then built a cabin and prepared to spend the winter at the diggings; but before snow closed them in, Littlefield and Schriver went to Walla Walla for supplies, which they planned to buy with their dust. Their trip was filled with adventure and hardships. On the way to Walla Walla they had to fight through a pack of wolves, and on the return journey snow lay fourteen feet on the trail. As they had no feed for their horse, they turned him loose and packed in the supplies on their own backs. The horse followed them into camp, living on twigs and the bark of trees.

In April, 1862, Littlefield stumbled on to a camp of prospectors from Walla Walla who were looking for the Powder River mines. These prospectors had been drawn to the mountains by stories of the wealth they contained. By June several hundred men had pitched their tents along the gulches, and every day brought new arrivals. On June 13th the town of Auburn was laid out as one long street, from Freezeout Gulch to Blue Canyon, with building lots set off on both sides of the winding thoroughfare.

Until William H. Packwood and Ed Cranston reached the mines, early in June, each with a stock of goods, only two makeshift stores served the mounting population—one at Blue Canyon and the other at Griffin's Gulch. The two men soon brought in another train of supplies and then drove cattle in from the valley and set up a meat market.

By the middle of June a mining district had been organized, and an informal election was held to select a recorder for it. The two candidates were Packwood and E. C. Brainard. When everyone was assembled, the chairman of the meeting told Packwood to stand on one stump and Brainard on another. "Now boys," he called, "all who want Packwood for recorder go over there, and all who want Brainard go over to him."

"Come on, all you Webfooters, here's our candidate," shouted an Oregonian.

"Over here, all you Tarheads and vote for this man," yelled a Californian.

The vote was taken, and Brainard won.

Water was scarce until the Auburn Canal Company's ditch brought plenty to the gulches, but the rate of 25 cents an inch was considered exorbitant. The canal company said they could reduce the rate if they sold more water, so in 1865 the miners voted on the question of admitting Chinese to the camp. The verdict was, "No Chinese." Later the issue was reconsidered, and the Chinese poured into the district.

As the town grew, every available piece of ground was staked off, and

1,270 claims were recorded within the first year. Forty stores and 500 cabins were built, all of logs. In the fall a sawmill was set up, and the price of lumber dropped from $100 to $60 per thousand. During that winter, when snow lay three feet deep on the trails, John Wilson, a freighter, was asked by the canal company how much he would charge to haul lumber from the sawmill to French Gulch. He replied $2.50 per thousand. The company thought the price too high and refused to give him the order. A few days later the company's agent again asked him his price. It had snowed in the meantime, and the trails were worse, so Wilson said $5. Again the agent left in a huff. A third price of $7.50 was turned down; but on the fourth visit, after more snow had fallen, a price of $9 was agreed upon. The canny freighter made $50 a day until the job was completed.

Many stories are told about the camp's early years. A young lady spent the last night before reaching Auburn at a ranch a few miles away. The next day she dressed in her best clothes so as to make a proper entry into the community, whose population exceeded that of Omaha, from which she had come. The first building she passed before reaching the town was a storehouse belonging to Iva Ward. Over its door a sign read, "I. WARD"; so she stopped at the next cabin and asked how far it was from there to the second Ward of Auburn. The men in the cabin roared with laughter and told her it was four miles, but they did not tell her that they were referring to Mr. Ward's son, Sam, who lived four miles away in Auburn. Later, at a party, he was introduced to her as the "Second Ward of Auburn."

Before Baker County was formed, miners' courts tried and settled criminal cases. Two partners who lived in a tent were poisoned with strychnine, which was found to have been mixed with the flour from which they made their bread. One of the men died, and suspicion rested on a Frenchman with whom they had quarreled. He was arrested, and since the nearest legal court sat at The Dalles, 250 miles away, the question arose as to where he should be tried. Public opinion decided that he was to be tried in Auburn. A court was set up, and in due time he was convicted and executed.

Another man killed his partner but claimed that he did it in self-defense. No one believed him, and when two men who were going to The Dalles offered to deliver him to the authorities there, their proposal was accepted. The men never reached their destination, but they were reported to have been seen mining together on the Salmon River.

By 1862 Auburn was the seat of Baker County, and by 1864, when its population reached 5,000, it was the second largest town in the state.

Instead of returning to the highway after leaving the site of Auburn, we went ahead on the old stage road over the mountain. Mr. Coombs knew every turn, for he had driven back and forth from Sumpter to Baker over this road in the years when he was Sumpter's dredge superintendent. He pointed out Poker Creek and California Gulch and Road Agent Rock, near Union Creek, behind which the bandits hid when they robbed the stages, and he slowed down when he reached the abandoned log station where the coaches stopped—their first halt out of Baker.

As we crossed Auburn Summit (elevation 5,000 feet), he told me about a rancher who used to live on this road and of the Chinese miner who had a placer claim near by. One night the rancher robbed his neighbor's sluice boxes and was caught red-handed by the owner. The enraged Oriental beat the man to death with a shovel. The murderer was never caught, and even the white men of the community said the thief had it coming to him.

After twisting through trees for several miles we left the timber and looked down on Sumpter Flat, a big dredged-out valley. Back of us were the Elkhorn Mountains and the lakes from which water was taken and ditched over the divide to Auburn, a gravity flow all the way.

SUMPTER

As we approached Sumpter, Mr. Coombs kept pointing out landmarks. "This valley used to be all pine trees," he said. "Now it's all dredged out. Everything was gold here. The tailings are two miles wide—the width of the valley. Two dredges went up the center of the creek, and a dragline worked the edges that the big dredge left. The Powder River Gold Dredging Company owned property along the river from Sumpter downstream for four or five miles. Their boat had a capacity of 5,000 to 6,000 cubic yards per day. Dredging recovered $12,000,000 from this valley alone.

"Where those stone foundations and that slag pile stand, on the far side of the valley, was a custom smelter. It was built in 1903 and ran until 1908. Then the cost of fuel and fluxes plus the high cost of labor forced it to shut down.

"Do you see the Huckleberry Pass road over the saddle of that mountain? Years ago I drove my mother over to Sumpter, and I pointed out that road to her and told her where it went. When I got through, she said, 'Son, I drove over that trail before you were born.' My mother came into this valley in 1867, from John Day on the way to the Coeur d'Alenes. She was one of the first women to go into that country. When she came in here, she was in a wagon; when she went back, she was on horseback and carrying a baby six weeks old."

In the fall of 1862 a small group of Confederate soldiers, on their way to California, found gold on the site of Sumpter. They built a log cabin and called it Fort Sumpter to commemorate the fall of the famous fort. Their discovery

MASONIC HALL AND SCHOOL (ALL THAT ESCAPED FIRE), SUMPTER

ORE MILL, HOMESTEAD, ON THE SNAKE RIVER

attracted others to the location, and a placer camp grew up along the banks of the stream. For years white miners cleaned the gravels and recovered quantities of gold. When they began to leave for richer diggings, hundreds of Chinese came in and worked the same glacial drifts that had yielded so many colors.

In the seventies and eighties the deep mines were discovered in the mountains above Sumpter, more miners came into the district, and Sumpter became a trade center as well as a placer camp. With the completion, in 1896, of the Sumpter Valley narrow-gauge railroad between Baker and the camp, mining operations increased; for the ores could now be shipped economically to the smelters. The next few years were the most productive for the area. During this period of prosperity Sumpter boomed and grew from a small camp of a few hundred to a town of 3,000. The year 1900 marked the peak of the boom, with an output of $8,943,486 from thirty-five mines. All this time dredging operations were being carried on in the Powder River valley and up Cracker Creek. The total yield from both placers and deep mines is set at $16,000,000.

When we drove into the town, Mr. Coombs showed me where the stage station had stood when three coaches left every morning for the camps of Granite, Canyon City, and Bourne, and where the *Sumpter News* had been published.

"We had two banks," he said proudly, "and each had its two-story brick building. We had an Opera House and a Masonic Hall and two hotels— the Capital and the Spencer—and twenty-seven saloons. The lumber mill cut 30,000 feet a day—the railroad handled as much timber as it did ore. Then came the big fire of 1916, and all the upper end of town went up in smoke. About all they saved was the schoolhouse and the hospital.

"I was working below town on the dredge when the fire broke out. As soon as word reached us, we stopped the dredge, and all of us men rushed up to help fight it. It started in one of the hotels from a cigarette, which the cook had been smoking when he fell asleep."

By this time we had driven above the town and were looking down over it. "Right down there was one of the water hydrants," he went on. "I saw the firemen couple two hoses on it, and just then the flames leaped across the street, burned the hoses off, and left the hydrant open; so the water supply was lost, and there was no way to control the blaze. They dynamited a few houses to stop it, and they thought they could save the big Lutheran church; but a spark caught the cupola. Whoosh!—the whole church was in flames. The schoolhouse was so near the church we had a hard time saving it; one side got a little scorched.

"After the fire a good many people moved away, and those that stayed tore down lots of old houses. The fire burned clear across the river," he added.

"We're going across the bridge, so you can see where Granite Creek and Mc-Cully Fork and Cracker Creek meet and form the Powder River.

"Before we leave here I'm going to take you up Cracker Creek aways. I want you to get some idea of the extent of placering in this area. These hills have been mined over more than once, and the tailings are ten to twenty feet deep. The dumps are overgrown with trees and bushes now, for work quit up here thirty to forty years ago; but every bit of this earth is pulverized dirt and rocks, stacked as you see it, by hand—it's not the work of a dragline. The Chinese worked down near the creek. The tailings on the other side of the road are their work.

"A saloon and a boardinghouse used to stand here, halfway between Sumpter and Bourne. Here's the hull of old No. 2 dredge, waterlogged in this shallow pool. I built this boat, and when the hull was finished and the floor boards planed smooth, we gave a dance on it."

Leaving Sumpter, we drove back to Baker over the abandoned narrow-gauge roadbed of the Sumpter Valley Railroad, now a well-kept highway.

"The next time you're over this way, go up to Bourne. It's six miles up in the mountains, and it was a lively gold camp in the seventies. After that the deep mines were discovered—the Columbia, the E. and E., the Golconda, and the Red Boy—but promoters ruined them, partly by distributing a newspaper that printed exaggerated descriptions of the properties to attract suckers to invest their money. Most of the mines were closed down by 1906. Than a cloudburst struck the town in 1937 and washed lots of buildings away, but there are still a few up there.

"Someday you should come back to Baker, and I'll take you south to Malheur City. It's in the middle of the barest, hottest desert you ever saw. But you ought to see the ditch they built in 1873—it's 101 miles long and hand dug. It had the largest channel of its kind in the west, big enough to float rafts of logs on for buildings at the mines. It carried 2,500 miners' inches of water, and it cost $250,000.

"The camp goes back to the sixties and seventies, when placer gold was discovered, but the last time I saw it there wasn't much left but a store and the post office; and Marysville and Eldorado, up the canyon from it, were completely gone. When the placers were going strong, the men used to give the kids pinches of dust for candy.

"Another old gold camp is Canyon City, in the John Day country, southwest of Baker. The placers on the John Day River were discovered in 1861 by a party from The Dalles. Half of them started back to The Dalles, but all but two were killed by Indians. The following year the rush to the placers began, and men came in from as far away as Washoe. A good many settlers came too and took up farms in the river valley. The miners built dams and rigged up pumps to get water to the gravel beds, and by 1866 the John Day mines had produced $1,500,000.

"John Day was a scout with the Astor party in 1811. When the expedition was working its way through the Snake River country, he got sick and had to stay behind with two men to look after him; but one of them died from exposure, and Day and the other man finally struggled through these Blue Mountains and followed a river west of here down to the Columbia. They were played out by then, and the trip was too much for Day. He went crazy and died soon afterwards. The river he traveled down to reach the Columbia was named for him, and so was the mining camp."

The next morning we again left Baker and this time headed into the sunrise over sage-covered hills until Mr. Coombs stopped the car on one of them.

"Look down there. See those ruts? They're the Old Oregon Trail where it first entered the Baker valley. The tracks are pretty hard to see, now that the sage is getting high, but you used to be able to trace them from here for about half a mile. Now look at the dump and mill on the right, on the shoulder of that hill. That's the Virtue mine, one of the oldest around here. Its total output ran to three millions, and it's been operating most of the time since its discovery in 1862. Four years later James Virtue bought it, and since then it's changed hands often. The Virtue Gold and Silver Mining Company put up a twenty-stamp mill, and there's an outfit doing some development work over there right now. There's gold in these dry hills; but it's in pockety shoots, and it's coarse grade. Three miles southeast of the Virtue is the White Swan mine. It worked well in the eighties, but it's been idle for a long time now. Lester Balliet became president and manager of the company in 1900. He was full of ideas and started the White Swan Concert Band. When the snappy green and white uniforms that he ordered for it arrived, he gave a champagne banquet for all thirty members."

When we entered the gorge of the Powder River, Mr. Coombs pointed to the narrow, winding stream and said, "Do you remember yesterday I showed you where Cracker Creek and McCulley Fork made the head of this river up at Sumpter, and how all the way back to Baker we rode beside it? Today you'll see the mouth of it at Robinette, where it joins the Snake."

We left the Powder just before its junction with the Snake and turned north into Pine Valley, a rich farming country developed by the Mormons. I'd been watching the high gaunt peaks ahead—the Wallowa Mountains, locally called the Eagle Mountains. As soon as we left the town of Halfway and turned north, we drove directly toward them. The last five miles were a 1,200-foot climb, with Pine Creek below and tall trees so close to the road that it was impossible to look far ahead to the rugged granite mountain tops.

OLD HOTEL, CORNUCOPIA

MAIN STREET, CORNUCOPIA

CORNUCOPIA

IN BOISE I had seen a picture of Cornucopia—a faded photograph that showed an almost vertical mountainside with a mine and its buildings stuck against it high above the timber. Far below, on a flat, lay a town of several streets and many buildings, all easily seen because there were so few trees. Another photo showed the main street full of people and buggies and wagons. I had also seen a copy of the Idaho *Weekly Avalanche* of October 2, 1875, which advertised:

Stage to Cornucopia

J. W. Moore has just put on a stage to Cornucopia and will carry passengers and freight between Silver City and that place and return. Fare $10. Mr. Moore guarantees grub for the trip by the payment of $15. The next trip to leave the 9th of Oct.

As we drove into the town we passed rows of gray, boxlike company houses, empty but so new that I was distinctly disappointed. Mr. Coombs kept on driving—across the creek, past a big mill, and back down the west side of the gulch to the original portion of the camp. On either side of the dirt road among the trees were frame houses, many with porches or surrounded by sagging picket fences. All of them looked weather-beaten, and all were empty. Several stores lined the street near a three-story false-fronted frame building, whose porch was so shattered that it looked as if a pile of jackstraws had been dumped in front of it. Some of these places must have been standing when *The West Shore—A Family Paper devoted to Literature, Science, Art and the Resources of the Pacific Northwest* described the camp in its September, 1885, issue by saying that it contained

"one nice frame house" and many "tents and log cabins, built rather hastily to accomodate the first rush. The town can boast of *five saloons, one store,* two restaurants, blacksmith shop, barber shop, butcher shop and livery stable; also a lodging house, which, while neatly kept for a young town, is hardly patronized enough, as the traveling class in such camps objects seriously to too close confinement and prefers camp life."

"I'm going to take you down to see Mr. Snyder," said Mr. Coombs. "He grew up here. He can answer all your questions."

We stopped at the far end of the street in front of a newly painted, two-story frame house, surrounded by a beautiful garden. While I admired the delphiniums that grew six feet high, Mr. Snyder talked about the camp as he had known it.

"I went to school here in 1912," he began. "The schoolhouse was an old saloon built up against the hill. Later on when the camp grew, they built a two-room school. Then in 1938, after the Cornucopia Gold Mines Company took over and all the new houses were put up, they built the school that you saw down on the flat. The old town was about a quarter of a mile from here. When I came here, the post office was where the barber shop is, and that three-story, false front up the road was the Keller Hotel.

"The Union and Companion claims were the first ones found around here, back in 1878, I think they said. The placer gold in Pine Creek was found about the same time, but most of the lode mines weren't discovered until the 1880's. All the mines and prospects were within four miles of camp, up the mountainsides or on branches of Pine Creek. You should see the prospect holes all over Granite Mountain and Red Mountain and in Norway Basin on Simmons Mountain. The Last Chance mine was higher than the Cornucopia— its outcrop lay at 7,000 feet."

Pointing as he talked, he showed me the location of each of the important mines—the Queen of the West, the Mayflower next to the Cornucopia, the Jim Fiske vein near it, the White Elephant, and the Wild Irishman.

"The boom years here were 1884 to 1886, when the Union Companion was the big gold property," he continued. "Besides the eighty or ninety men on the mine payroll, there were lots of woodchoppers cutting mine timbers and fuel for the boilers. Wherever you looked, you saw prospectors, like ants on an anthill. Their tents went all the way up against the mountain. There must have been 800 people in town then.

"The Cornucopia Mining Company bought the Union Companion for $60,000 in 1895, and they put up a twenty-stamp mill. The mine produced more than a million up to 1903, and the company put most of it right back into developing the property. It closed down right after that, and people moved away, until only about three hundred were left. It's been worked on and off ever since. There's one company here now, you know.

"Did you show her the Cornucopia Granites when you drove in?" he asked, turning to Mr. Coombs. "They're the big gray peaks back of the town. They're sure pretty in the winter after a storm. It snows about seventy-five inches a year up here. Seems that we used to have worse weather than we do now. I've heard about 'old time' winters when the snow piled up to 100 inches. Did you see the ladders nailed to all the cabin roofs? If you didn't shovel snow off them, they fell in from the extra weight."

HOMESTEAD

"WHICH road do we take to Homestead?" I asked, as we retraced our steps to the town of Halfway.

"We could go back the way we came and follow the Snake from Robinette," said Mr. Coombs, "but it's much longer. The road down Pine Creek was a bearcat the last time I drove it, but we'll try it."

The first five miles were fine, and then we saw the marker: NO CAUTION SIGNS BEYOND THIS POINT. "Just as I thought," said my driver, as we began the sixteen-mile stretch of one-way road. It squirmed beside Pine Creek all the way to the Snake River, not dangerous, just slow; and the more we dropped down toward the river valley the hotter it got. We passed six ranches, all but one deserted, and we saw nothing but dry hills and bare rock upthrusts as we neared the river. Time after time during our descent we flushed from their hiding places crested grouse, brush hens, mourning doves, and rabbits.

At Copperfield on the Snake River we left the country road and drove on an abandoned railroad grade to Homestead. When the tracks were torn up, the roadbed was turned into a highway, easy to drive and close enough to the river to give superb vistas of the grim vertical cliffs that hem in the banks, and of the high, rolling, green hills behind them, dotted with widely separated ranches.

The first signs of mining at Homestead were an empty mill beside the highway and a mine property with buildings and tram, set in a canyon up against the mountains to the west of the river. Broken machinery and more mine dumps lay within the town itself, but none of the people at the general store looked like miners, and I wondered when this camp had been active. "Here's a man who can tell you," said the storekeeper, introducing a lean rancher, who had driven in to see if the parts he had ordered for his tractor had arrived yet. From him I found that mineral deposits were known to exist in the vicinity in the early nineties, but that the Iron Dyke mine was not discovered until 1897. It was located originally as an iron mine to provide flux for the ores on the Idaho side of the river; but the iron was only a capping and below it lay the copper belt. Other copper deposits were then found near the surface in the exposed greenstones of the area, and several more properties were developed. The Koger group was found northwest of the Iron Dyke and only half a mile from town, while the MacDougal group of twenty claims was five miles north and 3,000 feet above the river. No quantity of ore was shipped out until 1909, after the completion of the railroad from Huntington to Homestead. During World War I the high prices paid for metals made the district boom, but since then its development has been limited by its inaccessibility, the hard basalt rock in which the deposits lie, and the present lack of railroad facilities.

SPARTA

As we neared a fork in the road which led back to Baker, my driver swerved to the right and started the long, hot, five-mile pull up to the Eagle valley in which the mining town of Sparta is situated. The hilltops were dry as tinder, the trees were few, and it was oppressively hot and dusty.

A Dutchman named Kooster struck pay dirt at the head of Maiden Gulch in 1863, and the camp that grew up nearby took his name. A rival camp called Gemtown was located a mile west of Kooster, but by 1870 Kooster had absorbed most of Gemtown and had changed its own name to Sparta.

The district, 1,600 feet above the Powder River, was full of quartz outcrops, some of which were "lousy with gold." One of the richest claims was on Shanghai Gulch and belonged to two brothers named Leikens, who worked their rockers and hauled their ore with oxen. At the end of two years they had cleaned up $35,000. Another lucky pair, the Harkleroder brothers, found $50 in their first pan and washed $10,000 from a piece of ground 200 feet by 60 feet.

Although all the gulches in the vicinity were auriferous, they were undeveloped as the men had to jack their dirt long distances to water and to their rockers. Then W. H. Packwood engineered the building of the Sparta Ditch to bring water from Eagle Creek to the mines. Charles M. Foster (United States surveyor), Jim Virtue, Bowen, and Cranston all helped with its construction. The ditch was twenty-seven miles long and was built to carry a capacity of 3,000 miners' inches of water. After its completion in 1871, the placers began to produce lavishly. It is estimated that $5,000,000 was taken from mines in the Sparta district. The richest placers were those in Shanghai, Moultrie, Maiden, Thorn, Blue, Murray, Rattlesnake, Sawmill, and Lion gulches, and these were worked by miners who tramped back and forth between Sparta and their diggings.

In the early eighties Postmaster C. W. Estabrook persuaded the merchants and some of the miners to send their gold dust through his office by registered mail. For more than two years $15,000 of dust was sent out by him each week. The many Chinese who mined near the camp sent their earnings to San Francisco through the mail, swelling the weekly shipment by $4,000.

When the gulch placers began thinning out, the men hunted for quartz veins, some of which had been found and worked in the early days by hand mortars and small arrastres. As mine shafts were sunk deeper into the earth, the country rock became harder, and it was almost impossible to separate the ore from it. As a result, fewer miners returned each season, and the newspaper inquired:

Where lie the lodes that fed the placers? Have the quartz ledges been pulled up by the roots and all the yellow fruit shaken off into the placers? Is there nothing left in the lodes? We shall see.

Very little is left of the town except a few houses and barns, a stone store built in the seventies, and the post office. The postmistress, Mrs. Mabel Binns, knows the history of the place and relates it vividly.

She spoke of the ditch and of how it was dug by 500 Chinese. She went to the door and, pointing out the sloping meadow where Chinatown had been, she said: "We had 3,000 people here once, and 1,000 were Chinese." She told how they had poured into the diggings after the richest placers were washed out and how they successfully scoured the bedrock. But the white population robbed and murdered them and finally drove them out. She mentioned the "lynching tree," and she produced a yellowed sheet from a storekeeper's ledger which showed what the customers wanted—the Chinese bought rice and gum boots, the white men bought gallons of whisky. Her lively description was in sharp contrast to the town before me, whose lodes are neglected and whose population has almost faded away.

Nevada

THE MINING state of Nevada has silver, gold, and copper camps tucked into every corner of its broken terrain. Some hide within the creases of its eroded, barren mountains; others sprawl over the baked and arid wastes of its deserts. Some, like Aurora, are old and deserted; some, equally old, like Austin, are busy towns with growing populations. Most were silver camps, like Tonopah; yet within twenty-five miles was Goldfield. The state's earliest camps, just east of the Sierra, have been called suburbs of California, because the discovery of precious metals in the area was made by prospectors who scrambled east from their California diggings in the ever-widening search for gold. At first the men were dissatisfied with the silver they discovered, but its later values surpassed their wildest dreams. Gold Canyon and Sun Mountain lured them on in the sixties; the Comstock lode made millionaires of them in the seventies; the stock market broke many of them in the eighties; and from then on, depleted mines, low-grade ores, and richer strikes in other parts of the state drew them away from the Washoe Valley. Today, huge copper properties have eclipsed the equally huge silver holdings of earlier decades; leasers rework many of the old mines successfully, and renewed activity is returning to more than one seemingly worked-out district.

I decided to "do" Nevada chronologically, beginning with the Virginia City area, the center of the earliest mining activity, then exploring Austin and Aurora, both camps of the early sixties; and finally visiting the desert towns of Tonopah, Goldfield, Rhyolite, and Searchlight, which were not developed until the first years of the twentieth century.

In Carson City we visited the Capitol, the State Library, and the defunct Mint, originally built to handle Comstock ore; it serves now as a unique historical museum, in which a realistic mine is "Exhibit A." Our first trip outside the city took us north to Washoe City, established during the winter of 1860-1861

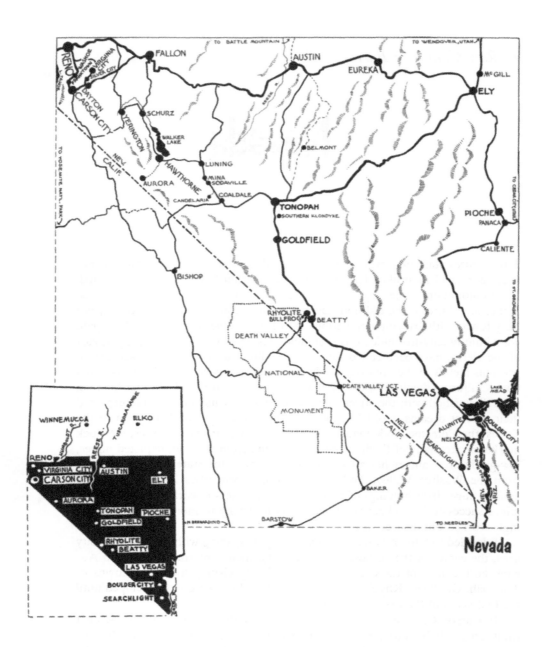

Nevada

and achieving a population of 2,500 by 1864. In 1951 a few farmhouses, a cemetery, a weed-grown stretch of railroad track, and the familiar brick Wells Fargo office with iron shutters and panelled doors were the only traces left. Only the foundations of a stamp mill, to which ore from Virginia City was hauled by the Virginia and Truckee Railroad, remain at the site of Ophir City, and Franktown has completely disappeared.

Close to the site of Franktown is the Bowers Mansion, a monument to Eilly Orrum and Sandy Bowers, whose mine at Gold Hill paid off so well that in 1862 the couple toured Europe and then returned to enjoy their new $300,-000 home. Neither was used to riches. In Gold Hill's early days, Eilly had run a boardinghouse and Sandy had been a miner; but their combined property, the Bowers mine, made them the first millionaires on the Comstock. Sandy died when he was thirty-five, and his widow lost not only their fortune but the mansion as well. When the new owner learned of her death in 1903, he arranged for her body to be placed beside her husband's and daughter's behind the still beautiful tree-shaded home.

VIRGINIA CITY

HAVING visited the landmarks close to Carson City, we approached famous Virginia City by the new well-graded road that twists and climbs the canyon to Mount Davidson. From the valley floor to the edge of the city, all that one sees are deep canyons, mine dumps with rusted shaft houses, and range upon range of distant mountains. Suddenly Virginia City appears, clinging to the side of the mountain, its widely scattered groups of buildings interspersed with crumbling dumps and bleached foundations. Directly ahead are the Fourth Ward school and C Street, the main thoroughfare. From one or two levels on the mountain above, Victorian houses peer primly through trees and shrubs. Below C Street the mines, more buildings, and the railroad tracks make up another group, and in the distance rises the spire of St. Mary's in the Mountains.

When we reached the city, hardly anyone was on the street; but before we left cars were parked bumper to bumper, the sidewalks of C Street were full of tourists, and little knots of visitors were exclaiming over "quaint" relics, taking pictures, and gravitating toward the raucous juke boxes in the bars and restaurants. Favorite sights are the *Territorial Enterprise* newspaper office, where Samuel Clemens became Mark Twain, and Piper's Opera House, where Modjeska and Lotta Crabtree played and sang before admiring crowds. One could spend days in Virginia City and still be reluctant to leave the picturesque historic shrine, whose very streets are paved with low-grade ore and whose fabulous Comstock lode yielded, between 1859 and 1938, over $900,000,000 —55 per cent of it in silver and the rest in gold.

The development of the Comstock mines at Virginia City was a natural sequel to the discovery of gold in California. The first find in the area was made in 1849 by a party of Mormons who panned a little gold at the mouth of a canyon on their way to California. In 1850 another group found colors in the same place and named the gulch Gold Canyon. The following year at least a hundred men crossed the Sierra from Placerville to prospect the same diggings. One of them, a Brazilian, recognized the presence of silver ore but was unable to make his companions understand what he had found. Then a bunch of Chinese began placering the gulch, and their camp, strung out along the canyon above that of the white miners, was called Johnstown.

The credit for the discovery of the Comstock lode belongs to Allen and Hosea Grosch, who in 1853 also crossed the Sierra and began placering in the same area. In the summer of 1856, the brothers found "quartz rotten with silver" and tested it in their small assay furnace; but they kept the location of their silver mine a secret. Then, in 1857, Hosea cut his foot with a pick and died of blood poisoning within a few days, and Allen froze his feet so badly in a Sierra blizzard that they had to be amputated. He died from the shock.

Henry T. P. Comstock, a shiftless sheepherder, who was better known as "Old Pancake" because he was too lazy to mix up sourdough bread, had reached Gold Canyon at about the same time as the Grosch brothers. The secrecy with which they worked irritated him, and he spent his time wandering up and down Gold Canyon, searching for the ledge from which they obtained the "blue dirt."

In the early fifties, while Hosea and Allen were exploring the canyon, another prospector known as "Old Virginny" had arrived in Gold Canyon, crossed Sun Mountain at the head of the gulch, and begun placering in Six Mile Canyon; but the pannings which he and the few who followed him found were so meager that the diggings were soon abandoned.

Early in 1859, after prospectors found a little gold high up Gold Canyon, the camp of Gold Hill materialized. Latecomers who could find no unclaimed ground went on to Six Mile Canyon and staked claims. Two Irishmen who tried their luck in the latter canyon were Peter O'Riley and Patrick Mc-Laughlin; since all the choice locations were taken by the time they arrived, they placed their stakes 500 yards higher up the mountain than the others. A day or two later they found a ledge of dark quartz rock on Sun Mountain and were already at work on it when Old Pancake appeared and announced that they were on his claim. In his attempts to ferret out the source of the Grosch silver ore, Comstock had gophered all over Sun Mountain; therefore, he insisted that everything of value on it was his. Although the Irishmen who discovered the ledge knew he was bluffing them about his right to the claim, they were alone in lawless country and were afraid to refuse his demand to be taken in on the discovery. O'Riley and McLaughlin were unaware that their discovery claim, the Ophir, was the first of the Comstock silver-lode properties; for the strange-looking quartz mixed with their gold ore was only a nuisance to them. Their find started a rush to Sun Mountain, and not only Comstock but all the Gold Canyon and Gold Hill prospectors were soon swarming over the peak, setting up location monuments.

As soon as a Californian named Stone saw the discarded ore which the miners cursed, he suspected that it was silver and sent samples to Nevada City and to Grass Valley, California, to be tested. The assay at the latter town ran $4,791 a ton in silver and $3,196 in gold. Atwood, the assayer, couldn't keep still and told a few close friends about the bonanza. As soon as the news was out, California's diggings were almost deserted, and the Washoe rush was on.

Old Virginny gave the new camp on Sun Mountain its name. He was weaving to his cabin one night, carrying a bottle, when he fell and the bottle broke. As the liquor sank into the ground, he bawled, "I christen this ground Virginia." Thereafter the camp was known as Virginia City.

During 1860 Gold Canyon and Sun Mountain (renamed Mount Davidson for Rothschild's representative in San Francisco) were covered with cabins, dugouts, and tents. The latter were torn to shreds or blown away by the blasts of wind, known as "Washoe Zephyrs," which raked the canyon as they crossed the "divide" between Gold Hill and Virginia City. By summer a road was under construction through Gold Canyon, and ore was packed down to Gold Hill and the quartz mills in the Washoe Valley. A telegraph line was extended from Genoa, in the Carson River valley to Virginia City, and real estate boomed. In July, 1860, the claims into which Gould and Curry had been pouring their capital struck bonanza ore. The next year, Gould and Curry built their million-dollar mill, complete with terraced lawns and artificial lake, and a million-dollar house as well, at the head of Six Mile Canyon.

Some of Jefferson Davis' camels, which had reached California in the late fifties, were used to haul salt from the marshes on the Humboldt River to the mills and arrastres. The animals delivered their loads at night in order not to terrify the pack mules and horses, which stampeded at the sight of them. They stalked silently up Six Mile Canyon, over stones and ruts, "leaving a trail of blood from their torn and mutilated feet."

Working conditions in the mines before ventilating systems and pumps were installed were unbearable; for the heat increased as the shafts sank deeper, and hot water on the lower levels added to the discomfort of the workers. The water in the bottom of the Yellow Jacket registered 170 degrees

Fahrenheit. Men worked stripped to the waist while water was sprayed over them. Later, those in the lowest levels, where the heat was greatest, worked a fifteen-minute shift and then stayed for forty-five minutes under cool-air blowers. The daily ice allotment to mines was prodigious—one property estimated that it allowed ninety-five pounds per day per man.

As the shafts sank deeper and drifts and stopes led off from them, cave-ins caused so many accidents that Philip Deidesheimer, a mining engineer, originated a plan of timbering that has been in use everywhere ever since. He built up an inner bracing of square-cut timbers wherever ore was stoped out; thus, a sturdy inner scaffolding supported the excavated walls and roofs at each level and prevented slipping and caving-in of unsupported earth. As both mines and city used great quantities of lumber, Mount Davidson was soon devoid of timber; logs were cut in forests over twenty miles away in the Sierra, moved by water flumes to the Washoe Valley, and then freighted to the fast-growing camp. During the 1860's all supplies were hauled by mule- and ox-teams from Sacramento, at first over the merest trails and later over the steep but more direct Geiger Grade.

Over this shelf road, with its 12 per cent grades and 2,000-foot rise in five miles, crawled long mule trains loaded with freight or bullion; on its narrow ledges Concord coaches lurched and swayed as their six-horse teams galloped toward Placerville. Occasionally a stage was blown over by the fierce Washoe Zephyrs, or horses and pack animals slipped off the edge after a blizzard had coated its surface with ice. In 1869, while the Virginia and Truckee Railroad was being built between Virginia City and Reno, a locomotive was hauled up this grade by thirty oxen. The railroad, when completed, formed a direct connection between Virginia City and the mills on the Carson River in the Washoe Valley. At one time the fifty-two-mile road ran fifty trains a day into Virginia City. In 1949 the road was abandoned, but its station is one of the city's landmarks.

During Virginia's early boom days, six men played especially prominent parts in the city's development. William M. Stewart, the lawyer for many of the big companies, formulated most of the mining laws; Adolph Sutro advocated and ultimately completed a drainage tunnel for the district; William Sharon, representative for the Bank of California, gained control of the milling and timber trade; George Hearst, father of William Randolph Hearst, invested heavily in mines; and John W. Mackay and James G. Fair became mining experts.

As the fantastic Comstock lode was explored, its mines were found to lie in three distinct zones. The discovery area was parallel with A Street, high on Mount Davidson. The ore streak dipped east from it, and a second zone full

4TH WARD SCHOOL AND MOUNT DAVIDSON, VIRGINIA CITY

LIBERTY ENGINE CO. FIREHOUSE, GOLD HILL (COLLAPSED WINTER, 1951).

of shafts paralleled D and E Streets. Later, groups of mines were developed near K and L Streets to make a third zone. In addition to these, the Combination property was off by itself in the southeast corner of the city. Besides the original Ophir bonanza, other properties produced sensational amounts of ore—the Sierra Nevada, Union, Mexican, Consolidated Virginia, Gould and Curry, Savage, Hale and Norcross, Chollar-Potosi, Belcher, Yellow Jacket, and Crown Point.

By 1864 or 1865 the bonanza ore had been skimmed off, and even the best properties stopped paying dividends. After yielding a total of $45,000,000, they closed down one by one, and the population of 15,000 that had crowded around them began to drift away. Part of this slump was the result of inaccurate mine surveys that failed to see available but undeveloped ore bodies, part was due to overlapping claims and subsequent expensive litigation, and part was caused by the fact that with production and transportation costs high only first-grade ore was sent to England to be milled. Second-grade ore was piled to one side, and low-grade ore was used to surface the streets. During these first years, the original mine owners sold out to gullible purchasers as fast as they could. Comstock and McLaughlin were among the first to part with their claims; O'Riley received $50,000 for his portion and went east. Only a few like Eilly Orrum and Sandy Bowers hung on; and they eventually received $15,000 a week from their combined properties.

In 1869, two experienced mining men named John W. Mackay and James G. Fair interested James G. Flood and William O'Brien, prosperous San Francisco saloon proprietors, in a scheme to run an underground exploration drift on the Comstock to "diagnose" where the vein's bonanza lay. By pooling their resources they secured control of the Hale-Norcross and Gould and Curry properties and a chain of mines which reached from the Ophir on the north to the Belcher on the south. This group they called the Consolidated Virginia.

The main vein, 150 to 320 feet wide and 400 feet deep, was discovered in March, 1873. It was the "Big Bonanza," the "Heart of the Comstock"! For the next four years, while the ore lasted, Virginia City went wild; for the gigantic lode continued to yield high-grade silver and gold on a scale that eclipsed all previous strikes. Virginia City was overrun with stock company offices and brokerage firms. Everyone owned stock and everyone played the market. Consolidated Virginia was quoted on the San Francisco Exchange at stupendous figures; since silver and gold continued to pour from the lode in undiminished amounts, branches of Pacific Coast banks opened in Virginia City, and the United States Treasury built a mint in Carson City (which operated from 1870 to 1893) to handle bullion from the great lode. The Consolidated Virginia and Consolidated California, which together owned the whole bonanza, had a stock value of $159,000,000 and for over three years paid monthly dividends which ran slightly over a million dollars. On December 31, 1877, an assay value of $1,110,000 was reported from an eight-day run of bullion from their mill.

By 1877, production had reached its peak and the city had 750 miles of underground workings; blasts continually shook the sturdiest buildings, doors and windows sagged and stuck as the earth shifted, and the din of hundreds of stamps from the mills was deafening. But after 1877 the mines bottomed, stocks fell, and serious litigation over surveys and boundaries tied up some of the best producers. In spite of Sutro's drainage tunnel, built in the face of criticism and without local support, the hot water in the mines was troublesome. Low-grade ore, instead of high-grade "picture rock," reduced profits so materially that Virginia City ceased to be the incredible mining center it once had been.

Books about the Comstock deal in detail with the city's fantastic financial life during the boom years, with the panic of 1875, with stock manipulations and tangled litigations, and with San Francisco's Nob Hill, which was built up with Comstock silver. But all the wealth was not shipped to California. A substantial and even pretentious city rose on the slopes of Mount Davidson; Gold Hill stood just across the ridge, or "divide," of the same mountain, and Silver City stretched down Gold Canyon to the Devil's Gate. Together they made a continuous five-mile stretch of buildings, where, during the seventies, 35,000 persons worked and gambled, made fortunes and lost them overnight in the mad whirl that was life on the Comstock.

Virginia City's growth might be divided into three periods: before 1863, after the fire of 1863, and after the fire of 1875. Although each blaze destroyed large sections of the city, new buildings, more imposing and more permanent, quickly replaced those that were lost. One of the earliest buildings was the one-story International Hotel, built in 1860 of lumber whipsawed in Six Mile Canyon. It was replaced in 1876 by a five-story brick and stone edifice with gas lights and an elevator, at that time the last word in elegance. It was also the largest building in the city. Rooms were engaged months in advance of the formal opening; one suite, engaged for a month by a mining engineer, cost him $1,500, and during that time he spent only one night in it. The hotel burned in 1914, and today its site is a vacant lot.

Another early building was the original office of the *Territorial Enterprise,* the vivid news sheet which Samuel Clemens made more vivid by the humorous sketches he signed "Josh." In 1862 Dan De Quille (really William Wright), who was on the paper's staff, wrote a witty jibe that was resented by a reader, and Dan took a hurried and indefinite vacation. During his absence Clemens was hired to "fill in." When De Quille returned after the unpleasantness blew over, Clemens was as much a part of the paper as he.

Two volunteer fire companies were organized in Virginia City in 1861, and by 1875 five more had been added. Virginia Engine Company No. 1 made an honorary member of Julia Bulette, a French Creole and one of the city's most seductive beauties, because during an epidemic in 1861 she had converted her house into a hospital, nursed the miners, and pawned some of her possessions in order to care for their families. Dressed in a striking costume, she attended all fires and not only worked beside the men at the stirrup pump but served refreshments to them afterwards. That was bad enough; but when she drove down C Street in her coach every afternoon and had her own opera box, the ladies of the city, who hated her blatant and bizarre appearances, tried to have her activities suppressed. To spite them, she gave more lavish parties and drew a still larger crowd of admirers to listen to her witty sallies and sample her excellent cuisine. When she was murdered for her diamonds by John Millain, in 1867, only the men of the city were upset. Her funeral procession, which extended for blocks, was led by a band playing "The Girl I Left Behind Me."

The fire of August, 1863, destroyed $7,000,000 worth of property in the business section; but the one in October, 1875, which broke out in Crazy Kate's lodging house on A Street, practically wiped out the town. A few hours after the flames broke through the flimsy roof, nearly 2,000 buildings were smoking ruins, and losses were estimated at $12,000,000. Business houses, dwellings, hoisting works, and mills disappeared in the blaze; quantities of blasting powder exploded and showered sparks of flaming debris in all directions. The fire was kept out of the mines by covering the mouths of the shafts with timbers and dirt; thus, although city business was suspended, the mines continued working.

Relief poured into the gutted city from all over the state. The Chinese of San Francisco sent a large donation "to be used for all sufferers regardless of race"; for a time, forty-five trains a day chugged up the long grade to the ruins, loaded with food and all manner of necessities. The city rebuilt at once, including among its new buildings a fire tower, or Corporation House (still standing), high on Mount Davidson. In it men watched twenty-four hours a day for a thread of smoke or burst of flame, ready to give an alarm and prevent another major disaster.

After 1875 C Street replaced B Street as the main thoroughfare; and as mine properties followed the eastern dip of the lode, A and B streets were no longer filled with headframes and dumps but became the residential section of the city. A surprising number of Victorian homes have survived, and the balustrades, gables trimmed with wooden lace, bay windows with lace curtains, terraced steps, and wrought iron fences and gateposts make endless subjects for photographers and artists. Not only private homes, but mine offices, schools, and public buildings are architectural gems. The red brick Gould and Curry office where John Mackay lived, with its white spindled porches and widow's walk on the roof; the sagging Savage mine office just below C Street, with mansard roof, first- and second-story porches encircling the building, ornate window trim, and carved cornice; the four-story Fourth Ward school of similar design; and the Storey County courthouse—all are gracious landmarks from the city's best days.

C Street is still lined with two- and three-story brick stores, in one of which Lucius Beebe and Charles Clegg have revived the city's famous paper, the *Territorial Enterprise*. Here the business houses are grouped within a few blocks—although Virginia no longer provides eighteen barbershops, four banks, and a "whisky mill every fifteen steps"; the "Sawdust Corner" and the "Howling Wilderness" are gone. Five breweries supplied its 100 saloons with 75,000 gallons of hard liquor and twice that amount of wine and beer during 1880. Today the Sazarac, the Crystal Bar, the Old Washoe Club, and similar establishments cater to thirsty patrons.

Virginia City had four churches, of which three remain. The white Presbyterian church on C Street is a vandal-wrecked shell, and the Episcopal church on F Street is closed; but St. Mary's in the Mountains continues to serve the community. The first Catholic church, a wooden structure, was blown down by high winds; later, Father Patrick Manogue reached the Comstock and built a Gothic church at E and Taylor Streets. Its silver bell, though cast in Spain, was made of bullion from Virginia's mines. In 1876, after the church was destroyed by fire, the present fine structure was built by the community; with its tall steeple and redwood columns, it stands on the site of the second church and dominates the city's skyline.

Entertainment in the early days of the city was both noisy and rough; in addition to the hurdy-gurdies and barroom specialties, it included dog and panther fights, bear and bull fights, and frequent cock fights. The first theatre in which plays were given was built on the corner of Union and D Streets by Tom Maguire and was known as the Melodian. Maguire soon took a partner, John Piper; and after the Melodian burned, they built a theatre called Piper's Opera House on the same site. It disappeared in the fire of 1875, and Piper rebuilt at Union and B Streets. This $50,000 hall burned in 1882, and its owner debated whether to try again or not; the citizens were so insistent that he decided to go ahead. The present Piper's Opera House, the third of that name, is still standing.

The weathered boards of the big playhouse are tinderdry, and the dark, rickety stairs that lead to the auditorium creak; but once inside the spacious auditorium one forgets everything but the days when Ada Menken as "Mazeppa" crossed the stage lashed to the back of a horse, when Edwin Booth and Lawrence Barrett played Shakespearean roles there, when Joe Jefferson was Rip Van Winkle, and when *Leah the Forsaken, The Two Orphans, The Ticket of Leave Man, The Black Crook,* and a troupe of Red Stocking Blondes all drew crowds to its doors. Appreciative audiences always threw silver coins to the performers. Later on, silver bricks were presented to stars. One such tribute was described as "of solid silver bullion, fifty ounces in weight, handsomely proportioned, polished and suitably engraved."

Virginia City is not only full of historic sites and buildings that have been reopened to give visitors a glimpse of past glories; it also has a small permanent population living in the Victorian mansions and over the stores in the brick buildings. While I was sketching one old house a man came out on the porch, and as I drew he told me about the drunk who sued Virginia City after he had fallen on its broken sidewalks. The defense objected to the suit on the grounds that the man was drunk at the time of the injury, but the judge ruled that a drunken man is as much entitled to good sidewalks as a sober man—and needs them far more.

GOLD HILL AND SILVER CITY

With so much to see, we were in no hurry to leave Virginia City. Reluctantly we drove back along C Street, past the Fourth Ward school, and then turned right to cross the divide and drop down the original steep grade through Gold Canyon, the scene of the earliest placering, to Gold Hill. During boom days, and especially before the railroad was completed to the Comstock, a continuous procession of mule trains packed ore from the mines to the quartz mills at Gold Hill, Silver City, and even the Washoe Valley along the Carson River. Gold Hill's solid mass of buildings used to extend to the fringes of Virginia City; but today the town consists of a mere handful of homes, a store and tavern, the old firehouse, and the site of the Bowers mine.

Farther down the canyon sprawls the husk of Silver City and the Devil's Gate, a break in the gorge so narrow that only a road and the creek can slip through. In the old days a toll gate stood at the Gate and a high railroad trestle bridged it. While low-grade mining is done in the canyon today, the big properties and the old mills are silent; and the days when rivalry among the three mining camps produced annual rock-drilling contests, wrestling matches, and other tests of brawn are over.

AUSTIN

ONE HUNDRED and sixty-five miles east of Virginia City, located almost in the geographical center of Nevada, is Austin, the center of the Reese River excitement in the early 1860's. The western approach to the city is across the Reese River Valley, an expanse of sagebrush so wide that distant ranches seem unreal. To the right of the highway at the edge of the town, Stokes Castle sits on top of a hill overlooking the vast valley; the bizarre ruin was built in 1897 as a summer home by Anson Phelps Stokes and J. G. Stokes of Philadelphia. A tall three-story stone chimney of a place, deserted for over thirty years and lacking even floors and stairs today, it is said to have been erected so that Stokes might keep an eye on his nearby mining properties. Its first floor contained a kitchen and dining room; its second, a living room; the third, two bedrooms; and the roof, a sun deck. The whole was approached by a circular drive from Austin. Today it is only a curiosity.

The Overland Stage route crossed the Reese River Valley, and William H. Talcott was the keeper of the station at Jacob's Springs. East of the station, a pass through the mountains was used as a cut-off by the Pony Express riders and called Pony Canyon. In May, 1862, while Talcott was hauling a load of wood through the canyon, one of the horses kicked up a piece of greenish, gold-bearing quartz. Talcott sent the sample to Virginia City, and the assay report showed it to be rich in silver.

Eight days later ten other men staked claims on the Pony Ledge. Pleased with their discoveries, they held the first meeting in the Reese River Valley on July 10, 1862, and organized a mining district. Although the rush to the district did not occur until 1863, the North Star, Oregon, and Southern Light lodes had been discovered by December, 1862, and news of the new silver field spread to other camps. The stampede began in January, 1863; since there was only one stone cabin anywhere near Pony Ledge, most of the men camped in tents or crowded into Jacobsville, the only village in the region. It was promptly declared the county seat, and an $8,440 courthouse was completed by March; but Jacobsville was too far from the mines, and its population soon dwindled to fifty. Clifton sprang up to the east around the cabin and mine of two prospectors, Marshall and Cole. Other miners gathered still farther up the canyon and made a third camp named Austin. At first its growth was delayed by the high cost of building a road to the site; then someone suggested that town lots be traded for road work, and by summer the camp had both a road and 366 houses. As Austin grew, Clifton shrank, until its population moved up the gulch in a body and Clifton and Austin became one.

In April, 1863, a second miners' meeting arranged an election to vote for county officers and a permanent county seat. Even though Jacobsville had just completed its courthouse, Austin won the vote. On the morning of September 21, the newly elected officials met in Jacobsville; but that afternoon the men and the courthouse itself moved the few miles up the canyon to Austin. Austin's present brick courthouse was built in 1869.

During 1863 people poured in so fast that in a single day 274 freight teams, 19 passenger wagons, 69 men on horseback, 31 on foot, and 3 pack trains entered the city. Two stage lines ran from Virginia City to the Reese River mines, and passage on every coach was booked for days in advance. As hundreds of men clawed at the mountains, searching for new claims, the hills became covered with prospect holes and ore dumps. Six mills and several arrastres reduced the ore; by August, David Buel's stamp mill had produced the first bullion. In 1864 nine camels padded regularly into town from the salt marshes near Walker Lake, bringing salt to the quartz mills. By 1867 eleven mills were in operation, and 6,000 mining claims had been recorded.

Saloons and hotels catered to the growing crowd which surged up and down the hilly streets and watched the erection of the International Hotel—a building which even then had a past. The hotel is still standing, and the bar and east side are part of the Original International Hotel of Virginia City. When a new hostelry was planned on the Virginia site, this frame structure was taken down and hauled 150 miles across mountain passes and deserts to Austin.

Water was scarce in the new camp, and a bath was described as "two inches of cold water in a big tub, a piece of brown soap, a napkin and a dollar and a half." Lumber was also scarce, but several firms made adobe bricks, and with them the town was so substantially built that it escaped serious fires. At first, although the mines provided plenty of gold, there was a dearth of silver coin, and merchants begged Nevada newspapers to print appeals to all newcomers to bring their money in small change. Austin's first paper, the *Reese River Reveille,* put the request simply: "Bring it in a bucket if necessary but bring it small."

Austin's most famous auction took place on April 20, 1864, as the outcome of a political bet. Reuel C. Gridley, a Missouri Democrat, and Dr. H. S. Herrick, a Republican, bet on the outcome of a local election. If the Republican won, Herrick agreed to carry a fifty-pound sack of flour from Clifton up to the east end of Austin. If the Democrats won, Gridley was to carry it down through the town. Gridley paid the bet, and the town turned out to watch the performance. A band led the procession, followed by the newly elected officials on horseback. Herrick came next, carrying Gridley's hat and cane, and Gridley, with the sack draped in Union flags, was last. When he set it down in front of the Bank Exchange Saloon, a mile and a half from the start of the procession, it was suggested that he auction it off for the benefit of the United

RUINS OF BRICK AND FRAME BUILDINGS, AURORA

CATHOLIC CHURCH AND STORES ON MAIN STREET, AUSTIN

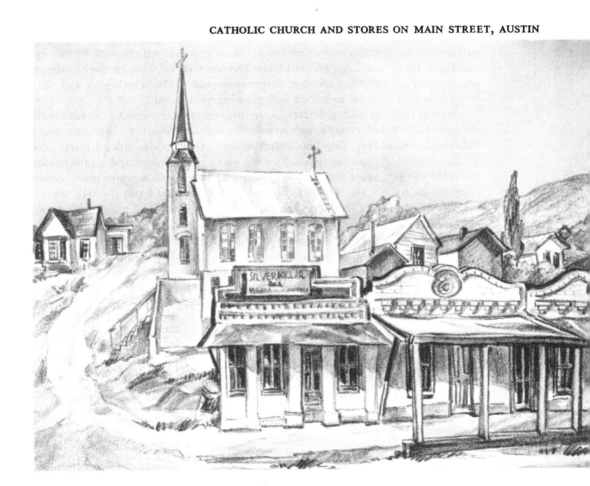

States Sanitary Commission (the Civil War equivalent of the Red Cross). The flour was sold again and again, and so successful was Gridley as an auctioneer that he began a tour covering several states, selling the same sack repeatedly and raising a total of $275,000 for the cause. Gridley's store, a small stone building at the east end of Austin, is still standing, and the flour sack is preserved in the Nevada State Historical Museum in Carson City.

All through the seventies Austin's mines were productive, but transportation costs ate up much of the profits. Austin hoped to be on the transcontinental railroad then under construction, but the survey, when completed, ran no nearer than Battle Mountain, 100 miles to the north. Austin's very life depended on economical hauling rates for its ore; the city was elated, therefore, when Mike Farrell got a construction subsidy of $200,000 from Lander County in 1875 to finance a narrow-gauge road from Austin to Battle Mountain.

The grant was to expire in five years. On August 30, 1879, Phelps-Stokes, an eastern syndicate, agreed to build the road and broke ground at Battle Mountain on September 1. By that time, the grant had only five months left to run. Work on the road was rushed at feverish pitch, although winter weather impeded top-speed construction. At noon on February 9, 1880, when only twelve hours of the subsidy period remained, the road was still two miles outside Austin, and the train carrying the rails was stalled up the line. That night the rails were laid on snow to within half a mile of the edge of town. To save the situation, the city council met and extended the city limits the necessary half mile. Ten minutes before midnight, the tracks crossed the new boundary and the subsidy was safe. The road, the Nevada Central, ran for twenty-seven years, not profitably but without suspension until 1938. During its last five years it is said to have averaged four passengers a month.

With a railroad to handle freight, mining boomed. In 1883, 29 mills with an aggregate of 444 stamps thundered away on ore from the Panamint, Paxton, Buel, North Star, London, Independence, Oregon, Isabella, Union, and Savage mines. At one time 69 shafts were being worked on Lander Hill alone, and 100 distinct veins were known to exist. The eighties contributed other color to the town's life. A murderer was quietly hanged from the balcony of the courthouse; and Emma Nevada (born Emma Wixom), a grand opera star who had grown up in Austin and had sung in the Methodist choir, insisted, while on a concert tour of the country, that her route include her home town so that she might sing to her old friends.

It is easy today to drive through Austin without stopping, for Highway 50 runs the length of the town, past the historic Lander County courthouse, the International Hotel, and Gridley's store. But to hurry through is to miss a glimpse of history, for, as Austin itself says:

Its population has shrunken to a fraction of what it once was, and many of its buildings have deteriorated and fallen down, but in most respects AUSTIN is much the same today as it was in the 'sixties.

It has not been "modernized" and its famous old Main Street is not lined with garish honkytonks. It is, in itself, an unspoiled relic of Nevada and the West in the days of their greatest fame and glory. [Leaflet sponsored by John F. Hiskey Unit, American Legion Auxiliary.]

AURORA

WHILE Austin has weathered booms and depressions and is a well-established town today, Aurora, another sensational camp of the sixties, skyrocketed to fame and fizzled out in less than ten years. To reach it we had to start from Hawthorne, at the southern tip of Walker Lake. Hawthorne is a supply town for the mines and smaller settlements around it and also serves as a Naval Ammunition Depot. As we drove down its main street, I looked at the mountain range behind it and wondered which zigzag trail climbed over Lucky Boy Pass to Aurora.

Rather than subject my car to thirty miles of rocks and ruts, I made arrangements with the Nevada Garage in Hawthorne to drive me to Aurora in a pickup truck. The driver brought with him for the trip former State Senator James Caughman, who as a mining man was not only familiar with all the landmarks of the region but could also identify for me the locations of the different strikes, the various mines, and the piles of rubble that had once been Aurora's buildings.

Late in August, 1860, E. R. Hicks, J. M. Cory, and James M. Brawley started prospecting northeast of Mono Lake, California. One day, while hunting for game, one of the men climbed over a hill and found a piece of quartz which so excited his companions that they located seven claims and then hurried to Monoville to report their discovery. On August 30, accompanied by a crowd of prospectors, they again climbed to their claims and laid out the ten-mile-square Esmeralda mining district. When the ore samples which the original discoverers sent to Carson City to be assayed were pronounced in the bonanza class, Monoville moved up in a body and put up tents and brush shelters on Esmeralda Hill. But the location was unsatisfactory, and the men moved down to a flat at the mouth of three gulches and laid out a new camp called Aurora. Although the winter was unusually severe, a few miners holed in near their properties; by the end of the spring rush to the district, the silver camp in the high mountain valley was crowded with miners.

Since the state boundary line between California and Nevada was not settled until September, 1863, Aurora's legal status was confused for over two years. Mono County was created by the California Legislature on March 24,

1861, with Aurora as county seat. Esmeralda County was set up by the Nevada Territorial Legislature in November, 1861, also with Aurora as county seat. Since California had acted first, it controlled elections until the boundary was determined. As the survey was not completed by election day, 1863, a novel plan was inaugurated to the satisfaction of everyone. Each county put up two full tickets and voters cast two sets of ballots, one at Armory Hall for Esmeralda officers and the other at the police station for Mono County nominees. By this device, both counties would have officers without a special election, regardless of where the survey line ran. On September 22 the line passed four miles west of Aurora, leaving it in Nevada. The newly elected officers of Mono County lost no time in piling the records in a wagon and taking them to Bodie, California, twelve miles west of Aurora.

All during the Civil War Aurora was such a "Union town" that those with Confederate leanings were forced by the Esmeralda rifle team to swear allegiance to the Union flag. To raise money for the Sanitary Commission, fairs and benefits were held in various towns, and although Aurora had no Gridley with a sack of flour, it did have Major E. A. Sherman with a piece of ore. A fifty-pound sample containing several hundred dollars' worth of free gold and silver was donated to the cause by the Wide West Mining Company, and the chunk of rock was sold at auction again and again until an amount greater than its value was added to the fund.

When the fairs were over no one claimed the heavy piece of stone, and Major Sherman, who was going east to Plymouth, Massachusetts, asked if he might take it with him and exchange it for a fragment of Plymouth Rock. The latter could be incorporated into a wall of Aurora's new brick courthouse, then under construction. He was given the specimen, and some time later a small piece of the famous rock was cemented into the courthouse wall.

Sherman was owner of the *Esmeralda Star,* the first copy of which appeared in May, 1862. He wrote in the *Inyo Register* of January 25, 1906, that the first few issues were printed on brown paper because the roads across the Sierra Nevada were blocked with snow until nearly July. Provisions got so low that "everyone had to live on beef straight—and not a few on the first cut behind the horns or above the hoofs."

Aurora was notorious for the number of crimes committed in or near it. In the spring of 1864, after a particularly flagrant murder, its solid citizens formed a Vigilance Committee, rounded up the desperadoes, and hanged four of them from a single gallows. When word reached Territorial Governor Nye that a group of men were about to be hanged, he wired one of the county commissioners that there must be no violence. The officer wired back, "All quiet and orderly. Four men will be hung in half an hour." Following the execution, Aurora was more law-abiding.

From 1861 to 1865 Aurora was a prosperous camp, where 175 stamps in 17 mills pounded out silver for bullion from the Aurora, Real Del Monte, Cortez, Coffee Pot, Antelope, and Wide West mines. By 1864, just as the population reached 10,000, the veins on Last Chance Hill began to thin out and some of the properties became involved in litigation; by 1869 many of the mines had shut down. Soon after Aurora lost the county seat. Nevertheless, 500 people still lived in the town in 1880; and the *Esmeralda Herald* for September 15, 1883, hopefully commented:

There is no star that sets, but that will rise again to illuminate another sky. Aurora is taking on new life. . . . Though the star of her glory went down to adorn the village on the lake; yet her ancient pride seems to be returning in the way of renewed activity in her mines. Work has been resumed on the Great Republic. The Silver Hill mill is working on Centennial and Garibaldi ore.

There has never been a lack of ore in Aurora; it has always been held back for want of capital and since the people can't get the mountain to come to them they have resolved to do the next best, work and prove their great worth. A contract to sink a shaft 100 feet deep on the Silver Lining, west of the Humboldt has been let. A few more pushers on the wheel and Aurora will resume her place of twenty years ago.

But two weeks later the paper said:

The few citizens of this place amuse themselves by going from store to store, saloon to saloon to tell each other how dull it is.

Between 1884 and 1914 Aurora dozed. From 1914 to 1918 the Aurora Consolidated Mines Company worked certain of the properties, but after its forty-stamp mill was hauled to Goldfield, Aurora fell back to sleep.

Unlike most mining camps, the town was built chiefly of brick, not locally made but shipped around the Horn and freighted over the mountains from Sacramento. For over eighty years these solidly built structures defied sun and and frost; recently, however, they were torn down, and their bricks were hauled away and sold in Reno for sixty-five dollars a thousand. As a result, only fragments of the larger buildings remain. Antelope Street and Silver Street are full of weeds; Wingate's office building, the imposing courthouse, and the Wells Fargo safe, from which $27,000,000 in bullion was shipped, are only memories. One sage-covered hill is crowned with the schoolhouse. Over the crest of the opposite hill are the town's two cemeteries, shaded by pines. Of the ten thousand people who had made Aurora a boom town in 1864, only one was left in 1930, and by 1952 the place was a ghost.

TONOPAH

FROM Hawthorne we drove southeast through a desert valley, rimmed by ragged and colorful mountain ranges, toward Tonopah, the boom silver camp which startled the mining world in 1900 and continues to dominate the area in which it lies.

A few miles east of Hawthorne we passed through Luning. It is a tiny place today; yet in 1879 it was a small trading center for the silver, lead, and copper mines located in the mountains beyond the town. Seven miles west of the highway, high in the mountains, is old Candelaria, a silver camp dating from 1864. A few miles farther south, the highway passes a dump, a ruined mill, and two or three shacks—the site of Sodaville, where all freight and passengers for Tonopah were unloaded before the railroad was extended farther south.

Stages met the trains at Sodaville, and the eager and impatient travelers began the long, dusty trip across the desert. One man insisted that at the end of the ride he had to use a shovel to determine which of the passengers in the coach was his wife! In those days freight was piled high at the Sodaville depot and everything was noise and confusion. Merchants, mining men waiting the arrival of machinery, and teamsters milled around among rigs, wagons, and pack trains as they sorted out the shipments, while alkali dust, churned up by the feet of men and beasts, filled the air and formed a white film on everything.

At Coaldale, another diminutive settlement, the mountains close to the highway are violently brilliant with red, pink, and green stratifications. Forty miles farther east lies Tonopah, crowded between the barren peaks of Mount Butler and Mount Oddie.

Outside the town are two cemeteries—the present one a green oasis filled with tamarisk trees, and the more interesting old one treeless and unkempt, its graves bordered by weathered picket fences. It was abandoned in favor of the new location when the tailings from the settling pond of a big mill threatened to engulf it. The pond and the charred ruins of the mill still remain.

Tonopah is a brisk place, with both new and old buildings crowding its streets. The main thoroughfare is flanked for blocks by two- and three-story commercial structures; a few, like the Mizpah Hotel, rise five stories. This main street gives a modern look to the busy town; to see what it was like when it was new, the visitor must walk up side streets or drive along the avenues that rise tier above tier on both mountainsides. There he will find not only the buildings that date from the early 1900's but also the mine properties that made the city.

If Jim Butler hadn't refused to get up early on May 19, 1900, when he and his partner William Hall were camping on the desert, he might never have found the outcroppings that started the silver stampede to the eroded mesas and volcanic hills in whose lap Tonopah hides. Butler, who lived on a ranch near the mining camp of Belmont, had persuaded Hall to accompany him on a prospecting trip to Southern Klondyke, and on the way there the men camped for the night at Tonopah Springs. As Southern Klondyke was fifteen miles south of the springs, Hall wanted to get an early start; but Butler was in no hurry to roll out of his blankets. Hall, in disgust, took his own burro and camp equipment and left.

When Butler did get up, his burros were gone, and he spent the rest of the morning hunting them. They had strayed four miles, and he found them grazing on a rocky hillside. As Butler climbed, he cursed the beasts and looked for rocks to heave at them. The first rock he picked up was a "likely looking quartz floater." Excited by its appearance, he climbed higher, guided by the outcroppings, until he reached the source of the vein. Here he selected samples of the ore, then caught his burros, packed them, and started south after his partner.

Southern Klondyke was not a very productive camp, and only a few prospectors were at work there. Among them were T. J. Bell and James Court, who had turned up the first specimens of copper-stained gold ore, Wilson Brougher, a miner from Belmont, and Frank Higgs, an assayer. Butler reached the camp the day after Hall and showed his ore to the men. They were unimpressed, and, as he had no money to pay for an assay, they threw aside the sample he gave them. On his way home Butler stopped to pick up more samples from the hillside, but he did not bother to stake the ground. When he reached his ranch in Belmont, he showed the samples of dark-streaked rock to his wife, who urged him to have them assayed. But Belmont had no assayer, and Jim was soon too busy with his ranch to bother. In August, however, Mrs. Butler got in touch with Tasker L. Oddie, a young attorney who knew ore, and with her husband's consent offered Oddie an interest in Jim's strike if he would have assays run.

Oddie sent the specimens to Walter C. Gayhart, who had a small furnace at Austin, promising him half of his own interest in Butler's find if the samples proved valuable. At first Gayhart thought the rock worthless; but the samples ran $175 to $500 a ton. Even so, Jim saw no reason to hurry back to the hill. His wife insisted, however, and to pacify her he hitched up the buckboard and started to the site of his unstaked claim. Some say that Oddie went with them and some say not. At any rate, when properties were laid out, one of the first eight claims was staked in his name. Mrs. Butler also staked a claim and named it the Mizpah, and this vein turned out to be one of the best properties of all.

While the Butlers were thus engaged, Frank Higgs, the assayer at Southern Klondyke, learned of Gayhart's assays and ran a test on the sample Jim Butler had left with him weeks before. Amazed that it showed a value of $500 to the ton, he scrambled into a wagon and streaked up the road to Tonopah Springs, only to find the Butlers covering the hill with stakes.

Wilson Brougher was taken into the partnership with Oddie and the Butlers because his wagon and mules were needed to haul ore to the nearest smelter, and by October, 1900, the four started work—Oddie digging, Brougher digging and hauling, Mrs. Butler cooking, and Mr. Butler directing the enterprise. The first load of ore was hauled to Austin, where the smelter reported an $800 value from the first ton. When miners from Belmont, Austin, and other camps rushed to the scene and asked for leases on the claims, Butler saw a way to develop his many holdings and gladly made contracts with them. He leased 112 claims, each lessee agreeing to pay 25 per cent of the proceeds to the owners and being allowed to select whatever ground he wished. The boundaries of each property were designated by rows of stones laid along the ground; leases were issued for short terms and expired on December 31, 1901. All agreements were made verbally, and each transaction was recorded simply by number and the lessee's name in a pocket memorandum book that Butler carried. By this arrangement several men made from $25,000 to $100,000 within the year.

Walter Gayhart laid out the town of Tonopah and watched it rise from the treeless, volcanic soil. Everything, including lumber and water, had to be hauled in from Belmont, fifty-five miles north, or from Sodaville, ninety miles west. Even the freight wagons had to carry hay and a barrel of water for each round trip. Every day streams of men poured in through the clouds of alkali dust, relieved to end their journey and pitch a tent, burrow into a dugout, or throw their blankets under a wagon—for tomorrow they would be rich. Everyone was in a hurry—to dig, to build, to sell, and to drink—and while water was scarce and sold for twenty-five cents a bucket, the liquor supply was abundant. Everybody ran a saloon, even Jim Butler. Lumber was almost unknown and outrageously costly; so empty bottles and oil cans became building materials. The bottles, set in adobe, formed walls; the cans, when pounded flat, made roofs and doors. Supplies were in such demand that goods, unloaded and piled on the boardwalks by the freighters, were sold before the merchant to whom they were delivered had a chance to carry them inside his store. No wonder that within a year the camp outgrew its plat and pushed up the barren slopes of newly named Butler, Oddie, and Brougher peaks!

Tonopah had a brief lull at the end of 1901, when the leases Butler had issued expired and many of the men who had held them left to spend their fortunes elsewhere. The camp's real boom came in 1902, after a Philadelphia corporation bought the eight discovery claims for $350,000 and organized the Tonopah Mining Company, with Oddie as manager. Following its example,

TONOPAH AND MINES ON MOUNT ODDIE

CATHOLIC CHURCH, GOLDFIELD (BURNED IN FIRE OF 1943)

the Tonopah-Belmont, the Montana-Tonopah, the Tonopah Extension, and other companies were set up.

The Crystal Water Company provided the town with adequate water, making unnecessary the sign over the door of a saloon which owned a small bathtub:

> First Chance $1, Second Chance 50 cents, All others
> 25 cents.

Within the year bigger and better buildings appeared and new streets crawled up the mountainsides, squirming past mine properties or coming to a dead end at some dump or hoist. The population grew to 20,000, and as long as silver poured from the mines Tonopah lived high. Restaurants served oysters, quail, and champagne and decorated their tables with flowers sent in from the Coast. The Tonopah Club became the city's rendezvous, and stakes at gambling rose to fantastic figures.

In spite of the 1903 rush to Goldfield, just twenty-five miles away, Tonopah held its own. In the fall of that year a raid on the Chinese quarter was reported by the *Jerome Mining News* of September 20:

> A mob of twelve to fifteen men invaded Chinatown yesterday afternoon and at the point of guns compelled a number of Chinamen to leave town at once. Several who did not comply at once were badly beaten and dragged to the outskirts of town and told to take the road to Sodaville. Later all the Chinese but one returned and notified the officers. . . . Ping Ling, a seventy-three year old man, the proprietor of a washhouse, was one of the victims. . . . His body was mutilated and found three miles west of town. The Chinese were also robbed of several hundred dollars. Eighteen men, mostly cooks and waiters, have been arrested and are now in jail. Among them is the president of a labor union.
>
> A meeting of the citizens of Tonopah was held at which resolutions denunciatory of the action of the mob were adopted.

In 1904 the Tonopah and Goldfield Railroad laid tracks across the desert from Sodaville and reached Tonopah on July 24. The first train was welcomed by the combined populations of Tonopah and Goldfield and by the Governor of Nevada. The locomotive was drenched with champagne by a white-robed beauty queen, a drilling contest was staged, and everyone celebrated the long-awaited event in his own way. In 1905 Belmont relinquished the county seat to Tonopah; but by 1913 the boom was over and production in the mines was beginning to decrease. By 1921 only four of the city's mines were listed among the twenty-five largest silver producers in the country. Gradually the properties shut down or were handled on a small scale by leasers, until by 1940 only leasers carried on. During World War II an air base was built on the fringe of the city, but today only concrete foundation posts and a few barracks show where it stood.

Tonopah was a busy place when we saw it. At sunset, when the rugged mountains surrounding the city are black silhouettes or tawny cones cut by deep blue-shadowed gorges, it is a dramatic place. Mine dumps and mills rise out of the midst of frame homes, and hoists stand like watchtowers above the many shafts. Anyone will point out the Montana-Tonopah, the Mizpah, the Valley View, the Desert Queen, and the Tonopah Extension. Look at the long, low, curving railroad station and picture the ore trains waiting to be loaded or stacked high with bullion. Visit the Tonopah Club, the Butler Theatre, and the Mizpah Hotel; and be sure to roam the streets of this city, which has produced between $200,000,000 and $300,000,000 of silver and gold and which is still the biggest little mining town on the desert.

GOLDFIELD

In the morning we started south just as the sun was gilding the tiny dome of the Nye County courthouse. Except for the paved black ribbon ahead of us leading straight to Goldfield, the desert was colorless in the early morning light. About halfway between the two towns we passed some diggings and a few ruined mine buildings—the remains of Southern Klondyke, the camp where Butler expected to prospect when he stumbled on his bonanza at Tonopah Springs.

Though Goldfield is surrounded by mountains, they do not press on the city as do those at Tonopah, nor are they so imposing. The town itself occupies a broad flat, once covered by a forest of Joshua trees but now barren and dusty. Columbia Mountain, where the mines were found, rises like a great cone from the desert floor, and long, high mesas, walled with black volcanic rock, stand just beyond the city limits. At first glance the town seems small, and its buildings seem to be concentrated within a few blocks; it was once larger, but the northern third was reclaimed by the desert after two huge fires swept away the buildings.

Goldfield's beginnings were certainly not sensational. Tom Fisherman, a Shoshone Indian, found the first specimen of ore in the area and showed it around Tonopah to anyone who would look at it. That city was at the peak of its silver boom, however, and few were interested except two local prospectors named Billy Marsh and Harry Stimler. They got a grubstake from Tom Kendall, the proprietor of the Tonopah Club, and started south to find the source of Fisherman's float. The men camped at Rabbit Springs, twenty-five miles south of Tonopah, and explored the ledges in the vicinity of Columbia Mountain. Here they found strings of gold, but, unable to trace the source, they worked northward and on December 4, 1902, located the Sandstorm lode. In spite of the fact that the ore assayed only $12.60 a ton, they continued prospecting and staked nineteen claims, elated that they had found gold in a region which heretofore had yielded only silver. But their news created no stir in Tonopah, and hardly enough prospectors joined them at the foot of Columbia Mountain to set up the camp of Goldfield.

In the spring of 1903 other prospectors arrived, and Marsh and Stimler, who had staked out more claims than they could work, let some of them lapse and pointed out the best locations to the newcomers. Charles Taylor relocated the Jumbo and, after working it unsuccessfully for several weeks, tried to sell it for $150; but no one cared to buy. He continued pecking at the unproductive ground, therefore, and struck a paystreak. In the end the mine brought him $1,250,000. Al Myers and R. C. Hart selected another of the abandoned claims, called it the Combination, and on May 24, 1903, struck the first rich lode in the district. By October the Combination Mining Company was formed, and when the first ore was shipped in December, even Tonopah was impressed. After George S. Nixon bought a claim for $10,000, men couldn't reach Goldfield fast enough. Although only trails and the roughest roads led to the camp, six-horse stages and sputtering automobiles ploughed through the dust, passing weary prospectors on foot and patient burros loaded with their gear.

Eleven of the first comers to Goldfield put up ten dollars apiece for a survey of a townsite, and within the next few months the camp became a city, real estate boomed, and choice lots sold for as much as $45,000 apiece. False-fronted two-story stores lined the principal streets, and men lived in anything— from tents to lodginghouses which advertised, "A Nice New Bed $7.50 a month or 50¢ a night." Eastern experts were called in to inspect mining properties; as a result of their favorable reports, the country round about was staked for miles.

By midsummer of 1904 the Jumbo, Florence, and January mines were shippers, and latecomers to the district were trying to buy claims from those already working them. Certain mines were developed by leasers, and, since the ore was close to the surface, many operators made fortunes within a few months. In 1905 the Red Top, Sandstorm, and Kendall joined the list of shippers. When the Mohawk shipped forty-seven tons of ore in 1907, on which the smelter returned a check for $574,958.39, Goldfield became hysterical. Men talked of nothing but "jewelry ore" and "picture rock" and willingly worked underground for $3.50 a day in order to "high-grade" chunks of the spectacular metal. A clever man could hide several hundred dollars' worth about him at a time. Mining stock sold as fast as new issues could be printed; and though some of it was sound, much was worthless. An investor who had been "taken in" on a deal wrote a letter to the editor of the *Mining and Scientific Press,* which appeared on June 1, 1907, under the title, "How to Wild-Cat."

Sir—Get a claim near some mine, give it a name. that can be mistaken for the adjacent property, leave a man there well supplied with telegraphic funds with instructions to use them prodigally; experience of mining is not necessary, provided he is prolific in mining lore, big imagination, and careless of telling the truth; form a company, get a lot of certificates printed, engage two or three brokers as fiscal agents and instruct them to go the gait; supply them with all the probable possibilities of your mine becoming a bonanza; in case of a lull in sales instruct your man at the front to make a strike, and in case he fails discharge him for incompetency; in replacing him be sure to get a man incompetent as to mining but well versed in geological gab; and just before your promised dividends are due let the control pass to someone else on whose shoulders you can shift the responsibility.

Though the mines seemed inexhaustible, they were shallow, and in time the veins pinched out and the jewelry rock was gone. But while they lasted money was plentiful, and muckers as well as millionaires drank champagne like water. Much of the champagne was consumed in Tex Rickard's elaborate saloon, The Northern, which opened with eighty bartenders in 1906, shortly after its owner returned from the Klondyke. Its patrons trusted Rickard; once, during a bank panic, they brought their deposits to him for safekeeping, unaware that he was returning the money they had just withdrawn to the bank via his back door, in an attempt to stop the run upon it.

It was Tex who thought up the Gans-Nelson "Battle of the Century" for the lightweight championship of the world, and held it in Goldfield on September 3, 1906. Nelson demanded a $30,000 purse; equal to any challenge, Goldfield raised $110,000 within twenty-four hours! On the great day, 50,000 people packed the town, arriving in all kinds of vehicles as well as by train (for the railroad had been extended from Tonopah to Goldfield in 1905). The contest lasted for forty-two rounds, and Gans emerged world champion.

The big hotel was built at a cost of $500,000 in 1910, when Goldfield's population was 30,000 and its mines were operating in three shifts. It was a sturdy four-story brick structure with mahogany woodwork, thick carpets, brass beds, and leather-covered furniture. On the night it opened, celebrities occupied its 200 rooms, and as the night wore on, champagne flowed through the lobby and down the steps into the street. It is still standing and was last used during World War II by aviators from the Tonopah Army Air Base.

The years 1910 and 1911 marked Goldfield's crest. Thereafter production began to drop, and even mines that had paid big dividends, such as the Florence-Goldfield and Mohawk, the Goldfield Combination Fraction, the Goldfield Consolidated, and the Jumbo Extension, tapered off and ultimately shut down. After 1918 valuable machinery was shipped away, buildings were razed, and Goldfield became a skeleton city. The picture rock was gone from the shallow deposits which had yielded an estimated $150,000,000 in fifteen years.

In 1923 fifty-two blocks of the business section burned, leaving crumbling walls and foundations filled with debris. In 1943 a seventy-mile wind fanned a small blaze in a frame house into a roaring inferno, scattered sparks for blocks, and destroyed quantities of buildings before it was brought under control. Although the Catholic church was gutted, most of the other stone buildings survived.

Goldfield produces a strange effect today, as it is alive and dead at the same time. From a distance its large buildings suggest a thriving city, yet its streets look deserted. Its few inhabitants are surrounded by empty houses and boarded-up stores, yet the Esmeralda County courthouse, an austere crenellated stone building, and the firehouse opposite it are in use. The Goldfield Hotel is boarded up, and at least one of the stone schoolhouses is closed; but Tex Rickard's home is well kept up, a modern motel is doing business, and an enterprising filling-station agent sells postcards, printed from old negatives, which show the city in its prime. In 1947 the old Florence mine was reopened by leasers, and a new 100-ton processing mill was built on the property; but the other mines are deserted. No trains puff into the station—the tracks are gone—and no customers lurch through the huge stone entrance arch, the sole remains of the Sideboard Saloon. Goldfield is a monument to a mining boom.

RHYOLITE AND BULLFROG

WE DROVE south of Goldfield seventy miles to an even ghostlier skeleton—Rhyolite. At Beatty we stopped to see W. H. Brown, a former sheriff of Death Valley, who told us how to reach Rhyolite and Bullfrog and drew a map showing the location of the principal mines. After a three-mile drive on the Death Valley highway, we turned right on an old railroad grade that led to the first of the two towns. The surrounding mountains were grim and bare, marbleized with streaks of red, brown, green, and ochre. On the left, at the base of Montgomery Mountain, were the foundations of a big mill, and ahead, on Ladd Mountain, stood the dumps of many mines. We spotted no town, however, until staring white concrete ghosts appeared above the desert growth, silhouetted against the barren hills.

The first building we came to was the railroad station, now called the Rhyolite Ghost Casino. Its dark, cool interior contains a bar in what was formerly the Ladies' Waiting Room, and its genial hosts, Bob and Paul Cornelius, are steeped in Rhyolite's history. While we refreshed ourselves, first one and then the other told us scraps of information.

Water, they said, had been so scarce in the first years of the camp that teams were constantly hauling it from the springs at Beatty at a cost of anywhere from two to five dollars a barrel. Ice was sold according to its weight as it left the icehouse in Goldfield; by the time it had been hauled across the desert, the twenty-five pound cake one had paid for might have melted to a small lump. After the entire population left in 1911, many of the buildings were torn down, moved out, or dynamited, and the excavations that remained contained all manner of discarded stuff. Only a year or two before our visit, some high buttoned shoes had been uncovered in the sagebrush behind the "cat house."

As we listened to our hosts and read from the several old newspapers they spread in front of us, we saw the Bullfrog mining district emerge from a desert waste known only to Indians and chance prospectors, and become first a group of tent cities and then the booming camp in whose depot we were sitting.

We could see Shorty Harris in August, 1904, as he crossed Daylight Pass from Death Valley into Nevada and came across the green bullfrog rock. He had been prospecting ever since 1878, following every strike but always missing the big money. He explored the hill and, in the greenish rock, found the big blowout of quartz full of free gold. Shorty showed his discovery to E. L. Cross; after the men were sure they had made a real strike, they set off for Goldfield to celebrate. Shorty got drunk and sold his share in the claim for $800; but Cross kept his portion and later got $60,000 for it. Their news started gold-hounds south on a new scent, and the rush to the Bullfrog Hills began.

Within three months people were living in canvas tents with cheesecloth or canvas partitions, or in wooden shacks with canvas tops, in the brand-new camp of Bullfrog. Men stood in line for hours waiting to be fed at lunch counters, and a correspondent from the *Jerome Mining News,* whose curiosity drew him to the camp, reported:

The first thing that struck my attention . . . was to see a bar right out in the open, with God's blue sky for a ceiling, and the surrounding sagebrush for walls.

Stage fare from Goldfield was eighteen dollars; automobile fare, twenty-five dollars. Colonel Mickey Hogan grubstaked the Iron-Gall Kid, the Big Nose Kid, and the Pecos Kid late in 1904 and sent them on a prospecting trip into Nevada. When he heard that the boys had struck it rich in Bullfrog, he bought an automobile and set out for the camp, making the trip

. . . from Las Vegas to Bullfrog in seven hours, slow time but the road is badly cut up with heavy freight wagons. Big Nose had a sale on for a sum written in six figures. . . . The Colonel says he saw Lordsburg, Hachita and Naco in their best days but they weren't in it a little with Goldfield and Bullfrog, which are red hot camps. [*Jerome Mining News,* June 24, 1905.]

Amargosa City, Jumpertown, and Bonanza, tent cities like Bullfrog, soon whitened the nearby hills close to the mines, but they were nothing compared to the one about to be born. In February, 1905, a townsite company laid out the streets of Rhyolite, and its boosters talked the men of the tent colonies into moving up to the new site in a body. Tempted by free lots, they made the move in a single day, and Rhyolite mushroomed overnight. As its population soared and the wooden shacks were replaced by concrete and brick buildings, plans were made for a $10,000 hotel, a $5,000 bath house, and an Opera House. The trickle of water known as the Amargosa River and a few springs in the vicinity were considered a sufficient water supply for the growing city, although to some they seemed more like a mirage which might disappear at any time and leave the city panting on the hot desert. But anyone looking at the magnificent $90,000 John S. Cook building, standing three stories high on the corner of Golden Street and Broadway, quickly forgot the water problem and the desert heat and admired the handsome quarters occupied by the First National Bank with its burglar-proof vaults.

Before the end of 1906 Rhyolite had 16,000 inhabitants, catered to by forty-five saloons, several gambling houses—one, called the Louvre, run by a woman—and a sporting section supplied with girls from San Francisco's Barbary Coast. From the residential part of town, known as Nob Hill, came the members of the Women's Rhyolite Society, the Women's Relief Corps, and the many committees which planned dances, socials, and bazaars for charitable purposes. At its peak the city had both a Presbyterian and a Catholic church, three daily newspapers, and the $130,000 station to which the Tonopah and Tidewater and Las Vegas and Tonopah railroads brought passengers and delivered freight.

The mines that caused Rhyolite to blossom in the desert were mere prospect holes until late in 1905, but their surface ore was richer than that at Goldfield. Shoshone Johnny discovered a mine and was just beginning to develop it, when Bob Montgomery came along and offered him a new pair of overalls in exchange for the hole in the ground. Johnny took the overalls, and Montgomery's purchase became the Montgomery Shoshone, the biggest producer of the camp.

As the district boomed, the hills surrounding Rhyolite were covered with mine dumps and the headframes of shafts. During 1906 speculation fever hit

BANK BUILDING, RHYOLITE

SEARCHLIGHT.
FIREWALL AT LEFT

EDGE OF TONOPAH

the district and sent Bullfrog mining stocks soaring to fantastic heights. Promoters who had learned the game in the Goldfield boom handled the town's publicity and watched with satisfaction as men and money poured into the district, attracted by their flamboyant stories. On the streets no one talked of anything but mines and investments: how much free gold had been found in the National Bank and Yankee Girl claims on Ladd Mountain; what rich deposits were constantly being uncovered in the Golden Sceptre, the Eclipse, and the Denver properties on Bonanza Mountain; how soon the Montgomery Shoshone mill would be completed; and what Tramp and Gibraltar stock were selling for that day.

For a time, sacked bullion accumulated faster than it could be shipped to San Francisco. In all, over $3,000,000 was taken from the mines of the district, and at the height of the boom over a thousand men were employed in the several properties.

Even the panic of 1907 failed to worry Rhyolite until money stopped pouring in. Rumors that the ledges contained only superficial bunches of rich ore and paystreaks were thinning out were disregarded, and for two more years the camp flourished. In March, 1909, Erle R. Clemens, editor of the *Rhyolite Herald,* published a special mining edition which boosted the district and told the world how rich the mines were. According to Clemens:

Mid-winter, 1909, four years after the Bullfrog excitement started, finds the district enjoying the greatest prosperity in its history from a standpoint of ore production and mine development. During the year 1908 the district marketed close to one million dollars' worth of gold-silver ores and bullion, and this was the first year that conditions had been favorable for production. . . .

The outlook for . . . the year 1909 is flattering in the extreme, and it is believed by many that the year's production will not fall short of two million dollars and perhaps reach much higher.

But in 1910 even the Montgomery Shoshone Mining Company stopped drilling, and as other mines ceased production, Rhyolite began to worry. The population shrank from 12,000 to 700, and then to a mere handful. By 1911 people were beginning to pull out as hastily as they had spilled into the incredible town, leaving houses completely furnished and offices fully equipped. Only eighteen children rattled around in the brand-new concrete schoolhouse. The *Herald* ceased publication, and the press was hauled away. Finally the last train pulled out, and salvage crews tore up the tracks. A few die-hards stayed on, but within a year or two everyone was gone, and the sagebrush and greasewood crept back over the desert and hid foundations of what had once been buildings.

The huge three-story concrete hulk of the First National Bank on Golden Street looms above all other ruins in the town. Its roof and floors are gone, its rear wall is demolished, and its steps lead to nothing. Another concrete skeleton is the two-story $20,000 schoolhouse, which was still under construction when it dawned on the citizens that the peak of production was over. Rhyolite's first school was a frame affair. It was built after a Mr. Smith, father of three children, demanded it. He was duly empowered by the town officials to buy equipment for it and hurried off to San Francisco, where he spent $650 and made arrangements for his purchases to be delivered C.O.D. Six weeks later they arrived by freight wagon and were dumped on the desert; for no one had started to build a school to put them in. In addition to the $650 to be collected, the freighter presented a bill of $378 for hauling charges. Fortunately, Mr. Smith and his family had left Rhyolite and were on their way to Oregon when the freight arrived. But the town was growing and the number of school-age children was increasing; so the citizens put up money for lumber, and by the time the school was completed 200 children were ready to enter it. No one had thought, however, to hire a teacher! By the time one arrived, 400 children were waiting for classes and a second teacher was needed. In 1907 bonds were issued for the big concrete building whose walls rise from the greasewood. It was never filled to capacity.

Since all but five or six buildings have been completely razed, and since the desert vegetation is low and evenly distributed over the ground, each of the cross streets—mere sand tracks today—is invisible until one reaches it. In every block a mass of cactus, sagebrush, and greasewood camouflages the broken foundation stones and cellar pits. Not even a tree breaks the monotony of the desert floor. At the end of a side street stands the shell of the jail; down Golden Street beyond the bank is the Bottle House, a strange creation whose walls are made of empty bottles laid in cement. In it live the Johnsons, who run a small museum for tourists. Beside it is a garden without flowers, ornamented with specimens of rock and fragments of colored glass laid out in patterns or grouped according to type.

Mr. Johnson showed us his collection of relics and then pointed down the hill to the site of Bullfrog and its few stone and adobe ruins, one of which was the old jail. All the rest of the town has disappeared.

Except for the wind that rattled through the greasewood, we heard no sound but our own muffled footsteps in the sand, and we saw no signs of life except darting lizards and desert quail zigzagging through the sage. Rhyolite, born in 1905 and dying in 1911, is an eerie ghost whose sand-filled skeleton buildings seem shockingly urban and out of place on the lonely, sun-bleached desert.

SEARCHLIGHT

FROM Rhyolite we returned to Beatty and then continued southeast through Las Vegas. South of Alunite, Highway 95 leads straight across the desert to Searchlight. It is a new-looking town, in which the older buildings hide on side streets or inside yards overgrown with cactus and Joshua trees. Too many of the false-fronted stores have been modernized for my taste with stucco and brick veneer, so I hunted up the postmistress and asked her where I could learn about the town's early history.

"That's easy," she said. "Just go up the street and see Ollie Thompson. He's in his eighties and he's been here since 1905. He'll be glad to talk to you."

She pointed to a small frame house with carved white pillars and an ornamental balustrade. On the porch sat Mr. Thompson. He motioned us to sit beside him in the porch swing and asked us where we were from. When we mentioned Colorado, his eyes lighted up. "I used to mine at Jimtown," he said. After we had chatted a while about places we both knew well, he began to tell me about Searchlight.

"The Searchlight mine was located in 1897," he began, "and there's two stories about how it got its name. The men who found it couldn't decide what to call it until one of them pulled a box of Searchlight matches out of his pocket, looked at the label, and said, 'Oh, let's call it the Searchlight.' The other story is that some men were panning for gold, and one of them yelled that he'd got colors. The rest didn't believe him, and one of the outfit looked into his pan and said, 'Fred, if you have colors there, you'll need a searchlight to find them.'

"Fred Coltin discovered the Duplex mine in 1898. The Searchlight, the original shaft, is part of the Duplex now. Some of the camp's richest ore came from stopes on the 200-foot level of the lode. The camp grew up around the Duplex, and you should have seen it when it had thirty-eight saloons, five of them on Hobson Street. Hobson was the Spanish-American war hero of 1898, the year this camp started; so the main street was named for him. The original road through town ran in front of those false-fronted stores you saw, but the new highway cuts through a different part of town."

"Which were the principal mines?" I asked.

"The Quartette's the big one over on the hill, and over there are the Duplex and the Searchlight. Then there's the Blossom and the Cyrus Noble.

"The Quartette was located in 1896 or 1897 by John Swickhart, who traded it to Ben McCready for five dollars, a team of mules, and a plug of tobacco. McCready took two partners, Fisher and Hubbard, and the three developed the prospect by sinking a shaft until they'd used up all their capital.

Still they hadn't struck the vein. So they held a final meeting before quitting; but the miners, who were working under Charles DePue, told McCready they believed the ore was there and that they'd like to continue digging without any assurance of pay and take a chance on striking a pay-shoot. They worked about a month, and in December, 1898, they fired their last round of shots. When the smoke cleared away, there was a streak of ore right across the face of the tunnel they'd been digging. Right after that Hubbard sold out his share in the mine, and Crocker and Hopkins bought into the property with McCready and Fisher. That made the Quartette. The company put up a twenty-stamp mill on the bank of the Colorado River and built their own seventeen-mile narrow-gauge single track to it. By 1903, after they'd struck enough water in the lower levels of the mine to pump and use for milling purposes, they built a forty-stamp mill on the property and abandoned the river plant. In 1915 the Quartette changed hands again, and the new owners took out nearly $100,-000 by cyanidizing the ore from the dump. The mine has produced several millions, and there's no reason why it shouldn't yield as much again.

"Searchlight was a boom camp from 1900 until 1906. That's why the Santa Fe began a survey up here, but the boom fizzled out. In 1912 we had a second boom when leasers came in to work the old properties. They found copper under the gold, silver, and lead and predicted that Searchlight would end up as a copper camp.

"In 1945 there was another boom—some kind of a scheme to make a resort town—and a dozen two-story Army surplus buildings were moved in. But there's not enough water here to attract tourists; so the scheme failed and they took the new buildings away. I can remember the days when money came easy around here. Once, I remember, men wagered a thousand dollars and mining claims on the outcome of a fight between two burros, Thunder and Hornet! Hornet won."

ELDORADO CANYON AND NELSON

"WHICH way are you heading when you leave here?" asked Mr. Thompson. "If you're going to Boulder Dam, turn off to the right before you get there and go to Nelson, in Eldorado Canyon. It's a gold and silver camp that dates back to the sixties, and it's named for an old fellow that was gophering around in the Canyon when the Indians got him.

"Nelson had a second boom between 1906 and 1913. That's when lots of the old places got torn down. The mining outfits that went in installed new machinery, and the camp buzzed for awhile. There used to be a camp near the river and an old cemetery on a ledge overhanging the water. It's crumbled into the Colorado by now. Some of the markers were put up in the eighties.

You might be able to find the foundations of a couple of old stone cabins on the site of the camp. I'm not sure what's there now.

"Eldorado Canyon's full of mines. The Quaker City, the Mocking Bird, and the Honest Miner are near the head of the canyon. The Wall Street, the Savage, and the Techatticup are nearer the river. If you're looking for stories, you find out all you can about the Techatticup."

Spanish explorers are said to have found gold in the canyon in 1775 and to have made a map of the region which they took with them when, loaded with nuggets, they returned to Mexico. Just 100 years later, in 1875, a party of Mexicans, also seeking gold, followed the trail marked on the old map. It led to the Techatticup mine. However, by the time they arrived, the mine was being worked and the whole district was active; for during the 1850's an Indian had shown the source of the canyon gold to prospectors, and by 1857 mining operations were under way. It was wild, lonely, outlaw country, in which desperate men found refuge and hostile Piute Indians harassed and killed those who had the temerity to explore the barren hills and canyons.

During the early sixties, Colorado River steamboats made regularly scheduled trips between Eldorado Canyon and Yuma, a distance of over 350 miles. Every five weeks these boats brought supplies, equipment, and miners to the canyon and took out the gold bullion which long trains of pack animals and freight wagons delivered to the boat landing. For the protection of the miners, a company of soldiers was stationed at the camp until 1863. After they were withdrawn, although miners "patrolled the hills watching for the approach of the bloodthirsty Piutes," no one dared explore the country or work a claim alone. Finally the Indians attacked, and the men escaped down the river on rafts to Fort Mohave.

But the mines were too tempting to be abandoned permanently, and the best properties were reopened during the seventies. By 1879, when the canyon was enjoying a boom, the Techatticup was sold to the Southwest Mining Company for $150,000. Between 1892 and 1895 this company, which worked not only the Techatticup but also other properties in the canyon, recovered $7,000,000 from its several holdings. The panic of 1895 paralyzed mining operations, and the combined properties were sold at a Sheriff's sale for $15,000. Joseph Wharton of Philadelphia bought them and immediately ran 1,000 tons of ore from the Techatticup dump through the mill. Only ore which brought $100 a ton was processed. Since 1906 spurts of mining have kept the canyon alive and even revived the camp of Nelson and the mines close to it.

No account of Eldorado is complete without the lurid tale of John Nash's connection with the Techatticup mine. The mine, whose Indian name means "plenty for all," has been worked intermittently ever since 1863 and is said to have produced $1,700,000. In the late 1860's it became the property of

John Nash, the organizer of the Eldorado Mining Company, who operated it until 1879. Adjoining it was the Queen City (or Savage) mine, owned by George Hearst. Nash wanted the Queen City, too.

In 1872 he hired three desperados to jump the mine and hold it for a stated time, promising to pay each man $5,000 for his services. When Hearst's agent next came to the premises to perform the annual development work, the gunmen ran him off and took possession of the property. Now that the job was done, Nash discharged the most dangerous of the three men after paying him his $5,000; but he talked the second gunman, a half-breed Indian named William Pirtle, out of his portion of the pay. The third accomplice, Jim Jones, who was also an Indian, held out for his money; and Nash, who had no intention of paying, circulated false stories about him until he was distinctly unpopular in the camp. Nash then ordered Pirtle to kill Jones. A few mornings later, while the unsuspecting Indian was bending over a washbowl outside the bunkhouse, Pirtle shot him in the back. Jones whirled around and beat his attacker over the head with a powder keg; then, grabbing his gun, he started down the trail to the Colorado River, pursued by most of the men in the camp. When he saw that the posse were about to capture him, he hid in a prospect hole and, as they drew near, killed one man and wounded another. While his pursuers retreated temporarily, Jones crawled from his hole, got the rifle belonging to the dead man, and crawled back to his hide-out. In spite of his wounds, he held off the men until the next afternoon, when, bleeding and half-crazed with thirst, he raised a handkerchief on his rifle as a token of surrender. "Water," he gasped, as one of the men rode up to him. A shot through the head was the answer. These tactics won for Nash undisputed claim to the Queen City, but they gave the mine a bad name, and even Nash was afraid to be caught near it after dark.

The following year, 1873, Nash's brother-in-law, Davis, reached Eldorado Canyon. Nash was building a mill near the river. Davis invested heavily in the Eldorado Mining Company's stock and persuaded a close friend named Fuller to join him in the venture. The combined capital set the mine on its feet. Davis became superintendent at the mill; and a man named William Piette was made superintendent at the mine, six miles up Eldorado Canyon. Soon an amazing body of rich ore, called the Bridal Chamber, was discovered; from this one chute, more than a million dollars was taken. Nash, greedy as ever, begrudged Davis and Fuller their share in this bonanza and plotted to get rid of them. His first move was to get Davis to inspect the new ore body. The honest superintendent rode up from the river, saw the ore, and at noon, instead of eating at the company boardinghouse, accepted Piette's invitation to have lunch at his cabin. After the meal Davis climbed aboard the ore wagon which had brought him up the canyon and started back to the mill. Within a few minutes he became violently ill and twelve hours later died of strychnine poisoning. Everyone knew what had happened, but no one dared hint that the death had been other than natural. A few days later, Piette visited Fuller's camp, several miles above the mill on the river bank. In June, when the Colorado is high, every outfit along the stream gathers its year's supply of fuel by snagging the driftwood that floats by, and Fuller, as usual, was busy directing a crew of Indians in catching wood. Piette stayed all night at the camp and left right after breakfast. Before noon Fuller died of strychnine poisoning.

In 1877, Piette and Hans Godsfritsen ran the company store at the river. They did not make a success of it and were glad to take as a partner Henry Warner, whose capital saved the business. Piette quarreled with Warner, but the latter stood up to the bully and made him back down before any shooting began. Then Warner disappeared, and no trace of him was ever found. The partners circulated a story that Warner had gone down the river with the firm's ready cash on a purchasing trip for the company; but no one believed them. Godsfritsen and Piette soon left the canyon, and the crimes ceased.

John R. Riggs concludes his "Story of Eldorado Canyon," which appeared on July 27, 1912, in the *Mohave County Miner* with these words:

The old Techatticup and Savage mines are silent—and have been for years, the habitat of bats, rats and owls. . . . The old mill is falling into decay . . . and a deep silence lies over all that once was a wild and lawless spot. A curse seems upon the place. Yet these mines contain millions of wealth and their product is estimated at above three millions of dollars.

10. The Army Turns Prospector

Utah

THE FIRST COMPANY of Mormons to look down over the vast mountain-locked plain where Salt Lake City stands were distinctly disappointed. They lacked the vision of their leader, Brigham Young, who surveyed the same arid waste, the meager stream meandering through it and the grim mountains surrounding it, and said, "This is the place." Two years later thousands of men off to the California gold fields wore trails across the Salt Lake valley, but the Mormons by then were busy building their new State of Deseret and paid little attention to them.

Brigham Young suspected the presence of minerals in the mountain ranges that towered above the many little hamlets and homesteads that were being coaxed into existence by the tireless efforts of his pioneers, and he feared what gold fever might do to his people. He therefore discouraged mining by saying:

We cannot eat silver and gold, neither do we want to bring into our peaceful settlements a rough frontier population to violate the morals of our youth, overwhelm us by numbers and drive us again from our hard-earned homes. [Kate B. Carter, *Heart Throbs of the West.*]

During the summer of 1849 he delivered a sermon which contained the following admonitions:

Do not any of you suffer the thought to enter your minds, that you must go to the gold mines in search of riches. That is no place for the Saints. Some have gone there and returned; they keep coming and going, but their garments are spotted, almost universally. . . . The man who is trying to gain for himself the perishable things of this world, and suffers his affections to be staid upon them, may despair of ever obtaining a cross of glory. This world is only to be used as

363

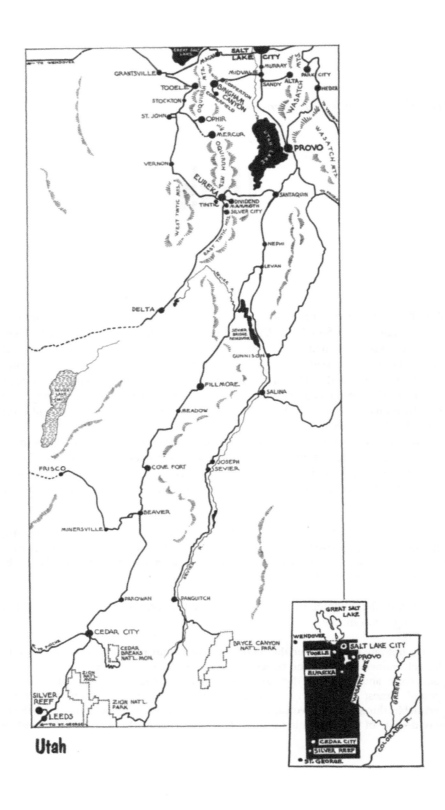

Utah

an apartment, in which the children of men may be prepared for their eternal redemption and exaltation in the presence of their Savior; and we have but a short time allotted to us here to accomplish so great a work. [Edward W. Tullidge, *History of Salt Lake City*.]

The Mormons, therefore, left the development of the mines to others; yet certain of their number were among the first to discover gold in California! As early as January, 1846, Brigham Young had offered President Polk the services of the Mormons for anything the government might need. As a result of his offer, the President asked for five hundred volunteers to assist in the war with Mexico. The Mormon Battalion left Fort Leavenworth, Kansas, July 19, 1846, and reached San Diego on January 29, 1847, only to find the Stars and Stripes flying over the fort. Since the army no longer needed them, the majority of the men started in the spring for Utah by way of Sutter's Fort. A number of them obtained work there, and nine of the Battalion accompanied James Marshall to the American River and were with him when he found gold on January 24, 1848. Henry W. Bigler, one of them, wrote in his journal, "This day some kind of metal has been found in the tail race that looks like gold." The men joined in the frantic placering which followed, until in June of the same year the Church recalled them to Utah, and they exchanged their picks and pans for shovels and hoes. Thereafter, the Mormons devoted themselves to agriculture and irrigation. Sporadic prospecting was carried on in southern Utah, but on so slight a scale that it did little more than confirm the fact that ore deposits lay in the mountains.

General Patrick E. Connor, the first man to exploit mining in the Territory, arrived in Utah in October, 1862, with a company of California volunteers and promptly established Fort Douglas east of Salt Lake City. He and his men were sent to the area by the Federal government, which had just passed a law prohibiting polygamy and suspected that the people in the Territory were defying it. Connor found that this was not so. But he hated the Mormons, who were in the majority and controlled the elections, and did everything in his power to lessen their control. His first plan to break their supremacy was to encourage his men, most of whom had mined in California, to prospect the canyons near Salt Lake, hoping that they would uncover mineral deposits which would attract non-Mormons to the area.

All through 1863 and 1864, while Connor was stationed at Fort Douglas, he and his men made strikes and organized mining districts in the Jordan and Tooele valleys. After organizing the West Mountain mining district in December, 1863, Connor published a circular that mentioned the evidence of mineral resources in the Territory and urged "opening up the country to a new, hardy, industrious population," who would prospect for the minerals. In

March, 1864, he issued a second highly colored bulletin, in which he offered army protection to prospectors and viciously attacked the Mormons, saying:

... my policy has been to invite hither a large Gentile population sufficient by peaceful means and through the ballot box to overwhelm the Mormons by force of numbers, and thus wrest from the church—disloyal and traitorous to the core— the absolute control of temporal and civic affairs. . . . With this in view I have bent every energy and means of which I am possessed, both personal and official, towards the discovery and development of the mining resources of the territory, using without stint the soldier of my command.

Connor's efforts were successful, and by 1869, when the first transcontinental railroad reached Salt Lake City and provided an outlet for its resources, mining was an established industry. Silver, gold, copper, lead, and zinc were found in Utah's ranges, with first one and then another metal producing sensational strikes. Just as silver and gold deposits built the early camps and copper the later ones, so the stamp mills that pounded out the precious metals were supplanted by cyanide plants and by the great copper smelters at Murray, Midvale, Garfield, Magna, and Tooele.

Most of Utah's mining camps lie in the Oquirrh, Tintic, and Wasatch ranges and can be reached by relatively short drives from Salt Lake City. Silver Reef, however, is close to the southern border of the state, near Zion National Park and the town of Leeds.

BINGHAM CANYON

As SOON as we reached Salt Lake City, my friend and I climbed the hill to the State Capitol. From the steps we looked out over the vast Salt Lake Valley and to the mountain ranges that encircle it. Far to the south the valley ends at the foot of the Tintic Range; to the east the rugged Wasatch Range rises sharply from the valley floor to its high snow-capped ridge; and to the west the top of the Oquirrh Range makes a jagged line against the clear blue of the desert sky. We could just make out on the slope of the Oquirrhs the white terraces of Kennecott Copper's tremendous open-pit plant at Bingham Canyon; and, as we looked back across the valley to the east, we tried to pick out which of the many gashes in the Wasatch Range was the entrance to twenty-mile long Little Cottonwood Canyon. As Bingham and Little Cottonwood canyons were the sites of the first mining in the state we decided to visit them first.

We started toward Bingham Canyon by rolling south on the broad Salt Lake-Provo boulevard as far as the smelter town of Midvale. Here we turned

INGHAM CANYON

MINE BUILDINGS, ALTA

west and drove straight toward the Oquirrh Mountains and the terraces, dumps, mills, and settlements that comprise Bingham Canyon. Copperton, at the entrance of the canyon, is a model town with shaded streets and green lawns; but just beyond and completely divorced from it, Bingham Canyon crowds in one interminable street along the bottom of a V-shaped gulch, whose sheer sides are terraced benches, rising tier above tier until they disappear from sight. The street is narrow, the sidewalks are narrow, and the houses press against the canyon walls so as not to encroach on the pavement. Some of them are freshly painted and have pocket-handkerchief garden plots, but most of them are weathered and dingy and monotonously gray. Power stations and mine buildings, schoolhouses and dreary concrete playgrounds enclosed by wire-mesh fences are crammed in tight between the houses. The high canyon walls, the forests of skeleton steel towers carrying long ribbons of electric wires, and the long shadows shrinking down the mountainside as the sun rose higher were both eerie and dramatic. A mile or two up the canyon the street widens slightly, and several blocks of stores make up the business section of the town. Here, too, is the entrance of the tunnel that dives through the mountain and emerges beside the vast open pit, with its twenty-three or more levels and its nearly ninety miles of track. The view from the observation platform into the pit is awesome, and the ore trains which crawl from level to level look like long, supple silver worms.

The town was small enough until copper took over about the turn of the century, but since then it has become more and more congested and for want of space to expand, it has pushed farther up the bottom of both forks of the squirming, narrow defile.

Fires have roared down the gulch, cloudbursts have flooded it, and landslides and snowslides have buried buildings from time to time; but as long as the electric shovels cut the hills into steps and the ore cars slide over the gleaming rails, Bingham Canyon remains a live, pulsing, boisterous mining camp, teeming with energy and turning out prodigious quantities of copper ore.

The steep sides of Bingham Canyon were covered with forests of red pine, maple, and scrub oak trees when, in 1848, Brigham Young sent Thomas Bingham into the hills to run a portion of the church cattle in the canyon. Bingham and his sons found pieces of ore in the gulch and showed them to President Young; but he said to forget them, as he feared that if the presence of minerals was generally known, men would desert their farms and head for the hills.

All during the fifties the Mormon loggers, who were lumbering in Bingham Canyon and cleaning off the forested slopes, often found pieces of ore exposed along the trails. Some of these pioneers, who had mined in California, were familiar with the appearance of gold ore; but they did not know silver. So, like many gold-hunters elsewhere (notably in Leadville, Colorado), they did not recognize the rich silver content of their heavy chunks of galena. Regarding the rock as lead, most of them ignored it, while a few melted it down and made bullets with which to hunt game.

As soon as the ex-miner troops under General Connor arrived at Camp Douglas, they showed as much interest in prospecting as in soldiering; and their leader encouraged them by granting long furloughs, so that they could explore the many canyons in the vicinity of the fort. Late in the summer of 1863, George B. Ogilvie, an employee at Gardner's sawmill on the Jordan River at the mouth of Bingham Canyon, while logging in the canyon, picked up a piece of rock, put it in his dinner bucket, and went on working. Just at this time General Connor was making arrangements to have a detachment of experienced miners drive a troop of cavalry horses to Bingham Canyon to graze. The miner-soldiers were to guard the horses and to prospect at the same time. At this juncture Ogilvie, who knew that Connor was interested in mining, arrived at the Fort with his specimen. Connor immediately had it assayed and learned that it was silver float rich in lead, gold, and silver. He, therefore, joined the prospecting-grazing party on its trip to the canyon, and there, on the Ogilvie ledge, the United States Army located the Jordan and other claims on September 17, 1863.

Connor announced this strike to the world, and the first rush to Utah was on. Shortly after the discovery a meeting was held at Gardner's sawmill to set up mining laws and to establish the Jordan Silver Mining Company; and on December 17, 1863, the West Mountain Mining District, which included Bingham Canyon, was organized. During the summer of 1864 the Jordan company began to work its claims in the canyon, although lack of transportation facilities and the high cost of supplies retarded any rapid development of the district. Before the end of the year, however, placer gold was discovered in the canyon, and for the next six to eight years Bingham was a gold camp. At first the richest diggings were on Clay Bar, from which $100,000 was washed by 1868. Then dust and nuggets were recovered from Bear Gulch, a tributary of Bingham Canyon; and by 1873, when placering was over, it was estimated that a total of $2,000,000 had been recovered from the gravels.

When in 1868 the first ore from Bingham was sent east to Maryland to be smelted, nearly one hundred properties yielding gold, silver, lead, and copper were under development; and their owners were anxiously awaiting the arrival of the transcontinental railroad, which reached Salt Lake City the following year and facilitated shipments to eastern plants. The completion of the Bingham and Camp Floyd railroad in 1870 renewed an interest in lode mining, and the scrawny camp of Bingham not only grew in population from

300 to 1,000 but also replaced its shacks and tents with more substantial frame buildings. Additional properties were located during the seventies; rich strikes were made in such mines as the Yosemite, Brooklyn, No-You-Don't, Highland Boy, and Boston Consolidated; and smelters were built in the district to handle the ores.

Between 1880 and 1893 the lead and silver mines flourished; but during the nineties the silver crash and the lowered market prices for silver, lead, and gold almost closed the camp. Copper deposits were known to exist in many of the properties, but their presence only hampered reduction of the silver, lead, and gold ores. No one at that time thought of mining copper except Colonel Enos A. Wall, who as early as 1887 had recognized the presence of the metal. A few years later he returned to Bingham and began to make secret tests of the ores, at the same time buying up copper holdings and relocating old claims. By 1896 he owned two hundred acres, he had spent $20,000 in exploration, he had obtained backers, and he was ready to develop his properties. Before going any farther, Wall and his associates hired Daniel C. Jackling and Robert C. Gemmell, exceptionally brilliant young engineers from Mercur, Utah, to examine the claims. As a result of their joint report, which was published in 1899, the history of copper mining was completely changed.

Both men believed that low-grade copper could be profitably mined if mass production methods were used and if the most recent findings in metallurgy were followed. This meant surface mining—the tearing down of the mountain and feeding it into mills properly equipped to separate the ore from the earth and waste rock. Captain J. R. De Lamar, the silver king, endorsed their plan but he could not afford to finance it. Jackling himself, therefore, bought an interest in the Wall property and procured as financial backers for the enterprise Charles MacNeill, Spencer Penrose, and R. A. F. Penrose of Colorado Springs. The Utah Copper Company, of which Jackling in later years became president, was organized in 1903 and erected an experimental mill at the mouth of Bingham Canyon. In 1906 the first steam shovel gouged a hole in the mineral-bearing earth, and by 1907 open-pit mining was in full swing. At first only ores which contained two per cent copper were processed; but as more advanced methods of production were perfected, ore carrying as little as one half of one per cent copper was handled profitably.

In 1907, after Jackling began his revolutionary experiment, Bingham Canyon became the largest open-pit copper mine in the country, and by 1927 the Utah Copper Company was the leader in production. Today the property is operated by the Kennecott Copper Company Corporation, and its mines are said to have sufficient ore bodies to keep them in operation until 1990. Over two billion dollars worth of copper has come out of Bingham Canyon, and General Connor's dream for Utah has been realized a thousandfold.

ALTA

FROM Bingham Canyon we retraced our steps to Midvale and then drove south to Sandy, where we turned east toward Little Cottonwood Canyon and the husk of the old camp of Alta.

The Little Cottonwood district was Indian hunting ground until the trappers discovered it in the 1830's, but few of them worked into its high, alpine valleys. It was left to restless General Connor and his miner-soldiers to explore thoroughly the long, narrow canyon, whose high, rocky walls shut in wooded green slopes and a tumbling stream. Connor liked to organize parties to go into the mountains and hunt for indications of mineral deposits. On such a trip, in 1864, he and his men found argentiferous galena in Little Cottonwood Canyon. One story credits the wife of an army surgeon with picking up the first piece of silver-bearing quartz and showing it to the men; another makes Connor himself the discoverer; but at the time the party was too busy staking claims to pay attention to such unimportant details.

The Wasatch mining district was immediately set up; but so little improvement work was done in it at first that by 1867 most of the claims had been jumped and the area was reorganized as the Mountain Lake mining district. The following year Camp Alta appeared as a few tents perched high on the side of Mount Baldy, but it was not until J. B. Woodman and his partners discovered the Emma mine in 1869 that the lofty settlement really boomed.

These men had been prospecting unsuccessfully in Little Cottonwood for some time and were about to give up, when two Salt Lake merchants, named Curtis and Hillyer, agreed to grubstake them. The men then returned through snow to a prospect hole they had previously opened and in 1868 began to dig again. There were no surface indications of its wealth or extent, but they doggedly sank a shaft ninety-three feet through solid rock and finally uncovered ore. This task had taken them ten months and had used up almost all their money; but the breast of silver they had exposed looked good, and they decided to hang on and develop their mine, the Emma. To raise money for further work they agreed to sell a fourth interest in the property for $3,000, but no one even nibbled at their offer. Finally, they "rawhided," or tobogganned the ore on cowhides, over the snow in the canyon to ox-drawn wagons, and sent it to Ogden to be forwarded by rail to San Francisco. From there it was shipped around the Horn to Wales. Some authorities state that the first shipment consisted of 4,200 tons, that from it $795,265 was recovered, and that, after transportation and smelting charges were deducted, the ore netted the owners $180 a ton.

Once the mine started to produce, Walker Brothers, bankers of Salt Lake City, bought a one-sixth interest for $25,000, and a Mr. Hussey bought a one-quarter interest for the same amount. Early in 1871 a new company was formed, controlled by Walker Brothers and called the Emma Mining Company of Utah. Next, Eastern investors examined the mine and paid $375,000 for an "undivided half interest," whereupon the property became known as the Emma Mining Company of New York. The size of the mine and its extraordinary richness gained it such an international reputation that British capitalists became interested and bought it in 1872 as the Emma Silver Mining Company, Ltd., of London, for a sales price of $5,000,000, half to be paid in cash and the rest in 25,000 fully paid shares. That same June a big stope, from which most of the ore came, caved in, and within two years, as the workings were extended deeper, the rich silver and gold vein pinched out against the smooth wall of a large fault, and the mine was worthless. England protested that the whole transaction had been a deliberate swindle, and relations between the two countries were so strained that an international investigation was arranged. The board found that, although the property had been over-evaluated at the time of the sale, no hint of the mine's true condition was known or anticipated.

As the discovery of the Emma brought men tumbling in to Alta, boom prices for commodities prevailed: a "house that accommodates 5 people" cost fifty dollars a month; water for the house was seven dollars; a gallon of whisky nine dollars and a box of two hundred candles six dollars. The town reached its peak in 1872 with a population of 5,000, with two breweries and six saw-mills running, and with twenty-six saloons interspersed between cabins, three-story lodginghouses, and stores. The *Cottonwood Observer,* a semiweekly paper, flourished; the Bucket of Blood and the Gold Miner's Daughter were the most popular saloons; and Alta Nell and Kate Hayes ruled the red-light quarter—Kate even having a mining claim named for her. Some reports say that more than a hundred men were killed in saloon brawls over mining claims and that in winter a much-used path was tunneled through the snow from the back doors of the resorts to the cemetery.

Even after the fiasco of the Emma, most of the miners remained in Alta; for enough other veins had been found on the rocky slopes to necessitate the subdivision of the mountain area into four mining districts, known as Little Cottonwood, Big Cottonwood, American Fork, and Uinta. Next to the Emma, the Flagstaff mine, located in 1869 by Groesbeck and Schneider and worked until 1873, was the most important of the early properties. Its history is similar to that of its rival; for it was purchased in 1872 by English capitalists for $1,500,000, and, as the Flagstaff Silver Mines Company of Utah (Ltd.), it was worked in a most extravagant way until December, 1873, when the visible ore bodies gave out. The company had completed a three-stack smelter at the mouth of Little Cottonwood just before the veins began to dwindle. Erwin Davis then took the mine and worked it for the English company until

1876, when he was dispossessed by order of the foreign directors. The property was put in litigation, and since then the Flagstaff has been worked only by leasers.

Alta's most productive years were those between 1871 and 1877, when first the Jones and then the Davenport smelters, four miles from the mouth of the canyon, ran on custom ores from the Wasatch, Alta Consolidated, North Star, South Hecla, Prince of Wales, Michigan-Utah, City of Rocks, Sells Albion, and Grizzly mines. Over $13,000,000 worth of ore was produced during the seventies, only $1,703,068 during the eighties, and barely $1,000,-000 in the nineties.

The demonetization of silver in 1893 hit the camp hard and caused mine after mine to close down, just as a railroad reached its outskirts. The road ceased operation a few years later, but in 1913 the grade was repaired and more rails laid. In 1917 a narrow-gauge extension ran almost to the outskirts of Alta. Today the old grade makes a fine highway to the camp.

Alta's steep mountainsides bred avalanches, and each year, when the snow ran, lives and property were lost. The slide of 1874 killed sixty men and buried much of the camp under tons of snow. On March 7, 1884, another crushing slide swept away the buildings at the new Emma mine, caused $15,000 worth of damage, killed two men and packed snow forty feet deep in the canyon cut. In 1885 the greatest avalanche of all ran over the town, killing 15 people, burying cabins, and causing a fire which destroyed most of the remaining buildings.

In 1904 an ore body was found on the Columbus property, a concentrating mill was erected, and Alta townsite replotted. Ground is still open to leasers in certain of the consolidated properties; but by 1937, when Alta was reborn as a ski playground, only a handful of faded, roofless shacks marked its main street.

It was early afternoon when we drove the eighteen miles up Little Cottonwood to see what was left of Alta. The road is excellent, for since Alta has become a center for winter sports, more people travel over it than ever did in the old days. The largest of the resorts, a three-story rustic lodge at the townsite, is built in part from rock taken from old mine buildings. The last of those on the townsite has disappeared, and only the weathered shafthouses and the big dumps on the mountains remain unspoiled. Where bucket trams brought ore to the mills, ski tows carry sport-lovers to the steep snow-packed ski runs. Alta is alive again, but it has a new outlook and a new goal.

After we had inspected the flat where the town stood, and had peered into a few of the old mine shacks near the dumps, we drove slowly down the canyon straight toward the sunset. Now that we had no townsites to hunt for, we could enjoy each mile of scenery. Stone parapets, whose bases were hidden in masses of trees, caught the sun's rays, and waterfalls cascaded from the highest rocks to the stream far below us. Near the canyon's mouth we passed the quarry from which granite for the Mormon Temple and for other civic buildings was obtained. In one day we had visited the first two mining districts in the state. Strangely enough, instead of dying, like so many other promising camps, Bingham Canyon and Alta have weathered depressions, legal entanglements, strikes, and changing industrial patterns. Both started as silver camps. Neither depends upon silver now. Both are modern, one being equipped with the highly developed industrial plant of a mechanized age, the other remodelled to provide an outlet for that most popular of sports —skiing. No other camps, we were sure, would offer such a fine study in contrasts.

STOCKTON

THE next day we drove west out of Salt Lake City on Highway 40, passed the big smelter at Garfield, whose lights we had seen twinkling in the distance the night before, turned south at Mills Junction, went through Tooele, where the International Smelter is in operation, and so reached the sleepy little town of Stockton.

Like many other mining towns in Utah, Stockton was a direct result of one of the prospecting trips of General Connor's Fort Douglas soldiers. They explored the canyons west of the Oquirrh Mountains and set up the Rush Valley mining district on June 11, 1864. Immediately afterward the General, with Major Gallagher and others, laid out the town and established it as the first Gentile community in Utah. Connor named it Stockton, for his former home in California, and built a smelting furnace to handle the ores brought in by his men from the mountains. Lieutenant James Finnerty and other officers also built small furnaces nearby, none of which was especially successful in reducing the ores. Nevertheless, in 1866 Connor built himself a home in the town he had created, and he watched with interest his volunteer soldiers turn prospectors in earnest after their discharges and start mining in the mountains. As camp after camp materialized, his dream of a mining industry conducted by Gentiles in Utah became a reality.

OPHIR

A MILE or two south of Stockton is the turnoff to Ophir. After the wide but barren Rush Valley, the drive up the deep, narrow canyon walled with high and ragged limestone cliffs was a pleasant contrast. The lower ledges of the rocks and the bottom of the canyon are almost choked with trees and bushes that shade not only the road but also the long line

CLIFFS AT OPHIR

MAIN STREET, MERCUR

of old and new, empty and occupied houses and sheds which stand on both
sides of the winding street. Here and there, above the homes, mine dumps and
shaft houses cling to the canyon walls; and now and then the sound of a
truck in low gear or the roar of rock released from an ore bin, rose above
the steady hum of our motor as it climbed the twisting gulch. Where the
ground leveled off the houses were thickest, and we stopped to look around.

One property was working, and miners' families filled many of the frame
cottages, made attractive by vine-covered porches and by colored glass insets
over windows and in door panels. Everyone talked to us, but all were newcomers to Ophir and knew nothing of its history. Hopefully, I entered the one
store; but the proprietor was too busy selling an inner tube to a miner and
bubble gum to his kids to tell me more than the names of the mines and the
fact that the present outfit was reworking the old Ophir property for silver
and lead.

When General Connor's soldiers heard, in 1865, that the Indians were
mining silver for bullets in a canyon east of Stockton, they explored the region
and discovered, in East Canyon on Treasure Hill, croppings of lead which
they named the St. Louis lode. Their good fortune attracted many others to
the canyon, and the Ophir, the Pocatello, the Wild Delirium, the Velocipede,
and the Miner's Delight claims were staked. As soon as the Ophir mining
district was organized in 1870, A. W. Morris laid out the town, and immediately tents and shacks for saloons and brothels were set up along the dusty
canyon trail. On August 23, 1870, horn silver was found on Silverado Hill,
and the Silveropolis, Chloride Point, and Shamrock lodes were staked. Old-
timers say that the first forty tons shipped from the Silveropolis netted $24,000
and that the ore averaged $6,000 a ton in ten-car lots. Shortly after these
discoveries, a dozen or more locations were made on Lion and Tiger Hills.

In 1871 the Pioneer Mill, erected by Walker Brothers of Salt Lake City,
began dropping stamps on twenty-five to thirty tons of ore a day from the
Zella, the Silveropolis, and the Tiger properties. The ores were well adapted
to milling, and before 1874, as the need arose, the Ophir and the Faucett
smelters and the Brevoort and the Enterprise mills were built. All during the
boom, ore was wagon-hauled across the range to Lehi, the nearest rail connection, or it was taken over Mack Gisborn's toll road to Stockton and from
there freighted to the Great Salt Lake, where it was reloaded on boats and
shipped up the Lake to the railhead at Corinne. For nearly ten years the camp
thrived; but in 1880 the initial Ophir boom was over, and the mines were all
but abandoned. Other booms have periodically revived the district, as copper
and zinc replaced silver in commercial importance and as deeper shafts and
drifts opened new deposits. The absence of underground water has also proved
a boon to mineowners, as shafts 1,000 feet deep remain dry.

During the camp's activity Senator W. A. Clark of Montana secured certain mines on Ophir Hill and worked them steadily for twenty-five years, and Marcus Daly, who staked the Zella mine, put its profits into Anaconda Copper. In recent years an increasing number of properties have been consolidated, and tailings and dumps of old mines have been reworked. In the 1930's the International Smelting and Refining Company built a 600-ton flotation mill at the mouth of the canyon to treat 400,000 tons of tailings from the Ophir Hill Mining Company, the property from which Clark had extracted such rich returns. Two piles of tailings just below the town mark its site.

On our way down the canyon we noticed the belfried firehouse and the tiny stone post office, and we got a better view of the castellated ramparts of Lion Hill, rising nearly 2,000 feet above the bed of the creek.

MERCUR

NOT far from the mouth of the gulch we again turned left into a road that for a while ran parallel to the foot of the Oquirrh Range. At the mouth of Lewiston Canyon it turned east and climbed for eight miles, getting narrower and rougher all the way. This was a dry canyon and lacked the high rock walls and the lush vegetation of the one we had just seen. Instead it offered only cactus and sagebrush-covered hills, rocky ledges, and a boulder-strewn creek bed.

The discovery of gold and silver near Camp Floyd brought prospectors to this canyon in 1869. L. Greenley found the first placer deposit and was the first to stake a claim. A few others washed dirt at the meager stream, but the scarcity both of gold and water put an end to the diggings. Nevertheless, the persistent prospectors organized the Camp Floyd or Lewiston mining district in 1870 and gophered the ridges until they uncovered silver lodes in the Sparrowhawk, Last Chance, Silver Cloud, Mormon Chief, Marion, and Grecian Bend mines; and the news of their success brought men stampeding to the new silver field.

To accommodate them a new camp, named Lewiston, sprang up along the gulch. But the real boom did not come until 1873, when Leandro Steele located the Carrie Steele and shortly afterwards shipped $80,000 from it. Stage companies ran six trips a day from the valley to the bonanza camp, and Lewiston's population swelled to 2,000; but by 1874 the richest ores were beginning to play out, and by 1880 the camp was deserted. Even its former existence was forgotten by the postal authorities, who gave its name to another community.

Arie Pinedo, a Bavarian prospector, drifted into the district just about the time the others had pulled out, and staked several gold-bearing claims within the next two years. In one he found traces of quicksilver and, believing he had located a vein of cinnabar, he named the claim the Mercur, the German word for cinnabar or mercury. Every assay showed gold in the ore, but neither he nor any of the other prospectors who were combing the hills for leads could pan any of it or separate it in arrastres or in mills. Completely disgusted, Pinedo and the others left the district.

In 1889 Joseph Smith rediscovered Pinedo's claim and was attracted by the gold carried in the vein. He "rawhided" it down the mountainside on dried skins to the amalgamating mill in the canyon; but again the tenacious rock refused to release the gold it contained. In 1890, when more rock containing small amounts of gold was found, prospectors, who remembered the 1870 gold placers at the mouth of the canyon, began to trickle back to the abandoned townsite. Since gold lay in the hills, some way to work it must exist. Optimistically, the men bought up the abandoned claims, including the Mercur, consolidated them into groups and formed mining companies to work them; and Arthur Murphy and C. L. Preble laid out on the old townsite of Lewiston their new camp—Mercur. Year by year its population grew: 400 at first, 6,000 after the coming of the railroad, and 12,000 in 1912 at the peak of the boom.

One party of men bought a mine for $15,000, built a $40,000 mill and, after dropping stamps for thirty days without recovering any bullion, were at a loss how to proceed. Not even the eminent chemists to whom they sent samples of the ore could tell them how to get at the gold. As a last resort, the owners sent a ton of ore to a plant in Denver that was experimenting with cyanide and found that most of the gold could be saved. After raising more capital, they built a cyanide and leaching plant at Mercur and ultimately recovered ninety per cent of the gold run through the mill.

By 1895 all the Mercur mines were successfully recovering the refractory gold by cyanidation, were producing millions in gold, and were paying substantial dividends to stockholders. Furthermore, the low-grade ores, which had previously been thrown aside as worthless, were being made to pay. When the owners of the Mercur mine were ready, in 1896, to build the Golden Gate mill, they put D. C. Jackling, the skillful young engineer from Cripple Creek, Colorado, in complete charge of its design and construction. Jackling analyzed the ore to be treated and decided to roast it before putting it through the cyanidation tanks. Since no one else had done this, he was laughed at for his idea; but he built his plant and found the process highly satisfactory. In 1900 the Delamar Mercur Mines Company and the Mercur Gold Mining and Milling Company combined and became the Consolidated Mercur Mines Company, and for thirteen years all ore was treated in their Golden Gate mill.

Up until 1895, when a pipeline from Ophir supplied the town, water was

MAMMOTH. RAILROAD TUNNEL PORTAL IN TINTIC MOUNTAINS

EUREKA AND ITS MINES

scarce; a man named John Nicholson hauled it from the only spring in the district and sold it by the cup, bucket, or barrel. Nicholson provided a month's supply of water free to every family with a new baby. In 1896 a narrow-gauge railroad reached the camp, and plans were made to incorporate the community on State admission day, January 6, 1896. Just before that date fire swept through the town and, as one old-timer put it, "left little to incorporate." The camp was rebuilt at once, only to be destroyed again in 1902.

When a circus was booked for Mercur, the advance agent failed to notice that the nearest standard-gauge track was five miles from the place. Since the circus train could not enter Mercur, the performance was held on a flat at the end of the main track, and those who went to it rode down the grade to the tent on flat cars, enveloped in cinders and sparks. Once, when bandits threatened to rob the town, two citizens hired a buckboard, put in it the $45,000 in gold which the robbers planned to seize, and drove off into the valley with the cache. When the trip got monotonous, they started chasing coyotes across the flats and used up all their ammunition. The heavy load of gold buckled the buckboard, and they had trouble reaching a blacksmith shop where it could be reinforced. Luckily the bandits never appeared.

Mercur boomed until 1913; then its ore deposits were said to be worked out. As soon as the Consolidated Mercur mine and the Golden Gate mill shut down, the town shrank quickly and residents tore down buildings, packed their belongings, and left the suddenly quiet camp. The following year the Salt Lake and Mercur railroad pulled its tracks; by 1925 "Mercur was only a memory."

But Mercur is like a jack-in-the-box—in 1931, when a group of local mining men formed the Sacramento Gold and Quicksilver Mining Company and obtained a bond and lease on certain properties, it came back to life. Next, the International Smelting Company reopened some of the old workings. Finally, in 1934, when Snyder Brothers located a rich claim in Horse Thief Gulch, the camp entered on its third boom. By 1937 Snyder's 1,000-ton mill was in operation with 150 men on its payroll, and as many more were treating the tailings from the Golden Gate and Mercur mills and exploring three miles of underground workings. Across the canyon the Geyser-Marion Gold Mining Company was operating an open-cut mine and a cyanide mill. As these two companies succeeded in treating the low-grade, complex Mercur ores by modern methods of metallurgical science, the recent ghost became the second largest gold-producing camp in the state.

In 1951, however, it was a ghost again. Scarcely any buildings were left, and the few that remained were either falling to pieces or were boarded up. Two stone walls beside the road once enclosed a store; two gasoline pumps in front of a shack seemed strangely out of place; and the huge circular cyanide tank foundations of one of the great mills were partly choked with tailings that had blown in from nearby dumps.

The place seemed completely deserted until I noticed smoke rising from 'the chimney of a house on top of a cliff. I climbed the cliff to the back door and knocked. There was no answer, but a radio blared inside the house. I knocked louder, then tried the door. It was unlocked, but the house was empty. Just as I again reached my car I noticed, farther down the street, a man walking toward me. He was Mr. Helmer L. Grane, the company watchman. Although he had lived in the deserted town only four years, he knew all about it.

"Mercur had everything," he told me. "The hill up there was full of houses, and before the last fire this street and the one that branches off from it at the fork were solid with stores and hotels and big boardinghouses. George Dern's big brick home stood on top of the hill up till just a few years ago. Dern was Assistant Manager of the Consolidated Mercur Mines Company before he was Governor of Utah. The old jail cage is over there, and an old vault too. This camp used to be the biggest in the state, bigger than Tooele, and there was talk of moving the county seat here. This camp shut down during World War II during the gold ban. But Mercur isn't through yet. She's about due to come back again."

THE TINTIC DISTRICT

FROM Mercur we drove back to the highway and continued south through Rush Valley to the silver camps of the Tintic mining district, which lie on the crest and on the western slope of the Tintic Mountains. All through the early fifties stockmen ran cattle in the lush valley below the mountains, although the Indians resented their use of the grazing land; and stage drivers whipped up their horses and hurried through it, glad if they escaped from well-aimed arrows. Chief Tintic, the Ute who claimed the mountains and the vast valley and who fought the few white men who crossed his land, died in 1859. Ten years later a cowboy, George Rust, while herding cattle in the Tintic Hills, picked up an odd-looking piece of rock and kept it as a curiosity. Later, tests showed that it contained silver. A party of prospectors returning from western Utah also gathered specimens of ore. But their finds failed to call attention to the wooded hills, for the strikes at Park City, Alta, and Cottonwood canyons were far more spectacular.

Although a mining district was organized in the spring of 1870, it was December before Steve Moore and his four companions bucked a snowstorm to stake the Sunbeam, the first recorded claim. According to his wife, on the other hand (in her *History of Eleanor Coltin Moore*), he and his companions were attracted to the ledge by the sun's rays glancing on the rock formation. He climbed to it in the morning and discovered the Sunbeam. She also tells the story of how some time later Moore and Brigham Young met. "I hear that you've been mining," said Brigham Young. "Don't you know that it's against my orders?"

"Yes," replied Moore.

"What do you intend to do?"

"Keep right on mining," said Moore. There was a pause. Then Brigham Young said, "Well, go ahead and may God bless you."

A month after the discovery of the Sunbeam, the Black Dragon was located north of the Sunbeam, and in February, 1871, the Eureka Hill and the Mammoth mines were staked. As more strikes were made, camps sprang up close to them, until the district contained Eureka on the north, next Mammoth and Robinson close together, Silver City over the hill in the next canyon, and Diamond still farther south.

SILVER CITY

JUST on the outskirts of Eureka we turned sharply to the right and drove four miles south to Silver City, the earliest of these camps. It was laid out in 1870 at the mouth of Dragon Canyon and was described as

a billiard saloon, blacksmith shop, grog hole, some tents, several drunks, a free fight, water some miles off, a hole down 90 feet hunting a spring without success, and any number of rich or imaginary rich lodes in the neighborhood. The owners are all poor, and the poor men work for them. By next spring the poor will be poorer. [I. E. Diehl, quoted in *Utah*, the *American Guide Series*, p. 413.]

In spite of this gloomy prediction, Silver City became the trading center for the Swansea and other mines and for the Black Dragon, which produced flux for the smelting works below the town. But when the miners struck water in the shafts and the cost of pumping became prohibitive, operations ceased, the population of 800 slipped away, and the city was virtually abandoned. In later years, William Hatfield took $700,000 of ore from below the water level of the Swansea, and his success encouraged others to reopen properties; but in 1951, when we turned on to the dirt street of the town, and drove past clumps of trees that almost hid the few tenanted frame houses, we saw no active mining—just foundations, a few old shafts, and the big golden mine dumps that surround the town and spill down the mountain ledges above it.

Diamond, in the next canyon south, had only half as large a population as Silver City though it, too, was laid out in 1870. By 1904, after the last mine closed down, most of the people moved away; in 1923 the last house was moved out.

MAMMOTH

WE TURNED back toward Eureka and stopped in the canyon north of Silver City, at Mammoth, third of the 1870 camps. Though the Mammoth mine was staked in 1871, it was 1873 before Charles Crismon and his associates began to work it; and even Crismon thought so little of the limestone deposit that he traded his share in it to Sam and William McIntyre for a herd of Texas cattle. The brothers were driving the steers to Salt Lake City to sell and were hunting good range land, when Crismon showed them the Tintic Valley and then offered to trade his mine for the stock. The Mammoth, under the direction of the McIntyres, became one of the bonanzas of the district. But in the eighties it and its twenty-two-furnace smelter suspended operations, and Sam McIntyre left his fine brick home in the town and moved to Salt Lake City. (The house was used by cowboys and ranchers until it was torn down in 1933.) After some years, the Mammoth was reopened under new management. The mine has continued to produce: one carload of ore in 1907 carried a value of $107,000, and its total output has exceeded $20,000,000.

We found Mammoth larger than Silver City and not quite so lonely. Mammoth's peak population of 1,000 had built over a wide area, as both old buildings and crumbling stone foundations testify. The big, boarded-up school, the concrete jail, two or three empty stores, and the mine buildings that fringe the community are no longer needed, but many frame houses are; and although the place is small today, we saw people on the street and heard children shouting at play. Perched high above the town, a giant black mouth on the edge of a mountain, is the portal of a railroad tunnel from which track and trestle are gone, leaving only the gaping hole, too big for a mine, to explain what it had been. Some mining is still going on; as we drove away, we watched a truck dump ore into a chute and listened to the clatter as the ore slid down into an empty freight car—one of a long line waiting to be loaded.

EUREKA

ONE mile north of Mammoth, near the entrance to the pass across the Tintic Range, we entered Eureka, the largest and most productive of the camps. Paul Schettler and George and Gotlieb Beck were gathering wood on the slope above the canyon where the town lies, one day in 1870, when they discovered ore upon the surface of the ground and quickly staked the Eureka Hill mine. The ore tested so well that Joab Lawrence bought the men's claims for $1,000 and organized the Eureka Mining Company. Lawrence and his partner found horn silver close to the surface and also in large boulders which they rolled down the hillside to ore wagons. The property looked so promising that in 1872 Captain E. B. Ward bought them out. Almost at once the vein pinched out, but by developing the mine to greater depths, he uncovered new and richer deposits. Claim-jumpers sometimes attacked the property, and to forestall a raid by an armed gang from the tough Nevada camp of Pioche, Watson Nesbitt, who was in charge at the time, built a stone fort, filled it with guards, and had all the cedar trees that surrounded the mine for a considerable distance cut down. Since this left them no shelter, the gunmen, when they did appear, were forced to withdraw.

During the seventies many mines were developed, and to handle the cascades of rich ore that streamed from them—some of it assaying $5,000 to $10,000 a ton—a number of mills were built in different parts of the district. As these were not successful in reducing the refractory ore, smelters were put up; and during the nineties new and more efficient mills and smelters were built. There was no water at Eureka; so wells were sunk at Homansville on the eastern slope of the mountain, and water for the mines and mills was piped to the several properties, while water for domestic uses was hauled to town and sold for ten cents a gallon.

The growth of the district was slow, until railroads reached the valley and provided cheaper transportation for the shipment of ore. The first of these to arrive was the Utah Southern in 1878; the second was the Oregon Short Line in 1883; and the last, and the most difficult to build, was the Rio Grande Western, which ran from Springville and reached Silver City in 1891. On August 24 Jay Gould arrived in Eureka in his special four-car train and, with his party, inspected the Bullion-Beck mine and the entire camp, to the surprise and delight of its citizens. He seemed duly impressed and described the district as containing "not only mountains of silver but valleys of silver."

We found Eureka a typical mining camp, full of buildings and activity but a little dingy. Mines and old mills, dumps, and long lines of houses and stores crowd between the hills that form the canyon. The city is honeycombed with mine tunnels, and in boom days its windows rattled with the constant blasting that went on underneath.

Tim Sullivan, sitting in front of a saloon, pointed out to us the Eureka Hill, the Centennial-Eureka, the Bullion-Beck, and the Gemini properties, and told us about the man who sold an option on a mine for $25,000 and refused to put the money in the bank. Instead, he asked to be paid in sacked gold, and when the specified amount was delivered to his cabin, he demanded that the Eureka police guard him and it indefinitely. In time he tired of the arrangement and went east, taking his boodle with him.

By 1910, when the Tintic-Standard, at the camp of Dividend, on the mountain about two miles east of Eureka, was the great producer, its big mill and two-story bunkhouse loomed above a swarm of new company houses. That same year many properties were consolidated either under the Tintic-Standard Company or under the Chief Consolidated Mining Company. By the twenties the mines were all tapping deep deposits reached by vertical shafts often 2,000 feet deep.

KNIGHTSVILLE

As WE LEFT Eureka and the Tintic Valley, we saw the site of Homansville, where the first mills were built in 1871 and where in later years, a well, a pumping station, and a lime hydrating plant supported a population of 300. We also found the site of Knightsville, just east of Eureka near the top of the pass through the mountains. Jesse Knight bought a tract of land in 1897, as soon as he saw that the mines in which he had interests—the Godiva, Uncle Sam, May Day, Humbug, and Yankee—were paying properties; and here he laid out Knightsville, a camp without a saloon. For his workmen and their families, many of whom were Mormons, he built houses made of vertical boards set up without foundations and roofed with shingles or tin. He also dug a well. As the camp grew he added a schoolhouse, a church, and a recreation center where dances, socials, and roller-skating parties could be held. In winter, when tobogganing was the popular sport, he arranged that those who sledded down the eight to ten miles of hill should be hauled back by a team of horses. Many stories are told of his interest in his workers. When an orchestra was needed for dances, Knight advertised that anyone who could play a musical instrument would be hired as one of his workmen. Young men about to go on a Church mission could always earn money for their pilgrimage by working for him. On their return their jobs awaited them.

When rich silver-lead ore was struck in the Beck tunnel in 1907 and a smelter was built, Knightsville boomed and its population of 300 rose to 1,000. But the boom faded; by 1924 most of the mines had closed; by 1940 only a handful of people were left; and today only the concrete foundations of the school remain.

SILVER REEF

As WE DROVE east across a low divide into the fertile Utah Valley, facing the imposing barrier of the Wasatch Range, we reached Santaquin. Here we turned south for the 233-mile drive to Silver Reef.

The camp, which lies in the extreme southwest corner of the state, did not receive its name of Silver Reef for some years after silver had been dis-

covered in the vicinity; the early references to the area speak instead of the
Harrisburg district, the Leeds claim, White Reef, and Bonanza City. Its mines,
which completely upset the theory of the geologists that "silver never occurs
in sandstone," flourished for ten years, and at the height of its boom the
camp's prosperity threatened the Mormon town of St. George in the race for
the county seat; then for another fifteen years it struggled along and, finally,
gave up.

John Kemple, a prospector, found the first indications of silver in 1866
when, while wintering at Harrisburg, he tramped over the surrounding country with his pick, pan, and assayer's kit. On a white reef, a few miles north
of the town, he noticed silver float in a sandstone vein, and although his tests
produced a small silver button, it was so minute that the following spring he
left the region and struck out for Nevada. But the presence of silver in a sandstone formation was so unusual that in 1870 he returned, with a few other
men, to file on the site of his earlier discovery. The men pitched their tents
on the reef, where they thought more silver might be hidden, and before the
end of the year they had organized the Harrisburg mining district.

Although John Kemple is believed to have made the initial strike, two
quite different stories are popularly accepted as describing the discovery of
silver in the district. One says that a stranger, who stopped on a cold night
at a house in Leeds, while warming himself by the fire, noticed something
oozing out of the stones lining the fireplace. He gathered several drops and
found that they were silver! The quarry from which the fire-back came was
a sandstone ledge in the vicinity.

The second story attributes the discovery of silver to Murphy, an assayer
in Pioche, Nevada, whose reports on samples of ore were so consistently high
that the miners distrusted him. One day Isaac Duffin of Toquerville, Utah,
who made grindstones out of rock quarried from a ledge north of Harrisburg,
took a load of his grindstones over to Pioche to sell. As he drove along the
street, some miners spied the grindstones and decided to test Murphy's hon-
esty. They bought one, pulverized it, sent a sample of the rock to the assayer,
and then waited expectantly to see what value he would put upon it. When
his report showed two hundred ounces of silver to the ton, the men were convinced of his dishonesty; but before they could expose him, Murphy was on
his way to Duffin's sandstone ledge to stake his claim. Another version of the
story names Alma T. Angell of Leeds as the maker of the grindstones; and
still another variant says that during a fight in Pioche a man was thrown
out the door of a saloon with such force that, when he collided with a
grindstone, it broke in pieces; and that a prospector, named Barbee, picked
up a fragment of the rock, found silver in it, and four days later was in Utah
testing the reef from which the grindstone came.

A few miners explored the area during the next couple of years; but no real interest was taken in the region until 1874, when Elijah Thomas and his partner John S. Ferris located the Leeds claim on White Reef, a sandstone ledge a short distance northwest of the town of Leeds, and sent a sample of the horn silver it contained to the Salt Lake City bankers, the Walker Brothers. After testing it, they outfitted William Tecumseh Barbee, Thomas McNally, and Ed Maynard, an assayer, and sent them to examine the claim. Barbee, the same man whom popular tradition connects with the grindstone story, was the most enthusiastic of the three and, when he found horn silver in petrified wood as well as in the sandstone, he located twenty-two claims and scurried back to Salt Lake City for more supplies. His reports were so glowing that men began to trickle south, and before long a small camp stretched along Quail Creek west of White Reef.

The others whom Walker Brothers sent to the silver field were less enthusiastic than Barbee, for they knew from geology that silver did not exist in sandstone. Upon receiving their unfavorable report, the Salt Lake City bankers refused to finance Barbee any farther and turned the mining claims over to him. Barbee's faith in the country was soon rewarded. In November, 1875, a wagonload of wood skidded while crossing Buckeye Reef and tore up the soft rock for a distance of several feet. Barbee examined the earth, found in it silver chlorides and horn silver, and immediately staked it as the Tecumseh claim. On a flat east of Tecumseh Hill he established a new camp called Bonanza City, and to acquaint others with the area and its assets he sent a series of letters to the *Salt Lake Tribune*. On December 13, 1875, he wrote:

We have an abundance of rich silver mines which your correspondent is now developing, and bringing to the surface their rich chlorides and horn silver—all in sandstone too.

Soon after the first letter he wrote that Bonanza City was

three weeks old and can boast an assay office, a blacksmith shop, a sampling works, a boarding house and several other wick-a-ups of smaller dimensions, and will soon have a miners' supply store.

On February 7, 1876, he continued:

This sandstone country beats all the boys, and it is amusing to see how excited they get when they go round to see the sheets of silver which are exposed all over the different reefs. . . . This is the most unfavorable looking country for mines that I have ever seen . . . but as the mines are here, what are the rock sharps going to do about it?

This last remark may refer to the letter that the Smithsonian Institute in Washington sent to Enos A. Wall in 1876. They courteously acknowledged the piece of petrified wood "shot through" with horn silver, which he had sent them, and described the sample as an "interesting fake as silver in nature is not formed in petrified wood." Barbee continued to write letters to the *Tribune* and brought thousands of miners into the district, attracted by such statements as:

Our mines are our capital; our banks are sand banks. We draw on them at will and our drafts are never dishonored.

Among the arrivals was Hyrum Jacobs, a Pioche merchant, who saw in the boulder-strewn ridge north of Bonanza City a more central location for a townsite. He returned to Pioche, packed his stock, loaded his store building in sections on a freight wagon, and started back. On the ridge he had picked out he set up his store; and since Buckeye, Middle, White, and East Reefs, where the miners were digging, all contained silver, he named his embryo camp Silver Reef. Jacobs then bought the Maggie mill at Bullionville, Nevada, and had it and its machinery moved to this new site. It was the first mill to treat the sandstone ores. Little by little the two camps became one, and Bonanza City was forgotten.

Silver Reef reached its peak between 1877 and 1880, and although its streets remained "paved by nature, just one boulder after another," they were lined with busy stores and hotels, a bank, a church, and a Wells Fargo office. A newspaper, the *Silver Reef Echo,* appeared early in 1877; and a brewery supplied the Elk Horn, the Capitol, and other saloons. Father Scanlan arrived during the summer; and through his efforts a church, a hospital run by Sisters, and a school were built. He immediately so endeared himself to the people of the entire district that not only was he invited to hold Mass in the Mormon Tabernacle at St. George, but the choir even learned the Latin chants so as to accompany the service.

Citizens Hall was the center for all social gatherings, as well as for Protestant services and Union Sunday School meetings. Hundreds of miners trudged up the trails to the mines each morning, worked ten hours, and trudged down again to spend their evenings milling about the busy streets, attending Lodge meetings, or celebrating in the brightly lighted saloons.

Silver Reef was a Gentile town, but its telegraph operator was a Mormon. The telegraph office in St. George was in a furniture store, and whenever Federal agents, on their way to the county seat to arrest polygamists, stopped off at the Reef, the operator would warn St. George by wiring for "two chairs" as soon as the officers appeared. When fire destroyed one-third of the business

RUINS AND DESERT FORMATIONS, SILVER REEF

FIREHOUSE AND HOSE TOWER, PARK CITY

section in 1879, the rest of the town was saved by men grabbing empty powder-kegs, filling them at the creek, and passing them from hand to hand in regular bucket-brigade fashion. A restaurant, scorched by the blazing building across the street, was saved by the Chinese cook, who kept its walls doused with milk.

During the boom, the din of dropping stamps merged with the shouts of freighters and the creaking of their wagons bumping over the rough, ungraded streets. To handle the ore from the many properties, the Christy, the Stormont, the Leeds, and the Barbee and Walker mills kept hammering day after day. The Tecumseh mine shipped silver as early as April, 1876; the Buckeye turned out a 1,000-ounce brick every day; and the Christy during 1878 milled 10,249 tons of ore valued at $302,597. By 1880 the best producers were consolidated and held by a few companies, each with its own amalgamating mill; but within a year the price of silver fell, water was encountered in the mines, and stock-holders, whose dividends were cut, demanded a cut in wages.

In protest against this demand more than three hundred miners organized a union and, when the new wage was announced as $3.50 per day instead of the former $4.00, the men refused to accept the terms, put out the fires at the reduction works, and left the mines. At the end of a month, when no settlement was forthcoming, sixty of the union men ran Colonel W. Allen, Superintendent of the Stormont Company, out of town. A Federal Grand Jury issued warrants for the arrest of forty of them, and a posse, led by the Sheriff, entered Silver Reef under cover of a snowstorm and easily found the men they were seeking. Since the jail was too small to hold so many, a stone dance hall was commandeered for the night. When the miners were at last imprisoned, some of the stores that had extended them credit were forced to close. The new workers, brought in to replace the strikers, were for the most part so inexperienced that as the real miners little by little pulled out of town, mines began to close and mills to shut down; until by February 4, 1884, the *Engineering and Mining Journal* remarked:

It would be difficult to imagine a more dull and lifeless mining camp than this place at the present time. The Barbee and Christy mills are both idle. . . . The Stormont continues running.

By 1891 all companies ceased operations. For a few more years local men leased some of the mines, and between 1892 and 1903 they shipped out $250,000 in bullion; but even a brief flurry of activity after World War I and the purchase of mining stock in 1928 by the American Smelting and Refining Company failed to bring the town back. Today the racetrack is an alfalfa field, the cemetery is neglected, the blocks of wooden sidewalks have rotted away, and only adobe and stone walls line the rocky, sage-clogged streets. The stone bank is a summer home, its vault torn off and flower beds bordering the building; for the townsite is now private property, and a barbed-wire fence posted with 'No Trespassing' signs surrounds the tract. Just inside the fence one large stone store, with iron shutters awry and dusty windowpanes, stands a glassy-eyed sentinel, brooding over the camp which squeezed $10,500,000 worth of silver from sandstone. Completely satisfied with our visit to such an unusual ghost town as Silver Reef, we returned up the long wide valley to Santaquin and then drove to Provo.

PARK CITY

THE next day we rolled through majestic Provo Canyon, admired Mount Timpanogos, and left the highway to visit Park City, another of the Utah towns that grew up around mines discovered by General Connor's soldiers in the late sixties. It is in the same mineral zone as Alta, and by airline is less than ten miles from that camp; but the high and rocky spine of the Wasatch Range separates the two settlements. Alta was a spectacular camp which rose like a rocket and then fizzled out; Park City, from the start, was a steady-going camp, never sensational, and still active.

It was Sunday morning when we drove into the city and church bells were ringing as we climbed the steep, terraced streets. Except for the bells, you could feel Sunday stillness, broken only occasionally by the noise of grinding gears or the distant barking of a dog. As we cruised up one street and down another, "spotting" the old buildings from among the newer crop, children, clutching their collection pennies, passed by on their way to Sunday school, climbing the steep grades or the long flights of steps from one level to the next. As I sketched the old firehouse with its weather-beaten wooden tower, a young woman stopped to watch; and when I commented upon the picturesque city in which she lived, she said, "What's picturesque about it? I never seen anything to look at. My husband works up at the mine and I'm stuck here. Give me Salt Lake City. There's a town for you."

After she had clicked down the street on her high heels, I took a second look at Park City. It is built in and on the sides of a hollow, beyond which the mountains rise rather steeply; and the brick, stone, and frame stores of the business section bunch close together at the mouth of the canyon. At the lower end of Main Street the mill of the Silver King Coalition Mines Company rises four stories high, big and black; and from the upper level of the building the spider-like threads of a bucket tramline hang above the road and stretch on up the mountainside to the high, invisible mines, from which they bring the ore. On either side of the main thoroughfare, row upon row of frame homes, surrounded with fences, terraces, and gay with gardens, stripe the canyonsides; above them the mountain slopes are green, except where mills, dumps, and tram towers break through the trees and the lush grass of the mountain meadows.

When Sam Snyder built sawmills at the lower end of the valley in 1853 and began to strip the hills of the biggest trees, this forested region was known as Parley's Park, and cattle grazed on these same high meadows. Not until three of Connor's soldiers stumbled onto outcroppings of quartz, about two miles south of the Park during the winter of 1869, marked the spot with a red bandanna, and found that the sample of ore they broke off assayed ninety-six ounces of silver, fifty-four per cent lead, and one-tenth ounce of gold, did anyone think of seeking minerals here.

With the opening of their mine, the Flagstaff, in 1870, however, a stampede to the district began, and a line of tents and shacks—the beginnings of Park City—took root along the bottom of the canyon. Prospectors like Rufus Walker and his partner Webster, who were the first to record their 1869 discoveries, staked claims all over the hills; but when the ores were found to run deep in the ground, the individual miners and small owners lacked sufficient capital to develop them. Claim holders, therefore, merged their properties and sank long drainage tunnels to unwater the deep workings.

It is not certain whether it was Hermann Budder or Rector Steen who made the original discovery of the Ontario, the mine that really made the camp. The stories are: 1. Budder, a former sailor and California miner who had heard of the Emma mine at Alta, wandered over the adjoining hills until, on July 19, 1872, he found a knob of rock which he believed contained silver. 2. Steen, also a California miner, had enlisted for service in Utah because he suspected that the mountains contained minerals. He camped in a brush shanty in Park Canyon for several months, waiting for the snow on the ridges to melt. On June 15 he and his friends, John Kain and Gus McDonnell, found a knob of rock projecting two inches above the ground, which, when scraped clean of dirt, "revealed a lead about fifty feet long." Steen broke off a fragment, had it assayed, and found that it ran one hundred to four hundred ounces to the ton in silver. He promptly staked the Ontario mine around the knob. On August 21 he and his associates sold their claim for $27,000 to George Hearst.

It was this coming in of capital, based on the fine prospects of the Ontario mine, that made the Park City mining district come to life in 1872 and enjoy a great boom. Eight years later 1,270 mining locations were registered and 500 were being actively worked. After Hearst's purchase, he and his partner Stanley developed the mine by digging tunnels, by installing giant pumps to remove the underground water, and by sinking three deep shafts. William Randolph Hearst, son of the owner, visited the mine just after his graduation from Harvard. While he was descending the shaft, the clutch which controlled the cage slipped, and the cage dropped sixty feet before it caught again. The operator turned green, but young Hearst merely asked the man if the hoist usually stopped that way!

As soon as the mine proved itself, John J. Daly acquired the ground adjoining the Ontario ledge and successfully developed it as the Daly, the Daly-West, and the Daly-Judge properties, all of which were operating on a big scale by 1886.

The growth of the city kept up with the development of its mines, and even the fires in 1882 and 1898—the latter a million-dollar blaze—failed to retard its progress for long. Its citizens were vigorous, brawny men, who enjoyed their beer as well as their wrestling matches and foot- and snowshoe-races, and who were the subject of complaint by the editor of the *Park Record* in 1884, because there was "too much promiscuous shooting on the streets at night." On the other hand, *Tullidge's Monthly Magazine—The Western Galaxy* in its issue of March, 1888, praises the camp by saying:

Society in Park City is as regular and respectable as in any manufacturing city, the habits and morals of the people as well ordered. . . . Indeed the Park City people can lay just claims to be a Christian society, and not, as in a primitive mining camp, a promiscuous gathering of stalwart adventurous sons of Christian parents. . . .

All through the eighties properties on Piñon Hill, Crescent Ridge, and Treasure Hill were worked, and the development of the mines was steady until the silver crash of 1893. This almost wrecked the camp and its population of 6,000. The camp never shut down, however, and by 1915 new mills were in operation. In recent years the mines have been owned and worked by the Park Utah Consolidated and the Silver King Coalition; and anyone visiting the city today will find a typical Western mining camp, which has produced more than $250,000,000 of gold, silver, copper, lead, and zinc, and which is still producing.

Park City was our last Utah mining camp; and, when we reached Kimball Junction six miles to the north, we turned right and headed for Colorado. All of Wyoming was ahead of us; and so, as we picked up speed and slipped across the wide stretches of rolling, sage-brush prairie, we watched for antelope and saw several of the alert, graceful creatures, grazing or poised for instant flight in case we came too near; we caught sight of a clumsy badger scuffling along the edge of the highway embankment; but most of the time we looked far ahead for the first glimpse of our home Rockies.

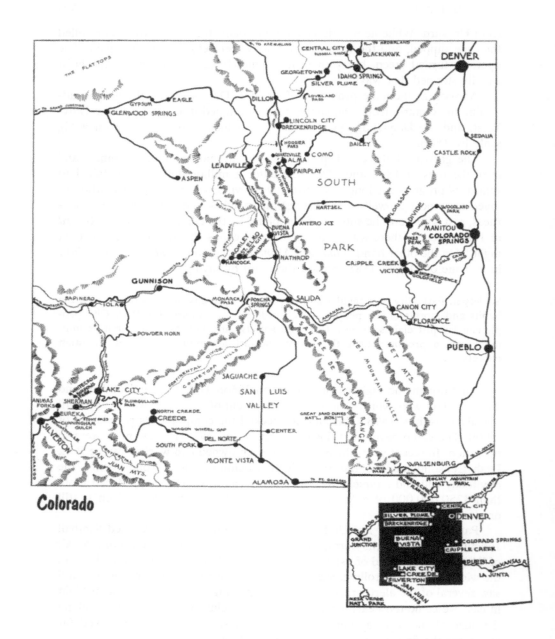

Colorado

11. *Stampede to Timberline*

Colorado

JUST TEN YEARS after California's gold rush, hundreds of prospectors began stirring up the stream beds and pecking at the rocks on the eastern side of the Continental Divide. Some of the men were greenhorns; others were experienced but disappointed miners returning from California. For them every stream and rocky outcropping held a promise of buried treasure. The initial gold strikes were made in 1858 and 1859 by George Jackson, John Gregory, and William Green Russell in what was at that time part of Kansas Territory, west of the present site of Denver. Idaho Springs sprang up close to Jackson's diggings; Central City and Black Hawk are memorials to Gregory; and Russell Gulch, located between the two places, still bears the name of its founder.

Colorado's mining booms occurred with regularity every ten years between the sixties and the early nineteen hundreds. Gold was discovered in the sixties; silver in the seventies; both gold and silver in the eighties and nineties; zinc, fluorspar, and uranium in the twentieth century. The silver crash of 1893 nearly finished mining in the state; but fortunately the Cripple Creek gold rush almost coincided with the silver panic, and the district's great gold mines averted a total collapse of the industry. Colorado's mines are still full of precious metals, but the richest of the pay ore has been removed. The reduced price paid for gold and silver today, combined with the rise in wages and production costs, has caused many properties to close down, and the camps near them have become deserted or at least less active.

These camps are spread from the front range of the Rockies to the jagged San Juan Mountains in the southwestern corner of the state. Central City started in 1859, with Fairplay and Breckenridge only months behind her; Silver Plume, Sherman and Whitecross, Eureka and Animas Forks, and the towns along Chalk Creek appeared in the seventies but continued to boom throughout the eighties; and Creede and Victor were the talk of the nineties.

CENTRAL CITY

CENTRAL CITY was my first mining town, and, in spite of the hundreds that I have seen since, it is still exciting and satisfying to me, for each visit is like going back home. My affection for it dates from the time of my first visit, when old Mr. Teller was still running the big hotel and George M. Laird, the affable veteran editor of the *Register-Call,* let me browse through the complete file of his paper and cull colorful bits of history and gossip from it. Every now and then he would look over my shoulder as I hurriedly copied notes from the faded sheets, chuckle, and say, "Bet you can't read 'em when you get home."

Those newspapers opened a new world to me, a world of living history, and through them I saw Central City from the time it was born—a straggling colony of crude shelters and log cabins, surrounded by mud and sluice boxes and nourished by the indomitable faith of the men who sloshed up and down the gulch panning gold from its muddy waters.

The climbing streets of this city still have an appearance of solidity. The two main thoroughfares consist of close-built rows of brick and stone business houses; space for the residences on the hillsides is gained by a series of massively stone-walled terraces. Many of the homes, and most of the mine buildings and mills, have been torn down since my first visit in 1926, but enough of the original town remains to put one easily into the atmosphere of the bustling camp of the seventies and eighties, when 7,000 people lived in its houses, dug in its mines, and swarmed in its narrow streets.

A monument beside the road marks the spot where John Gregory and his companions found gold on May 6, 1859. He washed the rich dirt, obtaining four dollars from the first pan, and then followed the "colors" up the gulch until he uncovered the Gregory vein. By September the tents and cabins of 900 prospectors covered the sides of the gulch, and an estimated $50,000 was cleaned up each week from the placers and lodes. Living was rugged and accommodations far from comfortable, as the following extract from a letter printed in the *Rocky Mountain News* shows:

It is quite cold here o' nights, and we have some threatenings of snow. There is an awful surplusage of ventilation about our cabin, and I have nightly misgivings that I shall be blown through the cracks, but Providence watches over us all.

As the population swelled, Gregory Point became Mountain City, and a second hamlet about a mile downstream was named Black Hawk. Near the close of the summer of 1860, Central City was platted a mile above Mountain City, and the following year it was designated the seat of Gilpin County.

Vestiges of its mines may still be seen on Quartz, Casto, and Gunnell Hills, where green-gold dumps and rusty shaft houses slump high above the city's streets. Just below the Gregory monument, on the south side of the highway, is the portal of the Bobtail tunnel, the oldest in Colorado. Hand-driven and opened in 1863, it was used for years to bring ore from the famous lode to the surface. The mine received its name because, before the construction of the tunnel, the pay dirt was loaded on a rawhide stretched between a forked stick and was hauled down the gulch to the sluices by a bob-tailed ox.

On the opposite side of the road from the Bobtail, on top of Bates Hill, the Ben Burroughs mine was discovered in 1859. Pat Casey was one of the miners who worked on the lode. He did some prospecting on his own and from time to time bought up claims from the Burroughs brothers. In 1862 an accidental cave-in on his property revealed a mass of exceptionally rich ore, and Pat became a wealthy and important man overnight, spending his money generously if not always wisely. The street leading from Central City to the Burroughs mine is called "The Casey" in his honor, and along its winding length the large force of miners known as "Casey's Night Hands" walked to and from work.

Once, when he had a bottle of whisky in his pocket and was in an expansive mood, Casey went to the shaft of his mine and yelled to the men below:

"How many of yez are down there?"

"Five," was the faint reply.

Casey pondered this a moment and then yelled again, "Well, half of yez come up and have a drink."

He bought a span of fine black horses for $1,500 and drove them around Central's steep streets. When the assessor asked their value, Casey, who was inordinately proud of them, said $2,500 and insisted on paying the tax at that rate. Once he took a trip to New York and stayed in one of the larger hotels. For fear that he could not find his room in the maze of corridors, he blazed a trail all the way from the lobby, and this cost him $2,000.

The placers and surface diggings "on the richest square mile on earth" were exhausted by the middle sixties, and mining slumped as soon as the oxidized ore was skimmed off. The district's sixty mills and arrastres were unable to extract gold from the harder complex deposits which lay beneath the layer of decomposed quartz. It was not until Nathaniel P. Hill's smelter at Black Hawk was blown in, and new and improved reduction processes were put into use, that the district perked up. The seventies and eighties were Central's best years; and since it was a gold rather than a silver camp, even the nineties proved productive. But by 1914 scarcely a mine was working, and since then only sporadic work has been attempted by leasers and one or two mining companies.

Mountain City had a newspaper, *The Rocky Mountain Gold Reporter,* which lasted for six weeks in 1859, but Central had no paper until Alfred Thompson brought a Washington hand press and type from Iowa and ran off the first issue of the *Miners' Register* (now the *Register-Call*) in July, 1862. With its first issue, the paper began its long cycle of reporting on the doings of Central and its mining neighbors in Gilpin County. The two-story Register Block was erected by the owners of the paper in 1862-63, and the paper is still printed on its second floor. A third story was added to the building when it was purchased by the Masons, and Lodge meetings are held to this day in its famous hall. In the early days the paper was sometimes printed on wrapping paper (and once on wallpaper), when the wagons crossing the plains from the East were burned by Indians and the shipments of newsprint destroyed. But its subscribers read the news, whether local or from the "States," with equal relish:

September 15, 1864
   An eastern mail is expected constantly. It is so long since we had eastern mail that we had forgotten almost that our correspondence lived.

December 4, 1864
   The Missouri River has been so full of ice for several days past that the mails could not be got over.

December 8, 1864
   The Down Coach was upset yesterday by running off the bridge at the Dickerson mill. It fell upon the top causing the passengers to fall on their heads. There were nine passengers inside. H. M. Teller was severely bruised and cut. . . . The driver . . . laid senseless for some time. He is now at the Pacific House and is recovering. The accident occurred because of the very slippery condition of the road.

November 5, 1864
   Madam Wright who has so long been the nuisance of Eureka Street, whose crib is just below the new Methodist Church, was arrested for larceny last night . . . and bound over to appear at the next term of the district court. . . . It is high time she were routed out from the place she occupies on one of the most public and respectable streets of our city. . . . Perhaps such creatures should be permitted to live in a community, but they certainly ought to be severely treated for their offenses against morality and law, and compelled to remove to some remote locality where their presence will not be so annoying.

   On April 16, 1865, a black-bordered paper printed the news of Lincoln's death. On April 15, when word of his assassination had reached Central by telegraph, William Taber, a Kentuckian recently arrived in town, had been overheard to say, "I'm glad of it. It served him right." As soon as this was reported, indignant men gathered in knots and talked of lynching the rebel at once. To prevent this, Bill Cozzens, Central's able sheriff, arrested Taber and put him in jail. But the angry men were not satisfied. A telegram was sent to Brigadier General Patrick E. Connor in Denver, asking what action should be taken, and Connor wired back, "Turn him over to the people to do with him as they please. If they do not want to deal with him send him here in irons."

By afternoon the grumbling crowd was so much larger that lawyer Henry M. Teller and the sheriff realized that the mob would rush the jail by night and lynch the prisoner. To avoid this "lasting disgrace on the town," Teller and the sheriff held a people's trial in the theatre, at which Teller, in an impassioned speech, "induced them to abandon their bloody purpose." Taber was then tried by a military court, and on April 27 the *Miners' Daily Register* reported that

Taber, the southern sympathizer, has been condemned at Denver and sentenced to carry a bag of sand weighing sixty pounds, six hours a day for thirty days.

The Teller House, the impressive four-story hotel on Eureka Street, opened on June 24, 1872. To celebrate the event, Bush and Company, the proprietors, sent out invitations

to nearly a hundred citizens of Central and vicinity. Most of them came, many with their ladies. After dinner the party assembled in the spacious parlors where a few brief speeches were made, garnished with exquisite music by Prof. Barnum's orchestra.

Across the main hall and opposite the office is the billiard rooms and bar . . . well supplied with things to cheer and inebriate.

All sleeping rooms to the number of ninety are tastefully fitted with all essential conveniences. The majority are . . . without transoms, ventilation being obtained by adjustable windows. Guests may therefore lie down to peaceful slumbers undisturbed by apprehensions of getting their heads blown off or valuables lifted by burglars.

When President U. S. Grant visited Central City in April, 1873, a pavement of silver bricks, valued at $12,000, was sent over from the Caribou mine, twenty miles away, and laid from the door of the hotel out to the street. The silver bricks were borrowed for the occasion because gold was too common in Central. The famous guest "was quite incredulous when told that the slabs were genuine silver; but had finally to accept the truth."

In 1873 Central City ranked next to Denver in size, yet within a year it was reduced to six buildings. The fire which destroyed it started in the Chinese quarter and quickly enveloped the entire city. The Register Block, the Wells Fargo office, and the Teller House served as firebreaks. The Register Block was saved by cutting away its wooden cornice and pouring water constantly on the roof. The windows of the Teller House were hung with wet blankets; nevertheless, the sashes and frames were charred, and every pane was broken or melted.

The town of Golden sent its fire-fighting apparatus to Central on the newly completed railroad, which ran as far as Black Hawk. The train carrying the fire company puffed up the canyon so fast that a fireman was shaken off, and the train traveled a mile up the heavy grade before it could stop and back down for him.

After the fire, Central rebuilt more solidly and reorganized its fire department. Of the city's three companies, the only remaining evidence is the bell tower of Alert Fire & Hose Co. #2, standing to the south of the highway near the site of Mountain City.

The Colorado Central Railroad was extended from Black Hawk to Central in 1878. Even now, though the tracks are gone, the grade can be traced along the side of the hills all the way from Black Hawk. Two years after its completion, George A. Crofutt, who toured Colorado and published the *Gripsack Guide of Colorado, A Complete Encyclopedia of the State,* visited Central and wrote:

The people are generally prosperous . . . the froth, scum and driftwood of civilization incidental to mining camps, has long since floated away to "new diggings" leaving a substantial class of citizens any one of whom will tell you with the greatest confidence "Gilpin County is good enough for me."

Even before the "froth and scum" had floated elsewhere, the people supported all manner of entertainments. The miners were Irish, Cornish, and Italian, and there were also many Germans in the city. As all these groups liked music, singing societies were organized and concerts were favorite diversions, as were wrestling matches and rock-drilling contests. The residents also went in for "culture," and many lecturers were brought to the city during its first years.

Artemus Ward, world renowned humorist and comic lecturer, arrived in Denver and on Thursday night will be with his mountain friends to "speak his piece" . . . and enlighten us on the mysteries of the show business and life in "Baldwins'-ville." The arrival of Louis Napoleon in the "Bey of Algiers" could hardly create a greater sensation in our mountain circles. [*Miners' Weekly Register*, February 24, 1864.]

Artemus Ward lectured to an immense audience. . . . The lecture was entertaining and replete with bright gems of eloquence. . . . He is a pleasing speaker to say the least. [*Register*, February 26, 1864.]

SILVER PLUME

TELLER HOUSE HOTEL, CENTRAL CITY, COLORADO,
AS SEEN FROM MASONIC HALL (LEFT).

OPERA HOUSE, CENTRAL CITY. BUILT IN 1878

A large congregation assembled at the Episcopal church last evening to hear Bishop Randall's lecture on the subject "The unity and antiquity of the human race considered in reference to the Darwinian Theory."

The Bishop took the ground that man came from the hand of his Creator a perfect man, destined to be the lord of earthly creatures, animate and inanimate, elemental and organic. [*Daily Central City Register,* May 14, 1872.]

Central's first theatre was the loft of a large log cabin near Mountain City, the "stage curtained from the auditorium and candles for footlights." Mme. Wakeley and the "fascinating Haidee Sisters" gave the first performances in it, and, since the troupe contained no men, Mlle. Haidee was forced to cast any men she could draft for the male roles. The People's Theater, the "first well ordered and respectable place for theatrical entertainment in the city," opened in 1860. The National, at the head of Main Street, was built in 1862 by George Harrison. He shot his competitor, Charley Switz, in the chest from the front balcony of the building, was tried for murder and acquitted and, after conducting a successful season of plays in Central City, went south and joined the Confederate army. Jack Langrishe and Mike Daugherty then acquired the theatre, changed its name to the Montana, and produced melodramas every summer for years to appreciative audiences.

Once Harry Richmond, Langrishe's leading man, was playing Maltravers in Bulwer-Lytton's *Alice or the Mysteries* and "with streaming eyes upturned toward the rafters exclaimed to the heroine in tones of agonized supplication, 'Alice, why don't you speak to me?' " Before Alice could reply, an astonished stage carpenter perched on a beam overhead, thinking that Maltravers was addressing him, shouted, "Damn it, Alice ain't up here!" When *Uncle Tom's Cabin* was presented for the first time on July 18, 1865, the *Miners' Daily Register* announced that "the machinery for this play . . . is said to be the finest ever brought into use here. The effect can be but beautiful." On July 21, in reviewing the performance, the *Register* commented on the excellent handling of the individual parts:

among these everybody has noticed that of Eva as personified by Master Benny Wheeler . . . with face upturned to heaven and eyes filling with tears, his appeals to his parent for the freedom of Uncle Tom is sublimely beautiful.

After the fire of 1874, the Belvidere Theater was erected; but it proved inadequate for a performance of *The Bohemian Girl,* and both music lovers and theatre patrons began to talk of an opera house. "Senator Henry M. Teller and Willard Teller were the heaviest contributors toward it, but we all chipped in," an old-timer told me one day. The imposing stone building was built with considerable dispatch and opened on March 4, 1878. Both the musical and the dramatic organizations of Central clamored for the honor of dedicating it, with the result that two formal openings were held, the music group appearing first.

During the seventies and eighties the Opera House drew to its stage the finest talent the country afforded. Emma Abbot, Mme. Janauschek, and Joe Jefferson gave spirited performances in its acoustically perfect auditorium. In the nineties traveling companies made one-night stands in Central, presenting minstrel shows and vaudeville acts. In one of these a female contortionist was the leading attraction. The following day's newspaper account was lavish in its praise of the lady's performance. Adjective after adjective described her suppleness and skill. Then in a burst of journalistic eulogy the editor wrote: "In fact, she was like a boned chicken." By the late nineties and early nineteen hundreds, however, the house was dark except for infrequent movies and school commencement programs.

Then in 1932 the heirs of Peter McFarlane gave the building to the University of Denver, and its restoration began. Every summer since then, with the exception of the war years, the Central City Opera House Association has held a festival, assembling notable producers, actors, and opera stars to perform in the historic theatre. At this time the restaurants and bars flourish, the antique shops and art emporiums attract curious customers, and even those churches which have been closed all year hold special Sunday services.

During the festival, Central City is gay and alive and recaptures a little of its former verve; but, except for the finished performances at the Opera House, much of the fanfare is a tinseled veneer. Central City itself carries on in its quiet way throughout the year; the festival is a summer jamboree.

Whenever I visit the city in the summer and find the streets full of tourists, I slip into the Gold Coin Bar on Main Street. Its dark, unspoiled interior has been left with its original fixtures and décor; and there I forget that this is 1952, and I almost hear the ore wagons rattling down the street to the Black Hawk mills and see the smoke from the train laboring up the grade to the station (which is still in Central City but lies buried under tons of tailings from the Chain-O-Mines mill). I admit that I am sentimental about Central, but then, of all the great mining camps whose glories have departed, I know it best.

CENTRAL CITY TO SILVER PLUME

BEYOND Central City is a long hill on which bits of the old wagon trail, with its steep grade, are still visible. Where the road levels off at the top of the hill, it pays to stop and look back, for there in the hollow lies the whole spread of Central City; radiating from it are the mine trails and roadways leading to the higher tiers of streets, the shaft houses, and the mine dumps.

They say that the roadbed between Central and Russell Gulch, three miles farther on, is made of gold, for it is surfaced from the dumps that piled up at the old mine properties before extracting processes were very efficient. The town of Russell Gulch lies below the level of the present road; so one sees only the roofs of stores and houses set close together on the terraced streets. Mine properties sprawl in all directions above and below the highway, and a frame church with a stained-glass oriel window sits primly beside the dusty thorough-fare.

Just beyond Russell, the highway turns sharply and approaches the brink of Virginia Canyon. The next few miles are full of scenery and thrills, for the road winds down the mountainside by curves and switchbacks and finally rolls along an incredibly steep street beside a gully into Idaho Springs. I can remember when the upper ledges of this shelf road were so narrow that every driver kept a sharp lookout for approaching automobiles and crawled into the first niche wide enough for passing; but today it has a two-way width for the entire distance. If you are the driver you will want to watch the road; if you are a passenger, you will enjoy the views of snow-capped Mount Evans across the valley and Idaho Springs far below, looking as tiny as a toy village. On the way down, the road passes many mine properties, whose gold-stained dumps of rock spill over the mountainside and are prevented from piling onto the highway by barricades of cribbing.

Idaho Springs has remained alive and active since George A. Jackson panned the first placer gold from Clear Creek in January, 1859, at a spot only a few hundred yards from the main highway. West of the town, the fourteen miles to Georgetown were once crowded with tents and cabins and were noisy with the thud of stamps as placer gold was washed from the streams and as gold and silver lode mines were developed in the nearby mountains. Nine miles west of Idaho Springs the road forks, Highway 40 continuing straight ahead and Highway 6 swerving left toward what seems to be a dead-end valley. At its end lies Georgetown, cupped at the bottom of the farthest mountain, and no Colorado mining town has more charm than this silver camp or more buildings that date from the seventies and eighties. Three of its five firehouses are stand-ing; the Clear Creek county courthouse is worth a visit; and Louis DuPuy's Hotel de Paris, built in 1875, with its Victorian bedrooms, diamond dust mir-rors, and walnut and maple inlaid floors, is a landmark to be admired. The present highway skirts Georgetown; but as it climbs toward Silver Plume, one can look down at Alpine Hose No. 2's tall tower, at the Hotel de Paris, at the Hammil House—built in 1880 for the city's mining millionaire—and at Grace Episcopal Church, whose separate, sturdy, rock-anchored belfry replaces an earlier steeple blown over by "mountain zephyrs."

It is also easy to trace the railroad bed of the once-famous Georgetown

Loop, the engineering sensation of the seventies. The old trestles and rails were removed after the road was abandoned in the 1930's, but the roadbed and the bridge abutments are visible below the highway. To reach Silver Plume, two miles beyond Georgetown and 1,000 feet higher, four miles of track were laid in a series of curves and overlapping loops, now close to the creek, now high above it, until by constant gyrations it squirmed into the high mountain valley where Silver Plume nestles at the foot of Sherman and Republican mountains.

SILVER PLUME

A NARROW gateway of rock, just wide enough to accommodate the old railroad grade, the cascades of Clear Creek, and the present highway, guards the approach to the town. Beyond the gate the Plume bursts into sight, silhouetted against the huge white dumps of the Pelican-Dives mines. To the right of the pavement a road meanders into its main street, whose false-fronted stores date from the boom days.

The town was given its picturesque name by prospectors whose first pay ore was in the form of leaf silver, shaped like a perfect plume or feather. Its first tents and cabins were perched on the mountainsides, for the valley floor was swampy and full of timber; but as soon as the flat was cleared and drained, homes and stores were built, and in 1870 the townsite began to take shape.

The richest of the mines were close by. They were reached by tortuous trails which zigzagged up the steep mountainsides to the many tunnel mouths. Silver, lead, zinc, copper, and gold-bearing lodes were found on Republican, Sherman, Brown, McClelland, and Leavenworth mountains, and the sacked ore from the many properties was packed down the trails by jack trains. Only a few of the mines are working today, but any resident will proudly show you the Pelican-Dives, the Payrock, the Corry City, the Dunderburg, the Burleigh, the Seven-Thirty, the Terrible, and the Mendota properties.

Owen Feenan discovered the Pelican mine in 1868; since he was working in another mine at the time and was unable to explore his prospect, he said nothing about it until he became desperately sick and feared he was dying. Then he described the location of his claim to two of his friends. Although critically ill for a long time, he recovered, only to find that the men had opened the mine and failed to include his name as joint owner.

The Dives mine adjoined the Pelican property and was believed to be on the same rich vein of silver ore. As the shafts of both mines were close together and tapped the same vein, a feud developed over the underground workings; each company accused the other of encroaching on forbidden territory. Experts hired at $100 a day reported that the original vein was diverted by a "horse," or mass of non-metallic rock; the vein continued on both sides of this obstruction and carried rich ore into both mines. This discovery in no way eased the tension between the companies, for each of them regarded the ore extracted by the other as stolen.

Lawsuits were filed to determine on which property the vein apexed. Since the whole population of the valley took sides on the issue, court hearings became so heated that Judge Belford was forced to keep a brace of pistols on his desk. Even with armed men guarding both mines, high-grading went on. One night a Denver undertaker was instructed to deliver six coffins to the Pelican for men who had been killed in the mine. These were lowered down the shaft and later drawn up with their heavy loads and hauled away. By the time it was found that the boxes contained stolen high-grade ore instead of bodies, the metal was being run through a smelter far from the Plume.

J. H. McMurdy was the resident manager of the Dives mine, and Jacob Snider was part-owner of the Pelican. One morning in 1875, Snider left the mine and started on horseback for Georgetown. On the outskirts of that city he saw Jack Bishop, one of McMurdy's armed guards, ambushed beside the road. Sensing danger, he tore into Georgetown with Bishop close behind him. Just as he was about to dash into a livery stable, Bishop overtook him, felled him with the butt of his pistol, shot him in the head, and escaped. A short time later McMurdy also died, and W. A. Hammill of Georgetown bought the Dives mine at a sheriff's sale for $50,000.

Although the railroad reached Georgetown in 1877, the famous Loop to the Plume was not completed until five years later. The road was built to move ore from the mines, but before long its passenger trains overflowed with tourists, drinking in the scenic wonders of the trip and freezing in terrified delight as the tiny cars crept over the high trestles. As excursion trains pulled into the station during the summer months, the hotels and restaurants placed tempting food on their tables and waited for the onslaught of the milling throngs.

My first trip to Silver Plume in 1926 was over the Loop. I spent several hours wandering through the town's winding streets, past houses with picket fences and lush green lawns, past pocket-sized gardens gay with mountain lupine and columbine, cultivated roses and delphinium. The diminutive stone jail, pressed close against the mountainside not far below the big, red schoolhouse, was empty; its grilled door stood slightly ajar so that I could peer into the dark, cobwebby interior. The frame city hall and firehouse, next to the rustic bandstand where miner musicians once gave concerts, was painted a gaudy red; and on the mountain slopes above the town, boardinghouses and shaft houses which have since disappeared stood beside the mine dumps.

To the west of the town is the site of Brownsville, a camp that was settled a year or two before Silver Plume and consisted at first of buildings connected with the mining properties on Brown Mountain, owned by William H. Brown. It was always considered a suburb of the Plume, and its days were cut short by a mudslide. It was never rebuilt. Looking up at the steep-sided mountains closing in the valley and at the long scars left by previous snowslides, it was easy to see how an avalanche of mud or snow could bury anything in its path.

Fire was also a menace to the camp. In November, 1884, a blaze started in a saloon in the middle of the night and consumed the greater portion of the business section before it could be controlled. According to the *Silver Plume Coloradoan,* which described the disaster under the caption, "The Smouldering Plume," "Everybody realized the town's helplessness in battling such a monster without waterworks, fire engines or hose company." A messenger was sent to Georgetown for aid; and while the town awaited the arrival of the Star Hook and Ladder Company's truck, "the destroyer was marching west on Main Street" and "citizens were heroically battling the fiery serpent which hissed defiance" at their efforts. The property damage was staggering. As the stricken merchants and householders began to dig into the smoking debris, "the charred remains of Patrick Barrett were found in the ashes of the building in which he was sleeping when the flames grappled him in their deadly embrace." The town rebuilt at once and even floated a bond issue to finance a waterworks and better fire protection. Although subsequent minor blazes have left gaping foundations and empty lots to show where buildings formerly stood, Silver Plume has never again been so nearly destroyed.

Each year, however, more old landmarks disappear. La Veta Hotel, which once served meals to hordes of hungry tourists, has been razed; the City Hotel, beside the Catholic church, was torn down to make way for a new building, and several private homes have lost their porches and the elaborate carved balustrades and pendants that adorned them. But the Windsor Hotel with its clean lace curtains is open, and Buckley's store and garage is run by the sons of one of the Plume's pioneer families. Only two years ago, I asked one of the Buckleys to identify the different mine properties for me; to my delight, he not only showed me the Ashby, Diamond, Burleigh, and Victoria tunnels, but pointed high up on Columbia Mountain, saying, "There's the monument at the Seven-Thirty." High above the town I saw the stone shaft that marks the grave of the Englishman Clifford Griffin, one of the first miners to come to the Plume. In prospecting on the mountainside in the late 1860's he discovered a mine, later known as the Seven-Thirty, which, when developed, revealed such rich deposits of gold and silver that he became the wealthiest mine owner in the camp. Close to the mine he built a cabin, and in front of it he hewed a tomb out of the solid rock.

Little was known about Griffin except that his fiancée had been found

dead in his room on the eve of their wedding, and that he had come to the
Rocky Mountains and become a miner in order to forget the past. As the years
went by he became a recluse, returning from work each day to his comfortable cabin and consoling himself with solitude, whisky, and music. A talented
violinist, he often stood in front of his cabin at sunset and played until dark.
At the first strains of music, the people in the town below would come out-
doors to listen, and at the close of the recital their applause would reverberate
against the rocky canyon walls.

He never played better than on the evening of June 10, 1887; his audience
listened spellbound as the last note died away. Then a shot broke the silence
and he fell forward. The miners rushed up the mountain trail and found his
body face down in the rock-hewn tomb, a bullet through the heart. In his cabin
was a note requesting that he be buried in the grave he had prepared. The
miners followed his instruction and erected over the grave a granite shaft with
the inscription:

Clifford Griffin
Son of Alfred Griffin, Esq. of
Brand Hall, Shropshire, England
Born July 2, 1847
Died June 10, 1887
and in Consideration of His Own Request Buried Here.

Silver Plume is gracious and unhurried, exuding the atmosphere of a quiet,
law-abiding town. On a recent visit I was shown a copy of the *Silver Plume
Coloradoan* dated March 25, 1882. As I turned the rattling brown sheets, I
paused at one short announcement:

Who shall we have for Mayor? Candidates are not very plentiful for City Fathers.
Some are afraid, others dare not.

The Plume must have waved more gaily in the eighties than it does today!

BRECKENRIDGE

WEST of Silver Plume a paved highway crosses the Continental Divide
at Loveland Pass, 11,992 feet above sea level, and drops down into
the valley of the Blue River. From Dillon, Highway 9 runs south along the
Blue to Breckenridge, one of the state's oldest mining towns and the seat of
Summit County.

Ruben Spalding and a party of thirty men were the first to prospect along the Blue in 1859. In the first pan of gravel dipped from the stream bed, they found particles of gold worth thirteen cents; a second pan contained values amounting to twenty-seven cents. Convinced that the river held pay-gravel, the men sunk holes three feet deep on a sandbar and whipsawed lumber for their sluices. At about the same time William H. Iliff, who was prospecting on the opposite bank of the river found "a pocket of auriferous gravel" worth two dollars a pan.

Fearful of the Ute Indians who roamed the area, the men built a block-house for protection and made no attempt to lay out a townsite until spring. The camp was named in honor of John Cabell Breckinridge, at that time Vice-President of the United States; but when he was found to favor the Confederacy at the outbreak of the Civil War, the Union miners changed the "i" to an "e" and wrote the name as Breckenridge.

Judge Silverthorn came to the camp in 1859 and held the first Miners' Court in the rough new settlement. He and his wife ran the Silverthorn Hotel, covering its walls with newspapers which the patrons read again and again, so hungry were they for news from the "States." The winters were too severe for the lady, and she spent the coldest months of each year in Denver. Each spring, when word reached Breckenridge that she was on her way back, the men would put on their snowshoes, meet her at the top of the range, and pull her into town on a sled.

The miners' cabins were crude affairs, often with dirt floors and sod roofs. One enterprising housewife covered her dirt floor with a thick layer of sawdust and over it laid a carpet made of burlap sacks sewed together. Another house had a floor made from discarded sluiceboxes. One miner had a cabin back of which ran a mountain stream. He finally went to town to have his shaggy hair cut. The barber snipped away for a while and then asked if his customer was a signpainter. "Hell, no," was the emphatic reply.

"Then how do you get so much gold-leaf on your scalp?" continued the perplexed barber.

"Gold leaf, is it?" cried the miner, rushing out of the shop and tearing up the mountain to his cabin. He knelt beside the stream, washed out a pan of gravel which contained a few grains of gold, and promptly staked a placer claim on his land.

From 1859 to 1863 the camp flourished. Then the placers washed thin and were abandoned as exhausted; and for fifteen years the little settlement was almost deserted.

In 1879, when Leadville's silver boom sent miners scurrying over the mountains hunting for quartz lodes, scores of prospectors worked their way over the passes or crossed the Ten Mile Range to gopher around on the slopes that rose above Breckenridge. With the discovery of rich lode mines in the early eighties, the town's second and biggest boom commenced; its streets were noisy with the sounds of hammers and saws as new two- and three-story frame buildings rose beside the cabins of the sixties. Whenever cellars were dug for new buildings, the excavated dirt was carefully washed and searched for nuggets before being hauled away. So rich was the placer ground on which the town was built that men even panned the dirt in the gutters and made a day's wages by doing so.

The railroad to the town was completed in 1883; it crossed the mountain range separating the valley of the Blue River from the eastern slope of the Rockies over Boreas Pass, and snaked its way into the camp past Windy Point. Even with a railroad, however, Breckenridge was often cut off from the rest of the world when deep snow drifted into cuts and stalled the trains that fought their way to the top of the windy summit. During the winter of 1899 Breckenridge was isolated for seventy-nine days. As supplies dwindled, hardy men mushed over Boreas on snowshoes to Como, on the eastern slope; they brought back food and one or two newspapers, which were eagerly read by the entire population. On April 25, when the first train, consisting of six engines and two coaches, made it over the range, the whole town turned out to watch it come in. Every bell in town clanged and every whistle tooted until it panted into the station.

In the middle nineties Breckenridge's third boom began when men talked of dredging the bed of the Blue. They believed that the placer deposits were not exhausted and that gold could be profitably recovered if the ground was worked on a big enough scale. Stanley Revett built the first gold-boat; as it gouged deep to bedrock and opened new pockets of pay gravel, more dredges were constructed and floated on artificially made ponds on both the Blue and its tributaries. By 1910 five dredges were operating in the Breckenridge area, digging their way through the gold-filled earth (which yielded twenty to thirty cents a cubic yard) and ejecting from the stacker a constant stream of worthless rock.

The channel of the Blue is walled for miles with the high mounds of stones and boulders discarded by the dredge. They are scoured so free of dirt that in only a few places has vegetation been able to find an earth-filled cranny in which to thrust an exploratory root. This man-made hill stretches behind Breckenridge's main thoroughfare right to the center of town, where one of the dredges rests in a pool of water, its long stacker extending out over a side street. The dredge is idle, but the rock piles in its wake form a wide, gray strip of debris through the otherwise green valley.

Some of the older town properties disappeared in the fire of 1896, and the firehouse, with its tall tower, has been replaced by an efficient but uninspired

FAIRPLAY. APPROACH BETWEEN DREDGE DUMPS IN THE SOUTH PLATTE RIVER

FIRST NATIONAL BANK, CENTRAL CITY

structure. Most of the buildings that remain, however, date from the second or third boom and are fascinating examples of late nineteenth-century Rocky Mountain Gothic.

LINCOLN CITY

FOUR MILES up French Gulch, east of Breckenridge, is the site of Lincoln City. So few of its buildings remain that today it can hardly be called a town. I had seen the dredging around Breckenridge, but I was unprepared for the extent of the operations that have literally turned the entire bed of the gulch into a gravel pit. The gulch is wide, and to cross it the road dips and twists in and out, around mounds of churned-up rock which in some places are higher than a car. One forgotten house stands stranded in the middle of the gulch, unfurnished and with floors that sagged and buckled under my feet. The only note of color left in its drafty interior was the faded green wallpaper that hung in limp shreds from the walls and fluttered in the slightest breeze.

Once out of the bed of the gulch, the road skirts the rock-piled channel and climbs the valley, past the Wellington mine with its many shops and sheds, past the Country Boy and the other mining properties, to the few scattered cabins and half-hidden foundations that today comprise Lincoln City. Like Breckenridge, it grew up in the sixties and reached its peak in the eighties, when pay dirt was discovered in the bedrock of French Gulch and lode mines were developed on Farncomb, Mineral, Nigger and Humbug hills.

During the peak of its boom it had two hotels, plenty of saloons, a post office and a school, a population of 1,500, and buildings which extended for some distance on both sides of the gulch.

Harry Farncomb came to Breckenridge as a young man and engaged in placer mining in French Gulch, at the base of the hill which he later acquired. The deposits of gold in the stream bed were so rich at this point that he decided to search for their source, believing it to be in the hill above the workings. He bought a few acres of the land and kept adding to his holdings until he owned a considerable portion of the hill. In prospecting its surface he discovered crystallized gold, which looked like matted, tangled wire, in such quantities that he was soon one of the wealthiest men in Breckenridge.

His discovery started a stampede to Farncomb Hill and to the Wire Patch, as the placer ground at its base was called; and before long the entire hillside was covered with claim stakes and miners feverishly gophering into its surface. The gold lay in rock crevices from fifteen to fifty feet beneath the surface and was found in such a pure state that the miners often carried it away in their handkerchiefs or in their boots for safety. Specimens of Farncomb Hill gold were sent to the World's Fair Exposition; one nugget from the diggings weighed almost fourteen pounds. Mining men still talk about Farncomb Hill and its riches, but all that tourists see are the tawny dumps forming terraces down to the boulder-strewn channel of French Gulch.

FAIRPLAY

IN 1859 thousands of men who had tried unsuccessfully to find gold along the eastern rim of the Rocky Mountains crossed the broad expanses of South Park to the banks of a creek in which they found the colors they were seeking. Here they made a camp, calling it Tarryall. So jealous were they of their location that they ran off all newcomers who tried to join them. In indignation, these late arrivals dubbed the flourishing camp Graball and, pushing on, found gold in the deep gravel bars of the South Platte River. A town of log cabins was hastily constructed along the river bank and was christened Fairplay by the still-indignant prospectors. As it grew in size, it became the important mining and trade center for the entire region. In recent years dredges have sucked gold from the channel of the South Platte and clawed away the banks that contained the coveted pay-gravel, but the town sits high above the trough of the river and looks much as it did in its prime.

Fairplay is 10,000 feet above sea level; in summer and winter alike, winds from the Continental Divide sweep down from the peaks just west of it and rush across the vast meadowland of South Park. Even in July and August the nights are so cold that water from lawn sprinklers freezes where it falls.

The most photographed building in the town is the white frame Presbyterian church. Built in 1874 by Reverend Sheldon Jackson, it is still a vital part of the community. Ben Graham, who made his strike in one of the district's mines, presented the church with a bell in 1875, and for years its mellow tolling served as both school bell and fire alarm.

Park County's two-story red sandstone courthouse, also built in 1874, is the oldest one still in use in the state; standing in the center of a block, surrounded by a lawn, it dwarfs the diminutive stone jail beside it. On the north side of the square stands its predecessor, a log building erected in Buckskin Joe, a nearby camp, and moved to Fairplay after the 1868 election.

In 1880 the present courthouse was the scene of a hanging. A murderer named Hoover was sentenced by Judge Bowen to life imprisonment. The inhabitants of the town, who had witnessed the cold-blooded killing, considered the punishment too light, so that night a group of Vigilantes went to the sheriff's house and demanded the keys to the jail. When he refused, they marched him to the jail, broke down the door, locked him in a cell, and rushed the prisoner out of the building. When Judge Bowen reached the courthouse the next morning, Hoover's body was dangling from a second-story window. Inside the building the Judge found a noosed rope on his bench and another labelled, "For the District Attorney." The two men lost no time in hiring a rig and driving the ten miles to Red Hill, where they caught the first train to Denver.

On Fairplay's main street, beside the Hand Hotel, stands the grave of Prunes, a burro who for sixty-two years worked in the mines around Fairplay and Alma. When he grew old he wandered about the alleys accepting any food given him, for he was too decrepit to forage for himself. He died in 1930, and his many friends decided to mark his grave with a suitable monument. A year after it was erected Rupert M. Sherwood, an old prospector and Prunes's last owner, died at the age of eighty-two. Toward the end of his illness, realizing that he would not recover, Sherwood requested that his body be cremated and buried beside Prunes, his faithful partner for so many years.

The first time I visited the grave, tall grass and wildflowers almost hid the low mounds which marked the location of the bones of the animal and the ashes of the man. Fastened to the iron fence surrounding the plot were the pick, shovel, and other tools which Rupe Sherwood used during fifty years of gophering in the vicinity. The gravestone is a concrete block surmounted by a bronze plaque depicting Prunes in his prime; until vandals pried them out, the animal's name was spelled out by colored marbles embedded in the concrete. Glass cases at the sides of the slab contained newspaper clippings and photographs of Prunes and Sherwood, and the stone was set with specimens of ore from each of the mines in which the burro worked; but during the last twenty years most of these colorful mementos have been pilfered by unscrupulous souvenir-hunters.

Prunes's descendants still wander Fairplay's streets and still need care. In a prominent location stands a barrel, with a sign on the side reading:

> THE MONEY DONATED
> IN THIS BARREL WILL
> BE USED TO FEED
> BURROS DURING BAD
> WEATHER. PLEASE HELP.

North of the town rises Mount Silverheels, a beautiful peak whose summit is snow-capped much of the year. Silver Heels was a dance-hall girl in Buckskin Joe who, because of her beauty, became the idol of the miners and the envy of the other camp women. In October, 1861, two Mexicans drove a flock of sheep into the camp and stayed until they had sold most of their animals for fresh mutton. Without warning, one of the men became violently ill and died, and before the startled miners were aware of what had happened, a smallpox epidemic was raging in their midst. Each day the living carried the dead to the little hillside cemetery and buried them under the aspens. Business was suspended and the dance halls were deserted. Nurses were scarce, and only two or three responded to a frantic telegram imploring help from Denver.

During those hideous days, Silver Heels nursed the sick and dying men until she too was stricken. Gradually the epidemic passed, and the survivors went back to mining. Silver Heels remained in her cabin, tenderly nursed by an old woman and slowly regaining her health. In gratitude to the girl who had willingly risked both life and looks to nurse the sick, the citizens made up a purse of $5,000, and a presentation committee took it to her cabin; but there was no response to their knocking. Silver Heels had disappeared, and all search for her proved fruitless. The bewildered committee returned the money to the donors, but, not to be thwarted in their gesture of gratitude, they named the mountain in her honor.

Years later a heavily veiled woman was seen weeping over the graves in the Buckskin Joe cemetery, but she slipped away before anyone could speak to her. Perhaps it was Silver Heels, whose beauty had been sacrificed during the plague and who thereafter shunned all her old admirers.

There are many old mining camps near Fairplay—some, like Mosquito and Buckskin Joe, only a mile or two from the highway, and others, like Horseshoe and Quartzville, hidden at the end of high mountain roads and trails, hard to reach but rewarding to ghost town addicts.

CHALK CREEK CANYON

THERE are also a number of old towns in the Arkansas River Valley, and no area contains more of them than does Chalk Creek Canyon near Buena Vista. The Chalk Creek road heads straight up a canyon formed by the sheer sides of Mount Antero and Mount Princeton. At the base of the latter are the spectacular Chalk Cliffs. The present auto road up the valley, which crosses the creek just below the cliffs, is the bed of the abandoned Denver, South Park and Pacific Railroad. It rises, therefore, on an easy grade, but it provides plenty of thrills in its steady climb up the canyon. At one point it crawls around the edge of a sheer cliff hundreds of feet above the valley floor, and in a couple of places it is so narrow that it would be difficult to pass a car; most of the way, however, it presents no hazards and simply twists between walls of rock or winds through groves of aspens which arch overhead. Beyond the cascades, the creek tumbles beside the road, while

above, on either side of the valley, steep cliffs shut out the sun and cast long
shadows on the opposite canyon wall.

ALPINE

THE trees beside the road have grown so tall that one has to keep a
sharp lookout for the brick smelter stack that marks the site of Alpine.
Just beyond the stack a road dips into the timber, crosses the creek, passes
one low, rambling building—the old stage station—and doubles back toward
the smelter. The few cabins along this once-busy "street" are summer homes
today, but even after necessary repairs they look much as they did in the days
when Alpine had five hotels, several restaurants and stores, twenty-three saloons, and a population of 5,000.

The first mineral discoveries in the Chalk Creek district were made in
1872, but Alpine did not materialize until 1875, after the discovery of the
Tilden mine. Its ore was packed on burros to Alpine, reloaded on wagons, and
hauled to Pueblo for smelting. The trip took eight days one way, but the Tilden
ore ran $1,500 a ton, and its owners made a profit of $36,000 on the property. After the discovery of the Murphy mines on Chrysolite Mountain in
1875, a small smelter was erected beside the creek at Alpine, and ore was
hauled to it in wagons. It was not a success, however, and later the plant was
converted into a sampling and concentrating works.

By 1879 Alpine was a lively camp supporting three banks and a dance
hall. It was undoubtedly to this building that Major Merriam of Centerville
brought "a flock of young men and maidens residing along Brown Creek";
he drove them "to Alpine—that romantically located town—where to the witch-
ing notes of entrancing music the nimble feet of the dancers kept time." It was
1881 before George Knox thought the toughness of the camp had toned down
enough to bring his wife and seven daughters there to live; and he not only
started the first school but also induced one of the ladies of the community to
conduct a Sunday School class. When she asked one of her pupils what Christ
was doing on the Mount, the boy replied, "I guess He was prospecting."

In 1880, when trains began running up the canyon as far as Alpine, it was
predicted that "so long as the railroad's end is here, Alpine will be a booming
city." But the road was pushed up the grade to Forrest City, and then to Hancock, and Alpine's best days were over. Years later, after the railroad was
abandoned, its population drifted away and most of its buildings were moved
to new locations. In 1949, Mr. and Mrs. H. O. Kullman bought the townsite,
and Helen J. Wright remodeled the old assay office next to the smelter chimney
and made it into a charming summer home.

On my first trip up Chalk Creek, I stayed overnight in a cabin camp near

Alpine. In the morning, as I ate breakfast at the camp store, the owner asked me where I was going that day.

"I'm off to St. Elmo, at the end of this road," I replied, looking at the highway map beside my plate.

"That ain't the end of the road," she said. "There's two ghost towns beyond it—Romley and Hancock—and you can drive to both of them and almost up to the tunnel."

ST. ELMO

THE approach to St. Elmo dips downhill from the railroad grade directly onto the main street, whose wooden sidewalks are splintered fragments beside empty stores. Nowadays business centers around one general-store-and-post-office run by the Starks, who were pioneers in the valley. Farther up the street and dotted through the trees along narrower avenues are dozens of frame houses—the homes of summer tourists and the small permanent population.

The town is located at the junction of five gulches and lies at the foot of four mineral-bearing mountains; it was originally called Forrest City, for when it was laid out it was necessary to cut away a heavy growth of spruce and pine trees and clear the ground of six feet of snow before any cabins could be built. When the town was incorporated in 1880, its name was changed to St. Elmo.

When the rush to the Gunnison and Aspen mining districts began in 1879 and 1880, hundreds of prospectors choked the crowded trails over the Continental Divide west of St. Elmo, carrying packs on their backs or prodding loaded jacks ahead of them. Even when toll roads were constructed across the range, and stagecoaches and freight wagons crowded past loaded pack trains on the trail, scores of men still struggled up the mountains on foot, or they rode hired horses or mules to the top of the pass, where they dismounted and sent the animals back down the trail to the livery barns at St. Elmo.

C. Thomas Ingham, whose book, *Digging Gold Among the Rockies,* is full of first-hand information about the early camps, reached St. Elmo when the camp was new and put up at the only hotel, which was still under construction. The proprietor ushered him into a large room partly filled with rows of cots and drew a chalk line around one of them in lieu of partitions.

On January 1, 1881, the *Chaffee County Times* described the camp as follows:

St. Elmo, the Child of 1880 in whose busy streets . . . the solitude of a primeval forest reigned one year ago, has grown to be a business and a mining center. . . .

Its society is very good for a mining town, many men of the highest standing
having located here, and brought their families to stay.

The town grew rapidly, and, as mining increased, its population reached
2,000. Before a church was built, services were held in a store or cabin whenever Father Dyer or Bishop Macheboeuf visited the camp. On one occasion
the Bishop held services in a bunkhouse and a high-backed rocker was brought
in to be used as a Bishop's Chair. After the schoolhouse was completed in
1882, services were held there.

In 1881 St. Elmo was the railhead of the Denver, South Park and Pacific
Railroad, which had been built up Chalk Creek from the Arkansas Valley.
The road reached Gunnison, on the western slope of the mountains, in September, 1882, after tunneling through the Continental Divide at Altman Pass
above St. Elmo; and every mile of construction was a fight against cold, snow,
and massive barriers of rock.

St. Elmo was the largest town on Chalk Creek; miners, freighters, and
railroad laborers swarmed to its saloons and dance halls on Saturday nights
to thaw out and celebrate after a week of grueling work in the mountains. Fire
swept the town in 1890, and two of the destroyed business blocks were never
rebuilt. Certain ore mills and one old saloon which I had seen on my first
visit in 1940 were gone last summer, when I again wandered through the picturesque streets. St. Elmo, once so vividly alive, is now placidly relaxed.

ROMLEY

For four miles the road beyond St. Elmo sweeps around blind corners
high above the valley and cuts a path through groves of quaking
aspens. Mine buildings and a group of red frame houses and sheds on a flat
meadow below the road mark the site of Romley. They were very much as they
had been twelve years earlier, though the post office and the tiny railroad station were rapidly disintegrating, and the mine office was now only a pile of
jumbled boards and broken plaster.

According to one account, John Royal and A. E. Wright are credited with
discovering the Mary Murphy mine, around which the town grew, sometime
in the 1870's. Another account says that a nameless prospector fell ill in the
early seventies, was sent to a Denver hospital, and while there was cared for
by a nurse named Mary Murphy. When he recovered and returned to the
mountains he discovered a lode which looked promising and, in gratitude to
the nurse, gave it her name.

Both the Mary and the Pat Murphy mines—parallel seams upon an immense lode—were developed by Royal and Wright and were finally sold by

OLD RAILROAD GRADE BETWEEN ROMLEY AND HANCOCK

BUSINESS CENTER, ST. ELMO

them for $75,000. The new owners were the same ones who had started the unsuccessful Kansas City smelter at Alpine. They sold out in 1880 to a St. Louis company, and under the new management the mine became the biggest producer in the district, with its best ore assaying $125 a ton in gold and silver. As soon as the railroad was completed to Murphy's Switch, as the town was first called, the ore was shipped down the canyon by rail instead of wagon.

During the nineties and until his death in 1903, Colonel B. F. Morley operated the mine with great success. It was while he was in charge of the property that the little town was renamed Romley, an inversion of the first three letters of his name. In 1909 the property was purchased by an English syndicate, which spent $800,000 in further development; but after 1917 the output decreased, and the mine finally closed down after having yielded a total of $14,000,000. Without the shipments from the Mary Murphy, there was no longer any need for the railroad, and in 1926 the tracks were torn up.

The mountainside, both above and below the railroad grade, used to be covered with cabins, for during its best days Romley had a population of more than a thousand. Several hundred miners worked in the labyrinth of underground tunnels and in the mills to which two aerial trams delivered buckets of ore in a ceaseless chain. The trams are idle today, and the shaft house in Pomeroy Gulch is empty. Romley is a true ghost town, and so is Hancock, two miles beyond it.

HANCOCK

THE townsite is a wide, marshy meadow on which a few sagging cabins lean at rakish angles. Only the stone foundations of the old red water tank that used to stand beside the track are left; beyond them the road is so full of ruts and quagmires that it is wiser to explore the place on foot. In one cabin a sheet of yellowed newspaper tacked to the wall caught my eye. The date was torn off, but on the stained and brittle page a woodcut of a man filled three columns. Under the portrait was printed: "Our Next President— William Jennings Bryan."

It was very quiet in Hancock, except for the stream gurgling through the meadow and the wind rustling in the trees; I knew it had been a noisy railhead town in 1881, with five stores, one hotel, two sawmills, and plenty of saloons for the 400 miners and the construction crews, but it was hard to imagine it as either rough or crowded. Where had the saloon stood in which, on December 28, 1880, "John E. Henry, a lumber gatherer, had an ear bitten off and his nose crushed" in a fight? In what part of town had the Wanner

House, the Clifton House, and the Miners' Home been located? Nothing today gives any indication of their whereabouts.

Prospectors discovered placers on the high mountain meadow in the summer of 1880, but it was 1881 before the Hancock Town Company platted the site and began to sell lots. During the construction of the railroad tunnel through the range, Hancock was a typical end-of-the-track construction camp, as well as the transfer point for freighters and passengers en route to Gunnison.

The laying of the rails up Chalk Creek was a fight all the way, as the sweating crews dug and blasted and ripped a path through the stubborn mountains. The boring of the Alpine Tunnel under Altman (or Alpine) Pass was the worst part of the undertaking, for the work was begun in the fall and carried on in spite of bitter weather and blizzard conditions.

The tunnel, 1,830 feet long, 12 feet wide, and 17 feet high, was lined with California redwood. It cost $120,000 and was completed in December, 1881; because of the snow, however, it was not used until the following spring. At its highest point it was 11,612 feet above sea level.

With the completion of the road to Gunnison, the company's headaches began. Rock slides sometimes buried the track and caused damage to rolling stock. But snow was the road's worst enemy, and even seasoned railroad men dreaded the winter months, when slides were a constant menace. Snowsheds crumpled and slid down the mountainside, engines were pushed off the track by the impact of tons of snow, and train windows had to be boarded up for the season to avoid breakage.

The stretch between the east portal of the tunnel and Hancock was the worst of all, for the snow lay deepest at that point and drifted back into the cuts made by the snowplows as fast as they were cleared. More than once an engine would start from the mouth of the tunnel at full speed and burrow under the snow for some distance "like a mole." If it got stuck, the fireman had to cut a vent through the snowy roof over the smokestack before the fumes suffocated the train crew. As one man told me, "It wasn't railroading in the winter, it was just fighting snow every inch of the way."

But in summer the ride through the canyon was one of exceptional beauty. E. Wilbur, roadmaster of the South Park, once took a flatcar to the top of the pass behind a passenger train and, when he was ready to return, rode the car downhill, using a brake club to control it. Mark Twain, who was visiting in the vicinity, heard of this trip and decided to do it too, in order to enjoy the scenery more than he could from a car window. The trip was wilder than he had anticipated, and when it was over he insisted that Wilbur must have tied a rope around an Irishman and thrown him off as a brake!

Before leaving Hancock I drove by the loading bins and under the trestles leading to the dumps of the Allie Bell and Flora Bell mines, and I wondered which of several properties high on the mountainside were the AA and XYZ lodes. On the way to the valley I rolled by St. Elmo without stopping and found the shelf road below Alpine just as thrilling on the down grade as it was on the up. The Chalk Cliffs, too, were more impressive in the afternoon light, when shadows modeled their ashy whiteness into fantastic domes and minarets. The whole Arkansas Valley seemed flat and tame after Chalk Creek's striking scenery and history-laden camps.

CREEDE

CREEDE, a mining camp in the southwestern corner of the state, is as quiet today as it was loud and tough in 1891, when miners and gamblers elbowed each other on its crowded main street and everyone packed a gun. The gulch at the foot of Campbell Mountain, where the camp took root, was far too narrow for the site of a city; after every inch of ground was covered with tents, cabins, and nondescript shacks, some buildings were crowded against the steep cliff walls and others were braced on stilts over the swift-flowing waters of Willow Creek. The camp then overflowed into the lower gulch, making one long street "rather straighter than a corkscrew," and sprawled over the flat below the narrow gorge in a suburb officially known as Jimtown, but referred to locally as Gintown.

When Nicholas C. Creede and his partner, George L. Smith, wandered through the high cliff gateway "to the junction of the Willows" in 1889, they found float along the banks of the stream; and Creede, tracing it to its source on Campbell Mountain, made a location and discovered a mine which he named the Holy Moses. The first ore he extracted carried native silver, horn, glance, and sulphuret, or amethyst quartz, and assayed eighty dollars a ton. The two men did some work on the claim that summer and then left the area until the spring of 1890.

David H. Moffat, president of the Denver and Rio Grande Railroad, and other wealthy men heard of this strike; after inspecting the property, they bought it for $70,000. As soon as it was learned that they were identified with the mine, prospectors rushed to Campbell Mountain, covered it with claim stakes, and then laid out the town of Willow (or Creede) at its foot.

In 1891 N. C. Creede located the Amethyst mine, from which a million and a half was realized, and in December of the same year the Denver and Rio Grande Railroad completed a branch line to Creede. The real rush then began; fifteen to twenty cars arrived each day at the station below the Cliff and as many pulled out, filled with ore for the smelters. Every train that arrived was jammed with passengers. As one newspaper correspondent put it:

Men sit on one another and on the arms of the seats, stand in the aisles and hang to the platforms. . . . At night there are no policemen to interfere with the vested rights of each citizen to raise as much Cain as he sees fit. Three-fourths of the population is of that kind which does see fit. . . .

Now and then a ten-ton load of ore in a ponderous sled comes thundering down the steep road with the driver pounding his horses lustily and shouting at the top of his voice. He is more afraid of sticking somewhere than of smashing all creation by colliding with it. Behind him come two or three more in the same style. . . . The sleighs whirl around with a tremendous swing when they reach the depot and unload into the cars. Down the trail from another direction has come maybe a train of fifty burros, each with 150 to 200 pounds of sacked ore on his back.

There were dozens of hotels, from board shanties with blankets for doors to the Cliff House—which was "conducted upon the advanced principles of the East with the warmhearted generousness of the West." There were never enough rooms available for the throngs that poured in daily; long before the population reached 10,000, all Pullman cars were kept on a siding at the station between runs and used as sleepers.

Henry Taber blew into camp in the fall of 1891 and started the *Amethyst,* the town's first newspaper; but before it was well established, along came Lute Johnson with a hand press and a hatful of type to start the weekly *Creede Candle.* The *Candle* became a permanent part of Creede, and its files contain a complete picture of the exuberant city; for, as the editor said:

Of course if you are a miner or in any way interested in mining you will want the *Candle.* For two silver discs you can have a new one every week for a year and may be lighted to a prospect that will return you thousands for one.

It is supposed that you understand that it takes "tallow" to keep a *Candle* going and that is what I'm here for.—Lute H. Johnson, Boss Trimmer [*Creede Candle,* January 7, 1892.]

Anything could happen in the fabulous camp of Creede. The friends of a certain gambler drank champagne at his grave and then, joining hands, marched around the mound of earth singing "Auld Lang Syne." One Easter the hotels and restaurants ordered an extra supply of fresh eggs. By noon the stock was exhausted, having been used, not for omelets, but for Tom and Jerries. For days after the first baby was born, crowds of rough men milled around J. S. McDonald's cabin to get a glimpse of the infant. They heaped gifts on McDonald and his wife, and they argued over a name for the child until someone in a burst of inspiration suggested Creede Amethyst McDonald. Even Nicholas Creede presented the baby with a gold ring, a pair of earrings, a hundred dollars' worth of toys, and the Daisy mine, a property close to his famous Amethyst.

The camp had its gamblers, fancy women, and tinhorns; as the *Candle* said:

Creede is unfortunate in getting more of the flotsam of the state than usually falls to the lot of mining camps . . . some of her citizens would take sweepstake prizes at a hog show. [April 29, 1892.]

Lulu Slain, a frail daughter laid aside the camellia for the poppy and passed into the beyond early Wednesday morning. She and the Mormon Queen had been living in a small cabin in upper Creede but the times grew hard and the means of life came not. They sought relief from life with morphine, the inevitable end of their unfortunate kind, a well-trodden path from Creede. Lulu's dead; the Queen lives. [September 15, 1893.]

Rose Vastine, known about camp as "Timberline," became weary of the trials and tribulations of this wicked world and decided to take a trip over the range, and to this end brought into play a forty-one calibre pistol. With the muzzle at her lily white breast and her index finger on the trigger she waited not to contemplate the sad result. A slight contraction of the muscles caused the gun to empty its contents into Rose, the ball passing through the upper portion of her left lung.

Medical attendants were at once summoned and the would-be suicide is in a fair way to recover. [February 3, 1893.]

Fire and flood have periodically destroyed whole sections of the city. The first fire raged through the newly built camp in 1892, another damaged it in 1895, and the most serious recent blaze occurred in 1936, when one-third of the business section was burned to a crisp. Floods sweeping down Willow Creek have washed away most of the old buildings in North Creede. Only five or six years ago the creek cut a new channel through the town, leaving a highway "Stop" sign marooned in midstream.

The mountains around Creede are full of mines approached by trails and steep "unimproved" roads; but except for work carried on by leasers and the Emperius Mining Company, whose mill dominates a hill below Jimtown, little mining goes on today. The present town lies on the flat, below the fantastic fingers of rock that rise above the forested mountain slopes. To visualize what Creede was like in its boom years, one must go through the narrow gateway between the vertical cliffs and drive as far up Willow Creek as he can. There in the gorge, hemmed in between narrow canyon walls, stood the boisterous camp where, as Cy Warman, the "Poet of the Cochetopa," wrote,

> It's day all day in the daytime
> And there is no night in Creede.

EMPTY MILL, NORTH CREEDE

MINE AT WHITECROSS

The road between Creede and Lake City follows the Rio Grande River for some twenty miles. Then it winds north through mountainous ranch country and crosses two passes; from the top of Slumgullion, the second pass, it dives into Lake City, an old mining town dating from 1874.

SHERMAN

LAKE CITY is the center of a mining district, and every road from it leads to one or more deserted camps. Henson, Capitol City, and the remains of the old stage station at Rose's Cabin are up Henson Creek. The road that skirts Lake Cristobal, three miles from Lake City, continues for twelve more miles to deserted Sherman; from there it goes on to Whitecross over the meanest and roughest road I have ever driven, and one which I do not recommend to anyone who values his car. A jeep takes it in stride, but not a low-slung automobile.

The approach to Sherman is through a sort of lane leading into a meadow, just before the road leaves the flat to climb Cottonwood Hill. There's not much left of the camp, but it's all ghost. Its rows of cabins are literally in the stream bed, surrounded by sand and water-worn boulders. Only a few buildings at the lower end of the town escaped the torrent, following a cloudburst, which recut the channel of the stream years after the place was deserted.

It was a new town in May, 1877, and its founders laid it out ambitiously, with streets 60 feet wide and blocks 300 by 400 feet. A dozen or more buildings were immediately thrown together beside hastily hacked out paths. Only a month later the Lake City paper, the *Silver World,* remarked:

Sherman is improving much faster than the most sanguine of its friends expected. Our butcher is erecting a good substantial slaughter house. . . . Last but not least, H. Deatherage keeps a tent where a drop of the crather can be had for the sum of twenty-five cents.

Hopes for Sherman were so high that even the Denver *Daily News* reported on June 11, 1880: "Sherman is going to make the boss camp of that section." The mines were not fully developed, however, until late that year, and it was 1881 before the Sherman House opened and a general store "tempted the one hundred citizens to spend their money at home."

Even though placer and lode mines were producing gold, silver, copper, and lead, the camp was dull in September, 1881, after most of the "boys" had gone out for the winter; "Saturday evening prayer meetings and Sunday extempore concerts at Mrs. Franklin's and Mrs. Wager's" were the only activities. The miners, however, were sure that by spring "business will revive and rush ahead like a burro with a light load on a down hill trail."

During the long winter months one miner composed a poem of twenty-two verses and sent it to the *Silver World* for publication. The first two stanzas were printed under the heading "Hang Him."

> The Spring, the spring, the beautiful spring,
> It's hurrying in like everything
> Today it shines, tomorrow it snows,
> And that's the way the wide world goes.
>
> The mountain tops are clothed in white
> The old prospector still gets tight,
> The burro winds around the hill,
> A carrying ores to Crooke's big mill.

As soon as the snow was melted sufficiently to enable them to work their claims, the miners who had left for the winter trooped back and continued to develop their properties—the George Washington, the New Hope, the Mountain View, the Minnie Lee, the Clinton, the Smile of Fortune, and the Monster. The best producer was the Black Wonder, and its ruined mill still stands beside capricious Cottonwood Creek.

On one visit to Lake City I talked with Mr. Ramsay, who had formerly worked at Sherman. "There was mining going on all through the nineties, and the Black Wonder was working as late as 1897," he told me. "I put in a dam for a company that was leasing the mines up there over forty-five years ago. It was to be over a hundred feet high, but by the time I'd built sixty-nine feet of it, the company was broke. Another outfit took over and had me go on with the work. Then the cloudburst came and ripped it out, and the town too, and left things the way you saw them."

WHITECROSS

THE shelf road to Whitecross switchbacks up the side of Cottonwood Hill above Sherman; then, high above the Lake Fork of the Gunnison River, it twists up the valley toward Cinnamon Pass. "The hill is now, was last summer, and always will be an intolerable nuisance," wrote the *Silver World* in 1877, and, having twice wound around its blind corners and over its rock-strewn surface, I am inclined to agree with the newspaper's description.

Even when nothing but a trail had been hacked along its side, the high valley at the head of the Lake Fork was known to contain mineral deposits.

On August 19, 1876, a letter from "An Old-timer" in Burrows Park, as the area was called, was printed in the *Silver World:*

> If things go on improving until Christmas the way they have the past two months up here, I would recommend that the unmarried good looking females East take the advice of that good old man Greeley to the young men, and come West; and there will be a good demand for wives.
>
> We want a postoffice; . . . the letters of my Betsy Susan are too long getting here without having to walk six miles. . . . Our first great want is a bank. If you know anyone who has lots of greenbacks and could advance liberally . . . send him up.

By November, 1876, a camp called Argentum had been laid out in the Park, and "about thirty people planned to spend the winter there." A half-dozen cabins not far away comprised the settlement of Burrows Park, and a third group of buildings, nearer the high peaks, was called Tellurium. On a mountain across the valley was a formation of white quartz in the shape of a cross, and the colony of cabins below it at the foot of the slope was soon known as Whitecross.

In 1881 a stage ran three times a week over a toll road between Lake City and the Park, and the district was lively. According to the Denver *Daily News* of June 8,

> buildings are going up all along the road. As a person rides along, the noise of the anvil and the crash and jar of the blasts tell him that old mines are being worked on all sides.

Each year the camps dotted throughout the valley grew larger as copper pyrites, argentiferous galena, and some gold ores were discovered in the Bald Eagle, Black Swan, Champion, Oneida Chief, Bon Homme, Monticello, and Silver Star mines. During the nineties the population of Whitecross reached 300, and in 1901 the Tobasco Mining Company built its mill high on the side of Cinnamon Pass.

One miner, about to go on night shift, wanted some coffee. In one of his two coffee pots he had stored four pounds of blasting powder. That was the pot he put on the stove!

The first time I went to Whitecross we drove to the head of the valley, past the few weathered cabins that still survive and the one or two small mills that cling to the mountain slopes. After leaving the last cabin, we climbed up Cinnamon Pass to timberline and to the skeleton of the Tobasco mill. From this vantage point we could look over the whole magnificent mountain valley which Charles Burrows prospected in 1873.

SILVERTON

TUCKED away in the Uncompahgre and San Juan mountains—the most rugged in Colorado—are a dozen or more ghost and semi-ghost towns, as well as several equally old but still active mining centers. Silverton, one of the largest of the latter, was laid out on Indian land even before the Brunot treaty with the Utes was signed in 1873. The town has a spectacular setting, for it lies at one end of Baker's Park, a mountain meadow through which flows the Animas River, and it is surrounded by towering peaks.

Just east of the town is the Shenandoah Dives mine and mill, the biggest enterprise in the area. The 10,000-foot tramway from the mine crosses the road at a height of fifty feet, delivering an endless chain of buckets into the maw of the mill; on the return trip, the empty buckets bob along on the cables till they seem to disappear up Arastra Gulch. On the south slope of King Solomon Mountain at the far end of the gulch, so high on the sheer mountainside that it seems pasted against the rock, is the main portal of the mine and the other end of the tram.

CUNNINGHAM GULCH

MOST of Silverton's buildings are old, but the place is alive; so I drove on past the Shenandoah Dives property to Howardsville, where I turned right into Cunningham Gulch. This gulch is of great interest, not only because it is filled with mines and mills, but also because in the seventies streams of prospectors came down its sheer sides from Stony Pass, the main route to Baker's Park. The trail crossed the top of the pass at an elevation of 12,090 feet, and the wagon road, when built, was 500 feet higher. The descent on the Howardsville side was very steep, dropping 2,300 feet in the first two miles.

The mines in Cunningham Gulch are a thousand feet above the road, and the mills are close to the creek. The property closest to its mouth is the Old Hundred. I remembered its skeleton mill between the road and the stream, and on my second trip to the gulch I planned to make a sketch of it; but it was gone, crushed by a mudslide.

Just beyond the Old Hundred is the Pride of the West property, one of the oldest in the San Juan. Ore from its mine was shipped by pack train over Stony Pass as early as 1874. The mine has been a steady producer and is still in operation, its new hundred-ton mill at Howardsville handling the present output. The third mill is the Green Mountain, which handled ore from a group of veins—the Leopard, the Osceola, the King William, the Old Hammer, and the Flat Broke. The most picturesque mill of all was the Highland Mary at the head of the gulch; but it too has disappeared, having burned in 1952.

On one trip to Cunningham I spent an entire afternoon sketching the different mills, each one dwarfed by the high mountain behind it. It was almost dark when I started back to Silverton. The mountain slopes were gray silhouettes; the rows of tram-towers marching up the slopes toward the mines were lost in the half-light, and everything was still. High on one rocky peak, like a star, shone a pinprick of light from some mine.

EUREKA

TEN MILES east of Silverton is Eureka, and four miles farther is Animas Forks—two ghost towns rich in mining history.

Baker (for whom Baker's Park is named) and his party of prospectors are believed to have spent the winter of 1860 in brush shelters at the point on the Animas River where Eureka now stands; but although they placered the stream, they found little gold. Prospectors who panned their way up the river more than a decade later had better luck, and by 1876 a small camp had been established at the same point.

Al Bernard was one of six men working in Eureka Gulch that year. Once, while going from his cabin to the mine, a slide started at his feet, swept him downhill over a sixty-foot bluff, and left him at the bottom, dazed, bruised, and half buried in snow. His companions rescued him and took him to a cabin where they found a bottle of whisky and some cayenne pepper. To warm him up, they rubbed him thoroughly with both of these products. This annoyed him, as he couldn't feel the pepper and lamented the waste of so much good liquor.

The *Silver World* describes a dance held at Eureka in April, 1877, to which "some damsels began to arrive on burros and more on foot." The music was provided by a fiddle and a banjo, and "the ball opened with the San Juan polka which resembled a Sioux War Dance. Soon the 'ironclads' of the miners began to raise the dust from the floor," so that "before long it was impossible to tell what was what." Toward midnight a supper was served, with ground hog and a "big ox" the main dishes. In addition, there was a quantity of "gravy, bacon, coffee, tea and a large variety of pies and cakes." After the food was consumed the dancing continued until morning.

By 1881, Eureka was a "village of two-score buildings" with one smelting works and a newspaper—the *San Juan Expositor*. The official plat of the town was prepared during that year, and the abstract of title states that "said town is found upon unsurveyed public lands." It was not until January 27, 1883, that the "United States of America" granted to W. R. Bowman, the county judge, a "Patent to the Townsite of Eureka, Colorado, containing 179.69 acres of

HOTEL, ANIMAS FORKS

EUREKA. SUNNYSIDE MILL (RAZED) IN DISTANCE

surface ground." The document was signed by "Chester A. Arthur, President."

The mountains above and beyond Eureka were full of mines. The Sunnyside and the Sunnyside Extension, the greatest producers of the area, were located in the early seventies, and a complete history of their development would fill an entire chapter. The Sunnyside was beside Lake Emma, well above timberline, and the first of its great mills was also built beside the lake. Its discoverers, the Thompson brothers, took John H. Terry as a partner in 1888, and much of the mine's success is due to his wise development and successful management.

Terry built a mill halfway between the lake and the town, and in 1894 he erected another mill at Eureka and completed a three-mile aerial tram between it and the mine. In 1910 Terry died, and seven years later his children sold the controlling interest in the property to the United States Smelting Refining and Mining Company for half a million dollars. The mill at Eureka burned just after the corporation completed remodeling and enlarging it; but a new one was constructed beside the ruined hulk. When the mine closed down in 1929 and the men and their families moved away, the town died; for 90 per cent of its population had worked for the Sunnyside company. The property was reopened for the last time in 1938; ten years later it was sold at auction. Some of its buildings were moved to Silverton and others to the Treasury Tunnel on Red Mountain.

On my first visit to Eureka, I found it a most satisfying ghost town. Its main street had well-preserved false-fronted stores. One gambling hall yielded a billiard ball for my collection of western Americana, and "Casey Jones," the "Goose," an old Cadillac equipped with cowcatcher and flange wheels, stood rusting beside the Sunnyside mill; for the railroad tracks between Silverton and Eureka had been torn up years ago, and sand from the banks of the Animas River had already buried much of the right of way. The mountains rise abruptly on either side of the town, but, high as they are, they could not dwarf the many-storied Sunnyside mill, the biggest I had ever seen. The mill was idle, for the mine which had produced fifty million dollars' worth of gold, silver, lead, zinc, and copper since its discovery was shut down. Today the mill is nothing but a mass of metal ribs looming above a few forgotten buildings.

ANIMAS FORKS

THE drive from Eureka to Animas Forks climbs the canyon, first on one side of the Animas River and then on the other. The four-mile stretch is thick with mines and the ruins of mills. Thread-like trails lead up the mountainsides to invisible tunnel openings; occasionally a truck in low gear grinds slowly up the trail to the mine and, loaded with ore, crawls cautiously down again.

The town of Animas Forks is more than 11,000 feet above sea level, and the mountaintops surrounding it are above timberline. Looking back toward the valley from its main street, a tremendous vista opens up as peak after peak and ridge after ridge interlock in one gigantic pattern of undulating rhythms, cut by the grooves of canyons and accented with patches of snow that never melts.

The mines in the district were first worked in 1875, and a mill was erected at the Forks to treat ore brought down from the Red Cloud property at Mineral Point. The townsite was not laid out until 1877. Lots were free to anyone who would "locate and build, parties selecting according to their own free will and choice." A trail connected it with Lake City (then more important than Silverton) by way of Burrows Park. As the camp grew it boasted that it was "without doubt the largest town in the United States at an altitude of 11,300 feet." Even its twenty-five-mile telephone line from Lake City crossed the Divide at a point 12,500 feet above sea level.

The first community Christmas celebration was held in 1881 in the dining hall of the Kalamazoo House. In addition to a tree and gifts for the children, there were speeches and toasts. The Mayor deplored the fact that "the timber south of us is being so rapidly destroyed as to endanger our town from sliding snows." As more and more trees were cut from the hillsides, the Mayor's warning was fulfilled. A slide came down Wood Mountain, jumped across Animas Canyon, and buried John Haw's cabin in fifty feet of snow. The terrific force of the snow burst in his door and filled the cabin in a moment. Three hours later he succeeded in digging himself out. A still larger slide came off Cinnamon Mountain and "after crossing the Animas River near the Eclipse smelter, ran up the other mountain, and then folded over and fell back like an immense wave." During the winter, when twenty-five feet of snow fell at the Forks, no cabin was safe from December to March, and the road to Eureka was often closed by slides.

The camp's best days lasted through the eighties, but once it began to fade "its decline was as rapid as its rise." The biggest mining property was that of the Gold Prince (also called the Sunnyside Extension), at the head of Mastoden Gulch. At the lower end of the main street, beside the river, stand the huge foundations of the Gold Prince mill. One glance at its size shows the scale on which mining was conducted at the Forks. After the mill was dismantled and moved to Eureka in 1917, Animas Forks was done for; by 1923 it was deserted.

Otto Mears, the Pathfinder of the San Juan, completed his Silverton Northern Railroad as far as Eureka in 1896, and he began extending the road to the Forks in 1903. This last stretch was the hardest to build and maintain because of the snowslides. The road was completed, however, and in 1906 Mears accepted a contract to ship ore from the Gold Prince mill throughout the winter. To keep the road open and minimize the constant hazard of slides, he designed an elaborate type of shed capable of resisting any amount of snow. Seven such sheds were to be placed between Eureka and Animas Forks, and a test shed was built near the Silver Wing mine, where the worst slides always ran. Mears prayed for a severe winter so that the shed would receive a supreme test. Before the season ended it was a jumble of rocks and kindling wood, smashed by a single slide. The other six were never built.

Animas Forks is lonelier and contains more empty houses than most ghost towns. Some are mere cabins, but a few are architecturally imposing structures with porches and bay windows. Trails from the town lead to Mastoden Gulch, to Mineral Point, and to Cinnamon Pass.

The canyon drive back to Eureka is always scenically magnificent. I have traveled it in the late afternoon, when shadows mould the slopes into sharp patterns, and I have seen it just before a thunderstorm sent sheets of rain slashing against the car. The most exciting ride was in an open jeep in August, in the midst of a snowstorm.

VICTOR

ANYONE with a car that will pull a hill can reach Victor, for the road to the mining camp is wide, and most of it is paved. Whichever route you choose out of Colorado Springs, you must climb one long hill before you can circle Pikes Peak and reach the town of Cripple Creek and the satellite camps that separate it from the "Core of the Rich Cripple Creek District," as Victor is sometimes called. Both Cripple Creek and Victor are gold camps of the nineties, and both are small but active towns today.

The best way to reach Victor from Colorado Springs is to climb Ute Pass, drive through Woodland Park, and turn south at Divide. Some miles before Cripple Creek the first signs of mining appear—a broken-down shaft house, yellow dumps, and the foundations of a mill—and just as you begin to wonder where the city is, a turn in the road opens up a whole new panorama, with Cripple Creek sprawled over the mountainside directly below.

Between Cripple and Victor one is never out of sight of the mines. The broad shelf of road cut into the mountains is the only interruption to the ore dumps, shaft houses, hoists, and railroad tracks that belong to the big properties which cover the entire six-mile stretch.

In the gully below Squaw Mountain, on the outskirts of Victor, are tier upon tier of foundations, the remains of the Economic Gold Extraction Company's mill. The Columbine Victor Tunnel, bored through Squaw Mountain in 1899, connected this mill with the Gold Coin mine in the nearby camp. Just around the shoulder of Squaw Mountain, as the highway passes through a deep, rocky cut, you suddenly see the city. Its mines, dumps, streets, and buildings cling to the side of a steep hill, and terraced dumps not only cover the mountainside but spill into backyards and choke alleys behind houses.

The Victor and other mines were located in 1891 and 1892, but the Woods Investment Company did not promote the town or locate it on the south slope of Battle Mountain until September, 1893. In March, 1894, while the Woods Company was excavating for the foundations of the Victor Hotel, a blast into the solid rock uncovered a vein of ore, and the usual stampede to a new gold field commenced. This vein, accidentally discovered, became the Gold Coin mine, which upon development paid over a million dollars. Its surface buildings stood in the center of the city, and those of the Strong mine were behind the railroad station. The Independence was nearby, and the Portland and the Ajax dominated the top of Battle Mountain. These mines really made Victor, with the Independence and the Portland the greatest of the five. By the time they were far enough developed to be ready for large shipments, a railroad had been built through the mountains and the camp became the transportation center for the whole district.

Winfield Scott Stratton staked the Independence on the Fourth of July, 1891. Stratton had prospected all over Colorado without striking it rich. He walked to Cripple Creek in 1891 to save stage fare, his prospector's outfit loaded on two burros. After wandering all over the hills of the region, he finally staked a claim near the base of Battle Mountain. It contained a rich vein, and in a short time he was a millionaire. The gross production of the Independence between 1891 and 1915 was $23,621,728!

James Doyle and James Burns had little success in their prospecting until John Harnan, an experienced miner, joined them. He discovered a mine near the top of Battle Mountain in January, 1893, which the men named the Portland; since their claim was not patented, they kept their strike a secret as long as they could, working at night and packing out the ore on their backs. In time they got a wagon and hauled the rich ore to Colorado Springs, where they disposed of it. With the proceeds from each trip they financed further development of their property. Finally their wagon broke down, and other prospectors, happening upon it, followed its tracks to the Portland. Speculators and owners of adjoining properties immediately began to make trouble for the men, and in desperation they went to Stratton, who by then had made his pile in the Independence, and asked him what they should do. He advised them to form a company and promised to take $75,000 worth of stock in it. In this way he provided them with the money they needed to fight their opponents. The men then bought up the adjoining claims, developed the mine, and found its ore to be so rich that single carloads worth $50,000 were not unusual.

Labor troubles upset the camp in 1894 and again in 1903, caused by clashes between the mine owners and the Western Federation of Miners, which was unusually strong in the district. Any old-timer will show you where the fort with its cannon stood on Bull Hill, where the Bullpen was located in Goldfield, and the site of the railroad station which the strikers blew up in the camp of Independence.

The city of Victor was well established and booming when a fire broke out in a Third Street dive on August 22, 1899, and in two hours wiped out fourteen blocks and the surface buildings of the Gold Coin mine. Losses were estimated at two million dollars; but new and more substantial buildings were immediately constructed to replace those lost in the flames, the mines continued to pour out gold, and even the Gold Coin, whose property was most heavily damaged, resumed operations.

By the time mining reached its peak, five railroads served the district. The Florence and Cripple Creek and the Midland Terminal were the first to reach the lofty city, 9,728 feet above sea level. The next to arrive was the Cripple Creek Short Line from Colorado Springs, which was financed by the mine owners to haul their ore to the valley. The last to be installed were two electric lines which ran between Cripple Creek and Victor—the High Line over the hilltops, and the Low Line around their shoulders.

As shafts were sunk deeper, water was encountered at the lower levels of the mines, and the Roosevelt Drainage Tunnel was constructed in an effort to empty the properties. It was satisfactory until the shafts and drifts were again sunk below the natural water table. The Carlton Tunnel was then bored to connect with the deepest shaft in the district, 3,460 feet below the ground. This seven-mile tunnel was completed in 1941 and has successfully cleared the active mines. The newest project to be completed in the district is the $1,500,000 Carlton Mill, which replaces the Golden Cycle mill at Colorado Springs. The new mill treats the ore at its source, and thus eliminates the expensive haul to the valley.

Victor is still a mining camp, but its properties nowadays are worked by lessees. Roads crisscross the hills to scores of mines, and anyone with a yen for ferreting out old places and old properties can explore the few square miles around the town and discover abandoned camps, famous shafts, and historic sites. If that is not enough, then drive back to Colorado Springs over the Gold Camp road. When the Cripple Creek Short Line ceased operations and its tracks were removed, the roadbed was turned into a scenic serpentine highway. It is full of thrills: it drops nearly 4,000 feet by a series of sweeping curves, loops, and ledge grades which shoot through tunnels or out over high trestles, until it reaches Colorado Springs far below.

South Dakota

THE BLACK HILLS of South Dakota rise out of grass-covered prairies and cover an area 75 miles wide and 150 miles long. They were important to the Indians because in them lived the great spirit of the Thunders, because from their forests came tepee poles, and, best of all, because the hills diverted the migrating buffalo herds to well-known trails where they could be easily hunted.

Admirers of Paul Bunyan boast that the Hills are really Babe, Bunyan's blue ox, who died as a result of eating a red-hot stove. Since it was impossible to bury a creature that measured forty-two ox-handles and a plug of tobacco between the eyes, Bunyan heaped earth and rocks over Babe, making an immense mound. In time the seeds which the winds and birds dropped covered the bare hummock with dense forests, and the grooves which the rains cut into its flanks became gulches in which yellow gold lay hidden. Bunyan shed so many tears over Babe that they ran down to the prairie and formed the Missouri River.

The Sioux knew of the gold in the Hills and had shown specimens of it to Father De Smet years before Custer's men washed particles of it from French Creek, but neither the Indians nor the priest would reveal the location. When the country was in the throes of the depression of 1873 and needed money, rumors became persistent that gold existed in the Black Hills. General Phil Sheridan had been advocating the establishment of military posts in the region to keep a closer watch over the Indians; in July, 1874, he sent General George A. Custer from Fort Abraham Lincoln, in Dakota Territory, to the Hills with orders to explore the country and report his findings. With Custer went 1,000 soldiers, correspondents, and Indian scouts, "led by a brass band mounted on white horses" and followed by a train of supply wagons. In August the cavalcade reached the prairie where the city of Custer now stands. While the soldiers were dashing over the country making the required "mili-

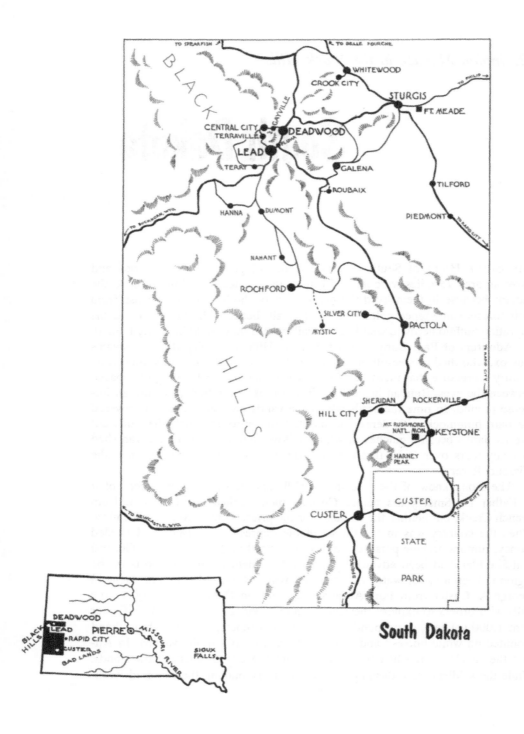

South Dakota

tary reconnaissance," H. N. Ross and McKay, two miners who had accompanied Custer, washed dirt from French Creek and discovered that it contained gold.

As soon as Charley Reynolds, one of Custer's scouts, reached Fort Laramie and sent a wire from General Custer announcing the discovery, men forgot that the gold lay in forbidden territory. They forgot that the Indians resented wagon wheels which crushed the grass and men who dug up the soil and destroyed timber; their eyes saw only a nebulous glitter in the west. The lure of gold was greater than the fear of death, and hundreds made hasty preparations to pull up stakes and head for the distant hills.

When Custer's men returned from the Hills, Charles Collins, a newspaper man, and T. H. Russell, a promoter, thought it a good time to organize a civilian exploring party to the same region. Their flamboyant advertising and the numbers of men who milled around their Chicago office caused General Sheridan to hear of their plan and refuse them permission to continue with it. Undaunted, they moved to Sioux City, Iowa, and continued their preparations in secret, assembling supplies and provisions and paying for them in cash in order to leave no records to betray them. Captain John Gordon was engaged to lead the expedition. On October 6 a party of twenty-eight slipped out of Sioux City without arousing government suspicion, ostensibly headed for O'Neil's Colony in Nebraska but actually making as quick a dash as possible for the Black Hills.

On December 23, 1874, Gordon's party reached French Creek, where the men built a stockade eighty feet square and eleven feet high; it had loopholes every six feet, and six cabins inside. Within this enclosure the adventurers spent the winter. In the Gordon party were the Tallents—David, Annie, and their nine-year-old son Robert. Annie D. Tallent was a true pioneer, equal to any emergency. When her shoes wore out on the long journey west, she made "packs" from gunny sacks and bound them on with cords; during the winter in the stockade, while the men were busy working gravel ledges, sinking pits on the flats and bars, and hunting game to eke out the provisions, she read Milton's *Paradise Lost*. In January, 1875, Captain Gordon started back to Sioux City with the gold that had been recovered from the creek and reported to Collins and Russell on the success of the expedition.

French Creek was on Indian land and by the terms of the treaty of 1868 was protected against white invasion; but the gold was a magnet which drew hundreds of men across the imaginary barrier and made them slip furtively across the plains and through the forests to the region, attempting to evade not only the Indians but also the U. S. troops who were beginning to scout the country looking for them. The Gordon party were discovered by the troops in April and removed from the Hills to Fort Laramie in Wyoming. Upon their release, Collins sent money for them to return to Sioux City; after they arrived, he staged a celebration and used their daring adventure to bolster his demands that the Hills be opened to the whites. His editorial cries started a movement which was taken up in city after city, but the immediate result was that thousands of men filtered into the Indian country without waiting for further treaties to be made or ratified in Washington.

The government, realizing that the more known about the region the better, sent Walter P. Jenney to the Hills with a geological expedition in the spring and summer of 1875. On June 17 Jenney reported to the Commissioner of Indian Affairs in Washington:

I have discovered gold in small quantities on the north bend of Castle Creek, in terraces and bars of quartz gravel. Arrived here yesterday. About fifteen men have located claims on the creek above here and have commenced working. Gold is found southward to French Creek at this point. The region has not been fully explored, but the yield of gold is small and the richness of the gravel has been greatly exaggerated. The prospect, at present, is not such as to warrant extensive operations in mining.

The miners who were pouring into the country thought differently. The government, as represented by General George A. Crook and his troops, arrived in the Hills in July and made perfunctory efforts to keep the men out until some sort of arrangement could be made with the Sioux. The treaty of 1868, which had created their reservation, could not be changed unless approved by three-fourths of the adult tribesmen; and the Indians were in no hurry to give up their land. Hounded and pressed from all sides, they had as their last hunting grounds only these hills and the surrounding prairies, and they were prepared to fight desperately to retain them.

The situation was an impossible one, and General Crook, knowing that treaty negotiations were under way and that the government could never succeed in keeping the miners away from the Hills, mingled with the men and even panned a little gold. He then issued a proclamation ordering all whites out of the area by August 15, 1875; but he suggested that, since some solution would ultimately be reached, the men hold meetings and organize mining districts before their departure. They laid out at least one townsite, Custer City, and then most of them left the area before the deadline. But the game of cat-and-mouse went on, and by fall many of the prospectors had sneaked back to their diggings. Before any treaty was concluded with the Sioux, the first bull trains were snaking across the plains toward the coveted territory. By December 1 all military restrictions were removed and the rush began. During the winter of 1875-1876, 11,000 men are said to have entered the Hills, most of them going first to Custer and from there fanning out in all directions in search of pay dirt.

After the battle of the Little Big Horn, which took place on June 25, 1876, the many hostile Indian tribes which had banded together to fight the white man scattered, and no other concerted attacks were made again. But even after September 26 of the same year, when the Sioux signed a treaty relinquishing their ancestral Black Hills to the greedy white man, small raiding parties continued to harass the settlers. Finally, in April, 1877, Chief Crazy Horse surrendered and active warfare ceased.

Actually, the territory had not been opened for legal settlement until February, 1877; but when gold was found in Deadwood Gulch and many other gulches north of Custer early in 1876, small camps sprang up at each discovery site. Some, like Custer, have become prosperous towns; others, like Rockerville, are ghosts; and Deadwood and Lead have grown into cities.

CUSTER

IN JUNE, 1951, I made a trip through the Black Hills for the purpose of visiting and sketching the many places which sprang up almost simultaneously during the middle seventies. As usual I took a friend along for the sake of companionship and to help with the driving. We went first to Custer, the oldest town in the Hills, and found it up-to-date and prosperous. One of its most noticeable features is its wide streets, said to have been planned so that bull trains could be turned without having to detour around an entire block. Not far from the town are the Gordon Stockade on French Creek and the site of the first miner's meeting, held on June 17, 1875.

The camp was laid out by a townsite company in July, 1875, and was named Stonewall in honor of Stonewall Jackson. One month later, on August 10, it was renamed Custer and was platted by Tom Hooper, who had only a pocket compass and a couple of picket ropes as equipment for the task and a small piece of birchbark on which to draw the plat.

During the first three months of 1876, when the initial rush to the Black Hills began, 1,400 buildings were erected on the townsite, and the nearby hills were black with men felling trees and dragging more lumber to the flat. Before spring the population reached 6,000! As parties of men and wagon trains of settlers arrived, enveloped in clouds of dust, the Indians became troublesome. They attacked small, unprotected groups of travelers coming to the Hills, and they lurked at the edge of Custer and stole the horses and stock which were pastured on the prairie. To combat their raids, a company of 125 citizens who called themselves "Custer Minute Men" was organized.

The group was directed by Captain Jack Crawford, a government scout, and, although they were often unable to recapture the stolen animals in their forays after the redskins, they no doubt reduced the number of thefts and atrocities.

HILL CITY

HILL CITY, north of Custer, is the second oldest camp in the Hills. Gold was found in the gulches and bars along Spring Creek during the summer and fall of 1875, but no permanent settlement could be made until the following spring; then cabins and tents jostled each other for a place on the flat where the townsite lay. No sooner had a camp been established than word of the Deadwood diggings reached it; and away went the population, on foot and on horseback, until only one man and a dog remained on the spot. Toward the end of the summer some of the adventurers drifted back, newcomers began to swarm over the bars and gulches, and even a few ranchers settled in the fertile valley. Placering continued, gold ledges were discovered nearby, and the town continued to grow. Then, in 1883, when the news was spread that tin had been found near Harney Peak, the Hills went wild. Some credit Dr. S. H. Ferguson with the discovery, saying that he noticed a strange mineral substance in his mica mine, the Etta, and, thinking that it might contain silver, sent a sample of it to be assayed. The test pronounced it tin. Others believe that George Coats and Joe McClure, while herding cows in the hills, found the first chunk of cassiterite on the ground and recognized it from a similar specimen they had seen in a mineral collection. Immediately after the discovery, claims were staked and a stock company was formed.

Some time later an English syndicate formed a corporation of American and English stockholders, the Harney Peak Consolidated Tin Company, and bought up all the likely prospects in the district. After a few months of successful operation in 1892, however, the plant closed, and even though several gold mines in the vicinity continued to be active, most of the population drifted away. Hill City is a modern town today; but tourists, not mines, provide the gold on which it thrives.

ROCKERVILLE

ROCKERVILLE, some miles east of Hill City, grew up along a gulch second only to Deadwood in the richness of its placers. William Keeler discovered the first gold there in 1876, during a late December snowstorm. He and his pack burros were taking a short cut through the hills when the storm struck, and he was forced to make camp. During this delay he prospected a little and found gold in a branch of Spring Creek. When the storm passed he went excitedly on his way, reinforced by an unexpected poke full of dust. Two experienced miners, Bart Henderson and D. G. Silliman, were the next to find colors in the gulch; and behind them came the usual stampede of men who, despite the lack of water, set up cradles and began feverishly to work the dry diggings.

Bedrock lay sixteen to twenty feet below the surface. When no water was available, the men piled their rockers (or cradles) and their dirt into hand-carts and trundled them to the nearest pool or stream, where they "rocked out their load" and often recovered $100 from a single trip. In the spring the swollen streams provided the needed water, and hundreds of rockers were agitated along the banks of Spring Creek, which by now was known as Rocker-ville Gulch.

The camp, according to Mrs. Tallent, was "the scene of mad excitement and reckless expenditure," where "gold dust and gold nuggets were plentiful, speculation was rife," and roulette wheels spun night and day. A miner named Spicer dreamed of a prospect hole on Spring Creek from which he dug glitter-ing gold. The next morning he searched for the spot, found a place that cor-responded to the one in his dream, dug a hole, and two feet below the surface uncovered a nugget worth thirty-eight dollars. Encouraged by this discovery, he formed a company which spent several thousand dollars building a flume and dam to bring water to the property. The following season both were com-pletely washed away in the first spring freshet.

Another miner, whose title to certain rich placer holdings was questioned, took his case into court. During the trial his lawyer advised him to smuggle into the court some Black Hills lightning, in order to keep the jury drunk for several days. While they were inebriated, the defendant was busily mining, and by the time the jury had sobered up and rendered a verdict, the ground under consideration was worked out and the miner had more than enough gold to pay his legal fees.

In 1880, when the camp had reached its peak, the Black Hills Placer Mining Company laid a flume to the diggings from a dam two miles above the town of Sheridan, a distance of seventeen miles. The flume had a capacity of 2,000 miners' inches of water; it was constructed of heavy planks, cut as needed by a portable sawmill that accompanied the construction crew, and was supported across deep gulches by substantial trestles. During the two years of its operation, $500,000 in gold was recovered. In 1881 the Rocker-ville Gold Mining Company built an 1,100-foot bedrock flume below the town, but it was not successful. By 1883 both ditches were empty, and mining had practically ceased. Only fragments of the big ditch, a few stone fireplaces, and one dilapidated cabin show the site of Rockerville. The rest of the buildings have been torn down.

KEYSTONE

KEYSTONE, another pioneer town founded in the late seventies, slumbered after its initial boom until December, 1891. Then William B. Franklin, Thomas C. Blair, and Jacob Reed located the Keystone mine and sold it to a group of St. Paul capitalists, who immediately built a twenty-stamp mill on the property. In 1894 the same men discovered another gold mine. The wife of one of the owners asked that it be named for her, whereupon her husband called it the Holy Terror. For a time its output averaged $70,000 a week, and for several years it paid substantial dividends.

During the nineties Keystone had 3 hotels, 25 business firms, 2 assayers, a newspaper, 2 churches, and a population of 1,500. Today the chief sources of income are the big feldspar mill and tourists en route to the great stone faces of Mount Rushmore National Memorial. The older part of the town follows the creek, and we drove from street to street picking out first one and then another landmark. At one spot I discovered several stone terraces and foundations, some holes that had once been cellars, crazy flights of steps leading nowhere, and piles of broken lumber and other debris. They were all old properties that had been razed only a month before.

SHERIDAN

SEVERAL miles south of Pactola the site of Sheridan, the third oldest camp in the Hills, moulders at the bottom of Sheridan Lake. Here, on July 18, 1875, Andrew J. Williams washed gravel from Stand-off Bar and then hurried to French Creek to report his good fortune to his partners. They returned with him at once, only to find that the claim had been jumped and most of the bar staked off by another group of prospectors. A month later all the miners were run out of the hills by General Crook. Before the end of October, however, they slipped back one by one and began to work again. They laid out a camp named Golden, later renamed in honor of General Phil Sheridan.

As the camp grew, many log cabins were built, some with portholes as protection against the Indians, who were extremely troublesome to the settlers. In April, 1877, Sheridan was made the temporary seat of Pennington County, and in October of the same year the first term of the Black Hills Circuit Court was held in the town's largest log building. In time other camps eclipsed it and its population dwindled. By 1900 only a handful of cabins and farmhouses and a schoolhouse marked its site; later a reservoir, known as Sheridan Lake, submerged it.

OLD HOUSE, SILVER CITY

RUINS OF OLD BUILDINGS, KEYSTONE

PACTOLA

DUE NORTH of Sheridan is Pactola. Prospectors were washing gold from Rapid Creek in July, 1875, before General Crook's cavalry discovered their whereabouts; they organized the Rapid Creek Mining District and called their diminutive settlement Camp Crook, in honor of the general with whom they were playing hide-and-seek. The industrious men were removed from the Hills by the soldiers in August, but in February, 1876, when the Hills were legally opened, they tore back to their diggings. In no time all the ground up and down the creek was taken, and miners jealously guarded their claims. James C. Sherman led a party of eighty men to the Hills in March, 1876, was caught in a blizzard at Camp Crook, and wisely decided to stay there until traveling was safe. Assured by the miners that placering was as good at Crook as at Deadwood, he remained in the camp permanently and became one of the most substantial promoters of the community.

When a post office was established in 1877, the miners at a mass meeting decided to call their camp Pactola, the name of the river from whose sands Croesus obtained his wealth. Soon afterward James Sherman built the Sherman House, the first hotel in the region. It immediately became a stopping place for the two stage lines which went to camps in the Hills. Several companies attempted to build ditches and flumes to the placer grounds, but the expense of construction soon caused them to give up. The most successful placering was done by individual miners. One false-fronted building in the meadow below the present highway is all that remains of early Pactola; a modern lodge, cabins, and a store form the nucleus of the town today.

SILVER CITY

SILVER CITY, founded in 1876 and described to me in 1951 as "ghost, except for tourists," lies four miles above Pactola on Rapid Creek. After the Gorman brothers—Jack, Tom, and Luke—struck rich silver deposits in the hills, seven men formed a company which platted the townsite of Camp Gorman. Several hundred persons swarmed to the spot. An eastern syndicate offered the Gorman brothers $300,000 for their claim, but they had set their minds on half a million. The company repeated its offer, and the brothers, who had no idea whether $300,000 was more or less than their demand, went home to talk the deal over. That night their cabin caught fire, and one of the brothers died of burns. The other two disappeared and were never heard from again.

The Scruton brothers also found gold in the nearby hills in the seventies and traded their yellow dust for grub and tools in Pactola. The location of their mine remains a mystery, however, for they died without revealing the location of their find.

Silver City has many new cabins and a trim white church today, and it was in this town that I had been told to look up Ted Brown. He was in Deadwood for the day, but his wife told me about the local mines. One was known as Duffy's Folly; two others, the Diana and the Lady of the Hills, produced silver combined with some gold. Mrs. Brown pointed out one picturesque old house, gray and weather-beaten, with a porch on three sides and an ornate balustrade. This relic of the old town is surrounded by brand-new cottages, but as part of an estate it cannot be touched.

"If my husband was here, he could tell you more than I can; but so can Sagebrush Jim," she said, as a well-dressed man with long hair and a beard came up the steps. "He's Mr. Cosgrove and he's mining near here. Show the ladies your gold, Jim," she urged.

From his pocket the man took a small bottle full of dust and turned it so that the grains shifted and gleamed; from a small pouch he pulled out nuggets and samples of gold and silver ore. Then, at Mrs. Brown's request, he showed us some "slickers"—pieces of smooth black iron rock which could be polished to a high luster.

"If you find slickers you may not find gold," he explained, handing each of us one of the shiny black stones; "but you can't find gold without slickers."

When we left he ran after us and gave us a piece of stone that was red and soft like chalk. "Paint rock," he called it—the kind the Indians used to decorate their bodies. Like the slickers, it was found in the hills near Silver City. "Come back and I'll teach you to pan gold," he called after us; "and don't forget about the slickers."

ROCHFORD

SOME miles north of Pactola a gravel road leads west to Rochford, winding through forested hills and following the wrigglings of Rapid Creek to the narrow gulch where the town lies.

Three hunters from Deadwood, M. D. Rochford, Richard B. Hughes, and William Van Fleet, accidentally discovered the gold-bearing rock on Montezuma Hill in August, 1876. A party of prospectors from Castle Creek made several locations the following March and, in order to record their discoveries, organized a mining district. After that, men from Lead and Central City poured into the area, staked locations on Little Rapid Creek and laid out a camp along the gulch in May, 1878. By December, Rochford's population was 500, and another 500 prospectors pitched their tents or built log shelters on the nearby hills.

By 1879 two twenty-stamp mills—the Evangeline on Irish Gulch and the Minnesota on Silver Creek—were clattering away; but no company with sufficient capital was interested in developing the low-grade ore on a big scale. The Standby mine, with its forty-stamp mill, specially constructed ditch, and large office-dwelling called "The Mansion," was the most extensively developed property and the best producer. When the mines were working to capacity, the camp was lively; men from Breakneck and Moonshine gulches and Gimlet Creek would come to town to clatter up and down the wooden sidewalks and lunge in and out of the Shamrock Dance Hall and the Irish Gulch Saloon. Over two hundred buildings made up the town, and a solid line of stores a block long, with connecting wooden canopies covering their sidewalks, comprised the heart of the community. The wooden awnings and the wooden sidewalks are gone, and only detached false-front stores and cabins are left to mark the bustling trade center.

A historical marker mentions the old Sullivan Trail, Reynold's Toll Road, which once served the town, and Lapp & Billup's Trading Post. It also states that Custer's troops camped near the site and that the area is filled with historic mine sites from the Gold Rush Days of '76. But my main interest was in seeing the modest, two-story frame structure which was once the home of Annie D. Tallent, the remarkable pioneer woman who in the eighties was Rochford's postmistress, schoolteacher, and superintendent of schools, and who wrote *The Black Hills, or the Last Hunting Ground of the Dakotahs,* the only complete history of the region.

In September, 1882, the *Black Hills Times* of Deadwood reported that her son, Robert E. Tallent, had visited their office and made the statement that Rochford "is showing signs of returning life and activity and will soon be fairly booming." It was not booming during our visit; only the Moonshine Saloon, the Irish Gulch Dance Hall, and one store seemed to be serving the eighty or more residents of the once pulsing camp.

A young couple, who had driven in for the day because their parents once lived in Rochford, stopped to chat and pointed out landmarks—the old post office, the site of the church, and the portion of the main street where the long line of stores used to stand.

"Don't miss the Standby Mill as you leave town," they said as we started back to the highway. "The mine office 'mansion' has been torn down but the mill is left, and they're keeping up the timbering in the mine. There's plenty of gold in it, but labor costs too much to work it now. This was all quartz mining around here. At Rockerville you saw what's left from placering."

ROCHFORD

BENTLEY HOUSE, GALENA

ROUBAIX

NOT FAR from the highway to Deadwood is Roubaix, counted on by its founders to be the great camp of the region. It did not pan out as expected, and only a handful of people, a few farmhouses, and some abandoned mine properties mark its site today. The camp, which was established in 1876, was first known as Perry. Gold was found on the banks of Elk Creek and was worked successfully in a one-stamp mill, which recovered $50,000 from the free-milling quartz within a year. The mine from which the gold came, later known as the Uncle Sam, changed hands several times; in 1880, after another spurt of production, it was finally closed and soon became filled with water. As a result of its shutdown and a subsequent forest fire which destroyed considerable town property, the camp practically disappeared.

The property was not developed further until Pierre Wibeaux, a wealthy Frenchman, came to the Hills in 1899 and obtained possession of the Uncle Sam. Under his management it was known as the Clover Leaf Mining Company, and it did well for several years. Wibeaux renamed Perry for his home town in France, Roubaix. The camp of 500 persons had stores, a post office, boarding and rooming houses, a barber shop, a hall, churches, a school, and a newspaper. Wibeaux put money into his property and took out $29,000 in a three weeks' run with his one-stamp mill and a water wheel. In another fifteen-day period, when he drifted into a rich vein, he took out $3,000 every twenty-four hours. Then, suddenly, the mine became flooded by underground water on the seventh level, and the shaft leading to the pump caved in. Since there was no other way to pump out water, the mine had to be abandoned; and again people moved away.

The property lay idle for a number of years, a fire swept the camp and destroyed many of its buildings, and most of the mine machinery was removed. During 1934 and 1935, when the Anaconda Copper Company became interested in the mine and began to drain it, a brief revival began, but before it was well launched the company stopped work. The mine was never operated again, and in 1947 it was sold for taxes.

GALENA

To REACH Galena, we left the highway about seven miles south of Deadwood and began climbing through a forest, so dense that only occasionally did we catch glimpses of prospect holes and tunnel openings high above on the hillsides. Roads to the mines broke off from the main highway and disappeared in the trees. We passed markers which identified some of the mine properties, and just at the outskirts of Galena a sign which read: "Pet Coyote. Do Not Shoot." We kept a sharp lookout for the creature as we drove the length of Galena's one street, but it never appeared.

The setting of the town is ideal. A stream borders one side of a meadow-townsite, and the few remaining houses, now summer homes, are surrounded by a grove of huge pines. Near the creek, we saw the foundations of several buildings and flattened piles of lumber that had once been cabins. The trees partly hide a schoolhouse and form a canopy over it and the adjoining residence, a long, low building with a porch and big yard, surrounded by a picket fence. While I was sketching the white schoolhouse, a lady appeared on the porch of the house next to it and called, "Are you from Rapid City?" When I answered that I was not, she said, "Good," and came down to watch me sketch.

"We don't like people to come in here. We like it the way it is," she said. "I'm Mrs. Charles Bentley," she continued, and then began to tell me about Galena.

"I was born in that very house," she said. "My mother was the first teacher in the schoolhouse. It was built in 1882. The little house next to ours is the assay office my father put up when he managed the Gilt Edge mine. The street below here used to be full of houses, and the mills of our two big mines were farther down the gulch. One family who lives here bought up the placer claims and tore down the old buildings near the creek. If you'd come here a few years back, you'd have seen what Galena really looked like."

Galena was settled by persistent prospectors who penetrated this remote, hidden valley in March, 1876. They did some placering, but instead of gold they found veins of silver-bearing ore and staked out two claims, the Florence and the Sitting Bull. Other men discovered the Merritt No. 1 and No. 2, the Cora, the Emma and El Refugio—mines that contained veins of almost pure metal. In September, 1876, Robert Florman, an experienced miner, bought the rich Florence mine from its discoverers and began to develop it. Next, Colonel J. H. Davey, who knew how to treat silver, acquired both the Florence and the Sitting Bull properties; in 1880 he enlarged the mill which Florman had built to twenty stamps and constructed a small smelter.

The camp in the meantime had taken shape, and although its growth was slow because of its isolation, it was soon the principal town of Bear Butte Creek. In 1880 a boom was reported by the *Black Hills Times* of March 10:

OUR NEW SILVER BONANZA

A gentleman from Galena, says people are wild with excitement over a new strike in the Cora mine . . . a piece of ore so lousy with wire silver that upon being broken in two, it was again stuck together quite firmly by inserting the sharp protuberances of the pure metal into the cavities of the rock from which they had been taken.

Galena's Fourth of July celebration of 1882 was reported to the *Times* as follows:

The Fourth here was ushered in by the booming of giant powder which shook the buildings from roof to basement. The fronts of most of the buildings were shaded by graceful firs, lending to our streets an appearance of comfort and grandure. The patriotic ladies had previously prepared large quantities of ice cream, cake, fruits and other delicacies of which the great, ugly male patriots partook freely and were made happy.

At 12:30 a large crowd gathered at the American House to witness the soup-eating contest between Sperindo Perrcri, superintendent of the Savage mine, and Defenbaugh, watchman at the Red Cloud, for the championship of the Hills and a silver-striking hammer.

A "grand display of fireworks in the evening in front of Hadley's place" and a dance in Brown's hall, which was "superbly decorated" and where "the light fantastic was tripped late into the night," closed the festivities.

Galena continued to grow from 1880, when Davey blew in his smelter, until the Richmond claim served an injunction on him, questioning his right to follow his "ledge on the dip beyond his side lines." The mine was forced to close down, and the case dragged on in court for several years. Finally Davey sold his property in disgust and left the Hills. During this period of stress, when both companies were tense, Frank Davey, the son of the Sitting Bull owner, and Billy Thatcher, the watchman of the property, got into a fight with a Richmond Company employee named Patrick Gorman. They shot Gorman to death. At the trial Thatcher claimed that he fired in self-defense and was acquitted, but he left the country at once and never returned. The legal tussle between the two big properties left them idle and killed the camp; except for a brief revival from 1895 to 1897, when silver prices were high, little work has been done in the immediate area. For a while it became a popular summer resort; but now only a few people enjoy its green retreat.

Deadwood and Lead are the cities of the northern Hills, but many small towns, scattered in the nearby gulches on Whitewood and Deadwood creeks, have retained their identity. Though we made Deadwood our headquarters, we visited the smaller places first before doing the cities.

CROOK CITY

FROM Deadwood we went north and east to Whitewood, a small, modern place, and from there turned back toward the Hills and Crook City. There we saw one heap of stones left from placering, a few farmhouses, barns, and sheds, and the deserted cemetery. Only one of the frame buildings dated from the seventies.

Crook City was named in honor of General Crook, who camped in the vicinity in 1875-1876. It was established in 1876, when the gravel bars of Whitewood Creek yielded large amounts of dust. The camp lay on the eastern edge of the Hills; separated from Deadwood and other camps by densely timbered ridges, it was isolated and open to Indian raids, which were frequent. During the summer of 1876, three members of the Wagner family were murdered and their bodies stripped; the pregnant wife of one of the men was scalped and mutilated by an ox goad driven into her abdomen. A mail carrier was ambushed and killed the same summer, and horses and stock were stolen as fast as they were brought in by the settlers.

At its peak, when men were shoveling and panning the stream bed, Crook City had 250 log and frame houses, a population of 2,000, and a newspaper, the *Crook City Tribune*.

For ten years the camp flourished, both through its mining activities and as a trade center, and when the railroad was being pushed toward Deadwood, Crook City looked forward to further prosperity. But the ridge between it and the larger city was a barrier the road could not cross, and an easier grade was discovered elsewhere. The new camp of Whitewood sprang up along the right of way, and as it grew Crook City dwindled into the ghost it is today.

As we got back near Deadwood we noticed an abandoned smelter on the far bank of Whitewood Creek, and at the edge of the city we passed the site of its once colorful Chinese section. Then we started off for Deadwood Gulch.

GAYVILLE

THE gulch was once a continuous string of settlements, each one started by a group of miners who had found good prospects in the gravels and bars at a certain spot. The oldest camp was Gayville; beyond it were South Bend, Blacktail, Central City, Anchor City, Poor Man's Gulch, Sheep Tail, and Golden Gate. Most of them have disappeared entirely, and all were once linked to Central City, the largest of the group. The first one up the gulch from Deadwood is Gayville.

Frank Bryant, prospecting with a small party, found indications of gold at the mouth of Whitewood Creek in 1875. William Lardner was also prospecting in the vicinity that same summer; but both had to leave almost immediately under General Crook's orders. They sneaked back in November, however, and on November 8 Bryant staked his first claim. The next day Lardner, with Alfred and William Gay, John B. Pearson, and others, found gold in an adjoining gulch, which was so choked with fallen timber that they named it Deadwood. They made their winter camp at the mouth of what is now Blacktail Creek and called it Gayville. In December, 1875, they made Lardner their recorder and organized the Lost Placer Mining District—the first in the northern Hills.

Captain C. V. Gardner, a prospector, built the first arrastre in Blacktail Gulch, to work ore from his Chief of the Hills property; in the fall of 1876 he installed the first quartz mill, but the latter was not a success. The first stamp mill in the region was built on the Alpha and Omega property, near Central City.

William Gay, one of the founders, was extremely jealous of his wife, and when he caught a messenger delivering a note to her from an admirer, he killed the boy. He was sent to the Penitentiary for a number of years but was pardoned after serving only three. When he returned to town, the Sheriff who had taken him to the Pen drove out in a buggy to meet the stage on which Gay was arriving, helped him into the vehicle, and pranced back to town, where a brass band welcomed him.

In its day the town had 250 homes, 30 business establishments, several quartz and sawmills, an assay office, and a brewery whose bottled beer sold for $4.50 a case and was advertised as "superior to any." Like all camps, Gayville had a bad fire; but, as the *Black Hills Times* of September 6, 1877, remarked, "A city destroyed by fire and rebuilt in two weeks would make the people in the States open their eyes." The camp flourished for ten years before the gulch claims began to play out. Today only one group of buildings—the Lawrence County Poor Farm, across the creek from the road—marks its location. One can imagine what the town must have been like in June, 1878, when the *Times* reported:

Times at Gayville are brightening. Two arrests were made there yesterday. Joshua Dunn drew a check on the banking house of Brown and Thum and was gobbled; and Miss Jessie Skinner was gathered in for selling fire water without a county license. When Charley Spencer started to make the arrest of the fair Jessie, he manifested considerable uneasiness . . . but . . . he encountered no trouble, . . . the fair budge vender succumbed without a kick.

CENTRAL CITY

A FEW MORE curves in the gulch road brought us to the outskirts of Central City, the camp which, it is said, might have become the key city of the Hills had its citizens been more enterprising; but they were too busy mining to form a town organization until January 20, 1877. A public meeting was then held, at which I. V. Skidmore, who had recently arrived from Central City, Colorado, proposed that name for the nucleus of camps close by. Thereafter they were known as Central City, and their combined population reached 10,000.

Central City proper soon had a population of 3,000 who lived along streets which were terraced on the sides of the gulch and who carried on active business in the solid line of false-fronted stores which lined the main thoroughfare. The noises of the town had a steady accompaniment in the clatter and thud of falling stamps from the sixteen mills which ran night and day during the boom years.

Four newspapers served the community: the *Herald* (1877-1881); the *Champion,* published for one year by the same Charles Collins who had boosted the gold rush so flamboyantly with the Russell party; the *Enterprise* (1881-1882); and the *Register,* which was still being printed as late as 1900.

Central was the first town in the Hills to make use of the public school system of Dakota Territory in setting up its school (although Crook City claims the same distinction); and its early religious services, conducted by Judge David B. Ogden of Anchor City, were held first at Golden Gate and then in Central's schoolhouse and Opera House, until a church structure was completed. Before 1880 Central offered diversions to its citizens in the form of lodges, clubs, and a fire company, all of which were eagerly joined and actively supported.

Then, in 1883, Deadwood Creek roared down the gulch, washing the placer workings away completely and demolishing everything in its path. The city had scarcely recovered from the flood when Lawrence Bellevue, who ran an eating house, left his restaurant for a few minutes to do an errand up the gulch. When he started back, he saw that his place was blazing. Terrified at what fire means in a wooden town, he raced away from the spreading flames and was never seen again. Much of the town was destroyed by the fire, and parts of it were never rebuilt.

Many empty, overgrown lots, some with deep stone foundations, are landmarks left by the fire. Nearly every street has several such gaps; but the buildings which survived—Victorian houses with wooden frills around their eaves—and the two-story brick and stone stores and office buildings that replaced the wooden matchboxes give to the city a look of belonging to the eighties which the other towns have not retained. One of the most interesting of the older structures is the false-fronted Central Golden & Terraville Hose Co. firehouse, full of old apparatus—two hosecarts, several long ladders, and a two-wheeled "dolly" on which equipment could be loaded and drawn to a blaze by members of the company. As I walked up the street, an old man sitting in front of his store pointed out a new hole in the ground, where until recently the brick bank had stood. He mentioned that inside the store he still had a supply of wagon hubs of assorted sizes, freighted in during the eighties, and a shipment of derbies.

"The big mill you passed on the way into town was the Blacktail," he volunteered. "The Father DeSmet mine was here in Central, and its mill stood at the foot of the hill near the Terraville road. Up the gulch beyond here is Golden Gate, but it's about gone now. There's new cabins there, but the old camp is torn down.

"Captain C. V. Gardner was one of the first men who mined in this gulch. Henry Keets was another. Have you heard about the Keets-Aurora fight? Along about June, 1877, Cephas Tuttle located the Aurora mine in Hidden Treasure Gulch, and its lines overlapped ground already located by Keets. The two men argued about the boundaries, until Tuttle decided to blow up the Keets property and began to lug boxes of powder toward the shaft. The two mines were connected underground by a long tunnel, and as soon as Keets saw what Tuttle was up to, he ordered his men out of the mine. All but a man named Norris got out as far as the blacksmith shop at the surface before Tuttle was through lowering powder into the shaft. He lighted a long fuse and threw it in after the boxes and beat it; but he didn't get far, for by that time, Keets's men and his own had built a kind of barricade and were sniping at each other. A couple were hurt and Tuttle was killed. Norris, who was still in the tunnel, was knocked out by the blast and was deaf the rest of his life. Some of the Keets men were arrested for Tuttle's murder, but you couldn't plant the blame, so they were released.

"There's another story about the Keets mine," said the old man, settling back and beginning to enjoy his reminiscing. "Once when the company missed sending the payroll, the employees grabbed the mine and moved into the tunnel with enough food and bedding to stay until the company came across. The owners of the mine were red hot about it and sent the sheriff to oust them, but they didn't budge. Then a company of soldiers were brought in from Camp Sturgis and they threatened to attack the mine if the men didn't surrender, but the men wouldn't budge. Finally the sheriff took an armload of stink bombs loaded with sulphur up to the airshaft of the mine and began dropping them down the hole. Next thing you knew, the men were high-tailing it out of the tunnel coughing and choking. That sulphur turned the trick.

SLIME MILL FOR HOMESTAKE MINE, DEADWOOD

CENTRAL CITY, GOLDEN & TERRAVILLE HOSE CO., CENTRAL CITY, SOUTH DAKOTA

"That's Terraville up on top of the hill in those trees. You ought to drive up there and go on to Lead over the mountain. The road's awful steep and it's slick if it's wet, but shucks, you can make it." He was right about the road, but we got to Terraville.

TERRAVILLE

THE town, which once had a population of 600, is on top of a mountain, between Central City and Lead. The gulch below it was the scene of much placering in the seventies and eighties. Its one street twists and humps its way over the summit, and from it branch many short spurs, which lead to individual houses above or below it, or down into the gulch, where big mill foundations are visible. Terraville is a woodsy place; its big trees shade cosy little homes, each with its flower and vegetable garden, and terraces and steps and steep paths lead in all directions from one level to another. Many of the houses have unique roofs, covered with what look like round gray shingles. Curious to know what they were, I spoke to a woman who was weeding her vegetable patch. "They're the lids of cyanide cans," she replied. "The plant down in the gulch was a cyanide mill, and there were always lots of empty cans lying around. The tops make good roofs. It's nice up here now, but we get snowed in solid in the winter. I wouldn't stay here all year, but the old folks wouldn't live anywhere else, and I can't leave them."

Clinging to the edge of the mountain a little farther up the street was a frame church with a cupola. Below it was a playground with swings and trapezes, enclosed by a heavy wire-mesh fence to keep children from tumbling down the cliff. While I was studying it, a man came across the street and asked if we would like to see the inside of the building. As he unlocked the door, he told us that it was a Methodist church and that the people were fixing it up with new wallboard, a coat of paint, and a picture window behind the pulpit. Standing at the window, he showed us the foundations of the Terra and Caledonia mills in the gulch, mills that had originally had 80 stamps each and employed 150 men. He pointed out other mines that were part of the Caledonia group—the Grand Prize, the Queen of the Hills, the Cornucopia, and the Monroe—and he explained that all the mines in Terraville and Central were now part of the great Homestake corporation, whose plant makes the city of Lead.

"If you didn't have that car you could go to Lead through the tunnel," he said, pointing to a dark hole in the far side of the gulch. "We use it all the time, and the kids go back and forth to the movies through it. It's three-quarters of a mile long and it's lighted with electricity. They used to run ore-cars through it, but not any more. It's a lot shorter than driving over the switchbacks. When you get to Lead you'll see the other end of it just behind the substation of the power plant. Terraville doesn't need stores any more. Lead is so close, any business we have can be done over there."

From Terraville we corkscrewed up to the top of the saddle between Deadwood and Whitewood gulches and then dropped down to the industrial city of Lead, as alive as Terraville was dormant. That evening back in Deadwood, as we leafed through old copies of the *Black Hills Times,* I found two items about Terraville. Both were from the issue of January 11, 1880:

The Emmett House at Terraville is enjoying a good run of custom because Mike O'Brien knows how to run a first class hotel.

Normoyle's is the only boarding house in the upper camp that can boast of not having a sick boarder this winter, and there are 73 boarding houses from Gayville to Pennington.

There was a raffle at the Daisy saloon last evening for a large, beautiful chromo, a view of Balmoral Castle in Aberdeen, Scotland. . . . Pat McHugh got away with the picture, throwing the highest number of dice, 38. By request, he puts it up again this evening.

Just before we put down the papers for the night I spied the following paragraph, dated May 20, 1878:

The boy who packs the Lead City part of the *Telegraph-Herald* to Central became lost in the snowstorm Saturday evening while crossing the range between the two towns, and remained out all night, reaching the Central office at 7 o'clock Sunday morning. He had a very hard time of it and frosted both of his feet, how badly we did not learn.

DEADWOOD

DEADWOOD is an exciting city to visit at any season, but in the spring, when the fruit trees are in bloom, it is a beautiful city as well. Built in a narrow gulch at the junction of two creeks, its brick business "blocks" are crowded into a compact area near the streams. Far above, the residential streets rise one above the other on the hillsides. Thickets of wild plum dot the hills, and cherry and peach trees hide the Victorian houses which they shade. Deadwood's development has been steady, from the time of its nebulous beginnings in 1875, on land belonging to the Sioux, to its present status. Together with the city of Lead, it forms a continuous line of buildings reaching for miles along Whitewood Creek.

The city is history-conscious; many sites and landmarks are labeled, and it is interesting to walk up one street and down another, locating the Chinese section, the site of the first gold discovery, the Gem theatre, and No. 10 Bar, where Wild Bill Hickok was murdered. The best account of Deadwood in its prime is given by Estelline Bennett in *Old Deadwood Days,* although many of the sights she describes have vanished. The Chinese truck gardens are gone, and no pig-tailed peddler in a blue blouse delivers vegetables in a horse-drawn cart. Indians no longer pitch their tepees at the edge of town, and the Gem theatre, which opened in the seventies and outlived all the others, is only a memory. But what tales it could tell—of the time in 1887, when the "Mikado" ran 130 nights; and of how, after the wooden chairs were pushed back in the smoky hall at the end of the evening's performance, the last dance was always the "Hack Drivers' Quadrille"!

Frank Bryant, John B. Pearson, and a party of others came into the northern Hills to prospect in August, 1875. Bryant found a little gold at the mouth of Whitewood Creek, named for the forest of silvery, fire-killed trees. He built a cabin there, but as General Crook's troops were ridding the Hills of miners, he left, barely escaping capture on the way out. On November 8, accompanied by Henry Coder and William Cudney, he returned and staked his Discovery claim east of his cabin. The very next day Lardner and his party staked their claims about a mile and a half up Deadwood Gulch and established Gayville.

In February, 1876, Bryant and his group created the Whitewood Mining District. The snow was deep all winter, but the men worked their claims steadily. In March, 1876, the news of their strike became known. Such a mad scramble to the diggings followed that the town of Custer lost all but one of its population overnight. Montana also heard the news; on March 20 a party of 200 men and 100 pack mules, followed by a train of supply wagons, left Helena and journeyed slowly eastward, keeping a close lookout for the Sioux, who were known to be on the warpath. The cavalcade reached the vicinity of Spearfish late in May, where, attracted by the country, most of the party remained to farm. Other Montana outfits arrived, in one of which was Seth Bullock, Deadwood's first sheriff.

Because of this rush, the army found it impossible to keep white men out of the Hills, even though no treaty rights had yet been settled with the Sioux. Streams of men and pack animals converged upon Deadwood and Whitewood gulches, the newest and richest of the gold fields. Some came down from Bismarck, Dakota; many others came up from Sidney, Nebraska; and the rest came from Cheyenne, Wyoming. Until the middle of 1876, when transportation companies were formed, individuals outfitting for the Hills paid freighters fifteen dollars a hundred pounds to haul supplies to Deadwood while they themselves walked beside the wagons and helped push them through muddy stretches.

The first men to discover gold dug above the mat of dead timber which filled the gulch, and before long they had staked off all the accessible ground. Late arrivals were therefore forced to clear the littered earth before they could work it. To their surprise they uncovered the richest placers. A townsite, called Deadwood, was laid out below Gayville on April 26, 1876, by J. J. Williams, Craven Lee, and Isaac Brown. Tents and log cabins immediately lined the stump-cleared trail that served as a street; some were set in clearings cut in the dense tangle of pines and fallen trunks. The camp's first newspaper, the *Black Hills Pioneer,* printed its first issue on June 8, 1876, commenting upon the event by saying:

We issue today only a HALF SHEET. Our regular issue will be just double the size of the present copy. But owing to the fact that we are working almost out of doors, with the elements apparently conspiring against us, it is impossible to fill the bill as we anticipated. Our material has been in Deadwood less than a week; our house is not up; it has rained two days during the time, and we think everyone who knows anything about the mechanical work of a printing office will appreciate our condition and bear for the present with the very best it is possible to do.

On June 24 it reported:

Six weeks ago the site of Deadwood City was a heavy forest of pine timber; now it extends nearly a mile along Deadwood and Whitewood, and contains nearly 2000 of the most energetic driving people on the continent. Every branch of business is represented, and many of them are overdone. Houses are going up on every hand, immense trains are constantly arriving, loaded with goods of all kinds, business is rushing, and bargains are driven here that would put Wall Street to the blush.

The first freight train of twelve wagons, drawn by forty-eight mules, reached Deadwood on June 28. On approximately the same date, the Cheyenne and Black Hills Stage Line was organized; but when Indians burned the relay stations, ran off the company's stock, and killed one of the agents, it ceased operations until the Indians became less of a menace.

From the opening of the Hills to white men in 1876 until the early eighties, Indians were the biggest problem that the settlers and miners encountered. Without exception, the Indian was looked upon as a constant menace, a usurper of land which the white man needed and was entitled to, and a foe to be exterminated. The initial issue of the *Black Hills Pioneer* stated the case forcefully and colorfully:

What We Want

To the Black Hiller there is a question that more nearly concerns him than all the gold he may gather. Is he to be always in dread of the murderous red man? Let us have this grand, and above all this, the most beautiful country that the eye of man ever beheld. . . . Is the red man to have this country, and are we to get down and out? Let this be settled and all is settled. There is but one policy that will forever put the matter at rest, and that is the same *old one* that ever gave the white man a foot of ground on the continent.

Let us educate him! What a grand idea. What a happy thought. Its source is purely eastern, and was conceived by a brain that is a *fac simile* of an ancient fossil. Nothing could be more absurd, nothing more ridiculous. A Sioux Indian takes education with the same will and spirit that his satanic majesty embraces the religion of Jesus Christ. . . . Let the noble white man have this country that is rich in silver and gold, a delightful climate, and whose valleys are covered with luxuriant grass, and beautiful beyond description, and whose lofty mountains tower far beyond the thunder's home.

D.D.T.

Even when the Indians were tending to their own affairs, the papers always insinuated that their intentions were evil. The *Black Hills Times* of May 17, 1878, reported that:

Geo. Adler, who was in town yesterday, says the prairies are alive with Indians, but as there have been no depredations committed yet, they are probably peaceably disposed hunting parties, looking after game and waiting for a good chance to lift hair when the weather gets more settled, for a Wild Indian can no more resist the temptation of taking a white man's top knot than he can of swallowing a glass of fire-water.

This attitude of intolerance is also shown in a *Times* headline of January 30, 1880: "Raiding Reds. Sitting Bull and Gang Again on American Soil." The article describes how the Indians, "driven by starvation to come south of the line" of their reservation, "propose to give themselves up" rather than eat their ponies. "If they surrender, the Government will feed them."

Even in 1883 the *Times* complains:

Our Red Brother

The Indian question like the ghost of Banquo pops up in unexpected times and places shaking its gory locks and in spite of cries of "that we didn't do it" points to an infamous record, including all crimes, from foul murder, high handed robbery, and sacrilegious hypocricy down to petty larceny. The Indians will forever be the skeleton in the nation's closet. Why not?

The Indians in general and the Sioux in particular fought every advance of the whites into their territory. Though they were engaged in a losing battle, they were determined to retain their rights as long as they were able to resist. When the Black Hills Telegraph Company began to build its line from Cheyenne to Deadwood in the summer of 1876, Indians attacked the linemen and tore down the wires as soon as they were strung, thus delaying the completion of the work until late fall. On November 30, the day of its arrival in Deadwood, the event was celebrated by a huge bonfire and thirty-nine salutes fired from anvils; the festivities closed with a ball given in the newly completed Grand Central Hotel.

By the summer of 1876 the first shipments of ore were sent east for treatment, for as yet no mills had been built. In July, 3,000 pounds of quartz were taken from the Inter-Ocean mine to Omaha, and in the fall such a large shipment of dust was sent out by Wheeler Brothers that a guard of twenty men accompanied the train as far as the railroad. Other mines along the line of march took advantage of the armed escort and added their gold until the total amount carried reached $500,000. By fall the need for mills was apparent, and one or more properties began their construction. The *Black Hills Pioneer* of October 14 announced with satisfaction the arrival of machinery "for the reduction of Alpha ore" and added, "Before many moons have waned the music of another quartz mill will gladden our ears. Tis well." The mill was completed in December, and a second mill began dropping stamps on ore from the Blacktail mine in April, 1877.

Excerpts from a letter written by Marshal Hollins to the editor of the Omaha *Herald* on December 18, 1876, sum up, at the year's end, the pioneer's attitude toward the gold rush and the feelings of the men who composed it:

GOLD

O powerful word, the incentive of man for gold must be vanquished to permit the golden treasures to remain in the bowels of mother earth. The American pioneer, who breaks the weeds for civilization, proposes to break open these vast gold fields which is to give employment to thousands and bring joy to the threshold of many a family. . . . The hazard, vicissitudes, and privations are great. However the legions who will pour into these hills when the truth is known cannot be intimidated by the proud, lousy, lazy, cunning, insolent savage warrior, or destroyed either by the seductions of fraud or the assaults of violence.

SERENADES

I have been honored every evening, by a serenade, since my occupation of this terrestrial abode. However, I do not reciprocate or return thanks for the melan-

choly notes from the throats of innumerable grey wolves and little coyotes. The
mountain lion joins in the howl with such energy you imagine the monster ser-
enades at your side. Not content with allowing a few moments for such recreation
they devote whole nights to us. You may imagine our minds are stretched on the
tender hooks of anxious suspense, and agitated by the fiercest extremes of hope and
fear. Such is not the case as our hairs have grown grey years ago, listening to the
coy minstrels. [J. H. Trigg, *The History of Cheyenne and Northern Wyoming,
Embracing the Gold Fields of the Black Hills.*]

    As early as July, 1876, Jack Langrishe, veteran comedian of many mining
camps, arrived with a wagonload of scenery and props and opened the first
legitimate theatre in the camp. The building had log and canvas sides and a
canvas roof. On July 22, the opening night, it was crowded to the doors. During the performance a drenching rain fell, to the discomfiture of the audience,
who nevertheless remained to the end of the program. As soon as lumber was
available, a solid roof was added to the log frame. Always generous, Langrishe
offered his theatre, the Bella Union, as a meeting place to church and civic
groups until more suitable quarters of their own could be provided. The trial
of McCall, the murderer of Wild Bill Hickok, was held in the building, as was
the first Masonic funeral. Other popular gathering places of noticeably less re-
finement were the Melodeon, a notorious gambling joint, and the Green Front,
in which hung a sign: "Gentlemen will not spit on the floor. Others must not."
    Two murders stunned the lusty new camp during its first summer. Rev.
Henry Weston Smith and Wild Bill Hickok had no more than settled in Deadwood than they were carried out of it feet first. Preacher Smith, a Methodist
minister who had come to the gulch with one of Captain Gardner's freight
outfits, worked during the week at mining, carpentering, and woodchopping.
On August 20 he set out for Crook City, where he planned to hold a service.
He was well liked in Deadwood, where he preached in the streets; and when the
men found that he was leaving for Crook City, they tried to stop him, for
the Indians had been making trouble and were known to be in the vicinity. He
left a note pinned to his cabin door which read, "Gone to Crook City to preach
and God Willing, will be back at 3 o'clock," and began his long walk through
the trees to the distant camp. Hours later his body was found in the road, not
far from Deadwood, his Bible clasped on his breast; and quite contrary to Indian practice he was unscalped.
    James Butler Hickok, the six-foot frontiersman, better known as Wild Bill
Hickok, had come to Deadwood with a varied and colorful past. He had been
a trapper, a freighter, a stage driver and station tender, an army scout, a Union
spy, and a buffalo hunter. He was known as the "Prince of Pistoleers" and
was said to have killed anywhere from fifteen to seventy-five men; but no one

questioned him as to the exact number. As a law-enforcement officer he had cleaned up more than one Kansas town, and the tough element in Deadwood was afraid that he might be made Marshal and attack their dives. Hickok arrived from Cheyenne only three months after his marriage to a circus rider, and prepared to make his stake in the roaring camp.

On August 2, 1876, Wild Bill, playing cards in Saloon No. 10, made the mistake of sitting with his back to the open door. Crooked Nose Jack McCall, who had agreed to rid the camp of the potential Marshal for $300, had tanked himself full of whisky to steady his aim and give him courage. Wild Bill was holding a poker hand consisting of black aces and eights—known since that day as a deadman's hand—when McCall slipped up behind him and shot him with a .45 in the back of the head. McCall was caught immediately and tried for murder before Judge W. L. Kuykendall. The trial was held in Langrishe's theatre before the assembled citizens; a packed jury freed him. Since no recognized law as yet governed the Hills, the case was not considered settled, and McCall was retried later in Yankton and hanged. Wild Bill—"the prettiest corpse I ever have seen," remarked Doc Ellis T. Peirce, who laid him out—was placed in the old burying ground above Whitewood Creek. When Mount Moriah Cemetery was opened, his remains were removed to the new site overlooking the city.

No account of Wild Bill can exclude Calamity Jane, who greatly admired him and whose grave, at her own request, is next to his. Calamity, born Martha Jane Canary, was as colorful a character as Wild Bill. Orphaned at an early age, she drifted west through army and mining camps, from Wyoming to Montana, usually dressed in men's clothes. One story connects her with the Jenney expedition to the Hills, and another describes how she smuggled herself into the territory with Crook's army, perhaps as the driver of a pack-train; both versions agree that her identity and sex were not discovered until she indiscreetly went swimming with the men and was discovered by one of the officers. She was good-hearted and utterly fearless. On one occasion she wrapped a blacksnake whip around a carter who was beating a weary ox, at the same time giving him such a tongue-lashing as only she could deliver. The *Pioneer* of July 13, 1876, mentions that

The man Warren, who was stabbed on lower Main St. Wednesday night, is doing quite well under the care of Calamity Jane, who has kindly undertaken the job of nursing him. There's lots of humanity in Calamity and she is deserving of much praise for the part she has taken in this particular case.

During a smallpox epidemic in 1878, she established a pesthouse in Spruce Gulch behind the White Rocks and cared for patients stricken with the disease. She was married more than once and had a daughter, whom she brought back to Deadwood some years later to place in a private school. The Green Front Saloon held a benefit to raise funds for the child's tuition; although some of the proceeds found their way across the bar, enough was salvaged for the child's education. Calamity died in 1903 at Camp Terry, but Deadwood claimed her at the end and gave her a funeral from the Methodist church.

Two other picturesque characters were Poker Alice and Deadwood Dick. The latter is the completely fictitious hero of numerous western dime novels. In 1924, when the annual "Days of '76" celebration was inaugurated, Deadwood needed someone to represent the daredevil Dick. Richard W. Clarke, an Indian scout and pioneer who was living near Whitewood, was chosen for the part and continued to act it with great gusto as long as he lived.

Poker Alice Tubbs was the camp's top gambler. She is said to have been a quiet English girl when she married her first husband; but when he died in Leadville, Colorado, and she needed ready cash, she discovered how to make it by gambling. Wearing a .38, smoking a long cigar, and always dressed in the height of fashion, she presided over many a gambling table, although she refused to play on Sundays. W. G. Tubbs, her second husband, is said to have retired from business upon discovering his wife's accomplishments.

Three churches were built during the year 1877. The history of the Congregational church is typical of all three. At first services were held in the International Hotel, with only a handful of worshipers present; later the dining room of the Centennial Hotel was used. An offer of Langrishe's theatre on Main Street was refused because it was unheated and it held Sunday night shows. Services were then conducted in a carpenter shop until a church was finished in July. After its completion, all denominations used it until their own buildings were ready, staggering services to accommodate everyone. Within the year the Methodists and the Roman Catholics built; the following year the Episcopalians erected a chapel.

The Reverend Molyneux, Rector of the Episcopal church, was on his way to a nearby camp to perform a wedding. On the way to the ceremony he was called in to see a miner who was dying. The sick man had already sent for his two partners and asked them to sit down, one on each side of his bed. From time to time they spoke to him, asking if he had anything to say or anything he wanted them to do, but he only shook his head. Finally one of them said, "Joe, have you anything on your mind?"

"Yes," he whispered, "I wanted to die like our Lord, between two thieves."

With the Gem, the Green Front, the Mansion, the Bella Union, the Eureka Hall, and the Montana saloons all serving liquor, not to mention the smaller dives, heavy drinking was common. The *Black Hills Times* of September 12, 1877, asked, " 'What will become of the sleeping drunkards we often see lying in the streets after night?' Echo answers, 'what?' " On September 23 the paper reported:

Among the passengers on the Cheyenne stage last evening was a young woman attired in male attire. She was from Hat Creek and immediately on arriving here she struck for a bar. In the course of time she got drunk, drunker than a biled owl, and kicked up a considerable of a rumpus on the streets. . . . Sheriff Bullock, he gobbled her and lodged her in jail, where she was sleeping off her drunk at last accounts. This is the first case of a woman being imprisoned in the Hills.

In a column of the *Times* headed "Gulch Hash," the following story appeared on May 15, 1878:

One of the new girls who arrived in this camp from Cheyenne this week, was out upon the street between two and three o'clock this morning with her little gun, aching to perforate the anatomy of a certain young man. She was gathered in by officer Graham and put in her little bed.

The same issue contained the announcement of Morton's New Club House on Lee Street:

Probably a more elegant clubroom is not to be found west of Chicago and the proprietor intends to keep it what it now is, a strictly private clubhouse—a resort for gentlemen. The "rounder" will find the gates of this temple closed.

As the town grew and its streets were improved, the *Times* of May 21, 1877, reminded its readers that

Coon Sing's washee-housee is still located in the middle of Deadwood St. . . . The residents on that street want to know how long it will be allowed to remain there?

Only a few months before the paper had asserted:

The miners who have been engaged in digging up Sherman St. have quit. They were convinced that business men and property owners had some rights that miners were bound to respect.

Although some varieties of game were becoming scarce, on November 14, 1879, the *Times* reported that:

Wagon loads of Blacktail deer saddles are becoming so numerous in Deadwood as to attract no more attention from the average citizen than a wagon load of sheep would in Chicago.

Phatty Thompson, who hauled freight between Cheyenne and Deadwood, brought in a load of animals in 1876 which did attract attention. Knowing that the miners were swamped with rats, and suspecting that the dance-hall girls liked cats, he paid urchins in Cheyenne two bits for every cat they brought him. Loading the creatures in his wagon, he set out for the Hills, where he quickly sold them all for five to ten dollars apiece.

During the seventies and eighties several hundred Chinese lived in the camp and engaged in a variety of occupations. They had their own section of town in the lower end of the gulch along Main Street, and their own stores, gambling and opium dens, and joss houses. Their celebrations were colorful affairs, with lanterns shedding soft light in the streets and firecrackers sputtering. Chinese funerals were impressive processions. As they marched all the men wore white robes and scattered thousands of little pieces of paper perforated with holes, in the belief that the devil would have to climb through each hole before reaching the soul of the deceased. The procession was always led by a brass band. At the cemetery a feast was spread, usually including a roast pig that had been carried in the procession, slung from a pole carried on the shoulders of two of the mourners. In case the pig arrived unroasted, a small building with a fireplace nearby stood conveniently in the burying ground on Mount Moriah. Every Chinese arranged in advance with an undertaker to send his bones back to China for final burial. Some time after interment, each body was removed from the ground, and the bones were wrapped in newspaper or muslin, placed in small zinc-lined boxes, labeled, sealed, shipped to San Francisco, and from there forwarded to China.

Dr. Von Wedelstadt, a well-known figure in Deadwood whom the Chinese called their "White Brother," organized a Chinese Masonic Lodge and always marched with them in their processions. The Orientals had their own uniformed fire and hose company, and their teams won many prizes in the annual races. The fire of 1879, however, destroyed most of their stores and residences, and many Chinese left soon afterwards. Those that remained contributed greatly to the city's color and to its industries. When their activities were reported in the papers, they were frequently described with an amazing lack of tact, as in this item in the November 27, 1882, issue of the *Black Hills Times:*

Several new gambling houses have opened in Chinatown and are nightly crowded with the almond-eyed gamblers tempting the Goddess Fortune with the enticing "Fan Tan." The noise the heathens make would drown a cowboy picnic.

In 1879, just as the town had outgrown its narrow canyon and was pushing up the sides of Deadwood and Whitewood gulches, fire broke out in the

Empire Bakery on Sherman Street and spread to some kegs of black powder in a nearby store. The explosion that followed scattered the flames, and four hours later the business section was in ashes; for the town had no water system and could not control the blaze. As a result of the fire, waterworks were constructed before the end of the year.

Deadwood rebuilt substantially after its big fire but was crippled again in May, 1883, this time by a flood which destroyed 150 buildings and took three lives. Melted winter snows had already filled both creeks even before a steady, warm rain began to fall. At 4:00 P.M. on the eighteenth, Whitewood Creek burst out of its banks and cut a broad channel through the city. Later that day Deadwood Creek, with waves ten feet high, roared down the narrow valley upon the town, piling up debris and taking out all the bridges in its path. The tollhouse on Whitewood Creek at the mouth of Gold Run was swept away and its three occupants drowned. The new schoolhouse, the Methodist church, and all placer equipment were destroyed.

The city slowly recovered from the disaster and even boomed in 1887, when a silver strike in the nearby camps of Carbonate and Galena started a rush to the district. Before 1890 most of the bullion recovered from the mines was obtained from free-milling ore which yielded to stamping and amalgamation processes of reduction. Bodies of rich ore combined with refractory minerals were allowed to remain in the mines or were discarded on the dumps, since no profitable method of treating such ore was known. With the invention of the chlorination and cyanidation processes for operating on low-grade deposits, a new era of mining began.

The Golden Reward Chlorination and the Deadwood and Delaware Smelting Company erected plants at the edge of town in 1887 and 1888 respectively, and ran with a combined capacity of 300 tons of ore per day. The Deadwood and Delaware Company's plant, which operated largely on custom ore, was burned in 1898; but it was immediately rebuilt and continued for some time to produce $2,000,000 a year in gold. After a third reduction works was built by the Gold and Silver Extraction Mining and Milling Company, a system of narrow-gauge railroads was constructed to bring ore from outlying districts to all three of the great mills. Although the silver depression of 1893 hit the city another staggering blow and its population dropped suddenly from 25,000 to 1,600, it held its own, thanks to the reduction works. By 1909 only the Golden Reward was operating; and today the city's mining income comes from the Homestake property at Lead, three miles away.

The last stagecoach rolled into town on December 28, 1890. The following day the Fremont, Elkhorn and Missouri Valley Railroad (now the Chicago and Northwestern) ran its first train into the city. Close on its heels was the Burlington and Missouri Railroad (now the C. B. & Q.), which reached Deadwood on January 21, 1891. With the arrival of the railroad, Deadwood's pioneer days ended. One old-timer remembers how he listened to the first train whistle echo in the canyon and watched the smoke come nearer and nearer. When the locomotive stood panting at the station, he turned to his wife and said, "Guess we'll have to lock our doors now."

PLUMA

AS WE DROVE away from Deadwood toward Lead, we passed through tiny Pluma (population: 12), where John Slaughter, the driver of the Cheyenne-Deadwood stagecoach, was killed by a shotgun blast late one moonlight night in 1877. The trip was nearly over, the coach was within two miles of Deadwood, and most of the passengers were asleep; suddenly five men rode from the shadows into the moonlight, and the leader called, "Halt!" Slaughter tried to stop the horses, but before he could do so a sawed-off shotgun "spoke," and he pitched to the ground. At the noise, the startled horses bolted, leaving the bandits in the road without the $15,000 which the strongbox contained. As soon as the careening coach dashed into Deadwood and the frightened passengers described what had happened, Sheriff Bullock and a posse galloped after the bandits; but they had scattered.

After several more holdups, the Black Hills Stage and Express Line built a special omnibus called the Treasure Coach. It was a large, lumbering vehicle, lined with steel plates five-sixteenths of an inch thick, with portholes in the doors and the strongbox bolted to the floor. In addition to the driver and the regular messenger, it carried extra armed guards who rode with their six-shooters across their knees; it carried no passengers. At least two such coaches were built; the first, called the "Iron Clad" or the "Monitor," was put in service in May, 1878, and the second, the "Johnny Slaughter" (named for the murdered driver) was completed in September.

These coaches made several trips safely between Deadwood and Sidney; but one day road agents staged a robbery at the Cold Spring Canyon station, a lonely stop in a wooded canyon, thirty-seven miles south of Deadwood. The stock tender at the station looked up when a stranger entered and asked for a drink of water. When he brought it in, he faced the barrel of a six-shooter. Half an hour later, when the Treasure Coach galloped up to the station, things were ominously quiet. Just as Big Gene, the driver, threw the lines to the ground and started to climb down, a volley of shots was fired at the coach. One man was killed, and a messenger named Gail Hill and one of the bandits were wounded. Scott Davis, a second messenger who was riding beside Big Gene, dashed for the timber, firing at the robbers so effectively that they hid behind Big Gene to force him to quit shooting. They pried open the treasure

STREET LEVELS, DEADWOOD

LUTHERAN CHURCH AND HOMESTAKE SHAFT, LEAD

box, which contained $45,000, stole the bullion, leaped on their horses, and disappeared down the road, leaving their wounded companion on the ground. The remaining messenger escaped injury and went to the rescue of the stock tender, who was found bound and gagged in the station. The wounded bandit, Big Nosed George, was so furious at being deserted that he told the messenger the names of his companions and where they could be found. Most of the gang were captured and much of the bullion recovered.

The Homestake sent regular shipments by the coach to Cheyenne. On clean-up days at the mine, the gold bricks were temporarily placed in a bank window under heavy guard until each was wrapped in canvas, sealed, and labeled; then they were loaded in the coach. A normal shipment would range from $95,000 to $148,000 in value. The largest shipment sent by the coach was $350,000. As agents were known to be active at the time, the normal guard of five men was increased to thirteen for this shipment, four of them mounted. A band of robbers was waiting to ambush the coach, but the unexpectedly large escort routed them.

Gold and valuables belonging to individuals were also sent by the coach, the owners following by regular stage. Passengers always hid their valuables when taking a trip, the women secreting rolls of bills in their elaborate coiffures and the men concealing gold in false-headed canes or in the soles of their shoes. Judge Bennett of Deadwood, a frequent passenger, was never in one which was held up. Years later he talked to a former highwayman and expressed surprise that the coach ahead of or behind his might be robbed, but never the one in which he was traveling.

"We knew which stage you were on every time, and we knew that if we were caught you'd be the judge that would try us. You might recognize us," said the man, "and we couldn't risk that."

LEAD

THE road up the gulch to Lead winds easily beside Gold Run, the stream which loses itself in Whitewood Creek at Pluma. Houses rise in terraces on either side of the gulch and spread over the tops of the hills; long, steep flights of steps, some of wood and some of concrete, connect one terraced street with the next, rising to the uppermost row of dwellings.

To the left of the road is the tremendous plant of the Homestake Mining Company, a city within a city, and on the right is the fabulous open cut, the man-made canyon from which ore was taken in the early days. The cut marks the site of the original ledge, discovered by the Manuel brothers, and the fenced-in meadow close to the present highway marks the site of Lead's first business section. Shifting ground and cave-ins caused the area to be condemned as unsafe; its buildings were razed, and a new center was built on firmer ground.

Lead's narrow main street, which slopes steeply up Gold Run, is built up solidly with stores, office buildings, a bank, a movie theatre, and a recreation building. Most of the city's residences are frame, and those perched on the hillsides are surrounded by trees. Lead's history, which is that of the Homestake mine, is one of continual growth and development, and since it is a booming industrial city today, it has no place in this book. Its early history, however, is bound up with that of Deadwood, Central City, and the other nearby camps.

In February, 1876, Thomas E. Carey, who had been placer mining in Deadwood Gulch, crossed over the divide which separated that gulch from Gold Run Creek; in the swollen stream and its tributaries he found still richer placer deposits than those he had been working, but he had no inkling that the greatest gold mine in the country lay hidden close by. He simply staked a claim and reported its location in Deadwood. Not long after his discovery, "Smoky Jones," accompanied by twenty miners, pushed through the dense pines. On July 10, 1876, they laid out a townsite along the gulch, just below the present Homestake substation, and named it Washington. They cut brush and trees and laid out lots fifty feet wide between the north and south forks of Gold Run; but, since twenty-five feet was sufficient land for a cabin, many of the men speculated by selling half of their property to newcomers. This accounts for the narrow frontages in the business section of Lead today.

By the spring of 1877, when the first attempts were made to reduce gold quartz, the town began to expand and outgrow its original survey. A new and larger townsite, which extended up toward the head of Gold Run and even spread over the tops of the nearest hills, was laid out and named Lead (pronounced Leed) because of the many leads or outcroppings of ore found in the surrounding hills. For several years after its establishment, Lead and Washington remained separate but adjoining communities.

The fifty or more mines which attracted prospectors to the gulch were discovered in 1876. Moses and Fred Manuel had already tried their luck near Custer and Hill City, but left because they were interested not in placering but in quartz mining. On April 9 they and their partners, Alex Engh and Henry Harvey, uncovered the ledge which became the greatest mine of them all. Other miners were finding promising locations, too; one of them said, "Sure, there's enough here for all of us to make a homestake in." The Manuels liked that idea and called their claim the Homestake. During the summer they developed the property and built an arrastre not far from it, near Pennington, another new, sprawling camp. Not satisfied with only one mine, the brothers searched the area for more leads and located the Old Abe, the Terra, and the

DeSmet. Later in the season the Giant, Pierce, Lincoln, Independence, Big Mission, and General Custer were discovered, as well as the Highland, located by M. Cavanaugh, and the Golden Star, located by "Smoky Jones."

To treat the ore from the many properties, two custom mills were built by the summer of 1877. As the gold continued to pile up under the noisy stamps, promoters and capitalists started to investigate the area from which such glowing reports were being circulated. By the time that representatives of wealthy companies arrived in Lead, the "city" had many business houses, four hotels, a newspaper (*Lead City Telegraph*), and a two-story Opera House, with a saloon on the main floor and a hall above; and it had held its first dance, at which seven women, the total female population, were present. By 1878, the newly organized Miners' Union had a hall for its meetings, and a year later Sam Wood opened a bank to handle the increasing business for which the mines were responsible. When Louis Janin, an engineer from San Francisco, came to the Hills to report on the mines, he was greatly impressed; the camp, he said, was not rough but "the most pleasant of all mining localities I have visited . . . and in no district is justice more ably administered or greater security afforded to life and property."

During the year 1877 the California capitalists Lloyd Tevis, J. B. Haggan (or Haggin), and George Hearst became interested in the mine and sent L. D. Kellogg, a mining expert, to investigate the property and to buy it if he found it as good as represented. He secured a short-option lease on the Homestake and returned to San Francisco to report to the syndicate. The next day he started back to the Hills, accompanied by Mr. Hearst, who purchased the mine for a sum quoted variously as $70,000 and $105,000. The new corporation bought an eighty-stamp mill in San Francisco and shipped it to Lead. The cost of freighting the mill and machinery from Sidney, Nebraska, to Lead was $33,000. Most of the machinery was delivered by January 1, 1878, but the portion freighted in by ox-team was delayed by a March blizzard near Crook City. Every animal in the train was frozen, and the shipment did not reach Lead until April.

With the installation of the stamp mill, the Homestake Company (with a nominal capital of $2,500,000) began operations. Year by year it acquired more mines—the Golden Star, the Highland, and the Old Abe in 1878, and the Deadwood Terra and the DeSmet in 1880. To provide logs for mine timbers and fuel, the company hired an army of woodchoppers, who hacked their way across the hills, felling trees and leaving behind them a wake of dead stumps. To bring the logs to the mine, a narrow-gauge railway was built and extended as needed to the ever-widening spread of lumber camps, circling the hills or crossing deep ravines on sturdy trestles to reach the loading platforms.

Lead is a city of contrasts, of old and new side by side; but dominating it are the many buildings which comprise the Homestake property. Close to Gold Run are old two- and three-story frame houses, propped up on the gulch side to keep them from slipping down to the water's edge; high above the city is the silvery Ross shaft of the mine, a gleaming monolith on top of a mountain; and in between is a city whose pulse is underground. The tremendous mine from which vast quantities of low-grade ore are taken each year is the biggest and most profitable gold mine in the United States, and most of the $550,000,000 which has been produced in the Black Hills since 1875 has come from its leads.

The rush to the Black Hills in search of gold was neither the earliest nor the latest to be made—California's gold was first washed in 1848 and Tonopah's in 1903—but the camps in the Hills retained their pioneer vigor and frontier ways longer than the others. Their remoteness, and the fact that they were on land which until 1876 was unknown to any but Indians, partly accounts for this. Years after trains on the Georgetown Loop were hauling ore to smelters from Silver Plume, tucked in at the foot of the Colorado Rockies, even after the Northern Pacific railroad had celebrated its completion by driving a golden spike at Gold Creek, Montana, Deadwood and Lead were still without rail connections with the outside world; and stagecoaches were dashing through their streets, weaving adeptly between freighters' wagon trains. For nearly fifteen years the towns in the Hills lived a frontier existence—lusty, exciting, discouraging, extravagant, and dangerous, but rewarding. As the *Black Hills Times* of December 15, 1877, put it:

Gold is here in great abundance but it does not grow on trees nor upon the surface of the ground. . . . If you come with the intention of mining come with an understanding that you have got to put in some of the hardest knocks of your life or else you must pay somebody to do the knocking for you. Here, if anywhere, is verified the old adage, "by the sweat of thy brow shalt thou eat thy bread."

In these camps fortunes were made and lost; towns were burned—and rebuilt while the charred walls were still warm; Indians killed from ambush, and road-agents killed in the open when their victims were uncooperative; the Chinese had their opium houses and the miners had their hurdy-gurdies. Tomorrow was always the day when the miner would strike it rich, and even if he didn't, his cronies were there to set him up to a glass of Black Hills lightning. And wherever men gathered there were whisky and stories, like the one about the miner who said to another:

"I can't touch your ground. It's in litigation."

"That's a damned lie," replied the man. "It's in porphyry."

Anyone who has read this far has covered with me the enormous stretches of mountains, valleys, deserts, and plains that comprise the twelve huge western states in which lie significant mining zones, full of camps both dead and alive, built by hardy pioneers who pushed their way across dangerous unknown terrain in search of gold. No attempt has been made to cover completely the mining towns of any state—to do so would require at least twelve separate volumes, each as large as this one—but by going to the places where the earliest discoveries of precious metals were made or to those where the richest strikes were found, I have gained some idea of the pioneering activity which touched off the development of the vast expanses of land west of the Rockies and made of it twelve great commonwealths. Now that I have seen these early towns, I am more keenly conscious of the indomitable courage and endurance of the men and women who surmounted unbelievable hardships in order to gain their most cherished desire—gold, and the ease and comfort they hoped it might bring. The towns and cities which are now nothing but ghosts, and the camps that have dwindled from active wealth to hopeful dearth, are to many people sad and depressing, but to me they are gallant monuments of faith and daring. Behind the present ruins I see the once bustling cities whose teeming life made possible the West of today.

A Glossary

OF THE MINING AND MINERAL INDUSTRY

by ALBERT H. FAY*

ADIT. A nearly horizontal passage from the surface by which a mine is entered and unwatered. A tunnel or drift.

ADOBE. A sun-dried brick. The mixed earth or clay of which such bricks are made.

AERIAL TRAMWAY. A system for the transportation of material, as ore or rock, in buckets suspended from pulleys or grooved wheels that run on a cable, usually stationary. A moving or traction rope is attached to the buckets and may be operated by either gravity or other power.

ALKALI FLAT. A sterile plain, containing an excess of alkali, at the bottom of an undrained basin in an arid region.

AMALGAM. In gold metallurgy, an alloy of gold and mercury, usually obtained by allowing gold-bearing minerals, after crushing, to come in contact with mercury in stamp batteries, sluices or mercury-coated copper plates.

AMALGAMATION. The process in which gold and silver are extracted from pulverized ores by producing an amalgam, from which the mercury is afterwards expelled.

APEX. The end, edge, or crest of a vein nearest the surface.

ARGENTIFEROUS. Containing silver.

ARRASTRE (or arrastra). Apparatus for grinding and mixing ores by means of a heavy stone, dragged around upon a circular bed. The arrastre is chiefly used for ores containing free gold and amalgamation is combined with the grinding.

ASSAY. To test ores or minerals by chemical or blowpipe examination. Gold and silver require an additional process called cupelling, for the purpose of separating them from the base metals.

ASSAY VALUE. The amount of the gold or silver, in ounces per ton of ore, as shown by assay of any given sample.

ASSESSMENT WORK. The annual work upon an unpatented mining claim in the public domain necessary under the United States law for the maintenance of the possessory title thereto.

BAR. Accumulation of gravel along the banks of a stream, which when worked by the miners for gold, are called Bar diggings.

BAR MINING. The mining of river bars, usually between low and high waters, although the stream is sometimes deflected and the bar worked below water level.

---

* Department of the Interior, Bureau of Mines. Bulletin 95. Washington, Government Printing Office, 1920.

BASIN. A large or small depression in the surface of the land, the lowest part of which may be occupied by a lake or pond. An area or tract having certain common features throughout, particularly a tract where the strata dip from all sides toward a center.

BATEA (Mexican). A wide and shallow vessel, usually of wood, used for panning ore.

BEDROCK. The solid rock underlying auriferous gravel, sand, clay, etc., and upon which alluvial gold rests.

BLOSSOM. The oxidized or decomposed outcrop of a vein.

BLOSSOM ROCK. The rock detached from a vein but which has not been transported.

BLOW-OUT. A large outcrop, beneath which the vein is smaller, is called a blow-out.

BONANZA. In miners' phrase, good luck, or a body of rich ore. A mine is in *bonanza* when it is profitably producing ore.

BREAST. The face of a working.

BULLION. Uncoined gold and silver. Gold and silver coined but considered simply with reference to its commercial value as raw material. Figuratively solid gold or silver . . . hence solid worth.

BULLION BAR. Unrefined gold or silver melted and cast into a bar.

BUTTON. The globule of metal remaining on an assay-cupel or in a crucible, at the end of the fusion.

CAGE. A frame with one or more platforms for cars, used in hoisting in a vertical shaft.

CARBONATES. Ores containing a considerable proportion of carbonate of lead.

CHIMNEY. An ore chute. A natural vent or opening in the earth.

CHISPA (Mexican). Ore containing visible gold. A nugget.

CHLORIDE. A compound of chlorine with another element or radical. A salt of hydrochloric acid.

CHLORIDES. A common term for ores containing chloride of silver.

CHLORINATION PROCESS. The process in which auriferous ores are first roasted to oxidize the base metals, then saturated with chlorine gas, and finally treated with water, which removes the soluble chloride of gold to be subsequently precipitated and melted into bars.

CHUTE. A channel or shaft underground, or an inclined trough above ground, through which ore falls or is "shot" by gravity from a higher to a lower level.

CLAIM. The portion of mining ground held under the Federal and local laws by one claimant or association, by virtue of one location and record. . . . The portion of land upon a gold field to which a miner is legally entitled.

CLEAN-UP. The operation of collecting all the valuable product of a given period of operation in a stamp mill, or in a hydraulic or placer mine.

COLEMANITE. A hydrous borate of calcium. . . . The commonest source of borax in the United States.

COLOR. The shade or tint of the earth or rock which indicates ore. A particle of metallic gold found in the prospector's pan after a sample of earth or crushed rock has been "panned out."

CONCENTRATE. That which has been reduced to a state of purity or concentration by the removal of foreign, nonessential or diluting matter.

CONCENTRATOR. An apparatus in which by the aid of water or air and specific gravity, mechanical concentration of ores is performed.

COUNTRY ROCK. The general mass of adjacent rock as distinguished from that of a dike, vein or lode.

CRIBBING. Close timbering, as the lining of a shaft.

CROSSCUT TUNNEL. A tunnel driven at approximately right angles to a main tunnel, or from the bottom of a shaft or other opening across the formation to an objective point.

CUPEL. A small, shallow, porous cup, especially of bone ash; used in assaying to separate precious metals from lead, etc.

CYANIDE PROCESS. The extraction of gold from finely crushed ores, concentrates and tailings by means of cyanide of potassium used in dilute solutions. The gold is dissolved by the solution and subsequently deposited upon metallic zinc or by other means.

DIGGINGS. Applicable to all mineral deposits and mining camps, but in usage in the United States applied to placer mining only.

DREDGE. A scoop or suction apparatus, operated by power, and usually mounted on a flat-bottomed boat. Extensively used in mining gold-bearing sand and gravel.

DRIFT. A horizontal passage underground. A drift follows a vein, as distinguished from a crosscut, which intersects it.

FACE. The surface exposed by excavation.

FAULT. A break in the continuity of a body of rock, attended by a movement on one side or the other of the break, so that what were once parts of one continuous rock stratum or vein are now separated.

FISSURE VEIN. A cleft or crack in the rock material of the earth's crust filled with mineral matter different from the walls and precipitated therein.

FLOAT. Pieces of ore or rock which have fallen from veins or strata, or have been separated from the parent vein or strata by weathering agencies.

FLUME. An inclined channel usually of wood and often supported on a trestle, for conveying water from a distance to be utilized for power, transportation, etc., as in placer mining, logging, etc.

FLUX. A substance as borax or as alkali that promotes the fusing of minerals or metals.

FREE GOLD. Gold uncombined with other substances.

FREE-MILLING. Applied to ores which contain free gold or silver, and can be reduced by crushing and amalgamation, without roasting or other chemical treatment.

GALENA. The commonest lead mineral.

GALLOWS. A frame consisting of two uprights and a cross-piece for supporting a mine roof.

GALLOWS FRAME. A frame supporting a pulley, over which the hoisting rope passes to the engine.

GIANT. A large nozzle used in hydraulic mining.

GIANT POWDER. A form of dynamite.

GLANCE. A term used to designate minerals having a splendent luster, as silver glance, lead glance, etc.

GOLD AMALGAM. A variety of native gold containing mercury.

GOLD DUST. Fine particles of gold, such as are obtained in placer mining.

GOPHERING. Prospecting work confined to digging shallow pits or starting adits. Term used from similarity of this work to the crooked little holes dug in the soil by gophers.

GRUBSTAKE. Supplies furnished to a prospector on promise of a share in his discoveries. So called because the lender stakes or risks the grub (food), etc., so furnished.

HEADFRAME. A structure erected over a shaft to carry the sheaves over which the cable runs for hoisting the cage. Called in England, Gallows frame.

HIGH GRADE. Rich ore. To steal or pilfer ore or gold, as from a mine by a miner.

HOIST. An engine for raising ore, rock, coal, etc. from a mine and for lowering and raising men and material.

HORN SILVER. Chloride of silver.

HORSE. A mass of country rock lying within a vein.

HYDRAULIC ELEVATOR. An elevator operated by the weight or pressure of water, especially an apparatus used in dredging and hydraulic mining which raises mud and gravel by means of a jet of water under heavy pressure inducing a strong upward current through a pipe.

HYDRAULIC HOSE. The flexible hose used to direct a stream of water against a wall or face of a drift.

HYDRAULIC MINING. A method of mining in which a bank of gold-bearing earth or gravel is washed by a powerful jet of water and carried with sluices, where the gold separates from the earth by specific gravity.

HYDRAULICKING. Washing down a bank of earth or gravel by the use of pipes, conveying water under high pressure.

INGOT. A cast bar or block of metal.

LEAD (pronounced *leed*). Commonly used as a synonym for ledge or lode.

LEDGE. A lode; a limited mass of rock bearing valuable mineral.

LEDGE ROCK. The true bedrock; distinguished from boulders or rock that has been moved.

LEVEL. A horizontal passage or drift into or in a mine. It is customary to work mines by levels at regular intervals in depth, numbered in their order below the adit or drainage level, if there be one.

LOCATION. The act of fixing boundaries of a mining claim according to law. The claim itself.

LODE. Strictly a fissure in the country rock filled with mineral. A tabular deposit of valuable mineral between definite boundaries.

MATTE. A product obtained in smelting sulphide ores of certain metals, as copper, lead or nickel. It is a crude metal combined with more or less sulphur and requires to be further purified.

LONG TOM. An inclined trough in which gold-bearing earth or gravel is crudely washed. It is longer than a rocker.

LOW-GRADE. A term applied to ores relatively poor in the metal for which they are mined; lean ore.

MILL. Any establishment for reducing ores by other means than smelting.

MILL SITE. A plot of ground suitable for the erection of a mill, or reduction works, to be used in connection with mining operations.

MILLING ORE. A dry ore that can be amalgamated or treated by leaching and other processes; usually these ores are low-grade, free, or nearly so, from base metals.

MINERS' INCH. Generally accepted to mean the quantity of water that will escape from an aperture one inch square through a two-inch plank, with a steady flow of water standing six inches above the top of the escape aperture, the quantity so discharged amounting to 2274 cubic feet in twenty-four hours.

MINING DISTRICT. A section of country usually designated by name and described or understood as being confined within certain natural boundaries, in which gold or silver (or other minerals) may be found in paying quantities.

MONITOR. In hydraulic mining, a contrivance consisting of nozzle and holder, whereby the direction of a stream can be readily changed.

MOTHER LODE. The principal lode or vein passing through a district or particular section of country.

NUGGET. A lump of native gold, silver, platinum, copper, etc.

OUTCROP. The coming out of a stratum to the surface of the ground.

PAN. To wash earth, gravel, etc., in a pan in searching for gold.

PATENT. Title in fee, obtained by patent from the United States Government when there has been done an equivalent of $500 worth of work on or for each mining claim.

PINCH. The narrowing of a vein or deposit.

PINCHED. Where a vein narrows, as if the walls had been squeezed in. When the walls meet, the vein is said to be pinched out.

PLACER. A place where gold is obtained by washing; an alluvial or glacial deposit as of sand or gravel, containing particles of gold or other valuable mineral.

PLACER CLAIM. A mining claim located upon gravel or ground whose mineral contents are extracted by the use of water, by sluicing, hydraulicking, etc.

PLACER MINING. That form of mining in which the surficial detritus is washed for gold or other valuable minerals. When water under pressure is employed to break down the gravel, the term *hydraulic mining* is generally employed.

POCKET. A small body of ore.

PYRITE. A hard, heavy, shiny, yellow mineral . . . generally in cubic crystals.

PYRITIC SMELTING. The fusion of sulphide ores by the heat generated by their own oxidation, and without the aid of any extraneous heat.

QUARTZ MILL. A machine or establishment for pulverizing quartz ore, in order that the gold and silver it contains may be separated by chemical means. A stamp mill.

REDUCTION WORKS. Works for reducing metals from their ores, as a smelting works, cyanide plant, etc.

REEF. A lode or vein. A word introduced into mining by sailors who left their ships to participate in the rush to Ballarat and Bendigo in 1851. To them a rock projecting above the water was a reef, and the term was therefore applied to quartz outcrops on land.

RIFFLE. The lining of the bottom of a sluice, made of blocks or slats arranged in such a manner that chinks are left between them.

ROASTING AND REDUCTION PROCESS. The treatment of lead ores by roasting to form lead-oxide, and subsequent reducing fusion in a shaft furnace.

ROCKER. A short trough in which auriferous sands are agitated by oscillation, in water, to collect their gold.

RUBY SILVER (Proustite). A silver-arsenic sulphide mineral.

SAMPLING WORKS. A plant and its equipment for sampling and determining the value of ores that are bought, sold, or treated metallurgically.

SINK. Any slight depression in the land surface, especially one having no outlet.

SKIP. A large hoisting bucket.

SLIME. A product of wet crushing containing valuable ore in particles so fine as to be carried in suspension by water.

SLUICE. A long, inclined trough or flume, usually on the ground, for washing auriferous earth.

SLUICE BOX. A wooden trough in which alluvial beds are washed for the recovery of gold or tinstone.

SLUMGULLION. A muddy, usually red deposit in the sluices.

SMELT. To reduce metals from their ores by a process that includes fusion. In its restricted sense, *smelting* is confined to a single operation, as the fusion of an iron ore in a shaft furnace, the reduction of a copper matte in a reverberatory furnace, and the extraction of a metal from sweepings in a crucible, but in its general sense it includes the entire treatment of the material from the crude to the finished metal.

SMELTER. An establishment where ores are smelted.

SMELTING WORKS. An establishment in which metals are extracted from ores by furnaces.

STACKER. A device fixed at the rear of a dredge and carrying a conveyor belt to stack the waste material behind the boat so that it will not interfere with navigation.

STAMP MILL. The building or apparatus in which rock is crushed by descending pestles (stamps) operated by water or steam-power.

STOPE. An excavation from which the ore has been extracted, either above or below a level in a series of steps.

TAILINGS. The worthless slimes left behind after the valuable portion of the ore has been separated by dressing or concentration.

TELLURIDE. A compound of tellurium with another element or radical. Often rich in gold and silver.

TRAM. To haul or push cars in a mine.

TRAMWAY. A suspended cable system along which material, as ore or rock, is transported in suspended buckets.

UNWATER. To pump water from mines.

VEIN (or lode) CLAIM. The terms "vein or lode" and "vein or lode claim" are used indiscriminately and interchangeably.

WIRE SILVER. Native silver in the form of wire or threads.

Selected Bibliography

GENERAL

Anderson, Alex D., *The Silver Country*. New York, 1877.
Bancroft, Hubert Howe, *The Works of* ——. 39 vols. San Francisco, 1882-1890.
Beebe, Lucius, and Clegg, Charles, *U. S. West, The Saga of Wells Fargo*. New York, 1949.
Browne, J. Ross, *Adventures in the Apache Country*. New York, 1869.
Carr, William H., *Desert Parade*. New York, 1947.
Corle, Edwin, *Desert Country*. New York, 1941.
Cozzens, Samuel W., *The Marvelous Country*. Boston, 1876.
Delano, Alonzo, *Across the Plains and Among the Diggings*. 1853; rev. ed. New York, 1936.
French, Joseph Lewis (ed.), *The Pioneer West*. Boston, 1924.
Fuller, George W., *A History of the Pacific Northwest*. New York, 1949.
Hill, James M., *The Mining Districts of the Western United States*. Washington, 1912.
Ingham, George Thomas, *Digging Gold Among the Rockies*. Philadelphia, 1888.
Lavender, David, *The Big Divide*. Garden City, 1948.
Lockwood, Frank, *The Apache Indians*. New York, 1938.
Morgan, Dale L., *The Humboldt*. ("Rivers of America Series.") New York, 1943.
Mullan, Capt. John (ed.), *Miners' and Travelers' Guide to Oregon, Washington, Idaho, Montana, Wyoming and Colorado*. New York, 1865.
Quiett, Glen Chesney, *Pay Dirt*. New York, 1936.
Shinn, Charles Howard, *Mining Camps*. New York, 1885.
Targ, William (ed.), *The American West*. New York, 1946.
Trimble, W. J., *The Mining Advance into the Inland Empire*. Madison, Wis., 1914.
U. S. Geological Survey, Reports, Bulletins, etc. Washington.
Wilson, Neill C., *Treasure Express*. New York, 1936.

> MAGAZINES: *American Institute of Mining Engineers, Bi-monthly Bulletin of; Desert Magazine; Engineering and Mining Journal; Ford Times; Lincoln-Mercury Times; Mining and Scientific Press; Mining World; The West Shore; Westways.*

ARIZONA

Arizona. ("The American Guide Series.") New York, 1940.
Burns, Walter Noble, *Tombstone*. Garden City, 1929.
Farish, Thomas E., *History of Arizona*. 8 vols. San Francisco, 1916.

Hall, Sharlot M., *First Citizen of Prescott, Pauline Weaver.* Prescott, n.d.

Hamilton, Patrick, *The Resources of Arizona.* San Francisco, 1884.

Hinton, Richard J., *Hand-Book to Arizona.* San Francisco, 1878.

History of Arizona Territory. San Francisco, 1884.

Lockwood, Frank C., *Pioneer Days in Arizona.* New York, 1932.

Martin, Douglas D., *Tombstone Epitaph.* Albuquerque, N. M., 1951.

McClintock, James H., *History of Arizona.* 3 vols. Chicago, 1916.

Myers, John Myers, *The Last Chance.* New York, 1950.

Wyllys, Rufus K., *Arizona, the History of a Frontier State.* Phoenix, 1950.

MAGAZINES: *Arizona Highways; Arizona Historical Review.*

NEWSPAPERS: *Arizona Republican,* Phoenix; *Arizona Silver Belt,* Globe; *Globe Chronicle; Jerome Mining News; Mohave County Miner,* Kingman; *Tombstone Epitaph; Weekly Arizona Miner,* Prescott; *Weekly Arizonan,* Tucson.

CALIFORNIA

Brockman, C. Frank, "A Guide to the Mother Lode Country," *Yosemite Nature Notes* (January, 1948).

Browne, J. Ross, *The Settlement & Exploration of Lower California.* New York, 1869.

————, "A Trip to Bodie Bluff," *Harpers Monthly* (August, 1865).

California. ("American Guide Series.") New York, 1939.

Caruthers, William, *Loafing Along Death Valley Trails.* Palm Desert, 1951.

Chamberlain, Newell D., *The Call of Gold.* Mariposa, 1936.

Davis, H. P., *Gold Rush Days in Nevada City.* Nevada City, 1948.

Death Valley. ("American Guide Series.") New York, 1937.

Dieter, Roy G., *First Annual Directory and Guide to the City of Nevada.* Nevada City, 1946.

Egenhoff, Elizabeth L., (ed.). *The Elephant As They Saw It.* San Francisco, 1949.

Glasscock, Carl B., *A Golden Highway.* Indianapolis, 1934.

Hall, Carroll D., (ed.). *Sutter's Fort.* Sacramento, n.d.

Hawthorne, Hildegarde, *Romantic Cities of California.* New York, 1939.

Hunt, Rockwell D., and Sanchez, Nellie Van De Grift, *A Short History of California.* New York, 1922.

Jackson, Joseph Henry, *Anybody's Gold.* New York, 1941.

Jenkins, Olaf P., (ed.). *The Mother Lode Country, Geologic Guidebook Along Highway 49.* San Francisco, 1948.

Johnston, Philip, *Lost and Living Cities of the California Gold Rush.* Los Angeles, 1948.

MacMinn, George R., *The Theater of the Golden Era in California.* Caldwell, Ida., 1941.

O'Brien, Robert, *California Called Them.* New York, 1951.

Paul, Rodman W., *California Gold.* Cambridge, Mass., 1947.

Rensch, Hero E., *Columbia, A Gold Camp of Old Tuolumne.* Berkeley, 1936.
Rider, Fremont, (ed.). *Rider's California.* New York, 1925.
Rourke, Constance, *Troupers of the Gold Coast.* New York, 1928.
Stellman, Louis J., *Mother Lode.* San Francisco, 1934.
Weston, Otheto, *Mother Lode Album.* Stanford, 1948.
White, Stewart Edward, *The Forty-Niners.* New Haven, 1921.
Wilson, Neill C., *Silver Stampede.* New York, 1937.

MAGAZINES: *Calico Print,* Twenty-nine Palms; *California Journal of Mines and Geology; Ghost Town News,* Buena Park.

NEWSPAPERS: *Calico Print,* Calico, later at Twenty-nine Palms; *Sacramento Bee; Stockton Record.*

COLORADO

Baskin, O. L., & Co., *History of the Arkansas Valley.* Chicago, 1881.
Colorado. ("American Guide Series.") New York, 1941.
Crofutt, George A., *Grip-Sack Guide of Colorado.* Omaha, 1881.
Fossett, Frank, *Colorado, Its Gold and Silver Mines.* New York, 1880.
Fowler, Gene, *Timberline.* New York, 1933.
Fritz, Percy S., *Colorado, The Centennial State.* New York, 1941.
Hafen, LeRoy R., *Colorado, The Story of a Western Commonwealth.* Denver, 1933.
Hall, Frank, *History of the State of Colorado.* Chicago, 1890.
Henderson, Charles W., *Mining in Colorado.* Washington, 1926.
Hollister, Ovando J., *The Mines of Colorado.* Springfield, Mass., 1867.
Karsner, David, *Silver Dollar.* New York, 1932.
Kemp, Donald C., *Colorado's Little Kingdom.* Golden, 1949.
Monroe, Arthur W., *San Juan Silver.* 1940.
Mumey, Nolie, *Creede, History of a Colorado Silver Mining Town.* Denver, 1949.
Ward, Louisa A., *Chalk Creek, Colorado.* Denver, 1940.
Willison, George F., *Here They Dug the Gold.* New York, 1931.
Wolle, Muriel Sibell, *Stampede to Timberline.* Boulder, 1949.

MAGAZINES: *Colorado Magazine,* State Historical Society; *Rocky Mountain Life.*

NEWSPAPERS: *Creede Candle; Cripple Creek Morning Times; Denver Daily News; Denver Post; Miners Daily Register,* later *Central City Register-Call; Rocky Mountain News; San Juan Prospector; Silverton Standard; Silver World,* Lake City.

IDAHO

Bailey, Robert G., *River of No Return.* Lewiston, 1947.
Butler, L. F., *The New Coeur D'Alene Gold Mines.* Chicago, 1884.

Defenbach, Byron, *Idaho, The Place and its People.* 3 vols. New York, 1933.
Donaldson, Thomas, *Idaho of Yesterday.* Caldwell, 1941.
Fisher, Vardis, *The Idaho Encyclopedia.* Caldwell, 1938.
Hailey, John, *History of Idaho.* Boise, 1910.
Idaho. ("American Guide Series.") New York, 1937.
McConnell, W. J., *Early History of Idaho.* Caldwell, 1913.
Smalley, Eugene V., "Coeur d'Alene Stampede." *Century Magazine* (October, 1884).
Stoll, William T., *Silver Strike.* Boston, 1932.

MAGAZINES: *Bi-Ennial Reports,* Idaho State Historical Department; *Scenic Idaho.*

NEWSPAPERS: *Boise News; Coeur D'Alene Eagle; Owyhee Avalanche,* Silver City; *Owyhee Nugget,* Marsing.

MONTANA

Campbell, William C., *From the Quarries of Last Chance Gulch.* Helena, 1951.
Dimsdale, Prof. Thomas J., *Vigilantes of Montana.* 12th rev. ed. Butte, 1950.
Fletcher, Robert H., *Montana Highway Historical Markers.* Helena, 1938.
Glasscock, Carl B., *The War of the Copper Kings.* New York, 1935.
Howard, Joseph Kinsey, *Montana, High, Wide and Handsome.* New Haven, 1943.
Leeson, Michael A., (ed.). *History of Montana, 1739-1885.* Chicago, 1885.
McPherren, Ida, *Imprints on Pioneer Trails.* Boston, 1950.
Marsh, George D., (ed.). *Copper Camp.* New York, 1943.
Montana. ("American Guide Series.") New York, 1939.
Thane, Eric, *High Border Country.* New York, 1942.

MAGAZINES: *Montana Magazine of History,* Historical Society of Montana, Helena.

NEWSPAPERS: *Columbus News; Great Falls Tribune; Missoulian; Montana Post,* Virginia City.

NEVADA

Beebe, Lucius, and Clegg, Charles, *Virginia and Truckee.* Oakland, 1949.
————, *Legends of the Comstock Lode.* Carson City, 1951.
Davis, Sam P., *History of Nevada.* 2 vols. Reno, 1913.
De Quille, Dan, *History of the Big Bonanza.* Hartford, Conn., 1876. Reprinted as *The Big Bonanza,* New York, 1947.
Drury, Wells, *An Editor on the Comstock Lode.* Palo Alto, 1936.
Emrich, Duncan, (ed.). *Comstock Bonanza.* New York, 1950.
Lillard, Richard G., *Desert Challenge.* New York, 1942.
Lyman, George D., *The Saga of the Comstock Lode.* New York, 1934.
Marye, George Thomas, Jr., *From '49 to '83 in California and Nevada.* San Francisco, 1923.

Nevada. ("American Guide Series.") Portland, 1940.
Pioneer Nevada. Harolds Club of Reno. Reno, 1951.
Twain, Mark, *Roughing It.* 2 vols. New York, 1871.

MAGAZINES: *Nevada Highways and Parks; Nevada Magazine.*

NEWSPAPERS: *Esmeralda Herald,* Hawthorne; *Hawthorne News; Reese River Reveille,* Austin; *Rhyolite Herald; Searchlight; Territorial Enterprise,* Virginia City.

NEW MEXICO

Anderson, John B., *A History of the Mogollon Mining District.* Albuquerque, 1939.
Fergusson, Erna, *Murder and Mystery in New Mexico.* Albuquerque, 1948.
Hough, Emerson, *Heart's Desire.* New York, 1905.
Jones, Fayette Alexander, *New Mexico Mines and Minerals.* Santa Fe, 1904.
Keleher, William A., *Maxwell Land Grant.* Santa Fe, 1942.
————, *Turmoil in New Mexico, 1846-1868.* Santa Fe, 1952.
McKenna, James A., *Black Range Tales.* New York, 1936.
New Mexico. ("American Guide Series.") New York, 1940.
Northrop, Stuart A., *Mining Districts of New Mexico.* Albuquerque, 1942.
Twitchell, Ralph Emerson, *The Leading Facts of New Mexican History.* 2 vols. Cedar Rapids, Iowa, 1912.

MAGAZINES: *New Mexico Highway Journal; New Mexico Magazine; New Mexico Miner and Prospector.*

NEWSPAPERS: *Golden 9; New Mexico Interpreter,* White Oaks; *Santa Fe Register.*

OREGON

Carey, Charles H., *General History of Oregon.* 2 vols. Portland, 1935.
Hastings, Lansford W., *The Emigrant's Guide to Oregon and California.* 1845. Reprinted Princeton, 1932.
Hiatt, Isaac, *Thirty-one Years of Baker County,* ed. Abbott Foster, 1893.
Judson, Katharine B., *Early Days in Old Oregon.* Portland, 1916.
Liebenstein, Charles, *Sumpter Goldfields.* 1902.
Lyman, Horace S., *History of Oregon.* 4 vols. New York, 1903.
Mineral Resources of Oregon, Oregon Bureau of Mines & Geology.
Mitchell, Graham J., *Minerals of Oregon.* Salem, 1916.
Oregon. ("American Guide Series.") Portland, 1940.
Rostel, Ernest A., *Historic Jacksonville.* Jacksonville, 1950.
Scott, Harvey W., *History of Oregon Country.* Cambridge, 1924.
Walling, A. G., *History of Southern Oregon.* Portland, 1884.

MAGAZINES: *Oregon Historical Quarterly.*

NEWSPAPERS: *Baker Morning Democrat; Grants Pass Courier; Oregon Sentinel,* Jacksonville.

SOUTH DAKOTA

Bennett, Estelline, *Old Deadwood Days*. New York, 1928.

Case, Lee, *Lee's Official Guide Book to the Black Hills and the Bad Lands*. Sturgis, 1949.

Casey, Robert J., *The Black Hills and Their Incredible Characters*. New York, 1947.

Collins, Charles, *Collins' Black Hills History and Directory for 1878-1879*. Central City, Dakota Territory, 1878.

Jenney, Walter P., *Black Hills of Dakota*. (Senate Exec. Doc. #51, 44th Congress, 1st Session, 1875.) Washington, D.C.: Government Printing Office, 1876.

McClintock, John S., *Pioneer Days in the Black Hills*. Deadwood, 1939.

South Dakota. ("American Guide Series.") New York, 1938.

Spring, Agnes Wright, *The Cheyenne and Black Hills Stage and Express Route*. Glendale, Cal., 1949.

Tallent, Annie D., *The Black Hills, or the Last Hunting Ground of the Dakotas*. St. Louis, 1899.

Trigg, J. H., *History of Cheyenne and Northern Wyoming, Embracing the Gold Fields of the Black Hills*. Omaha, 1876.

Williams, Albert N., *The Black Hills*. Dallas, 1952.

MAGAZINES: *The Black Hills Engineer,* Rapid City.

NEWSPAPERS: *Black Hills Pioneer* and *Black Hills Times,* later *Deadwood Pioneer-Times.*

UTAH

Carter, Kate B., *Heart Throbs of the West*. 10 vols. Salt Lake City, 1940.

Hunter, Milton R., *Utah, The Story of Her People*. Salt Lake City, 1946.

Rogers, Fred B., *Soldiers of the Overland*. San Francisco, 1938.

Skidmore, Charles H., *Utah Resources and Activities*. Salt Lake City, 1933.

Tullidge, Edward W., *History of Salt Lake City*. Salt Lake City, 1886.

Utah. ("American Guide Series.") New York, 1941.

MAGAZINES: *Tullidge's Monthly Magazine; Utah Historical Quarterly.*

NEWSPAPERS: *Deseret News; Park Record,* Park City; *Salt Lake Tribune.*

WASHINGTON

Bethune, George A., *Mines and Minerals of Washington*. Olympia, 1891.

Durham, N. W., *History of the City of Spokane and Spokane County*. 3 vols. Chicago, 1912.

Fuller, George W., *The Inland Empire of the Pacific Northwest*. 4 vols. Spokane, 1928.

Hines, Rev. H. K., *An Illustrated History of the State of Washington*. Chicago, 1893.

History of Klickitat, Yakima and Kittitas Counties, Washington. 1904.

Illustrated History of Skagit and Snohomish Counties. 1906.

Peattie, Roderick, (ed.). *The Cascades.* New York, 1949.

Spencer, Lloyd, and Pollard, Lancaster, *A History of the State of Washington.* 4 vols. New York, 1937.

Steele, Richard F., *History of North Washington.* 1904.

Told by the Pioneers. 3 vols. Washington Pioneer Project, 1937-38.

Trimble, William J., *The Mining Advance into the Inland Empire.* Madison, Wis., 1914.

Waring, Guy, *My Pioneer Past.* Boston, 1936.

Washington. ("American Guide Series.") Portland, 1941.

Whitfield, William, *History of Snohomish County.* 2 vols. Chicago, 1926.

Woody, O. H., *Glimpses of Pioneer Life of Okanogan County, Washington.* Okanogan, 1924.

MAGAZINES: *Northwest Mining Journal,* Seattle; *Northwest Mining News,* Spokane; *Pacific Northwest Quarterly,* formerly *Washington Historical Quarterly,* Seattle.

NEWSPAPERS: *Northport News; Okanogan Independent; Ruby Miner; Walla Walla Statesman.*

WYOMING

Bartlett, I. S., *History of Wyoming.* Chicago, 1918.

Burt, Struthers, *Powder River.* New York, 1938.

Coutant, C. G., *History of Wyoming.* Laramie, 1899.

Linford, Velma, *Wyoming, Frontier State.* Denver, 1947.

Mokler, James Alfred, *History of Natrona County, Wyoming, 1888-1922.* Chicago, 1922.

Morris, Robert C., (ed.). *Collections of the Wyoming Historical Society.* Cheyenne, 1897.

Trentholm, Virginia Cole, *Footprints on the Frontier.* Douglas, 1945.

————, and Carley, Maurine, *Wyoming Pageant.* Casper, 1946.

Wyoming. ("American Guide Series.") New York, 1941.

MAGAZINES: *Quarterly Bulletin,* State of Wyoming Historical Dept.; *Wyoming State Journal.*

NEWSPAPERS: *Casper Tribune; Cheyenne Daily Leader; Grand Encampment Herald; Rawlins Daily Times; Riverton Review; Rock Springs Rocket; Saratoga Sun; South Pass News; Wyoming Eagle,* Cheyenne.

Index

Proper names in the following categories are entered under their general heading: Bars, Canyons, Churches, Copper Cos., Counties, Creeks, Ditch Cos., Forts, Gulches, Hills, Indians, Lakes, Mills, Mines, Mining Cos., Mining Districts, Mountains, Newspapers, Passes, Peaks, Placers, Railroads, Rivers, Smelters and Smelting Cos., Theatres, Valleys.

Printed and bound by CPI Group (UK) Ltd, Croydon, CR0 4YY

13/04/2025

14656553-0002